7/2

BIBLE STUDY TEXTBOOK SERIES

# THE ETERNAL SPIRIT: HIS PERSON AND POWERS

". . . how much more shall the blood of Christ, who through the eternal Spirit offered himself without blemish unto God, cleanse your conscience from dead works to serve the living God?"

—Hebrews 9:14

". . . the Spirit and the bride say, Come. And he that heareth. let him say, Come. And he that is athirst, let him come: he that will, let him take the water of life freely."

—Revelation 22:17

## C. C. CRAWFORD, Ph.D.

College Press, Joplin, Missouri

# BIBLE STUDY TEXTBOOK SERIES

- ACTS MADE ACTUAL
- THE CHURCH IN THE BIBLE
- ROMANS REALIZED
- HELPS FROM HEBREWS
- THE GOSPEL OF JOHN VOLS. I & II
- GUIDANCE FROM GALATIANS
- THE GREATEST WORK IN THE WORLD
- PAUL'S LETTER TO TIMOTHY AND TITUS
- SURVEY COURSE IN CHRISTIAN DOCTRINE VOL. I
- SURVEY COURSE IN CHRISTIAN DOCTRINE VOL. II
- SURVEY COURSE IN CHRISTIAN DOCTRINE VOLS. III & IV
- LETTERS FROM PETER
- THINKING THROUGH THESSALONIANS
- STUDIES IN FIRST CORINTHIANS
- STUDIES IN SECOND CORINTHIANS
- THE SEER, THE SAVIOUR, AND THE SAVED IN THE BOOK OF REVELATION
- STUDIES IN LUKE
- JAMES AND JUDE
- THE GOSPEL OF MARK
- GENESIS VOLS. I & II
- HEREBY WE KNOW — THE EPISTLES OF JOHN
- STUDIES IN SAMUEL
- OLD TESTAMENT HISTORY

### Other Books by C. C. Crawford
Published by *DeHoff Publications*, Murfreesboro, Tennessee

- SERMON OUTLINES ON ACTS
- SERMON OUTLINES ON THE RESTORATION PLEA
- SERMON OUTLINES ON THE CROSS OF CHRIST
- SERMON OUTLINES ON FIRST PRINCIPLES

### Published by *The College Press*, Joplin, Missouri

- SURVEY COURSE IN CHRISTIAN DOCTRINE (in four vols.)
- GENESIS: THE BOOK OF THE BEGINNINGS (in four vols.)
- THE PASSION OF OUR LORD

### To be re-issued in the near future

- COMMONSENSE ETHICS

### Projected for future publication

- THE ETERNAL SPIRIT: HIS WORD AND WORKS

# CONTENTS

## Part Five
# THE NOMENCLATURE OF THE SPIRIT

## Part Six
# THE SPIRIT AND THE WORD

# FOREWORD

The first draft of this rather elaborate study of the Biblical doctrine of the Holy Spirit and His works was completed some twenty years ago—to be exact, in 1950. I am now presenting it in book form for the first time, after a thoroughgoing review of its content. I have intentionally allowed the material to have time to "jell," so to speak, to see whether on more mature re-examination I might find myself having made statements which I now have reason to restate or to reject altogether. I have found very little that needs to be omitted or even revamped. I have simply stated herein my personal convictions with respect to this fascinating, rewarding, and exceedingly important Biblical subject.

I have deliberately chosen to treat the subject before us from the point of view of the Bible as a whole, as a unity. This I have done simply *because the Bible is a unity.* It is a whole, complete, perfect, in content and in design, and therefore sufficient to furnish the man of God "completely unto every good work" (2 Tim. 3:17). This means, of course, that I have chosen to disregard the conjectures of much of modern Biblical criticism. For I am convinced that for the most part they *are* conjectures pure and simple, more often than not the products of prejudices and presuppositions which have no foundation in fact. They are the offspring of the ultra-analytical tendencies of the Teutonic mentality in which most of them had their origin, a mentality which for some two hundred years seems to have been incapable of seeing the forest for the trees, and which as a consequence has proved itself destructive in the extreme to both faith and morals. Incidentally, what is true of Biblical criticism in this respect is equally true of the critical theories of the texts of Homer, Plato, Aristotle and the other ancient writers. It is high time for pundits the world over, and the smaller fry as well, to return to sanity in this particular field as elsewhere. Besides, were these critical theories to be proven true beyond any reasonable doubt, the fact would still remain that the Bible is a unity. Regardless of the number of men who, theoretically, may have contributed to the writing of its component parts, the Bible is still *one* book, still *The* Book, the Book of the Spirit. Though a library of some sixty-six books, it is still a book with one theme from beginning to end. It begins with a picture of Paradise lost; it terminates with a picture of Paradise regained. It is not, never was designed to be, a textbook of science (even though it has often anticipated the findings of science). It makes no at-

1

tempt to present a system of philosophy, nor does it presume to give us a history of the human race. The Bible is simply the history of Redemption, and therefore of the Messianic Line through which the divine Plan of Redemption for man was worked out. It is this, and nothing more. It has one motif running throughout—the redemption of fallen man as effectuated through the offices and work of Messiah, Christ, the Son of God, and as achieved and realized by the continuing ministry of the Holy Spirit. If men would only accept the Bible and treat it as *the one book* which it really is, most of their false conclusions would disappear as chaff before the wind.

So-called "intellectualism," "secular learning," academic "scholarship," etc., has absolutely nothing to suggest that would discredit the Christian revelation of the living and true God, the Personal Absolute, the God and Father of our Lord Jesus Christ. The source of most of the antagonism to Biblical faith is clearly stated by the Apostle Paul when he tells us that the Gentiles—the pagan world—knew not God simply *because their senseless hearts were darkened.* "For," he writes, "the invisible things of him since the creation of the world are clearly seen, being perceived through the things that are made, even his everlasting power and divinity; that they may be without excuse: because that, knowing God, they glorified him not as God, neither gave thanks; but became vain in their reasonings, and their senseless heart was darkened. Professing themselves to be wise, they became fools, and changed the glory of the incorruptible God for the likeness of an image of corruptible man, and of birds, and of four-footed beasts, and creeping things." Hence, the Apostle adds, that "even as they refused to have God in their knowledge, God gave them up unto a reprobate mind," etc. (Rom. 1:20-23, 28). Is it not true in all ages that even when the Light shines in the darkness, "the darkness apprehends it not" (John 1:5)? It has always been true that men will not accept the Light simply because *they choose not to accept it.* They actually prefer to live in darkness, that is, especially in moral and spiritual darkness. *They voluntarily choose sin and reject righteousness.*

Why, for example, do the pseudo-pundits of this world attack the integrity and reliability only of the Scriptures? They make no such vicious attacks on the Vedas, the Avesta, the Koran, The Key to the Scriptures, the Book of Mormon, or other alleged "sacred" books of the cults and so-called "religions." No! It is

2

the Bible, and the Bible only, that is the butt of their supercilious attacks.

Again, why do the nit-picking "analytical critics" attack only the Genesis account of the Creation? They never attack the mythological Egyptian, Babylonian, Hindu, Greek, Roman, Amerindian, etc., cosmogonies. Why not? Because these are obviously mythological; their gods and goddesses are not personalities, but personifications of forces of nature. But the Genesis cosmogony patently is not mythological; it has not a single characteristic of the myth-form (*mythos*). The only way by which it might possibly be downgraded would have to be by efforts to show that it is not in harmony with human science, that is, not necessarily mythological, but *unscientific*. But the content of this Creation narrative in Genesis is so "sententiously sumblime" that it defies all human efforts to destroy its integrity.

Again, I have included in this work a few rather brief references to the correlations that exist between the more refined idealistic philosophical thinking, which, of course, is the product of man's reasoning powers alone, and the presentation of the doctrine of the Holy Spirit that we find in the Bible. These correlations (harmonies) *do exist*, and are also in accord with human experience itself. As a matter of fact, I know of no time in the entire history of human thought when scientific theory was in greater harmony with Biblical teaching than it is today. This, I think, is most significant.

Finally, it is my conviction that the church of the present day is relatively powerless, largely because professing Christians have lost their sense of the companionship of the Spirit of God. It is hoped that what is presented herein may serve in some measure to focus the attention of God's people upon this dire loss, and so awaken in them aspiration for a spiritual infilling of which they now seem to be pitifully unaware. May we all—we who profess to be Christians—open our hearts to the overtures of God's Spirit, that He may come freely into the interior life and abide there as a gracious Guest, Companion, Advocate, and Guide; filling us with that measure of His grace and power which He has freely promised to all obedient believers. For only by the continuing ministry of the Spirit can the Church, as the Temple of God, be kept strong and stedfast; as the Household of Faith, affectionate and tender; as the Body of Christ, harmonious and vitally active; as the Bride of Christ, chaste and devoted; and as the Army of the Great King, powerful and victorious. *May we not so much seek to possess the Holy Spirit as*

3

*to be possessed by Him,* that He may use us freely in the accomplishment of the task to which He has set Himself in this Dispensation as the true Vicegerent of Christ upon earth, viz., the preaching of the Gospel for a testimony unto all nations (Matt. 24:14). For not until this task shall have been accomplished will His work—and ours—have been gloriously consummated.

C. C. Crawford

Dallas Christian College
January 1, 1972

# PART ONE

# GENERAL
# INTRODUCTION

## 1. Definitions, Sources, Methods

By the term "Spirit," in the title which I have selected for this series of studies, I mean the Spirit of God, the Holy Spirit, of the Bible (except, of course, in instances in which I deal with the "spirit" that is in man: *e.g.*, Job 32:8, Eccl. 12:7, Gen. 2:7). By the term "cosmos" I mean the entire "natural" world, including what is designated in Scripture the "natural" man.

1 Cor. 2:14—Now the natural [*psychikos*, literally "soulish," rendered "natural," "sensuous," as distinguished from *pneumatikos*, "spiritual,"] man receiveth not the things of the Spirit of God. 1 Cor. 15:44—It is sown a natural body; it is raised a spiritual body. If there is a natural body, there is also a spiritual body. Gen. 2:7—And Jehovah God formed man of the dust of the ground, and breathed into his nostrils the breath of life; and man became a living soul![1]

"Man," writes Lecomte du Nouy, "is part of an immense cosmos and is capable, alone amongst the animals, of observing nature, of experimenting and of establishing relationships and laws between facts."[2] A scientist is reported to have said, "From the point of view of astronomy, man is just a speck upon a speck of the totality of being." To which reply was made, "Yes, but from the viewpoint of astronomy, man is still the astronomer." Man is, in fact, the only "frame of reference" to whom the fact of being-in-general could have any meaning.

I choose to treat man, as he is presently constituted, as an integral part of the cosmic environment generally designated as "nature," even though he does transcend it in many of his activities. (We should always keep in mind the fact that "nature" is not an entity, but only the name we give to observed phenomena.)

## 2. Christianity's Great Dynamic

Christianity is the world's unique religion in many respects. Its finality cannot successfully be contradicted. Both etymologically and literally it is the only system truly worthy of being designated a *religion* (from *religo, religare,* "to bind back," or "bind anew"): as Christians we are ready to defend the thesis at any time that the Christian Faith is the only true system of

1. For the sake of uniformity and clarity I am not enclosing in quotes, in the material in smaller type and extending from margin to margin, either passages from the Scripture or excerpts from the works of human authors. Personal comments I put in brackets, C.C.
2. *Human Destiny*, 12.

Divine-human reconciliation kown to man (cf. 2 Cor. 5:18-21, John 14:6).

It is unique in that it has at its heart and center the world's unique Personage, Jesus the Christ, the Son of the living God; Immanuel, the God-Man, *Theanthropos;* the Incarnate Word; the Mystery of Godliness; our Prophet and Priest and King. There are just two things to consider in Christianity: first, the Person; then, the System; and the System stands or falls with the Person. For Christ is Christianity, and Christianity is Christ.

Again, Christianity is unique in that it provides an adequate Atonement (Covering) for sin (John 1:29); an Atonement sufficient to vindicate the Absolute Justice of the Author of the moral order and to sustain the majesty of the divine law violated by human transgression (1 John 3:4). "To reconcile the forgiving goodness of God with His absolute justice," writes W. Robertson Smith, "is one of the highest problems of spiritual religion, which in Christianity is solved by the doctrine of the atonement."[1]

In the third place, Christianity is unique in that it displays before the world the challenge of the empty tomb. It is the only religion which claims an ever-living Person as its Founder, Head and Lord. The Lord Jesus Christ is as truly alive today as when He trod the storied hills of old Judea two thousand years ago. Buddha, Confucius, Mohammed, Zoroaster, and all the others, died—and death terminated their careers. But the Lord Jesus was raised up from the dead and is seated at the right hand of God the Father, alive forevermore (Rom. 8:34, 1 Pet. 3:22). This is the fundamental claim of the Christian religion, as stated by the Apostle Peter in his great sermon on the day of Pentecost: "This Jesus did God raise up, whereof we all [*i.e.,* the Apostles] are witnesses" (Acts 2:32). And this is the claim affirmed by the risen Christ Himself: "I am the first and the last, and the Living One; and I was dead, and behold, I am alive for evermore, and I have the keys of death and of Hades" (Rev. 1:17, 18). The *living* Creed of the *living* Church of the *living* God is the *ever-living* Christ.

We Christians make no pilgrimages to any shrine wherein molder the bones of the Founder of our faith. We worship a living Christ, who was raised up the third day from Joseph's new tomb, and made to sit at God's right hand in the heavenly places, "far above all rule, and authority, and power, and do-

1. W, Robertson Smith, *The Religion of the Semites: Fundamental Institutions*, 62.

minion, and every name that is named, not only in this world, but also in that which is to come" (Eph. 1:20, 21). We have an Intercessor *there*, at God's right hand; and we have also an Intercessor *here*, within our hearts, who "maketh intercession for us with groanings which cannot be uttered" (Rom. 8:26). The Intercessor *here* is the Holy Spirit. "O the depth of the riches both of the wisdom and knowledge of God! How unsearchable are his judgments, and his ways past tracing out!" (Rom. 11:33).

Finally then, in this connection, Christianity is unique in that it provides for all obedient believers a spiritual Dynamic who is precious beyond compare. That Dynamic is the Spirit of God, the Holy Spirit. The Spirit of God it is who energizes the Word, who vitalizes the Church, who indwells and strengthens the Christian with a spiritual might far transcending his own (Eph. 3:16). There is no Holy Spirit in Hinduism, Brahmanism, Buddhism, Confucianism, Taoism, Mohammedanism, or in any of the falsely so-called "world religions." True it is that in some of these esoteric cults we encounter the concept of "spirit" as what might be called a *metaphysical* influence or force of some kind—a strictly pantheistic notion; but in none of them do we find even an intimation of the *Holy* Spirit, that is, any suggestion of ethical or spiritual import attaching to the term. The Bible, however, is literally the Book of the Spirit: from first to last it bears the *imprimatur* of the Spirit of God. Had the Bible never been written, without doubt we should be in the same blind condition as those disciples whom Paul found at Ephesus, who confessed that they had never so much as heard "if a Holy Spirit is" (Acts 19:2).

The presence and power of the Holy Spirit in the Bible distinguishes it, sets it apart, from all other books. Scripture is *God-breathed* literature. The presence and power of the Holy Spirit in the Gospel sets it apart from all human messages, and makes it in truth "the power of God unto salvation to every one that believeth" (Rom. 1:16). The presence and power of the Holy Spirit in the Church of Christ sets it apart from all human institutions. The Holy Spirit does not indwell the club, the fraternal order, the ethical society, or any other community of human beings associated for human ends. The Spirit indwells the Church and the Church only. The Church alone is the "habitation of God in the Spirit, being built upon the foundation of the apostles and prophets, Christ Jesus himself being the chief corner stone" (Eph. 2:19-21). Because the Spirit comes to

8

indwell every obedient believer (1 Cor. 3:16-17, 6:19-20; Acts 2:38; Gal. 3:2-3), these obedient believers are said to be "living stones, built up into a spiritual house, to be a holy priesthood, to offer up spiritual sacrifices, acceptable to God through Jesus Christ" (1 Pet. 2:1-5).

The Holy Spirit is not a derivation from philosophical speculation nor from scientific theory. All branches of purely human wisdom are as silent as the grave with respect to His existence, His being, His presence and power. What we know of the Holy Spirit and His work we must learn from one, and only one Book —the Bible. The Bible is the Book which He Himself has given us. It is pre-eminently the Book of the Spirit.

Little wonder, then, in view of all these superlative excellences of the Christian faith, that Christianity is pre-eminently *the religion of joy*. At the background of its realism (it declares unequivocally that man is in sin, and in need of salvation, without which he is perishing in this world and in the world to come; never does it deceive him one whit) there is always the final optimistic note: "after the tribulation . . . then shall appear the sign of the Son of man in heaven . . . and they shall see the Son of man coming on the clouds of heaven with power and great glory" (Matt. 24.30). Whereas philosophical cults and Oriental mysticisms uniformly reek with pessimism, Christianity declares that *faith* is the victory "that hath overcome the world" (1 John 5:4).

Cf. Luke 2:10 [the words of the angel of the Lord to the shepherds], Behold, I bring you good tidings of great joy which shall be to all the people. John 15:11—These things have I spoken unto you, that my joy may be in you, and that your joy may be made full. John 16:24—Hitherto have ye asked nothing in my name; ask, and ye shall receive, that your joy may be made full. Acts 8:8—And there was much joy in that city [Samaria]. Acts 15:3—They passed through Phoenicia and Samaria, declaring the conversion of the Gentiles, and they caused great joy to all the brethren. 2 Cor. 7:4—I overflow with joy in all our affliction. Col. 1:11—strengthened with all power, according to the might of his glory, unto all patience and longsuffering with joy. 1 Thess. 1:6— having received the word in much affliction, with joy of the Holy Spirit. 1 Pet. 4:13—but inasmuch as ye are partakers of Christ's sufferings, rejoice; that at the revelation of his glory also ye may rejoice with exceeding joy. 1 John 1:4—And these things we write that your joy may be made full. [Cf. Acts 2:46, 47; Rev. 12:10-12; 19:6-8.]

## 3. The Book of the Spirit

God has written two Books—the Book of Nature, in which He has recorded the evidences of "his everlasting power and divinity" (Rom. 1:20), and the Book of Scripture in which He has unfolded the story of His gracious plan for the redemption of fallen man. There may be disagreements between Science, which is man's interpretation of the Book of Nature, and Theology, which is man's interpretation of the Book of Scripture; for where there is human effort, there is always imperfection and liability to error. Between God's two Books themselves, however, there are no disagreements, for the simple reason that Truth never contradicts itself.

*The Bible is the Book of the Spirit.* As. H. Wheeler Robinson writes:

> On its first page there is painted the impressive picture of chaos, when darkness was upon the face of the deep; but the Spirit of God was brooding, like a mother-bird, upon the face of the waters. From the last page there rings out the evangelical challenge of the Church to the world, "The Spirit and the bride say, Come." Between them there is the story of a divine evolution, which is from God's side, revelation, and from man's side, discovery.[1]

The presence and power of the Spirit in the Bible gives it a uniqueness all its own. Other great literary works may be the productions of human genius in its moments of loftiest flight, but Scripture is literature that is actually *God-breathed.*

God's revelation of His grace to man was wrought out, not in heaven, but on earth, in successive events in time, beginning with the creation of the Kingdom of Nature, and culminating in the Incarnation, Atoning Death, and Resurrection of Jesus Christ, and in the descent of the Holy Spirit and the incorporation of the Church of Christ on the great Day of Pentecost, A.D. 30. The accounts of these successive events, together with their significance for man, was made a matter of record in the sacred Scriptures, through the agency of the Spirit, for all subsequent generations to read and profit withal. In this work of revelation the Holy Spirit operated, as He seems to do invariably, through the instrumentality of inspired men. Thus did God take men into partnership with Himself in the unfolding of the divine Plan of Redemption. Both the revelation and the recording thereof were begun by the Spirit through "holy men of old" ("patriarchs," Acts 2:29, 7:9; Heb. 7:4), continued through the Hebrew prophets (2 Pet. 1:21, 1 Pet. 1:10-12), and concluded in the teaching of Jesus and the Apostles (2 Pet. 1:2-5).

1 Cor. 2:7-12. But we speak God's wisdom in a mystery, even the wisdom that hath been hidden, which God foreordained before the worlds unto our glory, . . . as it is written, Things which the eye saw

1. *The Christian Experience of the Holy Spirit,* 5

not, and ear heard not, and which entered not into the heart of man, whatsoever things God prepared for them that love him. But unto us God revealed them through the Spirit: for the Spirit searcheth all things, yea, the deep things of God. For who among men knoweth the things of a man, save the spirit of the man, which is in him? even so the things of God none knoweth, save the Spirit of God. But we received, not the spirit of the world, but the spirit which is from God; that we might know the things that were freely given to us of God. Which things also we speak, not in words which man's wisdom teacheth, but which the Spirit teacheth; combining spiritual things with spiritual words. Eph. 3:3-11—how that by revelation was made known unto me the mystery, as I wrote before in few words, whereby, when ye read, ye can perceive my understanding in the mystery of Christ; which in other generations was not made known unto the sons of men, as it hath now been revealed unto his holy apostles and prophets in the Spirit; to wit, that the Gentiles are fellow-heirs, and fellow-members of the body, and fellow-partakers of the promise in Christ Jesus through the gospel, whereof I was made a minister, according to the gift of that grace of God which was given me according to the working of his power. Unto me, who am less than the least of all saints, was this grace given, to preach unto the Gentiles the unsearchable riches of Christ; and to make all men see what is the dispensation of the mystery which for ages hath been hid in God who created all things; to the intent that now unto the principalities and powers in the heavenly places might be made known through the church the manifold wisdom of God, according to the eternal purpose which he purposed in Christ Jesus our Lord: in whom we have boldness and access in confidence through our faith in him. 1 Pet. 1:10-12, Concerning which salvation the prophets sought and searched diligently, who prophesied of the grace that should come unto you: searching what time or what manner of time the Spirit of Christ which was in them did point unto, when it testified beforehand the sufferings of Christ, and the glories that should follow them. To whom it was revealed, that not unto themselves, but unto you did they minister these things, which now have been announced unto you through them that preached the gospel unto you by the Holy Spirit sent forth from heaven; which things angels desire to look into. [Cf. John 3:34, Heb. 1:1-3; John 14:16-17, 14:26, 15:26-27. 16:7-15, 20:21-23; Acts 1:1-8; 1 Thess. 2:13, 2 Tim. 3:16, 2 Pet. 1:21, etc.]

What the Apostle Paul designates in his writings "the eternal purpose of God," "the mystery of Christ," "the mystery which for ages hath been hid in God," "the mystery of God's will," etc., was His purpose *from eternity* to send His Only Begotten Son "when the fulness of the time came" (Gal. 4:4) to make Atonement for sin and to conquer death, to establish the Church and publish the Gospel for a testimony unto all the nations (Matt. 24:14), and to unite both Jews and Gentiles in the one Body or Church of Christ; His ultimate end being that of preparing a holy, redeemed race or order of creatures sanctified by the Spirit and thus fitted to have fellowship with our holy God, and inhabiting a "new heaven and a new earth, wherein dwelleth righteousness," a state in which all that is mortal shall be "swallowed up of life."

11

See again Eph. 3:1-12. Cf. Eph. 1:3-11, Blessed be the God and Father of our Lord Jesus Christ, who hath blessed us with every spiritual blessing in the heavenly places in Christ: even as he chose us in him before the foundation of the world, that we should be holy and without blemish before him in love: having foreordained us unto adoption as sons through Jesus Christ unto himself, according to the good pleasure of his will, to the praise of the glory of his grace, which he freely bestowed on us in the Beloved: in whom we have our redemption through his blood, the forgiveness of our trespasses, according to the riches of his grace, which he made to abound toward us in all wisdom and prudence, making known unto us the mystery of his will, according to the good pleasure which he purposed in him unto a dispensation of the fulness of the times, *to sum up all things in Christ*, the things in the heavens, and the things upon the earth; in him, I say, in whom also we were made a heritage, having been foreordained according to the purpose of him who worketh all things after the counsel of his will. Gal. 4:4, 5—when the fulness of the time came, God sent forth his Son, born of a woman, born under the law, that he might redeem them that were under the law, that we might receive the adoption of sons. Matt. 24:14—And this gospel of the kingdom shall be preached in the whole world for a testimony unto all the nations; and then shall the end come. Matt. 5:48—Ye therefore shall be perfect, as your heavenly Father is perfect. Col. 1:22—now hath he reconciled in the body of his flesh through death, to present you holy and without blemish and unreprovable before him. Eph. 1:4—that we should be holy and without blemish before him in love. Heb. 12:14—Follow after peace with all men, and the sanctification without which no man shall see the Lord. 1 Pet. 1:15—be ye yourselves also holy in all manner of living. 1 Pet. 2:5—Ye also, as living stones, are built up a spiritual house, to be a holy priesthood, to offer up spiritual sacrifices, acceptable to God, through Jesus Christ. Heb. 12:23—the spirits of just men made perfect. 2 Thess. 2:13—for that God chose you from the beginning unto salvation in sanctification of the Spirit, and belief of the truth. Rom. 8:28-30, And we know that to them that love God all things work together for good, even to them that are called according to his purpose. For whom he foreknew, *he also foreordained to be conformed to the image of his Son*, that he might be the the firstborn among many brethren; and whom he foreordained, them he also called: and whom he called, them he also justified: and whom he justified, them he also glorified. 1 Cor. 3:16, 17 —Know ye not that ye are a temple of God, and that the Spirit of God dwelleth in you? If any man destroy the temple of God, him shall God destroy; for the temple of God is holy, and such are ye. 1 Cor. 6:19, 20—Or know ye not that your body is a temple of the Holy Spirit which is in you, which ye have from God? and ye are not your own; for ye were bought with a price: glorify God therefore in your body. 1 Tim. 6:14-16, until the appearing of our Lord Jesus Christ . . . who is the blessed and only Potentate, the King of kings and Lord of lords, *who only hath immortality, dwelling in light unapproachable;* whom no man hath seen nor can see: to whom be honor and power eternal. (Cf. 1 Thess. 5:23, Rev. 19:16; Rom. 2:7, 2 Tim. 1:10, 1 Cor. 15:50-56, 1 Thess. 4:7-8, Phil. 3:20-21). 2 Cor. 5:1-4, For we know that if the earthly house of our tabernacle be dissolved, we have a building from God, a house not made with hands, eternal, in the heavens. For verily in this we groan, longing to be clothed upon with our habitation which is from heaven: if so be that being clothed we shall not be found naked. For indeed we that are in this tabernacle do groan, being burdened: not for that we would be unclothed, but that we would be clothed upon, *that what is mortal may be swallowed up of life.* Rev. 22:10.11—Seal not up the words of th

12

prophecy of this book; for the time is at hand. He that is unrighteous, let him do unrighteousness still; and he that is filthy, let him be made filthy still; and he that is righteous, let him do righteousness still; and he that is holy, let him be made holy still.

Finally, in this connection, is it not in accord with the very nature of things that revelation should be, in a special sense, a work of the Spirit of God? How indeed could it be otherwise if our Heavenly Father is a personal God? "For," as the Apostle Paul puts it, "who among men knoweth the things of a man, save the spirit of the man, which is in him? even so the things of God none knoweth, save the Spirit of God" (1 Cor. 2:11). "For the Spirit searcheth all things, yea, the deep things of God" (1 Cor. 2:10). To the Spirit of God we are immediately indebted for all that is known, or knowable, of God, of the unseen world, or of the ultimate destinies of men. All that ancient or modern pagans pretend to have known or to know of these sublime topics, has either been borrowed from the oracles of the Revealer of secrets, or else is more conceit or conjecture of their own. The simple fact of the matter is, that the truth to be believed by man respecting his own origin, constitution, and proper end, could never have been known but by revelation of the Spirit. How profoundly thankful we should be, then, that our God has not left us in darkness, in that gross darkness in which heathen nations are still struggling and suffering; but has, by His Spirit, revealed His plan for our salvation so clearly that the wayfaring man, though a fool, need not err therein. "Now to him that is able to establish you according to my gospel and the preaching of Jesus Christ, according to the revelation of the mystery which hath been kept in silence through times eternal, but now is manifested, and by the scriptures of the prophets, according to the commandment of the eternal God, is made known unto all the nations unto obedience of faith: to the only wise God, through Jesus Christ [to whom?] be the glory for ever. Amen." (Rom. 16:25-27).

It is obvious that the revelation of this *mystery* in pertinent historical events, together with the account of the revelation as embodied in Scripture, has been in a special sense the work of the Holy Spirit, the One who "searcheth all things, yea, the deep things of God" (1 Cor. 2:10). Moreover, both the revelation and the record were vouchsafed *progressively*, that is, "precept upon precept, precept upon precept, line upon line, line upon line, here a little, there a little" (Isa. 28:10), embracing such events under the old Dispensations as the Call of Abraham,

13

and the Abrahamic Promise; the organization of the Hebrew Theocracy under Moses; and the work of the Hebrew Prophets, and especially that of John the Baptizer, in whom that illustrious line of "men of the Spirit" flowered and terminated (Luke 1:80). In a word, God spent four thousand years—and probably a great many more—preparing the world for the advent of Messiah, and building up a system of type, symbol, and prophecy, all designed to identify Him, beyond any possibility of doubt, upon His appearing in the world. Then "when the fulness of the time came, God sent forth his Son, born of a woman, born under the law, that he might redeem them that were under the law, that we might receive the adoption of sons" (Gal. 4:4-5, Rom. 8:14-17). Finally, when the Redeemer had accomplished the work for which the Father had sent Him into the world, both the revelation and the record thereof were brought to completion in the labors and writings of the Apostles, who served as the executors of His Last Will and Testament. *Revelation, inspiration, and demonstration then came to an end* with the termination of the Apostolic ministry: "all things that pertain unto life and godliness" were given (2 Pet. 1:3, Jude 3). No man has ever added, no man could ever add, one jot or tittle to the body of truth, moral and spiritual, set forth in the apostolic writings. They are in themselves sufficient to furnish the man of God "completely unto every good work" (2 Tim. 3:16-17). To every spiritually-minded person the finality of the New Testament revelation and record is self-evident. All subsequent alleged "special revelations"—all of which, incidentally, contradict one another—must therefore be rejected.

The Bible, from the first chapter of Genesis to the last chapter of Revelation, bears on every page the *imprimatur* of the Spirit of God. It is the account of God's progressive revelation to His rational creatures. This record has been given to mankind by the Holy Spirit through the instrumentality of inspired men. The revelation itself having been one, though progressive, revelation with one foreordained end or goal, it naturally follows that the record of the revelation is one. Hence, although some forty men, and possibly more, participated in the writing of the sixty-six component parts (books) of the Bible, nevertheless the finished product is one. The Bible is the history of redemption: it has one theme running throughout its length and breadth, namely, *redemption in and through Christ Jesus*. The Bible is one Book, even though it is a veritable library of books. It is a unity because basically it is the work of one Author—the Spirit of God.

## 4. Man's Ultimate Ends

*Man is a creature.* Individually or as a race he has nothing to do with his being in the world and very little to do with the time or manner of his going out of it (unless, of course, he resorts to suicide, the ultimate in sheer selfishness); and while he is in it, he is absolutely dependent on nature and on nature's God for the food that he eats, the water he drinks, the air he breathes, and even the very ground he walks on. No amount of self-pride or self-assertiveness on his part can alter these facts, now or ever.

*Man is a creature.* Neither as an individual nor as a race is he self-sufficient. Moreover, the unfailing criterion of a truly wise man is his own constant recognition of his creaturehood in all his dealings with his God and with his fellows. Humility, as Augustine was wont to reiterate, is the most essential condition to the acquirement of wisdom, wisdom being the constructive application of knowledge to the realization of man's natural and proper ultimate ends.

*Hence, as a creature, man, every man, every human being, has his own natural and proper intrinsic and extrinsic ends.* (*Intrinsic* ends are those realized within himself, the fulfilment of his natural potentialities; *extrinsic* ends are those served by him outside himself, in relation to the totality of being, specifically, in relations with his fellows and with his God.) (An *absolutely ultimate* end is defined *a priori* as that which leaves nothing further to be desired, that which is desired and sought for itself alone, and that which perfects (actualizes the potentialities of) his personal nature. In this last-named sense it is man's Highest Good, in Latin, the Summum Bonum.

*What, then, must be the natural and proper absolutely ultimate intrinsic and extrinsic ends of man,* the ends to which he is ordered by the Creator Himself, that is to say, the purposes for which He put him in the world? (Cf. Gen. 1:26-31). There can be only one truly satisfactory answer to each of these questions, as follows: *man's natural and proper absolutely ultimate intrinsic end is perfect happiness* (as designated by Aristotle, *eudaimonia,* and in Latin, *beatitudo*). Perfect happiness, heavenly joy, "exalted happiness," genuine *bliss,* obviously, is to be

15

realized *only in ultimate union with God.* variously designated
Seeing God Face to Face, Blessedness, The Beatific Vision, Life
Everlasting. (Note the following comment with respect to the
Beatitudes, (Matt. 5:3-10): "Beware of preaching the gospel
of temperament instead of the Gospel of God. Numbers of
people today preach the gospel of temperament, the gospel of
'cheer up.' The word 'blessed' is sometimes translated 'happy,'
but is a much deeper word; it includes all that we mean by joy in
its full fruition."[1] It strikes this writer that a more realistic
definition would be "bliss," "heavenly bliss," "rapture," etc.

*The natural and proper absolutely ultimate extrinsic end
of man is, of course, the glory of God.*

Isa. 46:9-11, Remember the former things of old: for I am God,
and there is none else; I am God, and there is none like me; declaring
the end from the beginning, and from ancient times things that are
not yet done; saying, My counsel shall stand, and I will do all my
pleasure. Isa. 45:25—In Jehovah shall all the seed of Israel be justified, and shall glory. Isa. 33:11—The counsel of Jehovah standeth fast
for ever, The thoughts of his heart to all generations. Phil. 2:9-11,
Wherefore also God highly exalted him, and gave unto him the name
which is above every name; that in the name of Jesus every knee
should bow, of things in heaven and things on earth and things under
the earth, and that every tongue should confess that Jesus Christ is
Lord, to the glory of God the Father. 1 Cor. 15:24-28, Then cometh
the end, when he shall deliver up the kingdom to God, even the Father;
when he shall have abolished all rule and all authority and power.
For he must reign, till he hath put all his enemies under his feet. The
last enemy that shall be abolished is death. . . . And when all things
have been subjected unto him, then shall the Son also be subjected to
him that did suject all things to him, that God may be all in all. Rev. 7:12
—[The song of the redeemed before the Great White Throne], Blessing,
and glory, and wisdom, and thanksgiving, and honor, and power, and
might, be unto our God for ever and ever. Amen. Rev. 21:23—And
the city hath no need of the sun, neither of the moon, to shine upon it:
for the glory of God did lighten it, and the lamp thereof is the Lamb.
1 Tim. 6:14-16, until the appearing of our Lord Jesus Christ, which in
its own times he shall show, who is the blessed and only Potentate,
the King of kings, and Lord of lords; who only hath immortality,
dwelling in light unapproachable; whom no man hath seen, nor can
see; to whom be power eternal. Amen.

In the Glorious Consummation of all things, the glory of
God will be seen to include redeemed humanity. Indeed Jesus
makes love for our fellows (mankind) an integral part of our
love for God.

Matt. 22:35-40, And one of them, a lawyer, asked him a question,
trying him: Teacher, which is the great commandment in the law?
And he said unto him, Thou shalt love the Lord thy God with all thy
heart, and with all thy soul, and with all thy mind. This is the great
and first commandment. And a second like unto it is this, Thou shalt

1. Oswald Chambers, *Biblical Psychology*, 116.

love thy neighbor as thyself. On these two commandments the whole law hangeth, and the prophets. [Cf. also Matt. 25:31-46, Deut. 6:5, Lev. 19:18, 1 John 4:7-11].

This cosmos in which man has his abode is neither *helio-centric, geocentric,* nor *anthropocentric*: it is *theocentric*. God Himself is the source and end of all things. His glory is the proper extrinsic end of His whole creation; any other end would be unworthy both of the Creator and of His creatures. But the ultimate intrinsic end of every human being—the end for which he has been put on the earth as its lord tenant—is *union with God*. This is evident from the fact that by his natural impulses he seeks happiness, or, specifically, that which he seeks as the ful-filment of a desire and which he considers to be a form of happi-ness. *Never does a human being seek to be permanently miser-able*: such an objective seems to be contrary to the very nature of man. The fact is not to be wondered at, therefore, that in all the higher systems of faith and practice ("religion") which have appeared in the course of human history, the concept of some kind of union with the Divine is envisioned as man's ultimate destiny. In Oriental systems this union is said to be reabsorption into Brahma, Tao, Unity, described by some as "the ocean of undifferentiated energy,"—after many reincarnations, of course; life is said to be "illusion" *(maya)*, and "salvation" is escape from it by the complete suppression of every aspect of individ-uality. Certainly, Nirvana is not thought of as a state of *personal* continuance beyond the grave. Someone has said rightly that *reincarnationism is not a hope, but a nightmare*. In Biblical re-ligion, however, this ultimate union is revealed as a never-ending *fellowship* with the personal living God who is the divine Other to all persons (others), and life is declared to be a divine gift and man's greatest good. This does not mean the suppression of individuality, but rather the enhancement of it, the self-realization of each person's potentialities by his sharing of the mind of Christ and the indwelling Spirit of God.

Phil. 2:5—Have this mind in you, which was also in Christ Jesus. 1 Cor. 2:16—But we have the mind of Christ. Rom. 5:5—the love of God hath been shed abroad in our hearts through the Holy Spirit which was given unto us. 1 Cor. 3:16—Know ye not that ye are a temple of God, and that the Spirit of God dwelleth in you? 1 Cor. 6:9—Or know ye not that your body is a temple of the Holy Spirit, which is in you, which ye have from God? and ye are not your own. 2 Cor. 6:16—And what agreement hath a temple of God with idols? for we are a temple of the living God, etc. Gal. 3:2—This only would I learn from you, Received ye the Spirit by the works of the law, or by the hearing of faith. Gal. 5:25—If we live by the Spirit, by the Spirit let us also walk. Rom. 8:11—But if the Spirit of him that raised up Jesus from the dead dwelleth in you, he that raised up Christ Jesus from the dead shall give life also to your mortal bodies through his Spirit that dwelleth in you.

Obviously, any syncretism of such antithetical—Oriental versus Biblical—concepts, is not only not desirable, but actually impossible.

In Scripture this ultimate union with God is described as seeing Him "face to face."

Matt. 5:8—Blessed are the pure in heart; for they shall see God. I Cor. 13:12—For now we see in a mirror, darkly; but then face to face: now I know in part; but then shall I know fully, even as also I was fully known. 2 Cor. 3:17, 18—Now the Lord is the Spirit: and where the Spirit of the Lord is, there is liberty. But we all, with unveiled face beholding as in a mirror the glory of the Lord, are transformed into the same image from glory to glory, even as from the Lord the Spirit. 1 John 3:2, 3—Beloved, now are we children of God, and it is not yet made manifest what we shall be. We know that, if he shall be manifested, we shall be like him; for we shall see him even as he is. 2 Pet. 1:3, 4—seeing that his divine power hath granted unto us all things that pertain unto life and godliness, through the knowledge of him that called us by his own glory and virtue; that through these ye may become partakers of the divine nature, having escaped the corruption that is in the world by lust. 2 Pet. 3:18—But grow in the grace and knowledge of our Lord and Savior Jesus Christ.

(It should be noted that "seeing God face to face" connotes not what we call physical "vision," but rather spiritual knowledge, illumination, by means of which we shall continue to grow as we are "transformed into the same image," that is, the image of Christ, "from glory to glory" (2 Cor. 3:18), and so become partakers of the divine nature. We must not lose sight of the fact that *the essential principle of life is growth*. Surely this growth will continue *spiritually* even in the experience of eternal life, in the Kingdom of Glory!)

In Scripture this ultimate Union with God, as we have noted, is described as seeing God "face to face" (Matt. 5:8, 1 Cor. 13:12, 1 John 3:2-3, 2 Cor. 3:18, Rev. 22:1-5). Such an ultimate oneness will surely consist of the complete union of the human mind with the mind of God in knowledge and the complete union of the human will with the Will of God in love, together with the accompanying illumination that such union can never be broken, that is, with the sense of its everlastingness. Again, since this occurs in God's realm, this experience—the Beatific Vision—is not just stretched-out time, but *timelessness*, and is therefore to our poor human minds inconceivable. Indeed, eye hath not seen, nor ear heard, neither has it entered into the imagination of man, to conceive of the things which God has

18

prepared for those who love Him (1 Cor. 2:9). This is—we repeat—the Vision of God, Beatitude, Blessedness, Perfection, Wholeness (Holiness), Life Everlasting (Matt. 5:48, John 5:48, John 3:16, Psa. 116:15, 1 John 5:18-20, Rev. 14:13, 21:1-4, 22:1-5). This final illumination surely will vouchsafe to God's saints the certainty of their own unalienable possession of God; not that they will be *as gods*—deity and humanity are necessarily of different *rank,* not just matters of degree—but that they will be partakers of the divine nature to the degree that they have made themselves partakers of the benefits of His grace (2 Pet. 1:4, Matt. 5:48, Eph. 5:1, Col. 1:28, Jas. 1:4, 1 Pet. 1:15, Rom. 1:4; Heb. 12:10, 14; 1 John 2:5, 4:12). In the final analysis, *Heaven is where God is, and Hell is where God is not* (2 Thess. 1:7-10). To these ultimate ends every human being is ordained by the Creator Himself. The only alternative view is that of the utter purposelessness and consequent futility of all existence, the view that

> The world rolls round for ever like a mill,
> It grinds out death and life and good and ill;
> It has no purpose, heart, or mind or will.[1]

To such an ultimate end, moreover, man has been disposed by the Divine implanting within him of a will that seeks only a good (in the broad sense, that which fulfils a desire) in its every activity. The human will was never known deliberately to seek ultimate and permanent evil (unhappiness). Even when it pursues an evil, it does so for the purpose of gaining what the person believes to be an ultimate good: the saint gives his body to be burned because he regards the temporary evil as a stepping-stone to ultimate bliss. Man errs when he mistakes and misuses *apparent* goods for *real* goods. *Spiritual discernment is the wisdom to put first things first.* Ignorance of his proper ends in life, and of the proper means of attaining them, is undoubtedly the prime source of man's faults and follies. (Cf. Matt. 6:33-34, John 8:31-32, Gal. 5:16-25).

Herein, too, consists the real meaning of *good* and *evil,* or *right* and *wrong.* Those human acts are *good* which perfect the character in virtue; those are *bad* which fail to do so (2 Pet. 1:5-9). Similarly, those acts of a man are *right* which tend to lead him toward the attainment of his proper ultimate ends, and those are *wrong* which lead him in the opposite direction or

1. James Thomson, "The City of Dreadful Night."

which keep him from attaining his proper ultimate ends (Matt. 7:13-14). *Goodness* has reference to *suitability* to the perfection of a person, to his growth in holiness; *rightness*, to the direction in which he is going morally and spiritually (Heb. 12:14, 2 Thess. 2:13, 1 Pet. 1:2), in relation to his ultimate ends.

Now it follows that, since man's ultimate end is union with God, in preparation for such an end he must be justified, purified, and sanctified, for the simple reason that a holy God (John 17:11) can have no concord with impurity of heart (Matt. 5:8). Indeed, in the very nature of things, only the pure in heart could ever hope to apprehend, to know, to realize the possession of, God. This, I repeat, is true because it is in accord with the very nature of things (Matt. 6:24, 1 Cor. 10:21, 2 Cor. 6:14-18). The "nature of things," moreover, is determined by the Will of God who is all-consistent, whose Will is the constitution of the universe—the cosmos—both physical and moral. Hence, it follows unquestionably that the God who, in Creation, determined man's ultimate ends and ordered him to the attainment of them, must have, by the same edict of His divine Will, and in the light of His omniscience, determined and ordered the necessary *means* to his attainment of these ends. For our God, the God of the Bible, is a purposeful God; and being omniscient, He knows perfectly how to adapt proper means to their respective ends. The whole cosmos is characterized throughout by this perfect adaptation of means and ends, even as it is characterized by mathematical exactness in all of its processes: or in the words of Pythagoras of old, "Things are numbers." (Cf. Isa. 46:9-11, Acts 17:24-31; Psa. 33:6-9, 148:5-6).

Therefore, on the principle of the perfect adaptation of means to ends, characteristic always of the activities of our living and true God, it follows that the one essential prerequisite of the individual man's attainment of his proper ultimate ends is *the life with the Holy Spirit.* Such a life is indispensable to the acquirement of that *holiness* or *wholeness* "without which no man shall see the Lord" (Heb. 12:14; cf. Eph. 4:24, 2 Pet. 1:4, Col. 1:12, Rom. 14:17). The same principle holds good in the present natural life: to be able to appreciate poetry one must cultivate this appreciation, to be able to enjoy a great symphonic production, one must cultivate the appreciation of this kind of music, etc. Similarly, to be able to appreciate ultimate Union with God, one must cultivate the Spiritual Life in the here and now. And, because appreciation in any area of human experience is necessarily based on *knowledge*, so appreciation of God, and

20

of Union with God, must be based on a person's cultivation of the Mind of Christ who is the revelation of God (Phil. 2:5, 1 Cor. 2:15-16; John 1:14, 14:6-9). No truer statement was ever uttered than the well-known saying that "heaven is a prepared place for a prepared people."

Now this Spiritual Life—the life that is "hid with Christ in God"—embraces three phases, as follows:

1. The *purgative* phase, as designated in its various aspects as conversion, remission, forgiveness, justification, regeneration, reconciliation, etc., the cleansing of the inner man from the body of the guilt of sin (which is spiritual circumcision, Col. 2:11-12, Rom. 6:1-14).

Acts 2:38—Repent ye, and be baptized every one of you in the name of Jesus Christ unto the remission of your sins; and ye shall receive the gift of the Holy Spirit. John 3:5—Except one be born of water and the Spirit, he cannot enter into the kingdom of God. John 5:24—He that heareth my word, and believeth him that sent me, hath eternal life, and cometh not into judgment, but hath passed from death into life. Rom. 6:4—We were buried therefore with him through baptism into death; that like as Christ was raised from the dead through the glory of the Father, so we also might walk in newness of life. 1 Cor. 6:11—but ye were washed, but ye were sanctified, but ye were justified in the name of the Lord Jesus Christ, and in the Spirit of our God. Eph. 2:8—for by grace have ye been saved through faith; and that [salvation] not of yourselves, it is the gift of God. Gal. 2:20—I have been crucified with Christ; and it is no longer I that live, but Christ liveth in me; and the life which I now live in the flesh I live by faith, the faith which is in the Son of God, who loved me, and gave himself up for me. Gal. 3:27—For as many of you as were baptized into Christ did put on Christ. 1 John 5:12—He that hath the Son hath the life; he that hath not the Son of God hath not the life. Heb. 9:14—how much more shall the blood of Christ, who through the eternal Spirit offered himself without blemish unto God, cleanse [A.V., *purge*] your conscience from dead works to serve the living God? 1 Cor. 5:7—Purge out the old leaven, that ye may be a new lump, even as ye are unleavened.

2. The *illuminative* phase: on the human side, this is *perseverance,* and on the divine side *sanctification.*

Rom. 12:2—Be not fashioned according to this world; but be ye transformed by the renewing of your mind, that ye may prove what is the good and acceptable and perfect will of God. Phil. 2:12—work out your own salvation with fear and trembling. 2 Pet. 1:10—give the more diligence to make your calling and election sure. 2 Pet. 3:18—But grow in the grace and knowledge of our Lord and Savior Jesus Christ. 2 Pet. 1:11—for thus shall be richly supplied unto you the entrance into the eternal kingdom of our Lord and Savior Jesus Christ. 2 Cor. 3:18—But we all, with unveiled face beholding as in a mirror the glory of the Lord, are transformed into the same image from glory to glory, even as from the Lord the Spirit. [Each human being—each person—is the image of God *personally;* the Lord Jesus, however, while in the flesh, was the "the very image of God's substance" (Heb. 1:3),

21

that is, not only the personal, but the *moral* image of God as well, that is, "one that hath been tempted in all points like as we are, yet without sin," Heb. 4:15]. 1 John 1:9—If we [as God's redeemed] confess our sins, he is faithful and righteous to firgive us our sins, and to cleanse us from all unrighteousness. [All Christians are sinners saved by grace.] 1 Cor. 15:58—Wherefore, my beloved brethren, be ye stedfast, unmovable, always abounding in the work of the Lord, forasmuch as ye know that your labor is not vain in the Lord. 2 Pet. 1:5—For this very cause adding on your part all diligence, in your faith supply virtue; and in your virtue, knowledge; and in your knowledge, self-control; and in your self-control, patience; and in your patience, godliness; and in your godliness, brotherly kindness; and in your brotherly kindness, love, etc. (Note that the eternal rewards are promised only to the Overcomers, Rev. 1:7, 11, 17, 26; 2:5, 12, 21.)

3. Finally, the *unitive*: as the final phase of redemption, the putting on of immortality (resurrection, transfiguration, glorification). This will surely include the union of the mind of the redeemed person with the mind of God in knowledge, and the union of his will with the will of God in love.

1 Thess. 5:23—And the God of peace himself sanctify you wholly; and may your spirit and soul and body be preserved entire, without blame at the coming of our Lord Jesus Christ. Rom. 8:28-30, We know that to them that love God all things work together for good, to them that are called according to his purpose. For whom he foreknew, he also foreordained to the conformed to the image of his Son. . . . and whom he foreordained, them he also called; and whom he called, them he also justified; and whom he justified, them he also glorified. 1 Cor. 15:54—But when this corruptible shall have put on incorruption, and this mortal shall have put on immortality, then shall be brought to pass the saying that is written, Death is swallowed up in victory. Rom. 8:23 —And not only so, but ourselves also, who have the firstfruits of the Spirit, even we ourselves groan within ourselves, waiting for our adoption, to wit, the redemption of our body. 2 Cor. 5:4—For indeed we that are in this tabernacle do groan being burdened; not for that we would be unclothed, but that we would be clothed upon, that what is mortal may be swallowed up of life. [Cf. 1 John: 3:2-3; Rev. 3:5, 3:12, 3:21, 21:1-7, 22:1-5.]

Finally, the beginning of this life with the Holy Spirit must be, in accordance with Scripture and again with the very "nature of things," in the change that is described as *union with Christ*, a change which is variously designated, in Scripture, from as many different points of view, conversion, regeneration, remission, justification, salvation, reconciliation, etc. Moreover, the New Testament teaches clearly that this change, this union with Christ, is consummated, for the repentant believer, in the institution of Christian baptism. Note the following: Rom. 10:10— "with the heart man believeth unto righteousness" (justification); 2 Cor. 7:10—"godly sorrow worketh repentance unto salvation"; Rom. 10:10—"with the mouth confession is made unto salvation"; Gal. 3:27—"for as many of you as were baptized into Christ did put on Christ." Hence, baptism—the baptism of the Great Commission (Matt. 28: 19-20) is Scripturally designated explicitly, "the washing of regeneration" (Tit. 3: 5-6; cf. John 3: 5, Eph. 5: 26, Acts 22: 16). In the sixth chapter of Romans, the Apostle makes this fundamental truth too clear for any possible misunderstanding by any person who is intellectually honest with God and with himself. "Are ye ignorant," says he, "that all we who were baptized into Christ Jesus were baptized into his death? We were buried therefore with him through baptism into death: that like as Christ was raised from the dead through the glory of the Father, so we also might walk in newness of life. For if we have become united with him in the likeness of his death, we shall be also in the likeness of his resurrection," etc. (Rom. 6: 4-7). It is in the *likeness* of Christ's death, that is, in baptism, which *most certainly* is a burial in water followed by a raising up therefrom—*and not anything less than this*—that the penitent believer is betrothed to Him, later to be literally married to Him, the Bridegroom, whose Bride the Church is (Rev. 19: 6-9).

2 Cor. 11:2—For I am jealous over you with a godly jealousy: for I espoused you to one husband, that I might present you as a pure virgin unto Christ. John 3:29—He that hath the bride is the bridegroom. Gal. 4:26—But the Jerusalem that is above is free, which is our mother. Eph. 5:22ff.—Wives, be in subjection unto your own husbands, as unto the Lord. For the husband is the head of the wife, as Christ also is head of the church, being himself the savior of the body. But as the church is subject to Christ, so let wives also be to their husbands in everything. Husbands, love your wives, even as Christ also loved the church and gave himself up for it, that he might sanctify it, having cleansed it by the washing of water with the word, that he might present the church to himself a glorious church, not having spot or wrinkle or any such thing; but that it should be holy and without blemish. Even so ought husbands also to love their wives as their own bodies. He that loveth his own wife loveth himself; for no man ever yet hated his own flesh, but nourisheth and cherisheth it, even as Christ also the church; because we are members of his body. For this cause shall a man leave his father and mother, and shall cleave to his wife; and the two shall become one flesh. This mystery is great: but I speak in regard of Christ and of the church.

There has been a tendency in all ages for unbelief to rail at the church. But the church, although made up of human beings, many of whom are at times decidedly *human*, still and all is a divine institution *per se*, with a divine foundation, a divine head, a divine fellowship, and a divine destiny: these are facts that nothing can change. It was not until Saul of Tarsus lay blinded and prostrate on the ground before the gates of Damascus that he realized for the first time that in persecuting the church he had been persecuting Christ (Acts 9:3-7, 22:6-16, 26:12-19). The simple fact is that, as Augustine has put it precisely, "He cannot have God for his Father who refuses to have the church for his mother."

Heb. 12:22—but ye are come unto mount Zion, and unto the city of the living God, the heavenly Jerusalem, etc. Also v. 23—to the general assembly and church of the firstborn who are enrolled in heaven, and to God the Judge of all, and to the spirits of just men made perfect, and to Jesus the mediator of a new covenant, etc. Rev. 3:12— I will write upon him [the Overcomer] the name of my God, and the name of the city of my God, the new Jerusalem, which cometh down out of heaven from my God, and mine own new name. Rev. 21:2—And I saw the holy city, new Jerusalem, coming down out of heaven from God, made ready as a bride adorned for her husband. Also vv. 9, 10— And he [the angel] spake with me, saying, Come hither, I will show thee the bride, the wife of the Lamb. And he carried me away in the Spirit to a mountain great and high, and showed me the holy city Jerusalem, coming down out of heaven from God, etc. (Cf. Gen. 2:20-24, Hos. 2:19. Heb. 11:8-10, 1 Thess. 4:13-17, 2 Thess. 2:13-15; Rev. 21: 11-27, 22:1-5). 2 Pet. 3:10-13, But the day of the Lord will come as a thief; in the which the heavens shall pass away with a great noise, and the elements shall be dissolved with fervent heat, and the earth and the works that are therein shall be burned up. Seeing that these things are thus all to be dissolved, what manner of persons ought ye to be in all holy living and godliness, looking for and earnestly desiring the coming of the day of God, by reason of which the heavens being on fire shall be dissolved, and the elements shall melt with fervent heat? But, according to his promise, we look for new heavens and a new earth, wherein dwelleth righteousness. [Cf. also Acts 3:19-21, Rev. 21:1, Rom. 8:21; Isa. 60:15-22, 65:17-25; also the entire Song of Solomon.]

Obviously, Christian baptism must embody a death and resurrection in order to serve as a complete testimony (witness) to the facts of the Gospel: cf. again Rom. 6:17 and 1 Cor. 15:1-4). Not that the water of baptism itself washes away sin—of course not; but that in baptism, as in every ordinance of God of a visible character, human faith meets Divine Grace in the appointment divinely designated; and where such a meeting takes place, the blessing connected by the word of God with the particular appointment is always conferred upon the obedient believer. This is *always* the case, for the simple reason that God keeps His promises. Now the divine blessing expressly connected by the word of God with Christian baptism, for the penitent believer, is remission of sins (Acts 2:38); and when sin is remitted—the pardon takes place, of course, in the Mind of God—then the union of the believer with Christ is the perfectly natural consequence. It is the blood of Christ, as the all-sufficient Atonement (Covering) that cleanseth from sin (1 John 1:7, Tit. 2:14, Heb. 9:14, Rev. 7:14, Rom. 3:26, John 1:29); the place divinely appointed for the believer to meet the efficacy of the Blood is the grave of water (John 3:5, 19:34; Tit. 3:5).

We therefore summarize here, as follows: 1. Man's ultimate intrinsic end, the end to which he is ordained by his Creator, is Union with God, Beatitude, Life Everlasting. 2. His ultimate extrinsic end is the glory of God (Matt. 25:34-40, Isa. 43:7, Rev. 4:11). 3. The one essential prerequisite or means to the attainment of these ends is the life with the Holy Spirit. 4. The beginning of this life with the Holy Spirit—the Spiritual Life— is in Union with Christ on the basis of the terms of pardon, namely, faith in Christ, repentance toward Christ, confession of Christ, and baptism into Christ. 5. The Spiritual Life embodies the three phases as described above—the *purgative*, the *illuminative*, and finally the *unitive;* and the end product is the fully redeemed person, redeemed in spirit and soul and body (1 Thess. 5:23). These five fundamental propositions, on which the Scriptures speak with uniform consistency and clarity, constitute the framework of the present series of studies of the Holy Spirit and His operations.

## 5. Difficulties of Our Subject

Certainly if the truth regarding the person and work of the Holy Spirit is to be preserved and disseminated at all, it will have to be done by the Church. The "world," said Jesus, cannot receive the Holy Spirit, "for it beholdeth him not, neither knoweth him" (John 14:17). The "world" simply is not interested in the Holy Spirit, in fact, the "world" cannot be expected to be interested in Him. Speculative theologians, analytical critics, demythologizers, and all their kind, like the disciples whom Paul found at Ephesus (Acts 19:2), seem not to realize that there is a Holy Spirit, or at least choose deliberately to ignore the claims He makes for Himself in Scripture. In the very nature of things, the Church alone—the true evangelical Church —can be looked to, to keep alive in the hearts of men whatever knowledge they may possess of the Spirit's being and activity (1 Tim. 3:15). Why, then, is the doctrine of the Holy Spirit so generally neglected by the Church of our time?

Undoubtedly one reason for this neglect is *the press of secularism on the spiritual life of the Church.* We are living in an age of things: gadgets of all kinds, visible and tangible things, physical things, mechanical things, things shaken up, pressed

25

down, running over. The circumstances of our mechanical and highly artificial civilization are surely anything but conducive to thinking in spiritual terms. The human race is so dominated at the present moment by *the sheer tyranny of things* that it stands in grave danger of losing its sense of the higher values of life, and hence the very music and dream of living. Somehow— perhaps through great suffering?—we shall have to learn anew the fundamental truth stated by our Lord, that "a man's life consisteth not in the abundance of the things which he possesseth" (Luke 12:15).

Another explanation, perhaps, of the Church's neglect of the doctrine of the Holy Spirit is in *the adverse reaction occasioned by the extravagances of those who carry the doctrine to such fanatical extremes.* The tendency on the part of certain sectists and cultists to ascribe to an operation of the Holy Spirit almost every impulse, emotion, and passion of the human soul, is derogatory to religion in general and most of all to the Spirit Himself. Such travesties on religion result not only in alienating thoughtful people from the Church, but also in discouraging intelligent churchmen from attempting to expound the doctrine of the Spirit lest they, too, fall into some grievous error. The ecstatic and orgiastic extravagances of so-called "Holiness" sects and mystic cults are anything but helpful to the spread of the Christian faith.

Then, again, *the obvious centrality of Christ in the Christian System, and in fact of the entire revelation of God to man, as recorded in the Bible,* may be cited as another reason for the prevailing tendency to overlook the Holy Spirit and His role in human redemption. The principal task of the Spirit in all ages, and especially in the present Dispensation, has been to testify concerning the Messiah. As Jesus Himself put it, in conversation with His disciples (the eleven) on the night of His betrayal, "Howbeit when he, the Spirit of truth, is come, he shall guide you into all the truth. . . . *He shall glorify me*: for he shall take of mine, and shall declare it unto you" (John 16:13-15). The Bible itself is the record of God's progressive revelation to man through the agency of the Spirit. This entire revelation centers in the person and work of the Messiah: in the Old Testament, the Messiah who is to come; in the New Testament, the same Messiah, who has come, who has died for our sins, been buried, and raised up from the dead, and exalted to the right hand of God the Father. The revelation, however, is the work of the Spirit of God. In the words of an eminent

26

writer on the subject, this—the glorification of Christ—is "the temporal mission of the Holy Ghost." In Scripture, we have the complete testimony of the Spirit regarding the mission and work of Messiah, the Great Demonstration that Jesus is the Christ, the Son of the living God (Matt. 16:16; John 20:30-31; Rom. 10:9-10). With becoming modesty, therefore, the Holy Spirit has kept Himself in the background. Nor has He indicated anywhere on the sacred pages that He would have men exalt and glorify Him; rather, He would have them honor, exalt, and glorify the Christ, the Anointed One. For in serving and glorifying Christ, they also exalt and glorify the Spirit who bears witness to Him. "He shall glorify me," said Jesus explicitly, of the Spirit.

Again, it seems evident that another prime reason for the neglect of the doctrine of the Spirit in our time lies *in the difficulties inherent in the nature of the subject itself.*

In the first place, in this connection, there is *the great difficulty of trying to apprehend, much more to comprehend, the being and nature of a Reality of whom it is impossible for us to get a mental image.* Human thought is carried on largely in terms of images in the mind and of the language (symbolism) by which the meaning of these images may be communicated; indeed it is doubtful that, without the power of receiving and retaining images, man in his present state would be able to think at all. By its very nature the human mind, unaided by divine revelation, is prone to conceive of God only in those forms of which mental images can be derived: hence the worship of the sun, moon, earth, and stars; of animals, plants, and even insects; and the worship of gross and gruesome idols. These are all things that can be seen, and men adhere instinctively to the things they can see. But the Spirit of God is not to be apprehended through the physical senses: His order of being lies beyond the physical (John 1:18, Exo. 33:20, Col. 1:15, 1 Tim. 6:16, 1 John 4:12, 2 Cor. 4:18). He is to be apprehended only through the intellect, affection, and will: that is to say, only through the "inner man" (2 Cor. 4:16). *And even this apprehension has to be intelligently examined and kept within proper bounds by what He has revealed about Himself in Scripture; otherwise, untold confusion is the result.* The difficulty here is precisely the difficulty involved in propagating a religion whose God is pure Spirit (John 4:24). This probably accounts for the fact that so many people—professing Christians though they may be—scarcely know that there is a Holy Spirit. They

27

seem incapable mentally of grasping the concept of an incorporeal Reality. This problem will always confront those who are trying to spread abroad in men's hearts a spiritual faith and life.

In the second place, there is the equally great difficulty of *the inadequacy of human language to communicate Divine thought and to bring Divine Realities down to the level of human comprehension.* This must have been the most profound problem encountered by our God Himself in His efforts to make known, through the Spirit, His Plan for the redemption of mankind. It accounts fully for the anthropomorphisms, types, symbols, metaphors, allegories, and parables of the Bible: to adapt His thoughts to our comprehension such devices are indispensable. The inadequacy of human language is the source of a great many of the problems which arise in our study of the Holy Spirit and His work. The profound mysteries of the subject, which are the mysteries of the very Being of God, and the mysteries of all other forms of being as well, appear to be shut out entirely from our human view: they are truths which simply lie too deep for words (Deut. 29:29). There are intimations in Scripture that the Spirit Himself labored under considerable difficulty in attempting to portray in words for future generations to read, some of the more profound events in the life of Christ and even some of the mysteries of His own operations in the created world. Perhaps, as Raymond Calkins has pointed out,[1] this difficulty is indicated by such words and phrases which occur not infrequently in the New Testament, as "like," "like as," "as if," "as it were," etc. Take, for instance, the scene at the baptism of Jesus: the opening of the heavens, the voice of the Father introducing His Only Begotten, and the descent of the Spirit upon the Son." "I have beheld," said John the Baptizer later, "the Spirit descending *as* a dove out of heaven; and it abode upon him" (John 1:32) This very simile shows that John found it difficult to describe the experience adequately in human language. Luke, who asserts in the prologue to his biography of Jesus, that he had obtained the information recorded therein from "eye—witnesses and ministers of the word" (Luke 1:2), clarifies the scene at the Jordan to some extent, but retains the simile. He says: "Jesus also having been baptized, and praying, the heaven was opened, and the Holy Spirit descended in a bodily form, *as* a dove, upon him" (Luke 3:21-22). Again, of the suffering of our Lord in Gethsemane, Luke writes: "And being in agony

1. *The Holy Spirit*, 105, 106.

28

he prayed more earnestly; and his sweat became *as it were* great drops of blood falling down upon the ground" (Luke 22:44). Luke is always precise in the use of language. Especially is this true of his description of the demonstrations which accompanied the descent of the Spirit upon the Apostles on the day of Pentecost. Luke was not there, of course, when it happened. He is relating what he has been told by others who were present on the occasion. "Suddenly there came from heaven," he tells us, "a sound *as of* the rushing of a mighty wind, and it filled all the house where they were sitting. And there appeared unto them tongues parting asunder, *like as of fire;* and it sat upon each of them" (Acts 2:1-3). Not a real wind, but the *sound* as of a mighty wind; not actual fire, but tongues parting asunder which had the appearance of flames of fire. These similes—and there are many others of like import throughout the Bible—all indicate how difficult it must have been for the Spirit, in preparing the permanent record of these earth-shaking spiritual experiences, to describe them adequately in human language. Of course, there is nothing surprising about this fact. The mysteries of the Being of God (the "ultimates") are facts which in themselves lie beyond the pale of human experience and are therefore always in some measure incommunicable to us; hence, they must be apprehended by faith (Heb. 11:6). We shall have to be content, therefore, with only partial knowledge, such knowledge as the Holy Spirit has seen fit to vouchsafe us, through the instrumentality of inspired men, in the Word of Life. For the fact remains that in this earthly life we do "see in a mirror, darkly." Our physical senses, instead of opening the real world to our view, actually shut it out. This of course is in adaptation to our present terrestrial environment. Only when we shall have laid aside the veil of this flesh shall we be able to discern Reality "face to face." This, moreover, will surely be a psychical rather than a physical vision. (Cf. 1 Cor. 13:12, 1 John 3:2, 2 Cor. 5:7, James 1:23, Phil. 3:12, Matt. 5:8). Hence, insofar as this present life is concerned we shall have to be content with what has been revealed (cf. again Deut. 29:29).

## 6. The Proper Approach to the Subject

How shall we approach the study of the Holy Spirit and His work? This is a matter of utmost importance.

In the first place, *we must come to our task in profound*

29

*humility and with profound reverence.* Jesus said on one occasion: "Every sin and blasphemy shall be forgiven unto men; but the blasphemy against the Spirit shall not be forgiven. And whosoever shall speak a word against the son of man, it shall be forgiven him; but whosoever shall speak against the Holy Spirit, it shall not be forgiven him, neither in this world, nor in that which is to come" (Matt. 12:31, 32). Certainly these words should be sufficient to impress upon our minds the deep seriousness of our subject. Let my right arm be withered, let my body be made impotent, let my tongue be silenced forever, ere I should speak or write a single word derogatory of the Spirit of God. I might in a moment of despair deny the deity of Jesus, but if I experience a change of heart, about face, and accept Him as the Son of the living God, I may enjoy the salvation which He offers on the terms of the Gospel. I may, as a member of His body, neglect His ordinances; I may forsake the assembly of the saints; I may turn my back upon Him in neglect and indifference; but if I come to myself and return to the fold in penitence and contrition, the Father will receive me back with outstretched arms (Luke 15:20). But if I as an alien blaspheme the Spirit, or as professing Christian do despite unto the Spirit of grace (Heb. 10:26-29), I am in grave danger of alienating myself forever from God's mercy. In view of these facts, therefore, one dare not approach the study of the Holy Spirit in a flippant or frivolous state of mind; the very gravity of the subject forbids such an attitude.

In the second place, *we shall have to decide at the very outset what sources of information we shall accept as reliable, and what sources we shall reject as unreliable, with respect to the Holy Spirit and His operations.* This is perhaps the most important decision we shall be called upon to make: in fact everything depends upon it. Now, as far as I know, there are only two sources to which we can appeal: 1. To human impulses, emotions and experiences. 2. To the Bible itself, which is the Book of the Spirit.

Are we justified in accepting human emotions and experiences as trustworthy sources of information regarding the Holy Spirit and His work? Time was, not so long ago, when prevailing systems of theology were prone to explain almost every emotional experience, within a "religious" setting, as an operation of the Holy Spirit. People were told that they could not come to God for salvation, but must work, watch and pray for God to come to them in some "extraordinary" manner. They were told that they were as dead spiritually as Lazarus was physically, and that as a special miracle was required to bring Lazarus forth from the grave, so a special "miraculous" manifestation of the Spirit was necessary to lift them out of the grave of moral corruption into which they, with all mankind, had fallen. The dogma of "miraculous conversion" was but the natural corollary of those of "total depravity," "original sin," and "baptismal regeneration" (as exemplified in so-called infant "baptism."). Hence they must hear the anthem of a choir invisible; they must see a ball of heavenly fire; they must be visited by an angel; or they must be caught and held in the grip of a mysterious and overpowering ecstacy, before they could be considered "elected" to receive the benefits of God's grace. Every conversion was looked upon as a "miracle"—a special act of Divine mercy, by which the sinful ("totally depraved") human heart was "fertilized," so to speak, by this special operation of the Spirit and thus made capable of attending to, and receiving, the Gospel call (2 Thess. 2:14, Rom. 1:16). Under this view, grace was defined as "a supernatural gift infused in the soul, making it pleasing to God." Thus conversion was described as *mystical*, and not *psychological* as presented in Scripture (Isa. 6:9-10, Matt. 13:14-15, Acts 28:25-27). "He that will, let him take the water of life freely" (Rev. 22:17) was a forgotten text.

Under this teaching alien sinners were exhorted to pray for the spirit to come upon them "with saving power." Some would pray for days at a stretch without receiving any unusual "experience," and failing to do so would give up in despair feeling themselves hopelessly lost. Others would become ecstatic: some going into trances, some even into a state of catalepsy. Others would roll on straw conveniently provided for the purpose, whence they were dubbed "Holy Rollers." And there were those who, though unable to attain to a state of emotional frenzy, would nevertheless experience an inward glow which they accepted as evidence of their divine "call." In some cases, on relating their "experiences," they were accepted as candidates for baptism by the vote of the local congregation; in others, the congregation, while not taking any formal vote, would accept them into fellowship according to the "rules of the church." Eminent revivalists would report some "converted"; others, "hopefully converted"; others, "joyously converted"; and still others, "gloriously converted."

I recall two cases in my own personal experience. A good woman told me on one occasion, in the course of a meeting I was holding for a church in Kentucky, that she was waiting to be "knocked down" like Saul of Tarsus was; short of that, she said, she could never consider herself genuinely converted. (To be sure, there was no likelihood of her ever being called to the apostleship; cf. 1 Cor. 9:1.) At another time I was holding a series of meetings in a small town in Indiana. A certain gentleman attended the meetings quite regularly, who had been born and reared a Quaker. One day he went home, became involved in an argument with his wife, which he finally settled by giving her a good trouncing. Later he told his neighbors that the "Spirit" had "moved" him to administer the "thrashing" as a corrective measure. This of course was one of the many cases in which individuals twist their "theology" to support their deeds instead of conforming their deeds to Bible teaching.

The Friends (Quakers), though dignified in their religious practice, and sane and honorable in their living, and for whose piety we have the highest regard, are nevertheless proponents of this type of theology. They meet for public worship, but neither say nor do anything until "the Spirit moves" someone to sing, pray or exhort. They reject water baptism altogether and claim Holy Spirit baptism. In this respect they are consistent, to say the least. The Apostle tells us expressly that there is "one Lord, one faith, one baptism" (Eph. 4:5). In the light of this assertion, obviously there cannot be two baptisms connected with Christian faith and practice: there must be only one. If therefore we are to experience Holy Spirit baptism, we should abandon baptism in water; conversely, if we are to be baptized in water, we should not expect to receive Holy Spirit baptism. This certainly is one point on which there can be no disagreement on the part of all who profess to follow the New Testament. What, then, did Jesus mean when He said: "Go ye therefore, and make disciples of all the nations, baptizing them into the name of the Father and of the Son and of the Holy Spirit"? (Matt. 28:19). Surely, the records of the conversions given us in the Book of Acts provide the correct answer to this question beyond possibility of reasonable doubt!

The question before us here is this: *Are we justified in accepting human emotions and experiences as reliable sources of information concerning the Holy Spirit and His work?* I answer emphatically, No: for the following reasons:

32

**1.** *There is no support for this type of "theology" in the New Testament.* There is not the slightest ground anywhere in Scripture for the assumption that the human mind itself is incapable of responding to the Gospel message; that is to say, that a special operation of the Spirit is required, in addition to the preaching of the Gospel, to quicken the mind into receptivity. On the contrary, we are told explicitly that "the gospel is the power of God unto salvation to every one that believeth" (Rom. 1:16); not just *a* power, mind you, nor *one of the* powers, but THE power of God unto salvation. Similarly we are told that "belief cometh of hearing, and hearing by the word of Christ" (Rom. 10:17). The whole Christian missionary enterprise has, from the very beginning, been predicated on the fact that where there is no Gospel message, no Bible to be read, no Gospel to be preached and heard, there can be no faith, no conversion to Christ. (1 Cor. 1:21, Rom. 10:14-15, 1 Thess. 2:13, etc.). Cf. Rom. 10:6-10: here we are told expressly that "the righteousness which is of faith" asks not for a special manifestation of Christ, either from heaven above or by a return from the dead, but trusts in the word of faith, which is always near at hand for reception into the heart (Cf. 1 Cor. 15:1-8, Luke 16:29-31). There is no evidence anywhere in Scripture to indicate that any faculties are imparted to the human mind in conversion, or any old ones annihilated. The renovation of the human intellect, or purification of the human heart, is not effected by the creation of new faculties or affections. What does happen in conversion is that a new Object (a Person, the Lord Jesus Christ Himself, the One Altogether Lovely) is presented to the faculties, affections, and volitions of men; this new Object apprehends and engages the powers of the human understanding, captivates the affection of the human being, and consequently directs or draws the whole man into new aims, endeavors, and pursuits. (Cf. John 12:32, Rom. 2:4, 2 Cor. 7:10). Whatever quickening of the mind or heart that may take place at the beginning of conversion is accomplished by the entrance of the Word, because the Spirit is in the Word and His Spirit-power is exercised through the Word. (Cf. Psa. 119:130, 119:105; John 6:63). There is not one iota of Scripture evidence that the Holy Spirit ever effected the conversion of a single soul *independently* of the preaching or hearing (or reading) of the Word; nor is there any evidence that, in conversion, the Holy Spirit is compelled to operate *in addition to* the Word. On the contrary, throughout the New Testament, the Gospel is presented as a great amnesty proclama-

33

tion to all people on specific terms. These terms are belief in Christ, repentance from sin, confession of Christ, and baptism into Christ (Matt. 16:16, John 20:30-31, Acts 16:31, Rom. 10:9-10, Luke 13:3, 2 Cor. 7:10, Matt. 10:32-33, Acts 2:38, Gal. 3:26-27, Rev. 22:17).

2. In the second place, observation proves *that this type of "theology" thrives largely among the more emotionally controlled persons.* The more ignorant a man is, the more superstitious he is; and the more superstitious, the more susceptible he is to all forms of religious fanaticism. Orgiastic and ecstatic cults have flourished in all ages, and particularly in the ancient pagan world (as in the Dionysiac, Orphic, and Mithraic "mystery religions"). So-called "Holiness" cults of modern times follow the same general psychological patterns of emotional intensity and frenzy.

3. In the third place, *modern psychic research has proved that the extremes of emotion oftentimes brought on by a undisciplined revivalism can be induced in a setting that is wholly non-religious in character.* The facts of hypnosis and auto-hypnosis are too well-known today to be questioned. Men do have the power to hypnotize other persons, even to reduce them to a state of catalepsy; and men do under certain psychological conditions hypnotize themselves. Such phenomena have been demonstrated independently of any religious setting. The simple fact is that the person who goes into a trance is self-hypnotized. As a matter of fact all the phenomena of emotional revivalism can be explained an purely psychic grounds.

4. *In the fourth place, persons who follow the leading of their emotions exclusively, in the matter of religious experience, soon become fanatics.* They become proud and puffed up in their own conceits, and utterly blind to their own faults. I knew a man one time who was a master at inducing trances in revival meetings, and who prayed at home so long and loudly that he kept his neighbors awake into the wee small hours of the morning. It was discovered later that he was responsible for the disappearance of a number of luscious hams from his neighbors' smokehouses. As a pioneer evangelist once put it: There are two classes of church members to be watched,—the *petrified* who are dried up and ready to be blown away, and the *sanctified* (that is, the "perfectionists"), who have quit worshiping God and gone to worshiping themselves.

5. In the fifth place, *there can be no reason for thinking that the Holy Spirit is the author of all the conflicting experi-*

34

*ences and "revelations" which men have claimed for themselves.*
Practically all the isms and cults abroad in the world to-day
are justified by their protagonists on the ground that they had
their origin in "religious experience," that is, in some special
"revelation" or "illumination" from the Spirit of God. If this
be true why in the name of reason are they so contradictory?
Surely the Holy Spirit does not "inspire" or "illumine" one man
to preach up Lutheranism for example, and another at the same
time to preach it down. Men who uphold the isms of denominational Christianity certainly are not prompted to do so by the
Holy Spirit. The Holy Spirit is the Author of order, not of dis-
cord or disunity. It is sheer blasphemy to attribute all the confusion and denominationalism of present-day Christianity to the
Spirit of God. The same argument holds good with respect to the
religious delusions and cults which are abroad in the earth; the
great majority of them have had their origin in alleged special
revelations from God. Joseph Smith, "the Prophet," claimed a
special revelation from God as a result of which we have the
Mormon hierarchy. Mrs. Ellen G. White claimed to have had a
special revelation in which she saw an angel pointing to the
Fourth Commandment; and on the strength of this alleged revo-
lation she founded Seventh-day Adventism. Mrs. Eddy was
forever hearing "voices," which, together with the manuscripts
of the professional mesmerist, Phineas P. Quimby, gave her inspiration to establish the system which she labeled "Christian
Science," and provided her as well with the content, substantially, of her textbook, *Science and Health*. (It is very doubtful
that Mrs. Eddy was sufficiently educated to have known that the
basic propositions of her system are Berkeleian and Hegelian.)
Emanuel Swedenborg claimed that when he was about 46 years
old (in the year 1744, to be exact) the perceptive powers of his
spirit were suddenly energized, and that from that time on until
his death in 1772 he enjoyed habitual intercourse with the spiritual world and its inhabitants. In his various works he has
given us elaborate descriptions of heaven, hell, and what he
calls the intermediate "world of spirits." All this, of course, is
in striking contrast to the reticence of Jesus respecting the
character and conditions of the after-life. As a matter of fact,
neither Jesus nor the Apostles had much to say about heaven
or hell, except to assert the fact of their existence; the former
they describe as a condition of union with God, and the latter
a state of complete separation from—or loss of—God (2 Thess.
1: 7-10). No doubt the reason for this reticence is the fact that

35

human language is utterly inadequate to depict either the remorse of hell or the bliss of heaven; hence in the rare instances
in which the New Testament writers do attempt to portray either
state, the Spirit resorts to "pictorializing": heaven is described as
the holy city, the city that lieth four-square, whose walls, foundations and gates are constructed of all manner of precious stones,
etc.; and hell, on the other hand, is pictured as "the lake that
burneth with fire and brimstone, which is the second death," etc.
(Rev. 21:8, 21:9-27, 22:1-5). (Of course, if this is "figurative,"
may our good Lord deliver us from the real thing!)

Mohammed, the camel driver of Mecca, was another who
claimed to have been the recipient of special revelations, the
first of which occurred in the year 610; he heard (so his disciples
were persuaded to believe), a heavenly voice commanding him
to convey a message. From that time on to his death, Mohammed,
we are told, never doubted that he was in immediate contact
with God, and whenever circumstances called for an authoritative word, revelations were forthcoming. Hence the *Koran*
(principal form of the verb, "recite thou," and meaning "that
which is recited"), the sacred book of Islam, is literally the col-
lection of the "inspired" utterances of the "Prophet," which he
was ordered by Allah to "recite" to his people. Dowieism, Spiritualism, "Pentecostal Missions," "Truth Centers," "Foursquare
Gospels," and like impostures are invariably founded on claims
of special operations of the Holy Spirit, special "inspiration,"
"illumination," or "revelation." It is sheer nonsense, I repeat,
if not actual blasphemy, to attribute all this confusion to the
Holy Spirit, who is the Author of peace and concord only. Besides, we are told explicitly, in the New Testament, that *revelation* ended with the Apostles, and that *demonstration* came to
an end along with it; that in the New Testament revelation, and
canon, "all things that pertain until life and godliness" (2 Pet.
1:3) have been given. The New Testament presents to our
minds and hearts "the faith which was *once for all* delivered
unto the saints" (Jude 3). All this being true, we may be certain, it seems to me, that any one who has come before the
world since the days of the Apostles, claiming to have been the
recipient of a special revelation from God, is an impostor on
the face of it.

For all these reasons, therefore, and others to which I shall
omit calling attention here, I reject human experience as a
proper source of information regarding the Holy Spirit and His

work. As the proper means to such an end human experience is simply unreliable.

We might ask, in this connection, What is a genuine Christian experience? To this question, I reply (1) that the fundamental criterion of such an experience is that it be in harmony with the teaching of the Word of God, and (2) that the essence of such an experience is in the joint testimony of the Divine Spirit and the human spirit. As the Apostle Paul puts it: "For as many as are led by the Spirit of God, these are the sons of God. For ye received not the spirit of bondage again unto fear; but ye received the spirit of adoption, whereby we cry, Abba, Father. The Sprit himself beareth witness with our spirit, that we are children of God: and if children, then heirs; heirs of God, and joint-heirs with Christ" (Rom. 8:14-17). Note well that the Spirit of God does not testify *to* the human spirit, but that the Divine Spirit testifies *with* the human spirit, to one and the same fact, viz., that the human individual is a child of God. This, again, is in harmony with the nature of things: "For who among men knoweth the things of a man, save the spirit of the man, which is in him? even so the things of God none knoweth, save the Spirit of God" (1 Cor. 2:11). The Holy Spirit testifies, as always, by means of the Word of God; in the Word, He makes overtures to us and states the terms whereby we may be received into covenant relationship with God the Father. The human spirit, that is, the human being, knows beyond peradventure, and testifies, as to whether or not he has complied with the terms. The Holy Spirit tells us to believe; man's spirit tells him whether he does believe. The Holy Spirit tells us to repent of our sins; man's spirit tells him whether he has repented. The Holy Spirit tells us to confess Christ and to be baptized into Christ; man's spirit tells him whether he has made the Good Confession, whether he has been obedient from the heart unto the pattern of teaching (Rom. 6:17, 1 Cor. 15:1-4), *i.e.*, baptism, which exemplifies before the world the facts of the death, burial, and resurrection of Christ. In the Word, the Scripture, the Holy Spirit tells man what to do to lead the Spiritual Life, and man's spirit tells him whether he is following the leading of the Spirit and the Word; that is, his spirit tells him this, on condition that he studies to show himself approved unto God, and so cultivates in himself the mind which was in Christ Jesus (Phil. 2:5, 2 Tim. 2:15, I Pet. 2:2, 2 Pet. 3:18). Studies what? The Word, of course. Knowledge of the Word as communicated by the Spirit will inform him as to the essentials of Christian worship and the fruit of the Spiritual Life (cf. Acts 2:42, Gal. 5:22-25, 1 Cor. 16:1-4) What more need he ask for?

For example, the Holy Spirit tells us, through the apostolic testimony, what to do to receive pardon, namely, to believe on the Lord Jesus, to repent, to confess Him before witnesses, to be baptized into Him for remission of sins. Acts 16:31—"Believe on the Lord Jesus, and thou shalt be saved," etc. On the great Day of Pentecost, some three thousand persons cried out unto Peter and the rest of the Apostles, asking what they should do to be saved. What was the answer? Acts 2:38—"Repent ye, and be baptized every one of you in the name of Jesus Christ unto the remission of your sins," etc. On condition of their meeting these terms they were also promised the indwelling Spirit Himself. *This, for the present writer, is sufficient*: it is the Word, authorized by the Spirit of God. Do I need, then, that the Lord send me a special telegram to convince me that the letter is genuine and that the promise of God will be fulfilled? I think not. Faith takes God at His Word. The sin of the church in all ages has been that of belittling, downgrading, even ignoring the Word of God. What a shame!

No man can deny the testimony of his own spirit. He may deceive his fellows, but he cannot deceive either the Spirit of God or the spirit that is within himself. Hence a genuinely Christian experience consists in the joint testimony of these two witnesses. And the joy which attends such an experience, and one's subsequent growth in grace and in the knowledge of our Lord and Savior Jesus Christ, rests upon a sure foundation. An experience contrary to the Word of God cannot be a true Christian experience.

*What, then, is the only reliable source of information for us respecting the Holy Spirit and His work?* My answer is: *The Bible and the Bible alone.*

The Bible is the Book of the Spirit. It is the *only* Book of the Spirit. In the Bible we find, not what men have written about the Holy Spirit and His work, but what the Holy Spirit Himself has seen fit to reveal to us respecting His being and His operations. "But we received," says Paul, "not the spirit of the world, but the spirit which is from God; that we might know the things that were freely given to us of God. Which things also we speak, not in words which man's wisdom teacheth, but which the Spirit teacheth: combining spiritual things with spiritual words" (1 Cor. 2:12, 13); that is, revealing spiritual realities in spiritual language. The Bible claims to be the record of a revelation from God, vouchsafed us by the agency of the Spirit through the instrumentality of men qualified (by inspiration of the Spirit) for the task thus set before them. This revelation, and the record of it, was begun through holy men of old, inspired by the Spirit; it was perfected in Jesus, the Incarnate Word, who possessed the Spirit without measure; and it was completed by the Apostles, who were guided into all the truth by the same Spirit "sent forth from heaven" (1 Pet. 1:12). As the Bible is the only book known to mankind claiming the Holy Spirit for its Author, we must certainly go to the Bible and the Bible alone for whatever knowledge we may have, or may hope to have, of the Spirit and His work. In fact, without the Bible, we should scarcely know that there is a Holy Spirit.

For the sake of emphasis, we repeat, is it not in accordance with the very nature of things as we know them that revelation should be, in a special sense, a work of the Spirit of God? How indeed could it be otherwise if our Heavenly Father is a personal God? "For," as Paul puts it,

who among men knoweth the things of a man, save the spirit of the man, which is in him? even so the things of God none knoweth, save the Spirit of God (1 Cor. 2:11).

Again: "For the Spirit searcheth all things, yea, the deep, things of God" (1 Cor. 2:10). To the Spirit of God we are immediately indebted for all that is known, or knowable, of God, of the unseen world, or of the ultimate destinies of men. All that ancient or modern pagans pretend to have known or to know of these sublime topics, has either been borrowed from the oracles of the Revealer of secrets, or else is mere conceit or conjecture of their own making. The simple fact is, that the truth to be believed by man respecting his own origin, constitution, and proper ends, could never have been known but by revelation of the Sprit. How profoundly thankful we should be, then, that our God has not left us in darkness, in that gross darkness in which heathen nations are still struggling and suffering, but has, by His Spirit, revealed His plan for our salvation so clearly that the wayfaring man, though a fool, need not err the rein!

Now to him that is able to establish you according to my gospel and the preaching of Jesus Christ, according to the revelation of the mystery which hath been kept in silence through times eternal, but now is manifested, and by the scriptures of the prophets, according to the commandment of the eternal God, is made known unto all the

39

nations unto obedience of faith: to the only wise God, through Jesus Christ, to whom be the glory for ever. Amen. (Rom. 16:25-27).

A final word here, in passing, regarding the significance of *feeling* in Christian faith and practice. Christianity is preeminently the religion of joy that comes from love and service toward God and toward our fellows. *He who puts feeling before the doing* puts the cart before the horse. We are reminded of the story of the farmer who, one wintry day, was passing his neighbor's stretch of timberland afoot, and seeing the latter standing knee deep in the snow at the base of a tree with an axe in his hand, shouted "Is there anything the matter, neighbor?" "nothing at all," was the reply. "Then why do you stand there in the snow doing nothing?" "Oh," replied the other, "I am waiting to get warm. When I do get warm, I'll cut down this tree." "Silly fellow," said the passer-by, after a pause, "Why don't you light in and start chopping, and you'll soon get warm!" The point is that both Scripture and experience confirm the fact that *feeling good follows the doing good*. Christianity, again we say, is *par excellence* the religion of joy; the Christian faith is the truly triumphant faith. "This is the victory that hath overcome the world, even our faith" (1 John 5:4). I do not find in Scripture any statement to the effect that "he that believeth and feeleth alright shall be saved." The question always asked is, "What must I do?" (Acts 2:38, 11:14, 16:30, 22:10). Moreover, in all these cases of conversion reported to us in Acts, in which special mention is made of *rejoicing,* it should be noted that the rejoicing is, without exception, said to have followed baptism (Acts 2:41ff.; 8:18, 12; 8:39; 16:14-15; 16:30-34; cf. 9:17, 18). Why so? Obviously, because it was made clear in apostolic preaching that pardon, remission, justification, etc., *follows, but does not precede, baptism.* Hence, in accord with John 3:3-7 and Matt. 28:19-20, Christian baptism is Scripturally designated the "washing of regeneration" (Tit. 3:5).

## 7. The Language of the Spirit

In the Book of Nature, as it has already been stated, we may find revealed God's "everlasting power and divinity."

Psa. 19:1, 2—The heavens declare the glory of God; And the firmament showeth his handiwork. Day unto day uttereth speech, and night unto night showeth knowledge. Psa. 8:3, 4—When I consider thy heavens, the work of thy fingers, The moon and the stars, which thou hast ordained; What is man, that thou art mindful of him? And the son of man, that thou visitest him? Psa. 89:5—And the heavens shall praise thy wonders, O Jehovah. Rom. 1:20—For the invisible things of him since the creation of the world are clearly seen, being perceived through the things that are made, even his everlasting power and divinity.

This natural revelation, however, is insufficient to meet all the needs of man's nature. Neither human reason nor intuition can throw much light on certain matters the knowledge of which is indispensable to man's quest for salvation and to his attainment of his natural and proper end, which is ultimate union with God in knowledge and love, Beatitude, the Life Everlasting. Among such matters are the following: the tripersonality of God, atonement, pardon or remission of sin, the proper means and modes of worship, survival after death, and personal immortality. Man is a creature. He has nothing to do with his being in the world, and very little to do with his going out of it; and while he is in the world, he is completely dependent upon Nature and Nature's God for the food that he eats, the water that he drinks, the air that he breathes, and even the very ground on which he walks. Moreover, man is imperfect; he is in sin, and he knows it; no honest person would ever think of denying the fact. Man is in sin, and natural religion is powerless to point the way out. The tenets of natural religion are at best but guesses at the riddles of the universe.

Natural revelation fails utterly to make known to us the higher attributes of Spirit. Professor Wm. James has well said:

> If there be a divine Spirit of the universe, nature, such as we know her, can not possibly be its ultimate word to man. Either there is no Spirit revealed in nature, or else it is inadequately revealed there; and, as all the higher religions have assumed, what we call visible nature, or *this* world, must be a veil or surface-show whose full meaning resides in a supplementary unseen or *other* world.[1]

In view, therefore, of the inadequacy of natural revelation, the special revelation of God's love and mercy, in the unfolding of the divine Plan of Redemption for man, became a necessity. This revelation complements, confirms, and enlarges the knowledge of God that is to be derived from nature. It remedies the defects of, and throws light upon, the problems of natural religion. The character of this final revelation was that of a continuous historical development; that is to say, it was—and is— progressive: "first the blade, then the ear, then the full grain

---

1. Wm. James, art., "Is Life Worth Living?" in *International Journal of Ethics*, Oct., 1895. Quoted by A. H. Strong, *Systematic Theology*, One-Volume Edition, p. 111.

in the ear" (Mark 4:28). In early ages, it was given only in germ, then was more fully unfolded as the race became better prepared to receive it. It will be consummated in the ultimate production of a holy redeemed race—the final phase of the whole Creative Process.

This revelation was wrought out first in the arena of human history. It embraced such events as the following: (1) the mysterious oracle that the Seed of the Woman should bruise the Serpent's head (Gen. 3:15),[1] (2) the lives and experiences of the antediluvians, especially those of the line of Seth, (3) the Call of Abraham and the Abrahamic Promise, (4) the organization of the Hebrew Theocracy under Moses, (5) the work of the Hebrew Prophets culminating in the ministry of John the Baptizer, (6) the sequence of typical and allegorical events and institutions of the entire Old Covenant which had only "a shadow of the good things to come, not the very image of the things" themselves (Heb. 10:1), (7) the Incarnation, Ministry, Miracles, Atoning Death, Resurrection, and Ascension of the Messiah, (8) the descent of the Holy Spirit on Pentecost and the incorporation of the Body of Christ, and (9) the subsequent preaching of the Gospel for a testimony unto all the nations (Matt. 24:14). Whereas the record of this revelation came to an end with the apostolic writings, the revelation itself goes on, in the lives of the saints. As the personal Christ was the incarnation of God in the world, so, throughout the present Dispensation, the Church is the incarnation of Christ. As Paul, writing of all Christians, puts it: "Ye are our epistle, written in our hearts, known and read of all men." To this he adds:

being made manifest that ye are an epistle of Christ, ministered by us, written not with ink, but with the Spirit of the living God; not in tables of stone, but in tables that are hearts of flesh (2 Cor. 3:2, 3).

Or, as some have stated the same fundamental truths, from Adam to Abraham we have the Gospel in the *purpose* of God, at best only in intimation; from Abraham to Isaiah, we have the Gospel in *promise*, that is, in the Abrahamic Promise; from Isaiah to Malachi, we have the Gospel in *prophecy;* throughout the personal ministry of Jesus, we have it in *preparation;* but since Pentecost A.D. 30, we have the Gospel in *fact*. The facts of the Gospel, we are told expressly, are the death, burial and resurrection of Christ (1 Cor. 15:1-4). These facts were proclaimed

---

1. Jesus of Nazareth is the only Person who ever came before the world claiming to be the Seed of a Woman exclusively. Never in all His teaching does he refer to anyone but God Himself as His Father.

for the first time *as facts* on the Day of Pentecost, at the inauguration of the New Institution, the Christian System (Acts 2:22-36). The truth to be remembered especially is that *all the events in this divine unfolding have been, or are being, wrought in the fields of human activity and history.*

Now in considering this progressive revelation, there is also the *record* of it to be considered. "Revelation" is a term which as we use it, may have reference either (1) to the series of pertinent events in themselves, that is, the events in the unfolding of the divine Plan of Redemption throughout human history; or (2) to the record which embraces the description of those events and the disclosure of their significance for man. This record, as it has already been made clear, has been embodied by the agency of the Spirit of God, through the instrumentality of inspired men, in written and accessible documents. These documents, some sixty-six in all, constitute our Bible. This we may properly designate the secondary or *documentary,* as distinguished from the *historical,* revelation.

This documentary revelation is, moreover, the product of *inspiration.* Inspiration is the name given to that activity of the Spirit whereby He has communicated to us the Thought of God (which is the expression of the Will of God) essential to our salvation and to the attainment of our ultimate end, and has in addition supervised the embodiment of that Thought in the written documents which make up our Bible, thereby guaranteeing the trustworthiness of those documents. The word "inspire" itself derives from the Latin verb, *inspiro,* the infinitive form of which is *inspirare,* meaning "to breathe into." The greatest literary works of all time are, despite their excellence, but the products of human genius. Scripture, on the other hand, is unique: it is *God-breathed* literature.

2 Tim. 3:16, 17—Every scripture inspired of God is also profitable for teaching, for reproof, for correction, for instruction which is in righteousness; that the man of God may be complete, furnished completely unto every good work. 1 Thess. 2:13—And for this cause we also thank God without ceasing, that, when ye received from us the word of the message, even the word of God, ye accepted it not as the word of men, but, as it is in truth, the word of God, which also worketh in you that believe.

It is not my intention to put forward here any particular theory of inspiration. That subject hardly comes within the scope of the present treatise. Suffice it so say, however, in this connection, that *inspiration* may, in the first place, have issued forth in the revelation of new truth to mankind. It may, in the second place, have brought about the quickening of men's minds to recall and to properly interpret truths already communicated. This latter phenomenon we call *illumination*. Both of these functions are clearly indicated in the words of Jesus to the Apostles:

But the Comforter, even the Holy Spirit, whom the Father will send in my name, he shall teach you all things, and bring to your remembrance all that I said unto you (John 14:26).

Again:

Howbeit when he, the Spirit of truth, is come, he shall guide you into all the truth; for he shall not speak from himself; but what things soever he shall hear, these shall he speak; and he shall declare unto you the things that are to come. He shall glorify me: for he shall take of mine, and shall declare it unto you (John 16:13, 14).

Or again, inspiration may, in the third place, signify only a *supervisory* activity sufficient to guarantee the inspired writer against error. In Luke's Gospel, for example, we have an instance of *supervisory* inspiration. Luke states expressly that his work is essentially a history; that he has obtained the material which he presents from those "who from the beginning were eyewitnesses and ministers of the word." And at the close of his Preface he vouches in no uncertain terms for the trustworthiness of what he writes. He says:

It seemed good to me also, having traced the course of all things accurately from the first, to write unto thee in order, most excellent Theophilus; that thou *mightest know the certainty concerning the things wherein thou wast instructed* (Luke 1:1-4).

In any case, inspiration is fundamentally the guarantee of trustworthiness, and is to be evaluated not so much from the viewpoint of method as from that of result. It is the warrant of the infallibility of the inspired writer and of the trustworthiness of his writings.

Obviously, then, it is in accord with the nature of things that both *revelation,* especially in its documentary form, and the *inspiration* whereby that revelation was handed down to man, should have been distinctively the work of the Spirit of God. Again, as the Apostle Paul puts it, "For who among men knoweth the things of a man, save the spirit of the man, which is in him? even so the things of God none knoweth, save the Spirit of God" (1 Cor. 2:11). Moreover, in the very nature of the case, the communication of God's Thought to man must have been accomplished through the medium of words, which, in their proper and meaningful arrangements, constitute language. Indeed, lan-

44

guage is the only known means of communication among persons, exclusive of course of such inferior and spatially limited means as facial expressions, gestures, etc. (It naturally follows that the Spirit of God, who is pure Person, *i.e.*, incorporeal, would not employ such means, because they are essentially of a corporeal character.) Even communication in the form of suggestion, from one subconscious mind to another, as, *e.g.*, from a hypnotist to his subject, has to be in words. The words or commands may be expressed vocally or sub-vocally: in any case the suggestion must be formulated in words. Hence, if Scripture was communicated to man by inspiration of the Spirit, that communication must have been made through the medium of words, and it follows that the language in which the revelation was given originally must have been *the language of the Spirit*. By the same token, it is the Word of God. This, precisely, is the claim which the Holy Spirit Himself makes for His own Book.

It is well and good to assert that by inspiration only the Thought of God was imparted. I am utterly at a loss, however, to understand how thought—on any level of being—can be communicated except by means of words. This is precisely what the Apostle Paul affirms:

> We [i.e., the Apostles] received, not the spirit of the world, but the spirit which is from God: that we might know the things that were freely given to us of God. Which things also we speak, not in words which man's wisdom teacheth, but which the Spirit teacheth; combining spiritual things with spiritual words (1 Cor. 2:12, 13).

That is to say, spiritual realities are made known to man, insofar as they can be made known in human language, by means of the proper words or symbols chosen by the Revealer, the Spirit of God. And is not this equally true of the converse operation of the Spirit? Are we not told that the Spirit of God, who indwells the Christian, takes the unutterable longings and petitions of the latter's spirit, bears them up to the Throne of Grace, and presents them to the Heavenly Father in the language appropriate to heavenly communication?

> Rom. 8:26, 27—And in like manner the Spirit also helpeth our infirmity: for we know not how to pray as we ought; but the Spirit himself maketh intercession for us with groanings which cannot be uttered; and he that searcheth the hearts knoweth what is the mind of the Spirit, because he maketh intercession for the saints according to the will of God.

In view of these facts, it must be concluded that the language in which God's revelation was embodied originally is the language of the Spirit and therefore the word of God. "No prophecy," we

45

are told, "ever came by will of man: but men spake from God, being moved by the Holy Spirit" (2 Pet. 1:21). And in this epistle addressed to the young preacher, Timothy, Paul affirms that "every scripture inspired of God is also profitable for teaching, for reproof, for correction, for instruction which is in righteousness, that the man of God may be complete, furnished completely unto every good work" (2 Tim. 3:16, 17). And to the Thessalonian Christians, the Apostle writes: "We thank God without ceasing that, when ye received from us the word of the message, even the word of God, ye accepted it not as the word of men, but, as it is in truth, the word of God, which also worketh in you that believe" (1 Thess. 2:13).

In view of all these Scripture passages, how important it is that Christians of both pulpit and pew should under all circumstances "hold the pattern of sound words," that is, call Bible things by Bible names, as the Apostle expressly charges them to do. "Hold the pattern of sound words," he says, "which thou hast heard from me, in faith and love which is in Christ Jesus" (2 Tim. 1:13). But—sad to say!—the Church on earth, though divinely obligated to be "the salt of the earth," "the light of the world," the "city set on a hill" (Matt. 5:13, 14), and "the pillar and ground of the truth" (1 Tim. 3:15), has failed to heed this apostolic injuction. For her history shows that in all ages she has been guilty of tampering with the language of the Spirit. The church has, in many instances, substituted *transliteration* for *translation,* thus obscuring the content of the original revelation; and she has repeatedly adulterated that content by "interpreting" it in terms and phrases of Greek philosophical thought. The net results are the creeds and divisions of modern Christendom.

Anyone familiar with the "gobbledygook" resulting from the early development of Christian "theology" knows that the favorite pastime of Latin writers, and of Latin ecclesiastical writers especially, was that of taking over words bodily, so to speak, from the Greek language into the Latin; whence by the same process these words ultimately made their way into English versions of the Bible. Take the Greek word *presbyteros,* for example. Anyone who has a smattering of Greek knows that this word never meant anything in that language but "an older man" or "elder." This is true of the word in both classical and ecclesiastical Greek. And it is so translated correctly, in Acts 11:30, Acts 20:17, 1 Tim. 5:19, and elsewhere. But for some strange reason, in 1 Tim. 4:14, the kindred word *presbyterion*

46

is rendered "presbytery." Here, obviously, the word is transliterated and not translated at all (probably as a concession to the Latin transliterated word, *presbyterium*). Had the word been translated it would read, as it should, the "eldership." There is really no justification for the appearance of the word "presbytery" in the New Testament. Another example of the case in point is the Greek word *episkopos*. This word derives from the verb *episkopeo*, which means literally, "I look out upon," or "oversee." Hence, *episkopos*, if translated, would simply mean "overseer," and nothing else. It was transliterated, however, into the Latin as *espiscopus*, then vulgarized into *ebiscopus*, whence in the course of time, and solely by the process of transliteration, by way of the Anglo-Saxon *bisceop*, arose our English word "bishop." A third and probably the most outstanding example of the substitution of transliteration for translation is in the case of the Greek verb, *baptizo*. It never means anything in Greek but "dip," "immerse," or metonymically, "overwhelm," and should be translated wherever it occurs. But, unfortunately, it was not translated, either into the Latin or into the English. In every case it has been transliterated, the Greek *baptizo* becoming the Latin *baptizo* (which appears frequently in Tertullian, Augustine, Hieronymus, and others), and ultimately our English word "baptize." The result has been untold, and wholly unnecessary, confusion and controversy.

Language is of course the only means of communication among persons. At the same time, however, the improper use of language is often a source of great confusion. And nowhere is this more obvious than in Christian theology. Take, for example, the Greek word *ekklēsia*. In the original it means "an assembly of citizens summoned [called out] by the crier." It is the word used invariably in classical Greek for the so-called popular assembly of the Greek city-state, of which the New England town meeting might be cited as the modern counterpart. It should therefore be translated the "assembly," "community," "society," etc. that is, of Christians. How, then, did the word "church" come to be used for the Greek *ekklēsia?* Evidently the word "church" came into our language from Teutonic sources (Old Teutonic, *kirika;* Old English, *cirice;* Modern High German, *kirche*). With the conversion of the Teutonic nations the word "church" was assumed as the proper equivalent of the Greek *ekklēsia* and Latin *ecclesia,* and therefore appears in all English versions of the New Testament. Fortunately, this happens to be a case in which the substitute word is not altogether unsatisfactory, although it must be admitted that the original *ekklēsia* had not the faintest connotation of hierarchical institutionalism which has come to be associated in denominational Christianity with the English word "church." A case may be cited, however, in which the appropriated word is very unsatisfactory, namely, that of the word "ghost," as in the "Holy Ghost" of the Authorized version. Now our English word "spirit" comes directly from the Latin *spiritus*, which the Latin writers used for the rendering of the Hebrew *ruach* and Greek *pneuma*. The word "ghost" is, however, from Teutonic sources (Old Frisian, *gast*; Old English, *gaest*; Old Dutch, *geest*; modern High German, *geist*.) The word was rarely used prior to the middle of the sixteenth century, but after that time came to be used in English versions as the conventional equivalent for the Latin *spiritus*, especially in passages in which the sense is that of a "blast" or "breath." But "Holy Ghost" is misleading as a name for the Spirit of God; hence the superiority of the American Revised Version with its rendering, "Holy Spirit."[1]

But perhaps the greatest iniquity committed by churchmen against the language of the Spirit has been that of corrupting it with terms and phrases borrowed from the ancient Greek philosophical systems, chiefly Platonism, Aristotelianism and Neoplatonism. This business began with Origen, who seems to have been as much of a Neoplatonist as a Christian. It was zealously pursued by Augustine, who was so enamored of Neoplatonism that he insisted upon "interpreting" Scripture passages in terms of the Neoplatonic nomenclature. The business reached its climax, however, in the Scholastic philosophy and theology of the Middle Ages, which was basically Aristotelian, even though clothed in the outer garments of Christian thought. The net result of all this intermingling of pagan and Christian thought was speculative theology, creed-making, apostasy, division and denominationalism, much of which survives to our own day. I am convinced that had the theologians heeded the injunction of the Apostle Paul to "hold the pattern of sound words," much of this confusion would have been avoided, and that to the unifying of the Church and to the glory of God.

Attention has already been called to the fact of the inadequacy of human language as a vehicle for divine revelation.

1. For the etymology of these words, see *A New English Dictionary: On Historical Principles*, edited by Sir James Murray. Clarendon Press, Oxford, 1888-1928. Commonly called "The Oxford English Dictionary."

And especially in the realm of pure Spirit, which is that of the very being of God, there must inhere a great many mysteries which lie too deep for words. How great, then, must have been the difficulties which the Holy Spirit faced when first He essayed to reveal to men something of the nature of His own being and activity! Obviously the communication had to be made, in the first place, in the language of the people to whom it was to be addressed. And in the second place it had to be made in words and terms sufficiently simple for them to comprehend, that is, if the revelation was to be of any value to them. Certainly there was one thing—be it said in all reverence—which the Holy Spirit could *not* do: He could not find a word in any language that would convey to their minds a mental image of Himself. For a mental image of a purely spiritual (*i.e.,* noncorporeal or nonphysical) entity would be a contradiction, both in terms and in fact. In view of this fact there seems to have been one course, and only one, open to Him: and that was to resort to metaphors, to metaphors that would have meaning, in the light of their own experience, for those receiving the revelation. This is precisely what the Spirit did. He selected words that would convey to their minds, in a metaphor, some conception, however inadequate, of the nature of His own being and activity. He selected the Hebrew word *ruach,* and later the Greek word *pneuma,* both of which in their crude meaning signify "wind" and "breath." These metaphors have no allusion of course to the Divine essence; they are but the imagery by which the Holy Spirit has seen fit to represent to us the character of His presence and approach to men.

By means of the metaphor, Wind, the Holy Spirit teaches us that His activity on occasion takes the character of an invasive energy sweeping in upon men from the supernatural realm. This was the character of His activity in the Creation, when He "moved upon the face of the waters." That is to say, by a "brooding" and "stirring," just like that of a great mother-bird, He energized and impregnated the hitherto lifeless primordial matter and brought it from chaos to cosmos. This was not infrequently the character of His activity when He "moved" or "came mightily upon" tribal and national leaders in ancient times, to qualify them with superhuman powers needed to meet emergencies.

E.g., Judg. 13:25—And the Spirit of Jehovah began to move him [Samson] in Mahaneh-dan. Judg. 14:6—And the Spirit of Jehovah came mightily upon him [Samson], and he rent him [a young lion] as

49

he would have rent a kid; and he had nothing in his hand. Judg. 14:19—And the Spirit of Jehovah came mightily upon him [Samson], and he went down to Ashkelon, and smote thirty men of them, etc. Judg. 15:14, 15—When he came unto Lehi, the Philistines shouted as they met him [Samson]; and the Spirit of Jehovah came mightily upon him, and the ropes that were upon his arms became as flax that was burnt with fire, and his bands dropped from off his hands. And he found a fresh jawbone of an ass, and put forth his hand, and took it, and smote a thousand men therewith. 1 Sam. 10:6—And the Spirit of Jehovah will come mightily upon thee [Saul], and thou shalt prophesy with them, and shalt be turned into another man. 1 Sam. 10:10—And when they came thither to the hill, behold, a band of prophets met him [Saul]; and the Spirit of God came mightily upon him, and he prophesied among them. 1 Sam. 11:6—And the Spirit of God came mightily upon Saul when he heard these words, and his anger was kindled greatly. 1 Sam. 16:13—Then Samuel took the horn of oil, and anointed him [David] in the midst of his brethren: and the Spirit of Jehovah came mightily upon David from that day forward.

This was likewise the character of His activity at the beginning of the Regeneration, on the Day of Pentecost. The Apostles "were all together in one place" somewhere in Jrusalem, probably in the Temple.

And suddenly there came from heaven a sound as of the rushing of a mighty wind, and it filled all the house where they were sitting. And there appeared unto them tongues parting asunder, like as of fire; and it sat upon each of them. And they were all filled with the Holy Spirit, and began to speak with other tongues, as the Spirit gave them utterance (Acts 2:1-4).

This was the fulfilment of the promise of Jesus: "Ye shall receive power, when the Holy Spirit is come upon you, and ye shall be my witnesses both in Jerusalem, and in all Judea and Samaria, and unto the uttermost part of the earth" (Acts 1:8). For the immediate result of this type of the Spirit's activity was invariably an energizing, either physical or mental or both. And under this metaphor the Spirit is to be apprehended as the Spirit of Power.

The metaphor, Breath, is especially meaningful. "The Holy Spirit," writes W. E. Biederwolf, "is called 'the breath of God' with reference to His mode of subsistence, proceeding from God as the breath from the mouth."[1] By this metaphor, too, the Holy Spirit makes it known to us that His activity is the source of life—of all life, natural, spiritual, eternal. As long as one continues to breathe, one is alive; but when breathing ceases, one dies. Although the breath is not the source of natural life, it is the manifestation or assurance thereof. But the activity of the Spirit, as the Breath of God, is the source, as well as the

1. *A Help to the Study of the Holy Spirit.* 18.

proof and pledge, of life on every level of being—in the Kingdom of Nature, in the Kingdom of Grace, and in the Kingdom of Glory. As Elihu said to Job: "The Spirit of God hath made me, and the breath of the Almighty giveth me life" (Job 33:4). The "life" alluded to here, of course, is the *natural* life which man enjoys in this present state. "He that hath the Son," writes John, "hath the life; he that hath not the Son of God hath not the life" (1 John 5:12). Jesus Himself said: "Verily, verily, I say unto you, He that heareth my word, and believeth him that sent me, hath eternal life, and cometh not into judgment, but hath passed out of death into life" (John 5:24). The "life" described in these texts is that divine gift which is possessed by the Regeneration, by those who have been "born again" into the Kingdom of Grace (John 3:3-5). This *spiritual* life, if properly cultivated and allowed to fructify, will ultimately bud and blossom into the life *eternal.* "He that soweth unto the Spirit," says Paul, "shall of the Spirit reap eternal life" (Gal. 6:8). Hence it is said of all the saints that they are "sealed with the Holy Spirit of promise," which is the "earnest" of their inheritance, that inheritance being the Life Everlasting (Eph. 1:13, 14). Thus the activity of the indwelling Spirit is the pledge or surety of man's attainment of his proper ultimate ends.

Now, in Acts 9:1, we read that Saul of Tarsus, prior to his conversion, was "breathing threatening and slaughter against the disciples of the Lord" in Jerusalem. Just *how* was Saul thus "breathing threatening and slaughter"? *In words,* most assuredly. Breathing necessarily accompanies the propulsion of words from the mouth; in fact the very breathing signifies that they are the living words of a living person. In like manner, the Breath of God issues forth *with,* and *in,* the living and life-giving Word that proceeds out of the mouth of God. The Spirit and the Word go forth together. It is the Spirit-power in the Word that makes it the living and life-giving Word. Hence, said Jesus: "The words that I have spoken unto you are spirit, and are life" (John 6:63). And to Satan, on the Mount of Temptation, He said, quoting Deuteronomy 8:3, "It is written, Man shall not live by bread alone, but by every word that proceedeth out of the mouth of God" (Matt. 4:4). And the writer of *Hebrews* tells us that "the word of God is living, and active, and sharper than any two-edged sword, and piercing even to the dividing of soul and spirit, of both joints and marrow, and quick to descern the thoughts and intents of the heart" (Heb. 4:12). In view of these Scripture affirmations, how meaningful becomes the act of Jesus that is narrated in the twentieth chapter of John's Gospel. Here we read that on the evening of that memorable first day of the week, the day of the Resurrection, Jesus appeared to the Eleven who, because of their fear of the Jews, were meeting behind closed doors. We read that

Jesus came and stood in the midst, and said, Peace be unto you. And when he had said this, he showed unto them his hand and his side. The disciples therefore were glad, when they saw the Lord. Jesus therefore said to them again, Peace be unto you: as the Father hath sent me, even so send I you. And when he had said this, *he breathed on them, and saith unto them, Receive ye the Holy Spirit;* whose soever sins ye forgive, they are forgiven unto them; whose soever sins ye retain, they are retained (John 20:19-23).

In this manner Jesus symbolically pointed forward to, and authorized, the subsequent descent of the Spirit on the Apostles to clothe them with authority and infallibility. Thus He *signified* (*e.g.*, *sign*-ified) that the Spirit at His coming on Pentecost would bring to them, and through them to all mankind, the living and life-giving Word that was designed to be inscribed upon the fleshly tables of the human heart (2 Cor. 3:3)—that Gospel which "is the *power* of God unto salvation to every one that believeth" (Rom. 1:16). Again we are reminded of certain fundamental truths, namely, that the Thought-power, Spirit-power, and Word-power of God are one; that the Spirit and the Word go forth together from the mouth of God; and that the Word of God is living and active and powerful because of the presence and power of the Spirit in it. The Word of God is the Seed of Spiritual Life; and the life principle in that Seed is the presence and power of the Spirit of God (Luke 8:11). All this is implied in the meaningful metaphor, the Breath of God. Under this metaphor, the Spirit is apprehended as the Spirit of Life and the Spirit of Truth.

Finally, in Ezekiel's famous Vision of the Valley of Dry Bones, we find these metaphors of the Spirit combined and intermingled in a manner that is most illuminating. Says the prophet:

The hand of Jehovah was upon me, and he brought me out in the Spirit of Jehovah, and set me down in the midst of the valley; and it was full of bones. And he caused me to pass by them round about; and behold, there were very many in the open valley; and lo, they were very dry. And he said unto me, Son of man, can these bones live? And I answered, O Lord Jehovah, thou knowest. Again he said unto me, Prophesy over these bones, and say unto them, O ye dry bones, hear the word of Jehovah. Thus saith the Lord Jehovah unto these bones: Behold, I will cause breath to enter into you, and ye shall live. And I will lay sinews upon you, and will bring up flesh upon you, and cover you with skin, and put breath in you, and ye shall live; and ye shall know that I am Jehovah. So I prophesied as I was commanded: and as I prophesied, there was a noise, and, behold, an earthquake; and the bones came together, bone to its bone. And I beheld, and, lo, there were sinews upon them, and flesh came up, and skin covered them above; but there was no breath in them. Then said he unto me, Prophesy unto the wind, prophesy, son of man, and say to the wind, Thus saith the Lord Jehovah: Come from the four winds, O breath, and breathe upon these slain, that they may live. So I prophesied as he commanded me, and the breath came into them, and they lived, and stood up upon their feet, an exceeding great army (Ezek. 37:1-10).

Fortunately, we are not left in any uncertainty as to the meaning of this vision. For the prophet goes on to interpret it for us:

Then said he unto me, Son of man, these bones are the whole house of Israel; behold, they say, Our bones are dried up, and our hope is lost; we are clean cut off. Therefore prophesy, and say unto them, Thus said the Lord Jehovah: Behold, I will open your graves, and cause you to come up out of your graves, O my people; and I will bring you into the land of Israel. And ye shall know that I am Jehovah, when I have opened your graves, and caused you to come up out of your graves, O my people. And I will put my Spirit in you, and ye shall live, and I will place you in your own land; and ye shall know that I, Jehovah, have spoken it and performed it, saith Jehovah (Ezek. 37:11-14).

H. Wheeler Robinson comments on this famous passage of Scripture most eloquently, as follows:

To the prophet of the exile there came a grim vision—a valley that was a charnel-house, full of the bones of the dead, from which the very flesh had long since rotted away. Then, at the prophetic word, a strange scene enacted itself before his horrified eyes—those ancient bones jarred and rattled from disorder into order, bone to his bone, and they became articulated, though unstrung, skeletons. The sinews were stretched upon them, the flesh was packed around these, and the skin drawn over each inanimate figure, but it remained a figure of death. Once more, at the word, a blast of wind swept through the valley and filled the bodies of the dead men and they lived and sprang to their feet, an exceeding great army, on an ancient battlefield which had once been the scene of their overthrow. The difference between death and life, the secret of vitality, was that 'wind' of God which in its Old Testament name cannot be distinguished from the 'Spirit' of God. To those men whose fathers had been desert-dwellers, the wind that swept the sand resistlessly before it was the very breath of God, and the power that so strangely moved men beyond their own power was the 'wind' of God. Whatever else the Spirit of God may mean in the Old Testament, it means the difference between death and life, it means vitality.[1]

A wind of God, an invasive energy having the sweep and onrush of a hurricane! The Breath of God, issuing forth in the Word—source, proof, and pledge of Life! Such is the activity of the Spirit. He is the Spirit of Power, the Spirit of Life, and the Spirit of Truth.

1. *Op. cit.*, 5, 6.

# QUESTIONS FOR REVIEW OF PART ONE

1. In what sense is the Bible *one* Book, and *The* Book?
2. What is the Apostle Paul's explanation of the sins of the pagan world?
3. Are we right in affirming that the United States is now a pagan nation, and that our secular educational system is pagan? Explain your answer.
4. Why do men attack the integrity of the Bible, but do not attack the "sacred" books of other so-called "religions"?
5. Why do men attack the Genesis cosmogony, but do not attack the heathen narratives of the Creation?
6. What is no doubt one of the main reasons why the church of our day is so spiritually powerless?
7. Define the terms "spirit," "Spirit," "cosmos," and "nature," as used in this text.
8. In what four respects especially is Christianity unique? Explain.
9. In what additional respect is Christianity especially unique?
10. What is Christianity's "Great Dynamic"?
11. What fact especially sets the Bible apart from all other books? That sets the Gospel apart from all messages? That sets the church apart from all other institutions?
12. In what sense is the church a "spiritual house"?
13. What is the only reliable source of our knowledge of the Holy Spirit and His works?
14. What distinguishes the Holy Spirit from a metaphysical concept of "spirit"?
15. Cite the Scriptures which assert Christianity to be a joyous faith. What facts serve to make it a religion of joy?
16. What two Books has God written for us and what is the principal aspect of God and His work that is revealed in each respectively?
17. What names to do we give to the human interpretations of these two Books respectively?
18. Why do we say that apparent discrepancies may exist between the interpretations, but cannot exist between the Books themselves?
19. In what way was God's revelation to man first given?
20. What is the essential character of the subject-matter of the Bible?
21. What, according to the New Testament, is the Eternal Purpose of God? What is the end ultimately to be realized by this Eternal Purpose?
22. What is meant by the revelation that the goal of the Eternal Purpose, insofar as the individual saints are concerned, is that each shall be "conformed to the image of God's Son"?
23. What is meant by the statement that God's over-all purpose is that "what is mortal may be swallowed up of life"?
24. Why is it in accord with "the nature of things" that revelation should be in a special sense a work of the Holy Spirit?
25. Distinguish between *revelation, inspiration,* and *demonstration* in reference to the progressive actualization of God's Eternal Purpose.
26. What is the over-all theme of the Bible from beginning to end?
27. How do we know that man is a *creature*? List the evidences of his creaturehood.
28. Explain what is meant by the natural and proper ends of man, by his ultimate ends, and by his intrinsic and extrinsic ends.
29. What would be the characteristics of an absolutely ultimate end?
30. Explain what is meant by the statement that the cosmos is not *heliocentric*, not *geocentric*, not *anthropocentric*, but *theocentric*?
31. Why do we say that man's ultimate intrinsic end is happiness?

Why do we say that it is *perfect happiness?* What does experience, as well as Scripture, teach us about this?

32. What is the designation given in Scripture to the experience of man's final union with God?

33. What does seeing God "face to face" essentially mean?

34. What significance does this phrase have with the respect to the character of the life after death?

35. What is the antithesis of this Biblical presentation of the character of the future life? What do we mean by pessimism, in this connection?

36. What is the necessary preparation for this ultimate union with God?

37. Explain the three phases of the Spiritual Life, and give the names of the divine operations associated respectively with these three phases.

38. How is redemption in all its phases described in Scripture? (See 1 Thess. 5:23).

39. What is the beginning of this life with the Holy Spirit? What are the Scriptural requirements for entrance upon the Spiritual Life?

40. What is the design of Christian baptism in relation to the beginning of union with Christ?

41. When does the Marriage Supper of the Lamb take place? (Cf. Rev. 19:6-9).

42. What is the testimonial aspect of baptism? Why does any act but immersion vitiate this testimonial aspect?

43. What great lesson did Saul of Tarsus learn, with respect to the church, by the Lord's brief conversation with him near the gates of Damascus?

44. Summarize our presentation of the truth with respect to man's ultimate intrinsic and extrinsic ends.

45. State the reasons why the doctrine of the Holy Spirit is so generally neglected by the modern church.

46. Explain the basic difficulties inherent in the nature of the subject itself.

47. What must be our proper approach to the doctrine subjectively, that is, in our attitude within ourselves? What warning did Jesus Himself give us respecting the sublimity of this subject?

48. What two sources do men appeal to, for information on this subject?

49. Why do we reject human emotions and alleged personal experiences as not sufficiently trustworthy in this area of Christian faith and practice?

50. What light has psychic research (parapsychology) thrown on the problem of the special phenomena of emotional revivalism?

51. On what grounds do we reject the claims of "special revelations"? List the more prominent of these alleged "special revelations."

52. What especially has God revealed, in the Book of Nature, about Himself and His works?

52. In what respect does so-called "natural religion" fail to meet the more profound needs of humankind?

53. In what sense does God's special revelation, of which the account is recorded in Scripture, the Book of Redemption, complement the general revelation that is given us in the Book of Nature?

54. List the events of human history through which this complementary progressive revelation has been worked out.

55. What is the relation between this revelation in history and that which is given us in Scripture.

56. Name the various Dispensations of divine revelation and state the essential character of each.

57. When and in whom was this progressive revelation brought to completion?

55

58. Distinguish between the *historical* and the *documentary* phases of revelation.
59. Distinguish between *revelation, inspiration,* and *illumination.*
60. Explain what is meant by *God-breathed* literature. What does the Breath of God allude to in Scripture?
61. What is meant by the phrase, "the language of the Spirit"?
62. What does the language of the Spirit express?
63. What is the common method of communication among persons? What light does this throw on the work of the Holy Spirit in revelation?
64. What does the injunction to "hold fast the pattern of sound words" mean?
65. Explain the difference between *transliteration* and *translation.* Cite the three instances specifically mentioned in our text as illustrations of the confusion caused by the substitution of transliteration for translation.
65. Explain the importance of "calling Bible things by Bible names."
66. Show how the improper use of language can cause great confusion.
67. Differentiate between *univocal* and *equivocal* uses of language.
68. Show how the language of the Spirit was corrupted by the attempts of churchmen to "interpret" Christian doctrine through the medium of Greek philosophical thought.
69. What Authorship does the Bible *as a whole* claim for itself?
70. What must have been the linguistic problem which the Divine Spirit encountered in communicating the thought of God to man?
71. What devices were often used by Him in making God's truth intelligible to man?
72. What must have been the Spirit's problem in attempting to convey to man any *mental image* of Himself or His work?
73. What does the term, Wind, signify as related to the Spirit and His work?
74. What does the term, Breath of God, signify metaphorically?
75. What is indicated by the truth that Spirit-power, Thought-power, and Word-power in God are essentially the same?
76. What according to the Scriptures is the essence of a genuine Christian experience?
77. What, therefore, do we accept (and why do we accept it) as the only reliable source of information concerning the Holy Spirit and His operations?

# PART TWO

# MATTER
# AND
# SPIRIT

## 1. The Mystery of Matter

Approaching our general theme from the points of view of human experience, science, and language, it is necessary, first of all, to inquire what is meant by "spirit." Does the word signify anything real; that is, for anything existing in fact, or not just as an idea in the mind?

In all ages there have been thinkers who have answered this question in the negative. Matter, they say, is the sole reality; everything in the universe is reducuble ultimately to matter and motion, or rather matter-*in*-motion. All such persons are commonly designated "materialists."

Obviously, the primary connotation of "spirit" is a negative one, in essence, namely, that of *immateriality*. Perhaps the best approach, therefore, to a satisfactory definition of "spirit" is by way of an understanding of what is meant by "matter."

Ordinarily, we define matter as anything that occupies space. Spirit, then, in the light of this definition, must be regarded as a something that transcends space altogether. Or, if matter is defined as something that affects one or more of our physical senses, then spirit becomes a something that transcends the physical senses, or that is not apprehensible by means of the physical senses. Cf. 2 Cor. 4:18, "the things which are seen are temporal; but the things which are not seen are eternal." As A. Clutton-Brock has written: "We are aware of matter with our senses; and, if we are aware of spirit at all, it is not with our senses."[1] Therefore there need be nothing surprising in the fact that, as the same writer puts it, "spirit is a name given to something the very existence of which is often denied, and those who believe in its existence often give an incredible account of it."[2]

What, then, do we mean by "matter"?

In common parlance we mean the *stuff* of things around us and in a sense, that of ourselves, or at least of our bodies. *Hyle*, the Greek word for "matter," used in that signification first by Aristotle, meant originally and primarily, "wood," that is, (1) a real wood, or forest; and also (2) wood cut down, firewood, etc.[3] Why Aristotle selected this particular word to signify the ultimate stuff of things is a mystery. The German word, *Stoff*,

1. Art., "Spirit and Matter," in a work entitled *The Spirit*, 309, edited by B. H. Streeter.
2. *Ibid.*, 309.
3. Liddell and Scott, *Greek-English Lexicon*, New Edition, by Stuart Jones and McKenzie, *s.v.*

is far more expressive than even our word, "matter," which derives from the Latin *materia*.[1] For matter is in fact the stuff of things. This, of course, is merely a substitution of one word for another; it does not tell us *what* the stuff of things is.

Now from ordinary observation we are led to classify the stuff of things in two general categories, namely, that of *living* (animate) stuff or matter, and that of *non-living* (inanimate) stuff or matter. Classification, however, gives little or no insight into the real essence of matter. Is matter ultimately homogeneous? If so, then what is it *per se,* that is, in its ultimate constitution? The answer to this question has been sought by scientists and philosophers in all ages and the quest is still going on.

Speculation regarding the ultimate constitution of all things physical—the ultimate ("irreducible") cosmic "substance"—had its beginning with the ancient Ionian "natural" philosophers, the first of whom was Thales of Miletos (c. 640-548 B.C.). Thales is alleged to have contended that *water* is the ultimate or primal substance. Just what Thales meant by "water," however, or whether he had reference to water ($H_2O$) as we know it, is problematical; he may have meant only that the primal stuff was of a fluid or plastic character. Again, Anaximander of Miletos (c. 610-547 B.C.), an associate of Thales, posited an ultimate matter undetermined in quality and scattered throughout infinite space, which he designated *To Apeiron,* that is, the Indeterminate or Undifferentiated, generally translated "The Boundless." Anaximenes (c. 598-524 B.C.), also of Miletos, put forward the view that the ultimate principle of all physical existence is *air,* by the thinning and thickening of which, fire, wind, clouds, water, and earth are formed. According to Herakleitos of Ephesus (c. 534-475 B.C.), the whole cosmos is a continuous flux, having for its mobile element *fire*. From the testimony of Aristotle it is evident that the Fire of Herakleitos was a very subtle substance of much the same character as the Air of Anaximenes. Indeed, fire, as we know it, is a *process* rather than an entity; and this may have been the meaning Herakleitos intended to convey by his use of the term. For reality was, for him, an ever-flowing stream, a ceaseless process of change, of becoming and ceasing to be—a view revived in recent years by the French philosopher, Henri Bergson. Empedokles of Akragas in Sicily (c. 495-435 B.C.) synthesized these earlier views into

1. The Latin word having the same original signification as the Greek *hyle*, was *silva*. *Harper's Latin Dictionary*, Lewis and Short, *s.v.*

the famous theory of the "four elements." The four bodies— water, air, earth, and fire—were named together by him as the elements constitutive of all things, the movements—dissociation and re-combination— of these elements being governed by the two forces of attraction and repulsion, which Empedokles poetic- ally termed Love and Hate respectively. This theory of the "four elements" was preserved by science as a sacred deposit down to the time of Lavoisier (c. 1790).

Demokritos of Abdera (c. 460 B.C.), or probably Leukippos of Miletos before him, was the first to put forward the so-called "atomic" theory. Demokritos proclaimed the homogeneous char- acter of all matter. According to his theory, corporeal things are made up of infinitely small, physically indivisible particles (*atomos* means literally "incapable of being cut," *i.e., indivisible*), full and solid, and eternally in motion. These atoms were con- ceived as differing in shape, size, weight, order and position, the soul being made up of fire-atoms of a more refined character than the atoms of gross matter. In reality, said Demokritos, nothing exists but atoms and the void, *i.e.,* empty space. In his theory, the birth and death of all material things is sufficiently explained by the association and dissociation of these atoms in the process of their whirling in all directions throughout space in response to the blind forces of impulse and reaction. The theory of Demokritos was subsequently championed by Epikouros (341-270 B.C.), with one important difference: whereas in the former theory the cause of all motion was assumed to be in the external movement of matter, in that of Epikouros the atom was conceived to be self-moving and self-determining. In later years this early materialistic theory was elaborately presented by the Roman philosopher-poet, Lucretius (98-51 B.C.) in his famed didactic poem, *On the Nature of Things*. This theory was so completely overshadowed, however, by the metaphysical systems of Plato and Aristotle that it made little headway among ancient thinkers.

Plato (427-347 B.C.) appears never to have given much thought, if any, to the problem of the constitution of matter. Indeed, as far as I am able to determine, he does not even use any Greek equivalent for our word "matter," but puts the main emphasis rather on the opposition between body (*soma*) and soul (*psyche*), a dualism which he seems to have inherited from Pythagoreanism. This dualism stemmed also from his basic conception of the universe as a Living Being, a World-Body animated by a World-Soul; a conception which he carried down and applied to all subordinate beings including even the heavenly bodies and man himself. In the *Timaeus,* a cosmological treatise in which it is impossible to determine whether Plato is presenting his own views or merely echoing those of contemporary Pythagoreanism, he describes the cosmos and its constituent creatures as having been carved out of empty Space—the Receptacle—by the Demiourgos, after the respective patterns provided by the eternally-existent Forms and according to strict mathematical relations. The Forms alone are declared to have real existence. Material things are but images, empty shadows, so to speak, of the eternal and immutable Forms. In fact, throughout his writings Plato denies any real existence to the material world; at best it is but the transitory, everchanging copy of the eternal pattern, the world of Forms; its sole reality inhering in the determinate geometrical configurations which the Demiourgos caused its four primary bodies—earth, water, air, and fire—to conform to, in the process of generating it. In Plato's thought, matter is relegated to the realm of non-being, or at best to that of pure becoming. In another dialogue, for instance, the *Theaetetus,* he tells us that the physical objects which give rise to our sensations and perceptions have no permanent qualities residing in them.[1] They are described as being actually "slow changes," that is, qualitative changes, or motions which produce sensations in a recipient. About the only thing we know, or can know, about them is that they have the power of acting on our sense organs and on one another.[2]

(Incidentally, John Locke, the English philosopher (1632-1704), showed that, after all, we do not know what the material substratum is in itself, but rather we know only our sensations of it; hence, he defined matter as "permanent possibility of sensation," as "something-I-know not what." This, as a matter of fact, is about as close as anyone has ever come to a "definition" of matter *per se.*)

Again, "soul," for Plato, was the source and cause of all motion. Hence, in the *Timaeus,* the World-Soul is pictured as the prime mover of the World-Body, the energizing and vitalizing principle of the cosmic Living Being. In this remarkable treatise, which is presented in the form of a "likely story," a typical Platonic *mythos* and nothing more, the Demiourgos apparently stands for the Divine Reason which is probably to be identified with the World-Soul itself and which is portrayed

1. Theaet., 155 D ff.
2. Vide F. M. Cornford, *Plato's Cosmology,* 204.

as working only for ends that are ultimately good. For Plato the physical world was not a reality but only an "image" of the real.

This conception of matter as essentially non-being was enlarged upon subsequently by Plotinus (c. A.D. 204-270) and became one of the principal tenets of Neoplatonism, the system sired by him. For Plotinus, matter was the principle of evil; he is said by tradition to have been ashamed that he had a body; he would never name his parents or remember his birthday. Moreover, in the theory of Creation by Emanation which he originated, matter was regarded as at the farthest remove from the One, the source of all being; and gross matter was identified with non-being wherein there is no reality at all. Incidentally, in this connection, the fact should not be overlooked that Neoplatonism was the system which exerted such a profound influence on the thinking of some of the Church Fathers, notably Origen and Augustine.

To Aristotle (384-322 B.C.), a pupil of Plato, must go the credit for having originated the first thoroughgoing metaphysical theory of matter, and by "metaphysical" I mean a conception arrived at primarily by inductive reasoning. Aristotle evolved what is known as the theory of Prime Matter, a theory which was incorporated and made basic in the Scholastic metaphysics of medieval times and which remains basic in the Neo-Scholasticism of our time. According to the Stagirite, two principles combine to give being to all things. The one, *prime matter*, is the passive principle; it is indeterminate, homogeneous in all bodies, and the permanent subject of all the changes effected in the physical world; obviously akin, by the way, to the *Apeiron* of Anaximander. The other, *substantial form*, is the active principle which resolves being into its different species of objects. All contingent things are, according to Aristotle, the product of the union of these two principles, matter and form; hence the theory is technically designated the *hylomorphic*, that is, *matter-form* theory. The reasoning which gives rise to this theory is, in my opinion, quite valid. It may be stated in a sentence or two as follows: In any substantial change as, *e.g.*, the change of a stick of wood into ashes by burning, there must be something which retains its identity throughout the change; otherwise there would be no change at all, but rather in every case of so-called change actually an annihilation followed by a creation. Hence there must be something that is ultimate and that persists throughout all change. That something, said Aristotle, is prime matter. Prime matter plus substantial form: this is the formula by which every contingent thing is to be accounted for. Perhaps it should be made clear too that the prime matter of this theory is not to be identified with gross matter, nor in fact with anything palpable to the senses, not even with the atom or any of its constituent parts. Prime matter lies altogether beyond the realm of sensible apprehension: it is the principle of pure passivity in things, but is always found in combination with substantial form.

Jacques Maritain, one of the foremost living Neo-Scholastic philosophers, states the Aristotelian view as follows:

> The Aristotelian philosophy recognises in corporeal substance two substantial principles: (1) *matter* (*first matter, materia prima*), which, however, in no way represents, as in the conception of the mechanists, the imaginable notion of extension, but the idea of matter (that of which something else is made) in its utmost purity—it is what Plato called a sort of non-entity, simply that *of which* things are made, which in itself is nothing actual, a principle wholly indeterminate, incapable of separate existence, but capable of existing in conjunction with something else (the form); (ii) an active principle, which is, so to speak, the living idea or soul of the thing, and which determines the purely passive first matter, somewhat as the form imposed upon it by the sculptor determines the clay, constituting with it one single thing actually existent, one single corporeal substance, which owes to it both that it is this or that kind of thing, that is to say, its specific nature, and its existence, somewhat as the form imposed by the sculptor makes a statue what it is. On account of this analogy with the external form of a statue (its accidental form) Aristotle gave the name of *form* (*substantial form*), which must be understood in a sense altogether special and technical, to this internal principle of which we are speaking, which determines the very being of corporeal substance. The Aristotelian doctrine, which regards a body as a compound of *matter* (*hyle*) and *form* (*morphe*), is known as *hylomorphism.*[1]

Thus it will be seen that whereas for Plato the Forms existed and functioned in a world apart, and material things only "participated" in them, an expression which Plato uses frequently but nowhere clarifies satisfactorily, in Aristotle's thought the Forms existed, it is true, but they existed only in combination with prime matter *in things.* According to Aristotle, says Nys,

> the two constitutive elements of the corporeal essence are real and intrinsically interdependent. According to Plato, mater is non-being and the forms alone have real existence. Platonic forms are ideal, self-subsistent types which, without impairing their character of universality, can project themselves into space and assume the appearance of sensible, mutable, and perishable things. Hence between these two conceptions of matter, a great and actual difference exists.[2]

Although Plato apparently never so states explicitly, he clearly intimates in the *Timaeus* that the Forms exist as eternal ideas

1. *An Introduction to Philosophy*, 166, 167.
2. D. Nys, *Cosmology*, II, 3, 4. Translated by Sidney A. Raemers.

or patterns in the Mind of Deity; hence they are the archetypes according to which the Demiourgos, or Divine Reason, created the various species of contingent things which go to make up our physical world. The concept is not far removed from the doctrine of the conjoint activity of the Spirit and the Logos in Creation, as that doctrine is presented in Scripture.

Gen. 1:1-3—In the beginning God created the heavens and the earth. And the earth was waste and void; and darkness was upon the face of the deep: and the Spirit of God was brooding upon the face of the waters. And *God said,* Let there be light: and there was light. Psa. 33:6, 9—By the word of Jehovah were the heavens made, And all the host of them by the breath of his mouth. . . . For he spake, and it was done; He commanded, and it stood fast. John 1:1-3—In the beginning was the Word [Logos], and the Word was with God, and the Word was God. The same was in the beginning with God. All things were made through him; and without him was not anything made that hath been made. Heb. 11:3—By faith we understand that the worlds have been framed by the word of God, so that what is seen hath not been made out of things which appear.

This theory of Prime Matter, as described in the foregoing paragraphs, was taken over by the Scholastic philosophers in medieval times and made basic in their metaphysic. It continues to be basic in the Neo-Scholastic philosophy of our own day. To quote again from Nys, a contemporary exponent of Neo-Scholasticism:

Whatever falls within the range of sense-perception is concrete and determined; and these phenomena of material substances, or, to be more exact, these compounds of substance and accident, are called *bodies.* . . . Prime matter exhibits none of these properties natural to bodies, hence it cannot be known by any one of our organic faculties. We know the existence of prime matter through reason alone, but even this faculty never affords us an exact and immediate conception of it. Since the intelligibility of a being is measured by the degree of actuality it possesses, it is evident that the purely potential eludes all direct perception. Consequently, it is by the route of reason and the analysis of substantial change alone that the intelligence of man arrives at some idea, partly positive, partly negative, of this principle of passivity, and is able to conceive it as the incomplete subject or permanent substratum of the specific types existing in the material world.[1]

It is a well-known historical fact, of course, that both Neoplatonism and Aristotelianism provided the foundations for the Jewish, Arabian, and Christian philosophical systems in vogue in the Middle Ages. Generally speaking, the Neoplatonist metaphysics was championed in Christian circles by the followers of Augustine, and the Aristotelian by Thomas Aquinas and his school. The medieval Arab philosophers followed Aristotle, as did also the Jewish philosophers down to the time of Spinoza.

1. *Op. cit.,* II, 18, 19.

Perhaps attention should be called here to a strangely up-to-date theory which sprang up in the thirteenth century, one of the most intellectually brilliant and prolific periods, by the way, in the history of human thought. The theory in question, which has been designated the "light metaphysics," was offered as supplementary to hylomorphism, which was in vogue everywhere. It was suggested, no doubt, by certain passages in the writings of Augustine, particularly by some of those in his treatise on the book of *Genesis*. The theory was developed by the English philosophers, Robert Grosseteste (died 1252) and Roger Bacon (1214-1294), and by the Italian mystic, Bonaventura (1221-1274). According to this theory, along with the creation *ex nihilo* of unformed matter, God brought into existence the first form, *lux spiritualis*. This *lux*, conceived, it would seem, as an extraordinarily rarefied form of corporeal light, something in fact which approximated spirit, originated space; and, as the form of corporeity in primordial matter, was the primary source and cause of all created things. As McKeon puts it:

The characteristic of all light is to engender itself perpetually, and diffuse itself spherically about a point in an instantaneous manner. Originally, the luminous form and matter were equally unextended, but the first form created by God in the first matter, multiplies itself infinitely, and spreads equally in all directions, distending thus the matter to which it is united and constituting thus the mass of the universe.[1]

Moreover, according to this theory, just as light is the power by which Pure Spirit produces the corporeal world, so too it is the instrument by which the soul comes into contact with the body and the things of sense; hence, viewed in this aspect, the *lux* becomes *lumen*. Commenting on Grosseteste's theory of *lux*, D. E. Sharp writes as follows:

It appears that Grosseteste experienced the same difficulties as modern physicists. The functions he assigns to light . . . show that he regards it as an energy; but his desire to speak of it as resembling body is strikingly like the present-day application of such terms as "wave lengths" and "rays" to the ether, which in itself is admitted to be imperceptible to the senses and is thought of only as the subject of activity or as that which is conserved throughout change. As a principle of unity in the universe, this light is comparable to the modern ether, which fills all space from the most distant stars to the interspaces of the atom. Again, Grosseteste's theory is not unlike the modern hypothesis of the convertibility of matter and energy. Lastly, we find something resembling the modern ethereal attributes of electricity,

1. Richard McKeon, *Selections from Medieval Philosophers*, I, 261. In the Modern Student's Library series.

65

magnetism, and chemical activities in his view of *lux* as the source of all movement and life and as the basis of sound.[1] [The concept of the ether has, of course, passed out of the most up-to-date physics. What this author has to say, however, about Grosseteste's difficulty in conceiving *lux* as energy and "body" at one and the same time, certainly reminds us of the difficulties encountered by modern physicists in attempting to describe the ultimate constitution of matter: they are at a loss whether to describe it in terms of "fields," "waves," "particles," "corpuseles," or what not.]

Two other pertinent facts should, I think, be pointed out in this connection, namely: (1) that Grosseteste's theory of *lux*, and its creative function is strikingly parallel to the tendency among present-day physicists to regard *radiant energy* as the ultimate form of matter,[2] and (2) that this "light metaphysics" is strikingly adaptable to the Biblical doctrine of the ultimate glorification of the bodies of the redeemed, and it was used by its formulators, especially by Bonaventura, to elucidate that doctrine. Grosseteste evidently thought of visible light as the primary phenomenon of *lux*.

Dan. 12:3—They that are wise shall shine as the brightness of the firmament; and they that turn many to righteousness as the stars for ever and ever. John 14:2—[Jesus speaking]: In my Father's house are many mansions; if it were not so, I would have told you; for I go to prepare a place for you. 2 Cor. 5:1—For we know that if the earthly house of our tabernacle be dissolved, we have a building from God, a house not made with hands, eternal, in the heavens. Rom. 8:22, 23— For we know that the whole creation groaneth and travaileth in pain together until now. And not only so, but ourselves also, who have the first-fruits of the Spirit, even we ourselves groan within ourselves, waiting for our adoption, to wit, *the redemption of our body*. Rom. 8:11— But if the Spirit of him that raised up Jesus from the dead dwelleth in you, he that raised up Christ Jesus from the dead shall give life also to your mortal bodies through his Spirit that dwelleth in you. Phil. 3:20, 21—the Lord Jesus Christ, who shall fashion anew the body of our himiliation, that it may be conformed to the body of his glory, according to the working whereby he is able even to subject all things unto himself. Rom. 8:29, 30—For whom he [God] foreknew, he also foreordained to be conformed to the image of his Son . . . and whom he foreordained, them he also called; and whom he called, them he also justified; and whom he justified, then he also glorified [*i.e.*, in His eternal purpose]. 1 Cor. 15:42-49: So also is the resurrection of the dead. It is sown in corruption; it is raised in incorruption: it is sown in dishonor; it is raised in glory; it is sown in weakness; it is raised in power: it is sown a natural body; it is raised a spiritual body. If there is a natural body, there is also a spiritual body. . . . The first man is of the earth, earthy: the second man is of heaven. As is the earthy, such are they also that are earthy; and as is the heavenly, such are they also that are heavenly. And as we have borne the image of the earthy, we shall also bear the image of the heavenly, etc. [Cf. also the glorified body in which Jesus was presented to the Apostles Peter, James, and John, on the Mount of Transfiguration

1. D. E. Sharp, *Franciscan Philosophy at Oxford in the Thirteenth Century*, 23.

(Matt. 17:1-8); also the glorified body (which outshone the brightness of the noonday sun) in which the risen Lord appeared to Saul of Tarsus before the gates of Damascus (Acts 26:12-15). Immortalization, according to Christian doctrine, seems to embrace the three processes of resurrection, revivification, *and glorification*.]

Modern philosophy is generally regarded as having had its beginning with Descartes (1596-1650). Gifted with an essentially mathematical mind, this French thinker attempted to construct a cosmology along strictly goemetrical lines. Hence, since geometry proceeds from the simplest propositions by a process of deductive reasoning to the most complex, Descartes sought among the attributes of bodies for the single attribute that is at once the most fundamental, most evident and most universal. This search led him to the conclusion that the essential property of material substance is *extension*. Now by extension is meant, according to Descartes, that property whereby (1) matter has parts, (2) the parts exist outside one another, (3) only one part can be in a given place at a given time, and (4) the whole is equal to the sum of the parts. Having established it to his own satisfaction that extension is the essence of matter, Descartes then denied to matter all properties which can not be deduced logically from an analysis of extension. One can see at a glance, of course, that the Cartesian theory of matter is at variance with the atomic hypothesis. For if mathematical extension is the essence of matter, then matter is divisible *ad infinitum*, and there simply can not be such a thing as an indivisible ultimate or atom. The theory, however, exerted considerable influence on subsequent scientific thinking about material substance, and was indirectly responsible for the "building-block" concept of the atom which came into vogue in the nineteenth century.

It was Robert Boyle, an English chemist, who introduced the modern period of the concept of matter by discrediting forever the long-standing theory of the "four elements." In his book, *The Sceptical Chymist*, published in 1661, Boyle formulated an entirely new definition of an element, describing it as a substance which cannot be decomposed into anything more ultimate. This was revolutionary. Over one hundred years later, in 1773 and 1774 to be exact, the independent experiments of Scheele in Sweden and Priestley in England resulted in the discovery of oxygen. Not long afterward, about 1790, the French chemist, Lavoisier, introduced the balance as an instrument of precision in the study of chemical processes, and as a result of his experiments discovered that in all chemical operations it is only the *kind* of matter that is changed, the *quantity* remaining the same. By this discovery of the principle of the conservation of matter, Lavoisier not only laid the foundation on which modern chemistry has grown to be an exact science, but also prepared the ground for the formulation of the scientific atomic theory. For, whereas the early Greek philosophers, Leukippos, Demokritos, and Epikouros developed the philosophic concept of the atom, it remained for the chemists of the nineteenth century to discover, by the scientific method, the scientific—or shall we say, *real?*—atom.

The modern atomic theory of the constitution of matter was first formulated, as a result of laboratory experimentation, by the great English chemist, John Dalton, of Manchester, between the years 1803 and 1808. In its simplest form, the theory is as follows: 1. Each element of matter is reducible to "ultimate particles" which can not be further subdivided. 2. The "ultimate particles" of the same element are all alike and of equal weight, while those of different elements are unlike. 3. Chemical combination takes place by the union of atoms of different elements in simple numerical proportions. Dalton pictured his "ultimate particles" or atoms as definite, concrete "grains" of matter, indivisible, and unaffected by the most violent chemical change. Dalton's work revolutionized the current conception of the constitution of matter and inaugurated the search for the chemical elements as we know them today. It was not until the year 1869, however, that the Russian scientist, Mendeleeff, first formulated with great completeness and gave to the world the Periodic Table of the elements, some ninety-two in all, of which all the myriad forms of matter in the world around us are composed.

The scientific world, however, inherited from Dalton what we now call the old "building block" or "billiard ball" concept of the atom. That is to say, atoms were conceived to be solid, inert, indivisible bits of matter, the bricks, so to speak, of which the whole material world is constructed. As Will Durant puts it:

The "matter" of Tyndall and Huxley was indestructible; it rested and slept, like the fat boy in *Pickwick Papers*, wherever it was put; and it resisted, with all the dignity of its volume and weight, every effort to set it moving, or to change the direction of its motion once it had condescended to move.[1]

This view prevailed throughout the greater part of the nine-

1. *The Mansions of Philosophy*, 61.

teenth century. Then came the more recent discoveries in the fields of electricity, magnetism, and radiation, realms so vast and so full of wonders that physicists now readily admit they have only begun to penetrate the mysteries of their amazing phenomena. The net result is that the old inert matter of the nineteenth-century physics is gone. We are now being told that the atom must no longer be regarded as a "substance" at all, that it is, rather, just a "field" in which "units," or perhaps only "waves," of energy are constantly playing; and that these units or waves of energy seem to be unrestricted by any of the conditions of distance or space. We are now told that an electric current is capable of traveling around the earth several times in a second; and that electrons can, like angels, move in all directions at once, and from one point to another without being found at any intermediate point. As a matter of fact, electrons seem to manifest some of the attributes which men have hitherto ascribed only to spirit.

We may summarize the conclusion of the latest physical science regarding the ultimate constitution of matter as follows: 1. The atom itself is no longer regarded as a compact something, a kind of building-block, but more properly as a "field" of energy. In the center of this field is a concentration of protons and neutrons (and interlocking mesons, according to the most recent pronouncements), the number of protons in each case specifying the particular element to which the atom belongs. Surrounding this concentration, which is designated the nucleus, is a kind of orbit in which electrons play (from 1 electron in the hydrogen atom up to 92 in the uranium atom), the number of electrons—which are negatively charged—corrsponding, in each atom, to the number of protons in the nucleus. Physicists generally speak of these ultimates of the stuff of things as "particles" of energy, although conceding that perhaps it would be just as correct to call them "waves" or "charges." The paradoxical nature of these particles consists in the fact that they can hardly be described as having spatial magnitude, and yet obviously they do have magnitude of a sort. For this reason physicists are at a loss to determine which of these designations—"particle," "wave," "charge," etc.—is precisely the proper one to indicate their essential nature. 2. In the general field of electromagnetic radiations, which includes all forms of radiant energy, such as light, heat, x-rays, gamma rays, cosmic rays, etc., the ultimates are pictured as discontinuous or discrete bits or "grains" of energy. In this field the waves of energy, we are told, travel throughout the cosmos, and frequently impinge upon the sense organs of percipients, in the form of what are usually designated "quanta" or "corpuscles." In a word, these radiations are essentially "corpuscular" as to nature. 3. In no sense can any of these ultimate bits of energy, either in the structure of the atom or in the electromagnetic field, be thought of as "substances" within the scope of the philosophical definition of that term. In a word, the ultimate constitution of matter has been found to be receding into the "immaterial." 4. Mass and energy are now shown to be equivalent. The property which hitherto has been called mass is now demonstrated to be concentrated energy. That is to say, matter is energy, and energy is matter; the distinction is simply one of temporary state. As Lincoln Barnett puts it, gross or solid matter is in reality only temporarily "frozen" energy.[1] And in addition to all this, we are told, the dissolution of matter into radiation and the dissipation of energy into empty space appears to be a fundamental cosmic process which now goes on without cessation. This means, of course, that the universe is slowly but surely moving toward a state of "maximum entropy," a state that may rightly be described as one of "perpetual and irrevocable stagnation" in which time shall be no more.[2] To offset this gloomy picture somewhat, there is a very great possibility, say some physicists, that somewhere out in the incalculable vastness of space— "somewhere beyond the blue"—matter is in the process of being formed anew. This notion, be it simply wishful thinking or not, gives us a faint ray of hope at least that the space-time continuum in which we now live and move and have our being may never actually become an unoccupied void.

Cf. in this connection 2 Pet. 3:1-13: This is now, beloved, the second epistle that I write unto you; and in both of them I stir up your sincere mind by putting you in remembrance; that ye should remember the words which were spoken before by the holy prophets, and the commandment of the Lord and Savior through your apostles: knowing this first, that in the last days mockers shall come with mockery, walking after their own lusts, and saying, Where is the promise of his coming? for, from the day that the fathers fell asleep, all things continue as they were from the beginning of the creation. For this they wilfully forget, that there were heavens from of old, and an earth compacted out of water, and amidst water, by the word of God; by which means the world that then was, being overflowed with water, perished; but the heavens that now are, and the earth, by the same word have been stored up for fire, being reserved against the day of judgment and destruction of ungodly men. But forget not this one

1. *The Universe and Dr. Einstein*, 59.
2. Barnett, *ibid.*, 100.

thing, beloved, that one day is with the Lord as a thousand years, and a thousand years as one day. The Lord is not slack concerning his promise, as some count slackness; but is longsuffering to youward, not wishing that any should perish, but that all should come to repentance. But the day of the Lord will come as a thief; in the which the heavens shall pass away with a great noise, and the elements shall be dissolved with fervent heat, and the earth and the works that are therein shall be burned up. Seeing that these things are thus all to be dissolved, what manner of persons ought ye to be in all holy living and godliness, looking for and earnestly desiring the coming of the day of God, by reason of which the heavens being on fire shall be dissolved, and the elements shall melt with fervent heat? *But, according to his promise, we look for a new heavens and a new earth, wherein dwelleth righteousness.* [Certainly the fiery destruction portrayed here could have reference to, and be fulfilled by, global atomic warfare.] Cf. Isa. 65:17—Behold, I create new heavens and a new earth; and the former things shall not be remembered, nor come into mind. Isa. 66:22—For as the new heavens and the new earth, which I will make, shall remain before me, saith Jehovah, so shall your seed and your name remain. Cf. Rev. 21:1, 2—And I saw a new heaven and a new earth: for the first heaven and the first earth are passed away; and the sea is no more. And I saw the holy city, new Jerusalem, coming down out of heaven from God, made ready as a bride adorned for her husband. Cf. also v. 3—And I heard a great voice out of the throne, saying, Behold, *the tabernacle of God is with men, and he shall dwell with them, and they shall be his peoples, and God himself shall be with them, and be their God.*

Some commentators have suggested that there may have been a "pre-Adamic" cosmos, which suffered a tremendous cataclysm of some kind; hence they describe the cosmogony that is given in *Genesis* as the "Adamic Renovation."[1] The excerpts from the Prophets and Apostles, quoted above, seem to indicate that the present cosmic age will terminate in a similar cataclysm, after which the Golden Age will be ushered in, with the banishment of sin and its consequences from the whole creation. *There is absolutely nothing in the Bible that can be construed as teaching the ultimate annihilation of matter.* I contend, moreover, that if matter is not to be annihilated, it is inconceivable that intelligent spirits or persons should suffer such an ultimate destiny. Indeed the Scriptures teach clearly that they are destined to live forever, either in eternal union with God, and clothed in immortal or ethereal bodies, which state is designated Heaven,—or in eternal separation from "the face of the Lord and from the glory of his might" (2 Thess. 1:8, 9), which is Hell, the penitentiary of the moral universe, originally "prepared for the devil and his angels" (Matt. 25:41). This is all in accord with the scientific laws of the conservation of matter and energy.

1. *Vide* R. Milligan, *Scheme of Redemption,* 23-30.

With regard to modern views of the ultimate constitution of matter, C. C. Furnas writes as follows:

> The atom which was once the very smallest bit of matter that could exist has now become a menagerie. It first resolved itself into a nucleus and a surrounding swarm of electrical charges. Now the nucleus is too large a unit to be final, so the greeting between physicists is: What's new in the nucleus? To explain the atom requires seven distinct fundamental physical entities: electron, positron, neutron, photon, proton, deutron, and alpha particles. Either that is not enough or it is too much, for the explanations of the atom are only as clear as a thick fog. Perhaps the atom is unexplainable but one hates to admit it.[1]

Again:

> Today the pure physicist seems to be reverting to metaphysics. He is always dabbling on the borderland of the unknowable and inconceivable. His idea of the atom is something that cannot be pictured. It is expressible as formulae, but it is something which our minds cannot visualize because it is not the kind of thing that can be visualized. Physicists have space that bends back on itself and universes that in some way expand without end. Energy sometimes acts like matter and matter is sometimes like energy. If it could be broken down it would release an enormous amount of energy for our own use, if we could catch it.[2]

To this we might add: Since these words were written, matter, that is, the atom, has been broken down. And what the future holds in store for man as a consequence, God alone knows!

The following excerpts from a volume entitled *The Advance of Science*, edited by Watson Davis, set forth clearly present-day conceptions of the constitution of matter:

> The atom has evolved from a little hard ball which was considered the ultimate particle of matter, into an entity so complex and multiplex that the best advice is not to try to visualize it. The components of atoms are at some times considered particles of matter and at other times, waves of energy. The picture of an atom as a heavy but minute kernel surrounded by circling bits of negative electricity—a nucleus of tightly packed protons and neutrons surrounded by orbital electrons, forming a miniature solar system with nucleus as sun and electrons as planets—has given way to a dim and indistinct mathematical entity that may best be visualized, if at all, as an equation.[3]
>
> Ernest Rutherford, now, as Lord Rutherford of Nelson, the presiding genius of the famous Cavendish Laboratory at Cambridge University in England . . . decisively blasted the idea that the atom was solid stuff. Some of the alpha particles flung at atoms bounced back, and from a study of the speeds of their recoil he showed that the atom is mostly space with its weight concentrated in an almost infinitesimal bit, with its diameter about one-one-hundred-thousandth of that of the atom itself.[4]

1. *The Next Hundred Years*, 187.
2. *Ibid.*, 186.
3. *Op. cit.*, 35.
4. *Ibid.*, 40.

Electrons have proved to be nearly omnipresent.[1]

Matter and energy are merely different aspects of the same thing. The famous principle of relativity, formulated by Professor Albert Einstein in 1905, included the idea of the equivalence of matter and energy. Lose mass and gain energy, or lose energy and gain mass. There is a very simple equation that allows the computation of just how much energy is equivalent to so much mass.[2]

Just because we may be practically interested in the obtaining of energy at the expense of matter, we must not overlook the importance of experiments that show the reverse process, the conversion of energy into the mass of matter. The discovery of what seems to be the creation of matter out of energy came in the train of research that followed upon the discovery of the positron. In many respects the making of matter out of energy is far more amazing and thrilling than the atom smashings that have liberated energy. The theory, well supported by experimental facts, is that *the positive electron is born out of radiant energy or "light" photons*. It is supposed that a highly energetic photon can transmute itself into a pair of electrons, one positive and one negative. Two particles of matter come into existence where only a bundle of energy existed before. That tested and famous Einsteinian equivalence of mass and energy tells us that the mass of two electrons at rest is equal to about one million electron volts. When this is put to the test by studying what happens in the formation of the electron pairs, it is found that the energy with a pair of electrons is moving after its formation is never within a million volts of the energy contained in the creating photon. This gives strong support to the idea that "light" is changing into matter.[3]

Attention has already been called to the striking correspondence between the "light metaphysics" of the thirteenth century philosophers, Grosseteste, Bacon, and Bonaventura, and the view expressed in the foregoing excerpt.

Physicists are now telling us that "cosmic rays bombard the earth from outer space every second of the day and night," that they "penetrate everything including our own bodies," that they "carry the mightiest packets of energy yet known to science," and that they "give rise to bursts of material particles."[4] The first scholar to put forward the view that these rays emanate from the depths of interstellar space was Madame Curie, who announced herself as suspecting the existence of a penetrating radiation disseminated throughout the universe. Some physicists have held that these rays are the super-radioactive outpourings of a primordial atom which Abbe Lemaitre considered to have formed the whole universe some ten thousand million years ago before it began to expand. The British physicists, Eddington and Jeans, think that cosmic rays result from the transformation of matter into radiation. Millikan, to the contrary, be-

1. *Op. cit.*, 53.
2. *Ibid.*, 71.
3. *Ibid.*, 73. Italics mine—C.
4. *Ibid.*, 26.

lieves that these strange rays are the "wailing cries" that attend the birth of matter from radiation. Harvey Brace Lemon writes:

It is with mixed emotions that we find ourselves getting far beyond our depth in the contemplation of the vast horizons to which we have been led by our simple curiosity about a leaking electroscope. . . . What story is further going to be decoded by the human mind as it goes on seeking further into these hidden matters, no man can now tell.[1]

Again, what is an electron? "Is it a bit of 'matter' manifesting energy," asks Will Durant, "or is it a measure of energy quite dissociated from any material substance? The latter is inconceivable to us."[2] It would no doubt be possible, writes Le Bon,

for a higher intelligence to conceive energy without substance . . . but such a conception cannot be conceived by us. We can only understand things by fitting them into the common frame of our thoughts. *The essence of energy being unknown, we are compelled to materialize it in order to reason about it.*[3]

Le Bon asserts, however, that "matter is a variety of energy."[4] "Some of the ablest men in the world at present," writes J. B. S. Haldane, "regard matter as merely a special type of undulatory disturbance."[5] Matter, says Eddington, is composed of protons and electrons, *i.e.*, positive and negative charges of electricity. What we call a solid body, he explains, is really empty space containing sparsely scattered electric charges. Concerning the "porosity" of the atom, he says:

The atom is as porous as the solar system. If we eliminated all the unfilled space in a man's body and collected his protons and electrons into one mass, the man would be reduced to a speck just visible with a magnifying glass.[6]

Whitehead writes:

The notion of mass is losing its unique pre-eminence as being the one final permanent quantity. . . . Mass now becomes the name for a quantity of energy in relation to some of its dynamical effects.[7]

John Dewey rightly concludes that "the notion of matter actually found in the practice of science has nothing in common with the matter of the materialists."[8]

1. *Cosmic Rays Thus Far*, 124, 125.
2. *The Mansions of Philosophy*, 62.
3. G. Le Bon, *The Evolution of Matter*, 13. Italics mine.
4. *Op. cit.*, 10.
5. *Possible Worlds*, 296.
6. *The Nature of the Physical World*, 1-3.
7. *Science and the Modern World*, 149.
8. *Experience and Nature*, 74.

In a word, "matter," in the sense of spatial or extended substance, has ceased to exist. The matter of the twentieth-century physicist has become at least *metaphysical,* if not ultimately immaterial. Sir James Jeans puts it as follows:

> Physicists who are trying to understand nature may work in many different fields and by many different methods: one may dig, one may sow, one may reap. But the final harvest will always be a sheaf of mathematical formulae. These will never describe nature itself, but only our observations on nature. Our studies can never put us into contact with reality; we can never penetrate beyond the impressions that reality implants in our minds.[1]

And Eddington seems to intimate that what we call "material things" are in reality only symbols by means of which intelligent beings or spirits communicate with on another. He says:

> That environment of space and time, of light and color and concrete things, which seems so vividly real to us is probed deeply by every device of physical science and at the bottom we reach symbols. Its substance has melted into shadow.[2]

Le Bon writes:

> The elements of atoms which are dissociated . . . are irrevocably destroyed. They lose every quality of matter—including the most fundamental of them all, weight. The balance no longer detects them. Nothing can recall them to the state of matter. They have vanished in the immensity of the ether. . . . Heat, electricity, light, etc., . . . represent the last stages of matter before its disappearance into the ether. . . . Matter which dissociates *dematerializes* itself by passing through successive phases which gradually deprive it of its material qualities, until it finally returns to the imponderable ether whence it seems to have issued.[3]

It should be noted, in this connection, that physicists are now prone to write about what they call the *dematerialization* of electrons. De Broglie, for instance, says:

> It has become tempting to imagine the photon as consisting of a corpuscle of negligible mass and charge obeying Dirac's equations, and associated with an anti-corpuscle of the same character. It is an attractive hypothesis, and from the mathematical point of view it can be completely worked out. It is easy to understand how a photon constructed in this way could be annihilated in the presence of matter by transferring to it the whole if its energy, a process analogous to the annihilation of a pair of electrons in the phenomenon of dematerialization. This annhilation—a quantum transition—would then constitute the photo-electric effect . . . and it ought then to be possible to define the electro-magnetic field as a function of this transition.[4]

Here, again, we have a clear intimation that light itself may be the primal energy.

1. *Physics and Philosophy,* 15.
2. *Op. cit.,* 37.
3. *The Evolution of Matter,* 14, 12, 7.
4. Louis de Broglie, *Matter and Light,* 159-160.

"Ether?—but what is this ether?" asks Will Durant, and goes on to say:

> The ether, said Lord Salisbury, is only a noun for the verb, to undulate;[1] it is a fiction created to conceal the learned ignorance of modern science; it is as mystical as a ghost or a soul. Einstein, by re-interpreting gravitation, deposed the ether; latterly he has decided to restore it for a while, with a limited sovereignty; whenever a physicist is puzzled, he answers, "Ether." The ether, says the latest authority, Professor Eddington, "is not a kind of matter"; it is "non-material."[2] That is to say, a non-material something, by certain mysterious contractions (vortices, as Lord Kelvin called them), transforms itself into matter; that which is without dimension or weight becomes, by adding bits of it together, spatial and ponderable matter. Is this theology restored, or a new Christian Science, or a form of psychical research? At the very moment when psychology is attempting by every presti-digitation to get rid of consciousness in order to reduce mind to matter, physics regrets to report that matter does not exist.[3]

Perhaps the latest word on the present-day view of the ultimate constitution of matter is contained in a little book, published several years ago, written by Lincoln Barnett, entitled *The Universe and Dr. Einstein*. This work is of special importance to us in view of the fact that its content bears the stamp of approval—the imprimatur, so to speak—of Dr. Einstein himself. (Barnett's book, published in 1948, contains a "Foreword" by Dr. Einstein himself, in which the latter expresses his personal approbation of the content of the book. This fact alone is sufficient to show that the volume contains the conclusions of the most up-to-date physics. This is the reason, of course, why I quote from the book rather freely in the present treatise. Its authoritative character can not be questioned.—C.) Concerning the subject before us— the ultimate constitution of matter, Barnett writes as follows:

> No one doubts today that all matter is made up of atoms which in turn are composed of even smaller building blocks called electrons, neutrons, and protons. But Einstein's notion that light too may consist of discontinuous particles clashed with a far more venerable theory that light is made up of waves. There are indeed certain phenomena involving light that can only be explained by the wave theory. . . . The phenomena—diffraction and interference—are strictly wave characteristics and would not occur if light were made up of individual corpuscles. More than two centuries of experiment and theory assert that light *must* consist of waves. Yet Einstein's Photoelectric Law shows that light *must* consist of photons [i.e., "particles" or "grains" of energy, discrete *quanta*, according to Planck's Quantum Theory]. This fundamental question—is light waves or is it particles?—has never

1. In William James, *The Meaning of Truth*, 19.
2. Eddington, *The Nature of the Physical World*, 32.
3. *The Mansions of Philosophy*, 63, 64.

been answered. The dual character of light is, however, only one aspect of a deeper and more remarkable duality which pervades all nature.[1]

The "duality" alluded to here is that of the apparent "particle" and "wave" structures which seem at one and the same time to characterize the ultimate stuff of things, both in the electro-magnetic field and in the basic structure of the atom. Hence Barnett goes on to say:

The first hint of this strange dualism came in 1925, when a young French physicist named Louis de Broglie suggested that phenomena involving the interplay of matter and radiation could best be understood by regarding electrons not as individual particles but as systems of waves. This audacious concept flouted two decades of quantum research in which physicists had built up rather specific ideas about the elementary particles of matter. The atom had come to be pictured as a kind of miniature solar system composed of a central nucleus surrounded by varying numbers of electrons (1 for hydrogen, 92 for uranium) revolving in circular or elliptical orbits. The electron was less vivid. Experiments had shown that all electrons had exactly the same mass and the same electrical charge, so it was natural to regard them as the ultimate foundation stones of the universe. It also seemed logical at first to picture them as hard elastic spheres. But little by little, as investigation progressed, they became more capricious, defiant of observation and measurement. In many ways their behavior appeared too complex for any material particle. . . . Shortly after De Broglie had his vision of "matter waves," a Viennese physicist named Schrodinger developed the same idea in coherent mathematical form, evolving a system that explained quantum phenomena by attributing specific wave functions to protons and electrons. This system, known as "wave mechanics," was corroborated in 1927, when two American scientists, Davisson and Germer, proved by experiment that electrons do exhibit wave characteristics. . . . But further surprises were in store. For subsequent experiments showed that not only the electrons but whole atoms and even molecules produce wave patterns when diffracted by a crystal surface, and that their wave lengths are exactly what De Broglie and Schrodinger forecast. *And so all the basic units of matter*—what J. Clerk Maxwell called "the imperishable foundation stones of the universe"—*gradually shed their substance. The old-fashioned spherical electron was reduced to an undulating charge of electrical energy, the atom to a system of superimposed waves. One could only conclude that all matter is made up of waves and we live in a world of waves.*[2]

Barnett then continues:

The paradox presented by waves of matter on the one hand and particles of light on the other was resolved by several developments in the decade before World War II. The German physicists, Heisenberg and Born, bridged the gap by developing a new mathematical apparatus that permitted accurate description of quantum phenomena either in terms of waves or in terms of particles as one wished. The idea behind their system had a profound influence on the philosophy of science. They maintained it is pointless for a physicist to worry about the properties of a single electron; in the laboratory he works with beams or showers of electrons, each containing billions of individual particles

1. *Op. cit.*, 19-21.
2. *Ibid*, 21-23. (Italics mine.—C.)

77

(or waves); he is concerned therefore only with mass behavior, with statistics and the laws of probability and chance. So it makes no practical difference whether individual electrons are particles or systems of waves—in aggregate they can be pictured either way. . . . Born took the mathematical expression used by Schrodinger in his equations to denote wave function and interpreted it as a "probability" in a statistical sense. That is to say, he regarded the intensity of any part of a wave as a measure of the probable distribution at that point. Thus he dealt with the phenomena of diffraction, which hitherto only the wave theory could explain, in terms of the *probability* of certain corpuscles—light quanta or electrons—following certain paths and arriving at certain places. And so "waves of matter" were reduced to "waves of probability."[1]

The same author then concludes:

It no longer matters how we visualize an electron or an atom or a probability wave. The equations of Heisenberg and Born fit any picture. And we can, if we choose, imagine ourselves living in a universe of waves, a universe of particles, or as one facetious scientist has phrased it, a universe of "wavicles."[2]

Again, concerning the reciprocal transmutation of matter and energy, as described by the Einsteinian principle of the equivalence of mass and energy, Barnett writes:

In the light of this broad principle, many puzzles of nature are resolved. The baffling interplay of matter and radiation which appears sometimes to be a concourse of particles and sometimes a meeting of waves, becomes more understandable. The dual role of the electron as a unit of matter and unit of electricity, the wave electron, the photon, waves of matter, waves of probability, a universe of waves—all these seem less paradoxical. For all these concepts simply describe different manifestations of the same underlying reality, and it no longer makes sense to ask what any one of them "really" is. *Matter and energy are interchangeable. If matter sheds its mass and travels with the speed of light, we call it radiation or energy. And conversely if energy congeals and becomes inert and we can ascertain its mass, we call it matter.* Heretofore science could only note their ephemeral properties and relations as they touched the perceptions of earth-bound man. But since July 16, 1945, man has been able to transform one into the other. For on that night at Alamogordo, New Mexico, man for the first time transmuted a substantial quantity of matter into the light, heat, sound, and motion, which we call energy.[3]

The "conclusion of the whole matter" is given by the same author in the following paragraph:

Yet the fundamental mystery remains. The whole march of science toward the unification of concepts—the reduction of all matter to elements and then to a few types of particles, the reduction of "forces" to the single concept "energy," and then the reduction of matter *and* energy to a single basic quantity—leads still to the unknown. The many questions merge into one, to which there may never be an an-

1. *Op. cit.*, 23-24.
2. *Ibid.*, 24.
3. *Ibid.*, 59. (Italic mine—C)

swer: what is the essence of this mass-energy substance, what is the underlying stratum of physical reality which science seeks to explore?[1]

Again, one of the most amazing facts about these discoveries of modern physics is that they were arrived at by the human mind, and not by the human eye or any other physical sense organ, by the way of mathematical formulae, many years before they were actually confirmed experimentally. To any thinking person, this mathematical accuracy points unmistakably to the Universal Intelligence and Will, to whom men in all ages have reverently given the name "God"—that Will which is the constitution of the cosmos. Moreover, with each succeeding discovery of modern physics, our world of the physical senses has lost more and more of its traditional character as the "real" world, and has become correspondingly a world of appearance, the *phenomenal* world. The real world has come to be more and more, in fact, that "region above the heaven" described by Plato as "the colorless, formless, and intangible truly existing essence, with which all true knowledge is concerned," which "is visible only to the mind, the pilot of the soul."[2] In short, it is the world of the Eternal Spirit, from whose very Being, perhaps, the phenomenal world has been projected and has taken shape before the eyes of created living beings. In this connection, I shall take the liberty of indulging another lengthy quotation or two from Barnett:

But the irony of man's quest for reality is that as nature is stripped of its disguises, as order emerges from chaos and unity from diversity, as concepts merge and fundamental laws assume increasingly simpler form, the evolving picture becomes ever more abstract and remote from experience—far stranger indeed and less recognizable than the bone structure behind a familiar face. For where the geometry of a skull predestines the outlines of the tissue it supports, there is no likeness between the image of a tree transcribed by our senses and that propounded by wave mechanics, or between a glimpse of the starry sky on a summer night and the four-dimensional continuum that has replaced our perceptual Euclidean space.

In trying to distinguish appearance from reality and lay bare the fundamental structure of the universe, science has had to transcend the "rabble of the senses." But its highest edifices, Einstein has pointed out, have been "purchased at the price of emptiness of content." A theoretical concept is emptied of content to the very degree that it is divorced from sensory experience. For the only world man can truly know is the world created for him by his senses. If he expunges all the impressions which they translate and memory stores, nothing is

1. *Op. cit.*, 59-60. *Vide* in a subsequent part of the present treatise a final word on the First Principle, the Principle of the Unity and Generation of all things.
2. *Phaedrus*, 247 C-E. Translation by H. N. Fowler, Loeb Classical Library Edition.

left. That is what the philosopher Hegel meant by his cryptic remark: "Pure Being and Nothing are the same." A state of existence devoid of associations has no meaning. So paradoxically what the scientist and the philosopher call the world of appearance— the world of light and color, of blue skies and green leaves, of sighing wind and murmuring water, the world designed by the physiology of human sense organs is the world in which finite man is incarcerated by his essential nature. And what the scientist and the philosopher call the world of reality—the colorless, soundless, impalpable cosmos which lies like an iceberg beneath the plane of man's perceptions—is a skeleton structure of symbols.[1]

## Again:

In the evolution of scientific thought, one fact has become impressively clear: *there is no mystery of the physical world which does not point to a mystery beyond itself.* All highroads of the intellect, all byways of theory and conjecture lead ultimately to an abyss that human ingenuity can never span. For man is enchained by the very condition of his being, his finiteness and involvement in nature. The farther he extends his horizons, the more vividly he recognizes the fact that as the physicist Niels Bohr puts it, "we are both spectators and actors in the great drama of existence." Man is thus his own greatest mystery. He does not understand the vast veiled universe into which he has been cast for the reason that he does not understand himself. He comprehends but little of his organic processes and even less of his unique capacity to perceive the world about him, to reason and to dream. Least of all does he understand his noblest and most mysterious faculty: the ability to transcend himself and perceive himself in the act of perception.

Man's inescapable impasse is that he himself is a part of the world he seeks to explore; his body and proud brain are mosaics of the same elemental particles that compose the dark, drifting dust clouds of interstellar space; he is, in the final analysis, merely an ephemeral conformation of the primordial space-time field. Standing midway between macrocosm and microcosm he finds barriers on every side and can perhaps but marvel, as St. Paul did nineteen hundred years ago, that "the world was created by the word of God so that what is seen was made out of things which do not appear."[2]

But is it necessarily true that man—a living, conscious spirit himself, created in the Divine image, we are told in Scripture, the noblest product of the Divine handiwork—is "merely an ephemeral conformation of the primordial space-time field"? Perhaps, after all, he, who has the power himself of transcending both space and time in his experience, has the possibility of a higher destiny than this world has to offer, by conforming his will to the will of the Divine, as he is urged again and again to do in the Word of God. Moreover, is it necessarily true, as this author seems to affirm, that the real world as envisioned by the present-day physicist, has no meaning for man? Certainly it has all the meaning which the human imag-

1. *Op. cit.*, 109-110.
2. *Ibid.*, 113-114. (Italic mine—C.)

ination is capable of grasping, for the man of the Spirit, who sees beyond the realm of flesh and sense. In fact, to him alone, it is the only world that can have fulness of meaning—simply because it is the abode of his God, and his God is Love (I John 4:7, 8). It is sheer presumption, sheer "earthboundness," to assert that sensory experience is the noblest and most satisfying of which man is capable. Such a view is derogatory of the very dignity and worth of the human individual; it is a view which spiritually-minded of all ages would repudiate and hurl back with scorn. To the man of the Spirit, the very hope of some day "seeing God face to face," of apprehending Him, that is, with the understanding and with the affections, is an infinitely greater source of pleasure even than the sensory apprehension of this present "world of light and color, of blue skies and green leaves, of sighing wind and murmuring water." Beautiful as this world is in many of its aspects, it can be only a shadow of that world which is filled with the presence of God, and is therefore filled with joy and thanksgiving and praise. And if the hope of such a state of spiritual satisfaction and peace is a source of great joy to the man of the Spirit, what indeed will the fruition be! It simply cannot be described in human language! Eye has not seen, nor ear heard, nor has it entered into the imagination of man to conceive the things which God has prepared for those who love Him. This Beatific Vision, Jesus tells us, is reserved only for the "pure in heart" (Matt. 5:8), for the obvious reason that it can be appreciated only by the pure in heart, by those who prepare themselves, by cultivating the fruit of the Spirit in themselves (Gal. 5:22-24), to apprehend and to appreciate it. Man's natural and proper end is the union of the individual mind with the Mind of God in knowledge, and the union of the individual will with the Will of God in love. In that heavenly state, what Spinoza has termed "intellectual love of God"[1] will indeed be realized to the full, but it will be supplemented by the blissful affection of Love which shall bind God and all His redeemed creatures in that everlasting holy fellowship which shall mark the consummation of the entire Creative Process. Small wonder that St. Paul was prompted to cry out at times, "For to me to live is Christ, and to die is gain" (Phil. 1:21), and again, "I am in a strait betwixt the two, having the desire to depart and be with Christ; for it is very far better; yet to

1. Spinoza, *Ethics*, Propositions XXV-XLII.

abide in the flesh is more needful for your sake" (Phil. 1:23, 24). No wonder he was prompted to shout, as his valedictory, "I have fought the good fight, I have finished the course, I have kept the faith; henceforth there is laid up for me the crown of righteousness, which the Lord, the righteous judge, shall give to me at that day; and not to me only, but also to all them that have loved his appearing" (2 Tim. 4:7, 8)!

Then, again, there is the mystery of Space, and the equally profound mystery of Time. The suggestion has been made in recent years that Matter might be an emanation from Space. Einstein predicted some years ago that the next forward step in science would be the attempt to solve the mystery of Space. He is reported to have said something to this effect: It appears that Space will have to be regarded as a primary thing with matter only derived from it, so to speak, as a secondary result. But—we may reasonably ask—what is Space to our minds but a possible location for matter in motion? This, however, is not in any sense a definition. The word "space" seems to convey the idea of an intangible something (or nothing?), let us say an expanse, that is everywhere, in whatever direction one might go and no matter how far in any direction one might go; a something that one could never leave behind, never get away from or out of; something akin, in its intangibility and every-whereness, to our notion of Spirit. One might well recall in in this context Pascal's statement: "The eternal silence of infinite space is terrifying." Or the cry of the Psalmist:

> O Jehovah, thou hast searched me, and know me.
> Thou knowest my downsitting and mine uprising;
> Thou understandest my thoughts afar off. . . .
> Whither shall I go from thy Spirit?
> Or whither shall I flee from thy presence?
> If I ascend up into heaven, thou art there;
> If I make my bed in Sheol, behold, thou art there.
> If I take the wings of the morning,
> And dwell in the uttermost parts of the sea,
> Even there shall thy hand lead me,
> And thy right hand shall hold me.
> (Psa. 139:1, 2, 7-10).

Is Space, then, a *sui generis* being, capable of indefinite extension in all directions, and, although completely independent of matter, yet the container—Plato, in the *Timaeus*, calls it the "Receptacle"—of the finite world of material objects? Are these so-called "material" objects, after all, in a state of continuous flux, and hence only illusory changes? Newton, Clarke, and Fenelon, for example, identified absolute Space with the Divine immensity or ubiquity; and Spinoza regarded Space as the extension of the Divine Substance, and essential attribute of the Divine Being. Or, on the other hand, is Space merely an ideal being, a concept of the human mind, purely subjective in character? Kant, the German philosopher, for example, explained both Space and Time as "forms of perception" inherent in the perceiving mind, forms which the mind itself brings to bear upon the raw material of sensation. Leibniz, while rejecting the innateness of the idea, nevertheless regarded Space as a subjective representation formed in the presence of, or under the impact of, external objects. And Bergson held that Space is "an ideal scheme or a symbol appended to matter to render the latter divisible and subject to our conscious actions."[1] Bergson says:

> The glance which falls at any moment on the things about us only takes in the effects of a multiplicity of inner repetitions and evolutions, effects which are, for that very reason, discontinuous, and into which we bring back continuity by the relative movements that we attribute to "objects" in space. The change is everywhere, but inward; we localize it here and there, but outwardly; and thus we constitute bodies which are both stable as to their qualities and mobile as to their positions, a mere change of place summing up in itself, to our eyes, the universal transformation.[2]

For Hegel, Space was the *exteriorization of the Absolute* (whatever this phrase may mean!); and for Herbert Spencer it was an abstract concept of all the relations between co-existents, real space itself being unknowable. And so the problems attached to the term persist in persisting: Is Space one? Is it absolute or relative? Is it mobile or immobile? Is it finite or infinite? Is it a vacuum or a plenum (and if the latter, is it filled with ether?)? Are there intervals in the cosmos that are empty of all matter? Is Space homogeneous or heterogeneous? And the basic problem of all: Does Space exist objectively, or is it merely an idea in the human mind? About all that can be said in answer to any of these questions is: Who knows?

(It is interesting to note at this point how many of our "modern" pundits have been indulging the pastime of poking fun at the medieval scholars who are said to have spent much

1. *Vide*, D. Nys., *Cosmology*, II, 347-432.
2. Henri Bergson, *Matter and Memory*, trans. by Paul and Palmer, 277.

time in discussing the problem as to *how many angels could dance on the point of a needle*. The modern theologian might reply in kind by asking the scholars of our day, *How many atoms can dance on the point of a needle?* We must remember, of course, that the medievals were dealing with the problem as to how a spiritual (non-corporeal) entity could be thought of as occupying space. In our time, such questions as, In what sense does an atom occupy space, or, Does it occupy space in any sense of the term? are apparently as insoluble.)

Or, take the mystery of Time: what is it? "Time," said Plato, "is the moving image of eternity." That is to say, the things of sense-perception, the "objects" of our phenomenal world of Becoming, are but copies, and copies in a state of continuous flux, of the fixed, unchangeable, and eternal Forms of the world of true Being. Says Plato, by the mouth of his Pythagorean spokesman, in the *Timaeus*:

> Time came into existence along with the Heaven, to the end that having been generated together they might also be dissolved together, if ever a dissolution of them should take place; and it was made after the pattern of the Eternal Nature, to the end that it might be as like thereto as possible; for whereas the pattern is existent throughout all eternity, the copy, on the other hand, is through all time, continually having existed, existing, and being about to exist.[1]

Time, therefore, being cotemporaneous, so to speak, with the Creation itself, God the Creator must transcend all Time and indeed all Space as well. Or, as Scripture puts it: "One day is with the Lord as a thousand years, and a thousand years as one day" (2 Pet. 3:8). But what is Time *per se*? It was St. Augustine who wrote, centuries ago: "What is time? If nobody asks me, I know; but if I were desirous to explain it to one that should ask me, plainly I know not."[2] Is Time simply duration, a duration that is *felt* rather than measured, as Bergson contended?[3] Is it merely the measure of the relative imperfections of human beings? Is Time strictly identical with movement or change? Is it reversible or irreversible? Is it absolute, or relative? Did it have a beginning? Will it come to an end? Is such a distinction as that of *real* time and and *mathematical* time legitimate? Is time an objective element in the scheme of things, or again is it merely subjective, an idea that the human mind imposes upon the facts of experience? Again,

1. *Tim.* 37 D ff. Trans. by R. G. Bury, Loeb Classical Library Edition.
2. Augustine, *Confessions*, XI, ch. 17. Pusey translation, Everyman's Library Edition, 262.
3. Bergson, *Time and Free Will*.

about the only honest answer we can give to any of these questions is: Who but God knows?

Suffice it to say that the tendency among physicists at present is to unite Space and Time in theoretical wedlock, so to speak; that is to say, to regard Space-Time as one, as fourth dimensional. As Lincoln Barnett puts it:

Since time is an impalpable quantity it is not possible to draw a picture or construct a model of a four-dimensional space-time continuum. But it can be imagined and it can be represented mathematically. And in order to describe the stupendous reaches of the universe beyond our solar system, beyond the clusters and star clouds of the Milky Way, beyond the lonely outer galaxies burning in the void, the scientist must visualize it all as a continuum in three dimensions of space and one of time. In our minds we tend to separate these dimensions; we have an awareness of space and an awareness of time. But the separation is purely subjective; and as the Special Theory of Relativity showed, space and time separately are relative quantities which vary with individual observers. In any objective description of the universe, such as science demands, the time dimension can no more be detached from the space dimension that length can be detached from breadth and thickness in an accurate representation of a house, a tree or Betty Grable. According to the great German mathematician, Herman Minkowski, who developed the mathematics of the space-time continuum as a convenient medium for expressing the principles of Relativity, "space and time separately have vanished into the merest shadows, and only a sort of combination of the two preserves any reality."[1]

This author continues:

It must not be thought, however, that the space-time continuum is simply a mathematical construction. The world *is* a space-time continuum; all reality exists both in space and in time, and the two are indivisible. All measurements of time are really measurements in space, and conversely measurements in space depend on measurements of time. Seconds, minutes, hours, days, weeks, months, seasons, years, are measurements of the earth's position in space relative to the sun, moon, and stars. Similarly latitude and longitude, the terms whereby man defines his spatial position on the earth, are measured in minutes and seconds, and to compute them accurately one must know the time of day and the day of the year. Such "landmarks" as the Equator, the Tropic of Cancer, or the Arctic Circle are simply sundials which clock the changing seasons; the Prime Meridian is a co-ordinate of daily time; and "noon" is nothing more than an angle of the sun.

Even so, the equivalence of space and time becomes really clear only when one contemplates the stars. Among the familiar constellations, some are "real" in that their component stars comprise true gravitational systems, moving in an orderly fashion relative to one another; others are only apparent—their patterns are accidents of perspective, created by a seeming adjacency of unrelated stars along the line of sight. Within such optical constellations one may observe two stars of equal brightness and assert that they are "side by side" in the firmament, whereas in actuality one may be 40 light years and the other 400 light years away.

1. *Op. cit.,* 64.

Obviously the astronomer has to think of the universe as a space-time continuum. When he peers through his telescope he looks not only outward in space but backward in time. His sensitive cameras can detect the glimmer of island universes 500 million light years away—faint gleams that began their journey at a period of terrestrial time when the first vertebrates were starting to crawl from warm Paleozoic seas onto the young continents of Earth. His spectroscope tells him, moreover, that these huge outer systems are hurtling into limbo, away from our own galaxy, at incredible velocities ranging up to 35,000 miles a second. Or, more precisely, they *were* receding from us 500 million years ago. Where they are "now," or whether they even exist "now," no one can say. If we break down our picture of the universe into three subjective dimensions of space and one of local time, then these galaxies have no objective existence save as faint smudges of ancient enfeebled light on a photographic plate. They attain physical reality only in their proper frame of reference, which is the four-dimensional space-time continuum.[1]

After all, is there not an obvious kinship between this Space-Time continuum of the twentieth-century physicist and the connotations of the term "Spirit"? Not only with respect to the *everywhereness*, but also with respect to the *inexhaustible-ness*, of both. And would it be too far-fetched to regard Matter, that is, in its ultimate character of, perhaps, radiant energy, as a projection of Space-Time or Spirit? Bergson certainly approximates this view in his presentation of the *Elan Vital* as a Cosmic Consciousness—in one or two instances he speaks of it as "Spirit"—ever pushing its way upward like a fountain that gushes higher and higher, and of which the particles that fall back toward the source of the movement constitute what we call "matter."[2]

Mr. Walter Russell, then President of the Society of Arts and Sciences, was quoted in the daily press a few years ago as saying, in an address delivered in New York City:

The question arises, Is there any line of demarcation between a spiritual and a physical universe? And have we not been calling the invisible universe "spiritual" just because we could not see it? We have begun to see something tangible and inspiring beyond place, mass, and dimension. There must be a limitless source of static energy somewhere back of all this dynamic expression.

Speaking with reference to the ultimate particles of which matter is composed, which seem to constitute light, and which carry energy, scientists, said Mr. Russell, find them all acting suspiciously like some of the processes of human thought. He then added:

Tomorrow physics will undoubtedly divorce energy from matter and give it to space. . . . What we call the spiritual universe may

1. *Op. cit.*, 65, 66.
2. H. Bergson, *Creative Evolution*. Trans. by Arthur Mitchell.

## MATTER AND SPIRIT

prove to be the static source in space of electric energy. If Einstein's prophecy is fulfilled it would cause a far greater upheaval in science than Copernicus caused in the concept of Ptolemy. Basic conclusions of today would be either reversed or discarded entirely, for if energy belongs to space as the new cosmogony suggests, light would belong to space, as Jesus inferred. When energy is found to belong to space, light will be understood to be an emergence from space, and God will be found to be what Jesus said He was—Light. As we study Jesus' teaching from the point of view of science, we become convinced that He understood light, energy, motion, and space, and knew what filled space. Jesus taught that life is eternal, that there is no death. Science may prove this to be literally true, and that the body, like all other material phenomena, merely registers the intensity of the thinking of a Supreme Intelligence. If science proves this, it will give meaning to the words of Sir James Jeans that "matter may eventually be proved to be pure thought."[1]

As we read these excerpts in which are set forth the views of the most distinguished physicists of our day, the words of the first three verses of the Bible come to mind:

In the beginning God created the heavens and the earth. And the earth was waste and void; and darkness was upon the face of the deep; and the Spirit of God was brooding upon the face of the waters. And God said, Let there be light; and there was light.

In the light, therefore, of the most recent scientific view of the essential constitution of matter, are we not justified in believing that creative activity began with the initial putting forth of radiant energy as a result of the activity of the Divine Spirit? And that this projection of primal energy resulted in the vast accumulation of matter: the stuff of which the Spirit of God, through the instrumentality of successive fiats of the Divine Word, subsequently moulded, arranged and constituted our cosmos? We may well ask then: Was this primal energy inherent in the Being of God? Or was it a *primary* creation, what theologians have termed a creation *ex nihilo*? Science has no answer for this question, and probably never will have one. Faith, however, answers that it was, in some sense, a primary creation. "By faith we understand that the worlds have been framed by the word of God, so that what is seen hath not been made out of things which appear" (Heb. 11:3). "By the word of Jehovah were the heavens made, and all the host of them by the breath [spirit] of his mouth. . . . For he spake, and it was done; he commanded, and it stood fast" (Psa. 33:6, 9). *All of which boils down to the fact that pure Spirit-Power, which is pure Thought-Power, is capable of generating what we call "physical" power: a fact of which, as we shall see later, we have*

1. I have misplaced the original of this press story. However, I vouch for the accuracy of the excerpt presented here.

*an imperfect analogy in the powers of the pure spirit of man.*
As Dr. Michael I. Pupin has said:

> Sixty years ago, Clerk-Maxwell, the great electrical mathematician, spoke like a prophet when he made the startling announcement that . . . radiation of light is a manifestation of moving electricity. The most precious among the fruits of this discovery of Maxwell is that the origin of all light radiation is in the motion of the tiny electrons, which are, as far as we know, the unchangeable, primordial building stones of the material universe. Everything that moves seems to be deriving its breath of existence from the electrical forces which have their origin in these tiny electrons. These little workers, infinitely small, but infinitely numerous, by their combined activities make up the larger activities of that stupendous thing which we call the universe. And this busy little worker, the electron, is the most law-abiding creature in the universe. It loves, honors and obeys the laws, and its eternal mission is to serve. God employed the heavenly host of electronic workers to build the atoms, the molecules, and the galaxies of burning stars. These celestial furnaces, throbbing with the blazing energy of the electronic host, are moulding all kinds of planetary castings, and tempering them so as to be just right for organic life. One of these planetary castings is our Mother Earth. It is a mere dust speck in the universe, but this dust speck is the home of the soul of man, and this lifts our tiny earth to a place of honor near the throne of God. The soul's very breath of life is the beautiful electronic music, and to be thrilled by the melody of that cosmic song is the highest aim in our study of electrical science.

Again:

> What is the only mystery today in electrical science? It is this: Where, when and how did the electron come into existence? The sensible man will answer; God created the electron, and therefore only God knows where, when and how. This eliminates the mystery at once. The rest we can see for ourselves. God created a host of electrons to be His assistants in building the universe. And when science discovered the electrons and learned to use them in man's service, it was our first glimpse of the method of creative operation.[1]

There are those "unbelieving" scientists, of course, who dislike the name of God, and who choose to begin with electrons and atoms (or some other kind of particles of primal energy), holding these to be the unoriginated First Principle (or Principles) of all things. Under such a view, of course, it becomes necessary to conclude that these primal particles—whatever name may be given to them—have always contained, and still contain, within themselves the potentialities of all the higher phenomena of human experience, such as life, consciousness, thought, conscience, personality, and the like. Is it not obvious, therefore, that such a Primal Energy as the First Principle, that is, one embracing the potentialities of life, consciousness, and thought, certainly approximates what is designated "God" in the vocabu-

1. Quoted by A. E. Wiggam, *Exploring Your Mind*, 385-407.

lary of the Christian? Obviously, there must be an unoriginated or self-existent First Principle of all things—a Someone or Something that has always been and will always be, that is without beginning or end; the human mind revolts against the notion that Something could ever have been generated by an "eternal Nothing." It is to just such a First Principle that religion applies the name "God." And no matter how zealously the scientist tries to avoid this designation, the fact remains that his Primal Energy bears the same relation to the Cosmos and its processes as does the believer's God. I therefore affirm that there are no actual atheists in the world; those who profess to be "atheists" are simply hiding behind a mass of verbiage. Every thinking person is compelled by both logic and common sense to accept the fact of a First Principle, either monistic, dualistic, or pluralistic in character. Therefore, the question primarily is not, Where did God come from?—but, Why is there Something instead of Nothing? And, secondarily, What is the nature of this Someone or Something that is without beginning or end, which is the Source of Cause of the whole Creation? Now if the First Principle be Primal Energy of some kind—radiant, electronic, atomic, or what not—that Primal Energy is God. This is the long of it, the short of it, and the all of it. There is simply no getting away from an eternal Something.

The difference, then, between the "non-believer" and the believer is that, whereas the former holds the First Principle of all things to be the nature of matter or energy (materialism), the believer holds that the First Principle is of the nature of Spirit or Person (theism). The "non-believer" bows in adoration before electrons, atoms, and molecules; the believer worships the Eternal Spirit, the Eternal Spirit of the Bible. For Jesus Himself tells us that "God is a Spirit, and they that worship him must worship in spirit and truth" (John 4:24). The whole issue boils down, therefore, to this: Which view—laying aside the claim of revelation altogether, for the moment—is the more reasonable, and which is more in accord with human experience?

I choose, for strictly experiential reasons, to take my stand for the Eternal Spirit of the Bible—the Spirit of God or Holy Spirit. In the first place, science has not one iota of evidence to offer in support of the hypothesis that pure energy or matter has within itself the powers of producing life, consciousness, or thought. The gaps between these successively higher phenomena are just as great as they ever were: not one of them has even been begun to be bridged. Neither life, consciousness, or thought has ever been reduced to purely physiochemical or even cellular activity; all assertions to the contrary that one may read occasionally in textbooks are sheer bravado. In the second place, the essentially mathematical structure, and the obviously theological aspects (in the form of adaptation of means to ends), of the Cosmos and its processes, both point unmistakably to Spirit, that is, to Universal Intelligence and Will, rather than to unthinking, purely chance-operative particles of energy. Besides all this, the application of energy, in the form of force, to any particular end, as occurs constantly throughout Nature, presupposes the exercise of a Sovereign Will,—that Will which is the constitution of the universe. There is no accounting for the framework of Order which Nature presents to our view, and without which there never could have been a science, without a Sovereign Orderer. As the Psalmist puts it: "God spake, and it was done; He commanded, and it stood fast" (Psa. 33:9). I contend, therefore, that it is far more reasonable, and more in accord with human experience, to begin with Pure Spirit as the First Principle, as the One who embraces within Himself both potentially and actually all these higher phenomena, and who has infused them, one by one, progressively, into the Creative Process. It is far more reasonable to begin with the all-pervading Spirit as the Source of all orders of Being—electronic, atomic, vital, conscious, rational, moral, and spiritual—than it is to begin with nothing but irrational "waves" or "particles" of "brute" force. The former view accounts for all known phenomena of experience; the latter, one might well say, for none. If called upon to make the choice between the Eternal Spirit, on the one hand, and purely chance-operative particles of non-thinking, amoral particles of primal energy on the other hand, as the First Cause of all things, it seems to me that any intelligent person would take his stand on the side of Spirit. For man *knows*—if he will but look into himself—that he is infinitely more than an aggregate of physiochemical processes; that he is, in a word, a being who has been created "in the image of God" (Gen. 1:27).

To summarize: It must have become perfectly apparent by this time that is speaking of "matter" we may have, primarily, either of two *referents* in mind: (1) gross matter, the matter of everyday experience, palpable to the senses; or (2) ultimate matter, that of the present-day physicist, which is essentially energy rather than extension, and which, though none the less real, is intelligible only in terms of mathematical formulae. There is a third sense too in which we may speak, secondarily, of "matter," namely, as designating the imperceptible, unknowable cause of our sensations: a universal substratum, a support "we know not what" which "is the same everywhere," to use John Locke's phraseology. This is a view which has prevailed quite generally throughout the history of philosophic thought, the *Apeiron* of Anaximander oft repeated. And finally, we may use the word "matter" merely to signify a something that is the opposite of "mind" or "spirit." It is with this signification, perhaps, that the word is most commonly used in everyday speech.

What practical conclusions are to be drawn, from this excursus into the history of the concept of matter, for our present purpose? I suggest the following lines of thought:

In the first place, At what point is the line of demarcation between matter and spirit to be drawn, or perhaps it would be more correct to say, between the ontological *referents* designated by the words "matter" and "spirit"? Where shall we find—or locate—the line that divides the "material" from the "non-material" or "immaterial"? Does such a line of demarcation actually exist? Or, is this an antithesis, like that perhaps of "natural" and "supernatural," probably formulated and arbitrarily imposed upon reality by the human mind itself? Perhaps the Totality of Things is, after all, a *continuum*, with the "material" shading into the "non-material," and vice versa, at certain points and under certain conditions. We might, for instance, approach the solution to this problem by asking, What is the essential property of matter? That is, what is the characteristic of matter lacking which it would not be *matter*? A great many thinkers, following Descartes, have contended that the essential property of matter is *extension;* others, the Neo-Scholastics, for example, say that it is *divisibility*. Now these conclusions may be true of gross matter, the matter common to our everyday experience. But they simply cannot be true of the ultimate matter as it is described by our present-day physicists. The ultimate "particles" which go to make up the atom can hardly be said to have spatial magnitude at all, and yet, paradoxically, they must have spatial magnitude of a sort. Moreover, as previously stated, the word *atomos* means "indivisible"; hence, the moment the atom is postulated as the ultimate *unit* of matter, the bridge has been crossed from the realm of the divisible and "material" into that of the indivisible and hence by definition "immaterial." The same reasoning applies to the proton, neutron, electron, and like subordinate particles of the atom. The issue is not resolved in any respect by conceiving the atom as a "particle," "wave," or "field" of energy. As a matter of fact, the atoms of the new physics are not in the strictest sense indivisible; rather, they are found to be composite and occasionally to lose or gain their "parts," and even to change their nature. But in view of the fact that these "parts" ("particles" or "charges"?) are themselves indivisible, our argument still stands. If the essential property of matter is divisibility, there can be no ultimate indivisible unit at all, for the obvious reason that any indivisible unit would be not-matter or "non-material." We must therefore conclude that matter is not indivisible *ad infinitum*: that there is a point at which, by definition, the "material" becomes "immaterial."

Are we not justified in concluding, therefore, that matter, in its ultimate form has to be, in that form at least, "immaterial," that is, *qualitative* rather than *quantitative*? To put the same proposition in another form: In the realm of matter, we say, the whole is equal to the sum of the parts. But in the realm of spirit, any "part," speaking by way of analogy, is "equal" to the "whole." Why is this true? Because in the realm of spirit we are in the qualitative again rather than in the quantitative. The life that pervades a human organism, for example, is equally and qualitatively present in all parts of that organism. It simply can not be divided into "parts" as we divide a material object, nor can it be analyzed or measured quantitatively. More than this, it is an *inexhaustible* something. We are safe in saying then, it seems to me, that if the essential property of matter be divisibility, the essential property of spirit is *inexhaustibleness*. No matter how much of spirit-power is expended, the source of supply is never exhausted, nor even diminished. But here again we are speaking qualitatively rather than in terms of quantity.

In the second place, if by this process of regression we actually pass from the "material" into the "immaterial" or "non-material"—not only logically, but ontologically as well—it naturally follows that the opposite may well be true, namely, that matter, in its ultimate form, perhaps that of radiant energy, is either a creation of, or an emergence from, the "non-material," that is, from the activity of Pure Thought or Spirit. And certainly the tendency among physicists of the present day is toward the adoption of this view. As Sir James Jeans says:

Today there is a widespread measure of agreement which on the physical side approaches almost to unanimity, that the stream of knowledge is heading toward a non-mechanical reality; the universe begins to look more like a great thought than like a great machine.[1]

## Again, the same author says elsewhere:

To my mind, the laws which nature obeys are less suggestive of those which a machine obeys in its action than of those which a musician obeys in writing a fugue, or a poet in composing a sonnet. The motions of electrons and atoms do not resemble those of the parts of a locomotive so much as those of the dancers in a cotillion. And if the true "essence of substances" is for ever unknowable, it does not matter whether the cotillion is danced at a ball in real life, or on a cinematograph screen, or in a story of Boccaccio. If all this is so, then the universe can best be pictured, although still very imperfectly and inadequately, as consisting of pure thought, the thought of what, for want of a better word, we must describe as a mathematical thinker. . . . Creations of an individual mind may reasonably be called less substantial than creations of a universal mind. A similar distinction must be made between the space we see in a dream and the space of everyday life; the latter, which is the same for us all, is the space of the universal mind. Again we may think of the laws to which phenomena conform in our waking hours, the laws of nature, as the laws of thought of a universal mind. The uniformity of nature proclaims the self-consistency of this mind. . . . If the universe is a universe of thought, then its creation must have been an act of thought. Indeed the finiteness of time and space almost compel us, of themselves, to picture the creation as an act of thought; the determination of the constants such as the radius of the universe and the number of electrons it contained imply thought, whose richness is measured by the immensity of these quantities. Time and space, which form the setting for the thought, must have come into being as a part of this act. Primitive cosmologies pictured a creator working in space and time, forging sun, moon and stars out of already existent raw material. Modern scientific theory compels us to think of the creator as working outside time and space, which are part of his creation, just as the artist is outside his canvas. It accords with the conjecture of Augustine, "*Non in tempore, sed cum tempore, finxit Deus mundum.*"[2] Indeed, the doctrine dates back as far as Plato: "Time and the heavens came into being at the same instant, in order that, if they were ever to dissolve, they might be dissolved together. Such was the mind and thought of God in the creation of time."[3] And yet, so little do we understand time that perhaps we ought to compare the whole of time to the act of creation, the materialization of the thought.[4]

Obviously, the Biblical presentation of the Spirit of God as the energizing and vitalizing Agent in the Creation—in a word, as the Spirit of Power—is in harmony with these conclusions of the latest physics. We need not be surprised, therefore, to read in Scripture of instances, as we have already seen,

1. *The New Background of Science*, 158.
2. "Not in time, but with time, God fashioned the world."
3. *Vide Timaeus*, 37 D ff.
4. Sir James Jeans, *The Mysterious Universe* (New Revised Edition, 1943), 167-168, 175, 181-182.

in which the Spirit of Jehovah "came mightily upon" certain divinely appointed individuals (e.g., Samson, Saul, David, etc.), to clothe them with extraordinary physical and mental powers for special divine ends. Nor is there anything incredible about this, for it is a well-known fact that psychic power is capable of greatly intensifying the physical powers of the human organism under certain conditions. This is true even in cases of insanity: the abnormal physical strength of frenzied persons is a well-known fact, and has been known for ages. (*Vide* especially the *Bacchae* of Euripides. Phenomena of this kind have always characterized orgiastic "religions.") Hence we may reasonably conclude that the operation of the Divine Spirit at the very lowest level of being, produces energy (shall we call it "physical"?), which has the inherent power to build itself up into the gross matter, with its manifold representations, of our present physical world. The transmutations of energy into matter and of matter into energy are now known to be ontological facts.

Dr. Harold Paul Sloan seems to have given us the "conclusion of the whole matter" quite forcefully, in these words:

> The new science itself is now pointing us to philosophy. It is now affirming that the ultimate ground of objective things is spirit. Matter, these leaders say, is not *stuff;* it is force; it is a complex of interacting forces; and these forces seem to resolve into mental values— into the "mathematical formulae" of Jeans—into ideas of an Infinite Mind.[1]

## 2. The Mystery of Sensation

Some further light is thrown upon the problem of the ultimate constitution of matter by a study of the phenomenon of sensation as experienced by sentient beings.

Alexander Polyhistor, a writer of the first century B.C., has put posterity everlastingly in his debt by his formulation of a brief account of the metaphysical cosmogony of the ancient Pythagoreans, in a treatise no longer extant, entitled *Successions of Philosophers*. Fortunately, however, this account has been preserved by another writer, Diogenes Laertius, in his work written in the early part of the third century of the Christian era, a work entitled *Lives and Opinions of Eminent Philosophers*.[2]

1. *He Is Risen*, 127.
2. This work, in two volumes, may be found in the Loeb Classical Library, Harvard University Press. Translation by R. D. Hicks.

The first paragraph of Alexander's account, as reproduced by Laertius, tells us that the Pythagorean cosmogony went as follows:

> The first principle of all things is the One. From the One came an Indefinite Two, as matter for the One, which is cause. From the One and the Indefinite Two came numbers; and from numbers, points; from points, lines; from lines, plane figures; from plane figures, solid figures; from solid figures, sensible bodies. The elements of these are four: fire, water, earth, air; these change and are wholly transformed, and out of them comes to be a cosmos, animate, intelligent, spherical, embracing the central earth, which is itself spherical and inhabited round about.[1]

In this connection, it should be explained, perhaps, that the Pythagoreans appear to have conceived the cosmos as being constructed ultimately of primary entities, a kind of atoms, to which they applied the term "numbers"; the celebrated dictum, "Things are numbers," is quite generally attributed to Pythagoras himself. According to the clear testimony of Aristotle, these "numbers" were conceived as having spatial magnitude, *i.e.*, as extended unit-points—the ultimate stuff of the whole physical universe.[2] The arithmetical or numerical process seems to have been regarded by the Pythagoreans, at least by those of the fourth century B.C., especially Philolaus and his contemporaries, as having been paralleled by the cosmogonical process; they attempted to describe at one and the same time both the formation of the number system (as symbols) and that of the physical universe (as made up of the entities thus symbolized); the construction was a parallel one, in terms of the ideal and the concrete, of symbol and reality. It appears too that they conceived the whole cosmogonical process as partaking of the character of the growth and development of seeds; that is to say, as some sort of an essentially dynamic, generative, or life process.[3] This, of course, was in strict harmony with the Pythagorean conception of the Cosmos as a Living Being. According to other ancient writers, notably Sextus Empiricus and Proclus, they were wont to describe their extended unit-points as "flowing" into lines, the lines as "flowing" into plane figures, the plane figures as "flowing" into solid figures, and the solid figures as

1. Diogenes Laertius, *op. cit.*, VIII, 25. Translation by F. M. Cornford; *vide* Cornford, *Plato and Parmenides*, 3.
2. Aristotle, *Metaphysics*, I, v, 986a ff.; I, viii, 989b 3 ff.; XIII, vi, 1080b 1 ff.; XIII, viii, 1083b 8 ff.; XIV, ii, 1090a 22 ff.; XIV, iii, 1090a 32 ff.; also *Physics*, III, iv, 203a 6.
3. Aristotle, *Metaphysics*, XIV, iii, 1091a 15 ff.; also *De Anima*, 409a 4.

"flowing" into sensible bodies.[1] All this suggests the concept of an essentially dynamic or generative process.

Now the one aspect of this cosmogonical theory which provoked the criticism of Aristotle more than any other,[2] and the one which has been a subject of great difficulty to all subsequent thinkers, was that which had to do with "sensible objects" and the phenomenon of sensation. The problem may be stated thus: *How did the Pythagoreans effect—theoretically, that is —the transition from geometrical solid to sensible body? Or, to put it in another form: How did these geometrical magnitudes ontologically transform themselves ("flow") into the objects of sense-perception?*

Obviously, any attempt to answer this question necessarily plunges us into one of the profound mysteries of being—the mystery of sensation or sense-perception—which, up to the present time, has refused to yield up its secrets either to the physicist or to the psychologist. We know but little more today about the process of sensation in a sentient being than did the Pythagoreans of twenty-six centuries ago. Again I shall quote at some length from Barnett, who states the problem so clearly that it would be impossible to improve upon his presentation. He writes as follows:

In accepting a mathematical description of nature, physicists have been forced to abandon the ordinary world of our experience, the world of sense-perception.. To understand the significance of the this retreat it is necessary to step across the thin line that divides physics from metaphysics. Questions involving the relationship between observer and reality, subject and object, have haunted philosophical thinkers since the dawn of reason. Twenty-three centuries ago the Greek philosopher Democritus wrote: "Sweet and bitter, cold and warm as well as all the colors, all these things exist but in opinion and not in reality; what really exists are unchangeable particles, atoms, and their motions in empty space." Galileo also was aware of the purely subjective character of sense qualities like color, taste, smell, and sound, and pointed out that "they can no more be ascribed to the external objects than can the tickling or the pain caused sometimes by touching such objects."

The English philosopher, John Locke, tried to penetrate to the "real essence of substances" by drawing a distinction between what he termed the primary and secondary qualities of matter. Thus he considered that shape, motion, solidity and all geometrical properties were real or primary qualities, inherent in the object itself; while secondary qualities, like colors, sounds, tastes, were simply projections upon the organs of sense. The artificiality of this distinction was obvious to later thinkers.

"I am able to prove," wrote the great German mathematician, Leibnitz, "that not only light, color, heat, and the like, but motion,

1. *Vide* F. M. Cornford, *Plato and Parmenides*, 10-20.
2. *Vide* Aristotle, *Metaphysics*, XIII, vi, 1080b 18 ff., also XIV, iii, 1091a 12 ff.

shape, and extension too are mere apparent qualities." Just as our visual sense, for example, tells us that a golf ball is white, so vision abetted by our sense of touch tells us that it is also round, smooth, and small—qualities that have no more reality, independent of our senses, than the quality which we define by convention as white.

Thus gradually philosophers and scientists arrived at the startling conclusion that since every object is simply the sum of its qualities, and since qualities exist only in the mind, the whole objective universe of matter and energy, atoms and stars, does not exist except as a construction of the consciousness, an edifice of conventional symbols shaped by the senses of man. As Berkeley, the archenemy of materialism, phrased it: "All the choir of heaven and furniture of earth, in a word, all those bodies which compose the mighty frame of the world, have not any substance without the mind. . . So long as they are not actually perceived by me, or do not exist in my mind, or that of any other created spirit, they must either have no existence at all, or else subsist in the mind of some Eternal Spirit." Einstein carried this train of logic to its ultimate limits by showing that even space and time are forms of intuition, which can no more be divorced from consciousness than can our concepts of color, shape, and size. Space has no objective reality except as an order or arrangement of the objects we perceive in it, and time has no independent existence apart from the order of events by which we measure it.[1]

Certainly it cannot be doubted that sensation, of whatever kind it may be, is physiologically subjective. On the other hand, common sense tells us that our sensations must have their causes; that if there were not something in the world around us or within our own bodies—forces of some kind impinging upon our neural system—we simply would not experience sensations at all. It was this reasoning, no doubt, or to be more exact, this fact of experience, which led John Locke to define matter as "permanent possibility of sensation" and as "something-I-know-not-what." This is, of course, no definition at all. However, it is about as near as anyone has ever come to a "definition" of matter *per se;* for the simple fact is that we do not "know" objects in themselves, we "know" only our sensations of those objects. And even if matter be defined as energy, we still have the problem, *What is energy?* The undeniable truth is that we cannot apprehend or know matter *per se* through the avenue of the physical senses; we know, I repeat, only our sensations of material objects. This is the reason why the physicists of the present day resort to mathematical symbols and formulae in order to apprehend and to describe the ultimate stuff of the Cosmos, and in most cases the intuition of the formula has preceded by several years the empirical verification. It must not be supposed, of course, that these formulas are mere abstractions; they are not; they have been experimentally demonstrated to

1. *Op. cit.,* 10-12.

be accurate interpretations of natural processes; they bespeak
the mathematical orthodoxy of the Cosmos itself. As Barnett
puts it: "In physics and equation is never a pure abstraction;
it is simply a kind of shorthand expression which the scientist
finds convenient to describe the phenomena of nature." The
fact must not be overlooked that these "shorthand expressions"
do actually describe natural (*i.e.*, physical) phenomena. And in
virtue of the very fact that they lead us at last to "a final fea-
tureless unity of space-time, mass-energy, matter-field—an ultimate, undiversified, and eternal ground beyond which there appears to be no progress," they simply serve to prove that the
world of the physical senses is a prison-house—to use Plato's
own term—in which man finds himself incarcerated for the
tenure of his existence in this present state of being. This is
designated "the egocentric predicament."

Now, as previously stated, sensations in living beings certainly must have their causes. What, then, are the physical
forces or forms of physical energy which, by impinging upon the
neural system, give rise to sensations in human beings and in
the lower animals as well? Suppose we take, for example, sensations of the configurations of objects, of the relations of such
configurations in space, and the sensations of color. All such
sensations depend upon the human sense—and sense-organs—of
vision. The sense organ for vision is, of course, the eye with
its various parts plus the optic nerve; and the stimulus for
vision is radiant energy, which is in turn one of the forms of
electromagnetic energy. The electromagnetic spectrum, we are
told, includes cosmic rays, radio waves, infra-red rays, visible
light, ultra-violet rays, x-rays, and gamma rays. All of these
are differentiated one from another by respective *wave lengths*.
The human organism has no sense organs, however, which are
sensitive to any except those radiant vibrations within the
range of sensual vision; that is, between the wave lengths that
produce the sensation *red* at one end of the visible spectrum and
those which produce the sensation *violet* at the other end. Radiation of various wave lengths between these two extremes produce
our sensations of all other colors. And just above this range are
the wave lengths which produce the ultra-violet, and just below
it are the infra-red wave lengths. As Barnett puts it, "From the
standpoint of physics, the only difference between radio waves,
visible light, and such high-frequency forms of radiation as x-rays

1. *Op. cit.*, 49, 111

and gamma rays lies in their wave length." (Again): "It is evident . . . that the human eye suppresses most of the 'lights' in the world, and that what man can perceive of the reality around him is distorted and enfeebled by the limitations of his organs of vision. The world would appear far different to him if his eye were sensitive, for example, to x-rays."[1] All of which goes to show that man's "physical" senses are specifically adapted to his needs in this present world only. As the Apostle puts it: "The things which are seen are temporal, but the things which are not seen are eternal" (2 Cor. 4:18). Moreover, the physical senses, in thus adapting man to his present environment, actually shut off from his perception the vaster area which extends illimitably throughout the vast reaches of this phenomenal world.

Thus it becomes obvious, in the light of modern physics, that man's visions of all "objects" in space, of their shapes, relations as to distance, colors, etc., are produced by these "wave lengths" of energy as they impinge upon his organs of vision. But what this process of sensation is *in itself* remains inscrutable. Space is "simply a possible order of material objects," and time is "simply a possible order of events." "What we call an hour is actually a measurement in space—an arc of fifteen degrees in the apparent daily rotation of the celestial sphere. And what we call a year is simply a measure of the earth's progress in its orbit around the sun."[2] Light waves, we are told, have maximum velocity of 186,000 miles *plus*, per second; nothing in the universe moves faster. Radio waves travel at the same speed as light waves. These and all other phenomena of electromagnetic radiation are measured by the modern physicist in terms of *wave lengths* and *frequencies*. Wave lengths of *what*? Of *something*? Or of nothing? The physicist answers: Wave lengths of quanta ("corpuscles," like bullets from a machine gun), that is, *quanta of energy*. Yet this energy in its ultimate form can hardly be said to have spatial magnitude, in the strict sense of that phrase. As one author puts it: "Electromagnetic energy is radiated or absorbed in discrete quanta . . . and the size of one quantum is directly proportional to the frequency with which it is associated."[3] Thus the "quantum" takes the place of "spatial magnitude," "extension," and "divisibility," in modern physics.

"Radiant energy," writes Barnett, "is emitted not in an unbroken stream but in discontinuous bits or portions" called

1. *Op. cit.*, 13.
2. Barnett, *op cit.*, 40, 41.
3. William H. Michener, *Physics for Science and Engineering*, 532.

(first by Planck) quanta. Again: "Einstein postulated that all forms of radiant energy—light, heat, x-rays—actually travel through space in separate and discontinuous quanta."[1] Incidentally, the sensation of sound is the effect of the same wavelike kind of movement, with the difference of course that sound waves are transmitted by the air or some other medium, whereas electromagnetic waves are conceived as traveling through empty space. The sensation of sound is produced by the impact of these wavelike movements upon man's organs of hearing. And finally, in this connection, sensations of touch, taste, and smell— indeed all other kinds of sensations—are produced by the impact upon various parts of our neuro-sensory system of those basic atomic and molecular movements by which matter is described as differentiated into its three fundamental forms, namely, gases, liquids, and solids, all of which now pictured as forms of more or less "congealed" energy.

Thus, according to the picture which is given us by the most up-to-date physics, the ultimate dynamic "building stones" of the Cosmos are these "particles" of energy which go to make up the structure of the atom, and the quanta or "corpuscles" of wavelike energy which, similarly, go to make up all the forms of electromagnetic radiation. The effort has been made by Dr. Einstein, we are told, to bring all these ultimate "bits" or "portions" of energy into a unity, that is, to interpret them as being ultimately of the same essential stuff, as "parts" or "aspects" or manifestations of a Primal Dynamic Unity.

The thing that is of special significance to us here, however, is the fact that it is by the co-operation, that is to say, by the action and reaction of these particles or corpuscles of primal energy on the one hand, and the human sense organs on the other hand, themselves apparently corporeal and hence no doubt the products of the same primal forces, that *sensible objects are thus brought into phenomenal existence, or at least into the range of human experience; or, to put the same fact in ancient Pythagorean terminology, that geometrical magnitudes—mere configurations—"flow" into the objects of sense-perception.* This does not mean, of course, that the quantum of the present-day physicist is to be conceived as a geometrical magnitude; on the contrary, it seems to be something essentially qualitative, an entity characterized by the property of *inexhaustibleness* rather than by that of extension; it is the entity which, in modern

1. *Op. cit.,* 16, 17.

physics, replaces the geometrical magnitudes of ancient and medieval philosophers, as the ultimate of "material" stuff. Nor does this mean that the ancient Pythagoreans attained to any of these concepts of modern physics. It means simply that the Pythagoreans, by a sort of intuition, hit upon one of the secrets of the Cosmos, a secret which is made just a little less mysterious by the light shed upon it by the discoveries of our modern physicists. We are justified, I should say, at least in pointing out the correspondences between those "flowing" unit-points postulated by the Pythagoreans, and the "particles" or "corpuscles" of primal energy known to us today as *sensa,* which by impressing themselves upon our sense organs *actualize for us all sensible objects.*

To summarize: *What is sensation?* In modern terms, it is the effect of an impingement upon the neuro-sensory system of a percipient, a *living* creature, of forces external to that system, forces operating both outside and inside the particular organism. How can these various forms of energy which undoubtedly provoke the phenomena commonly designated "sensations," be reduced to quantities of any kind? *Obviously, we ourselves, the percipients, know only the sensations.* We can "know" the causes of these sensations only in terms of atomic changes, molecular movements, chemical affinities, vibrations, intensities, frequencies, etc., most of whcih are reducible, apparently, to mathematical formulae, just as Pythagoras himself discovered with reference to the perfect consonances in music. Hence, it seems to be in these mathematical terms alone that we can ever know what "things-in-themselves" are. Yet these very forces, interpretable only mathematically, just as the atom is interpretable only in mathematical terms, "fill in" the geometrical configurations, so to speak, and by their impingement upon the sense organs of the living organism, actualize sensible objects. Indeed all the sensations known to psychology—visual, auditory, gustatory, cutaneous, olfactory, organic, visceral, kinesthetic, static, or what not— may properly be said to be the effect of the impact of such primal forms of energy—emanating from outside or from within the organism—upon the neuro-sensory system of the living recipient.

All this emphasizes one fact, however, namely, that even though we do have a partial understanding at least of the *how* of sensation, certainly we are as much in the dark as ever regarding the *what* of the phenomenon. What sensation is *in itself,* no one knows. For sensation involves, in some inscrutable manner, the additional and accompanying phenomena of *perception,* of *consciousness* of the sensation and of the sense-perceived object, and of the *meaning* which thought, by the aid of memory, may attach to the sensation, and even the utilization of the word or *symbol* which linguistic convention has associated with that particular meaning. Not one of these attendant phenomena can be identified strictly with the sensation itself, yet all of them are, in some unexplainable manner, bound up with it. This is especially true in the experience of a *person* or *spirit.* We shall therefore look into these accompanying phenomena further, in a subsequent examination of the processes of thought. For sensation undoubtedly provides the raw material for thought.

## 3. The Mystery of Consciousness

The phenomenon of sensation is inextricably interwoven with those of *perception* and *consciousness,* and all three are related to the greater and over-all phenomenon of *meaning.*

A sensation is an event in the neurosensory system. It is a *physiological* event. Undoubtedly the raw material of knowledge is provided by *sense-perception.* Faith itself, we are told by the Apostle, "cometh of hearing, and hearing by the word of Christ" (Rom. 10:17). "It was God's good pleasure through the foolishness of the preaching to save them that believe" (1 Cor. 1:21). The psychological sequence is clearly stated in Scripture in different places, first in Isa. 6:9-10, as seeing with the eyes, hearing with the ears, understanding with the heart, and turning again: that is, seeing and/or hearing the Gospel message leads to understanding, understanding leads to believing, and believing in turn leads to turning again (repentance), and the entire process culminates in remission, justification, forgiveness, etc., ("turn again, and be healed"). Scripturally speaking, conversion is not mystical—it is definitely psychological. (Cf. Matt. 13:14-15, John 12:40, Acts 28:25-27, Rom. 11:8, etc.). Direct contact with the Word of the testimony, by seeing, hearing, etc., is the first step in conversion. The Gospel is not *a* power, nor *one of* the powers, but it is *"the power* of God unto salvation to every one that believeth"* (Rom. 1:16). Hence it follows that "whosoever shall call upon the name of the Lord shall be saved." "How then shall they call on him in whom they have not believed? and how shall they believe in him whom they have not heard? and how shall they hear without a preacher? and how shall they preach,

102

except they be sent?" (Rom. 10:13-15). The whole missionary and evangelistic enterprise of the church is predicated upon the fact that the raw material for thought, and hence in the spiritual realm for faith, is provided by sense-perception (*i.e.,* sensations): as Aristotle put it long ago (in substance), Nothing is in the intellect that was not first in the sense, that is, that did not have its beginnings in sense-perception. This view was maintained by Thomas Aquinas in medieval philosophy, and in modern philosophy by John Locke and Immanuel Kant. This view was again reaffirmed by Alexander Campbell in his debate with the Communist, Robert Owen, held in Cincinnati, in April, 1829. In this debate, Campbell spoke as follows:

Now it is only necessary to name these five senses, and their respective uses, in order to discover in them all that beneficence, wisdom, and design which suggest the idea of a supremely intelligent First Cause, manifesting its wisdom and benevolence in the animal organization of man, to discover that man has been endowed by his Creator with an organization which enables him to elicit every valuable property of matter. [The five senses indicated here, as specifically named by Mr. Campbell, were the traditional ones, viz., sight, hearing, smell, taste, and touch.] We discover an admirable adaptation of these senses to the conception of all ideas of colors, sounds, odors, tastes, and tacts; and that all our intelligence on these subjects is derived through these five channels. The conclusion, therefore, from these premises, is, that a man born without any one of these senses, must ever remain destitute of all ideas derivable through it; that a man born deaf, dumb, blind, and without tactability, has all these avenues to intelligence closed up, and must therefore remain an idiot all his lifetime.

After developing this conclusion specifically with reference to each sense named, Campbell concludes:

The mind forms ideas in accordance with the sensations impressed upon the brain. The mind is perfectly conscious of the existence of these impressions; they are communicated directly to the *sensorium;* and here begins the intellect process of reflecting upon, comparing, and recalling them; then presenting them in different views, separating, abstracting, combining, and generalizing them. All this is in the natural operation of the intellect on the objects presented to it by sensation. Thus it is that we derive our ideas of sensible objects, and thus we begin to reason upon them.[1]

It was Mr. Campbell's thesis in this debate that man has no power *per se to* originate the basic ideas of religion. It was his twofold task, he affirmed, in this debate, to demonstrate "philosophically" two propositions: first, "that it is impossible for man to originate any of those supernatural ideas which are developed

1. *Campbell-Owen Debate,* 149, 151. Published by McQuiddy Printing Co., Nashville, 1957. First published by Standard Publishing Co., Cincinnati, under the title, *Evidences of Christianity.*

in the Christian religion," and, second, that the central point at issue is, "whether we have reasonable grounds to believe the truth and certainty of the apostolic testimony." His contention was that man could never have invented the "ideas of a God, a Spirit, a future state, or of any of the positive institutions of religion . . . the ideas inseparably connected with the words *priest, altar, sacrifice,* etc. . . . . ergo, that these ideas and the words used to express them are derivable only from an immediate and direct revelation, man having no power, according to any philosophic analysis of his intellectual powers, to originate any such ideas."

It will thus be seen that the Restoration movement definitely has a philosophical background. Having previously taken the position that sense-perception, by means of which men may apprehend the truth communicated in the "apostolic testimony," and by obedience to which, as the Last Will and Testament of Our Lord and Savior Jesus Christ, we obtain justification, sanctification, and immortalization—redemption of "spirit and soul and body" (1 Thess. 5:21)—it follows that sensory experience originally could not have been the source of divine revelation as communicated by inspiration of the Spirit through patriarchs, prophets, and Christ and His Apostles; however, this revelation, or rather the record of it, having been made complete in the apostolic testimony (2 Pet. 1:3, Jude 3), therefore "to the law and the testimony" we must go for our knowledge of God's will for our lives. The Word of God, therefore, as read (seen) or preached (heard), hence as presented to our minds through the senses, must be the source and basis of Christian faith and practice. This all points up the fact that *the Restoration Movement does have a philosophical background. In its positive emphasis on the all-sufficiency of the Word, negatively it repudiated all the vagaries and excesses of mysticism.* To the extent that it repudiates feeling states as evidences of regeneration and sanctification and urges fidelity to "the living oracles" as apprehended by sense-perception, it may truly be designated an *empirical* movement, that is, a movement belonging, like the political philosophy of the Declaration of Independence, in the empirical tradition set by Aristotle and repeated in modern times especially by John Locke. The present writer is in complete agreement with this emphasis. Why, in the name of reason, in view of God's having provided us, by inspiration of the Spirit, a "letter," so to speak, to tell us what to do and how to live, should we call on the same Spirit for additional evidence in the form of a telegram, to support the content of the letter? I Pet. 4:11—"if any man speaketh, speaking as it were oracles of God." Acts 7:38—"our fathers who received living oracles to give unto us." (Cf. Rom. 3:2, Heb. 5:12). 2 Tim. 1:13—"Hold the pattern of sound words." 1 or. 2:13—"combining spiritual things with spiritual words." Luke 16:29—"They have Moses and the prophets; let them hear them." Rom. 10:8—"The word is nigh thee, in thy mouth, and in thy heart: that is, the word of faith, which we preach." (Cf. Rom. 10:17, 1 Cor. 1:21, Rom. 1:16, Matt. 7:24-27, John 6:63, Luke 21:33, Heb. 4:12, etc., etc.).

We are now ready to inquire: What is the relation between *sensation* and *perception* in man? A very significant series of statements, again from Alexander Campbell, is illuminating, at this point:

Objects of senses are presented to the infant mind, it perceives them, begins to reflect upon them, and after exercising its power of discrimination, it arrives at certain conclusions about them. And this leads us to notice the intellectual powers of man. 1. *Perception,* by which we become acquainted with all things external. 2. *Memory,* by which we are enabled to recall things past. 3. *Consciousness,* which acquaints us with all things internal. Perception has present sensible objects for its province. Memory is the record which we have of the past. But consciousness has respect only to things present, I perceive a numerous assemblage now before me, and I am *conscious* of my own thoughts at the time, I *remember* that there were such and such persons here yesterday. These three powers of perception, memory, and consciousness, are the primary powers of the mind.[1]

But—how is sensation related to perception? A sensation, we repeat, is a physiological event, in the neurosensory system. Sensations, moreover, are *atomistic,* that is, each originates through *its own* channel of excitation. (One does not hear by way of the optic nerve, nor does one see by way of the auditory nerve.) Vision is effected by means of the optic nerve; sound, by way of the auditory nerve endings; touch, by means of the thousands of nerve endings (receptors) scattered over the surface of the skin; smell, by means of receptors in the nasal cavity; taste, by means of taste buds on the tongue. In addition to these, there are innumerable kinesthetic receptors, pain receptors, cold and warmth receptors, and millions of internal sense receptors scattered throughout the inner linings of the body. What, then, is the mysterious power in man which gathers up these different excitations of the nervous system and unifies them into the *perception* of a thing as an *object,* preserves the perception in the form of an *image,* and in addition to all this,

1. *Op. cit.,* 153

vests the whole process with *meaning?* It would seem to be a process, like the vital process, designed to be experienced only but never to be defined. (Who can define the infinitive "to be"? "To exist," do you say? But this is only a synonym, not a definition.) Aristotle called this power, "active intellect." The process, however named, is conclusive proof of the unceasing activity of mind.

Sensations provide the raw material for this elementary kind of "knowledge," which is to conceive (form in the mind) an idea in which one preceives or apprehends ("seizes," "takes hold of") something. It is to think, *e.g., "apple, "man," "chair," "red," "soft,"* etc. Our mental powers are awakened, directly or indirectly, by sensations; our first acquired ideas thus have reference to sensible objects; these primary ideas become the occasions for, and the antecedents of, other ideas and emotions which derive from our higher rational and moral nature. But, it must be remembered, sensations are in themselves operations of the individual neurosensory system, separate impressions of different aspects (qualities) of the thing producing them. (Obviously, then, there must be an external something—which becomes the *object* of cognition—to produce these sensations, or they would not occur. Therefore, we must accept the fact of the existence of the external (physical) world, as a matter of necessary inference; negatively, we must deny the notion that it is illusion.) (Even an illusion must be an illusion of *something,* as a figure, a symbol, an emblem, must be, in any case, a figure or symbol or emblem of *something.* An illusion of nothing is inconceivable.) Physicists would describe these motions in matter which cause sensations in the percipient, by their impact on the nervous system, as *sense data,* or *sensa:* vision, for example, is produced by the refraction of quanta of radiant energy, sound by vibrations in a medium, etc. It seems to lie beyond the possibility of man to determine what the nature of the contact is, between the impinging *sensum* (stimulus) and the responsive nerve-endings of the recipient, in instances of touch, taste, and smell. This is the mystery of the relation between the psychical and the physical (or physiological), a mystery which no doubt will always remain a mystery.

For example, let us imagine an apple lying on the table before us. On looking at it, we experience a sensation of color ("redness"), another of configuration ("roundness"); if we touch the apple, we experience another sensation( that of a certain quality of "hardness" or "softness," depending on how "ripe" the apple is); and if we bite into the apple, we experience another kind of sensation, that of a certain quality of pleasantness or unpleasantness to the taste ("sweet," "sour," "bitter," and the like). But, obviously, in order to perceive the thing (the apple) *as an object,* some activity within each of us must—and indeed *does*—unite these sensations into the perception of the object *as a whole.* As Gestalt psychologists contend, no analysis of separate percepts can account for the total experience. This internal activity of weaving into a whole the sensations produced by a thing in becoming an object of cognition is properly designated one's *perception* of the object. Now the sensations themselves may be explained as activities, or at least as the result of the activities, of brain and nerve cells. But certainly the perception of the object, the process in which these sensations are unified, cannot be explained solely in terms of cellular processes.

Again, on perceiving an object, one immediately attaches the proper word-symbol (in this case, "apple") to it, the symbol attached by social usage. This, of course, is a phase of the actual perception of the apple, or other object, whatever it may be. This attachment of a word-symbol becomes an elaboration of the perception by a phenomenon known as *consciousness.* This attachment of the conventional word-symbol that serves as identification, simply cannot be explained on the ground of any cellular or other physiological process, for the use of language involves memory and memory images, and in addition gives *meaning* to the perception. It is utterly inconceivable that cells should remain in juxtaposition themselves over a period of years in such a manner as repeatedly to produce the same memory images. Hence, we must conclude that neither the retention of memory images nor their recall can be identified with any cellular process exclusively, and that the phenomena of perception, retention and recall, and the more significant fact of *meaning,* are properly described as "mental" rather than "physical." As the psychologist McDougall has expressed it: "There is no correlate in the brain for meaning in thought."

The jump from sensation to consciousness is the great mystery involved here. D. Elton Trueblood calls it "the leap of faith." It is the leap from the physiological stimulus to the mental interpretation or response. In terms of the sciences involved, it is the leap from physiology to psychology. We affirm, in this connection, that there is no way, that there will never be found a way, by which psychology can be identified with sheer physiology. Brain and mind are correlated, of course, but they cannot be *identified* as one and the same thing, no matter how desperate may become the efforts of materialists the world over to effect this identification, or to conjure up a name which they can find usable in deceiving mankind into thinking that the human being is *animal only;* when as a matter of fact he may be animal as pertaining to his body ("earthly tabernacle") but he is surely animal *plus* as pertaining to his higher thought processes. *Sensation is not consciousness.* The relation between sensation and consciousness is an inscrutable mystery. And this being true, surely the relation between sensation and *meaning* is one of the most amazing of all the phenomena of human existence!

A distinguished writer in the field of psychology has presented this problem clearly as follows:

Psychologically, a fine discrimination is made between the processes of sensation and perception. *Sensation*, we have said, is the act of receiving a stimulus by a sense organ. *Perception* is the act of interpreting a stimulus registered in the brain by one or more sensations. . . . To illustrate the difference between sensation and perception, a common analyogy compares a *photograph* of a scene with an artist's *painting* of the scene. The photograph would record the scene as the sense organ *receives* it, whereas the painting depicts the scene as the artist *perceivs* it. Succintly stated, we might say, the eye "receives" while the mind "perceives." Instances of pure sensation in human experiences are rare. If you hear a strange noise, no matter how unusual, you immediately associate it with something familiar. If you see a completely strange and foreign object, you unconsciously attempt to relate it to some form or shape you have seen before. The nearest circumstance to a pure sensation might be the instant in which a color is presented for the first time to a person who has been blind from birth and suddenly gained the power to see. No one of us can look at an object, hear a voice or taste food, and receive these sensations without projecting into them some facet of past experience. At whatever age, the accumulations of a lifetime of all sensory experiences go into our perceptions. An orange might be perceived by an infant as just another colored ball with which to play. To an adult in the United States at this time, it represents a commonplace breakfast fruit served usually in the form of juice. To some youngster in Great Britain during World War II when oranges were very scarce, it would have represented a curiosity and a luxury to be enjoyed in its entirety as a rare treat. Thus, in describing the phenomena of perception, we come to the psychological truism aptly stated by the philosopher Immanuel Kant: "We see things not as they are but as we are." Stated differently, *perception represents our apprehension of a present situation in terms of our past experiences.*[1]

1. Abraham P. Sperling, *Psychology Made Simple*, 38.

Obviously, this author is thinking of *perception* as having meaning, in whatever situation it may occur, of a *functional* rather than *essential* (ontological) character. In this respect his analysis is acceptable. However, existentially considered, an orange, or any other entity, *as such,* in whatever part of the world it may be perceived as an existent and to the extent it is perceived as an existent, will have the same meaning, no matter by what linguistic symbol it may be designated. In any case whatever, *perception* involves *meaning.* Perception as apprehension of a present *object,* therefore, has meaning in terms of our past perceptions of the same object; moreover, in any case whatever, the fact of meaning certainly brings in activity that is beyond the physiological, activity that can truly be defined only as mental. All this accounts for the fact that the mind-body problem is just as pertinent today as it has ever been in the history of human thought. It is the acceptance of this fact which accounts for the rise of *psychosomatic* treatment, in recent years, of many human afflictions. As the late C. E. M. Joad, onetime professor of philosophy, the University of London, has written:

> Common sense holds that a human being is not exclusively a body. He has a body, but he is, it would normally be said, more than his body; and he is more, in virtue of the existence of an immaterial principle which, whether it be called mind, soul, consciousness, or personality, constitutes the reality of his being. This immaterial principle, most people hold, is in some way associated with the body—it is frequently said to reside *in* it—and animates and controls it. . . . Mind and body continually interact in an infinite number of ways: in fact, mind influences body and body mind at every moment of waking life. If I am drunk, I see two lamp-posts instead of one; if I fail to digest my supper, I have a nightmare and see blue devils; if I smoke opium or inhale nitrous oxide gas, I experience celestial visions, pass into a state of beatitude, and discourse with the Almighty and His angels. These are instances of the influence of the body upon the mind. If I see a ghost, my hair stands on end; if I am moved to anger, my face becomes red; if I receive a sudden shock, I turn pale; if I am in dread of a coming ordeal, my mouth becomes dry and the palms of my hand moist. These are instances of the influence of the mind upon the body. The examples just quoted are only extreme and rather obvious cases of what is going on all the time. Many psychologists, indeed, assert that there can be no event in the mind which is not accompanied by some corresponding event in the body, and vice versa, although the corresponding event in the body may be too small to be perceptible by such recording instruments as we at present possess. The apparent interaction between mind and body is, at any rate, a fact beyond dispute.[1]

The interaction is beyond dispute, even though the method of this interaction eludes man's ability to apprehend and explain it. No matter that psychologists take the organismic approach

1. *Guide to Philosophy,* 499-500.

(treating the human being as an integrated whole), they then proceed to classify his motives and acts as "viscerogenic" and "psychogenic." But what do these high-sounding terms designate but *physiological* and *psychological* respectively. Apparently, science has yet to learn that *naming* an event is not *explaining it*. (Theologians seem to be very prone to commit the same fallacy also.)

This interaction, as pointed out in the foregoing excerpt, takes place in other most significant ways. The student, for example, does not leave the room after class until he "makes up his mind" to propel his feet toward the door; the baseball pitcher throws the ball if and when and how he "makes up his mind" to throw it in relation to the body of the man at bat. One's feet do not *per se* move one's body across the floor; they move only when something within—call it soul, mind, will, or self, as you will—*moves them*. As Dr. Rudolph Otto has written:

> For a manifestation of the influence exerted by the psychical upon the physical we need in fact go no farther than the power of our will to move our body—the power, that is, of a spiritual cause to bring about a mechanical effect. This assuredly is an absolutely insoluble riddle, and it is only the fact that we have grown so used to it that prevents it from seeming a "miracle" to us.[1]

Gen. 2:7—"Jehovah God formed man of the dust of the ground, and breathed into his nostrils the breath of life; and man became a living soul." Here we have it—the organismic approach to the study and understanding of man (the *vogue in psychology everywhere today*): we find that this organismic approach is in harmony with the Scripture. Yet as man he is an integrated unity of matter, the dust of the ground (the same elements of which all things material are constituted) and spirit, the Breath of God); moreover, as a unity, a body-spirit unity, he is to be known as a *living soul;* the saints, moreover, will be individual body-spirit unities in heaven, the only difference being that they will be clothed in "spiritual" bodies as a result of resurrection, revivification and glorification (cf. 1 Cor. 15:35-56, 2 Cor. 5:1-10; Rom. 2:7; 8:11, 8:23; Phil. 3:20-21, etc.). Rev. 20:4 —"I saw the souls of them that had been beheaded for the testimony of Jesus, and for the word of God," etc. Note that, at the Marriage Supper of the Lamb, the redeemed shall be clothed in "fine linen, bright and pure; for the fine linen is the righteous acts of the saints" (Rev. 19:8, 14).

In a word, to recap this phase of our subject, it is absurd

1. *The Idea of the Holy*, 214.

to insist that *sensation* and *consciousness* are identical. Our personal experience makes it obvious that this cannot be true: to the contrary, sensation is physiological, whereas consciousness is psychological; sensation is event A, but consciousness is event B. And in some inscrutable manner, sensation, consciousness, *and meaning*, are all interwoven in *perception*. No amount of wishful thinking will—or can—reduce consciousness or meaning to sheer sensation.

## 4. The Mystery of Life

"And he showed me," writes John the Revelator, "a river of water of life, bright as crystal, proceeding out of the throne of God and of the Lamb" (Rev. 22:1). From what primary Source indeed can the River of Water of Life emanate, but from the one self-existent Living Being, — God?

According to Aristotle,[1] the Totality of Things constitutes a hierarchy of being; our world is a terraced world, so to speak, and not a continuum. At the lowest level is the inanimate creation, the physiochemical foundation of things. At the next level is the plant world, which has this physiochemical basis, *plus* vegetation, *i.e.*, the cellular processes or processes of growth. At the third level is the animal creation, which has the same physiochemical basis and cellular processes, *plus* sensitivity and locomotion. At the highest level is the rational creature, man, characterized by the same physiochemical basis (which he shares with all physical existents), the same cellular processes (which he shares with plants and animals), sensitivity and locomotion (which he shares with the animal orders only), *plus* rationality or reason, which specifies him as man. In Aristotle's own terms, the plant is characterized by "vegetative *psyche*" ("soul"), the animal by "sensitive *psyche*," and man by "rational *psyche*." And above the whole is God who, says Aristotle, must be defined probably as pure Self-thinking Thought.[2] General observation and experience would seem to confirm, in its bold outlines at least, this Aristotelian picture of the Cosmos.

The first step upward in the scale of created being is the step from the level of "non-living" (inanimate, inorganic) substance to the level of "living" (animate, organic) substance.

1. *De Anima.*
2. *Metaphysics,* XII, vii, 1072b 15 ff.

111

Here we encounter the greatest mystery of all—the Mystery of Life itself, and in some inscrutable manner this mystery is embodied,—or perhaps it would be more correct to say, *enacted*,— in the living cell.

The cell is the ultimate or basic unit of every "living" entity. "True," writes Nordenskiold,

ultra-microscopical technics have given us some insight into the composition of the living substance over and above what the microscope has been able to provide, but no one has succeeded in isolating any vital unit in this way, and up till now the cell, with all its complications, remains the smallest form under which the living substance has been found to exist by itself and independently of other living entities.[1]

"The fundamental substance of the cell," adds this author, "has remained in its innermost essence undiscovered."

"To *metabolize*, to *move*, to *grow*, to *reproduce*, to *adapt* to the environment, and to have *organization*," writes a contemporary biologist, "is to be alive."[2] The same author tells us that the secret of life itself—and indeed all scientists would agree—is contained within the protoplasm of cells. He writes as follows:

The bodies of human beings, as well as those of other animals and of plants, are composed of a substance called *protoplasm*. This basic, living material is not homogeneous, but varies among organisms and among the different organs of a single animal or plant. From time to time, even a single organ may change in composition. All the many kinds of protoplasm share certain physical and chemical characteristics, however, and whatever the secret of life may be, it is well hidden in this exceedingly complex substance.[3]

Again,

The protoplasm of the human body, and of all plants and animals, is nowhere present in a single large mass, but exists in tiny discrete portions called *cells*. These are the units of structure of the body, just as bricks may be the units of structure of a house. But they are more than mere building blocks; each is an independent, functional unit, and the processes of the body are the sum of the coordinated functions of its cells. The units vary considerably in size, shape, and function. Some plants and animals have bodies made of just a single cell; others, such as man or an oak tree, are made of countless billions fitted together.[4]

1. Erik Nordenskiold, *The History of Biology*, 539. Trans. from the Swedish by Leonard Bucknall Eyre.
2. Claude A. Villee, *Biology: The Human Approach*, 28.
3. *Ibid.*, 21.
4. *Ibid.*, 34. *Protoplasm*, from the Greek *protos*, "first," and *plasma*, "anything formed or moulded"—the latter derived in turn from *plassein*, "to form" or "to mould"—is obviously just a name for this ultimate living substance, which is itself largely unknown. Certainly the secret of life itself has never been fathomed.

All cells, we are told, both plant and animal, although varying in many aspects, have several features in common, as follows: (1) All are completely enclosed by a *plasma membrane* which is made of protoplasm and which functions importantly in regulating the content of the cell; (2) Each contains a small, usually spherical, body, which is known as the *nucleus,* which functions to direct cellular activity and which contains the hereditary factors in both plants and animals; (3) In each cell, the *nucleoplasm* or protoplasm of the nucleus is separated from the surrounding protoplasm by a *nuclear membrane;* (4) Running through the nucleus of each cell are strands of a deeply staining protoplasmic material, which is known as *chromatin,* and when cell division takes place, these strands form *chromosomes,* rod-shaped bodies which in turn bear the hereditary units, known as *genes;* (5) In each cell, the protoplasm outside the nucleus is known as cyptoplasm, which contains other specialized structures to perform specific functions, that is, in relation to the biochemistry of the cell as a whole.

Plant cells differ from animal cells chiefly in three respects, as follows: (1) Plant cells, excepting those of higher plants lack the *centriole,* a dark staining structure which is found in the cytoplasm of all animal cells; (2) Plant cells, but not those of animals, have plastids in the cytoplasm. These plastids are small protein bodies. One type of plastid, called a *chloroplast,* contains the pigment *chlorophyll,* which is responsible for the green color of plants, and which is best known for its mysterious action in *photosynthesis.* This is the complicated and subtle process in which green plants convert the energy of the sun's rays into stored food energy. Science has never been able to break the process down and to discern exactly how it works, but it has long been known that without chlorophyll, neither plants nor animals (including human beings) could live. Thus it becomes obvious that solar energy is a prerequisite of plant life, just as plant life is a prerequisite of the various forms of animal life. Were it not for the constant transformation of light energy into potential chemical energy, and the constant replenishing of the supply of oxygen in the atmosphere, by this process of photosynthesis in plants, no living thing could exist. These, as we shall see later, are important facts to be considered in relation to the order of Creation that is given in the first chapter of *Genesis.* (3) In the third place, a plant cell has a stiff cell wall of cellulose which prevents its changing shape or position, whereas animal cells usually have only the thin plasma membrane on the outside and thus are able to move and to alter in shape.[1]

There are fundamental differences too in the atomic bases of plant and animal life. On this rather important aspect of the subject, De Nouy writes as follows:

It is very likely that evolution had an extremely elementary point of departure common to all living beings animals and vegetables. But from the very beginning we observe at the same time a relationship and a profound difference between the two. The active base, the nutritive liquid of the animals, is the blood, and that of the superior animals contains a fundamental substance, the red pigment called hemoglobin, which transports oxygen to the cells so as to oxydize, or burn, the refuse. The molecule of hemoglobin is very large and highly complicated; its structure varies from one species to another (mean molecular weight: 69,000).

Chemically, this hemoglobin is fairly close to the circulatory pigment of plants and algae, chlorophyll (molecular weight. 904). There is, therefore, a relationship, but whereas hemoglobin is characterized by the presence of one atom of iron in its molecule, chlorophyll, which is much simpler, is built around an atom of magnesium. To complicate the problem further, the blood of certain arthropods and mollusks, inferior animals which preceded superior animals, contains a pigment with a molecular weight varying, according to the species, between 400,000 and 6,700,000, and containing an atom of copper instead of iron or magnesium. [Certain snails, for instance.]

How was the chemical transition from one to the other accomplished? Honestly speaking, it is impossible to conceive it, and yet the hypothesis of a sudden appearance is not satisfactory. Some kind of transition must have taken place. We may never know how.[2]

Indeed, many of the secrets of the life process seem to be utterly impenetrable. (May I state, at this point, that I myself do not accept evolutionism either as being proved or even as provable scientifically. My position is clearly stated in the Addendum on the subject to be found at the end of this volume. C.C.C.)

Now the ultimate unit of the human organism, as of every other living thing, is the cell. Every individual, writes Dr. Jesse F. Williams,

is a mass of cells, microscopic units too small to be seen by the unaided eye. It is estimated that the body is composed of a total of 26,500,000,-000,000 cells. This enormous number, too large to be comprehended easily, grew from one cell, the ovum which was produced by the ovary of the mother and fertilized by the spermatozoon of the father. The statement that a new individual derives from a single cell is almost as unbelievable as the number of cells of which he is composed. The facts, however, are well established, and students of anatomy and physiology accept them. They remain, none the less, sources of wonder and even awe.[3]

1. *Vide* Villee, *op cit.*, 34-38, 54-58.
2. Lecomte De Nouy, *Human Destiny*, 58-59.
3. *A Textbook of Anatomy and Physiology*, Seventh Edition, 1.

# H. G. Wells, Julian Huxley, and G. P. Wells in a collaborated work, write as follows:

We may compare the body to a community, and the cells to the individuals of which this vast organized population is composed. . . . Single cells can be isolated from the rest of the body, and kept alive. . . . The size of this object is such that about 2,500 laid side by side would measure an inch. And it is itself separately and independently alive. Such is the stuff that man and all his life is made of. [I feel obliged to object to this statement: as far as we know, it is man's corporeal life only, and not his higher thought processes, that is the direct result of cellular activity. This, however, may be what these authors mean.] In our bodies there are millions of such individual cells, inherent and necessary parts of us. They are not dead like the bricks in a wall; they can be persuaded by the arts of Dr. Strangeways to desert! Then they will move by themselves, take nourishment, absorb oxygen, exude waste matters. They can be starved or suffocated. Not only will they move about as free individuals, but they will reproduce themselves. . . . The number of cells in the reader's body is staggering. In the blood of an average man there are over fifteen million million cells in the blood alone; his brain system contains nearly two thousand million; and the total number in the human body is over 1,000,000,000,-000,000—a thousand billions (and English billions, not American ones). They serve the body community in various ways and have various appropriately specialized forms. Some are of service because they can actively change their shape—such as muscle-cells; others, the nerve-cells, are drawn out into enormously long, thin threads, and are like living telephone wires; others, more cubical, serve by exuding special chemical substances—such as the cells of the salivary or thyroid glands. We need not catalogue all the possible varieties, but can content ourselves with stating that there are well over fifty distinct kinds of cells to be found in every man's body.[1]

## Again, from the same authors:

From the green scum on a dank garden path to Solomon in all his glory, from the tree to the tiger, from the swarming millions of germs in a poisoned finger to the tame elephant in the Zoological Gardens, from intestinal worm to rosebud, and from lichen to whale, life plays in endless variations that drama of movement, metabolism, and reproduction which marks it off from the mineral kingdom and from all the interplay of inanimate Nature. And, perhaps, in endless variations it plays also upon the themes of conscious and sub-conscious life, it dreams and slumbers in the plant or in the motionless fish, or drinks deep of contentment or flashes into frenzies of desire and delight and terror in hunter and hunted, in basking snake or playing cub or singing bird. And the writing and reading of this book and the thought-process behind these things are life also.[2]

The basic cellular processes of the human organism, starting with the fertilized ovum, are those of *segmentation* (or multiplication, and hence growth, for where there is life, there is growth), *differentiation* (of structure), and *specialization* (or alteration of function, which accompanies differentiation). (In-

1. *The Science of Life*, I, 40, 43, 46.
2. Wells, Huxley, and Wells, *op cit.*, I, 16.

cidentally, when a group of cells multiply only, and thus "run wild," so to speak, but fail to differentiate and to specialize, a cancer is formed in the given area.) Williams writes:

This development of different functions by different groups of cells is not the sudden acquisition of a new power nor an unusual capacity only possible in certain cellular elements, but rather an emphasis of one of several functional abilities common to all embryonic cells. This change, called specialization, means that certain cells take over and lift to a higher level of performance a particular function which all cells at one time possessed. Specialization of cells in the human organism has the same meaning that it has in human society. The more exquisitely a cell is adapted to one function, the less capable it is of performing all functions which it exercised formerly. . . . These changes, segmentation, differentiation, and specialization go on to some extent at the same time. In a precise manner of speaking there is probably no differentiation without specialization, and vice versa. Whether structure makes function or function makes structure is not determined by the above facts. In the embryo, function is at a minimum, and yet structure increases rapidly; on the other hand, after birth, function frequently determines structure. It should be remembered that structure and function are two aspects of the same thing— organization of protoplasm. Those who see in structure or in function a greater importance fail to recognize the essential unity of the whole organism.[1]

Thus the human organism is composed of differentiated and highly specialized aggregations of cells—each of which is "living" *per se*—built up hierarchically into tissues, organs, and systems, in the order named, and finally into the unity or whole, the organism itself. Science tells us, moreover, that these billions of living cells of various kinds and functions which constitute the organism as a whole, are in a state of constant flux; that, in fact, the human body undergoes a complete cellular transformation every four years or so. That is to say, the cells which go to make up my body at this moment, will have sloughed off and been replaced by an entirely new aggregation of cells some four years from this date. Through all this flux of cellular change, however, the *life* of the organism goes on undisturbed. *Memory* also, and *self-consciousness*, and *personal identity*, persist through all this flux: I am the same I, basically, at ten, twenty-five, fifty or seventy years of age. The memories I cherish are *my* memories—they can belong to no other; the images I retain in my "mind" are *my* images—I can not transfer them to anyone else; the essential self that I know is the self of *me*. I am the same person throughout the span of my earthly life, and I *know* that I am the same person. No getting around this fact!—that is, if I am a normal human being. Does not this persistence of

1. Dr. Jesse F. Williams, *op cit.*, 14-16.

personal identity through some fifteen or twenty complete cellular transformations in the course of a lifetime, point forward unmistakably to my personal survival of the last great change—the change which occurs in connection with the "death" of the body?

In the light of all these facts, one can only cry out with the Psalmist, in wonder and awe:

> I will give thanks unto thee; for I am fearfully
> and wonderfully made:
> Wonderful are thy works;
> And that my soul knoweth right well.
> (Psa. 139:14)

The evidence seems to be quite conclusive that the Mystery of Life resides in the protoplasm of the living cell. Protoplasm is described as a semifluid, jellylike substance possessing not only physical and chemical characteristics, but also such definitely physiological functions as growth and repair, liberation of energy from food, sensibility or irritability, and reproduction. These are all characteristics of what we call organic or "living" substance. But what is this force—or process—this phenomenon itself that we call "life"? Obviously, it is something essentially qualitative rather than quantitative—but what is it? Whence came it? What is that elusive something within the living cell that causes it to be "alive," and distinguishes it from the non-living atom? Is the secret of life inherent in the physiochemistry, perhaps in the juxtaposition of the atoms, within the cell? Biologists as a rule think so. Villee, for example, writes:

The unique property of protoplasm, its aliveness, does not depend upon the presence of some rare or unique element. Four elements, carbon, oxygen, hydrogen and nitrogen, make up about 96 per cent of the material of the human body. Another four, calcium, phosphorus, potassium and sulfur, constitute 3 per cent of the body weight. Minute amounts of iodine, iron, sodium, chlorine, magnesium, copper and perhaps other elements complete the list. All these elements, and especially the first four, are abundant in the atmosphere, the earth's crust, and the sea. Life depends upon the complexity of the interrelationships of these common, abundant elements.[1]

This last statement, however, is purely gratuitous; certainly it has never been proved experimentally, that life has its explanation in the complexity of the interrelationships of the elements, nor even of the atoms within the elements, here enumerated. Consequently there have been thinkers in all ages who

1. *Op. cit.*, 21-22.

have held that Life is a force superposed upon, or added to, the physiochemical bases of living organisms. Again I quote from Villee:

Most present-day biologists agree that vital phenomena, though more complex, are reducible to the same basis as nonliving phenomena, that both are explainable in terms of chemistry and physics. This is called the *mechanistic* theory. A corollary of this view is that if we knew everything about the chemistry and physics of vital phenomena, we would be able to synthesize life. An opposing school of thought, *vitalism*, states that some unique force, not reducible to the terms of chemistry and physics, controls the activities of life and differentiates living from nonliving things. Vitalists believe that no matter how great our knowledge of the physics and chemistry of protoplasm may be, we shall never understand life or be able to create it artificially.[1]

One thing is sure, however, with reference to the issue stated here, and that is, that science does not, *as yet* have the answer. Up to the present moment no one has penetrated the Mystery of Life itself. As one of the most distinguished of modern biologists puts it:

We do not know what life is. No one has yet observed a transition from inanimate to animate nature, nor has any theory been proposed which successfully explains the origin of life on the earth. We must remain satisfied with the fact of life's existence, without being able to explain it or even describe it clearly.[2]

The Mystery of Life *per se* remains as inscrutable as the mysteries of matter, consciousness, and personality. It is but one of the many mysteries which seem to remain impenetrable to human science—in spite of its boasted self-sufficiency—in a world that is full of mysteries, and of mysteries that become more mysterious and more numerous as the horizon of human knowledge is extended.

Is there any evidence anywhere in Nature, as we know it, that inanimate matter has the inherent power to produce life? Modern science answers this question firmly in the negative: "spontaneous generation," it says, does not occur. But, strange as it may seem, the theory of spontaneous generation was held quite generally, by non-churchmen and churchmen alike, throughout ancient and early medieval times. Several of the early Church Fathers, notably Ephrem, Basil, Gregory of Nyssa, and John Chrysostom, in the East, and Ambrose and Augustine in the West, clearly interpreted the *Genesis* account of Creation as teaching that originally-created inorganic matter was really

1. *Op cit.*, 28-29.
2. Fritz Kahn, M.D., *Man in Structures and Function*, I, 5. Trans. from the German and edited by George Rosen, M.D.

endowed by the Creator, from the moment of its creation, with the power of producing living beings. This view was fully developed by St. Augustine, Bishop of Hippo, in his celebrated theory of "seminal reasons," namely, that the inorganic elements, God's primary creation, contained in themselves, from the beginning, the "seminal reasons" of all living things, *i.e.*, the powers necessary to the generation of living things. He states expressly that, at the proper moment in the Creative Process, the earth (not *seeds* in the earth, mind you!) was given the impetus to produce life.[1] According to Augustine's interpretation, all species of plants and animals were created potentially from the very beginning, in that their causes or principles were implanted in matter when it was created; therefore, the account·of the Creation which appears in the first chapter of *Genesis* is but the record of the progressive actualizing, *by the Word of God*, of those powers which hitherto had existed potentially in the inorganic elements. In a word, according to this theory, the creation of inorganic matter by the Deity was a *primary* creation (that is, no secondary causes, or what we call "laws of nature," were involved), whereas that which followed in the successive epochs ("days") of Creation was the result of the cooperation of the Creator with secondary causes—causes proceeding from the waters, the earth, etc.

Cf. Gen. 1:11—And God said, Let the earth put forth grass, herbs yielding seed, and fruit trees bearing fruit after their kind, wherein is the seed thereof, upon the earth: and it was so. Also v. 20—And God said, Let the waters swarm with swarms of living creatures, and let birds fly above the earth in the open firmament of heaven, etc. Also v. 24—And God said, Let the earth bring forth living creatures after their kind, cattle, and creeping things, and beasts of the earth, after their kind: and it was so. [Incidentally, does not modern science hold that animal life existed *first* in the water, *then* in the air, and finally on the land?]

I might add here that a plausible argument certainly can be made at any time in support of this Augustinian interpretation.[2]

But present-day science, on the whole, rejects the theory of spontaneous generation. The modern view seems to be that Pasteur, by proving conclusively that "microbes have parents," demonstrates once and for all that the generation of life by inanimate matter does not take place in nature. C. C. Furnas declares that "Pasteur effectively silenced all spontaneous gen-

1. *De Genesi ad litteram*, Lib. V, 4. *Vide* Migne's Edition.
2. For an excellent presentation of the teaching of the Church Fathers on this subject, *vide* Ernest C. Messenger, *Evolution and Theology.*

eration advocates with an air-tight set of data."[1] Wells, Huxley, and Wells testify as follows:

Life seems always to be produced by pre-existing life. It presents itself as a multitude of individuals which have been produced by division or the detachment of parts from other individuals, and most of which will in their time give rise to another generation. . . . It is accepted now by all biologists of repute that life arises from life and in no other way—*omne vivum ex vivo*. Life as we know it flows in a strictly defined stream from its remote and unknown origins, it dissolves and assimilates food, but it receives no living tributaries.[2]

All living things take their origin in pieces of living substance detached from the bodies of other living thngs. . . . Every living cell arises from a pre-existing cell.[3]

One fact remains, that all the life we know is one continuing sort of life, that all the life which exists at this moment derives, so far as human knowledge goes, in unbroken succession from life in past time, and that the unindividualized non-living world is separated from it by a definite gap.[4]

It seems that life must once have begun, but no properly informed man can say with absolute conviction that it will ever end.[5]

So, generally speaking, conclude the scientists of our day. The mysteries of life, of the origin of life, of the living cell, remain impenetrable to science.

There is an occasional exception, however, in so far as the origin of life by spontaneous generation is concerned. For example, Dr. George W. Beadle of Stanford University, in an address before the George Westinghouse Centennial Forum, held in Pittsburgh, Pennsylvania, in May, 1946, explicitly defended the possibility of spontaneous generation. Among other things, he said:

It is a fascinating diversion to speculate on the manner of the origin of the first living thing on earth and to wonder what its nature could have been. Although the complete answers can never be known, it is nevertheless of interest to see how plausible a hypothesis can be built up in terms of our present knowledge. One of the questions that one soon faces in any attempt of this kind is the simple one: what constitutes a living system compared with a non-living one? Not everyone will give the same answer; indeed, in giving any at all one runs the risk of stimulating violent argument. Let us assume for purposes of our particular kind of speculation that the decisive step was taken when the first chemical combination capable of self-duplication came into being. By self-duplication I mean that process of replica formation that occurs regularly *only* in the presence of a model. To state it differently, once the first living unit appeared by chance, then and

1. *The Next Hundred Years*, 22.
2. *Op. cit.*, 4-5.
3. *Ibid.*, 459.
4. *Ibid.*, 6.
5. *Ibid.*, 13.

only then could more units of the same kind appear with regularity. In the present state of this world, organic molecules are—as the term itself implies—almost invariably synthesized by living beings. It is often supposed, therefore, that they were not present before life arose. If this were true, life must have come about by some lucky chance combination of inorganic molecules that possessed the property of catalyzing further combinations of the same sort. While the probability of such a combination would be exceedingly small, that is not a valid objection to assuming its occurrence since it need have happened only once. But this theory can be disposed of on logical grounds by a simple argument. The fact that life arose at all is itself sufficient grounds for concluding that it did not happen in one step from inorganic molecules. This follows from the consideration that if anything as complex as a self-duplicating organic molecule could arise in a single step, then it is infinitely more probable that simpler organic molecules without the power of self-duplication would have arisen. If these arose spontaneously, then they, rather than inorganic molecules, certainly would have served as the precursors of the more complex combination that was the first living unit. The thesis that organic molecules were present in great variety in the pre-life world is defended in a book entitled *The Origin of Life* by the Russian biochemist Oparin. His assumption that organic molecules could be formed spontaneously in a lifeless world is one against which the average person tends to rebel violently at first. On second thought, however, one is inclined to concede that with the infinite variety of combinations of molecules and reaction conditions that must have existed on earth before life was present, organic molecules would have had a slight but real probability of being formed by chance. . . . Assuming, then, the existence of endless kinds of organic molecules of varying complexities, it becomes possible to imagine the spontaneous origin of a combination, like a present-day protein molecule, which possessed the power of directing the formation of more molecules like itself from precursors like those from which it first arose. In the absence of competition for its components, such a simple being could have enjoyed a quite peaceful existence, forming descendants like itself whenever and wherever it found the right combination of raw materials. It would have mattered little if the happy opportunity of making a replica occurred only once in a thousand or million years. Actually we know of the present-day existence of molecules with the essential properties that we have ascribed to the protogene. As first shown by Stanley, many viruses are crystallizable nucleoproteins that have the property of automultiplication in an environment in which all the component parts are present under the proper conditions. The principal difference between the present-day virus and the postulated protogene is that the protogene was free-living while the virus is parasitic on a living cell. Considering that the environment in which the protogene is assumed to have arisen was like the interior of a living cell in containing a vast array of organic molecules, this certainly is not a profound difference.[1]

Dr. Beadle then goes on to suggest the possibility that "reaction chains" of protogenes were "built up through mutation and natural selection in a way in which every single step would

1. George W. Beadle, "High-Frequency Radiation and the Gene," *Science and Life in the World*, Vol. II, The George Westinghouse Centennial Forum Series, in three volumes, 1946. McGraw-Hill.

have conferred a selective advantage over the previous condition," the ultimate result being, of course, life in its various forms and degrees of complexity.

Now the eminent doctor of biology, self-admittedly, is "speculating," "assuming," "imagining"—in a word, guessing—throughout this entire presentation. The argument itself, however, proves that the ghost of spontaneous generation stalks the halls of science once more, and is remindful of the age-old creed of materialism:

> Once nothing arrived on this earth out of space;
> It rode in on nothing; it came from no place;
> It landed on nothing—the earth was not here—
> It worked hard on nothing for year after year.
> It sweat over nothing with mighty resolve;
> But just about then things began to evolve.
> The heavens appeared, and the sea and the sod;
> This Almighty Nothing worked much like a god.
> It started unwinding without any plan,
> It made every creature, and ended with man.
> No God here was needed—there was no Creation;
> Man grew like a mushroom and needs no salvation.
> Some savants say this should be called evolution,
> And ignorance only rejects that solution.[1]

And no doubt there are some scientists who would shout with ill-concealed glee, "Exeunt the spirits!" (Dr. L. T. Hogben, for example, writes of carbon compounds as "the last resting place of spirits."[2]) All this, however, is only wishful thinking, no matter if it should turn out to be "scientific." All that the revival of the spontaneous generation theory accomplishes is to push "spirit" back a step or two in the developmental scale of total being. All self-styled naturalistic scientists should familiarize themselves with the writings of the Church Fathers cited in a foregoing paragraph. For, in the final analysis of the case, whether the *life principle* was incorporated in matter from the beginning (or, to speak more precisely, in certain *relations* existing within matter itself), or whether it was superimposed upon matter from without, is not a matter of too great significance after all. The author of a recently-published textbook on geology has summarized the point at issue very sensibly, as follows:

Two views that are at least partially opposed to one another may be advanced concerning the origin of life. (1) Life is the result of special creation; the existence of plants and animals on the earth

1. I have never succeeded in identifying the author of these lines. —C.

2. L. T. Hogben, *Science for the Citizen.*

122

depends on the creative act of a Deity. (2) Life is the result of certain physiochemical conditions; the introduction of these conditions and the properties of matter that are involved depend on "laws" of nature, which in turn are an expression of inherent characters of the universe. All of these are conceivably the result of an initial divinely established order; otherwise there is no understandable beginning or end.[1]

And one of the most ardent of contemporary evolutionists, Earnest A. Hooton, writes in a similarly restrained vein:

One cannot conclude a volume of facts, reflections, and speculations concerning the course of human evolution without asking himself if there is any place for a guiding intelligence in this marvelous progression of organic events. However you look at him, man is a miracle, whether he be a miracle of chance, of nature, or of God. Further the whole sequence of evolutionary development is such an astounding and incomprehensible concept that it baffles explanation. That evolution has occurred I have not the slightest doubt. That it is an accidental or chance occurrence I do not believe, although chance probably has often intervened and is an important contributing factor. But if evolution is not mainly a chance process it must be an intelligent or purposeful process. ["Chance," of course, is best defined as essentially a *non-purposeful* something or event.] It seems to me quite immaterial whether we believe that the postulated source of the intelligence or purposeful causation is a divine being or a set of natural "laws." ["Laws," however, presuppose a Lawgiver, a Sovereign Will, for all law is essentially the expression of will. Science, therefore, by its use of the term, "laws" of nature, either wittingly or unwittingly recognizes the Will of God as the Constitution of the universe.] What difference does it make whether God is Nature or Nature is God.? [The Scriptures clearly teach that God is the Author and Creator of Nature.] The pursuit of natural causes either leads to the deification of Nature, or to the recognition of the supernatural, or to a simple admission of ignorance, bewilderment, and awe. It should arouse the feeling of reverence in any one who attempts to grasp the central phenomenon which emerges from the vast assemblage of organic facts. I venture to assert that the concept of organic evolution is one of the grandest and most sublime which can engage the attention of man. Whether man arose from the apes or was made from mud, he is in a sense a divine product. Organic evolution is an achievement not unworthy of any God and not incompatible with the loftiest conception of religion. But if it were conclusively demonstrated tomorrow that man has not evolved from anthropoid ancestors, if it were finally proven that the species had not been derived one from the other, but had been separately created, the anthropologist would still face the dawn with equanimity and with eager anticipation of new scientific visits. Theories of origin and causation are often transient and evanescent; life itself can never fail to command the interest and evoke the inquiry of human minds.[2]

Again I quote from Lincoln Barnett's book, in this connection:

Cosmologists for the most part maintain silence on the question of ultimate origins, leaving that issue to the philosophers and theology. Yet only the purest empiricists among modern scientists turn their

1. Dr. Raymond C. Moore, *Historical Geology*, 102.
2. E. A. Hooton, *Up from the Ape*. 604-605.

backs on the mystery that underlies physical reality. Einstein, whose philosophy of science has sometimes been criticized as materialistic, once said:

"The most beautiful and most profound emotion we can experience is the sensation of the mystical. It is the sower of all true science. He to whom this emotion is a stranger, who can no longer wonder and stand rapt in awe, is as good as dead. To know that what is impenetrable to us really exists, manifesting itself as the highest wisdom and the most radiant beauty which our dull faculties can comprehend only in their most primitive forms—this knowledge, this feeling is at the center of true religiousness."

And on another occasion he declared, "The cosmic religious experience is the strongest and noblest mainspring of scientific research." Most scientists, when referring to the mysteries of the universe, its vast forces, its origins, and its rationality and harmony, tend to avoid using the word God. Yet Einstein, who has been called an atheist, has no such inhibitions. "My religion," he says, "consists of a humble admiration of the illimitable superior spirit who reveals himself in the slight details we are able to perceive with our frail and feeble minds. That deeply emotional conviction of the presence of a superior reasoning power, which is revealed in the incomprehensible universe, forms my idea of God."[1]

And so, again, we are back to the only possible logical startingpoint: Either intelligent Spirit or unintelligent atoms (or energy) must be the unoriginated First Principle of all things. He who holds the former view is a *theist;* he who holds the latter view, a *materialist.* There is, of course, an alternative position, namely, that of the *dualist,* who holds that both Spirit and Matter are eternal or unoriginated. But, would it not be unphilosophical to postulate *two* self-existent First Principles when *one* alone is sufficient? And this is precisely the claim that is made for the Eternal Spirit throughout this treatise.

Getting back to the theory of spontaneous generation, Dr. A. H. Strong has written—to my mind—conclusively on this subject, as follows:

If such instances [for spontaneous generation] could be authenticated, they would prove nothing as against a proper doctrine of creation—for there would still exist an impossibility of accounting for vivific properties of matter, except upon the Scriptural view of an intelligent Contriver and Originator of matter and its laws. In short, evolution implies previous involution—if anything comes out of matter, it must first have been put in. . . . This theory, if true, only supplements the doctrine of original, absolute, immediate creation, with another doctrine of mediate and derivative creation, or the development of the materials and forces originated at the beginning. This development, however, cannot proceed to any valuable end without guidance of the same intelligence which initiated it. The Scriptures, although they do not sanction the doctrine of spontaneous generation, do recog-

1. *Op. cit.,* 105-106.

nize processes of development as supplementing the divine fiat which first called the elements into being.[1]

It must be remembered that whether God operates primarily and directly, or through secondary causes ("natural laws"), it is He who, as the First Cause or Principle, is back of, and responsible for, the whole life process. The same measure of creative power is required equally for a creation by emanation, or a creation by evolution, or a direct and instantaneous creation. The problem involved here is not that of *method*, but that of *power*—it is the problem of the *Elan Vital*—to use Bergson's well-known designation. As a matter of fact, it was Bergson himself who first called attention to the inadequacy of the traditional theories of evolution; they postulated methods only, said he, but failed to take into consideration the Life Force itself, the Vital Impetus which has ever surged onward and upward in the myriads of living species, the Force which *actualizes* all methods which may be involved in the ongoing of the life process; methods are, in fact, but evidences of the operation of this basic Life Force. The universe and its creatures, said Bergson, are the embodiment of this immanent principle of living change and creativity; it is one continuous flow, evolution being only the movement of the flow. Underneath the conflict of the *Elan* with the living forms in which it is compelled to concrete itself in order to find proper expression,—for the very impetus of Life consists in the need for creation—there is a fundamental spiritual unity which is the rhythm of the mobility of Life itself. This mobility, moreover, is essentially the stuff of duration, which is *real* time (*i.e.*, time, as experienced by a spirit or spiritual being), as distinguished from *mathematical* time, which is a form of measurement arbitrarily imposed upon reality by the human intellect.[2]

It is to the *Elan*, therefore, according to Bergson, that we must look for the answer to the problem of the origin of species. It is useless to look to mere physiochemical forces for this solution; we shall not find it there. Something more is needed to explain the Mystery of Life and of living forms than the operation of either physical or chemical forces or even of both together. The ultimate source of the evolution of life must be Something of the nature of consciousness, of duration,—in a word, of Spirit. As a matter of fact, Bergson's *Elan Vital* is a *conscious* Life

1. *Systematic Theology*, One-Volume Edition, 390.
2. *Vide* Henri Bergson. *Creative Evolution*, authorized translation by Arthur Mitchell.

Force. It is a universal principle or power which transcends the present moment, and must needs transcend any factual embodiment of itself at any time. It is infinite in the sense of being *inexhaustibly creative*. And, paradoxical as it may seem, the self-manifestations of the Infinite must needs be first, simply because it *is* infinite in the sense of being inexhaustibly creative. It is because of the inexhaustible richness of life itself, that it is alway developing in the direction of such great variety and multiplicity. Thus it must be obvious to any thinking person that Bergon's *Elan* has practically all the properties traditionally ascribed to the Spirit of God. In fact, the property most characteristic of Spirit is *inexhaustibleness*. This is always true, whether the Spirit be regarded as operating in the realm of power, or in that life, or in that of thought.

The Mystery of Life is still a mystery—as great a mystery as it ever was. Dr. Alexis Carrel, formerly of the Rockefeller Institute, kept a piece of the heart-muscle of a chicken alive and pulsing and growing for more than twenty years. Cutting off a bit of the heart of a live, unhatched chicken, he placed the fragment in a glass tube in which it was supplied a constant bath of liquid food which included blood. The bit of "flesh" grew, and from time to time it had to be trimmed down to fit the receptacle in which it was contained. Remarkable as this experiment was, it served only to accentuate three great "unknowns": (1) What was the something in that particle of living tissues that caused it to continue to be "alive"? (2) What is it that keeps the heart, or any other organ, of a live chicken from growing beyond proper bounds, as this piece did? (3) What is the mystery in blood that endows it with power to sustain life, power that obviously cannot be created from pure chemicals? *No chemist has ever synthesized a living cell in the laboratory. No man has ever created a seed.*

Cf. Lev. 17:11—For the life of the flesh is in the blood; and I have given it to you upon the altar to make atonement for your souls: for it is the blood that maketh atonement by reason of the life. Cf. also Luke 24:39—[the words of Jesus, after His resurrection]: See my hands and my feet, that it is I myself: handle me, and see; for a spirit hath not flesh and bones, as ye behold me having. [Evidently the blood—the principle of *animal* life—was gone from His resurrection body.]

Then, again, what is the secret of the mystery of the propagation of life? Scientific experiment has proved the fact beyond any possibility of doubt that the mystery of the *life process* is bound up, in some inscrutable manner, with the chromosomes and genes of the reproductive cells. Not only are physical characteristics, but temperamental and intellectual endowments as well, transmitted through such media from one generation to another. But precisely what this relation is, continues to be a secret apparently as impenetrable as the comparable mystery of the relationship existing between brain and "mind." These mysteries, of course, are to be expected, if life is essentially a metaphysical or spiritual force—a conclusion which, in the view of thinkers who are not predisposed to an absolutely materialistic interpretation of the universe, can hardly be avoided.

That life is more than a mere physiochemical phenomenon seems to me too obvious to be questioned. I can see no alternative, either from the viewpoint of reason or from that of ordinary common sense, but to accept the fact of a basic, essentially non-material Pure Activity or Creative Spirit, which contains within itself (or, speaking precisely, who contains within Himself) all the actualities of energy, life, consciousness, personality, and holiness, *i.e., wholeness*. Such are the actualities of the Spirit of God as He is presented in Scriptures. He is revealed as the Source of Power, Life, Light, Truth, Law, Love, and Wholeness; apart from Him there is only impotence, death, darkness, error, license, hate and disunity.

Just as at the lowest level of the Totality of Being, the inorganic level, the Spirit operates to produce energy and is therefore the Spirit of Power, so at the next level of being, the organic level, He operates to generate life and is the Spirit of Life. Life in all its forms is a Divine Gift—the gift of the Spirit of God.

In the first place, the Spirit is the Giver of the natural or physical life which we enjoy here and now.

Acts 17:24-25: The God that made the world and all things therein, he, being Lord of heaven and earth, dwelleth not in the temples made with hands; neither is he served by men's hands, as though he needed anything, seeing he himself giveth to all life, and breath, and all things. Job 33:4—The Spirit of God hath made me, and the breath of the Almighty giveth me life. Job 27:3—For my life is yet whole in me, and the spirit of God is in my nostrils. John 6:63—It is the spirit that giveth life; the flesh profiteth nothing. Gen. 2:7—Jehovah God formed man of the dust of the ground; and breathed into his nostrils the breath of life; and man became a living soul.

In the second place, the Spirit is the Giver of the spiritual life which we may enjoy here and now, in the Kingdom of Grace, through Christ the Word.

John 1:1-4—In the beginning was the Word, and the Word was with God, and the Word was God. . . . In Him was life; and the life was the light of men. John 6:35—Jesus said unto them, I am the bread of life: he that cometh to me shall not hunger, and he that believeth on me shall never thirst. John 14:6—Jesus saith unto him, I am the way, and the truth, and the life. 1 John 5:12—He that hath the Son hath the life; he that hath not the Son of God hath not the life. Eph. 2:8—For by grace have ye been saved through faith; and that [i.e., that salvation] not of yourselves, it is the gift of God. Eph. 2:4, 5—God, being rich in mercy . . . made us alive together with Christ (by grace have ye been saved). John 3:5, 6—Jesus answered, Verily, verily, I say unto thee, Except one be born of water and the Spirit, he cannot enter into the kingdom of God. That which is born of the flesh is flesh; and that which is born of the Spirit is spirit.

In the third place, the Spirit is the Giver of eternal life, that life which the saints shall enjoy in the Kingdom of Glory, which is mediated through Christ the Word, and which shall consist in ultimate union with God in knowledge and love. One of the concomitants of that life, moreover, shall be a redeemed or spiritual body.

John 3:16—For God so loved the world, that he gave his only begotten Son, that whosoever believeth on him should not perish, but have eternal life. John 11:25, 26—Jesus saith unto her, I am the resurrection and the life. . . . whosoever liveth and believeth on me shall never die. 2 Cor. 3:6—the letter killeth, but the spirit giveth life. Rom. 6:23—For the wages of sin is death; but the free gift of God is eternal life in Christ Jesus our Lord. Rom. 8:11—But if the Spirit of him that raised up Jesus from the dead dwelleth in you; he that raised up Christ Jesus from the dead shall give life also to your mortal bodies through his Spirit that dwelleth in you.

Every year, in the springtime, noiselessly and without effort, the earth blossoms into beauty and melts into fragrance. As the poet has written,

> Whether we look or whether we listen,
> We hear life murmur, or see it glisten;
> Every clod feels a stir of might,—
> An instinct within that reaches and towers —
> And, groping blindly above it for light,
> Climbs to a soul in grass and flowers.

What is this never-failing awakening of life, year after year, but a gracious providential operation of the Spirit of God? In the words of the Psalmist, referring to all living creatures: "Thou sendest forth thy Spirit, they are created; and thou renewest the face of the ground" (Psa. 104:30).

Life is not a creation—it is a Divine Gift. We ourselves were born, not made; our parents were born of their parents; and so on, back to the beginningless Fountain of Life. That Fountain, the Scriptures tell us, was the very Being of God

Himself; first life was enjoyed by man as the result of a Divine Inbreathing. Gen. 2:7 again: "Jehovah God formed man of the dust of the ground, and breathed into his nostrils the breath of life; and man became a living soul." How fitting that the very Name of our God is I AM, HE WHO IS, the Ever-Living One! Exo. 3:14—"And God said unto Moses, I AM THAT I AM: and he said, Thus shalt thou say unto the children of Israel, I AM hath sent me unto you." John 4:24, the words of Jesus: "God is a Spirit: and they that worship him must worship in spirit and truth."

The Breath of God is the outgoing of the Spirit of God, and it is the Spirit that giveth life. Our God IS a Spirit, and they who worship Him must worship Him in spirit and according to the Truth.

The Stream of Life flows ever onward and upward in this present world, from the lowliest plant form to the highest, thence upward through all creatures of water, air, and land, finally to attain its highest manifestation in human personality. The red River of Life has flown out from Someone, Somewhere, for ever! And it will continue to flow—even beyond the grave— where in the redeemed and immortalized saints, its red shall have been transformed into crystal purity and brightness. "And he [the angel] showed me," writes the Seer of the Apocalypse, enraptured, "a river of water of life, bright as crystal, proceeding out of the throne of God and of the Lamb" (Rev. 22:1). "Out of the throne of God and of the Lamb"—note it well!

Ah, sweet Mystery of Life, precious gift of the Spirit of my God. As Tennyson has expressed it, so exquisitely:

> Flower in the crannied wall,
> I pluck you out of the crannies,
> I hold you here, root and all, in my hand,
> Little flower—but *if* I could understand
> What you are, root and all, and all in all,
> I should know what God and man is.

## 5. The Mystery of Thought

Is there anything in the universe—any entity or activity— that is not matter or not material? Can everything that exists be reduced ultimately to matter in motion? Is thought, for example, but a manifestation of electronic, atomic, or some other—possibly as yet unknown—form of "physical" energy? There have been those in all ages who have stubbornly insisted

129

that our universe is ultimately a universe of matter and of matter only; there are those today who would so affirm; we call them "materialists." They insist that we have no knowledge of anything except by means of the senses, and that even we ourselves are constitutionally material; hence, that all our knowledge is simply knowledge of matter by matter. Obviously, however, in stating their position, materialists overlook the fact that they are talking about two separate things, namely, (1) about everything, including themselves, all of which they affirm to be matter, and (2) about their *belief* that everything is matter, which they affirm to be the *truth* about the world we live in. But any person of ordinary common sense should be able to see that by no stretch of the imagination can any *belief* or *theory* or alleged *truth* about matter be identified with matter itself. The arrangement of cells in the brain is one thing; a belief, theory, or alleged truth is quite another thing. It has been rightly said that the materialist can explain everything but his own theory: *that,* obviously, is not "material."

We recall the theory of the "conditioned reflex" developed by the Russian school and especially by Pavlov, soon after the turn of the present century. This came to be the basis of what was called "the dog-and-drool" psychology, and finally of what came to be elaborated as "behaviorism," first by Dr. John B. Watson of the University of Chicago and later of Johns Hopkins University. Watson repudiated the traditional conception of the mental processes and interpreted "thinking" as subvocal "conditioning." This caused Dr. Will Durant to quip that "Dr. Watson had made up his larynx that he did not have a mind." "Behaviorism" in its various forms ran rampant for half a century, until a measure of sanity began to assert itself in psychology departments of our universities. Behaviorism of our day and age is not that which was advocated by Watson. At any rate these facts serve to show how desperately men in psychology have tried to downgrade the human race into an animal species, disregarding altogether the essential facts of person and personality, and thus relieve themselves of all moral responsibility or at least to reduce what has been called morality to sheer meaningless relativism. Naturally this kind of propaganda became a bulwark of materialism. It is being kept alive to some extent in our day by the psychologist B. F. Skinner. Materialism, however, is so absurd, so contrary to the higher outreaches of man, that about all it is doing now is to drive them into the opposite extremes of orgiastic and ecstatic emotional outbursts, into various diabolical cults such as fatalism, spiritualism, divination, witchcraft, black magic, libidinism, homosexuality, and even devil-worship itself. The following clear statement of fact is pertinent here (from Claude Tresmontant, French Professor of the Philosophy of Science in the Sorbonne, Paris):

> The discoveries of modern science have made it easier to prove the existence of God than it used to be. Those who find no place for God in their philosophy must be prepared to affirm that mindless, inanimate matter has been able to organize itself, to become animated, and to endow itself with consciousness and thought. . . . If the material universe is to be regarded as the only reality, matter must be credited with all the attributes that theologians specify as belonging to God, including supreme intelligence, creative power, and eternal autonomous existence. [When asked if the emergence of life could not be attributed purely to the laws of chance over a very long period of time, this scientist said]: It may be theoretically possible, but mathematically it is so extremely improbable that only a very few scientists now seriously think that pure chance can be put forward as an explanation of the emergence of even the simplest living organism. [In Shar Salom Publication tract entitled "So You Are an Agnostic!" by Harry Bucalstein, 236 West 72nd Street, New York, N. Y., 10023].

These words remind us of the notion put forward in the heydey of Darwinism that if a monkey were placed at the keys of a typewriter, given a sufficient time, by just pounding the keys at random it could hammer out one of Plato's dialogues. Frankly, it takes more faith to accept this argument than to believe in a Creator-God.

The case against materialism is stated so clearly by Mr. A. Clutton-Brock that I feel justified in re-presenting his argument here at some length. He writes as follows:

> We are aware of matter with our senses; and, if we are aware of spirit at all, it is not with our senses. The first question is, then, Are we aware of anything not with our senses? Of ourselves, perhaps; but those who believe that matter is the sole reality must believe also that self-consciousness is an illusion. For them there is no self but merely matter in certain formal arrangements functioning, they say; and self-consciousness is but an effect of that functioning. They insist that we have no knowledge of anything except with our senses, and that this knowledge is all knowledge by matter of matter.
> Yet all the senses in combination applied to some one particular object could not produce any conclusion about that object, could not even tell us that it was an object. Smell by itself does not tell me that what I smell is also that which I touch and see; nor do simultaneous smell, sight, and touch tell me that. A creature with only sense-perceptions could not go beyond them; there would be nothing in it to conclude that it was smelling, touching and seeing the same object. It would in fact *consist* only of sense-perceptions and would have no notion of external reality at all; and it may be that there are creatures which do consist only of sense-perceptions and have no notion of external reality. But man is not one of them; he is aware of an

131

object over and above his sense-perceptions of it; and he calls that which is aware the self.

But still the question remains whether this self can be aware of anything but matter. Assuming, as we must, that the self is not merely a combination of sense-perceptions, is it still only matter, by some means which we cannot yet understand, aware of the existence of other matter? Now the man who believes this believes also something more, namely, that it is the truth about matter. For him, therefore, besides matter there exists the truth about matter, which itself clearly is not matter and is not perceived with the senses. He may say that the truth about matter is a product of that matter which is his own mind, and exists only in his mind. But, if the truth is that and merely that, it is not the truth to him, and he cannot believe it. Truth means to us, not a product of our minds, but that which exists independently of them, that which would exist if we were not. The very word truth implies its independent existence; the value for truth, to which we all appeal when we use the word, implies its independent existence. If we could believe that we had made truth ourselves, we should no longer value it, and it would not be truth to us. [That is to say, Truth is *discovered*, not formulated, by man. It is essentially being, and the relations within the Totality of Being. The truth of electricity is cotemporaneous with the universe itself; it existed long, long before Benjamin Franklin flew his kite. The truth of the ingredients of the atom bomb has existed in the cosmos from the beginning, yet only recently has it been discovered and utilized by man. The quest of science is essentially the quest for truth—the truth of the relations which obtain within the cosmos]. When we speak of a bitter truth, an unwelcome truth, we imply that it exists independently of us and compels our recognition of its existence. If it did not, why should we not make for ourselves truths only comforting to ourselves? The answer is that we could not believe them. Belief implies that what we believe in exists independently of our minds. So the truth about external reality exists independently of our minds; it is not matter, though it be about matter, nor is it perceived by the senses. . . .

So, to one who says that he believes only in the existence of matter, one may put it that that belief is inconsistent with his other belief that he has attained to the truth about matter, is indeed inconsistent with belief of any kind, and so even with itself. For if only matter exists, the truth about matter does not exist for us; it is merely an effect produced by matter upon matter; belief is an effect produced by matter upon matter. But he who believes that cannot believe anything else, or even that.

Mr. Clutton-Brock goes on to show that the same reasoning applies to our perceptions of beauty and goodness:

Turn now from truth to something which can be much more easily confused with matter; something which most people suppose they perceive with their senses, namely beauty. To us the truth about objects is not the objects themselves; but we may suppose that the beauty of an object is the object itself, and that we perceive it with our sense of sight or hearing. The beauty of a tune is the tune; and we hear that beauty. Yet it is possible to hear the notes without hearing the tune and so the beauty. The beauty of the tune does not consist merely of the pleasant sound of the individual notes. Play the same notes in another order and there is no tune and no beauty of the tune. The tune is something we cannot perceive without the sense of hearing; but that which perceives it, and the beauty of it, is not the sense of hearing.

132

And, though the notes themselves are merely sounds, and material, the tune is not material; it is something beyond matter and informing it. It is that relation of material things which we call beauty, and which, though it consists of material things, is itself not matter nor perceived with the senses.

And the perception of truth and beauty is a perception of—what? not particular objects perceived with the senses, but universal relations not perceived with the senses, although we can be aware of them only through the medium of the senses. And spirit is the name given to that in us which is aware of these universals; and they themselves, since they are not matter, though always perceived in or to matter, are said to be spiritual. The word spirit is an acknowledgment of their existence, and of the existence of something in ourselves, not sense, which perceives and values them.

And there is another universal, another relation, in our own actions, which is spiritual and perceived by spirit, not by sense—that relation which is called righteousness. We are aware of it only in men and in their conduct; yet it is also to us a universal relation like truth and beauty. It does not consist merely in particular thoughts of our own as we are aware of them. It consists in the relation of action, speech, or thoughts to circumstance. Righteousness, in fact, is a certain arrangement of actions, speech, or thought, though we cannot be aware of it apart from these. So we say that righteousness also is spiritual, and that spirit is aware of it. There is this difference between it and beauty or truth, that it is a universal we are aware of only in human beings, and perhaps sometimes in animals. We are not aware of it in mere phenomena or in inanimate objects. . . . So there seems to us to be two kinds of reality, a reality of matter, of particulars, perceived by the senses, and a reality of spirit, of universals, perceived through the senses but by spirit.[1]

This author goes on to attribute this seeming duality of the Real to our inability to attain to any fulness of perception of it. He concludes:

> So this fulness of perception is always a matter of degree for us, and always we fall short of completeness. That is why we make our division of spirit and matter, a division not in reality itself, but only in our fragmentary perception of it.[2]

That is to say, could we but look upon the Totality of Being *sub specie aeternitatis*—to use Spinoza's well-known phrase— no doubt it would manifest itself to us as one, as basically monistic. From such a point of view, however, finite beings are excluded, in their present state of existence.

That the individual human being as presently constituted is partly matter or "flesh," no sane person doubts. Correlation of brain and mind has never been seriously questioned, as far as we know. However, correlation is not *identity*, and the mind-body problem is still with us, despite the efforts of materialistic

1. A. Clutton-Brock, "Spirit and Matter," in a work entitled *The Spirit*, 309-316, edited by B. H. Streeter.
2. *Op. cit.*, 316.

psychologists to ignore or to deny the fact. The following statement, by W. R. Hess, of the University of Zurich, Nobel Prize-winner in Medicine in 1949, is pertinent:

> From clinical experience as well as experiments on animals, we know that certain behavior patterns are associated with well-defined areas in the brain. Through electrical stimulation of the brainstem and contiguous areas we can elicit the reactions of defense, flight and hunger; through stimulation of higher levels, a compulsion to laugh; through stimulation of the cortex, visual and auditory reactions, among others. The results of this kind of research on the brain . . . are fascinating but we must realize that they are hardly even a beginning. The great gap to be bridged in our knowledge of the mind remains this: how are the actions of the nervous system translated into consciousness?[1]

It can hardly be doubted that there is some subtle and impenetrable interaction of body and brain on the one hand, and of the mental processes on the other, taking place all the time in the human individual. It can hardly be doubted, moreover, that the penetration and description of this interaction lies forever beyond the ability of the intellect to fully comprehend it. Nor again—let me say parenthetically—does this obvious interaction of body and mind militate in any way against the belief that the mind or spirit of a human being will survive the death of his body. For the Christian doctrine is, clearly, in the words of St. Paul, that "if there is a natural body, there is also a spiritual body," and that as we—i.e., the saints of God—"have borne the image of the earthy" here, "we shall also bear the image of the heavenly" hereafter (1 Cor. 15:44, 49). It is an undeniable fact of human experience that when the breath or spirit of life departs from the human body, the body dissolves, that is to say, it is resolved into its original elements. Undoubtedly this proves that *spirit* is the unifying principle of the organism, even in his present life; in other words, that the body is simply the tabernacle in which the real person, self, or spirit dwells for a brief time upon this earth. Hence if spirit can attract to itself and unify the constituent elements of the natural body, the body which is adapted to man's needs in his present environment—much in the same manner, let us say, that a magnet attracts to itself and binds together a quantity of iron filings—certainly it follows logically that the same spirit, endowed additionally, as the spirit of every saint will be, with the regenerating and sanctifying graces of the Holy Spirit which are imparted in the Kingdom of Grace, will have abundant power to attract

1. From *The Mind*, A Life Science Library book, Introduction, 1964, 1971.

to itself and to bind together the constituent elements of a spiritual (ethereal?) body, a body constituted of a kind of matter more refined or attenuated in texture, a body that will be adapted to the needs of the redeemed person in the ages to come and on the next higher level of being, the Kingdom of Glory. "For we know," writes Paul, "that if the earthly house of our tabernacle be dissolved, we have a building from God, a house not made with hands, eternal, in the heavens" (2 Cor. 5:1). It may well be that the constituent elements of the spiritual body are even now present in the natural body, and that they will need only to be sifted out and re-assembled in the processes of resurrection and glorification—that is, in the putting on of immortality. Certainly there is no indication in Scripture that the saints will be *bodiless* in eternity; the notion of "disembodied spirits" is an inheritance from Oriental and Platonic philosophies. Every human being in this present earthly state is, according to Scripture, a body-spirit unity, a living soul (Gen. 2:7). There is every reason for believing that every redeemed person will continue to be, in the heavenly state, a body-spirit unity, and a living soul, but of course with a body constituted of a more attenuated form of matter. "And I saw thrones," writes the Revelator, "and they sat upon them: and I saw the *souls* of them that had been beheaded for the testimony of Jesus, and for the word of God" (Rev. 20:4). It must be clearly understood, in this connection, however, that *interaction* does not indicate *identity* of body and mind, either in the here or in the hereafter. Man's higher thought processes simply cannot be reduced to purely physiochemical or physiological phenomena.

Therefore, while it can not be doubted that man, as he is presently constituted, is partly matter or "flesh," neither can it be doubted by any thinking person that he is *more than* matter or "flesh." Man is more than a brute animal; he is a *rational* animal. He is specified *as man*, that is, set apart from the lower orders as a separate and distinct species, as *homo sapiens* (to use a strictly scientific term), by his power of reason. His higher thought processes embrace (1) the power of thinking in abstract terms—in letters, words, and figures, all of which serve as symbols, and even in explicit terms that symbolize, not things, but relations, such as justice, love, freedom, and the like; (2) the power of creative imagination, which is the mainspring, not only of human art, but of all human science as well; and (3) the power of evaluation, or a sense of values, which lies at the root of all human society, morality, and law. There is no evidence whatever that such exalted powers exist within or among the lower animals. Biologists who insist upon treating man as a mere animal are largely responsible for the present-day confusion in the realm of morals. For, even granting that creation was by a process of evolution of which man is the end product thus far, the fact still remains that, being man, he has evolved *from* or *beyond* the mere animal level: he is, to say the least, animal *plus*. And the *plus* is identical with his power of reasoning, the power which specifies him as man. This fact is proved every time a scientist theorizes about human nature and its origin; no matter how strenuously he may insist that man is animal and nothing more, he cannot presume to affirm that the process by which he has arrived at this conclusion is a process characteristic of a brute. The brute follows its instincts, but it gives no evidence of inherent power to think connectedly, from *this* to *that*, and so on. No man on earth would be so foolish as to try to teach his old dog Rover the Ten Commandments. Scientists would contribute greatly to general clarity of thought if they would eschew the use of such terms as "mind," "personality," "psychology," and the like, with reference to brute animals. These terms have legitimate reference only to human capacities and powers.

Every human being in this present earthly state is a body-spirit unity—a living soul. This is the teaching of the Bible. "And Jehovah God formed man of the dust of the ground, and breathed into his nostrils the breath of life; and man became a living soul" (Gen. 2:7). According to this Scripture, a living soul is a material body informed by the Breath of God. That is to say, the Breath of God infused into the material formed of the dust of the ground (the chemical elements, we would say) the added increment of *personal* life, or, strictly speaking, all the potentialities of a person. And the Breath of God, we must remember, is the outgoing of the Spirit of God. This is not only the teaching of the Bible; it is the conclusion as well of sound thinking and of plain common sense. Every sane man *knows* that he is infinitely more than mere physiochemical elements and processes.

"Man consists of all his actual and potential activities," writes Dr. Alexis Carrel.[1] This is a truism all too frequently ignored in our age of ultra-specialization in the physical and biological sciences. Man's history upon the earth shows that

1. Alexis Carrel, *Man the Unknown*, 119.

from the remotest times, simultaneously with the physio-chemical, biochemical, and general physiological activities carried on more or less automatically by the organism, he has manifested other and higher activities which are commonly designated mental and spiritual. These are essentially activities of the spirit which is in him, which was breathed into him in creation. These higher reaches—or perhaps it would be more correct to say *out-reaches*—of the human being are directed toward the attainment of the supreme values in life. These supreme values are generally conceded to be Truth, Beauty, Goodness, and Holiness; and the higher mental activities by which the quest for these values is pursued are designated, respectively, intellectual, esthetic, moral, and religious. The object of intellectual activity is Truth; that of esthetic activity is Beauty; that of moral activity, Goodness or Righteousness; and that of religious activity is Holiness. Holiness is, in essence, *Wholeness* (from the Greek *holon,* meaning "whole," "entire," "perfect," "complete,") and is to be equated therefore with Being, or fulness of Being. The ultimate intrinsic natural and proper end to which man is ordered by his Creator is Wholeness or real Being (entire sanctification) to be achieved ultimately in the putting on of immortality. Reality, in any case, is IS-ness; that which IS, and to the extent that IT IS, is real.

"There is a spirit in man, and the breath of the Almighty giveth them understanding," said Elihu to Job (Job 32:8). Man's intellectual activity—thought—is empirical proof of this passage of Scripture. Thinking, according to John Dewey, is problem-solving. This is true no doubt, in so far as the function of thought is concerned,—but what is thought itself? What is this activity designated "thinking," the activity by which man is specified as man? I quote again from Dr. Carrel:

What is thought, that strange being, which lives in the depth of ourselves without consuming a measurable quantity of chemical energy? Is it related to the known forms of energy? Could it be a constituent of our universe, ignored by the physicists, but infinitely more important than light? The mind is hidden within living matter, completely ignored by physiologists and economists, almost unnoticed by physicians. And yet it is the most colossal power of this world. Is it produced by the cerebral cells, like insulin by the pancreas and bile by the liver? From what substance is it elaborated? Does it come from a preexisting element, as glucose from glycogen, or fibrin from fibrinogen? Does it consist of a kind of energy differing from that studied by physics, expressing itself by other laws, and generated by the cells of the cerebral cortex? Or should it be considered as an immaterial being, located outside space and time, outside the dimensions of the cosmic universe, and inserting itself by an unknown procedure into our brain, which would be the indispensable condition of its manifestations and the determining agent of its characteristics? At all times, and in all countries, great philosophers have devoted their lives to the investigation of these problems. They have not found their solution. We cannot refrain from asking the same questions. But those questions will remain unanswered until new methods for penetrating more deeply into the consciousness are discovered.[1]

The basic thought processes—operations of the intellect—are three in number. The first is *simple apprehension*—the act by which the mind grasps or perceives something without affirming or denying anything about it. It is to conceive or form in the mind an idea in which one perceives or "apprehends" something. As explained heretofore in the present text, it is to think, *e.g.*, "apple," "man," "chair," "red," "soft," etc. Sensations, of course, provide the raw material for this kind of knowledge. It must be conceded, I think, that in the vast majority of instances our mental powers are awakened and excited, directly or indirectly, by sensation; and that our first acquired ideas have reference to sensible objects; and that, further, these primary ideas become the occasion for, and antecedents of, other ideas and emotions which derive from our higher rational and moral nature.[2] (By these statements I do not mean to deny *in toto* the possibility of intuition as a mode of receiving knowledge. It has been rightly said that suddenly seen facts are but discoveries of what has been there all the time. Man discovers truth; he does not create it or formulate it: physical truth is written into the structure of the cosmos, moral truth into the structure of human nature and human natural relationships. Intuition, in this sense, is not mysticism.) But sensations are, in themselves, distinct operations of the individual neurosensory system, separate impressions of different qualities in the thing producing them. For example, there is an apple on my desk.[3] On looking at it, I experience a sensation of color ("redness"), another of configuration ("roundness"); if I touch the apple, I experience a third sensation, that of a certain quality of "hardness" or "softness"; and if I bite into the apple, I experience a fourth sensation, that of a certain pleasantness to the taste, a sensation probably difficult to name. But, obviously, in order to perceive the object *as an object*, some activity of my mind must unite these sensations into a whole. Aristotle called this power the active intellect; Kant called it the synthetic unity of

1. *Op. cit.*, 118-119.
2. *Vide* R. Milligan, *Scheme of Redemption*, 31.
3. I repeat here for emphasis.—C.

apperception, which is practically the same thing. At any rate, the result of this activity of some power within me, which from want of a better word must be designated "mental," in weaving these sensations into a unity, is my *perception* of the object—the apple—as a whole. Now the sensations of themselves may be explained as activities, or at least as the result of the activities of brain and nerve cells. But certainly the perception of the object, the perception in which these sensations are unified, cannot be explained, at least not exclusively, in terms of cellular processes. Nor can my attachment of the conventional word-symbol—in this case, "apple"—to the perceived object, the symbol established by social usage, be explained on the ground of any cellular or other physiological process, for the use of language involves memory and memory images, and in addition gives "meaning" to my perception. It is utterly inconceivable that cells should remain in juxtaposition over a period of years in such a manner as to reproduce memory image. As a matter of fact, as it has been stated heretofore, scientists now tell us that all the cells of the human body are replaced by new cells every four years or so. Hence, neither the retention of memory images nor their recall can be identified with any cellular process.

The second operation of the intellect is a *judgment*. A judgment is an act of the mind by which it unites two concepts by affirming or separates them by denying. In forming a judgment, as, *e.g.,* The apple is red, or, Man is mortal, I give assent mentally to what I believe to be an ontological relationship and thus declare myself in possession of the truth on this or that point. A judgment logically expressed is a *proposition,* and grammatically expressed, is a *sentence.*

The third operation of the intellect is *reasoning,* or thinking connectedly, that is, from *this* to *that,* and so on. Formal reasoning involves the syllogism, the classic example of which is the following:

> All men are mortal. (Major Premise)
> Socrates is a man. (Minor Premise)
> Therefore, Socrates is mortal. (Conclusion).

Maritain writes:

Reasoning is the most complex operation of our mind; it is by reasoning that we go from what we know already to what we do not yet know, that we discover, that we demonstrate, that we make *progress in knowledge.*[1]

1. Jacques Maritain, *An Introduction to Logic,* 2.

In inductive reasoning, the mind moves from the sensible to the intelligible level. In deductive reasoning, the mind moves purely on the intelligible plane. Incidentally, these mental processes are all implicit in the words of Jesus, quoted by Him from the prophet Isaiah (6:9-10):

> By hearing ye shall hear, and shall in no wise
>     understand;
> And seeing ye shall see, and shall in no wise
>     perceive;
> For this people's heart is waxed gross,
> And their ears are dull of hearing,
> And their eyes they have closed;
> Lest haply they should perceive with their eyes,
> And hear with their ears,
> And understand with their heart,
> And should turn again,
> And I should heal them.
>
> (Matt. 13:14-15).

Sensations, I repeat, may be mere cellular processes. They may, and undoubtedly do, serve to awaken consciousness. But what is "consciousness"? Should anyone answer, Consciousness is *awareness,* I should reply that "awareness" is merely a synonym for, not a definition of, consciousness. What consciousness is in itself, no one knows, and there is no indication at present that any man will ever know. Sensations, however, do not provide meaning, understanding, belief or truth. These are facts and values characteristic of a higher level of being than the mere physiochemical or biological. By no stretch of the imagination is any unbiased person able to identify these higher thought processes—simple apprehension, judgment, retention and recall of memory images, and inductive and deductive reasoning—with the shuffling and re-shuffling of brain cells. These are activities of the spirit that is in man, powers that were originally imparted to him by the Breath of God.

Moral activity in man is also a historical fact. The fact that individuals and peoples, no matter how primitive their culture, have always been known to make distinctions of some sort between right and wrong, good and bad, in human conduct, can hardly be refuted. Even though anthropologists may designate such distinctions, in their most elementary form, as "customary" law, the fact remains nevertheless that the distinctions are made, and made universally. Moreover, although different reasons have been assigned for these distinctions, in diverse social structures, and by different systems of ethics, the fact of the universality of the distinction is historically established.

The distinction between right and wrong is a universal judgment of the race; as one author has put it: "The feeling of obligation is an ineradicable element of our being."[1] This fundamental distinction between right and wrong, good and bad, has been found to be so general that by many philosophers it is designated the Ethical Fact. Moral activity—the quest for Goodness, for the answer to the question, What is the Good Man? —is another manifestation, obviously, of the *spirit* that is in man.

The same is true of the esthetic and religious activities which have characterized the life of man upon earth from the very earliest times. Esthetic activity manifests itself in the quest for Beauty, and in the creation and contemplation of Beauty; and the crude, but graphic, paintings on cave walls, uncovered by the archaeologists, prove that the esthetic sense existed in the most primitive human beings as well as in the most civilized. Religious activity too is just as real in human history as esthetic activity. The religious consciousness of man has manifested itself, in all ages, and among all tribes and peoples, in a great variety of forms, depending of course upon the standard of revelation by which it was guided, from the crudest animistic beliefs and the ritualistic worship of gods who were but personifications of the forces of Nature, up to that pure Love for God and man which fills the heart of the spiritually-minded person for whom true religion is the constant communion of the human spirit with the Divine Spirit. It is doubtful indeed that any people ever existed without some consciousness of their human frailty and need of strength to be gotten from a source or sources higher than themselves, and without a sense of sin, a sense of the need of salvation and of prayer, and a dim longing for an expectation of survival beyond the grave. It has been rightly said that man learns to pray before he learns to reason; that he feels the need of supplication long before he begins to argue from effects to causes. I am reminded here of Bergson's thrilling words:

1. George P. Fisher, *The Grounds of Theistic and Christian Belief*, 19.

Beings have been called into existence who were destined to love and be loved, since creative energy is to be defined as love. Distinct from God, Who is this energy itself, they could spring into being only in a universe, and therefore the universe sprang into being. In that portion of the universe which is our planet—probably in our planetary system—such beings, in order to appear, have had to be wrought into a species, and this species involved a multitude of other species, which led up to it, or sustained it, or else formed a residue. It may be that in other systems there are only individuals radically differentiated—assuming them to be multifarious and moral—and maybe these creatures too were shaped at a single stroke, so as to be complete from the first.[1] On Earth, in any case, the species which accounts for the existence of all the others is only partially itself. It would never for an instant have thought of becoming completely itself, if certain representatives of it had not succeeded, by an individual effort added to the general work of life, in breaking through the resistance put up by the instrument, in triumphing over materiality—in a word in getting back to God. These men are the mystics. They have blazed a trail along which other men may pass. They have, by this very act, shown to the philosopher the whence and whither of life.[2]

The mystics see, says Bergson, that "the very essence of divinity can be both a person and a creative power." That power is Love. "God is love, and the object of love: herein lies the whole contribution of mysticism."[3] (This does not mean, however, that feeling is an acceptable substitute for an intelligent faith.)

Let it never be forgotten that intellectual, moral, esthetic, and religious activities are facts of human experience and of human history from the most remote times. They are proofs conclusive that man is not *all* matter—that there is a spirit in him and that the Breath of the Almighty—the outgoing of the Divine Spirit—has given him understanding. They are proofs conclusive that man was created in the image of God.

Materialism is a faithless, hopeless, lifeless creed. To summarize in the words of C. E. M. Joad:

Inconsistent with ethics and esthetics, and owning an inadequate basis in physics, materialism is indefensible in logic. More precisely, in so far as it establishes the conclusions which it asserts, it robs these conclusions of any possibility of being true.[4]

In a purely material world there can never be such a thing as *oughtness* or *value*. Truth, Beauty, and Goodness simply do not exist for anyone in a world that is nothing more than an aggregation of atoms and cells.

1. Does Bergson have any reference here to *angels?*
2. Henri Bergson, *The Two Sources of Morality and Religion*, 245-246; translated by Audra and Brereton.
3. *Op. cit.*, 240, 241-242.
4. *Guide to Philosophy*, 539.

## 6. The Mysteries of the Subconscious

Spirit in man, however, embraces many activities, many phenomena, many mysteries even more profound than the mysteries of the operations of the intellect. It embraces not only the phenomena of the conscious mind, as outlined in the preceding chapter, but the phenomena of the Subconscious as well —those which lie far below sense-perception, hence beyond any necessarily permanent relationship with matter.

The Subconscious is an aspect of the human individual which has been quite generally ignored by scientists until recent years. This neglect may be attributed chiefly: (1) to the concentration of scientific attention and effort upon the study of the external world and its phenomena—the investigation of matter and its combinations, the analysis of the atom, and especially of late the exploration of the whole field of electrical energy; and (2) to the similar concentration of science upon the study of the purely biological aspects of the human organism, a concentration activated largely by the rise and spread of the evolution hypothesis. As a matter of fact, every branch of orthodox science was so thoroughly impregnated with crass materialism, throughout the post-Victorian era, that it was prone to ignore and even to scorn any alleged phenomenon to which the label "physical" could not be attached. As Dr. J. B. Rhine puts it:

The mechanistic biology of Dr. Jacques Loeb and the behavioristic psychology of Dr. John B. Watson, set against the backdrop of a simplified mechanistic universe popularized in such works as Professor Ernest Haeckel's *The Riddle of the Universe*, were typical of common scientific thought through the early decades of the present century. For a psychologist to have published evidence of telepathy in those days would would have taken exceptional courage.[1]

Then too, in addition to the skepticism of science, there has been a popular notion abroad in the world for a long time, that all so-called psychic phenomena are but the offspring of an unholy alliance of trickery, fraud and "magic" with human ignorance and superstition. And so the man on the street, susceptible to suggestion at all times, and especially to the voice of authority with which "experts" are assumed to speak, pooh-poohed the possibility of telepathy, clairvoyance, prescience, and like phenomena, as emphatically—and as dogmatically—as did the intelligentsia.

During all this time, however, a small group of courageous scientists, men of high standing in their respective fields, per-

1. J. B. Rhine, *The Reach of the Mind*, 20.

sisted, in spite of the skeptical attitude of their fellows, in a thoroughgoing investigation and analysis of the *subliminal* self. The result has been the accumulation of a body of facts of far-reaching significance. New reaches and vistas of the human person have been brought to light. The Subconscious has been explored and has been found to be a vast laboratory in which all sorts of elements are gathered, compounded, and stored away. And in the light of this additional information, we are now able to comprehend, to a greater extent than ever before possible, the mighty sweep of the truth stated in the book of *Genesis* that man was created "in the image of God" (Gen. 1:26-27).

The British Society for Psychical Research was founded in London in 1882, under the presidency of Henry Sidgwick, then Professor of Moral Philosophy at the University of Cambridge. In the announcement made by the Society at the time of its organization, it was explained that its work would be "to make an organized and systematic attempt to investigate that large group of debatable phenomena designated by such terms as mesmeric, psychical and spiritualistic." "The task of examining residual phenomena," the announcement went on to say, "has often been undertaken by individual effort, but never hitherto by a scientific society organized on a sufficiently broad basis." The membership of the British Society has included, in addition to that of Henry Sidgwick, its first president, the names of such distinguished scientists as A. J. Balfour, W. F. Barrett, William Crookes, Lord Rayleigh, and Alfred Russel Wallace. Canon A. W. Robinson writes:

For many years this body, which was founded in 1882, was not regarded very seriously by the orthodox exponents of science. Its business was more or less privately to collect and sift evidence relating to spiritualism, and to ghostly apparitions, in the hope of discovering what lay behind it and of reducing it to some order. This, the original purpose, has been rewarded with a fair measure of success, but in the course of the search more important discoveries have been made. A strict examination into the phenomena of hypnotism, clairvoyance, clairaudience, and suggestion, with the accompanying conditions of abnormal apprehension, the heightening of ordinary powers, and the sometimes alarming evidences of what looks like a disintegration of personality, has disclosed what may prove to be new reaches and vistas of the mind and soul.[1] ["Metapsychic" means, literally, "along with," "after" or "beyond" the "mind." The corresponding term in use generally today is "parapsychology."]

In 1884 the American Society for Psychical Research was formed. It was incorporated with the British Society in 1890,

1. *The Holy Spirit and the Individual*, 36-37.

but became separated from the latter again in 1906. Similar societies were formed in Germany and in other countries. In 1919 an International Institute of Metapsychics was established in Paris with the approval of the French Government, and under the auspices of the distinguished physiologist, Charles Richet, the discoverer of anaphylaxis, and of the learned physician, Joseph Teissier, Professor of Medicine at the University of Lyons. Among the members of the Committee of Administration were a professor at the Medical School of the University of Paris, and several physicians. Its president, Charles Richet, has written a comprehensive treatise on metapsychics,[2] entitled *Thirty Years of Psychical Research,* and the Institute itself publishes the *Revue Metapsychique.* Records of the work and findings of these various Societies are sufficient to fill several volumes of "Proceedings" and "Journals."

Interest in the investigation of psychic phenomena was greatly stimulated by the tragic experiences of the first World War. Research in this field, especially in that of telepathy, was carried on by different individuals in different parts of the world—by the German physician, Dr. Karl Bruck, and science teacher, Professor Rudolf Tischner; by the French engineer, Rene Warcollier; and by the distinguished American novelist, Upton Sinclair. Both William McDougall, the psychologist, and Albert Einstein, the physicist, were sufficiently impressed by the results of Sinclair's experiments to appeal to the scientific world to give his book, *Mental Radio,* an unprejudiced hearing. Hans Driesch was enthusiastic in his praise of Tischner's work, and Gardner Murphy introduced to American readers a translation of Warcollier's book, *Experiments in Telepathy.* Then, during the nineteen-twenties, two significant series of experiments in telepathy, in which new techniques were employed, were carried out in two psychology laboratories, one in Europe at the University of Groningen in Holland, the other in the United States at Harvard University. The European work was done by Dr. H. J. F. W. Brugmans, under the sponsorship of the eminent Professor G. Heymans; the American research work was done by Dr. G. H. Estabrooks, under the supervision of Professor William McDougall, who had just transferred to Harvard from Oxford University.[1] Both series of experiments undoubtedly yielded positive results. Yet, although very little criticism was leveled at the techniques employed, or even at the results announced, practically nothing was heard of them; they

1. *Vide* J. B. Rhine, *The Reach of the Mind,* 13-24.

were simply ignored by the "scientific" world in general. Commenting on this fact, Dr. J. B. Rhine says:

> In looking back over these experiments today, it is difficult to see how a properly scientific mind could have been indifferent to the challenge which the work of Estabrooks and Brugmans presented. One can only conclude that Science, too, can be functionally blind when it would shock her complacency to see. Science can be *very* human.[1]

How true!

As a matter of fact, the prejudice of "orthodox" scientists has been the greatest obstacle, perhaps, which experimenters in the field of the Subconscious have been compelled to overcome. Not only did the "straight line" scientists for many long years persistently refuse to acknowledge that such phenomena as telepathy, clairvoyance and the like, occur, or even *could* occur, but they actually closed the pages of standard scientific journals to the reports of experiments in these fields. Indeed, many able research workers in what is called "metapsychics," or more recently "parapsychology," have been reluctant to announce their findings or to state their convictions, lest they lose their standing in the scientific world and even become objects of ridicule. This attitude of "conservative" scientists toward psychic experimentation is reminiscent of the treatment at one time accorded osteopaths and chiropractors by the orthodox medical men. While physicists, generally speaking, have not been unsympathetic toward psychic research, the prejudice of biologists, psychologists and sociologists against it has been amazing. The attitude of these "scientists" has been almost anything but scientific; they seem to have closed their minds completely and to have kept them closed. One is reminded of the words of Victor Hugo: "Some men deny the sun: they are the blind." Obviously this bias was, and still is, in many cases, engendered largely by personal antipathy toward any new light that might prove to be confirmatory of the spiritual interpretation of the universe. It is similar to that of the Communists, the vast majority of whom are Communists, not because of any deep overwhelming love for their fellow-men, but because of their intense hatred of religious faith or practice in any form—hatred arising from their own perverted wills rather than from rational consideration of the nature and destiny of man. The attitude in general toward psychic research seems to be just another case in which the wish is father to the thought; our materialistic scientists do not want, in fact will not admit, evidence that

1. *Op. cit.*, 25.

would break down their cherished mechanistic picture of the universe,—a picture which has become to them a veritable object of worship in itself. (It must be understood, of course, that in dealing with the phenomena of parapsychology, we are not in the area of occultism at all. Occultism embraces such matters as witchcraft, wizardry, spiritualism, divination, sorcery, necromancy, voodooism, etc.)

That picture has been broken down, however, if not completely shattered, in recent years. It has been shattered by attacks from three directions: (1) from discoveries in the field of atomic physics, which, as we have already seen, tend to point to a reality that is of the character of pure Thought; (2) from the "Heracleitean" philosophy of Henri Bergson, with its basic concept of the *Elan Vital* or Life Force; and (3) from recent experiments in the field of parapsychology itself. The most significant experiments in this field were initiated at Duke University in 1930, under the direction of four members of the Duke department of psychology staff, namely, Professor William McDougall, Dr. Helge Lundholm, Dr. Karl E. Zener, and Dr. J. B. Rhine. Experiments in extra-sensory perception (telepathy, clairvoyance, prescience, etc.) and in psychokinesis (the movement of matter by pure thought) have been carried on by these men (some of whom are now deceased) and their associates subsequently added to the staff, throughout all the intervening years, and are still in progress. The outcome was the setting up of a Department of Parapsychology at Duke, and the launching of the *Journal of Parapsychology*, published by the Duke University Press. (Two other journals are published regularly covering the work done in the field of psychic research—the *Proceedings of the Society for Psychical Research*, published in London; and the *Journal of the American Society for Psychical Research*, published in New York City.)

Dr. Rhine has presented to the public the methods and findings of the Duke experiments in a series of books. The first, published several years ago, was entitled *Extra-Sensory Preception;* the second, published in 1937, *New Frontiers of the Mind.* In one of his latest works, *The Reach of the Mind*, published late in 1947,[1] Dr. Rhine has summarized the results of all the research work which had been done at Duke up to that time. He affirms unequivocally that the Duke experiments have proved the fol-

1. A condensation of this book appeared in *Reader's Digest*, issue of February, 1948.

147

lowing: (1) that telepathy—communication of one mind with another without the media of the physical senses—is a fact, (2) that clairvoyance—the power of the mind to perceive events and to locate physical objects, likewise without the use of the physical senses—is also a fact; (3) that distance has no effect on the functioning of these powers; (4) that time likewise apparently has no effect upon either, at least in some persons—hence there is such a thing as *precognition* or *prescience;* and (5) most remarkable of all, that there is a force inherent in the mind, a force of a non-physical order, which can produce a physical effect upon a physical object, and furthermore, that apparently there is no correlation between the effectiveness of this force and the size or number of the objects. Telepathy, clairvoyance, and prescience are all included by Rhine and his co-workers under the designation, *extra-sensory perception;* and the power of thought to effect the movement of ponderable bodies is named *psychokinesis.* (By earlier writers on the subject of psychic phenomena, this was called *telekinesis.* The well-known phenomenon of *levitation* belongs, of course, in this category.)

With reference to Dr. Rhine's presentation, one reviewer writes as follows:

These proofs are revolutionary. They alter the basic scientific concepts of the world. Man has believed similar things from time immemorial, but he has never known them. Science has not believed them and has not attempted to know them. It is now, however, evident that there is an active factor in man which is not controlled by physical laws governing time, space, mass and number.[1]

To these statements I should like to add that personal experience should convince any man of ordinary common sense that all this is true; any normal person should be able to realize that "mind" is something which transcends all the limitations of space and time. Nor is there any ground whatever for assuming that "mind" is something confined within the body.

In summarizing the implications of these findings, Dr. Rhine himself makes two or three statements of far-reaching significance, as follows:

The establishment of the mind as different from the brain in some fundamental respect supports the psychocentric view of man. This means that the mind is a factor in its own right in the total scheme of personality. The personal world of the individual is therefore not centered completely in the organic function of the material brain.[2]

1. Quoted from the review appearing on the jacket of Dr. Rhine's book, *The Reach of the Mind.*
2. *The Reach of the Mind,* 205-206.

Now, too, psychology will have its own distinctive realm of study. It will no longer be merely an extension of physiology. The science of the psyche has its own peculiar principles, its own definite boundaries, its uniqueness. Its true domain begins where sensorimotor physiology leaves off, though what its full extent and outer bounds may be, no one can at present conjecture.[1]

Thus far the influence of parapsychology on religion has been constructive. As far as it goes, the discovery of evidence that man is something more than a physical being gives support to the most basic and general of all religious doctrines, namely, that man has a spiritual nature.[2]

The research in parapsychology even now touches other great issues of religion. If the mind of man is nonphysical, it is possible to formulate a hypothetical picture of a nonphysical system or world made up of all such minds existing in some sort of relationship to each other. This leads to speculative views of a kind of psychical over-soul, or reservoir, or continuum, or universe, having its own system of laws and properties and potentialities. One can conceive of this great total pattern as having a transcendent uniqueness over and above the nature of its parts that some might call its divinity.

It is, however, on the problem of immortality that religion and parapsychology have most often met. . . . If logic alone could be trusted, the evidence of ESP would go far to establish the survival hypothesis on logical grounds. As will be recalled, when ESP was found to function without limitation from time and space, this discovery was taken to mean that the mind is capable of action independent to some degree of the space-time system of nature. Now, all that immortality means is freedom from the effects of space and time; death seems to be purely a matter of coming to a halt in the space-time universe. Therefore the conclusion that there is at least some sort of technical survival would seem to follow as a logical derivation from ASP research. . . . There is another relation of ESP-PK to survival that is important. If there were no ESP and PK capacities in human beings it would be hard to conceive of the possibility of survival and certainly its discovery would be impossible. As it is, nonphysical activity of the mind is demonstrated. The only kind of perception that would be possible in a discarnate state would be extra-sensory, and psychokinesis would be the only method of influencing any part of the physical universe. Even for an incorporeal mind to communicate with the living would probably involve PK. Telepathy would seem to be the only means of intercommunication discarnate personalities would have, with either the living or the non-living. . . . The survival question must be kept open for investigation by scientific method. We dare not neglect an issue of such consequence.[3]

The name most prominently associated with the investigations conducted by the British Society for Psychical Research is that of F. W. H. Myers, who died in 1903, leaving an elaborate work in two volumes, entitled *Human Personality and its Survival of Bodily Death,* in which he set forth the mass of evidence that had been obtained together with such conclusions as he thought justified therefrom. The following is his own

1. *Op cit.,* 208.
2. *Ibid.,* 209.
3. *Ibid.,* 211, 213, 214, 216.

statement of what is generally regarded as the most striking of these conclusions:

> The conscious self of each of us as we call it—the empirical, the supra-liminal self, as I should prefer to say—does not compromise the whole of the consciousness or of the faculty within us. There exists a more comprehensive consciousness, a profounder faculty, which for the most part remains potential only so far as regards the life of earth, but from which the consciousness and the faculty of earth-life are mere selections, and which reasserts itself in its plenitude after the liberating change of death. . . . I find it permissible and convenient to speak of subliminal Selves, or more briefly of a subliminal Self. . . . I conceive that no Self of which we can here have cognizance is in reality more than a fragment of a larger Self—revealed in a fashion at once shifting and limited through an organism not so framed as to afford it full manifestations.[1]

Professor William James did not hesitate to speak of this "discovery that, in certain subjects at least, there is not only the consciousness of the ordinary field, with its usual centre and margin, but an addition thereto in the shape of a set of memories, thoughts, and feelings which are extra-marginal and outside of the primary consciousness altogether, but yet . . . able to reveal their presence by unmistakable signs," as "the most important step forward" that had occurred in psychology since he had become a student of the subject. "This discovery," he went on to say, "has revealed to us an entirely unsuspected peculiarity in the constitution of human nature."[2]

Canon Robinson summarizes these discoveries in the psychical field as follows:

> According to the new theory, human personality, as it has developed, has become differentiated into two phases. One of them is the self known to the ordinary consciousness, which is easiest for us to observe in action, and which has been evolved mainly to correspond with our material environment. The other is a deeper capacity or faculty of semiconsciousness, and even of unconsciousness, which lies below the threshold of the familiar waking life and thought. This is a storehouse into which is accumulated all that has ever passed through the avenue of sense. What is thus stored, abides, and although it may not always be recoverable at will, is never lost. Moreover, the subconscious mind is a workshop in which new combinations are effected and new products are fashioned, almost as if they had been subjected to chemical change. Through the subconscious mind the soul is kept in touch with the spiritual region, from which messages can be received, and out of which can be drawn the succors and forces that account for exceptional activities, as, for example, those of genius, which Mr. Myers defined to be "a capacity for utilizing forces that lie too deep for the ordinary man's control." It is in this direction that we are bidden to look for the explanation of much that is puzzling in connection with

1. *Op. cit.*, 12-15.
2. Wm. James, *Varieties of Religious Experience*, Modern Library Edition, 228.

mind-healing, faith cures, and kindred phenomena. Already a change can be observed in the attitude adopted by the scientific mind toward these experiences.[1]

The tendency no longer exists among truly great scientists to blindly discredit the facts which have been brought to light in the field of psychic research. In evidence of this fact I might cite an illuminating article by Mr. George Kent, which appeared in a well-known monthly magazine some years ago,[2] in which the author gives an authentic description of the life, work, and views of Dr. Alexis Carrel, then of the Rockefeller Institute. The heading of the article was: "Dr. Alexis Carrel Believes That We Can Read Each Other's Thoughts." The subhead: "In the Uncharted Realm of the Human Mind Lie the Great Discoveries of the Future, Says the Rockefeller Institute's Miracle Man of Science." Among other things, the writer said:

A wizard in all things that concern the body, Dr. Carrel has now startled the medical world with his avowed belief in the extraordinary powers of the human mind—mystic, immeasurable powers that, until today, lacked the endorsement of a great man of science. He is convinced that most of us possess, in some form or another, the ability to transfer thought from mind to mind at a distance. He believes that there are clairvoyant men and women who can know and tell the past and future, whose minds travel as easily in time as the rest of us travel in space. Orthodox scientists do not like these views overmuch, and have been looking slantwise at our good genius—but they haven't said a lot. Once before, some years ago, they attacked him, sneering at his "acrobatic surgery" . . . and were forced to eat their words. These acrobatics of the operating room are now used, in one form or another, whenever a surgeon goes to work.

Again,:

As a student, Carrel was at times a sober investigator of the ordinary subjects, and at other times a hunter for the truth that lay behind things like telepathy, clairvoyance, miracles. We do not understand these things, so we consign them to side-show promoters, carnival touts, and other merchants of the hocus-pocus. Carrel tried to separate the fake from the little that was real. He came to the conclusion then that in these things there was an element of truth which could be gotten at, if science would quit being high-hat about it and give the subject honest attention. This is his conviction after thirty-five years' study.

As a matter of fact, Dr. Carrel confirms these statements in his own book, *Man, the Unknown*, in which he frankly declares his acceptance of psychic phenomena such as suggestion, telepathy, clairvoyance, and the like, as established facts. Mr. Hamlin Garland testifies in similar vein, in his book, *Forty Years of*

1. *The Holy Spirit and the Individual*, 39-40.
2. In *The American Magazine*, March, 1936.

*Psychic Research,* which came from the press not so long ago. Concerning this book and its author, one reviewer writes:

Hamlin Garland was one of the small group who fifty years ago founded the American Society for Psychical Research. He himself was decidedly skeptical of the apparently fantastic business, as were several of his associates. This group of professional men and scientists was organized to investigate psychic phenomena. It was Mr. Garland's duty to record all experiments, which were conducted under the strictest conditions the group was able to devise. But, as seems always to happen as a result of systematic investigation in this particular field, he and his co-workers soon lost all their doubts as to the actuality of the phenomena. The author's intense interest has continued, and what we have in this book is taken from his records of hundreds of experiments concerned with all known phases of the subject. Those who are more or less familiar with the records of the British Society, or with any of the major works on the subject, of which Myers' *Human Personality* is still perhaps the most impressive, will find nothing new here. But they will find a wholly unprejudiced and unemotional presentation of the phenomena. Comprehensive studies are introduced in this book, of clairvoyance, clairaudience, slate-writing, direct-voice seances, trumpet seances, and the production of ectoplasmic forms. Ectoplasm is described by Mr. Garland as an elementary substance given off in varying degrees by the human body. According to his conception, it is ideoplastic, capable of being moulded by the mind of the psychic or the sitter. The most sensational evidence introduced by Garland was in regard to an ectoplasmic hand. The manifesting intelligence was directed to dip the hand into hot wax, which was then cooled. Fingerprints, differing from fingerprints of the psychic and the sitters, were obtained. Mr. Garland will convince you that the possibility of fraud did not exist! Whence the fingerprints? The readers of this book will discover for themselves that the author is not credulous. Nor is he a spiritualist in any sense of that term. Therefore, he is proved to be an unusually reliable witness of supranormal occurrences. Fortunately, Mr. Garland has been permitted to work with various mediums who were willing to give their time and energy, and who agreed to submit themselves to the most humiliating control-conditions. Thanks to the cooperation of these singularly gifted people, Hamlin Garland and his associates were able to gather evidence which should challenge the biochemist just as it fascinates the layman. It is clear that the author is not moved by wishful thinking. . . . His only insistence is upon the actuality of the phenomena and their fundamental importance in any attempt to extend our understanding of ourselves.[1]

Intimations of the inner aspect of the self, or perhaps it would be proper to say, of the inner self, which has been opened to view by psychic research, may be found in two of the most common facts of human experience, namely, the subconscious association of ideas and the subconscious maturing of thought, as illustrated in the sudden appearing, in a dream or in a dreamlike moment of waking, of the solution of a problem which has

---

1. I have misplaced the original of this excerpt and cannot name the reviewer. The review itself, however, is an accurate one.

occupied and vexed the mind in the hours of objective awareness and reasoning. Jastrow writes:

All this points to the fact that the large stores of accumulated learning which we carry in our heads lie in part near the focus of interest that occupies our immediate attention, in greater part lie in ever widening areas—all permeated by an intricate network of highways and byways, along which the goods of our mind come floating. . . . There exists in all intellectual endeavor a period of incubation, a process in great part subconscious, a slow, concealed maturing through absorption of suitable pabulum.[1]

Schopenhauer called this activity "unconscious rumination." Ernest Dimnet writes:

Psychologists speak of the "mental stream," and this expression alone has meant an immense progress in the domain of interior observation as compared with the misleading division of the soul into separate faculties. In reality, the flux in our brain carries along images—remembered and modified—feelings, resolves, and intellectual, or partly intellectual, conclusions, in vague or seething confusion. And this process never stops, not even in our sleep, any more than a river ever stops in its course. . . . Our soul is an ocean. Its possibilities, its receptivity and elasticity are mysterious and seldom within our ken, but they cannot be doubted. What it stores up during our life is as mysterious, but it as undoubtedly vast. . . . Who has not been amused or puzzled by the reviviscence of an utterly indifferent sentence, heard years before, caused by a few syllables bearing a faint resemblance to it? The forgotten words fall on our ear, eerie but unmistakable. A strain of music, the odor of a mignonette, will unexpectedly revive in us states of mind from which, in childhood or adolescence, we shook ourselves free because their vague pregnancy made them as hard to sustain as their poignancy made them exquisite. Inspiration, the highstrung condition in which emotion, eloquence, music or merely strong coffee can place us, reveals to us whole regions in our souls which have nothing in common with the sandy barrenness of our daily existence. Often, too, in our lives, but more frequently at certain intervals than others, we are conscious that our intellectual vision is keener than people, or even than we ourselves, supposed. We hear a conversation and, as the words cross one another, we register people's motives as if we were reading them. We go to a lecture and we appreciate or criticize as it goes on, as we seldom did before. We are conscious of all that flashes through our minds. Meanwhile we know that other, less perceptible, gleams may gather light if we watch them without pretending to do so, and a rare illumination will follow.[2]

The unconscious, writes Ernest R. Groves, "may be the source of energy, the origin of inspiration, and even, as comes out so clearly in the case of genius, a means of insight so direct and penetrating that we commonly call it intuition."[3] Suggestions of this general view may be found as far back as Plato, but Leibnitz, the German philosopher, born in 1646, seems to

1. J. Jastrow, *The Subconscious*, 95-99.
2. *The Art of Thinking*, 183-184.
3. *Understanding Yourself*, 172.

have been the first to think of a part of the self as functioning outside ordinary consciousness. It was another German, Von Hartman, born two centuries later, who, in his book entitled *The Philosophy of the Unconscious,* developed the notion of a dynamic self-life outside what we now know as consciousness. William James had glimpses of the importance of the Unconscious (or Subconscious) as the source of available energy that could be drawn upon by the self, especially in times of stress: the concept, in fact, lay at the root of the "stream of consciousness" psychology which he originated. Freud, of course, developed the concept of the Id, and the corollary notion of the ceaseless conflict between the Id and the Super-Ego (environmental forces), at the center of which the Ego, according to his system of psychology, finds itself throughout life, but it is difficult to determine whether Freud's Id was psychological or physiological. As a matter of fact, endocrinologists would be inclined, I think, to regard it as more or less identical with the activities of the hormones of the endocrine glands. Henri Bergson, the distinguished French philosopher, contended that within each of us there are "two different selves, one of which is . . . the external projection of the other, its spatial and, so to speak, social representaton." Only the inner or "fundamental" self, he contends, is free; the other unfolds in space, because we live for the external world rather than ourselves. This inner self, he affirms, is practically unlimited in it powers. "Considered in themselves," he says, "the deep-seated conscious states have no relation to quantity, they are pure quality."[1] Similarly, Abbe Dimnet holds that the inner self is the seat of pure thought. He writes:

We have an idea that thought—as diamonds are wrongly supposed to do—can exist in a pure state, and is elaborated without images. We feel sure that we are not infrequently conscious of conclusions, practical or speculative, arrived at without the help of images.[2]

Aristotle, it will be recalled, defined God as Pure Thought Thinking Itself; and there are well-defined correspondences between Aristotle's "active intellect" in man and the subconscious of modern psychology.

This *subliminal* (i.e., below the threshold of consciousness) association of ideas and maturing of thought, which may be going on all the time regardless of the state of the body, is in itself an unfailing evidence of a subconscious aspect of person-

1. H. Bergson, *Time and Free Will,* Pogson translation, 231 137.
2. Ernest Dimnet, *The Art of Thinking,* 11.

ality which needs looking into. By some writers this subliminal aspect of the Self is designated "the Unconscious," by others "the Subconscious." Personally, I prefer to equate this inner, subliminal, subconscious aspect of the Self with the "spirit" in man, that is, speaking in ontological terms, and the outer or conscious aspect of the self with "mind." The practical consideration in which we are especially interested here, is that there is a dynamic "part" of the Self, the "inner man," which is always alert, which is never at rest, which never "sleeps." This fact alone exposes the fallacy of all such notions as those of "soul sleeping," "total unconsciousness," "ultimate annihilation," "the oblivion of Nirvana," and such like. Incidentally, if there is any form of survival in store for man that will have any meaning for him, certainly it will have to be a *conscious* existence of some kind. I fail to see how "total unsconsciousness" could be any kind of existence at all—for a *person*.

The conclusions of the men who have devoted their lives to the study of the phenomena of the Subconscious may be systematized as follows:

1. The human person is a house, so to speak, with two rooms in it: a front room which faces the external world and through which impressions from that world make their entrance by way of the "physical" senses. This room is commonly designated the "objective" (conscious, supra-liminal) aspect of the self, or the "objective mind." Also a back room in which the impressions which have entered by way of the front room find a permanent abiding-place. This back room is commonly designated the "subjective" aspect of the Self, the "subliminal self," or the "subjective mind." It is this back room to which we refer when we speak of the Subconscious.

In general terms, the attributes of man's two "minds" or "selves" may be differentiated as follows: The *objective* part takes cognizance of the external world; its media of observation are the physical senses; it is the outgrowth of man's physical necessities, his guide in his process of adaptation to his present environment. Its highest function is that of *reasoning*. The *subjective*, on the other hand, takes cognizance of its environment by means independent of the physical senses; it perceives by intuition; it is the storehouse of memory; it performs its highest functions when the objective senses are in abeyance.

In a word, it is that intelligence which makes itself manifest in a hypnotic subject when he is in a state of somnambulism. In this state

155

many of the most wonderful feats of the subjective mind are performed. It sees without the use of natural organs of vision; and in this, as in many other grades, or degrees, of the hypnotic state, it can be made, apparently, to travel to distant lands and bring back intelligence of the most exact and truthful character. It also has the power to read the thoughts of others, even to the minutest details; to read the contents of sealed envelopes and of closed books. In short, it is the subjective mind that possesses what is popularly designated as clairvoyant power, and the ability to apprehend the thought of others without the aid of the ordinary objective means of communication.[1]

This subjective mind, or subliminal self, seems to be unlimited by any of the objective concepts of distance, space or time. It has all the appearance of a distinct entity, with independent powers and functions, having a mental organization of its own, and being capable of sustaining an existence independently of the body. *It is, in its ultimate aspect, the ontological Self; the real, essential being of the human individual.* Whereas the custom of most students of psychic phenomena is to speak of this subliminal self as the "soul," I think it would make for clarity to designate it the "spirit," and the objective or conscious self the "mind," in man. [For want of more precise language, I am compelled to speak here in dualistic terms. It is to be understood, however, that the line of demarcation between the "objective" and the "subjective," within the Self, cannot be exactly determined.]

It follows quite logically from the foregoing description, that as long as the *spirit*, which is the real You, the real I, the real *being*, is housed in a physical body—a matter of necessity to man's adaptation to his present environment—it must relate itself to the external world through the medium of the objective faculties, chiefly through the physical senses. For, contrary to the popular view, as indeed Bergson has pointel out in his work entitled *Matter and Memory*, the physical senses do not disclose the real world to our apprehension; on the contrary, they shut it out.[2] They reveal to us only the phenomenal world, the world that is ever changing, ever in a state of flux. Think, for example, what the effect would be in man, had he the highly developed sense of smell that a dog has; or if he had a visual apparatus like the lens of a high-powered microscope, so that every time he took a drink he could see the microbes playing around in the water; or if he had an auditory mechanism, say,

1. T. J. Hudson, *The Law of Psychic Phenomena*, Thirty-second Edition, 29-30. McClurg, Chicago, 1909. This book can be obtained only at secondhand book stores.
2. *Vide supra*, 104-115.

of the character of a radio receiving set, so that all the sound waves in the external world around him would beat constantly upon his ear-drums! Life would be intolerable, if not actually impossible! The physical senses function to adapt man to his present or earthly environment. "Mind,"—or speaking more precisely, "spirit"—is not something to be thought of as enclosed within a body; as a matter of fact, its activities transcend all corporeal limitations. In an ordinary dream, for instance, while a man's body reposes on his bed at home, in a definite location, he himself may be a thousand miles away, bathing in the surf at Atlantic City, or driving an automobile up Pike's Peak. Or, indeed, completely unlimited by either time or space at the given instant, he may be a child again, in his dream, picking strawberries on the farm on which he grew up, perhaps in some other part of the world. Who has not re-lived many of the experiences of childhood in his adult dreams? Or again, in a dream, one may re-live the experiences of an entire period of one's life, in the time required for a clock at one's bedside to tick out a few mathematical seconds. These dream experiences of one's sleeping hours, moreover, are just as vivid, just as real oftentimes as the experiences of one's waking hours. The essential human being—the spirit which is in man—simply knows no restrictions of distance, space or time. Hence, it follows that once the spirit is liberated from the earthly body in which it is temporarily housed, and is clothed upon with an ethereal body, a body of finer texture, in adaptation to the higher order of being, it will be completely free from all limitations of time and space.

[Compare, for example, the "movements" of Jesus and Satan in the Temptation Experience]: Then the devil taketh him into the holy city, and he set him on the pinnacle of the temple. [Again]: The devil taketh him unto an exceeding high mountain, and showeth him all the kingdoms of the world, and the glory of them, etc. [Matt. 4:5; 8]. [Cf. again 2 Cor. 5:1-4]: For we know that if the earthly house of our tabernacle be dissolved, we have a building from God, a house not made with hands, eternal, in the heavens. For verily in this we groan, longing to be clothed upon with our habitation which is from heaven; if so be that being clothed we shall not be found naked. For indeed we that are in this tabernacle do groan, being burdened; not for that we would be unclothed, but that we would be clothed upon, that what is mortal may be swallowed up of life.

Again, as it has been pointed out heretofore, spirit, the life principle which, in man, includes all the potentialities of personal life and experience, obviously is that which unifies and vitalizes the constituent parts of the natural or animal bod-

This is evident from the fact that when the life principle leaves the body, in death, the body disintegrates, *i.e.*, it is resolved into its original elements. Now if spirit can attract to itself and unify the constituent parts of a body adapted to its present terrestrial environment, is it not reasonable to conclude that the same spirit will have power to attract to itself and to unify the constituent parts of an ethereal body adapted to its future celestial environment? This celestial body, moreover, will be essentially a *spiritual* body, *i.e.*, a body formed by a spirit that will itself have been made holy by growth in holiness or sanctification. Undoubtedly, too, such a body will possess and manifest a certain measure of glory, in proportion no doubt to the degree of holiness which the informing spirit itself will have acquired through its being indwelt and possessed by the Spirit of God. This, precisely, is the substance of Paul's argument with respect to the resurrection of the body, in the fifteenth chapter of *First Corinthians*. He says:

> All flesh is not the same flesh: but there is one flesh of men, and another flesh of beasts, and another flesh of birds, and another of fishes. There are also celestial bodies, and bodies terrestrial; but the glory of the celestial is one, and the glory of the terrestrial is another. There is one glory of the sun, and another glory of the moon, and another glory of the stars; for one star differeth from another star in glory. So also is the resurrection of the dead. It is sown in corruption; it is raised in incorruption: it is sown in dishonor; it is raised in glory; it is sown in weakness; it is raised in power; it is sown a natural body; it is raised a spiritual body. If there is a natural body [literally, a *psychikos* or "soulish" body, *i.e.*, a flesh-and-blood body informed by natural spirit, the principle of personal life], there is also a spiritual body [literally, a *pneumatikos* body, a body of finer texture of matter, assembled and informed by the spirit as the principle of holiness, and hence in a real sense by the Holy Spirit, and glorified to the degree that the Holy Spirit shall have possessed and moulded the human spirit]. So also it is written, The first man Adam became a living soul [*i.e.*, a natural body-spirit unity]. The last Adam became a life-giving spirit [in the sense that the Spirit of Christ, being essentially the Holy Spirit, will give *life* to the bodies of the saints, that is, clothe them in immortality]. Howbeit that is not first which is spiritual, but that which is natural; then that which is spiritual. The first man is of the earth, earthy; the second man is of heaven. And as is the earthy, such are they also that are earthy; and as is the heavenly, such are they also that are heavenly. And as we have borne the image of the earthy, we shall also bear the image of the heavenly (2 Cor. 15:39-49).

Finally, in this connection, it is obvious that if the Subconscious—the spirit that is in man, the essential being—functions, in its present relations with the body, independently of the latter, as it must do in all cases of telepathy, it is only reasonable to think that it can and will continue to function, in

158

the exercise of its higher powers and faculties, after the physical body shall have been resolved into its original elements and all the limitations of the flesh shall have been removed. In a word, these facts of the Subconscious certainly provide a scientific foundation for our confidence in the personal survival and immortalization of God's saints.

2. Phenomena of the Subconscious, which go to prove the independence, transcendence, persistence and imperishability of the subsistent human being, are (1) telepathy, (2) perfect memory, (3) perception of the fixed laws of nature, (4) suggestion and auto-suggestion, and (5) thought energy, thought projection, and thought materialization.

3. From the fact of telepathy we derive the truth that intellectual converse between persons, in its purest form, is not contingent upon the functioning of fleshy media, but is carried on independently of body activity and without regard to such objective concepts as position, distance, space, or time.

Telepathy is an activity of pure personal being. The fact of telepathy, moreover, provides a scientific basis for the doctrines of Divine inspiration and revelation. (1) Telepathy is defined as the transmission of thought from one person to another without communication through the physical senses. Telepathy in its pure form is intelligible communion between the subjective self of one person and the subjective self of another. When any two persons are in such a state of subjective or subconscious communion, they are said to be *en rapport*. (2) The facts regarding telepathy may be summarized as follows: (a) There is inherent in man a power which enables him to communicate his thoughts to others, under certain conditions, independently of objective means of communication. (b) Telepathy is primarily the communion of subconscious selves, or rather it is the normal mode of communication between persons in their subconscious states. (c) A state of perfect passivity on the part of the recipient is the most favorable condition for the reception of telepathic communication. The more perfectly the objective intelligence is held in abeyance—its functions suspended—the more perfectly will the Subconscious perform its functions. (d) This condition of passivity obtains either in induced sleep (hypnosis) or in natural sleep, and more perfectly perhaps in the latter state than in the former. Natural sleep is said to be the most perfectly passive condition attainable. (e) Although suggestion does make its impression upon the objective mind, yet the essential condition to the most successful telepathic communication is that both communicator and recipient be in their subconscious states. (f) Distance has no effect on, nor relation to, telepathic intercourse. As has already been stated, apparently neither Space nor Time exists for the Subconscious.

[Cf. Kant's theory, that Space and Time are "forms of perception" inherent in the mind, modes of objective thought, but not characteristic of Reality]. Cf. also 2 Pet. 3:8—Forget not this one thing, beloved, that one day is with the Lord as a thousand years, and a thousand years as one day. [That is to say, Time does not exist for God; or, to put the same truth in philosophical terms, mathematical time is an arbitrary human concept and not a feature of Reality at all. It follows also that, because man was created *in the image of God*, there must be in him powers that transcend all the objective concepts of distance, space and time.]

The only obstacle in the way of successful telepathy between persons at a great distance from each other is our human habit of thinking. We are accustomed to regard space as being essentially a hindrance to long-distance communication; hence, our faith in telepathy is in inverse proportion to the distance involved. And so we fail in telepathic intercourse, as in many other things, primarily through our own lack of faith. Besides, the average Westerner goes through life without ever attempting to develop the powers of his subliminal self, in fact oftentimes in complete ignorance of them; our Western culture prides itself chiefly on turning out a race of "go-getters"; on the whole we of the Occident are extroverts *par excellence*.

Obviously, the phenomenon of telepathic communication provides a scientific basis for our acceptance of Divine revelation and inspiration as historical facts. For, if men in their subconscious states can communicate thought to each other apart from the media of the physical senses, certainly the Divine Being, who is pure Spirit, can in like manner communicate Divine Thought to the spirit of man. Jesus tells us that "God is a Spirit, and they that worship him must worship in spirit and truth" (John 4:24). *Inspiration is the breathing of eternal Truth into the spirit of man by the Spirit of God.* This eternal Truth is the Thought of God; naturally, then, the communication of this Thought is the work of the Spirit of God. This is the Truth, moreover, which makes men free—free form ignorance, superstition, error, prejudice, malice, hate, sin, and ultimately from death itself. As Jesus Himself puts it: "If ye abide in my word, then are ye truly my disciples; and ye shall know the truth, and the truth shall make you free" (John 8:31-32). Or, as He testified to Pilate, the Roman governor: "To this end have I been born, and to this end am I come into the world, that I should bear witness unto the truth. Every one that is of the truth heareth my voice" (John 18:37). Truth, moreover, to be intelligible to man, must be communicated in words which he can understand. Hence, even as in telephathic communication by *suggestion*, that which is communicated is expressed *in words* (that is, if it is an intelligible communication and not mere empathy or *en rapport*-ness of feeling), subvocally, of course, but in words, nevertheless, which are expressions or revelations of the communicator's thought and will; so, likewise, the communications of eternal Truth from God are embodied in words, that is, in a form not only intelligible to the immediate recipients but designed as well for preservation for subsequent generations. Divine Truth is the Word of God; it is the expression or revelation of the Thought and Will of God; hence the communication of the Word is invariably attended by a *proceeding forth* of the Spirit from the Divine Being. The Scriptures make it clear, as we shall see later, that in the various Divine operations the Spirit and the Word go together and act together. Jesus said: "The words that I have spoken unto you are spirit, and are life" (John 6:63).

Now the Bible is the record of the progressive communication or revelation of this eternal Truth or Word to man, through the agency of the Spirit; hence, Scripture is God-breathed literature.

[Cf. again 2 Cor. 2:9-13]: As it is written, Things which eye saw not, and ear heard not, and which entered not into the heart of man, whatsoever things God prepared for them that love him: unto us God revealed them through the Spirit; for the Spirit searcheth all things, yea, the deep things of God. For who among men knoweth the things of a man, save the spirit of the man, which is in him? even so the things of God none knoweth, save the Spirit of God. But we received, not the spirit of the world, but the spirit which is from God; that we might know the things that were freely given to us of God. Which things also we speak, not in words which man's wisdom teacheth, but which the Spirit teacheth; combining spiritual things with spiritual words. [It must be understood, of course, that by the pronouns "we" and "us" in this passage, Paul has reference to the *apostles*, himself included.]

A specific example of the Divine mode of revelation and inspiration may be found in Matt. 16:15-17. Here Jesus is represented as asking the Twelve, "Who say ye that I am?" and Simon Peter answered immediately, "Thou art the Christ, the Son of the living God." To this Jesus replied as follows: "Blessed art thou, Simon Bar-Jonah: for flesh and blood hath not re-

vealed it unto thee, but my Father who is in heaven." That is
to say, the sublime truth to which Simon Peter gave expression
on this occasion—the truth of the Messiahship of Jesus, the
fundamental truth of Christianity—was not a creation of Peter's
own thought, not a figment of his own human imagination, nor
had he derived it from any other human source; on the contrary, it was a truth communicated, obviously not by means of
sensible media at all, but breathed into Peter's mind, flashed
upon his consciousness, in just so many words, directly from
God the Father in Heaven. In a word, this truth, as to its nature,
was an eternal truth; as to its source, it was a direct revelation
from God; as to its mode of communication, it was God-breathed,
*i.e.*, communicated by the Divine Spirit to the human spirit
who voiced it. An even clearer case of the mode of Divine
revelation and inspiration is described in the second chapter of
*Acts,* in which we find the account of the events of that memorable first Pentecost after our Lord's resurrection, events beginning with the descent of the Holy Spirit and closing with the
incorporation of the Church of Christ. Here we read that the
immediate effect of the Spirit's descent in baptismal measure
upon the apostles was that "they were all filled with the Holy
Spirit, and began to speak with other tongues, *as the Spirit
gave them utterance"* (v. 4). That is, they were not delivering
a message which had its origin in their own minds, or which
they had received from any source by means of sensible media.
No,—they were delivering a God-breathed message, a message
communicated to them *in words* by the Spirit of God. Speaking
by way of analogy from our present understanding of the subconscious and its powers, they were like men in a state of
hypnosis delivering a message that was being communicated
to them by suggestion; they were but giving voice to the words
that were being put upon their lips by the Holy Spirit Himself.
In a word, they were acting simply as mouthpieces of the Spirit
of God. That they did not themselves comprehend the full
import of the revelation that was being communicated through
them to all mankind is evident from the context. In closing his
sermon, for instance, Peter is represented as saying: "For to
you is the promise [*i.e.*, the promise of remission of sins in the
name of Jesus Christ], and to your children, and to all that are
afar off, even as many as the Lord our God shall call unto him"
(v. 39). Obviously the phrases in this statement, "to all that
are afar off, even as many as the Lord our God shall call unto
him," included the Gentiles as well as the Jews. Yet for many

years after Pentecost, neither Peter nor any other Apostle, as far as we know, preached the Gospel to a single Gentile; and a sequence of providential acts became necessary, some eight or ten years later, to break down the prejudice in Peter's heart and teach him that "God is no respecter of persons, but in every nation he that feareth him, and worketh righteousness, is acceptable to him" (Acts 10:34-35). Thus it was, on the day of Pentecost, that the facts, commands and promises of the Gospel were breathed into the subconscious minds of the Apostles—in words, of course—and thereafter communicated by the latter to all mankind. The apostolic testimony is recorded in the New Testament canon, once for all time, for all men to read, hear and understand. As Jesus Himself stated expressly to the Apostles themselves: "Ye shall receive power, when the Holy Spirit is come upon you; and ye shall be my witnesses both in Jerusalem, and in all Judea and Samaria, and unto the uttermost part of the earth" (Acts 1:8).

Inspiration, in the primary sense of the term, is the communication of truth without the use of sensible media, by the Divine Spirit to the human spirit; and the truth so communicated is the Word of God. *Inspiration* has reference primarily to the mode of communication, and to the agency of the Spirit therein; *revelation,* on the other hand, has a twofold reference, namely, (1) to the source, and (2) to the matter or content, of the communication. The prerequisite of both operations is *en rapport*-ness of the Divine Spirit, the communicator, with the human spirit, the recipient. And the operation itself is essentially a subconscious one, especially in so far as the recipient is concerned.

4. The Subconscious is the storehouse of all the impressions that are received in the course of a lifetime. It is the seat of perfect memory. Perfect memory, moreover, provides the scientific basis for the doctrine of sanctions in the universal order, *i.e.*, future rewards and punishments.

In his epoch-making book, *The Unconscious,* Dr. Morton Prince describes case after case of perfectly normal persons in whom the recovery of details of inconsequential experiences of everyday life was brought about simply by inducing states of *abstraction* in them. He writes:

It is often astonishing to see with what details these experiences are conserved. A person may remember any given experience in a general way, such as what he does during the course of the day, but the minute details of the day he ordinarily forgets. Now, if he allows himself to fall into a passive state of abstraction, simply concentrating

163

his attention upon a particular past moment, and gives free rein to all the associative memories belonging to that moment that float into his mind, at the same time taking care to forego all critical reflection upon them, it will be found that the number of details that will be recalled will be enormously greater than can be recovered by the voluntary memory. Memories of the details of each successive moment follow one another in continuous succession.

To this Dr. Prince adds:

This method requires some art and practice to be successfully carried out. In the state of abstraction, attention to the environment must be completely excluded and concentrated upon the past moments which it is desired to recall.[1]

This process of recovery, while one is in a state of abstraction, itself usually involves dipping into the storehouse of the Subconscious. But in both natural and induced (hypnotic) sleep, and in the latter state especially, memory becomes far more vivid, and recovery far more comprehensive, than is ever possible in a mere state of abstraction. Professor E. R. Groves affirms that free abstraction, i.e., allowing the Subconscious to have free reign independently of the objective faculties, brings out the fact that in the subjective self there is perfect memory, memory even of the unpleasant things and experiences of life. He says:

It is clear that we do not succed in driving all our unpleasant past away, for everyone has some memories that seem constantly intruding, although they are frowned upon and are never welcomed to consciousness. Undoubtedly there are a great many more that we have thoroughly eliminated, so it would seem, since they do not appear in memory. That they are not reall out of the life is proved when attempting to explore the past we dig them up and bring them again to recollection.[2]

Again:

Since free association has become the method of tapping the unconscious, the question naturally arises, Do dreams also provide channels for the coming out of unconscious energy? It is the belief of many psychologists and psychiatrists that they do.[3]

Waldstein has written as follows, in his work entitled *The Subconscious Self*:

One fact it is necessary to insist upon, that, in whatever degree or manner . . . perceptions may have been received, they are registered permanently; they are never absolutely lost. We cannot, it is true, recall at will every impression which has been received during the

1. *Vide* Dr. Morton Prince, in *An Outline of Abnormal Psychology*, edited by Gardner Murphy, Modern Library Edition, 193-195, 203 ff.
2. *Understanding Yourself*, 174.
3. *Ibid.*, 179.

course of our own existence; but the countless instances of the reappearance of the most feeble impressions, coming up again after many years, should make further proof unnecessary. Impressions that have been registered in early childhood, for instance, reappear involuntarily, thus showing their original tenacity at a period of life when no selective process of reason for remembering or forgetting, can possibly have been at work. . . . Impressions once received have a great quality of permanence, and when taken together constitute the elements of what we call memory.

It is not until we begin tapping the Subconscious, however, that we begin to realize that memory is so vast it comprehends all the thoughts, ideas and impressions of one's total experience. All, I repeat: all, without exception! As T. J. Hudson writes:

In all degrees of hypnotic sleep, the exaltation of the memory is one of the most pronounced of the attendant phenomena. This has been observed by all hypnotists, especially by those who make their experiments with a view of studying the mental action of the subject. Psychologists of all shades of belief have recognized the phenomena, and many have declared their conviction that the minutest details of acquired knowledge are recorded upon the tablets of the mind, and that they only require favorable conditions to reveal their treasures. . . . All the facts of hypnotism show that the more quiescent the objective faculties become, or, in other words, the more perfectly the functions of the brain are suspended, the more exalted are the manifestations of the subjective mind. Indeed, the whole history of the subjective phenomena goes to show that the nearer the body approaches the conditions of death, the stronger become the demonstrations of the powers of the soul [spirit?]. The irresistible inference is that when the soul is freed entirely of its trammels of flesh, its powers will attain perfection, its memory will be absolute.[1]

Sir William Hamilton has written:

The evidence on this point shows that the mind frequently contains whole systems of knowledge which, though in our normal state they have faded into absolute oblivion, may in certain abnormal states— as madness, febrile delirium, somnambulism, catalepsy, etc.—flash out into luminous consciousness, and even throw into the shade of unconsciousness those other systems by which they had, for a long time, been eclipsed, and even extinguished. For example, there are cases in which the extinct memory of whole languages was suddenly restored; and, what is even still more remarkable, in which the faculty was exhibited of accurately repeating, in known or unknown tongues, passages which were never within the grasp of the conscious memory in the normal state.[2]

Now it must be obvious to any intelligent person that this perfect memory of the Subconscious provides a scientific basis for the doctrine of future rewards and punishments. Who knows but that memory—by which the Self preserves the record of its own acts, both good and evil—may prove to be the worm that

1. *Op. cit.*, 40, 47.
2. *Lectures on Metaphysics*, 236 ff. Quoted by Hudson, *op. cit.*, 41.

shall never die, and conscience the fire that shall never be quenched? In the only glimpse into the world beyond the grave which Jesus gives us in His teaching—in the narrative of Lazarus and the Rich Man—the fact stands out clearly that the *law of memory* operates in that world to punish transgressors of the Divine Law. As the story is told by Jesus, Lazarus, the beggar, died and was carried away by the angels into Abraham's bosom. The Master then adds (Luke 16:22-24):

> And the rich man also died, and was buried. And in Hades he lifted up his eyes, being in torments, and seeth Abraham afar off, and Lazarus in his bosom. And he cried and said, Father Abraham, have mercy on me, and send Lazarus, that he may dip the tip of his finger in water, and cool my tongue; for I am in anguish in this flame.

May it not be reasonably assumed that the memories of his past utterly selfish and irreligious life, neglected as it had been of the better things, the higher values, stoked the fires of this great anguish of soul which the Rich Man was now—justly —experiencing? So it would seem, for we read that, in response to his petition, "Abraham said, Son, *remember* that thou in thy lifetime received the good things, and Lazarus in like manner evil things; but now here he is comforted, and thou art in anguish" (Luke 16:22-25). "Son, remember!" Whatever else the Rich Man may have taken with him into the next world, one thing is sure: he took his memory. As Alexander Maclaren has put it: Memory will embrace all the events of the past life, will embrace them all at the same moment, and will embrace them continuously and continually. Memory is a process of self-registry. As every business house keeps a copy of all letters sent or orders issued, so every man retains in memory the record of his sins. The mind is a palimpsest; though the original writing has been erased, the ink has penetrated the whole thickness of the parchment, and God's chemistry is able to revive it.[1] It is significant, too, that memory is individualistic. As William James says, "Memory requires more than the mere dating of a fact in the past. It must be dated in *my* past." The law of memory seems to be the guarantee of personal identity and of individuality as well.

Now of course someone may be objecting that, if this reasoning is true, the saints themselves will suffer in the world to come, from the memories of sins they have committed in this present life both before and after conversion, and suffer perhaps

---

1. *Vide* A. H. Strong, *Systematic Theology*, One-Volume Edition, 1026. A. Maclaren, *Sermons*, I, 109-122.

even more poignantly by virtue of their more profound appreciation of holiness and consequent greater capacity for suffering, even as Jesus the Holy One, in the Garden of Gethsemane, suffered to the extent that drops of His blood mingled with His sweat to sanctify the ground beneath the olive trees, suffered more excruciatingly than a mere man could ever suffer and continue to live. For, is it not true that we have all sinned and fallen short of the glory of God (Rom. 3:23)? To this objection, I reply that God's grace is sufficient to meet every need of His saints and that the blood of Christ is an all-sufficient covering (Atonement) for their sins. God's clear promise, uttered in olden times, was that under the New Covenant—after the Atonement had been provided—He would forgive the iniquity of His people and remember their sin no more (Jer. 31:34; Heb. 8:12). In the words of the Psalmist:

> For as the heavens are high above the earth,
> So great is his loving kindness toward them that fear him.
> As far as the east is from the west,
> So far hath he removed our transgressions from us.
> Like as a Father pitieth his children,
> So Jehovah pitieth them that fear him.
> For he knoweth our frame;
> He remembereth that we are dust.

(Psa. 103:11-14).

Difficult as it may be for us poor mortals to comprehend, the fact is, nevertheless, that *when God forgives, God forgets*. Hence forgiven sins will never be brought up in the Judgment, neither from any source external to the individual saint nor from any law operating within his own being. Herein perhaps consists the metaphysical aspect of the salvation in Christ; it is tied up somehow with the process of immortalization. According to Scripture, the redeemed will appear in the Judgment clothed in glory and honor and immortality, in order that the infinite goodness and mercy of God may be made manifest to all intelligent creatures—both angels and men—in the greatness of the salvation then and there to be revealed. For the ultimate function of the final Judgment will be the vindication not only of God's past dealings with His moral creatures (both angels and men) but of His determination of their future destinies as well. And the salvation to be made manifest on that last great Day will be so indescribably glorious that even though only one human creature should be found worthy of receiving it, this one instance, nevertheless, would be found sufficient to convince both angels and men of the wisdom and goodness of God, and

167

sufficient also to demonstrate the successful consummation of the Divine Plan of the Universe. For just as the value of a life is determined not by its quantity, or length in years, but by its quality; so the success of God's plan for His creatures will be determined, not by the number saved, but by the greatness of the salvation that will finally be revealed.

With reference again to the metaphysical aspect of the problem under consideration here, I take it that the remembrance of his past sins by a saint of God will be dimmed as a result of his progressive infilling with the Spirit of God and consequent growth in holiness, in this present life. Moreover, the saint's progressive sanctification in the present terrestrial order can lead to but one outcome in the future celestial order, for which it is indeed the necessary preparation; that outcome will be the putting on of immortality, the redemption of the body. Thus the saved person will not only outgrow, so to speak, the practice of sin, in sanctification, in this life, but he will ultimately lose even the remembrance of his sins in the final transmutation of his physical into his spiritual body in the life to come. It could hardly be otherwise with respect to a holy race that is to be fitted ultimately for fellowship with our holy God. For ultimate holiness will surely be, if anything, *wholeness*—a literal wholeness in which all the marks, including even the vestigial ones, of sin will have been blotted out by the chemistry of the Spirit of God.

To the wicked, disobedient and neglectful, on the other hand, no promise of immortality is held out in the Bible. With what manner of body they will come, we are not told in Scripture, and hence we do not know. We are told by Jesus Himself that "the hour cometh, in which all that are in the tombs shall hear his voice, and shall come forth: they that have done good, unto the resurrection of life; and they that have done evil, unto the resurrection of judgment" (John 5:28-29). What form this final punishment will take, in so far as the body is involved, we do not know. But we may be certain that the *law of memory* will be functioning as it has never functioned in this present life. We may be sure, too, that when the wicked shall come face to face with Infinite Holiness, their own wickedness will stand out in such execrable contrast that their anguish will be unspeakable; so terrible will it be that the inspired writers are compelled to resort to poetic imagery to describe it. The lost, they tell us, will cry out "to the mountains and to the rocks, Fall on us, and hide us from the face of him that sitteth on the throne, and from the wrath of the Lamb: for the great day of their wrath is come; and who is able to stand? (Rev. 6:16-17). No anguish experienced in this life can be comparable to the ultimate anguish of a lost spirit, a spirit conscious of its own "eternal destruction from the face of the Lord and from the glory of his might" (2 Thess. 1:9). For just as Heaven will be essentially the union of the human spirit with God in knowledge and love; so Hell, whatever else it may be, will surely be the human spirit's absolute loss of God for ever and ever. Its population will take in all those wicked and neglectful ones whom the Spirit will have irrevocably turned over to their own wickedness. The Judgment will be the day of final reckoning; on that great Day, Christ the Judge, we are told, "shall say unto them on the left hand, Depart from me, ye cursed, into the eternal fire which is prepared for the devil and his angels" (Matt. 25:41). As St. Chrysostom puts it: Hell was prepared for the devil and his angels; if men go to Hell, it will be because they cast themselves into it.

O sinner friend, to be without God, without Christ, without the Holy Spirit, for ever and ever!—what an awful and tragic destiny! Turn ye, turn ye,—for why will ye die?

Thus it will be seen that related to the *law of memory* is the *law of conscience* by which men voluntarily anticipate punishment for their vices and sins. As Wordsworth has written:

For, like a plague will memory break out,
And, in the blank and solitude of things,
Upon his spirit, with a fever's strength,
Will conscience prey.

### The Scriptures tell us that

in the day of wrath and revelation of the righteous judgment of God, he will render to every man according to his works; to them that by patience in welldoing seek for glory and honor and incorruption, eternal life; but unto them that are factious, and obey not the truth, but obey unrighteousness, shall be wrath and indignation, tribulation and anguish, upon every soul of man that worketh evil, of the Jew first, and also of the Greek [Rom. 2:5-9].

For the wicked, the neglectful, the proud and the apostate, there can be only "a certain fearful expectation of judgment, and a fierceness of fire which shall devour the adversaries" (Heb. 10:27) in that final reckoning, in which every human spirit, judged by his own works, will go to his own proper place—the place which he shall have prepared for himself by the kind of life he has lived on earth. Dr. A. H. Strong tells of a man who was converted in Whitefield's time by a vision of the Judgment, in which he saw all men gathered before the Throne, and each one coming up to the book of God's law, tearing open his heart before it "as one would tear open the bosom of his shirt," comparing the content of his heart with the things written in the book, and then according as that which was disclosed in his heart agreed or disagreed with that standard, either passing triumphantly to the company of the blest, or going with howling to the company of the damned. Not a word was spoken; the Judge sat silent; the judgment was strictly one of self-revelation and self-condemnation.[1] Just as in the well-known case of Judas, conscience sent each man to *his own place* (Acts 1:25). For all those ultra-wise persons, therefore—the wise in their own conceits—who are inclined to scoff at the notion of a "physical hell," I would say by way of warning that there are forms of punishment infinitely more terrible than physical suffering. As a matter of fact, there is no form of anguish comparable to mental anguish, and certainly there is no conceivable form of mental anguish that would be more terrible than mental anguish occasioned by the loss of *all good.* Hence it may be that memory is the worm that shall never die, and conscience the fire that shall never be quenched. Moreover, the individualistic character of both memory and conscience would seem to substantiate the fact of the individualistic character of the final judgment: that is, that it will be an accounting in which every man will be judged according to *his own* deeds. This is precisely what the Bible teaches.

Matt. 16:27—For the Son of man shall come in the glory of his Father with his angels; and then shall he render unto every man according to his deeds. Rom. 2:6—[God] who will render to every man according to his works. Rev. 20:12—and the dead were judged out of the things which were written in the books, according to their works.

In any case, all Nature bears out the fact that our world—the Kingdom of Nature—is an individualistic world; we come into it one by one, and we go out of it one by one. In like manner, according to the teaching of Jesus, we come into the Kingdom of Grace by being "born again" one by one, "born of water and the Spirit" (John 3:3-5). And so shall we be "born from the dead" one by one, into the Kingdom of Glory, "the eternal kingdom of our Lord and Savior Jesus Christ" (2 Pet. 1:11), after having rendered our proper accounting, each person according to his own works. There is no such thing in the Christian System as either salvation *en masse* or salvation by proxy. In-

1. A. H. Strong, *op. cit.,* 1026.

170

cidentally, the prime fallacy of all totalitarian systems—both ecclesiastical and political—is their failure to take into account the glory, dignity, and *priority* of the individual in the Plan of the Universe. That priority obtains, however, and no scheme of man will ever change it.

Finally, there is a third law which is inevitably linked up with the laws of memory and conscience, namely, the *law of character,* according to which every thought and deed in the course of a lifetime makes an indelible impress upon the moral nature of the individual human being. Now it is a law of nature that a man cannot enjoy what he has not trained himself to appreciate; hence, it is obvious that no man could possibly enjoy Heaven in the next world, who has not, by opening his heart to the abiding presence of the Spirit *here,* by presenting his body as a living sacrifice *here,* prepared himself in knowledge, in affection, and in desire, for full participation in, and enjoyment of, the fulness of fellowship with God hereafter. As one of the older Catechisms puts it: *Man's end in life is to love God and serve Him here, that he may enjoy Him hereafter.* This is literally and naturally true. Man builds in this present life for eternity. By cultivating the Mind of Christ, by living the life with the Holy Spirit, in a word, by growth in holiness, he builds for a life of ultimate and complete union with God— the Life Everlasting. On the other hand, by living here for himself and for himself alone—the essential principle of all sin is selfishness—he prepares himself for the awful destiny of complete separation from God, of absolute loss of all good, in the world to come. He had no time for God, no desire for God, no love for God, here; hence he cannot expect to acquire that desire and love "in the twinkling of an eye" hereafter; moral character, including holiness, is not so acquired. And not only will he discover that he cannot suddenly and mysteriously acquire love for God after he shall have crossed "the great divide," but he will find himself, no doubt, so steeped in self that he will be wholly lacking even the desire to acquire it; the habits he has built up through the years all tend in the opposite direction,—away from God. As a matter of fact, he will even find himself miserable in the presence of Infinite Holiness. How could it be otherwise? One cannot conceive of an environment more repugnant to the devil and his angels, creatures who are totally depraved, nor an environment in which they would be more miserable, than Heaven, filled as it is with the presence of God. Undoubtedly, the same reasoning holds good with respect to the destiny of all lost human spirits. There simply can be no other proper habitation for them, none other suited to their moral status, than Hell, the association of their own kind. To speak in the scientific terms: *every human being has this choice to make—the choice between growth in godliness on the one hand, and atavism on the other, reversion to animal type.* Conscience, moreover, will tell each lost spirit, in the final adjudication, precisely where he belongs, what his proper place is. In a word, our individual destinies hereafter are determined by the characters, made up of thoughts, affections, habits, and dispositions, which we build up in this present life. The most fundamental ethical and religious truth of all time and eternity, a truth embodied in the very structure of the universe, a truth which applies equally to all men everywhere and in all ages, was enunciated by Jesus in these words: "He that findeth his life shall lose it; and he that loseth his life for my sake shall find it" (Matt. 10:39). Second only to this truth is the corollary truth as stated by St. Paul: "Be not deceived; God is not mocked: for whatsoever a man soweth, that shall he also reap. For he that soweth unto his own flesh shall of the flesh reap corruption; but he that soweth unto the Spirit shall of the Spirit reap eternal life" (Gal. 6:7-8).

The point is, I repeat, that a man's ultimate destiny is determined by the character which he builds in this present life. As the poet has written:

> Heaven is not reached at a single bound;
> But we build the ladder by which we rise
> From the lowly earth to the vaulted skies,
> And we mount to its summit round by round.

"Round by round"! *All life is growth;* the Christian life is growth —growth "in grace and knowledge of our Lord and Savior Jesus Christ" (2 Pet. 3:18). Moreover, the individual destiny thus determined is determined for ever; it is fixed for all eternity. So Jesus Himself teaches, quite clearly—again in the narrative of Lazarus and the Rich Man. Said Father Abraham to the latter: "And besides all this, between us and you there is a great gulf fixed, that they that would pass from hence to you may not be able, and that none may cross over from thence to us" (Luke 16:26). That is to say, the gulf between these two persons, Lazarus and Dives, in the world beyond the grave, the gulf between Abraham's Bosom and Hades, was impassable; it was a great gulf *fixed.* Why so? Because it was a gulf of char-·cter which had been fixed by the contrary lives—lives of diametrically opposite ideals, habits, and ends—which the two men had lived; by the entirely different character-structures which they had erected. To use Jesus' own analogy: one, Lazarus, had built his house upon the rock; the other, Dives, had built his house upon sand (Matt. 7:24-27). The one had lived a life of humility and faith, and thus had builded for eternity; the other had lived a life of utter selfishness, building only for time. Dives had sought all his heaven in this world; and that being the only heaven he desired, that was all he received. And now, on the other side, the one was enjoying rest and peace in Abraham's bosom, but the other was in Hades, in anguish, tormented in the flames of remorse and despair. Jesus was not drawing upon His imagination here. He was presenting truth; hence the portrayal is in perfect harmony with the nature of things. It would no more have been possible for either Lazarus or the Rich Man to have acquired the moral status of the other after death, than it would be possible for a grain of corn in the earth to metamorphose itself into a watermelon seed. The contrary moral characters of the two men fixed the gulf between them and fixed it for ever. There is not the slightest intimation here of any possibility of post-mortem repentance or salvation, nor is there any intimation of such a doctrine anywhere else in Scripture. The verdict of the final judgment will be explicit and irremediable: "He that is unrighteous, let him do unrighteousness still; and he that is filthy, let him be made filthy still; and he that is righteous, let him do righteousness still; and he that is holy, let him be made holy still" (Rev. 22:11).

Here, then, are three fundamental *natural* moral laws—the laws of memory, conscience, and character. These laws operate in their own right; nothing can prevent their operation; they belong to the very nature of things and of man. And they all have their confirmation scientifically in the phenomena of the Subconscious.

5. Another power of the Subconscious is that of perception of the fixed laws of Nature. The operation of this power indicates clearly that when the Self shall have been freed from the limitations of its objective environment, it will be able to perceive and to know all truth intuitively.

Three sub-classes of subjective mental phenomena which belong in this category are manifested in mathematical prodigies, in musical prodigies, and in those rare persons who are able to transcend all time-measurements. These phenomena do not depend upon the raw material which comes into the mind through sensation and which is retained therein, in some mysterious manner, in the form of images; sensation, image-ing, and reasoning belong to the objective mind. No one can, of course, without an objective education, become a financier, an orator, a statesman, or a practical man of affairs. But one can be a mathematician or a muscian independently of any objective education, that is, by the exercise of the powers of the subjective mind alone. Many instances could be cited to show to what a prodigious extent the mathematical and musical faculties—for music is basically mathematical—manifest themselves in persons who are not only without objective training but who in some instances are lacking even the capacity for any considerable objective education. Rzeszewski, for example, moved his chessmen to a world's championship before he was ten years old. Mozart, at the age of four, amazed his family by going into the garret and playing on the spinet, without having received any instruction, and some of his compositions were written in his childish hand at the age of five. The cases might be cited, too, of Zerah Colburn, the mathematical "genius," and Blind Tom, an imbecile who, without any objective training whatever, was able to reproduce the most difficult classical compositions with accuracy. Blind Joe was a similar character who appeared in vaudeville. As a matter of fact, cases of idiot-savants are rather numerous.[1] And most of us have at some time in our lives met up with mathematical and musical prodigies—"lightning calculators," musical improvisers, individuals with "perfect pitch," and the like. Undoubtedly these are all examples of the manifestations of powers which inhere in the Subconscious, power which, for aught we know, may be latent, though in varying degrees perhaps, in all men.

Creativity, no doubt, also has its roots in the subliminal self. Probably the "genius" of a William Shakespeare, of a Michelangelo, or of a Louis Pasteur, for example, should be placed in this category. Pasteur, writes R. J. Williams, the biochemist,

seemed to be able again and again to arrive at valid conceptions long before he had experimental proof. His creativeness lay in his ability to formulate hypotheses that turned out on the basis of his own hard work and enthusiasm to be tremendously productive.

The same author goes on to say:

1. See R. J. Williams, *The Human Frontier*, 152-156. Material on "idiot-savants" has been collected from several sources; an important source is D. C. Rife and L. S. Snyder, *Human Biology*, 3, 547, 1931.

For the purposes of this discussion and avoiding all theological disputation, we may say that Jesus' teaching arose by intuition. . . . Even if we recognize and exaggerate the opportunities which he had for learning from his forebears and others, his selection and enunciation of the fundamental laws of life indicate an ability to draw upon a Universal Mind, which does not fall within the abilities previously considered. The universality is the feature which makes the ability of such outstanding importance—the fact that after many centuries, minds of the highest quality still pore over his words and obtain from them ideas that are applicable to modern life.[1]

The late Gandhi, for example, admitted that he had gotten the inspiration for his sacrificial life from the Sermon on the Mount. We must not overlook the fact, however, that according to Scripture, Jesus was the Incarnate Word, the expression or revelation of Universal Mind Himself. His own testimony is: "Heaven and earth shall pass away, but my words shall not pass away" (Matt. 24:35).

The power to transcend mathematical time—and perhaps even real time— seems also to exist in the highly-developed Subconsciousness alone. The only means available to the objective mind for the measurement of time, are the physical senses, in the observation of the movements of the heavenly bodies or of some mechanical instrument, such as a clock, which objective experience has proved to be an accurate device for such measurement. The subjective mind, on the other hand, possesses the inherent power of measuring time accurately, independently of objective aids or of the exercise of reason. The subliminal self, in fact, manifests inherent power not only to measure accurately the lapse of time, but even to transcend all such measurements by projecting itself either into the past or into the future. There can be little doubt, it seems to me, that the phenomenon of *prescience* (literally, "to know beforehand"), not infrequently exhibited by historical personages, is the result of the contact of the Subconscious within them with the Universal Mind, the Mind of God, to whom all the events of history are known from the beginning. (Cf. Isa. 46:9-10: "I am God, and there is none like me, declaring the end from the beginning, and from ancient times things that are not yet done.") Obviously, these "prophetically illumined" persons who have appeared in history from time to time were persons who were subconsciously *en rapport* with the Universal Mind, and who were thus able to foreknow events, that is, to "know" those events prior to their occurrence in time as we measure it objectively. This is true of the Biblical prophets in a special sense,

1. *The Human Frontier*, 140.

for they were instrumentalities *divinely chosen and called* for the communication of *evidential* truth to mankind. However, as stated in a foregoing paragraph, it is now claimed that the Duke University experiments have provided conclusive evidence of the existence of the power of prescience, on a small scale at least, in the ordinary run of human individuals. Be that as it may—whether the power is common to all men or not—the very existence of the phenomenon affords a scientific explanation of the fact of prophecy.

Finally, this subconscious power of intuiting the fixed laws of nature is a clear intimation of the method by which the saints will apprehend eternal Truth in its fulness in their ultimate union with God,—the Beatific Vision. On this point Dr. Hudson sums up as follows:

We have seen that certain phenomena depend for their perfect development upon objective education, and that certain other phenomena are exhibited in perfection independently of objective education. In other words, certain powers are inherent in the subjective intelligence. These powers appear to pertain to the comprehension of the laws of Nature. We have seen that, under certain conditions, the subjective mind apprehends by intuition the laws of mathematics. It comprehends the laws of harmony of sounds, independently of objective education. By true artists the laws of the harmony of colors are also perceived intuitively. These facts have been again and again demonstrated. It would seem, therefore, to be a just conclusion that the subjective mind, untrammeled by its objective environment, will be able to comprehend all the laws of Nature, to perceive, to know all truth, independently of the slow, laborious process of induction. We are so accustomed to boast of the "god-like reason" with which man is endowed, that the proposition that the subjective mind of man is incapable of exercising that function, in what we regard as the highest form of reasoning, seems, at first glance, to be a limitation of the intellectual powers of the soul, and inconsistent with what we have been accustomed to regard as the highest attributes of human intelligence. But a moment's reflection will devleop the fact that this apparent limitation of intellectual power is, in reality, a god-like attribute of the mind. God himself cannot reason inductively. Inductive reasoning presupposes an inquiry, a search after knowledge, an effort to arrive at correct conclusions regarding something of which we are ignorant. To suppose God to be an inquirer, a seeker after knowledge, by finite processes of reasoning, is a conception of the Deity which negatives his omniscience, and measures Infinite Intelligence by purely finite standards. For our boasted "god-like reason" is of the earth, earthy. It is the noblest attribute of the finite mind, it is true, but it is essentially finite. It is the outgrowth of our objective existence. It is our safest guide in the walks of earthly life. It is our faithful monitor and guardian in our daily struggle with our physical environment. It is our most reliable auxiliary in our efforts to penetrate the secrets of Nature, and wrest from her the means of subsistence. But its functions cease with the necessities which called it into existence; for it will be no longer useful when the physical form has perished, and the veil is lifted which hides from mortal eyes that world where all truth is revealed. Then it is that the soul [spirit?]—the subjective mind—will perform its normal functions, untrammeled by the physical form which imprisons it and binds it to earth; and in its native realm of truth, unimpeded by the laborious processes of finite reasoning, it will imbibe all truth from its Eternal Source.[1]

In the well-known words of the Apostle Paul:

For we know in part, and we prophesy in part; but when that which is perfect is come, that which is in part shall be done away. . . . For now we see in a mirror, darkly; but then face to face: now I know in part; but then shall I know fully even as also I was fully known [1 Cor. 13:9, 10, 12]. [Cf. 1 John 3:2]—Beloved, now are we children of God, and it is not yet made manifest what we shall be. We know that, if he shall be manifested, we shall be like him; for we shall see him even as he is.

This ultimate apprehension will surely be that of every form of Truth, not only of what we call "physical," "psychological," and "mathematical" truth, but of all moral and spiritual truth as well. In the presence of Absolute Holiness, all men will "see" —that is, *understand*—themselves exactly as they are, and each will know as a result of this vision what his proper destiny must be.

6. There also resides in the inner self a psychic power over the functions of the physical body, a power which can be invoked, under proper conditions, to alleviate the ravages of disease. The majority of persons, however, are unmindful of these inherent psychic powers which the Creator has endowed them with for their own use and benefit. The facts of suggestion and auto-suggestion are fairly conclusive proof that the "inner man"—the spirit—unifies and controls the physical organism. Thus the truth of the pre-eminence of Mind over Matter is well established.

The healing power of suggestion, either from an external source or from one's own mind, is now recognized by all reputable physicians and psychiatrists; mental therapeutics has, in fact, become a legitimate phase of scientific medicine. It is a matter of general agreement among scientists that nothing is so conducive to the general health of the organism as a healthy mental outlook on life. Indeed these general principles are now being successfully utilized in as important a function as childbirth.[2] Moreover, a proper mental outlook on life is more often provided by a genuine religious faith than by any other factor. As Dr. G. W. Allport writes:

1. *Op. cit.*, 72-74.
2. *Vide*, for example, Grantly Dick Read, *Childbirth Without Fear*, published in England under the title, *Revelation of Childbirth*.

177

Religion is the search for a value underlying *all* things, and as such is the most comprehensive of all the possible philosophies of life. A deeply moving religious experience is not readily forgotten, but is likely to remain as a focus of thought and desire. Many lives have no such focus; for them religion is an indifferent matter, or else a purely formal and compartmental interest. But the authentically religious personality unites the tangible present with some comprehensive view of the world that makes this tangible present intelligible and acceptable to him. Psychotherapy recognizes this integrative function of religion in personality, soundness of mind being aided by the possession of a completely embracing theory of life.[1]

## Dr. R. J. Williams writes in like vein:

While psychologists, psychiatrists, and students of mental hygiene could not unanimously endorse theology as a beneficent agent in human life, they would be practically unanimous in their endorsement of religion if they could specify that the religion must be the kind that engenders in human beings the triad of *faith*, *hope*, and *love*, of which the greatest is love. These three are probably the most important mental medicines, and their opposites—fear, despair, and hate—are among the worst mental poisons.[2]

From the viewpoint of psychic research, the fundamental principles which underlie the practice of mental therapeutics may be summarized as follows: 1. The subjective mind exercises a general control over the sensations and functions of the body. 2. The subjective mind is at all times amenable to control by suggestions of the objective mind. 3. These two propositions being true, the conclusion is obvious, namely, that the sensations and functions of the bodily organs are subject to control by suggestions from the objective mind. As a matter of fact, both trances and cures often occur as a result of *auto-suggestion*. 4. These suggestions, however, must be strongly and repeatedly willed, and decreed, either orally or mentally, in words. 5. In all cases, passivity on the part of the patient is necessary to favorable results.

That bodily sensations are subject to control by suggestion is proved by the phenomenon of catalepsy, a condition in which the subject is immunized to physical pain of any kind. It is further proved by the not infrequent use of hypnotism for anesthetic purposes in surgical operations. Again, with reference to the bodily functions, Bernheim, Moll,[3] and others may be cited as authority for the fact that symptoms of disease (fever, rapid pulse, flushed cheeks, etc.), partial or total paralysis, pains

1. G. W. Allport, *Personality: A Psychological Interpretation*, 226.
2. *The Human Frontier*, 182.
3. *Vide* H. Bernheim, *Suggestive Therapeutics*, translated by Christian A. Herter, recently reprinted by the London Book Company, Woodside, New York. Also A. Moll, *Hypnotism*.

in the body, hemorrhages, bloody stigma, and even structural changes have been produced in various subjects by means of suggestion. This being true, how much easier it should be to alleviate the symptoms and ravages of disease by the same method: it is well known that Nature *per se* is constitutionally constructive and restorative. Hudson writes:

At the risk of repetition, the self-evident proposition will be repeated, that the instinct of self-preservation is the strongest instinct of our nature, and constitutes a most potent, ever-present, and constantly operative auto-suggestion, inherent in our very nature. It is obvious that any outside suggestion must operate with all the greater potentiality when it is directed on lines in harmony with instinctive auto-suggestion. It follows that normal conditions can be restored with greater ease and certainty, other things being equal, than abnormal conditions can be induced. And thus it is that by the practice of the various systems of psycho-therapeutics we find that the most marvelous cures are affected, and are again reminded of the words of Paracelsus: "Whether the objects of your faith be real or false, you will nevertheless obtain the same effects."[1]

Again:

The faith required for therapeutic purposes is a purely subjective faith, and is attainable upon the cessation of active opposition on the part of the objective mind. And this is why it is that, under all systems of mental therapeutics, the perfect passivity of the patient is insisted upon as the first essential condition. Of course, it is desirable to secure the concurrent faith both of the objective and subjective minds; but it is not essential, if the patient will in good faith make the necessary auto-suggestion, either in words, or by submitting passively to the suggestions of the healer.[2]

Suggestion, it must be understood, supplemented by faith on the part of the recipient is the all-potent factor in the production of phenomena of this kind. Dr. Phineas P. Quimby, for example, a self-styled "free-thinker," by means of suggestion cured Mary Baker of neurotic disorders several years before she wrote and published her *Science and Health*. By means of suggestion and auto-suggestion, so-called "miracles of healing" have been effected in all ages and in all parts of the world, and not infrequently apart from any kind of a religious setting. As a matter of fact, these two phenomena have played an important role in the science of medicine from its earliest beginnings; indeed, they figured significantly in the art of healing developed under Asklepios (who later became the Greek god of medicine) several centuries before Christ. Undoubtedly, too, they play the determining role in present-day "miracles" of the kind, such as,

1. *Op. cit.*, 154-155.
2. *Ibid.*, 156.

for example, those wrought at Lourdes, France. In a word, the facts of suggestion and auto-suggestion account for the successes of "faith healers," "divine healers," "mental healers," "magnetic healers," "mesmerists," and the like, in all ages of the world's history. Christian Science practitioners are particularly efficacious in the exercise of these subconscious powers, the therapeutic values of which are available to all men. That all do not benefit therefrom is simply due to the fact that the vast majority of persons go through life totally unmindful of the existence of these natural powers and functions within them; hence, through ignorance, failing to develop or to utilize them, they suffer unnecessarily a multitude of ailments, both mental and physical. It is quite probable too that Jesus Himself made use of these powers of the Subconscious in performing many of His miracles, especially His miracles of healing. He, being Himself the Author of Nature—for "all things were made through him, and without him was not anything made that hath been made" (John 1:3)— certainly possessed complete knowledge and control of the operations of Nature's laws. In fact, in the *variety* of His miracles (miracles of healing and of exorcising demons—miracles of benevolence; miracles of raising the dead; miracles of judgment, as the blasting of the fig tree; miracles showing His control of the natural elements, as the stilling of the tempest; miracles of creation, as the feeding of the five thousand with a few loaves and fishes, etc.), He demonstrated His absolute control of Nature at every point and in every phase of her workings. One must not, however, positively identify the power by which the miracles of the Bible were wrought, with the powers of the Subconscious in man by which the "miracles" of strictly human agency have been performed. The latter are, to say the most, but feeble reflections of the former, even as man himself is— in the potencies of his person—but the image or likeness of God. The miracles of the Bible are to be distinguished from the "miracles" wrought exclusively by human agency, in three respects in particular: (1) in their *timeliness*, that is, in relation to the unfolding of the Divine Purpose; (2) in their essentially *evidential function*; and (3) in the fact that the Word of God itself entered, either directly or indirectly (in the form of a symbol of the Word, as, for example, Moses' rod), into the performance of them. Bible miracles are in a separate—and higher —category from any event wrought exclusively by human agency.

Finally, all this evidence with respect to the powers of the

Subconscious proves, of course, that the "inner man," the sub-liminal self, the spirit, unifies, dominates and controls the physical organism in which it is temporarily domiciled, and that Mind is superior to, and exercises sovereignty over, Matter. Indeed, it is only through the avenue of Mind that we can even know Matter or know that Matter exists.

7. Psychokinesis (or, as it is sometimes called, telekinesis) is proof that *the thoughts of the Subconscious are capable of self-transmutation into "physical" energy.*

8. Ectoplasms, spirit materializations, phantasms, etc., are evidence that *the thoughts of the Subconscious are capable of embodying themselves in visible form.*

9. *Thoughts are entities which impress themselves upon their surroundings. Thoughts are indeed things.*

10. In the existence and exercise of these powers, man re-veals the spark of the Infinite that is in him, and himself gives evidence of having been created in the image of God. *For, is not the Cosmos itself a constitution of the Divine Will, a projection of the Divine Spirit, an embodiment of the Divine Thought?*

Charles Richet writes as follows:

1. There is in us a faculty of cognition that differs radically from the usual sensorial faculties (cryptesthesia). 2. There are, even in full light, movements of objects without contact (telekinesis). 3. Hands, bodies, and objects seem to take shape in their entirety from a cloud and take all the semblance of life (ectoplasms). 4. There occur premonitions than can be explained neither by chance nor by perspicacity, and are sometimes verified in minute detail. Such are my first and explicit conclusions. I cannot go beyond them.[1]

Hudson writes: "The subjective mind, or entity, possesses physical power; that is, the power to make itself heard and felt, and to move ponderable objects."[2]

Again:

There are several ways by which the operations of the subjective mind can be brought above the threshold of consciousness. When this is done by any one of the various methods, a phenomenon is produced. . . . The leading phenomena are clairvoyance, clairaudience, telepathy, mesmerism and hypnotism, automatic writing, percussive sound (spirit-rapping), movement of ponderable bodies (table-tipping), and phantasmic appearances.[3]

*Clairvoyance* is the power of discerning objects which are not

1. *Thirty Years of Psychical Research,* 596-597. Translated from the French by Stanley DeBrath.
2. *Op. cit.,* 208.
3. Hudson, *op. cit.,* 219.

present to the senses but which are regarded as having objective reality. Dr. Rhine says:

Clairvoyance perception is the awareness of objects or objective events without the use of the senses, whereas telepathy is the awareness of the thoughts of another person, similarly without sensory aid.[1]

*Clairaudience* is defined as "the power of hearing the spoken words of a human soul." It is the faculty which enables a man's objective mind to receive communications from his own or another's subjective mind by means of intelligible words. *Automatic writing* consists in holding a pencil in one hand and letting it write; the subjective mind assumes control of the nerves and muscles of the arm and hand, and propels the pencil, the objective mind being perfectly quiescent, and often totally oblivious of what is being written . *Levitation* is not, as often defined, the *illusion* that a heavy object is suspended in the air without visible support: it is the actual thing. *Psychokinesis* is the designation now given to any form of movement of ponderable objects by thought power alone; attention has already been called to the positive results of the Duke University experiments in this field.

*Ectoplasm* is defined by Mr. Hamlin Garland as an elementary substance given off by the human body in varying degrees. He conceives it to be *ideoplastic*, that is, capable of being moulded into various shapes by the mind of the psychic or that of the sitter. *"Spirit materializations"* are said to be *thought projections* of the Subconscious. As Hudson puts it:

The power resides in the subjective mind of man to create phantasms perceptible to the objective senses of others. Again it seems to be well established by experiment that some persons have the power not only to create such phantasms but also to endow them with a certain degree of intelligence and power.[2]

**Again:**

The medium goes into a trance, or hypnotic state, and projects the shapes of various persons, generally of the deceased friends of some of those present. A good medium will produce any number of visions, of any number of persons, men and women, large and small.[3]

In fact it is thought that a good medium is capable of extracting any image (that is, of a loved one or friend) that may be in the mind of any sitter, and of projecting that image in a manner perceptible to the latter's physical senses.

1. *The Reach of the Mind*, 27.
2. *Op. cit.*, 289.
3. *Ibid.*, 291.

From these facts it is fair to conclude: 1. That the power to create phantasms resides in and is inherent in the subjective mind, or personality, of man. 2. That the power becomes greater as the body approaches nearer to the condition of death; that is, the subjective, or hypnotic, condition becomes deeper, and the subjective personality in consequence becomes stronger in its sphere of activity. 3. That at the hour of death, or when the functions of the body are entirely suspended, the power is greatest. . . . All that we know is that phantasms are created by some power inherent in the subjective personality of man. They may be called "embodied thoughts," as man may be called the embodied thought of God. . . . It is fair to presume that that part of the Infinite which is embodied in each of us must partake, to a limited extent, of His power to create. Experimental psychology suggests that we have that power, and that it is thus that phantasms are produced.[1]

Thoughts are entities which impress themselves on their surroundings. Truly, *thoughts are things*. All this is in perfect harmony with Scripture, which teaches clearly that the Will of God is the constitution of our universe both physical and moral, that is to say, the Will of God is that which constitutes it and *constitutes it to be what it is*. But the Will of God is expressed by the Word of God (which is the revelation of the Thought of God), and is realized through the activity of the Spirit of God. To God the Father, we are indebted for *faith;* to God the Word or Son, we are indebted for *doctrine;* and to God the Holy Spirit we are indebted for *evidence* or *proof*. The Father *originates,* the Son *executes,* the Spirit *applies* and *realizes*. Hence, the Cosmos is presented in Scripture as the creation or projection of the Divine Spirit and the embodiment or materialization of the Divine Word.

Psa. 33:6, 9—By the word of Jehovah were the heavens made, and all the host of them by the breath of his mouth. . . . For he spake, and it was done; he commanded, and it stood fast. Heb. 11:3—By faith we understand that the worlds have been framed by the word of God, so that what is seen hath not been made out of things which appear. John 1:1-3: In the beginning was the Word, and the Word was with God, and the Word was God. The same was in the beginning with God. All things were made through him; and without him was not anything made that hath been made. Cf. also v. 14—And the Word became flesh, and dwelt among us (and we beheld his glory, glory as of the only begotten from the Father), full of grace and truth. Acts 17:24-25: The God that made the world and all things therein, he, being Lord of heaven and earth, dwelleth not in temples made with hands; neither is he served by men's hands, as though he needed anything, seeing he himself giveth to all life, and breath, and all things. Psa. 148:1-6: Praise ye Jehovah. Praise ye Jehovah from the heavens; Praise him in the heights. Praise ye him, all his angels; Praise ye him, all his host. Praise ye him, sun and moon; Praise him, all ye stars of light. Praise him, ye heavens of heavens, And ye waters that are above the heavens. Let them praise the name of Jehovah; For *he commanded*,

1. Hudson, *op. cit.,* 293-294.

*and they were created. He hath also established them for ever and ever; He hath made a decree which shall not pass away.*

Students of psychic phenomena also write of what they designate the Superconscious, Edith Lyttelton, for example, says that the Superconscious is a term used to designate the "enlarged faculties of intellect, perception, and intuition, of which the ordinary conscious mind is not aware."[1] She goes on to explain that the forms of superconscious power exhibiting knowledge which the conscious mind does not possess, are (1) knowledge of either past or current events or facts, which has not been acquired normally by the individual percipient; and (2) knowledge of future events, *i.e.*, prescience. "Inspiration," she says, "is another word for a message from the superconscious part of mind, which has contact with a wider world than has the conscious mind."[2] Again:

> The deduction to be drawn . . . may be that the superconscious part of a man's mind is in contact not only with the conscious and superconscious parts of other living minds, but also with another field of existence where time is different from our time, and is thus enabled now and then to see the future as if it were past, as if it were the inevitable scene of a drama in which we play our already destined and rehearsed role. . . . In the course of evolution the unconscious elements in our being have been largely despised and ignored. In primitive times men were ruled almost entirely by their instincts, passions, and terrors, and the path of progress has lain along the way of suppression of these unreasoning rulers. Probably this was a necessary process, for the conscious intellect of man needed time to develop. But just as the intellect in our early primitive history was subordinated to the instincts, so in our later development the instincts have been subordinated to the intellect; or, in other words, the conscious has ignored the unconscious. Then came the work of studying the subconscious, and the tendency was to believe that all the unconscious part of the mind was in that region. Now we are beginning to understand that we have a superconsciousness as well, and that within the compass of our own being we have powers of contact with a far greater and wider life than we know here.[3]

Along the same general line is Lecomte du Nouy's thesis, in his recent work, *Human Destiny.* Biological evolution, he contends, is giving way to higher moral and spiritual evolution, as the enlargement of man's powers, especially those of the brain (to which the conscious mind seems to be closely related) produces in him greater freedom of action and hence accelerated progress. All future "evolution," he holds, will be in the realm of the moral and spiritual. Similarly, L. Ron Hubbard, in his book, *Dianetics*, makes the point that men as a rule utilize only

1. *Our Superconscious Mind,* 5.
2. *Ibid.,* 36.
3. *Ibid.,* 257-258.

a small fraction of their individual brain power in their daily life and activity, and hence fail to make the advancement (by eliminating the unconscious impressions ("engrams") which hang over them from the past) of which they are inherently capable. One is reminded, in this connection, of those memorable words of St. Paul:

> Now the Lord is the Spirit: and *where the Spirit of the Lord is, there is liberty.* But we all, with unveiled face beholding as in a mirror the glory of the Lord, are transformed into the same image from glory to glory, even as from the Lord the Spirit (2 Cor. 3:17-18).

And the Apostle tells us elsewhere that it is God's eternal purpose that those who are called through the Gospel and justified by the obedience of faith in Jesus Christ, shall ultimately be glorified—*i.e.,* redeemed both in spirit and in body—and thus conformed to the image of His Son (Rom. 8:29-30). May we not reasanably conclude, therefore, that the "far greater and wider life" alluded to in the foregoing excerpt, is in truth the life of the Being of our God, the life of the Spirit of God?

11. In a word, the phenomena of the Subconscious would seem to compel us to reject the notion that Spirit is but an "epiphenomenon" of Matter, and to conclude, rather, that Matter is a creation, or projection, of Spirit.

12. We conclude, in the second place, that the Subconscious aspect of the Self is identical ontologically with what we speak of as "spirit" in man. If so, the objective or conscious aspect of the Self must be identical with what we speak of as "mind." Mind is, then, the medium through which the spirit, the real being, relates itself to the environment in which the human organism, as it is presently constituted, dwells and functions.

13. We necessarily conclude, in the third place, that there is a personal life in man which is carried on even in this present world more or less independently of the physical organism and on a higher (metaphysical) order of being than the psycho-biological life of the organism itself; in a word, that the body is, in the words of the Apostle, merely "the earthly house of our tabernacle" (2 Cor. 5:1) in which this real self—the onto-logical man—is temporarily domiciled. In view of the fact, then, that such a personal life is carried on here to some extent independently of the body—as we know from the phenomena of the Subconscious that it is—who is able to gainsay the conviction that this personal life will persist, and persist for ever, beyond the dissolution of the body; and, provided it shall have

been possessed and moulded by the Spirit of God in this present world, that it will not only persist but also enlarge—everlastingly —in knowledge and love, clothed in glory and honor and immortality, in the very presence of God? This personal life is designated in Scripture as the life of the spirit that is in man. In the words of the "writing" of Hezekiah, the great reformer-king of Judah, "O Lord, by these things men live; and wholly therein is the life of my spirit: wherefore recover thou me, and make me to live" (Isa. 38:16). "By these things men live," that is, "the things which thou speakest and doest" (v. 15); "wholly therein is the life of my spirit." "Man shall not live by bread alone, but by every word that proceedeth out of the mouth of God" (Matt. 4:4; Deut. 8:3). The personal life of man—the life of the spirit that is in him—was breathed into him at creation; that is to say, it was imparted to him by the procession of the Spirit from the Being of God. It is an endowment of the Breath of God. God is a Spirit, and man is essentially spirit; he is therefore the image and likeness of God. But, as Bergson has put it, man in his present state is only "partially himself." He is the *personal*, but not yet wholly the *moral*, image of his Creator. The true Food, therefore, for the spirit that is in him— the Food by partaking of which constantly he may become god-like, and therefore wholly himself—the Food by partaking of which he may attain "unto a fullgrown man, unto the measure of the stature of the fulness of Christ" (Eph. 4:13) who is Himself "the effulgence of God's glory, and the very image of his substance" (Heb. 1:3)—that true Food is the living Word of the living God. By partaking of that Food, digesting it, assimilating it, making it the very warp and woof of his character, he grows in grace and in the knowledge of God, he is possessed by the Spirit of God, he lives in this present world the life of the Spirit, and ultimately attains holiness—wholeness— in the very presence of God. This—Beatitude, the Life Everlasting—is man's natural and proper ultimate end; and the attainment of this end by the saints of God will mark the culmination and the consummation of the whole Creative Process.

## 7. The Mystery of the Person

At the lowest or inanimate level of being, the procession of the Spirit from the Being of God brought into existence *energy* —the first form of which was, in all probability, radiant energy or light—which transmuted itself into matter in motion. In modern physics, as we have already seen, there is no "solid matter." If a material object looks "solid" to us, it does so only because the motion of its matter is too rapid or too minute to be sensed. It is "solid" only in the sense that a rapidly rotating color chart is "white" or a rapidly spinning top is "standing still."

At the second level, as we ascend in the scale of total being, the procession of the Spirit resulted in the implanting of the life principle in the first plant form. This remains true just the same, whether this life principle was a something *added to* the basic physiochemical processes, or whether is consisted in *the effectuating of a certain arrangement* between the basic physiochemical units or elements.

At the third level of being, the procession of the Spirit added to the life (vegetative) principle in the plant the powers of sensitivity characteristic of animal life, those powers which make consciousness possible. Thus the writer of *Ecclesiastes* differentiates between the "spirit of man" and the "spirit of the beast." In a mood of depression he exclaims:

> For that which befalleth the sons of men befalleth beasts; even one thing befalleth them: as the one dieth, so dieth the other; yea, they have all one breath; and man hath no preeminence above the beasts: for all is vanity. All go unto one place; all are of the dust, and all turn to dust again. Who knoweth the spirit of man, whether it goeth upward, and the spirit of the beast, whether it goeth downward to the earth? (Eccl. 3:19-21).

In a subsequent chapter, however, in contemplation of death the same writer's faith emerges in a triumphant answer to his own question: "the dust returneth unto the earth as it was, and the spirit [of man] returneth unto God who gave it" (Eccl. 12:7). That is to say, man is more than animal: he is animal *plus*.

And so, at the fourth level of being, the procession of the Spirit added to all previously imparted powers the attributes and potencies of a *person*. The result was a human being created "in the image of God." Hence it is expressly asserted in Scripture (1) that there is a spirit in man, and (2) that God is, in a strictly natural sense of course, the Father of our spirits.

> Job 32:8—There is a spirit in man, and the breath of the Almighty giveth them understanding. Zech. 12:1—Thus saith Jehovah, who stretcheth forth the heavens, and layeth the foundation of the earth, and formeth the spirit of man within him. Heb. 12:9—Furthermore, we had the fathers of our flesh to chasten us, and we gave them reverence; shall we not much rather be in subjection unto the Father of spirits, and live?

187

Now it seems quite probable that, speaking ontologically, the spirit in man embraces essentially all the powers of the Subconscious. In this present state, however, it embraces also the operations of the intellect, affections, and will, by means of which it—the ontological being—relates itself to its present environment. This latter aspect of spirit, which I have chosen to designate the *mind*, will, of course, have been left behind for ever when the spirit *per se*—the true "inner man"—shall have been freed from the limitations of time and space as a result of the dissolution of the physical form in which it is now tabernacled. Again, as man is presently constituted, all his characteristically spiritual powers or faculties are also comprehended in the term *person*, the designation by which, for centuries, man has been specified in the language of human thought. Those natural attributes which distinguish spirit in man from spirit in beast are (1) reason, (2) self-consciousness, (3) self-determination, (4) the subconscious powers previously described, and, in consequence of all these (5) the potentiality of holiness. All these may also rightly be said to be the essential attributes of a person. Thus either the *spirit*, or the *person*, or even the *self*, may be said to be the carrier, so to speak, of the personality. That is to say, all three terms designate the same reality which survives all change. Whether named the "spirit," the "person," or the "self," or even the "inner man," it is the essential or ontological human being that is designated. Therefore all these terms shall be used interchangeably in the present treatise.

Thus every normal human being *as such* is from the time of his conception, either in potency or in actuality, a *person*. This is his specific designation—that which specifies his position in the scale of total being, and which at the same time signifies the aggregate of all those attributes heretofore mentioned which differentiate him from the lower orders. I think that the great majority of scientists would agree to this designation and to the implications here stated as suggested by it.

In so far as his adaptation to his present environment is concerned, however, man is specified, *i.e.*, set apart as a species, especially by his power of reason. Although he shares with the sub-human orders the vegetative, sensory, and locomotive powers, it is the faculty of reason which sets him apart from the rest of creation and gives him a standing and dignity all his own. Indeed this fact is implicit in the present-day scientific use of the term *homo sapiens*. Whether he makes proper use of the power or not—and in many cases it must be admitted that he does not, but allows, rather, his reason to be controlled by his emotions, ambitions, and prejudices—nevertheless he does possess the power and possess it obviously to a far greater degree than any brute possesses or ever could possess it. The brute, of course, is governed by instinct, but instinct is quite another thing from intellection. As a matter of fact, no one knows what instinct really is: someone has rightly called it "the great sphinx of Nature." In its qualities of adaptation and unerringness it would seem to best explained as the providential operation of Universal Intelligence, the means by which God cares for His non-rational creatures. The power of reason characteristic of man, however, is something else altogether. It is the power (1) of thinking connectedly, or from *this* to *that*, etc., and (2) of thinking purposefully, that is, toward foreknown and forechosen ends; as Dr. John Dewey would have it, real thinking is problem-solving. Now this power of reason is that specific power which differentiates a *person* from all other creatures of earth. Hence Boethius' classic definition of a person as "an individual substance of a rational nature" is perhaps the best, from the metaphysical point of view, that has ever been formulated. [*Persona est substantia individua rationalis naturae.* Boethius was a Roman philosopher who lived about 484-520, and who became a convert to Christianity. His philosophy was fundamentally Aristotelian.]

Even granting the validity of the hypothesis that man is the end-product of a long-drawn-out process of organic,[2] the fact still remains that he has advanced beyond the level of the brute. This has to be true, if biological evolution has actually taken place; that is to say, if man has really *evolved from* the brute, he is *more than* brute; he is, so to speak, animal *plus*. And the plus would seem to consist essentially in his power of thinking connectedly or reasoning in terms of his own experience. This is a truth which seems to have been overlooked all too frequently by the biologists; their tendency to treat man as an animal, and as an animal only, has brought about untold confusion especially in the field of morals. Man is not merely an animal; he is, as Aristotle said many centuries ago, a *rational* animal, and no amount of "scientific" casuistry will ever alter the fact. [My personal objections to the evolution hypothesis are stated at the end of this volume.]

I should like to take the opportunity at this point to protest strenuously against the all too general tendency that has prevailed in scientific circles recently to try to reduce man to the status of the brute. Psychologists, physiologists, neurologists, and especially endocrinologists, have put forward the most fantastic conclusions and claims in recent years—claims based entirely on the results of experiments with animals. As a consequence of their too ready application to human beings of the results of such experiments, these experimenters have shown themselves unduly prone to fall into certain very grave errors, as, *e.g.*, that of making an omnibus term of the word "personality," and that, consequently, of confusing personality with temperament. The behavior of animals may indeed show a variation in temperamental characteristics, but to speak of their having "personality traits" is certainly an illegitimate extension of the term "personality," an extension that is justified neither by the exigencies of language nor by the facts in the case. Temperament is not personality, either in animals or in man. This error of attributing "personality" to the brute, however, is one that occurs in many current scientific textbooks. Even the term "animal psychology" is misleading, to say the least. These facts lead me to observe, in passing, that a great deal of confusion could be avoided in modern education if scientists in general would only familiarize themselves with, and follow, the Socratic twofold injunction to all thinkers, namely, (1) first to define the terms they propose to use in any field of scientific investigation, and (2) having defined those terms, to use them univocally thereafter. Words are, of course, the means of communicating thought among persons; only persons are *known* to have evolved language. But at the same time words can, and often do, become prolific sources of mental confusion as a result of equivocal usage. And through the overlapping of terms, modern scientific "universe of discourse" has in many instances become a veritable Babel. "Personality," for example, is a term that should be confined strictly to human beings. Animals, of course, appear to manifest certain forms of behavior which are commonly thought to be characteristic of a person. This is true especially of their "emotional" reactions (whatever the term "emotion" may signify: it has never been clearly defined). But—I repeat—it is an illegitimate extension of the term "personality" to speak of any single animal—and personality is a mystery that is invariably tied up with individuality—as being a "personality," or as having "personality" or "personality traits." By no stretch of the imagination can a brute animal properly be designated a person; and only a person—that is, if we are going to speak univocally—can rightly be considered a carrier of personality.

I should like to point out too that even among human beings "personality types" become more clearly differentiated only in the field of abnormal psychology; and, as a matter of fact, psychologists themselves have never been able to agree upon any such differentiation among normal persons, among whom it seems likely that no such precise differentiation exists. Moreover, this view of man as a sort of "glorified brute" is, as previously stated, largely responsible for the current world-wide confusion in ethical theory and practice. Indeed it is frequently offered as an alibi for looseness in morals; we should not hesitate, we are told, to give free expression to our "natural" impulses and desires. And thus human morality is prostituted into "barnyard morality," which, if universalized, would destroy the race. Devotion to this Cult of Self-Expression may explain why some of our modern writers have expressed themselves in such illiterate language, as, for example, Theodore Dreiser; it may explain, too, some of the terrible gobs hanging on the walls of our art galleries today. They are supposed to be artistic expressions —but one wonders, of what? I commend Oedipus' terrific oracle to all those who hold this brute interpretation of man: "May'st thou ne'er know the truth of what thou art!"

Man is characterized by self-consciousness and self-determination, and by the capacity for holiness, the properties of a *person*. Hence no society regards the brute as a person, for the obvious reason that no brute animal manifests these characteristics, at least not in sufficient degree to be regarded as a person. True, a parrot can be taught to vocalize "I" but no mere animal was ever known to say of its own accord, meaningfully to itself, "I am a parrot," or "I am a pig," etc. If it could, it would no longer be a parrot or a pig. Moreover, no can can ever know to what extent an animal "thinks" or "feels," for the obvious reason that no man can "put himself into an animal's skin," so to speak, in such a manner as to know what the experiences of an animal are. A thoroughgoing comparison of animal and human experience simply cannot be obtained. But every man can, by looking into himself, know what he thinks and feels and wills. And every man can and does know that he cannot teach his old dog Rover, or his old horse Dobbin, either the Ten Commandments or the elementary theorems of plane geometry. In view of all these facts, it must be obvious that such terms as "animal mind," "animal personality," "animal psychology," and the like, are not only misleading but downright illegitimate.

Psychologists seem never to have awakened to the fact that

before there can be such a thing as "behavior" or "adaptation," there must be an entity capable of "behaving" and of "adapting" itself. Hence the need of a widespread revival of what is called "personalistic psychology" at the present time—a psychology which returns to the fundamental concept of man as a *person* and treats him as such. This is as it should be, for the simple and obvious reason that man *is* a person.

Dr. Gordon W. Allport summarizes the arguments put forward by personalists in psychology to support their position, as follows:

1. Without the co-ordinating concept of person (or some equivalent, such as Self or Ego), it is impossible to account for, or even to depict, the interaction of mental processes upon one another. Memory affects perception, desire influences meaning, meaning determines action, and action shapes memory; so on, indefinitely. This constant interpentration takes place within some *boundary*, and the boundary is the Person; it occurs for some purpose, and the purpose can be represented only in terms of service to the Person. 2. The phenomenon of mental *organization* can have no significance unless it is viewed as taking place within a definite framework. Mental states do not organize themselves nor lead independent existences; their arrangement always constitutes part of a larger arrangement—the personal life. "Everything mental is a totality or a part of a totality." 3. Such concepts as *function*, *adaptation*, *use*, and *adjustment*, are of no significance without reference to the Person. An adaptation must be the adapting *of* something *to* something: so with adjustment. Use and function likewise imply an interested personal agent. 4. Above all, it is in immediate experience that the case for a central co-ordinating agent becomes unanswerable. The central position of Self is implied in all states of consciousness.. Descartes' dictum, *Cogito ergo sum*, can hardly be refuted. This argument, though cast in metaphysical terms, has psychological support in the vivid sense of the self present in experiences of strain, conflict, and choice. 5. Another argument stresses the *creative* properties of the Person or Self. Every system of thought originates with someone. The most objective of scientists, no less than philosophers, ultimately create or "will" the canons of their own science. Disagreements result in the last analysis from the individuality of their own minds. So too with psychologists. If they embrace a nomothetic positivism and empty the personality of all its bothersome individuality, they do so ultimately because they *want* to. Thus a prior act of volition is responsible for the austere limits they place upon their own speculation. We all build our scientific world from the symbols taken from our own personalities. Which then is the prior fact, the creative person or the creed he creates?[1]

Personalistic psychologists, Allport goes on to say, agree that *psychology,*

whose task it is to treat the whole of mental life, cannot possibly discharge its duty without relating the states and processes it studies to the Person who is their originator, carrier, and regulator. There can

1. G. W. Allport, *Personality: A Psychological Interpretation*, 550-551.

be no adjustment without someone to adjust, no organization without an organizer, no memory without self-continuity, no learning without a change in the person, no knowledge without a knower, and no valuing without someone possessed of desires and the capacity to evaluate. Psychology must take seriously James's dictum that every mental operation occurs in a "personal form," and must take it more seriously than James himself did.[1]

The Self is, of course, a mystery. Are "Self," "Ego," "Person," all synonymous terms? Is the Self made of body-mind? Is the real Self identical with "spirit" in man? Is it exclusively "spiritual," and dwelling in a body? I quote again from Allport, whose analysis is most penetrating and difficult to improve upon:

> To be sure, the sense of self is a peculiarly elusive datum for introspection. To catch it for direct examination seemed to James like trying to step one's shadow. In Brentano's terms, the Self, though ever present, is a matter of "secondary" awareness. Primarily I am conscious of the object to which I attend: a tone, a landscape, a menacing gesture; only secondarily am I aware that it is *I* who am apprehending, admiring, or fearing these objects. The situation becomes even more elusive when the Self is regarded not only as Knower (reflected to itself somehow in a "secondary awareness"), but also as the *ground* for that which is known. I not only know that it is *I* who perceive an object, but I feel that this object has some special significance for *me*. The intimacy of the whole conscious process is baffling, a cause of consternation to philosophers and psychologists alike. The point is that this very intimacy is one of the chief arguments in support of personalistic psychology.[2]

Again:

> The Person, like the Self, is *persistent; changes* as it develops; is *unique; is many-sided;* is the *groundwork of all its own experiences;* and *is related to its physical and social environment.*[3]

Although personality is the one fact with which we are most intimately acquainted, at the same time it is the most mysterious thing we know. The following exquisite bit of literature from the pen of Ernest Dimnet is especially pertinent at this point:

> "*Something mysterious in being a person! Why, I never thought there was anything mysterious about that. Yet I have been a person for some time.*
> "Are you sure that you have never felt the mysteriousness of being a person? Didn't you, as a child, ask questions which showed that you really did feel it?
> "*Oh! You mean the silly questions which children do ask; Why am I Johnny and not Tommy?—Why am I not a tree?—Couldn't I have*

1. *Op. cit.*, 551-552.
2. *Ibid.*, note 2.
3. *Ibid.*, 557.

*been one?—How can I be anybody with God being everywhere? All
children say these absurd silly things.*

"They are not silly, Heaven knows! When children sound silly,
you will always find that it is in imitation of their elders. But even
grown-ups will sometimes be conscious of the strangeness of being a
person. It may only be a few times in their lives, and it may only be
in flashes, but practically everybody has had that experience, and most
people are awed by it. Have you never been conscious of the space
occupied by your body and how inconsiderable it is?

*Oh! Of displacing that little space with me, as I walk and of
being shut up in it? Why, many times!*

"That is the sensation I mean. You are then within an ace of
realizing that you are an exceedingly fragile bundle of phenomena,
supported, in some unaccountable way, by a centre, a core which you
cannot locate, your Ego.

*"Why, I realize that very well, and it IS frightening. All the
strength we might derive from the consciousness that we are ourselves
is paralyzed by the realization that what makes us a person is, as you
say, so slender and impalpable. The more we think of it, the more it
seems to shrink INTO itself, till we are afraid to see it thinning into
nothing. I know that feeling of evanescence very well.*

"No doubt, for you describe it pretty well, too.

*"But why is it frightening like that?*

"Probably because it is the foretaste of our death. What is death?
The completeness of the phenomenon you describe. The support of our
personality vanishes, and suddenly it is independent of its familiar
phenomena. The simile of the soap-bubble is well chosen. The more
we think of our personality, the more afraid we are to see the bubble
dissolve into the brilliant morning.

*"Yes, evidently we dread to move from the outside world which
supports us, so far inward that we shall be conscious of nothing but
our ephemeral selves. I once met at a gloomy boarding-house near the
British Museum, a weird old sea-captain whom what we are saying
causes me to remember. He had never known, he assured me, anybody
brave enough to go to a lonely place at night, and to call his own name
out loud three times. Realizing one's own personality in that way, no
matter how simple, he thought was beyond human endurance."*[1]

It should be remembered, however, that this moving from the
outside world which supports one, into the inner world of the
Self is, in fact, a moving out of the limited world of more or
less illusion into the apparently illimitable world of reality.
As stated heretofore, the physical senses limit one's experience
to the circumstances of the external environment. Once the
person (spirit) is liberated from this objectivity, he is free to
"roam the universe," so to speak. Intimations of the illimit-
ableness of this inner world may be found in dreams, in which
the dreamer often re-enacts, in an instant or two of mathematical "time," the experiences of a whole period of his life,
or travels from one locale to another far distant without any
sense of intervening distance or space whatsoever. Even in one's
waking hours, one's thoughts transcend both time and space.

1. Ernest Dimnet, *What We Live By*, 16-17.

When I look at a distant star, for example, at what point in space does the perception take place? Does it take place within me, or does it take place where the light from the star is, at the moment of my seeing it? Or does it take place in space at all? Is "mind" a something necessarily confined to body, or is it an activity of the person that outreaches all measurements of time, distance, and space? Obviously, there is but one answer: The "inner man"—being himself the image of God—knows none of the limitations of the physical world. And death is, in the final analysis, but the stepping out of the limited illusory world of the flesh, into the unlimited real world of the spirit.

1. *A person is, in the first place, a unity.* Illingworth writes:

> The fundamental characteristic of personality is self-consciousness, the quality in a subject of becoming an object to itself, or, in Locke's language, "considering itself as itself," and saying, "I am I." But as in the very act of becoming thus self-conscious I discover in myself desires, and a will, the quality of self-consciousness immediately involves that of self-determination, the power of making my desires an object of my will, and saying, "I will do what I desire." But we must not fall into the common error of regarding thought, desire, and will, as really separable in fact, because we are obliged for the sake of distinctness to give them separate names. They are three faculties or functions of one individual, and, though logically separable, interpenetrate each other, and are always more or less united in operation. I cannot, for instance, pursue a train of thought, however abstract, without attention, which is an act of *will*, and involves a *desire* to attend. I cannot desire, as distinct from merely feeling appetite, like an animal, without *thinking* of what I desire, and *willing* to attain or abstain from it. I cannot will without *thinking* of an object or purpose, and *desiring* its realization. There is, therefore, a synthetic unity in my personality or self; that is to say, not a merely numerical oneness, but a power of uniting opposite and alien attributes and characteristics with an intimacy which defies analysis.[1]

Cases of so-called multiple personality are probably not, after all, what the name implies, but are, rather, instances of disconnected allotments of experiential data which need reintegration to effect a restoration of the original unity. About one hundred such cases have been reported at widely separated times and in different parts of the world, the most celebrated of which perhaps was the case of Sally Beauchamp, reported by Dr. Morton Prince in his book entitled *The Dissociation of a Personality,* published in 1920. The basic problem involved in this phenomenon is that of how suggestion becomes so effective and dissociation so complete in these individuals. Two contemporary psychologists have this to say on the subject:

1. J. R. Illingworth, *Personality, Human and Divine,* Shilling Edition, 28-29.

If, by way of analogy, one conceives of consciousness as being made up of many interlacing streams of thought, then some of these may meet obstacles in the form of emotional conflicts or fixations and form whirlpools which separate from the main currents of thought. When large and powerful, they may assume the form of secondary personalities, any one of which may become dominant under certain conditions.[1]

Whatever the true explanation of this phenomenon may be, the fact remains that it belongs to the field of *abnoraml* psychology, whereas we are considering here normal persons only. (It will be remembered that Dr. Prince was himself successful in re-integrating the personality of Sally Beauchamp.) Besides, even in cases of "dual" or "multiple" personality, the subliminal self may remain unified beneath the phenomena of exterior dissociation. Moreover, we must not lose sight of the distinction between the person as the ontological being, and the personality which is constructed out of hereditary and environmental factors and the personal reactions thereto; the former is, in the nature of the case, one, whereas the latter may indeed exhibit lack of integration or evidences even of disintegration. A person is essentially a unity.

2. *A person is, in the second place, a persistent unity.* The "I" persists through all changes, physical and mental. As Illingworth goes on to say:

This unity is further emphasized by my sense of personal identity, which irresistibly compels me to regard myself as one and the same being, through all my changes of time and circumstance, and thus unites my thoughts and feelings of today with those of all my bygone years. I am thus one, in the sense of an active unifying principle, which can not only combine a multitude of present experiences in itself, but can also combine its present with its past.[2]

Memory seems to be both the basis and the guarantee of personal identity. Remembering, as William James put it, is something more than the mere dating of an event in the past; it is the dating of an event in *my* past. As St. Augustine wrote, centuries ago:

I come to the fields and spacious palaces of my memory, where are the treasures of innumerable images, brought in from things of all sorts perceived by the senses. . . . Nor yet do the things themselves enter in; only the images of the things perceived are there in readiness, for thought to recall. . . . It is I myself who remember, I the mind. . . . Great is the power of memory, a fearful thing, O my God, a deep and boundless manifoldness; and this thing is the mind, and this am I myself. What am I then, O my God? What nature am I? A life various and manifold, and exceeding immense![3]

1. Carney Landis and M. Marjorie Bolles, *Textbook of Abnormal Psychology*, 98.
2. *Op. cit.*, 29-30.
3. *Confessions*, Pusey translation, Everyman's Library, 210-219.

One inescapable fact of human experience is that personal identity persists through all changes in the organism, a fact which confirms our faith that it will survive the last great change, the dissolution of the body.

3. *A person is, in the third place, a unique unity.* Says Illingworth:

At the same time, with all my inclusiveness, I have also an exclusive aspect. "Each self," it has been well said, "is a unique existence, which is perfectly impervious to other selves—impervious in a fashion of which the impenetrability of matter is a faint analogue." Thus a person has at once an individual and a universal side. He is a unit that excludes all else, and yet a totality or whole with infinite powers of inclusion.[1]

Allport writes:

The outstanding characteristic of man is his individuality. He is a unique creation of the forces of nature. Separated spatially from all other men he behaves throughout his own particular span of life in his own distinctive fashion. It is not upon the cell nor upon the single organ, nor upon the group, nor upon the species that nature has centered her most lavish concern, but rather upon the integral organization of life processes into the amazingly stable and self-contained system of the individual living creature. . . . The *person* who is a unique and never-repeated phenomenon evades the traditional scientific approach at every step. . . . Whether he [the scientist] delimits his science as the study of the mind, the soul, of behavior, purpose, consciousness, or human nature—the persistent, indestructible fact of organization in terms of individuality is always present.[2]

J. C. Smuts has this to say:

Personality is the latest and supreme whole which has arisen in the holistic series of evolution. It is a new structure built on the prior structures of matter, life, and mind. . . . Mind is its most important and conspicuous constituent. But the body is also very important and gives the intimate flavor of humanity to Personality. . . . The ideal Personality only arises where Mind irradiates Body and Body nourishes Mind, and the two are one in their mutual transfiguration.[3]

Nature is individualistic: we come into the world *one by one,* and we go out of it *one by one;* and while in it, each human individual is a unique one. As Emerson has said: "Nature never rhymes her children nor makes two men alike." My potentialities, thoughts, memories, desires, decisions, likes and dislikes, all belong to *me;* in the very nature of the case I cannot transfer them to anyone else. Nature's provision, moreover, is directed primarily toward the welfare of the individual; even the state, in the Providence of God, exists to benefit the individual. Hence,

1. *Op. cit.,* 30.
2. *Op. cit.,* 3, 5.
3. *Holism and Evolution,* 261, 262.

said Jesus, one human life is of infinitely greater value than the whole material world: "For what shall a man be profited, if he shall gain the whole world, and forfeit his life? or what shall a man give in exchange for his life?" (Matt. 16:26). The reason for this high evaluation of a human soul is obvious: every person is an image and likeness of God.

4. *A person is, in the fourth place, a transcendent unity.* A person, in knowing and evaluating and utilizing material things, however imperfectly, transcends the whole material order. Despite shallow and thoughtless observations to the contrary, the fact remains that our world is, and will always be, anthropocentric; anthropocentric, that is, in the sense that every person is the center of his own world, the world of his own experience. [Actually, the Totality of Things may best be described as *theocentric.*] And there is no evidence that any other creature of earth possesses the ability to reflect upon, or to resolve the problem—for himself at least—of his place in, or relation to, the Totality of Things. *Adaptation to environment,* for man, means infinitely more than mere adaptation to one's immediate family, neighborhood, state or nation: it means, for the thinking person, adaptation to the Universal Order, that is, a satisfactory philosophy of life. Man alone is capable of evolving for himself a *Weltanschauung.* Again I quote from Illingworth:

Personality is the gateway through which all knowledge must inevitably pass. Matter, force, energy, ideas, time, space, law, freedom, cause, and the like, are absolutely meaningless phrases except in the light of our personal experience.[1]

And again:

Now the significance of all this is that we are spiritual beings. The word spirit is indeed undefinable and may even be called indefinite, but it is not a merely negative term for the opposite of matter. It has a sufficiently distinct connotation for ordinary use. It implies an order of existence which transcends the order of sensible experience, the material order: yet which, so far from excluding the material order, includes and elevates it to higher use, precisely as the chemical includes and transfigures the mechanical, or the vital the chemical order. It is thus synonymous with supernatural, in the strict sense of the term. And personality . . . belongs to this spiritual order, the only region in which self-consciousness and freedom can have place.[2]

Personality, that which fills the capacities and actuates the potentialities of the person, is the supreme mystery of being, yet the most real thing in human experience. Nothing can ever be

1. *Op. cit.,* 25.
2. *Ibid.,* 45.

quite so real to me as my own thoughts, my own desires, my own will.

Thus it will be seen that spirit in man includes at least the following: (1) all the powers of the Subconscious, (2) the objective power of reason, (3) self-consciousness, memory, and personal identity, (4) self-determination, and, in consequence of all these powers, (5) the capacity for holiness, for man's becoming *entirely himself*.

A word is in order here about the relation of the person's power of self-determination—freedom of will, as it is commonly called—to his attainment of holiness. Dr. Glenn Negley says:

> The individual is both a Physical Man and a Social Man, and he cannot ignore either area of his existence. It is precisely the adjustment of these two factors into a harmonious unity that describes what is meant by personality, and the final category of the Individual aspect may be called *Person*.[1]

He then adds:

> I suggest that *Liberty* is the concept most appropriate to Person. As a value principle Liberty means, briefly, the guarantee to individuals of as much freedom of thought and action as is consistent with the exercise of an equal freedom by other men.[2]

But what, precisely, is self-determination, freedom of will, liberty?

Freedom of will, of course, definitely is *not* action without motive; on the contrary, human action invariably proceeds from motives. Free will, moreover, is always exercised within a framework of heredity and environment. The extent of a person's knowledge is necessarily determined by his environment; certainly he cannot will to achieve an end which is utterly unknown to him. An African pigmy, for example, who has never heard of ice, who knows nothing at all about ice, certainly would never think, wish or plan to go skating. Alternative choices are presented to the person by the circumstances of his environment, and the ends for which he strives necessarily lie within the circumference of the knowledge afforded him by that environment. Free will means, in a word, *immunity from necessity within the framework in which choice can be made;* it means that the person who chooses to pursue one course of action could have elected either not to act at all or to pursue an alternative course of action. It means simply that *the motive which prevails, out of two or more alternative and perhaps con-*

1. *The Organization of Knowledge*, 79.
2. *Ibid.*, 85.

*flicting appeals, is the motive that is more closely in harmony
with the individual will.* In every choice, three factors are
present: that of heredity, that of environment, and that if the
personal reaction. Determinists, of course, are those gentlemen
who are *determined* (*i.e.,* necessitated) to deny the operation
of the last-named factor; in short, those who are *determined* to
be *determinists.*

Now the question has often been asked: Why did God so
constitute man as to endow him with the potentiality of evil as
well as of good? Or, to put it in a simpler form, Why did He
not create man incapable of sinning? Frankling admitting that
this problem involves a basic element of mystery that perhaps
will never be penetrated by human intelligence in its present
state—the age-old mystery of the origin of evil—I answer, however, that one fact stands out as obvious, namely, that had
the Creator brought into existence a creature incapable of sinning, *that creature would not have been a person.* Sin, of
course, is choosing to disobey, rather than to obey, the Word of
God; it is choosing one's own way above God's way of doing
things. 1 John 3:4—"Sin is lawlessness." Now a creature incapable of making such a choice simply would not be a man, for
self-determination is specifically the property of a person, and
man is a person. Hence, we can only conclude that man was
constituted a person by the Creator for a specific Divine purpose or end. That Divine end, the end which was known to
God from the beginning, the end which every human being is
ordered by the Divine Thought, Love, and Will to attain, the
only end which can fully satisfy all his capacities and potencies,
is ultimate union of the human will with the Divine Will in
knowledge and love. This is man's absolutely ultimate natural
and proper intrinsic end, and his ultimate real Good. As his
ultimate intrinsic *perfective* Good, it is Wholeness or Holiness;
as his ultimate intrinsic *delectable* Good, it is Beatitude or
Blessedness. In the never-to-be-forgotten words of St. Augustine:
"Thou awakest us to delight in Thy praise; for Thou madest
us for Thyself, and our heart is restless until it repose in Thee."
This is not only the testimony of the most profound human
thought, but the clear teaching of the Scriptures as well.

But what is holiness, and how is man to attain it? For
one thing, holiness is not innocence. Innocence is a *negative*
condition of complete inexperience of temptation and sin, a
state of untried childhood, to speak by way of analogy. Holiness,
on the other hand, is a condition of experienced but *positively*

200

repudiated temptation and sin. It is a life *actively* lived in conformity with the Word of God, motivated solely by one's love for God. It is the life of the Spirit—the life of the human spirit yielded in loving obedience to the guidance of the indwelling Holy Spirit. Holiness, in short, presupposes the power of self-determination actively exercised in the direction of righteousness, and righteousness is simply doing right, doing what God would have us to do. Holiness is the cultivation, actively, of a disposition to please God in all things, purely out of the love for God in one's heart. Hence it is obvious that a necessary connection exists—that of *means* to *end*—between freedom of will and holiness; furthermore, that only a *person* can become or be holy in the strict sense of that term.

Plato, in his great cosmological treatise, the *Timaeus*, pictures the Demiourgos, the Divine Reason, as having overruled Necessity (which he designates the Errant Cause) by persuasion, rather than by compulsion, in the process of fashioning the Cosmos. The Divine Reason, in other words, was confronted by a factor which was not wholly under His control and which partly thwarted His benevolent purpose. Indeed it is difficult to see how it could be otherwise in any undertaking that is *purposive;* purposiveness *necessarily* embraces the adaptation of indispensable means to given ends. As Dr. F. M. Cornford writes, in commenting on this Platonic conception:

> The necessity lies in the links connecting the purposing will at the beginning of the chain with the attainment of the purpose at the end; we need not think of it as extending further in either direction. Reason and will are conditioned by this concatenation of indispensable means. So it is with the craftsman. If I wish to cut wood, I must make my saw of iron, not of wax. Iron has certain properties of its own, indispensable for my purpose. On the other hand, I can take advantage of this very fact to attain my end. I can make use of those properties to cut wood, though the iron in itself would just as soon cut my throat.[1]

All this implies, of course, that even Omnipotence, in any ordered system, is limited to some extent by purposiveness; the prerequisite of the achievement of a purpose is the indispensability of specific means to the forechosen end. Now as Christians, our conviction, justified both by reason and by Scripture teaching, is that God created the world and man purposefully; that the Divine end in creation is the ultimate establishment of a holy redeemed race of immortals in the new heavens and new earth

Confessions, I, 1, Pusey Translation, Everyman's Library.
1. *Plato's Cosmology*, 174.

wherein dwelleth righteousness (2 Pet. 3:13)—a race fitted to have fellowship with Infinite Holiness Himself. Granting, then, that the glorified and immortalized saint is the end-product of the whole Creative Process, the end-product divinely foreseen and foreordained from the beginning, it is difficult to see how even Omnipotence Himself could have achieved the production of this end-product without having created the natural person endowed with self-consciousness and self-determination, *the indispensable means to sainthood.* In a word, the relation between freedom of will and holiness is that of the indispensable means to a divinely predetermined end. Hence, our God created man first a person, in order that he might become a saint, and, in addition, provided him with all the necessary means of achieving sainthood. Therefore, although a person must "work out his own salvation with fear and trembling," at the same time "it is God who worketh in him both to will and to work, for his good pleasure" (Phil. 2:12-13). The result is that man alone, of all creatures of earth, is capable of ultimate union with God, ultimate holiness, Everlasting Life.

## QUESTIONS FOR REVIEW OF PART TWO

1. What is our approach to an understanding of the term "spirit"?
2. List some of the more common definitions of matter.
3. In what two categories do we classify "the stuff" of things?
4. Explain what is meant by the cosmic "substance."
5. State some of the earliest concepts of the cosmic "substance."
6. What was the ancient theory of the four "elements"?
7. State the theory of Demokritos and Epikouros.
8. State what is meant by Plato's dualism.
9. State the main features of Plato's story of the Creation.
10. What was the theory of matter held by Plotinus? What is meant by Creation by Emmanation?
11. State Aristotle's *hylomorphic* theory.
12. Explain (1) *materia prima* and (2) "substantial form."
13. Explain the "light metaphysics" of the early Oxford philosophers.
14. What are the three processes involved in immortalization? Explain.
15. What is the essential property of matter, according to Descartes?
16. What were the discoveries of Boyle and Lavoisier?
17. Explain the "building block" theory of the atom. Who originated it?
18. What is the present-day theory of the atom?
19. State the conclusions of the latest physical science in regard to the constitution of matter.
20. Explain what is meant by the Einsteinian theory of energy and matter.
21. Explain what is meant by "maximum entropy."
22. What is meant by the "ether"? What is the present-day view about it?
23. What is the quantum theory?
24. What significance is there in the fact that our most modern con-

cept of the atom is arrived at, first of all, by the way of mathematical formulas?
25. Does the Bible teach the doctrine of annihilation? Explain.
26. Explain Madame Curie's discovery.
27. Explain how the present-day concept of the atom is more metaphysical than physical.
28. Explain: "There is no mystery in the physical world which does not point to a mystery beyond itself."
29. Is sensory experience the noblest and most satisfying of which man is capable? Explain.
30. Explain what is meant by the "mystery of space."
31. Explain what is meant by the "mystery of time."
32. State the current theory of the Space-Time dimension.
33. What correspondences do we find between Spirit and Space?
34. Discuss *everywhereness* and *inexhaustibleness* in relation to both Spirit and Space.
35. What additional phenomena must be accounted for by those who would contend that atoms were the first forms of being?
36. In this area of thought what distinguishes the "non-believer" from the believer?
37. Why do we accept the view that Pure Spirit is the First Principle of all things?
38. Explain how that in the realm of Spirit we are dealing with the *qualitative* rather than the *quantitative*.
39. Show how the Biblical presentation of the Spirit of God as the energizing Agency of the Creation is in harmony with the latest conclusions of physical science.
40. What significant conclusions may we draw from this excursion into the study of the constitution of matter?
41. Explain the Pythagorean theory of the Cosmos.
42. How explain the notion of the "flowing" of a geometrical configuration into a sense-perceivable body?
43. What kind of phenomenon is sensation? By what are sensations originated and in what media do they manifest themselves.
44. To what function especially are man's physical senses adapted?
45. What are the ultimate kinds of energy that make up the structure of the atom?
46. To what does the term *sensa* refer?
47. For what reasons do we say that the raw material of knowledge is given us through sense-perception?
48. What does the Bible teach regarding the source of our faith?
49. Show that the Scriptures teach that conversion is *psychological* and not mystical.
50. State Alexander Campbell's view of this problem of the primary source of knowledge and faith.
51. What is the philosophical background of the Restoration movement?
52. Can feeling states be reliable as evidences of salvation? Explain your answer.
53. What do we mean by the statement that sensations are "atomistic"?
54. What occurs in perception, in relation to the sensations which produce it?
55. How is consciousness related to sensation and perception? Explain how consciousness brings in the problem of *meaning*.
56. Why is the jump from sensation to consciousness called "a leap of faith"?
57. Where does the distinction between physiology and psychology become apparent in the over-all process of cognition?
58. Is it possible in fact to reduce psychology to sheer physiology? Explain your answer.

59. Explain what is meant by the term "psychosomatic." How does this accord with Genesis 2:7?
60. What is the mind-body problem?
61. "Scientists make the mistake of assuming that by naming a phenomenon they explain it." Give some examples of the truth of this statement.
62. What evidence do we have in daily living that the psychical in man can move, direct, and control the physical?
63. Man is a "living soul." What does this phrase indicate with respect to the state of the redeemed both now and hereafter?
64. Is it possible to explain consciousness in terms of pure sensation, that is, in terms of the activity of brain cells?
65. State Aristotle's doctrine of the hierarchy of being.
66. What is the basic unit of every "living thing"?
67. What are the over-all characteristics of living things?
68. Describe the structure of the cell. How do plant cells differ from animal cells? What is protoplasm? What is the mystery of protoplasm?
69. What is *photosynthesis?* What great function does it serve in nature?
70. Define the cellular processes of segmentation, differentiation, and specialization. What causes cancer?
71. How is the persistence of personal identity to be explained? What does point to, in relation to human destiny?
72. What is self-consciousness?
73. Distinguish between the mechanistic and vitalistic theories of life.
74. What is meant by "spontaneous generation"? How was it regarded in earlier times? How do scientists regard it today?
75. What is the significance of Pasteur's research in this area?
76. Explain what is meant by *theism, materialism, dualism.*
77. How does Strong deal with the problem of the method of the Creation?
78. Explain Bergson's doctrine of the *Elan Vital.*
79. What is the mystery of the life process? Explain the significance of the phrase, "River of Life."
80. Why must we insist that life in *every* form is a divine gift?
81. How is the Divine Spirit related to all forms of life, both temporal and spiritual?
82. Explain the Conditioned Reflex and Watson's Behaviorism.
83. Explain what is meant by psychological materialism or materialistic psychology.
84. What is the special significance of the swing of the pendulum in our day away from materialism to extremes of cultism, mysticism, and even occultism?
85. Summarize Tresmontant's statement of the case against materialism.
86. Summarize Clutton-Brock's statement of the case against materialism.
87. Summarize the statement of Dr. Hess concerning the mind-body problem.
88. Explain how we know that truth is discovered—not formulated—by man?
89. What is the problem involved in the interaction theory of mind-body relationship?
90. Show how interactionism is in harmony with the Christian doctrine of immortality.
91. What mean we by affirming that man is more than body or "flesh"?
92. What is meant by the Breath of God in Scripture revelation? Cf. Gen. 2:7.
93. What does this Breath of God add to the being of man?

94. State Dr. Carrel's affirmation about the transcendence of man. What are man's *outreaches* and from what internal source do they come?
95. Explain what is meant by *holiness* in Scripture. Explain *Reality* and *Real Being*. How may man ultimately attain Real Being?
96. Explain again the relation between sensations and perception.
97. Explain what is meant by *simple apprehension*, the first "operation" of the intellect.
98. Explain what is meant by a *judgment*, the second "operation" of the intellect.
99. Explain what is meant by *reasoning*, both inductive and deductive.
100. List the higher activities of man which are not reducible to matter-in-motion but which transcend all his physical activities.
101. State Joad's final statement of the case against materialism.
102. What are the proofs that man was created in the image of God?
103. Explain: "In a purely material world there can never be such things as values."
104. To what may we attribute the reluctance of the academic world to explore the powers of the Subconscious in man?
105. Explain what is meant by each of the following terms: parapsychology, extrasensory perception, telepathy, clairvoyance, prescience, telekinesis, psychokinesis.
106. What is the correlation between discoveries in this field and (1) the traditional concept of the mind (or soul), and (2) the traditional concepts in the area of religious thought and life.
107. What is indicated by such phenomena as the subconscious association of ideas and the subconscious maturing of thought?
108. Summarize Ernest Dimnet's discussion of the powers apparently inherent in the Subconscious.
109. Summarize Bergson's theory of the "two selves." Distinguish between "subliminal" and "supraliminal."
110. State and discuss the interpretation of the "two selves" suggested herein.
111. With what may we correlate "mind" and "spirit," respectively?
112. What is indicated to be the *real* spirit in man?
113. Discuss the powers of the *subjective* as distinguished from the *objective* in man.
114. What is the special function of the physical sense in man?
115. Give examples to show that the powers of the subliminal self in man transcend space and time.
116. What is one of the essential functions of *spirit* in man? How may it be related to the putting on of immortality?
117. How are the facts stated here, related to the Scripture doctrines of survival and immortality?
118. What important evidence is provided by the Subconscious to prove the essential independence and imperishability of the substantial human being?
119. What evidence have we from the study of the Subconscious to authenticate each of the following: (1) the Scripture doctrines of inspiration and revelation, (2) eternal rewards and punishments, (3) progressive sanctification, (4) the law of memory, (5) the law of conscience, (6) the law of character, (7) creativity in man (mathematical prodigies, music prodigies, "idiot-savants," etc.), (8) prescience in man, (9) psychotherapeutics (physical healings, etc.)?
120. From what we know of the powers of the Subconscious, what may truly be the final state of the redeemed, known as "holiness" or "entire sanctification"?
121. According to one of the old Catechisms, what is man's end in life?

122. Explain what is meant by man's choice between growth in holiness on the one hand, and atavism on the other? What is atavism?
123. What is the essential property of life? What does this mean with respect to the Spiritual Life?
124. What are the lessons to be derived from the Narrative of Lazarus and the Rich Man?
125. What is meant by perception—by the Subconscious—of the fixed laws of nature?
126. What light do these phenomena throw upon the nature of the Beatific Vision?
127. What consequences are indicated from the healing power of suggestion and auto-suggestion?
128. Summarize Allport's evaluation of the function of religion.
129. What are the fundamental principles which underlie the practice of "mental therapeutics"?
130. How are the miracles of the Bible—especially those wrought by Christ Himself—to be distinguished from the alleged "miracles" wrought by human agency?
131. What must be our conclusion regarding the powers of the Subliminal Self?
132. Explain what is meant by psychokinesis. What are the conclusions to be made with respect to the various aspects of this phenomenon?
133. Explain the statement that these specific powers serve to prove the spark of the Infinite in man and to authenticate the Biblical teaching that he was created in God's image.
134. What is catalepsy? What fundamental fact is inherent in this phenomenon?
135. Explain Richet's analysis of the phenomena which he attributes to "a faculty of cognition that differs radically from the usual sensorial faculties."
136. How does Hudson explain what he calls the "physical power" of the subjective mind?
137. Explain ectoplasms, phantasms, automatic writing, levitation. How account for these phenomena?
138. How does Hamlin Garland account for ectoplasms?
139. Explain the statement, "Thoughts are things." How is this related to God's method of Creation?
140. Explain Lyttelton's analysis of the powers of the "Superconscious." What is meant by the term?
141. State Hubbard's theory of "engrams."
142. What is the general conclusion to be drawn from this particular phase of our subject, with reference to the Spirit of God?
143. What light does this study of the powers of the Subconscious throw on the relation between Matter and Spirit?
144. What conclusion can we draw with respect to the nature of man and the development of the Spiritual Life?
145. What is the type of being found at the lowest level?
146. What kind of being do we find at the second level and what are the specific powers which are added at this level?
147. What kind of being do we find at the third level and what are the specific powers added at this level?
148. What kind of being do we find, and what powers are added, at the fourth level?
149. What are the characteristics or powers comprehended in the term *person?*
150. What attributes in man distinguish "spirit" in man from "spirit" in beast?
151. Distinguish between *person* and *personality.*
152. What are the characteristics of the power of *reason?*

153. Distinguish between *instinct* and *intellection.*
154. What do we mean by saying that man is animal *plus?* How did Aristotle distinguish man from the lower animals?
155. State Boethius' definition of a person.
156. Describe the confusion that is caused by present-day attempts to reduce man to the animal status, that is, to treat him as a "glorified brute."
157. Why do we insist that such terms as "person" and "personality" must be restricted to human beings?
158. Explain what is meant by *self-consciousness.*
159. What was the Socratic injunction to all thinkers?
160. Can there be any "behaving" or "adapting" apart from a *being* capable of doing these things?
161. How explain the tendency in modern psychology to ignore the significance of the Self and selfhood?
162. What is "personalistic psychology"?
163. State Allport's analysis of the evidences of the Person or Self.
164. What are the characteristics of the Person or Self, according to Allport?
165. In what respects does the mind of man transcend time and space?
166. Explain how, according to Illingworth, a person is (1) a *unity,* (2) a *persistent* unity, (3) a *unique* unity, (4) a *transcendent* unity.
167. Explain what is meant by the dissociation of a personality?
168. Explain the case of Sally Beauchamp, as described by Dr. Prince. What is, perhaps, the explanation of cases of "dual" or "multiple" personality?
169. What is the significance of memory in the person? What did William James say about *remembering?*
170. Why do we say that the world is *anthropocentric?* Why do we say that is might better be described as *theocentric?*
171. Summarize all that "spirit" in man embraces.
172. What is meant by *self-determination?*
173. Explain: Freedom of will is not action without motive. Is there any such thing as *motiveless* action? What is the definition of freedom from a negative point of view?
174. In what "framework" is freedom of choice necessarily exercised?
175. How can we account for the fact that man was created with the potentiality of doing wrong? What might well have been the divine purpose in this?
176. Explain: "The price that man pays for his personal freedom is the possibility of evil."
177. What, again, are man's ultimate intrinsic and extrinsic ends?
178. What is his ultimate intrinsic *perfective* good? What is his ultimate intrinsic *delectable* good?
179. What is *holiness?* How does it differ from *innocence?*
180. Explain how the characteristics of the person are indispensable to *sainthood.* How does the power of love fit into this over-all picture?
181. In what sense does the activity of the Holy Spirit play an indispensable role in God's purpose for His saints?
182. What, according to Scripture, is God's Eternal Purpose for His redeemed? (Cf. Rom. 8:29 and 2 Cor. 5:4).

# PART THREE

# THE HIERARCHY
# OF BEING

# 1. Recap: Man's Ultimate Ends

The word "hierarchy" originates from the Greek *hierarches,* and this in turn from *hieros,* "sacred," and *archos,* "leader" or "ruler," from *archein,* "to rule." The term is used (1) to specify an ascending series of orders of holy beings, as the *celestial hierarchy* ("the angelic orders collectively"); (2) to designate a series of ecclesiastics "disposed organically in ranks and orders, each subordinate to the one above it," and (3) "a series of objects or items divided or classified in ranks or orders, as in natural science or logic."[1] With reference to the Totality of Being, as used here, the meaning of the word embraces especially the first and last of these definitions, that is, it takes in all ascending orders and ranks of being, both physical and spiritual, including both the "natural" and "supernatural."

We have emphasized previously, under various headings, that *man is a creature.* Individually or as a race he has nothing to do with his being in the world, and very little to do with the time or manner of his going out of it; and while he is in it, he is absolutely dependent on Nature and Nature's God for the air that he breathes, the water he drinks, the food he eats, and even the very ground he walks on. No amount of self-pride or self-assertiveness on his part can substantially alter these facts, now or ever.

*Man is a creature.* Neither as an individual nor as a race is he self-sufficient. Moreover, the unfailing criterion of a truly wise man is his own constant recognition of his creaturehood, in all his dealings with God and with his fellow-men. Humility, as St. Augustine was wont to reiterate, is the most essential condition to the acquirement of wisdom. This is a lesson which our age needs desperately to learn.

Again, as a creature, man—every man, every human being— his his own proper ultimate end, the end to which he is ordered by the Creator Himself, the purpose for which He put him in the world. What is the proper ultimate end of man? There can be but one genuinely satisfactory answer to this question, namely, man's ultimate intrinsic end is *union with God.* His ultimate extrinsic end is, of course, God's own glory. This universe of ours is neither heliocentric, geocentric, nor anthropocentric: it is *theocentric.* God Himself is the source and end of all things. His glory is the proper extrinsic end of His whole creation. Any other end would be unworthy of both the Creator and His

1. *Webster's New Collegiate Dictionary,* Second Edition, s.v.

creatures. But the ultimate *intrinsic* end of every human being is union with God. Ths fact is not to be wondered at, therefore, that basic in all systems of faith and practice which have emerged from the religious consciousness of humankind is the concept and hope of ultimate union with the Divine. No matter how divergent these systems may be as to the means and methods by which this union is to be achieved, the fact remains that they uniformly envision union with God as the ultimate goal of individual human attainment.

In Scripture this union with God is described as seeing God "face to face." "For now we see in a mirror, darkly; but then face to face; now I know in part; but then shall I know fully even as also I was fully known" (1 Cor. 13:12). "Beloved, now are we children of God, and it is not yet made manifest what we shall be. We know that, if he shall be manifested, we shall be like him; for we shall see him even as he is. And every one that hath this hope set on him purifieth himself, even as he is pure" (1 John 3:2-3). Such an ultimate oneness with God will surely consist of the complete union of the human mind with the divine Mind in knowledge, and the complete union of the human will with the divine Will in love, together with the accompanying illumination that such union can never be broken, that it is indeed everlasting. This is the Vision of God. This is Beatitude. This is the Life Everlasting. I am unable to conceive of eternity as merely stretched-out time, so to speak; I must think of it rather as illumination,—illumination that embraces the sense of unending duration, and that will bring to the saint the certainty of his own inalienable possession of God. For, in the final analysis of the case, *Heaven is where God is, and Hell is where God is not.*

To such an ultimate intrinsic end every human being has been ordered by the Creator Himself. The only alternative view is that of the utter purposelessness and consequent futility of all existence; the view that

> The world rolls round for ever like a mill,
> It grinds out death and life and good and ill;
> It has no purpose, heart, or mind or will.

Unfortunately for man this is the view which has permeated all too generally the literature of the past half-century; this despite the fact that it is a view which finds little support in human observation, experience or science.

To such an ultimate end, moreover, man has been disposed

by the Divine implanting within him of a will that seeks only a good in its every activity. The human will was never known to seek complete ultimate evil. Even when it pursues an evil, it does so for the purpose of gaining what the individual conceives to be an ultimate good; the saint who gives his body to be burned does so only because he regards the temporary evil as a stepping-stone to ultimate bliss. Man errs only when he mistakes and misuses *apparent* goods for *real* goods. Ignorance of his proper end, and of the proper means of attaining it, has always been, is yet, and probably always will be, the prime source of man's faults and follies. As Jesus Himself states expressly: "If ye abide in my word, then are ye truly my disciples; and ye shall know the truth, and the truth shall make you free" (John 8:31-32). (Cf. Matt. 7:24-28; 6:19-22, 6:33; Rom. 2:4-11).

Herein, too, consists the real meaning of "good" and "evil," and of "right" and "wrong." Those acts of a human being are naturally *good* which perfect his character in virtue; those are *bad* which tend to destroy his character and standing as a man. Similarly, those acts of a man are *right* which tend to lead him toward the attainment of his natural and proper ultimate end; and those are *wrong* which lead him in the opposite direction, or which tend to prevent his attainment of his proper ultimate end. *Goodness* has reference to the perfection of the human character in virtue; *rightness,* to the directionality of his activity and life.

Now it follows that, since man's proper ultimate end is union with God, in preparation for such an end he must be justified, purified, and sanctified, for the simple reason that a holy God can have no concord with impurity of heart. "Blessed are the pure in heart; for they shall see God" (Matt. 5:8). Indeed, in the very nature of things, only the pure in heart could ever hope to apprehend, to know, to realize the possession of, God. This, I repeat, has to be true because it is in accord with the very nature of things. The "nature of things," moreover, is determined by the Will of God who is all-consistent; His will is the constitution of the universe both physical and moral. Hence it follows inevitably that the God who, in creation, determined man's proper ultimate end and ordered him to the attainment of it, must have, by the same edict of His Divine Will, in the light of His Divine Intelligence, determined and ordered the necessary means to his attainment of that end. For our God, the God of the Bible, is a purposeful God. And being omniscient, He knows how perfectly to adapt proper means to their respective ends. He Himself tells us: "I am God, and there is none else; I am God, and there is none like me; declaring the end from the beginning, and from ancient times things that are not yet done; saying, My counsel shall stand, and I will do all my pleasure . . . yea, I have spoken, I will also bring it to pass; I have purposed, I will also do it" (Isa. 46:9-11).

On the principle then of the perfect adaptation of means to ends, always characteristic of the activity of our Creator, it follows that the one essential prerequisite of the individual man's attainment of his proper ultimate ends must be *the life with the Holy Spirit.* Such a life is indispensable to the acquirement of that holiness, which is *wholeness,* "without which no man shall see the Lord" (Heb. 12:14). Only by the life with the Holy Spirit can the creature "put on the new man, that after God hath been created in righteousness and holiness of truth" (Eph. 4:24). Only by the life with the Holy Spirit can men become in fact "partakers of the divine nature, having escaped from the corruption that is in the world by lust" (2 Pet. 1:4). Only by the life with the indwelling Spirit of God can men be made "meet to be partakers of the inheritance of the saints in light" (Col. 1:12). There is no other way. "For the kingdom of God is not eating and drinking, but righteousness and peace and joy in the Holy Spirit" (Rom. 14:17). How exceedingly important, then, that we frail mortals understand what the life with the Holy Spirit is and how it may be engendered within us, in order that we may live it and experience its joys, and attain its crowning recompense—Beatitude!

Finally, the beginning of this life with the Holy Spirit must be in *union with Christ,* that process which in Scripture, viewed from the standpoint of the new principle of spiritual life which is implanted in the natural heart, is described as *regeneration.* This new increment of power implanted in the human heart by the Spirit, in conversion, is the living Word of God, the Seed of spiritual life, in short, the Gospel which is the power of God unto salvation to everyone that believes. This Gospel or Word of God is "living, and active, and sharper than any two-edged sword" (Heb. 4:12)—a savor of life unto life to one who accepts it, but a savor of death unto death to one who rejects it (2 Cor. 2:16)—because the Holy Spirit is in it and exerts His regenerative power through it.

Luke 8:11—The seed is the word of God.—John 3:6—That which is born of the flesh is flesh; and that which is born of the Spirit is spirit. John 1:12-13—But as many as received him [the Logos], to them gave he the right to become children of God, even to them that believe on his name: who were born, not of blood, nor of the will of the flesh, nor of the will of man, but of God, Rom. 1:16—For I am not ashamed of the gospel: for it is the power of God unto salvation to every one that believeth. 1 Cor. 4:15—For in Christ Jesus I begat you through the gospel. Jas. 1:18—Of his own will he brought us forth by the word of truth, that we should be a kind of first-fruits of his creatures. 1 Pet. 1:23—Having been begotten again, not of corruptible seed, but of incorruptible, through the word of God, which liveth and abideth. Phil. 2:5—Have this mind in you, which was also in Christ Jesus. John 6:63, [the words of Jesus]: the words that I have spoken unto you are spirit, and are life. Col. 3:16—Let the word of Christ dwell in you richly. 1 John 5:12—He that hath the Son hath the life; he that hath not the Son of God hath not the life.

Again, the Scriptures teach clearly that the prerequisites of *union with Christ* are some four or five in number, as follows:

1 *The preaching and hearing of the Gospel.* This Gospel, moreover, consists of (1) three facts to be believed (namely, the death, burial and resurrection of Christ); (2) three commands to be obeyed (the commands to believe, repent, and be baptized); and (3) three great promises to be enjoyed (remission of sins, the gift or indwelling of the Holy Spirit, and eternal life). The whole Christian missionary and evangelistic enterprise is predicated upon the obvious fact that men must first hear the Word of the Gospel in order to believe; that where there is no preaching and hearing of the Gospel, no contact with the Gospel message by physical sense, certainly there is no operation of the Spirit, and consequently no conversion.

Acts 15:7—Brethren, ye know that a good while ago God made choice among you, that by my mouth the Gentiles should hear the word of the gospel, and believe. Rom. 10:14, 15, 17—How then shall they call on him in whom they have not believed? and how shall they believe in him whom they have not heard? and how shall they hear without a preacher? and how shall they preach, except they be sent? even as it is written, How beautiful are the feet of them that bring glad tidings of good things! . . . So belief cometh of hearing, and hearing by the word of Christ. 1 Cor. 1:21—For seeing that in the wisdom of God the world through its wisdom knew not God, it was God's good pleasure through the foolishness of the preaching to save them that believe. Matt. 24:14—And this gospel of the kingdom shall be preached in the whole world for a testimony unto all the nations; and then shall the end come.
[The fundamental facts of the Gospel are that Christ died for our sins, that He was buried, and that He was raised up on the third day and crowned Lord of all, that is, both Lord and Christ: Lord of the Universe, and Absolute Monarch of the Kingdom of God.] 1 Cor. 15:1-4 Now I make known unto you, brethren, the gospel which I preached unto you, which also ye received, wherein also ye stand, by which also ye are saved. if ye hold fast the word which I preached unto you, except ye believed in vain. For I delivered unto you first of all that which also I received: that Christ died for our sins according to the

scriptures; and that he was buried; and that he hath been raised on the third day according to the scriptures, etc. Acts 2:32—This Jesus did God raise up, whereof we all are witnesses. Acts 2:36—Let all the house of Israel know assuredly, that God hath made him both Lord and Christ, this Jesus whom ye crucified. [Upon these fundamental *facts* rests the fundamental *truth* of the Gospel, namely, that Jesus is the Christ, the Son of the living God.] Matt. 16:16—And Simon Peter answered and said, Thou art the Christ, the Son of the living God. [Jesus was His name; Christ is His title. This title, *Messias* in Hebrew, *Christos* in Greek, means literally "The Anointed One." Three classes of leaders were officially anointed into office in olden times: prophets, priests, and kings. To accept Jesus as the Christ, therefore, is to accept Him as *prophet*, to whom we go for the words of eternal lfie; as *priest*, who intercedes for us at the Throne of Grace; and as *king*, who has all authority over our thoughts and lives. Moreover, according to this Confession, He is not only the Christ, but the Son of the living God as well. Not *a* son, as all human beings are, in a natural sense, but *the* Son of God in a special sense—the Only Begotten Son of God, begotten by the "overshadowing" of the Holy Spirit and born of the virgin Mary.] John 3:16—For God so loved the world, that he gave his only begotten Son, that whosoever believeth on him should not perish, but have eternal life. John 1:14—And the Word became flesh, and dwelt among us. Luke 1:35—And the angel answered and said unto her [Mary], The Holy Spirit shall come upon thee, and the power of the Most High shall overshadow thee: wherefore also the holy thing which is begotten shall be called the Son of God. Gal. 4:4-5—But when the fulness of the time came, God sent forth his Son, born of a woman, born under the law, that he might redeem them that were under the law, that we might receive the adoption of sons.

[The commands and promises of the Gospel are clearly set forth in the following Scriptures]: Rom. 2:8—unto them that are factious, and obey not the truth, etc. 2 Thess. 7:8—at the revelation of the Lord Jesus from heaven, with the angels of his power in flaming fire, rendering vengeance to them that know not God, and to them that obey not the gospel of our Lord Jesus. [*Any message that is to be obeyed must have commands.*] Cf. *Acts* 16:31—Believe on the Lord Jesus, and thou shalt be saved, thou and thy house. Acts 2:38—Repent ye, and be baptized every one of you in the name of Jesus Christ unto the remission of your sins; and ye shall receive the gift of the Holy Spirit. [Here we have the promises of remission of sins and of the indwelling of the Spirit.] Rom. 5:5—the love of God hath been shed abroad in our hearts, through the Holy Spirit which was given unto us. 2 Cor. 1:22—God, who also sealed us, and gave us the earnest of the Spirit in our hearts. Eph. 4:30—Grieve not the Holy Spirit of God, in whom ye were sealed unto the day of redemption. Rom. 6:23—For the wages of sin is death; but the free gift of God is eternal life in Christ Jesus our Lord. [Thus we can readily see that the precious and exceeding great promises (2 Pet. 1:4) of the Gospel are remission of sins, the indwelling of the Spirit, and eternal life.]

2. *Faith (belief) in Christ,* or that Jesus is the Christ, the Son of the living God. The active principle of justification, regeneration, and sanctification in man, is faith actively exercised in conformity to the Will of God. For faith without works of faith is dead (James 2:17).

John 14:1 [the words of Jesus]: Believe in God, believe also in me. Heb. 11:6—without faith it is impossible to be well-pleasing unto him [God]; for he that cometh to God must believe that he is, and that he is a rewarder of them that seek after him. Rom. 5:1—Being therefore justified by faith, we have peace with God through our Lord Jesus Christ. John 20:30-31—Many other signs therefore did Jesus in the presence of the disciples, which are not written in this book: but these are written, that ye may believe that Jesus is the Christ, the Son of God; and that believing ye may have life in his name. Acts 8:12—But when they beileved Philip preaching good tidings concerning the kingdom of God and the name of Jesus Christ, they were baptized, both men and women. Acts 16:31—Believe on the Lord Jesus, and thou shalt be saved, thou and house. John 3:18—He that believeth on him is not judged; he that believeth not hath been judged already, because he hath not believed on the name of the only begotten Son of God. John 3:36—He that believeth on the Son hath eternal life; but he that obeyeth not the Son shall not see life, but the wrath of God abideth on him.

3. *Repentance toward Christ,* that is, "turning from darkness to light and from the power of Satan unto God" (Acts 26:18).

Luke 13:3 [the words of Jesus]: Except ye repent, ye shall all in like manner perish. Acts 17:30—The times of ignorance therefore God overlooked; but now he commandeth men that they should all everywhere repent. Acts 2:38—Repent ye, and be baptized every one of you in the name of Jesus Christ unto the remission of your sins. Acts 3:19—Repent ye therefore, and turn again, that your sins may be blotted out, etc. Acts 26:19-20—Wherefore, O king Agrippa, I was not disobedient unto the heavenly vision: but declared both to them of Damascus first, and at Jerusalem, and throughout all the country of Judea, and also to the Gentiles, that they should repent and turn to God, doing works worthy of repentance. 2. Cor. 7:10—For godly sorrow worketh repentance unto salvation, a repentance which bringeth not regret: but the sorrow of the world worketh death.

4. *Confession of Christ,* that is, confession *with the mouth* that Jesus is the Christ, the Son of the *living* God. Not the Son of a dead god (of wood or stone), but the Son of the *living* and true God. The *living* Creed of the *living* Church of the *living* God is the *ever-living* Christ.

Matt. 16:16—Simon Peter answered and said, Thou art the Christ, the Son of the living God. John 9:22—the Jews had agreed already, that if any man should confess him to be the Christ, he should be put out of the synagogue. Matt. 10:32-33: Every one therefore who shall confess me before men, him will I also confess before my Father who is in heaven. But whosoever shall deny me before men, him will I also deny before my Father who is in heaven. Rom. 10:9-10—If thou shalt confess with thy mouth Jesus as Lord, and shalt believe in thy heart that God raised him from the dead, thou shalt be saved: for with the heart man believeth unto righteousness; and with the mouth confession is made unto salvation. 1 John 4:15—Whosoever shall confess that Jesus is the Son of God, God abideth in him, and he in God.

5. *Baptism into Christ.* The Scriptures clearly teach that union with Christ is consummated for the *penitent believer—*

216

and, I should add, only for the *penitent believer*—in the ordinance of Christian baptism. For this reason baptism is explicitly designated "the washing of regeneration": "according to his mercy he saved us, through the washing of regeneration and renewing of the Holy Spirit, which he poured out upon us richly, through Jesus Christ our Savior" (Tit. 3:5-6). (Cf. also John 3:5, the words of Jesus to Nicodemus: "Verily, verily, I say unto thee, Except one be born of water and the Spirit, he cannot enter into the kingdom of God.") Hence, too, the whole Church of Christ or Christian Church—these are interchangeable names—is said to have been cleansed "by the washing of water with the word" (Eph. 5:26). The Apostle elsewhere makes this basic truth too clear for any possible misunderstanding. "Are ye ignorant," says he, "that all we who were baptized into Christ Jesus were baptized into his death? We were buried therefore with him through baptism into death: that like as Christ was raised from the dead through the glory of the Father, so we also might walk in newness of life. For if we have become *united with him in the likeness of his death*, we shall be also in the likeness of his resurrection" (Rom. 6:4-5). That is to say, in baptism, which pictorializes the facts of the Gospel— the death, burial, and resurrection of Christ—the penitent believer literally dies to sin and arises in Christ, to walk in newness of life. Hence, asks the Apostle: "We who died to sin, how shall we any longer live therein?" (v. 2). (Cf. also 2 Cor. 5:17—"Wherefore if any man is in Christ, he is a new creature: the old things are passed away; behold, they are become new." Also Rom. 8:1—"There is therefore now no condemnation to them that are in Christ Jesus.") It is in his conforming to the *likeness* of Christ's death and resurrection, in the ordinance of baptism, that the penitent beiliever is united with Him, literally betrothed to Him, the Bridegroom, whose Bride the Church is. "For ye are all sons of God, through faith, in Christ Jesus. For as many of you as were baptized into Christ did put on Christ" (Gal. 3:26-27). Language could hardly be plainer. Jesus Himself envisioned this union of the believer with Christ in baptism, in the giving of the Great Commission. He said: "Go ye therefore, and make disciples of all the nations, baptizing them [*i.e.*, those who have been made disciples, believers, followers] into the name of the Father and of the Son and of the Holy Spirit; teaching them [*i.e.*, those who have been baptized into Christ, and who therefore belong to Christ and are entitled to the name Christian] to observe all things whatsoever I commanded you: and lo, I am with you always, even unto the end of the world" (literally, unto "the consummation of the age" or dispensation, Matt. 28:19-20). Not that the water of baptism itself washes away sin: obviously it does not. But that in baptism, as in every ordinance of God of a visible character, human faith meets Divine Grace in the appointment divinely designated; and where such a meeting takes place, the blessing connected by the Word of God with that particular appointment is always conferred upon the believer. This is *always* the case, I repeat, for the simple reason that the Word of God never fails. Now the divine blessings expressly connected by the Word of God—which is the Word revealed by the Spirit—with the ordinance of Christian baptism, for the penitent believer, are remission of sins and the indwelling presence of the Holy Spirit. "Repent ye, and be baptized every one of you in the name of Jesus Christ unto the remission of your sins; and ye shall receive the gift of the Holy Spirit" (Acts 2:38). Moreover, when his sins are remitted, the beginning of the union of the penitent believer with Christ is the perfectly natural result. Thus through faith in Christ, repentance toward Christ, confession of Christ, and baptism into Christ, one who has heretofore been an alien to the commonwealth of God is *betrothed to Christ* and begins his *life with the Holy Spirit.*

Cf. Rom. 5:5—the love of God hath been shed abroad in our hearts through the Holy Spirit which was given unto us. 1 Cor. 3:16—Know ye not that ye are a temple of God, and that the Spirit of God dwelleth in you? 1 Cor. 6:19—Know ye not that your body is a temple of the Holy Spirit which is in you, which ye have from God?

Thereafter the Christian life is a growth: growth "in the grace and knowledge of our Lord and Savior Jesus Christ" (2 Pet. 3:18). "For the kingdom of God is not eating and drinking, but righteousness and peace and joy in the Holy Spirit" (Rom. 14:17). It is the life of the saint who "continues stedfastly," one whose human spirit is indwelt by the Holy Spirit; one in whom this life *with* the Spirit becomes in truth the Life *of* the Spirit, as the human spirit becomes *possessed* more and more by the Spirit of God. The final recompense is Holiness, Beatitude, the Life Everlasting—man's natural and proper ultimate intrinsic end. (The actual consummation of the betrothal occurs at the Marriage Feast of the Lamb (the Heavenly Bridegroom), at which the actual, permanent—*eternal*—complete Union takes place. (Cf. Matt. 22:2-13; Eph. 5:22-32; 2 Pet. 3:10-13; Rev. 19:7-9, 21:1-4.)

## 2. The Hierarchy of Being

Attention has already been called to the fact that the interpretation of the Cosmos as a Hierarchy of Being—*i.e.*, as a Totality whose constituent forms of existence are organized according to rank and therefore function on separate and progressively higher levels of being—originated with Aristotle. According to Aristotle, the various kinds of soul (*psyche*), ranked according to the level of being on which each exists and functions, are the vegetative, sensitive, and rational, respectively; and over all is God, who is pure Self-thinking Thought. This view has persisted, though in somewhat different forms, throughout the entire history of human thought. Alfred Russel Wallace, for example, a contemporary and close friend of Charles Darwin, held that there were three distinct breaks in the continuity of the evolution of life upon earth, namely, (1) the appearance of life, (2) the appearance of sensation and consciousness, and (3) the appearance of spirit. (It will be remembered that Darwin himself closed his first book, *The Origin of Species*, with the frank declaration that life, with all its potencies, was originally breathed by the Creator into the first forms of organic being. The last sentence of the *Origin* reads as follows:

There is grandeur in this view of life with its several powers, having been originally breathed by the Creator into a few forms or into one; and that, while this planet has gone circling on according to the fixed law of gravity, from so simple a beginning endless forms most beautiful and most wonderful have been, and are being evolved.

Obviously, these breaks in the Creative Process correspond to the beginnings of vegetable, animal, and human life, respectively. Wallace held that while natural selection may account for man's place *in* nature, it cannot account for his place *above* nature, as a spiritual being. The introduction of life (vegetable form), he declared, of consciousness (animal form), and of intellection (human form), points clearly to a world of spirit, to which the world of matter is subordinate; man's intellectual and moral faculties could not have been developed from the animal, but must have had another origin, for which we can find an adequate cause only in the world of spirit.[1] It will be recalled that both Wallace and Darwin, unknowingly to each other, had been thinking along the same general lines; that in fact Wallace had arrived at the evolution hypothesis in its broad outlines *before*

1. A. R. Wallace, *Darwinism*, 445-478. Quoted by A. H. Strong, *Systematic Theology*, One-Volume Edition, 473,

Darwin; but that when Darwin published his *Origin of Species,* Wallace hastened to make his acquaintance and became thereafter his staunch friend and supporter. Wallace may in all truth be said to have been co-author with Darwin of the theory of Natural Selection. (As a matter of fact, it was neither Darwin nor Wallace, but the German, Ernst Haeckel, who tried to develop the theory of evolution so as to make the postulate of a Creator superfluous. Haeckel (in his work, *The Riddle of the Universe*) was the exponent especially of what is properly called *materialistic evolution* (*i.e.,* evolution by *chance,* starting from forms of "energy"). He constructed his "Tree of Life" by adding a superfluity of "missing links," simply by drawing on his storehouse of fantasy. His "Tree" is generally looked upon as a joke today, even among biologists themselves.)

The same general view of the Cosmos as a Hierarchy of Being is implicit in the conception of evolution put forward by Hermann Lotze in his great work, *Mikrokosmus,* published in three volumes, 1856-1864. According to Lotze, *new increments of power came into the life process at different stages, by direct impartation from the Divine Being Himself.* Lotze's position is summarized by Dr. A. H. Strong as follows:

That great philosopher, whose influence is more potent than any other in present thought, does not regard the universe as a *plenum* to which nothing can be added in the way of force. He looks upon the universe rather as a plastic organism to which new impulses can be imparted from Him of whose thought and will it is an expression. These impulses, once imparted, abide in the organism and are thereafter subject to its law. Though these impulses come from within, they come not from the finite mechanism but from the immanent God. Robert Browning's phrase, "All's love, but all's law," must be interpreted as meaning that the very movements of the planets and all the operations of nature are revelations of a personal and present God, but it must not be interpreted as meaning that God runs in a rut, that He is confined to mechanism, that He is incapable of unique and startling manifestations of power. The idea that gives to evolution its hold upon thinking minds is the idea of continuity. But absolute continuity is inconsistent with progress. If the future is not simply a reproduction of the past, there must be some new cause of change. In order to progress there must be either a new force, or a new combination of forces, and the new combination of forces can be explained only by some new force that causes the combination. This new force, moreover, must be intelligent force, if the evolution is to be toward the better instead of toward the worse. *The continuity must be continuity not of forces but of plan.* The forces may increase, nay, they must increase, unless the new is to be a mere repetition of the old. There must be additional energy imparted, the new combinations brought about, and all this implies purpose and will. But through all these runs one continuous plan, and upon this plan the rationality of evolution depends. A man builds a house. In laying the foundation he uses stone and mortar, but he makes the walls of wood and the roof of tin.

220

In the superstructure he brings into play different laws from those which apply to the foundation. *There is continuity, not of material, but of plan.* Progress from cellar to garret requires breaks here and there, and the bringing in of new forces; in fact, without the bringing in of these new forces the evolution of the house would be impossible. Now substitute for the foundation and superstructure living things like the chrysalis and the butterfly; imagine the power to work from within and not from without; and you see that *true continuity does not exclude but involves new beginnings. Evolution, then depends on increments of force plus continuity of plan.* New creations are possible because the immanent God has not exhausted Himself. Miracle is possible because God is not far away, but is at hand to do whatever the needs of the moral universe may require. Regeneration and answers to prayer are possible for the very reason that these are the objects for which the universe was built. If we were deists, believing in a distant God and a mechanical universe, evolution and Christianity would be irreconcilable. But since we believe in a dynamical universe, of which the personal and living God is the inner source of energy, evolution is but the basis, foundation, and background of Christianity, the silent and regular working of Him who, in the fulness of time, utters His voice in Christ and the Cross.[1] [Italics mine—C. C.]

It will be noted that this analysis of the Creative Process resembles Bergson's portrayal of the operation of the *Elan Vital* in certain respects. Bergson would say, of course, that the successive increments of power postulated by Lotze—the sources ontologically of the progressively advanced types of existents—were contained within the *Elan* itself and put forth by it (or Him?) at different stages in the ongoing of the life process. Now if it were possible to identify Bergson's *Elan* with the Divine Spirit—which it is not, precisely—such a position would be in accord with the thesis which is being suggested in this treatise.

*My own thinking may be stated as follows, in a nutshell: Whereas evolution (i.e., variation, either upward or downward) may conceivably have taken place on each of the various levels of being themselves, the fact remains that the bridges or gaps between those levels have never been successfully bridged, nor do they give any evidence whatever of ever being successfully bridged, multitudinous conjectures to the contrary notwithstanding, by any purely naturalistic theory of evolution. The gaps, for example, in the Totality of Being, between (1) the inanimate and the animate, (2) the unconscious and the conscious, and (3) the conscious and the self-conscious or personal, have never been accounted for, not even remotely so, by any naturalistic evolution hypothesis. The suggestion of the present treatise is, therefore, that it was at these intervening points or gaps that*

1. A. H. Strong, *Christ in Creation*, 163-166. Cf. Lotze, *Mikrokosmus*, II, 479 ff.

*new increments of power, as postulated by Lotze—that is, that new and successively higher powers and functions, namely, those designated in the aggregate by the terms "life," "consciousness" and "person"—may have been introduced into the Creative Process at successive intervals, the introduction of each new set of powers or functions thus marking the beginning of a new and higher level of existence; and that these successively higher increments of power may have been imparted to the Creative Process by the the Divine Spirit from the very Being of God Himself. The final result is, and will be, when the Creation shall have been consummated, a Hierarchy of Being. Evolution, as a matter of fact, is a faith, based entirely on inference, and on inference that is, in many respects, very questionable.*

On the other hand, should it turn out eventually that these breaks or gaps in the scale of total being could be bridged by any theory of natural evolution or development (*i.e.*, according to Le Conte, continuous progressive change, according to fixed laws, by means of resident forces), the fact would still remain that all those potencies actuated and revealed at subsequent stages in the Creative Process *must have been inherent originally in the first existing forms.* "In order to progress there must be either a new force, or a new combination of forces, and the new combination of forces can be explained only by some new force that causes the combination." There is simply no getting around the fact of an all-embracing First Principle, that is, One who is the source and cause of all powers and functions inherent in the Cosmos and its creatures as we know them. No theory of evolution can dispense with Creative Power; and when scientists and philosophers talk about Creative Power, they simply mean that Power whom Christians reverently designate as God. All this boils down to the fact that most of the controversy alleged to have prevailed in recent years between scientific and religious thought has been pretty much a business of thinking and talking in circles.

Again, it is quite generally agreed today, I think, that *mutations* constitute about the only satisfactory ground on which the *arrival* of a new species can be accounted for. But what are mutations? And what causes mutations? Cosmic rays, it may be? But who or what causes cosmic rays? And who or what has caused the obtrusion of cosmic rays into the Creative Process, especially in such a manner as to account for the origin *progressively* of the phenomena of life, consciousness, mind, self-consciousness, and so on? Would not such a *progressive* sequence of mutations, that is, a sequence resulting in such progressively higher types of existences, necessarily presuppose a guiding Intelligence? Can any thinking person attribute such an orderly procedure to mere chance? In a word, if cosmic rays were back of the mutations, and these mutations back of the various levels of phenomena which constitute our Cosmos, then we must conclude that Universal Intelligence and Will directed the application of those primal cosmic rays to the Creative Process, in such a manner and at such well-chosen intervals, as to build up the ordered Totality of Being with which our human science makes us, partially at least, familiar. For, that there has been a Creation, certainly cannot be denied logically or experientially; that there was a time when man did not exist, and indeed an earlier time when neither plant nor animal existed, is implicit in the evolution hypothesis. Then how came all these phenomenal creatures into existence? Whether by mutations or what not, they came into existence by the operation of the Creative Power (Efficient Causality) which is the First Principle of all things. Creation did take place, whether by emanation, by evolution, or instantaneously. We Christians believe, and have every good reason to believe, that the Creative Power is Spirit, He whom we revere and worship and adore as God. It is impossible to rule Intelligence, Purposiveness, and Order—in a word, God—out of the Scheme of Things.

Again, the hierarchical conception of the Cosmos is implicit in the current philosophy of Holism, according to which the Creative Process concretes itself in increasingly complex *wholes* which mark off the different levels in the total structure of being. General J. C. Smuts, for example, defines Holism as

the ultimate synthetic, ordering, organizing, regulative activity in the universe which accounts for all the structural groupings and syntheses in it, from the atom and the physicochemical structures, through the cell and organisms, through Mind in animals, to Personality in man. . . . The all-pervading and ever-increasing character of synthetic unity or wholeness in these structures leads to the concept of Holism as the fundamental activity underlying and co-ordinating all others, and to the view of the universe as a Holistic Universe.[1]

Again he says:

The New Physics has traced the physical universe to Action; and relativity has led to the concept of Space-Time as the medium for this Action. Space-Time means structure in the widest sense, and thus the universe as we know it starts as structural Action; Action which

1. *Holism and Evolution*, 317.

is, however, not confined to its structures, but continually everflows into their "fields" and becomes the basis for the active dynamic Evolution which creatively shapes the universe. The "creativeness" of evolutionary Holism and *its procedure by way of small increments or instalments of "creation"* are its most fundamental characters, from which all the particular forms and characteristics of the universe flow.[1]

## And again:

There is a progressive grading of this holistic synthesis in Nature, so that we pass from (a) mere physical mixtures, where the structure is almost negligible, and the parts largely preserve their separable characters and activities or functions, to (b) chemical compounds, where the structure is more synthetic and the activities and functions of the parts are strongly influenced by the new structure and can only with difficulty be traced to the individual parts; and, again, to (c) organisms, where a still more intense synthesis of elements has been effected, which impresses the parts or organs far more intimately with a unified character, and a system of central control, regulation, and co-ordination of all the parts and organs arises; and from organism, again on to (d) Minds or psychical organs, where the Central Control acquires consciousness and a freedom and creative power of the most far-reaching character; and finally to (e) Personality, which is the highest, most evolved whole among the structures of the universe, and becomes a new orientative, originative centre of reality. All through this progressive series the character of wholeness deepens; Holism is not only creative but self-creative, and its final structures are far more holistic than its initial structures. Natural wholes are always composed of parts; in fact the whole is not something additional to the parts, but is just the parts in their synthesis, which may be physio-chemical or organic or psychical or personal. As Holism is a process of creative synthesis, the resulting wholes are not static but dynamic, evolutionary, creative. Hence Evolution has an ever-deepening inward spiritual holistic character; and the wholes of Evolution and the evolutionary process itself can only be understood in reference to this fundamental character of wholeness. This is a universe of whole-making. The explanation of Nature can therefore not be purely mechanical; and the mechanistic concept of Nature has its place and justification only in the wider setting of Holism.[2]

"Personality," writes Smuts, "is the latest and supreme whole which has arisen in the holistic series of Evolution. It is a new structure built on the prior structures of matter, life, and mind."[3] This "holistic" interpretation implies, unmistakably, a hierarchical organization of the Cosmos.

The same general view is implicit in the following excerpts from the pen of W. P. Montague, who writes, in summarizing a part of his excellent treatise, *The Chances of Surviving Death:*

I have tried to show (1) that the phenomena of life and mind are not susceptible of a mere mechanical interpretation; (2) that the factor that must be admitted to supplement the atoms and their motions, though psychical in nature and possessed of memory, organicity, and

1. *Op. cit.*, 318. Italics mine.—C. C.
2. *Ibid.*, 86-87.
2. *Ibid.*, 261.

purposiveness, is yet itself describable in physical terms as a field of forces or potential energies; (3) that these fields or systems of the traces of the past are of four successively emergent types or grades: the inorganic, the vegetative, the animal, and the personal; and (4) that in the evolutionary ascent from the lower and earlier to the later and higher fields, the constituent forms of energy seem to become more and more different in quality from the matter and motion of their bodily matrices, and therefore more and more likely to survive the dissolution of those matrices.

Again:

With the dawn of man a new level of life is achieved. The traces of the past stored up in memory attain sufficient strength to function in and for themselves, rather than as mere guides to bodily conduct. Instead of the past and the future and the imagined being utilized only for present action, present action is utilized for them and their enjoyment. Instead of mind as organ of the body, body becomes an organ of the mind, and the whole material set-up is, or may be, treated as the means and the occasion for personal and cultural ends. Fancy, freed from the fetters of present bodily needs, presents us with a world of waking dreams, with promises that far outrun performance and make us humble and ashamed at what we are when thought of in the light of what we might be. The human mind thus constitutes a field of forms in which there is the possibility continually present, however seldom used, of building an interpersonal community, in which the duties are to help others and ourselves to live more richly, and to grow indefinitely in every sort of power. Nor is this all, for there are intimations (and some would say far more than intimations) of *a chance of union with a higher or the highest life.* If we could share in that, our own lives, finite at their best, might be transfigured and gain a new and different prospect of continuance.

Dr. Montague describes the forward steps in the Creative Process as follows:

To us it does seem a moment in evolution when fields of potentiality attain through protoplasm the power not only to induce or reproduce their own patterns in neighboring matter (magnetic, electric, and other inorganic fields can do as much as that), but to induce those replicas with no diminution of intensity; so that life once started ramifies and spreads over the planet, conserving the cumulative heritage of its increasing past, and by that heritage evolving new forms for its future. These new forms, added to the old which still continue, make the phylogeny of life no less increasingly diversified than its ontogeny. . . . The second moment of life's evolution comes when protoplasm takes to mirroring the distant and remembering the past and thus builds up within a nervous system a private history of its own adventures by which reactions to the here and now are modified and guided. The sensory consciousness and intelligent conduct that come to supervene upon the merely vegetative seem certainly to be a definite advance. . . . The third great moment comes, and man emerges from the merely animal stage and gains a figurative freedom from the whole material world, which then becomes a footstool for his spirit and a means for realizing his ideals. . . . The personal or rational stage of evolution brings with it not only increased opportunities for life's enrichment but increased responsibility for using them. The principle of *noblesse oblige* applies to man's status as compared with that of the animal. And as between the human being who fails to use his great occasion

225

and the brute who does rise to his small occasion, the award for superiority in essential value must go to the latter. The love of a dog for his master, surmounting the sad barrier of species and of rank that separate the two, has in it an absolute and poignant beauty that exceeds the value of any far-flung human plan in which the quality of love, or some equivalent or coordinate ideal, is lacking. And there would be more point in the continuance through eternity of the poor brute being who, despite the limitations of his mental span of comprehension, could go through pain and death for loyalty than there would be in the eternal continuance of the cleverest human rogue who ever lived. These ethical comparisons of animal and human values may not be so irrelevant to the hard world of fact as they might seem. For if we translate the idealistic language of evaluation which we have just been using into the physical or materialistic language in terms of which our main discussion has been conducted, we can say that there well may be a chance that the *moral* qualities of a psychic field would be less easily reduced to mere material motions than would the *intellectual*, and therefore more likely to survive. In short, the simple goodness which animals and men can both *acquire* (rather than the rationality which man alone *inherits*) may be the main determiner of whether life continues after death, or at least of whether such continuance would hold that promise of unending progress lacking which eternity would pall.[1]

In a word, according to this author, the "fields" of existence which, in addition to the inorganic, make up the Totality of Being, are, in the order of their ascending complexity and corresponding liberation from matter and its motions, the vegetative, the animal, and the personal. Moreover, the final argument advanced by Dr. Montague, namely, that a *person's* attainment of the higher order of being which awaits him at the death of his body, depends on his cultivation of such spiritual values as faith, hope, and the greatest of all, love, — in a word, the life of the Spirit, in Biblical terms—is precisely the view that is being put forward in the present treatise. Lecomte du Nouy presents the same general thesis in his work, *Human Destiny*, namely, that the Creative Process—he calls it "evolution," of course—has passed and is passing, in the main, through some four stages: the physiochemical, and biological, the intellectual, and finally the moral or spiritual. It is difficult to see how any thinking person could come to any other conclusion.

Therefore, I should like to point out here, again, that the "union with the highest life," envisioned as a possibility for man by Dr. Montague, is precisely what the Bible teaches to be man's natural and proper ultimate intrinsic end, the end to which he is ordered by his Creator. This union, as we have already stated, will consist essentially of the union of the human

1. W. P. Montague, *The Chances of Surviving Death*, reprinted by permission of the publishers, Harvard University Press, in *Basic Problems of Philosophy*, edited by Bronstein, Krikorian, and Wiener, 614-627.

mind with the Mind of God in knowledge and the union of the human will with the Will of God in love; and the necessary preparation for such union is the life of the Spirit in the individual believer. *Heaven is a prepared place for a prepared people*: in the very nature of things, it could not be otherwise; only the pure in heart can hope, or expect, to see God. The highest achievement of the Spirit of God in the Totality of Being is the nurture of the individual person in that holiness or sanctification "without which no man shall see the Lord" (Heb. 12:14), that holiness necessary to fit him for "the inheritance of the saints in light" (Col. 1:12). *At the lowest level of Being, the inorganic, the Spirit operates as the Spirit of Power; at the second level, the organic, He operates primarily as the Spirit of Life; at the third level, that of the person whom He has endowed with the capacity for seeking and finding Truth, He operates as the Spirit of Truth; and at the highest level, that of sainthood, He operates as the Spirit of Holiness. Sainthood is fulness or wholeness of individiual personal being.* This fulness of being begins to be achieved here, in this present life, in union with Christ, who is the Divine Mind, and in the life with the Holy Spirit, who is the Divine Heart of Love. It will be fully realized in the life to come in one's complete personal union with the wholeness of the Divine Being. This is the Life Everlasting.

Moreover, even though we may be able to discern the activities of the Spirit as the Spirit of Power and the Spirit of Life, from the dim light of so-called "natural religion," not until we open the pages of the Bible do we come to know Him as the Spirit of Truth and the Spirit of Holiness. And especially is our knowledge of the Spirit as the *Holy* Spirit mediated to us through the Bible. Indeed, without the Bible, it is doubtful that we should even so much as know that there is a *Holy* Spirit.

I have shown, with some degree of conclusiveness I think, that both scientific and philosophical thought tend toward the hierarchical interpretation of the Totality of Being. The vast majority of evolutionists, and the advocates of "emergent" evolution in particular, would agree, I am sure, that there are at least four fairly well-defined levels of natural existence—those of matter, life, consciousness, and personality, respectively. As yet no theory of evolution has successfully bridged the gaps between (1) the inanimate and the animate, (2) the unconscious (plant) and the conscious (animal), although the latest

227

science draws the line very thin at this point, and (3) the conscious and the self-conscious or personal. As a matter of fact, the evolution hypothesis as a whole, despite dogmatic assertions to the contrary, is still a hypothesis; indeed it is doubtful that any naturalistic view of Creation could, in the very nature of the case, ever be anything more than a hypothesis. Of course, if these gaps should eventually be closed, that would only prove the Cosmos to be a continuum instead of a hierarchy; in either case it could be accounted for only on the ground of creative Force. As Ernest Dimnet has written: "If the evolutive theory, in spite of the strong scientific objections to it, is the most satisfactory, the elemental formless creatures in which life was first manifested contained the germ of what we now witness."[1] Indeed a feeble analogy of the operation of such primordial potencies or "seeds" might be traced in the power of such submicroscopic "blobs" as chromosomes and genes to contain and to transmit, in some manner wholly incomprehensible, physical and temperamental characteristics, and even mental endowments and aptitudes, from a parent to his offspring. The mystery of heredity is equally as profound as the mystery of creativity; it is, in fact, but another mysterious phase of the total Mystery of Life.

I now call attention to the fact that the Bible not only supports, but actually supplements and perfects, this hierarchical interpretation of the Cosmos that is suggested by science and philosophy. The teaching of the Bible is that the Creation was —or speaking more precisely, is—a progressive development, *with new increments of power—impartations from the Divine Being, mediated by the Divine Spirit and Logos—coming into the Creative Process at successive intervals, thus endowing the recipient creature in each case with higher and nobler faculties than its predecessors had possessed, and thus also clearly marking off the various grades or levels which constitute the Totality of Being.* All this is clearly indicated by the verbs used in the *Genesis* narrative of the Creation. To be explicit, the Hebrew language has three verbs to indicate the general idea of bringing into existence something which had not previously existed. First, there is *yatsar*, which means to "form" or "fashion." Second, there is *asah*, which means to "make" or to "do." Both *yatsar* and *asah* indicate the fashioning or arranging of previously created substances into new forms. Then, third, there is the verb *bara*, which invariably conveys the idea of an *absolute* or *pri-*

1. *What We Live By*, 21.

*mary* creation; that is, a creation without the use of pre-existing materials. And in the some forty-eight instances in which *bara* is found in the Hebrew Scriptures, whatever its object may be, it always has God for its subject.[1] Now the verb used in *Genesis* 1:1, translated "created," is *bara*: "In the beginning God *created* the heavens and the earth." This points to the primary creation of matter, in all probability the first putting forth of primal energy from the Being of God. The subsequent transmutation of this primordial energy into gross matter, and the arrangement of the cosmic mass into our physical universe—all as a result of the "brooding" of the Spirit of God—is described in subsequent verses. Now the word *bara* occurs again just two times in the same chapter. It occurs in verse 21, to indicate the transition from the vegetable (unconscious) to the animal (conscious) level: "And God *created* the great sea-monsters, and every living creature that moveth, wherewith the waters swarmed, after their kind, and every winged bird after its kind," etc. It occurs again in verse 27, to indicate the advance from the animal (conscious) to the human or personal (self-conscious) level: "And God *created* man in his own image, in the image of God created he him; male and female created he them." It is significant, too, that the two verbs, *bara* and *asah*, are used together in *Genesis* 2:3: "And God blessed the seventh day, and hallowed it; because that in it he rested from all his work which God had *created* and *made*." Does not the use of the two verbs, side by side, in this passage clearly differentiate *primary* creation from creation through *secondary* causes? In short, "create" is the term used to describe the introduction of an element or increment of power which cannot be explained by what had gone before. Intermediate acts may have been of an "evolutionary" character, that is, the readjustment of material already present to form new combinations; hence the verb used to describe them is not "create" but "make."

Thus it will be seen that at least three stages in Creation are clearly marked out in the Biblical narrative. These are the beginnings (1) of matter, (2) of conscious life, and (3) of self-conscious life. For some strange reason, the transition from the inorganic to the organic is not as clearly indicated in the Biblical account. Does the Divine command, then, in verse 11: "Let the earth put forth grass, herbs yielding seed, and fruit-trees bear-

1. Robert Young, *Analytical Concordance to the Bible*, Twentieth American Edition, Revised Throughout (Twelfth Printing) by Wm. B. Stevenson. *s.v.*

ing fruit after their kind, wherein is the seed thereof, upon the earth," etc., indicate the cooperation of God with secondary causes proceeding from the earth, or from matter (spontaneous generation), as many of the Church Fathers believed? On the face of it, it would seem so. At any rate, it is quite clear that at each of the three successive advances clearly marked out—the beginnings of matter, of conscious life, and of self-conscious life, respectively—new increments of power came into the Creative Process from the Being of God, imparted as we shall see later by the activity of the Spirit in conformity with the edict (Word) of the Divine Reason. Thus the Spirit brooded over empty illimitable Space at the "beginning" and the energy was produced which transmuted itself into matter in motion. (It is significant, I think, that the Greek word *Chaos* meant originally "empty, immeasurable space." Hesiod, who personifies the concept, represents Chaos as the first state of existence, the rude and unformed mass out of which the universe was created.[1] Thus did early tradition support the Biblical revelation.) At the next forward step in the Creative Process, the Breath of God, in conformity with the Word as always, issued forth to implant the vital principle, the principle of vegetation, in the first plant form. This remains true whether this vital principle imparted by the Spirit was a *new* increment of power, an added vital force, or whether it was the result of a recombination of atoms in such a way as to actuate potencies which had been implanted in them originally. For "in order to progress there must be either a new force, or a new combination of forces, and the new combination of forces can be explained only by some new force that causes the combination." Besides all this, plant life had to come before animal and human life, for the simple reason that the latter forms subsist on it. This is in accord with the very nature of things as we know them.

At the third advance, the Breath of God issued forth again, in conformity with the Word, the edict of the Almighty, to implant the principle of consciousness in the primordial animal form.

Gen. 6:17, [the words of God to Noah]: And I, behold, I do bring the flood of waters upon the earth to destroy all flesh, wherein is the breath of life, from under heaven, etc. [Similarly, in Gen. 7:21-22, we read that in the Great Deluge in Noah's time] all flesh died that moved upon the earth, both birds, and cattle, and beasts, and every creeping thing that creepeth upon the earth, and every man; all in whose

1. *Theogony*, 116.

nostrils was the breath of the spirit of life, all that was on the dry land, died.

Obviously, in the case of the animal, the "breath" or "spirit" of life includes consciousness, in addition to the purely vegetative life (the cellular processes which contain the secret of growth) of the plant.

[Cf. Eccl. 3:21]—Who knoweth the spirit of man, whether it goeth upward, and the spirit of the beast, whether it goeth downward to the earth?

And finally, at the next advance in the Creative Process, after all things had been made ready for the new creature who was to take his place upon the earth as lord tenant, the Breath of God accompanied by the Word issued forth again, this time to endow the natural man with all the potencies of person and potentialities of personality. "And Jehovah God formed man of the dust of the ground, and breathed into his nostrils the breath of life; and man became a living soul" (Gen. 2:7). Thus did "God create man in his own image, in the image of God created he him" (Gen. 1:27). As the patriarch Job put it: "For my life is yet whole in me, and the spirit of God is in my nostrils" (Job 27:3). And the Psalmist writes in like vein, with reference to the Creation as a whole: "By the word of Jehovah were the heavens made, and all the host of them by the breath of his mouth. . . . For he spake, and it was done; He commanded, and it stood fast" (Psa. 33:6, 9).

Now some very important questions arise at this point: Is the human (personal) order the last and highest level in the Totality of Being? Is the natural man the final product of the activity of the Divine Spirit? Did the Creative Process come to an end with the breathing of the spirit of life into the first human form? I can see no necessity for answering these questions in the affirmative. As a matter of fact, it is at this point especially that the Bible supplements science and brings to completeness the true picture of the total Life Process. It is my conviction that what is called "regeneration" in Scripture is, after all, but *the second stage*—or shall we say *fifth—in the whole Creative Process*, the stage provided for in the Plan of God, no doubt, in conformity with the Divine foreknowledge of man's fall into sin; that above the level of the "natural" man is that of the "spiritual" man—*the order of sainthood*, the highest level attainable by any creature in the Totality of Being, and *the ultimate goal of the whole Creative Process*. In a word, the order of progression for man, as willed by the Creator, is from

231

the Kingdom of Nature, through the Kingdom of Grace, into the Kingdom of Glory.

The thesis of this work is that God planned from before the "foundation" of the world the building of a holy race fitted to have perfect fellowship with Him ultimately in an environment purged of all evil. For it must be remembered that only a holy being *could* have unhindered access to, and fellowship with, our holy God. "Blessed are the pure in heart; for they shall see God" (Matt. 5:8). God has ordained us *as persons* to ultimate union with Himself in knowledge and love, and this union is possible of realization only as a result of our living the life with the Holy Spirit (that is, unbroken companionship with Him as our ever-present indwelling Advocate, Guide, and Sanctifier), and thus becoming—each of us—"partakers of the divine nature" (2 Pet. 1:4). This life with the Spirit (or *of* the Spirit, in the sense and to the extent that the Holy Spirit possesses the human spirit) begins, as we have already made clear, in our union with Christ in faith, repentance, confession and baptism.

Rom. 6:4-5 again: "We were buried therefore with him through baptism into death; that like as Christ was raised from the dead through the glory of the Father, so we also might walk in newness of life. For if we have become united with him in the likeness of his death, we shall be also in the likeness of his resurrection. 1 John 5:12—He that hath the Son hath the life; he that hath not the Son of God hath not the life. 1 John 1:3—yea, and our fellowship is with the Father, and with his Son Jesus Christ. John 17:3—[the words of Jesus Himself]: And this is life eternal, that they should know thee, the only true God, and him whom thou didst send, even Jesus Christ. 2 Cor. 11:2—For I am jealous over you with a godly jealousy: for I espoused you to one husband, that I might present you as a pure virgin to Christ.

From baptism on to the death of the body, this Life with the Spirit is a process of continuous growth "in the grace and knowledge of our Lord and Savior Jesus Christ" (2 Pet. 3:18), which is equivalent to that "sanctification without which no man shall see the Lord" (Heb. 12:14). Thus by the processes Scripturally designated *regeneration* and *sanctification,* men are redeemed from both the guilt and the practice of sin. Then, according to the teaching of the Scriptures, *the ultimate phase of the Creative Process* will take place in the redemption of the body from the consequences of sin, namely, physical disease, suffering, and death, in the putting on of immortality.

Rom. 8:22-23: For we know that the whole creation groaneth and travaileth in pain together until now. And not only so, but ourselves also, who have the first-fruits of the Spirit, even we ourselves groan within ourselves, waiting for our adoption, to wit, the redemption of our body. Phil. 3:20-21: For our citizenship is in heaven; whence also we wait for a Savior, the Lord Jesus Christ: who shall fashion anew the body of our humiliation, that it may be conformed to the body of his glory, according to the working whereby he is able even to subject all things unto himself. 2 Cor. 5:1-4: For we know that if the earthly house of our tabernacle be dissolved, we have a building from God, a house not made with hands, eternal, in the heavens. For verily in this we groan, longing to be clothed upon with our habitation which is from heaven: if so be that being clothed we shall not be found naked. For indeed we that are in this tabernacle do groan, being burdened; not for that we would be unclothed,, but clothed upon, that what is mortal may be swallowed up of life. Now he that wrought us for this very thing is God, who gave unto us the earnest of the Spirit. Rom. 8:11—But if the Spirit of him that raised up Jesus from the dead dwelleth in you, he that raised up Christ Jesus from the dead shall give life also to your mortal bodies through his Spirit that dwelleth in you. 1 Cor. 15:44-58: If there is a natural body, there is also a spiritual body. So also it is written, The first man Adam became a living soul. The last Adam became a life-giving spirit. Howbeit that is not first which is spiritual, but that which is natural. The first man is of the earth, earthy: the second man is of heaven. As is the earthy, such are they also that are earthy: and as is the heavenly, such are they also that are heavenly. And as we have borne the image of the earthy, we shall also bear the image of the heavenly. Now this I say, brethren, that flesh and blood cannot inherit the kingdom of God; neither doth corruption inherit incorruption. Behold, I tell you a mystery: We all shall not sleep, but we shall all be changed, in a moment, in the twinkling of an eye, at the last trump: for the trumpet shall sound, and the dead shall be raised incorruptible, and we shall be changed. For this corruptible must put on incorruption, and this mortal must put on immortality. But when this corruptible shall have put on incorruption, and this mortal shall have put on immortality, then shall come to pass the saying that is written, Death is swallowed up in victory. O death, where is thy victory? O death, where is thy sting? The sting of death is sin; and the power of sin is the law. But thanks be to God, who giveth us the victory through our Lord Jesus Christ. Wherefore, my beloved brethren, be ye stedfast, unmovable, always abounding in the work of the Lord, foreasmuch as ye know that your labor is not in vain in the Lord.

The consummation of the Creative Process, indeed of the Divine Plan of the Ages, will be realized in the ultimate conformity of God's saints to the image of His Son.

Rom. 8:28-30: And we know that to them that love God all things work together for good, even to them that are called according to his purpose. For whom he foreknew, he also foreordained to be conformed to the image of his Son, that he might be the first-born among many brethren: and whom he foreordained, them he also called; and whom he called, them he also justified; and whom he justified, them he also glorified.

And thus at the end of the age, "the spirits of just men made perfect" (Heb. 12:23), that is, clothed in "glory and honor and incorruption" (Rom. 2:7)—in a word, the immortalized saints of God—will take their rightful place in "new heavens and a

233

new earth, wherein dwelleth righteousness" (2 Pet. 3:13). Then, the wicked also having gone to their proper place, the place of eternal segregation "prepared for the devil and his angels" (Matt. 25:41)—the penitentiary of the moral universe—this renovated earth will have been purged for ever of every form of sin and death: mortality itself will have been "swallowed up of life" (2 Cor. 5:4). Then indeed will that glorious vision which was vouchsafed the beloved John on the barren isle of Patmos, be actualized.

> And I saw a new heaven and a new earth: for the first heaven and the first earth are passed away; and the sea is no more. And I saw the holy city, new Jerusalem, coming down out of heaven from God, made ready as a bride adorned for her husband. And I heard a great voice out of the throne saying, Behold, the tabernacle of God is with men, and he shall dwell with them, and they shall be his peoples, and God himself shall be with them, and be their God; and he shall wipe away every tear from their eyes: and death shall be no more; neither shall there be mourning, nor crying, nor pain, any more: the first things are passed away. And he that sitteth on the throne said, Behold, I make all things new, and he saith, Write: for these words are faithful and true (Rev. 21:1-5).

Faith proclaims this to be, in Tennyson's well-known words, that

. . . . one far-off divine event,
To which the whole creation moves.

This, I firmly believe, is the will and plan of our God; and because it is His will, it will be done. "For," says He, "I am God, and there is none else; I am God, and there is none like me; declaring the end from the beginning, and from ancient times things that are not yet done; saying, My counsel shall stand, and I will do all my pleasure. . . . Yea, I have spoken, I will also bring it to pass; I have purposed, I will also do it" (Isa. 46:9-11).

*On the basis of this Weltanschauung, the fundamental facts of the Christian religion—the Incarnation, the Atonement, and the Resurrection—are integral parts, or events, of the total Plan of the Universe. And Redemption is but the consummating phase of the total Creative Process.*

On this view too, just as the Bible teaches, new increments of power come into the Life Process, by the agency of the Spirit and through the instrumentality of the Word, the incorruptible seed which "liveth and abideth" (1 Pet. 1:23), by which the "natural" man is regenerated and raised to the status of the spiritual man. By the reception of the living Word into his heart—the Gospel which is "*the* power of God unto salvation

234

to every one that believeth" (Rom. 1:16), because the life-giving power of the Spirit is in it and is exercised through it—the natural person is elevated to the level of sainthood, the highest level in the total Hierarchy of Being; he is literally "the new man, that after God hath been *created* in righteousness and holiness of truth" (Eph. 4:24). "For we are his workmanship, created in Christ Jesus for good works, which God afore prepared that we should walk in them" (Eph. 2:10). "Wherefore if any man is in Christ, he is a new creature: the old things are passed away; behold, they are become new" (2 Cor. 5:17). The natural man can no more transform himself into the spiritual man by merely tugging at his own bootstraps, so to speak, than the grain of wheat can, by any power of its own, transform itself into a watermelon seed. As in the biological realm, wheat begets wheat only, and barley begets barley, and so on; so in the moral realm, only the Spirit of God can beget that which is Spiritual. "Each after its own kind" (Gen. 1:11, 21, 25) is as truly a law of the moral world as it is a law of the natural world. As Jesus Himself put it, in His conversation with Nicodemus: "That which is born of the flesh is flesh; and that which is born of the Spirit is spirit. Marvel not that I said unto thee, Ye must be born anew" (John 3:6-7) Thus by the process known in Scripture as *regeneration*, a new life is born, a new *kind* of life, spiritual life, which, if properly nurtured by the means appointed by Divine Grace, will enlarge and deepen into the Life Everlasting in the very presence of our God.

Thus it will be seen that the highest level in the total Hierarchy of Being is that of *sainthood*. All Christians were known as saints, in apostolic times.

Acts 9:13—But Ananias answered, Lord, I have heard from many of this man, how much evil he did to thy saints at Jerusalem. Rom. 1:7 —Paul . . . to all that are in Rome, beloved of God, called to be saints. 1 Cor. 1:1-2: Paul, called to be an apostle of Jesus Christ . . . unto the church of God which is at Corinth, even them that are sanctified in Christ Jesus, called to be saints, with all that call upon the name of our Lord Jesus Christ in every place, their Lord and ours. 2 Cor. 1:1—Paul, an apostle of Christ Jesus through the will of God . . . unto the church of God which is at Corinth, with all the saints that are in the whole of Achaia. Eph. 1:1—Paul, an apostle of Jesus Christ through the will of God, to the saints that are at Ephesus, and the faithful in Christ Jesus. Phil. 1:1—Paul and Timothy, servants of Christ Jesus, to all the saints in Christ Jesus that are at Philippi. Eph. 1:18—what the riches of the glory of his inheritance in the saints. Col. 1:12—giving thanks unto the Father, who made us meet to be partakers of the inheritance of the saints in light. 1 Cor. 6:2, 3— Know ye not that the saints shall judge the world? . . . Know ye not that we shall judge angels? 2 Thess. 1:10—when he shall come to be glorified in his saints, etc., etc., etc.

The saints of God—sons and daughters of the Almighty (2 Cor. 6:18), heirs of God and joint-heirs with Christ (Rom. 8:17)— constitute "the general assembly and church of the firstborn who are enrolled in heaven" (Heb. 12:23).

[Again] Phil. 3:20-21: For our citizenship is in heaven; whence also we wait for a Savior, the Lord Jesus Christ: who shall fashion anew the body of our humiliation, that it may be conformed to the body of his glory, according to the working whereby he is able even to subject all things unto himself.

And on this level of sainthood, the Spirit of God operates, in regeneration and in sanctification, as the Spirit of Holiness. Holiness is Wholeness. And it is the task of the Spirit of God to make the world and man *whole,* so that in the finality of things God may look out upon His creation, as He did at the beginning, and pronounce it *good.* In the words of Paul:

For as in Adam all die, so also in Christ shall all be made alive. But each in his own order: Christ the firstfruits; then they that are Christ's, at his coming. Then cometh the end, when he shall deliver up the kingdom to God, even the Father; when he shall have abolished all rule and all authority and power. For he must reign, till he hath put all his enemies under his feet. The last enemy that shall be abolished is death. For, He put all things in subjection under his feet. But when he saith, All things are put in subjection, it is evident that he is excepted who did subject all things unto him. And when all things have been subjected unto him, then shall the Son also himself be subjected to him that did subject all things unto him, that God may be all in all [1 Cor. 15:22-28].

I feel that I should comment briefly at this point on *evolution* and *evolutionism.* The former word, of course, is used to designate the alleged *process;* the latter, to designate the *hypothesis.* The chief protest by Christians with respect to evolutionism is a protest against the blowing up of the theory into a dogma. A dogma is a proposition to be accepted on the ground that it has been proclaimed by the proper authority; in this case, of course, the "proper authority" is human science. (We must not forget that science becomes at time *very, very human.*) Evolution is presented in many high school and college textbooks as an *established fact;* and in others, the inference that it is factual is expressed by innuendo, with the accompanying inference that persons who refuse to accept it are naive, childish, or just plain ignoramuses. It seems to be assumed by the devotees of the cult that they have a monopoly of the knowledge of this particular subject. The fact is that much of the material appearing in these textbooks is simply "parroted" by teachers who are so ignorant of Biblical teaching they are not even remotely qualified to pass judgment on the matter. Unfortunately too many persons of eminence in certain highly specialized fields are prone to break into print on various aspects of Biblical doctrine only to prove by their statements that they are completely uninformed on the subjects on which they choose to expatiate. Pernicious fallacies, based on the authority of a great name, thus have a way of persisting from generation to generation even though they have been shown many times to be fallacies. (In logic, this is known as the *argumentum ad verecundiam.*) I would have believed, in earlier times, almost anything Henry Ford the First said about the production and marketing of an automobile. But when he broke into print on matters of politics or religion, I would not believe anything he had to say on these subjects: by his very statements he demonstrated his colossal ignorance of both. The theory of the "big lie" has merit, undoubtedly, as first proclaimed by Thrasymachus in Plato's *Republic,* and by Adoph Hitler in his *Mein Kampf;* that is, if you want people to accept any—even the most absurd—proposition, state it vigorously and *repeatedly,* and the power of suggestion will eventually elevate it to a matter of faith and *stamp it in,* so that no one will dare to question it. This, of course, is the danger of present-day "brainwashing" under totalitarian systems. This is precisely what is being done to the hypothesis of evolutionism (as LeConte has put it, the notion of "continuous progressive change, according to fixed laws, by means of resident forces"). As a matter of fact, evoluton is *not* a fact—it is still a *hypothesis,* a kind of "sophisticated guess." Evidence to support it is derived not from *established fact*—that is, by the testimony of eye-witnesses—but on evidence that is *inferential* in character. The important questtion, therefore, is this: Is the inference drawn from alleged phenomena in this field *necessary inference*—that is, inference, the opposite of which is inconceivable? Or does much of it savor of little more than conjecture? Dr. James Jauncey states the case clearly in these words:

Of course you will often hear from some enthusiastic evolutionists that evolution is now indisputable, that is has been proved beyond doubt, and that anyone who disputes this is an ignoramus or a fanatic. This is jumping the gun, to say the least. The vehemence of such statements makes one suspect that the speakers are trying to convince themselves. When a scientific theory crystallizes into law, such as that of relativity, it speaks for itself. All we can say at the moment is that evolution is generally accepted, possibly because of the lack of any scientific alternative, but with serious misgivings on the adequacy of some aspects of it. As for the kind of rigorous proof that science

237

generally demands, it still isn't there. Indeed, some say that because of the philosophical aspects of the theory, that proof will never be possible.[1]

A clear example of the "blind spots" which seem to characterize the devotees of evolutionism is the title of an article which appeared not too long ago in a well-known periodical, (*Reader's Digest*), viz., "Can Science Produce Life?" This title is misleading, to say the least: life never was produced (created) by human agency. This fact, the author of the article in question, seems to realize. Toward the end, he writes, with reference to *microspheres* ("proteinoids" formed by the fusion of amino acids):

> Although these spheres are not true cells—they have no DNA genes and they are simpler than any contemporary life—they do not possess many cellular properties. They have stability; they keep their shapes indefinitely. They stain in the same way as the present-day protein in cells, an important chemical test. But the real significance of these microspheres is that scientists do not *synthesize* them piece by piece, they simply set up the right *conditions*—and microspheres produce themselves.

Thus it will be noted that the eminent scientist-author of this article flatly contradicts the import of the title, by stating that man can only set up the conditions necessary to the production of microspheres but cannot himself do the "producing." The title of the article is, in fact, an excellent example of the manner in which careless use of language can spread confusion. Man indeed sets the precondition, but only the God of nature, as the cosmic Efficient Cause, can actualize the life process.

Nor should we overlook the *practical* ("pragmatic") effect of evolutionism. This is so clearly stated by one of my ministerial colleagues that I feel justified in presenting here what he says regarding this aspect of the subject, as follows.

> Why do some have so little regard for life? Why are the rebels so careless with their own lives and the lives of others? Why do some think so little of their lives as to ruin their health in dissipation and drugs? One reason is faith in evolution. To the evolutionist life is no more than a tiny step in a long process of happenstance. There is no purpose for it and no plan, since there is no planner. One simply exists under prevailing conditions, and has no obligation to the past or hope for the future. His life is an accident, an interval, and with no intrinsic meaning. After millions of years perhaps a better breed and better condition might happen, but then that is of no value to our present generation. No wonder that so many young people, under this depressing conviction, space out on drugs, cop out and foul up their lives in sin. They do not love life! They may love pleasure, but have no love for living, and the things they may do in this frame of mind tend to destroy chances for a good lfe.[2]

1. *Science Returns to God*, 57.
2. Curtis Dickinson, *The Witness*, March, 1972, Lubbock, Texas.

## 3. God's Ministering Spirits

The presentation here of the Totality of Things as a Hierarchy of Being would be incomplete without the inclusion of a word regarding angels. Although, as Strong puts it,

the scholastic subtleties which encumbered this doctrine in the Middle Ages, and the exaggerated representations of the power of evil spirits which then prevailed, have led, by a natural reaction, to an undue depreciation of it in more recent times.[1]

the fact remains neverthless, that the activity of angels plays a very important role in the Bible record of God's dealings with men. Indeed, angels figure prominently in the unfolding of the Plan of Redemption from beginning to end. Reason, moreover, supports this Biblical presentation in pointing to the need of an order of creatures intermediate between God, who is pure Spirit, and man, who in his present state is a body-spirit unity, a living soul. Without such an intermediate order, there would be a very noticeable gap in the Creation. Now, according to Scripture, it is the angelic order—an order of beings possessed of superhuman, yet finite, intelligence and power—which fills this gap, in the total structure of Reality. Thus with the angels the hierarchical picture of the universe becomes complete.

Scripture teaching regarding the angelic order and their function may be summarized briefly as follows:

1. *Angels are created beings.*

Psa. 148:2, 5: Praise ye him, all his angels; praise ye him, all his host. . . . For he commanded, and they were created. Col. 1:16—for in him [Christ] were all things created, in the heavens and upon the earth, things visible and things invisible, whether thrones or dominions or principalities or powers; all things have been created through him and unto him." 1 Pet. 3:22—Jesus Christ, who is on the right hand of God, having gone into heaven; angels and authorities and powers being made subject unto him.

God alone is The I AM, HE WHO IS, the uncreated and eternal One.

2. *Angels are older than, and distinct from, man.*

1 Cor. 6:3—Know ye not that we shall judge angels? [that is, we, the saints of God]. Heb. 1:14—Are they [angels] not all ministering spirits, sent forth to do service for the sake of them that shall inherit salvation? Heb. 2:16—For verily not to angels doth he [Christ] give help, but he giveth help to the seed of Abraham. [Authorized Version]— For verily he took not on him the nature of angels, but he took on him the seed of Abraham. [*Angels are not glorified human spirits, i.e.,* spirits of the righteous dead. Heb. 12:22-23—here the *innumerable hosts of angels* are distinguished clearly from *the general assembly*

1. A. H. Strong, *Systematic Theology*, One-Volume Edition, 443.

*and church of the firstborn,* and also from *the spirits of just men made perfect.* That angels existed prior to man is evident from the various passages which clearly imply that the fall of Lucifer took place before the fall of man, *Vide* Gen. 3;1, John 8:44, 1 Tim. 3:6, 2 Cor. 11:3].

3. *Angels are personal* (*i.e., intelligent and voluntary*) beings. Being personal, and hence possessed of the power of self-determination, they were capable of disobeying God, and indeed some of them did rebel against the Divine government, under the leadership of Satan, and did in this manner fall from their original estate.

(1) [Angels have intelligence and will.] 2 Sam. 14:20—my lord is wise, according to the wisdom of an angel of God, to know all things that are in the earth. Luke 4:34—[here an evil spirit—fallen angel— is represented as saying], What have we to do with thee, Jesus thou Nazarene? art thou come to destroy us? I know thee who thou art, the Holy One of God. James 2:19—Thou believest that God is one; thou doest well: the demons also believe and shudder [cf.Matt. 8:29-31; Mark 1:24, 5:7; Acts 16:16-18, 19:15, etc.]. 2 Tim. 2:26—and they may recover themselves out of the snare of the devil, having been taken captive by him unto his will. Rev. 12:12—Woe for the earth and for the sea; because the devil is gone down unto you, having great wrath, knowing that he hath but a short time.

(2) [Angelic power and intelligence, however, though superhuman, have fixed limits.] Matt. 24:36—But of that day and hour knoweth no one, not even the angels of heaven. 1 Pet. 1:12—these things, which now have been announced unto you through them that preached the gospel unto you by the Holy Spirit sent forth from heaven: which things angels desire to look into. Eph. 3:9-10: to make all men see what is the dispensation of the mystery which for ages hath been hid in God who created all things; to the intent that now unto the principalities and the powers in the heavenly places might be made known through the church the manifold wisdom of God. [Here the phrase], the principalities and the powers in the heavenly places, [evidently alludes to the angelic host, whose natural habitat is heaven, the presence of God.]

(3) [Power seems to be the outstanding attribute of the angelic nature, rather than intelligence or beauty.] Psa. 103:20—Bless Jehovah, ye his angels, that are mighty in strength, that fulfill his word, hearkening unto the voice of his word. 2 Thess. 1:7-8: at the revelation of the Lord Jesus from heaven with the angels of his power in flaming fire,, rendering vengeance to them that know not God, and to them that obey not the gospel of our Lord Jesus. 2 Pet. 2:11—whereas angels, though greater [than men] in might and power, etc. [Power is the attribute ascribed in Scripture to evil spirits especially, as evident from such characteristic phrases as "the prince of this world" (John 12:31), "the god of this world" (2 Cor. 4:4), "the prince of the powers of the air" (Eph. 2:2), "the power of darkness" (Cor. 1:13), "the great dragon" (Rev. 12:9), etc.] Cf. Eph. 6:12—For our wrestling is not against flesh and blood, but against the principalities, against the powers, against the world-rulers of this darkness, against the spiritual hosts of wickedness in the heavenly places. 1 Pet. 5:8—Be sober, be watchful: your adversary, the devil, as a roaring lion, walketh about, seeking whom he may devour. [Satan, we are told, in trying to seduce Jesus] taketh him unto an exceeding high mountain, and showeth him all the kingdoms of this world, and the glory of them;

and he said unto him, All these things will I give thee, if thou wilt fall down and worship me (Matt. 4:8-9). [And Jesus Himself teaches His disciples to pray]: Bring us not into temptation, but deliver us from the evil one (Matt. 6:13). [Even Satanic power, however, is definitely limited by the Will of God, and its exercise will be completely thwarted by the power of God in Christ.] [Thus, in the Prologue to the book of *Job*, Satan, always the "accuser of our brethren" (Rev. 12:10), is represented as appearing in the presence of God to make accusation that the patriarch Job was a man who served God solely for the material benefits which he received in return for such service; in a word, said Satan, Job was simply "feathering his own nest." This was a direct—and most impudent—challenge of the veracity of the Almighty, who had just spoken in praise of Job saying,] There is none like him in the earth, a perfect and upright man, one that feareth God, and turneth away from evil (Job 1:8). [God perforce accepted the challenge]: And Jehovah said unto Satan, Behold, he is in thy hand; only spare his life (Job 2:6). [That is to say, the devil was permitted to destroy Job's material possessions, to bring about the death of Job's children, and even to afflict the patriarch himself with a sore disease, but that was the limit to which he was allowed to go; the exercise of his diabolical power was circumscribed by the Will of God. So it has always been, and in the end Satan will suffer complete and ignominious defeat—nothing short of eternal segregation in hell with all his rebel host—at the hands of the Son of God, Lord and Christ, who now has "all authority in heaven and on earth" Matt. 28:18]. Heb. 2:14-15; Since then the children are sharers in flesh and blood, he [Christ] also himself in like manner partook of the same; that through death he might bring to nought him that had the power of death, that is, the devil; and might deliver all them who through fear of death were all their lifetime subject to bondage. Eph. 1:19-22: according to that working of the strength of his might which he wrought in Christ, when he raised him from the dead, and made him to sit at his right hand in the heavenly places, far above all rule, and authority, and power, and dominion, and every name that is named, not only in this world, but also in that which is to come; and he put all things in subjection under his feet, and gave him to be the head over all things to the church, which is his body, the fulness of him that filleth all in all. Phil. 2:9-11: Wherefore also God highly exalted him, and gave unto him the name that is above every name; that in the name of Jesus every knee should bow, of things in heaven and things on earth and things under the earth, and that every tongue should confess that Jesus Christ is Lord, to the glory of God the Father. 1 Cor. 15:25-26: For he [Christ] must reign, till he hath put all his enemies under his feet. The last enemy that shall be abolished is death. Rev. 20:10— And the devil that deceived them was cast into the lake of fire and brimstone, where are also the beast and the false prophet; and they shall be tormented day and night for ever and ever.

(4) [Angels being personal, hence voluntary beings, we have in Scripture the doctrine of both good and evil angels. The good angels, we are told, are confirmed in goodness; the evil angels are equally confirmed in evil; that is, Satan and his rebel host, *not* the descendants of Adam, are totally depraved.] Luke 10:18—[the words of Jesus], I beheld Satan fallen as lightning from heaven. John 8:44. [again the words of Jesus]: Ye are of your father the devil, and the lusts of your father it is your will to do. He was a murderer from the beginning, and standeth not in the truth, because there is no truth in him. When he speaketh a lie, he speaketh of his own: for he is a liar, and the father thereof. 2 Pet. 2:4—For if God spared not angels when they sinned, but cast them down to hell, and committed them to pits of

241

darkness, to be reserved unto judgment, etc. Jude 6—And angels that kept not their own principality, but left their proper habitation, he hath kept in everlasting bonds under darkness unto the judgment of the great day. Matt. 25:41—Then shall he say also unto them on the left hand, Depart from me, ye cursed, into the eternal fire which is prepared for the devil and his angels." [Satan is invariably designated "the evil one" in Scripture (Matt. 5:37; 6:13, 13:19; 1 John 2:13, 5:18, 19, etc.): that is, he and his rebel host are wholly confirmed in evil; hence, for them there can be but one end—"the lake of fire and brimstone," Rev. 20:10]. [The good angels, on the other hand, are equally confirmed in good.] 2 Cor. 11:14—Even Satan fashioneth himself into an angel of light, [thus implying that there are angels of light] Psa. 89:7—the council of the holy ones. Mark 8:38—For whosoever shall be ashamed of me and of my words in this adulterous and sinful generation, the Son of man also shall be ashamed of him when he cometh in the glory of his Father with the holy angels. Matt. 18:10: [here Jesus says, concerning little children]: I say unto you, that in heaven their angels do always behold the face of my Father who is in heaven. [And so Jesus teaches His disciples to pray]: Thy kingdom come, Thy will be done, as in heaven, so on earth (Matt. 6:10).

4. *Angels are ethereal beings,* that is, neither, on the one hand, completely bodiless, nor on the other hand, clothed in physical bodies such as human beings have. They are clothed, rather, in bodies of a very rarefied form of matter, of a texture perhaps approximating radiant energy or light, which may best be described as ethereal. Here again we encounter the limitations of human language: the term "ethereal" is used perforce in lieu of a more precise designation.

Though described as "ministering spirits" (Heb. 1:14), there is no evidence in Scripture that angels are completely bodiless. Indeed, the notion of an "immaterial soul" or "disembodied spirit," in the case of created beings, is foreign to the Bible; it is a Platonic concept pure and simple. According to Scripture, as we have already seen, even the redeemed saints themselves will be clothed in "spiritual" (ethereal?) bodies, bodies of a finer texture of matter, in the next world.[1] As Professor Albert C. Knudson writes:

> Spirit, as we find it in the Scriptures, was a rarefied form of matter. But this fact, while interesting from the philosophical point of view, did not seriously affect the distinction made between the material and the spiritual. Matter in its sublimated or spiritual form was so different from matter in its ordinary manifestations that there was felt to be a virtual antithesis between them.[2]

An ethereal form of this kind is not localized of course; hence, in certain Scripture passages the idea is implicit that evil spirits—the fallen angels—are possessed of an instinct or long-

1. *Vide* again 1 Cor. 15:35-58.
2. *The Religious Teaching of the Old Testament,* 94.

ing to incarcerate themselves in a physical body, even in the body of an animal, in order to secure a certain measure of respite from their ceaseless wanderings "to and fro in the earth . . . and up and down in it."

Job 1:7—And Jehovah said unto Satan, Whence comest thou? Then Satan answered Jehovah, and said, From going to and fro in the earth, and from walking up and down in it. [Paul describes Satan as "the god of this world" who has "blinded the minds of the unbelieving," 2 Cor. 4:4; that is to say, Satan is the "god" of the kingdom of this world, as by way of contrast with the Kingdom of Christ.] Matt. 8:31— And the demons besought him [Jesus] saying, If thou cast us out, send us away into the herd of swine [cf. Mark 5:1-17, Luke 8:26-37]. Matt. 12:43 [the words of Jesus]: But the unclean spirit, when he is gone out of the man, passeth through waterless places, seeking rest, and findeth it not.

*Only God Himself may properly be designated Pure Spirit.* As Jesus Himself stated expressly: "God is a Spirit; and they that worship him must worship in spirit and truth" (John 4:24). (Cf. Heb. 9:14—"the eternal Spirit.")

Angels are represented in Scripture as completely lacking the attributes or propensities that characterize a physical body such as human beings have in their present environment. Paul states explicitly that "flesh and blood cannot inherit the kingdom of God, neither doth corruption inherit incorruption" (1 Cor. 15:50). That is, (1) fleshly or natural birth cannot give one entrance into the Kingdom of Grace, for one must be born anew, born of water and the Spirit, to enter into that kingdom (John 3:3-6); (2) and neither can flesh and blood literally, nor flesh and blood relationships, in the very nature of the case enter into the Kingdom of Glory. All such natures and relationships are of the earth, earthy; they are left behind by the saints in the putting on of immortality. Jesus Himself made it clear that His resurrected body was one of "flesh and bones"; that is, the blood—the seat of animal life—was gone. "See my hands and my feet, that it is I myself: handle me, and see; for a spirit hath not flesh and bones, as ye behold me having" (Luke 24:39). This means too that He was not a mere ghost or phantasm; He was there in the presence of His disciples in a substantial form. If this be true of the saints, that they will not possess the qualities of physical life in the celestial world, how much more so of angels, whose natural habitat is that world. Jesus makes this crystal clear in one of His controversies with the Sadducees, the materialists among the Jews of His day.

Matt. 22:23-30: On that day there came to him Sadducees, they that say there is no resurrection; and they asked him, saying, Teacher,

Moses said, If a man die, having no children, his brother shall marry his wife, and raise up seed to his brother. Now there were with us seven brethren: and the first married and deceased, and having no seed left his wife unto his brother; in like manner the second also, and the third, unto the seventh. And after them all, the woman died. In the resurrection therefore whose wife shall she be of the seven? for they all had her. But Jesus answered and said unto them, Ye do err, not knowing the scriptures, nor the power of God. For in the resurrection they neither marry, nor are given in marriage, but are as angels in heaven.

That is to say, the immortalized saints shall be, like the angels of God, without sex distinctions, and hence without flesh and blood relationships, in the spiritual world, the difference being of course that whereas angels are *by nature* without these fleshly attributes and powers, the saints will have laid them aside on the exchange of their physical for spiritual bodies; they will be simply "sons and daughters of the Almighty" (2 Cor. 6:18). In a word, angels, not having physical bodies, know nothing of birth, growth, sex, age, or death.

Being without powers of physical reproduction, angels therefore constitute a company rather than a race.

Luke 20:34-36: And Jesus said unto them, The sons of this world marry, and are given in marriage: but they that are accounted worthy to attain to that world, and the resurrection from the dead, neither marry, nor are given in marriage: for neither can they die any more: for they are equal unto the angels; and are sons of God, being sons of the resurrection.

## As Dr. A. H. Strong puts it:

We are called "sons of men," but angels are never called "sons of angels," but only "sons of God." They are not developed from one original stock, and no such common nature binds them together as binds the race of men. They have no common character and history. Each was created separately, and each apostate angel fell by himself. Humanity fell all at once in its first father. Cut down a tree, and you cut down its branches. But angels were so many separate trees. Some lapsed into sin, but some remained holy.[1]

"Sons of God" is a term used in Scripture sometimes to designate angels (Job 1:6—"Now it came to pass on the day when the sons of God came to present themselves before Jehovah, that Satan also came among them"), sometimes to designate righteous men (Gen. 6:2—"the sons of God [pious Sethites] saw the daughters of men [the irreligious Cainites] that they were very fair, and they took them wives of all that they chose"). "Sons of God" is a common designation for the members of God's household, whether they be angels or righteous

1. *Systematic Theology*, One-Volume Edition, 447-448.

men (Eph. 3:15). However, because angels are a company, as distinguished from a race, we never read of "sons of angels" in Scripture.

5. *As to their number, angels are of the great multitude.*

Heb. 12:22—to innumerable hosts of angels. Deut. 33:2—Jehovah came . . . from the ten thousands of holy ones. Psa. 68:17—The chariots of God are twenty thousand, even thousands upon thousands. Dan. 7:10—thousands of thousands ministered unto him, and ten thousand times ten thousand stood before him: the judgment was set, and the books were opened. Matt. 26:53—Thinkest thou that I cannot beseech my Father, and he shall even now send me more than twelve legions of angels? Jude 14—Enoch, the seventh from Adam, prophesied, saying, Behold, the Lord came with ten thousands of his holy ones. Rev. 5:11—And I saw, and heard a voice of many angels round about the throne . . . and the number of them was ten thousand times ten thousand, and thousands of thousands. 1 Sam. 1:11—Jehovah of hosts. Gen. 32:2—God's host. 2 Chron. 18:18—all the host of heaven. Luke 2:13—And suddenly there was with the angel a multitude of the heavenly host. Rev. 19:14—the armies which are in heaven.

Angels, moreover, are presented in Scripture as having an organization.

1 Kings 22:19—And Micaiah said . . . I saw Jehovah sitting on his throne, and all the host of heaven standing by him on his right hand and on his left. 1 Thess. 4:16—the voice of the archangel. Jude 9—Michael the archangel. Col. 1:16—thrones or dominions or principalities or powers. Matt. 25:41—the devil and his angels. Eph. 2:2—the prince of the powers of the air. Rev. 19:13-14: and his name is called The Word of God. And the armies which are in heaven followed him upon white horses, clothed in fine linene, white and pure.

6. *As to function, angels are minister's of God's providence.*

Psa. 103:20-21: Bless Jehovah, ye his angels, that are mighty in strength, that fulfill his word, hearkening unto the voice of his word. Bless Jehovah, all ye his hosts, Ye ministers of his, that do his pleasure. Heb. 1:14—Are they not all ministering spirits, sent forth to do service for the sake of them that shall inherit salvation?

In the presence of God, the good angels worship Him without cessation:

Psa. 29:1, 2—Ascribe unto Jehovah, O ye sons of the mighty, Ascribe unto Jehovah glory and strength. Ascribe unto Jehovah the glory due unto his name; Worship Jehovah in holy array. Psa. 89:6, 7—Who among the sons of the mighty is like unto Jehovah? A God very terrible in the council of the holy ones. Rev. 5:11—And I saw, and I heard a voice of many angels round about the throne . . . saying with a great voice, Worthy is the Lamb that hath been slain to receive the power, and riches, and wisdom, and might, and honor, and glory, and blessing.

The good angels rejoice in God's works:

245

Job 38:7—When the morning stars sang together, And all the sons of God shouted for joy [that is, at the Creation of the world.] Luke 2:13, 14—And suddenly there was with the angel a multitude of the heavenly host praising God, and saying, Glory to God in the highest, and on earth peace among men in whom he is well pleased [on the night of the Christ-Child's birth]. [Luke 15:10—There is joy in the presence of the angels of God over one sinner that repenteth.]

## Good angels execute God's will, in nature and in history:

Psa. 104:4—Who maketh his angels winds, His ministers a flaming fire. [Matt. 28:2—the descent of an angel caused the earthquake on the morning of Christ's resurrection.] [Acts 12:7—an angel struck the chains from Peter's limbs and delivered him from prison.] Dan. 12:1—And at that time shall Michael stand up, the great prince who standeth for the children of thy people, etc. [2 Thess. 1:7-8: at the end of our age or dispensation, the Lord Jesus shall be revealed from heaven] with the angels of his power in flaming fire, rendering vengeance to them that know not God, and to them that obey not the gospel of our Lord Jesus.

## Good angels minister God's providence in a special sense to individual believers:

[1 Kings 19:5—an angel ministered to Elijah under the juniper tree]: Behold, an angel touched him, and said unto him, Arise and eat. Psa. 91:11 [a Messianic prophecy] He will give his angels charge over thee, To keep thee in all thy ways. They shall bear thee up in their hands, Lest thou dash thy foot against a stone. [cf. Matt. 4:6]. Dan. 6:22—My God hath sent his angel, and hath shut the lions' mouths, and they have not hurt me. Matt. 4:11: [here we read that following the Temptation of Jesus] angels came and ministered unto him. Matt. 18:10: [the words of Jesus concerning little children]: See that ye despise not one of these little ones: for I say unto you, that in heaven their angels do always behold the face of my Father who is in heaven. Luke 16:22—And it came to pass, that the beggar died, and that he was carried away by the angels into Abraham's bosom.

## Good angels minister God's providence also by punishing His enemies:

2 Kings 19:35—And it came to pass that night, that the angel of Jehovah went forth, and smote in the camp of the Assyrians a hundred fourscore and five thousand. [As in several instances in the Old Testament, the "angel of Jehovah" here may have been the Logos in one of His pre-incarnate manifestations.] Acts 12:23—And immediately an angel of the Lord smote him [the wicked Herod], because he gave not God the glory; and he was eaten of worms, and gave up the ghost.

These are but a few of the many instances in Scripture of angelic ministration of Divine Providence.

The doctrine of fallen angels is linked up in Scripture with the inspired account of the primary origin of evil (in Satan's pre-mundane rebellion against the Divine government), a subject which does not come within the scope of the present treatise. To me it seems too obvious even to be questioned that

246

our moral universe is essentially a struggle between the forces of good and the forces of evil for the spirit of man. Let it not be forgotten, either, that the New Testament promises the ultimate and complete triumph of the good. I could no longer forbear, sent that I might know your faith, lest by any means the tempter had tempted you, and our labor should be in vain. Heb. 2:14-15: Since then the children are sharers in flesh and blood, he [Christ] also himself in like manner partook of the same; that through death he might bring to nought him that had the power of death, that is, the devil; and might deliver them who through fear of death were all their lifetime subject to bondage.

[Cf. Job. 1:6-12, 2:1-7] Zech. 3:1—And he showed me Joshua the high priest standing before the angel of Jehovah, and Satan standing at his right hand to be his adversary; Matt. 13:39—and the enemy that sowed them [tarco] is the devil [John 8:44-45] 1 Pet. 5:8—your adversary, the devil, as a roaring lion, walketh about, seeking whom he may devour; Rev. 12:10—the accuser of our brethren is cast down, who accuseth them before our God day and night; Matt. 17:15-18; Mark 3:7-12; Mark 5:5-20; Luke 8:26-39; Luke 10:17-20; Luke 13:10-17; Acts 10:38—Jesus of Nazareth . . . who went about doing good, and healing all that were oppressed of the devil; Acts 16:16-18; 2 Cor. 12:7—there was given me a thorn in the flesh, a messenger of Satan to buffet me, that I should not be exalted overmuch; Eph. 6:11 12, Put on the whole armor of God, that ye may be able to stand against the wiles of the devil; for our wrestling is not against flesh and blood, but against the principalities and powers . . . in the heavenly places; 1 Thess. 2:18—we fain would have come unto you . . . and Satan hindered us. 1 Thess. 3:5—For this cause I also, when I could no longer forbear, sent that I might know your faith, lest by any means the tempter had tempted you, and our labor should be in vain. Heb. 2:14-15: Since then the children are sharers in flesh and blood, he [Christ] also himself in like manner partook of the same; that through death he might bring to nought him that had the power of death, that is, the devil; and might deliver them who through fear of death were all their lifetime subject to bondage.

The Scriptures teach that evil angels, being totally depraved, that is, wholly confirmed in evil (Matt. 25:41, 2 Pet. 2:4, Jude 6, Rev. 20:1-3, 7-10), strive constantly to defeat the will of God, and to hinder man's temporal and eternal welfare. Yet in these nefarious activities, evil angels—in spite of themselves, and perhaps unwittingly, for angels are limited both in knowledge and in power—minister God's providence by illustrating His unfailing justice; either directly or indirectly they execute His plan of chastening the good and punishing the ungodly; and they illustrate also the nature and destiny of evil. A God who is all love would be a God unjust. This age certainly

247

needs to learn that righteousness and justice are the foundation of His throne (Psa. 89:14).

The role of angels in the Drama of Human Redemption that is disclosed to mortal view on the pages of Scripture is indeed a paramount role. To remove it from the Bible would denude the drama, and the Biblical record as well, of a major portion of its mystery and power. According to the teaching of the Scriptures, at every important advance in the unfolding of the Plan of Redemption, the activity of angels rose to a high point. Hence, we read of their presence and activity at the completion of the Creation (Job 38:7); at the giving of the Law at Mount Sinai (Acts 7:53; Gal. 3:19, Heb. 2:2); at the birth of the Anointed (Luke 2:8-15); at the Temptation of Christ, in the Wilderness and again in Gethsemane (Matt. 4:11 Luke 22:43); at the empty tomb, on the morning of the Resurrection (Matt. 28:1-7); at the Ascension (Acts 1:9-11); and at the Last Judgment (Matt. 25:31, 2 Thess. 1:7-10).

The angels, as has already been stated, occupy the position in the Hierarchy of Being intermediate between God and man. Psa. 8:3-6: "When I consider thy heavens, the work of thy fingers, The moon and the stars, which thou hast ordained; What is man, that thou art mindful of him? And the son of man, that thou visitest him? For thou hast made him but little lower than God (Hebrew *Elohim*: A.V. rendering, "the angels"), And crownest him with glory and honor. Thou makest him to have dominion over the works of thy hands." In this passage, writes Knudson,

> *Elohim* is commonly rendered "angels," and it is quite possible that the term was used in this sense; for in several instances it has the general meaning of "a godlike being."[1] But in this particular passage *Elohim* probably means neither "angels" nor "God" exclusively, but both. It is divine beings generally, than whom man has been made but a little lower.[2]

In a word, man lives and moves and has his being on the highest level of existence possible to a creature of earth. Though in his present state clothed in a physical body, he is himself, in his essential and imperishable nature, the image of God, and he has inherently the capacity to become, by means of the knowledge of Christ and the life of the Spirit, a partaker of the divine nature.

2 Pet. 1:2-4: Grace to you and peace be multiplied in the knowl-

1. *E.g.*, 1 Sam. 28:13, Exo. 4:16, 7:1.
2. *Op. cit.*, 193.

edge of God and of Jesus our Lord: seeing that his divine power hath granted unto us all things that pertain unto life and godliness, through the knowledge of him that called us by his own glory and virtue; whereby he hath granted unto us his precious and exceeding great promises; that through these ye may become partakers of the divine nature, having escaped from the corruption that is in the world by lust.

In knowledge and power, angels are *superhuman* beings of course. But—are they "supernatural" beings? Obviously, the answer to this question depends entirely on one's definition of the word "nature." I am reminded here of the words of Stuart Chase:

> When one says—as I have often said—"We must plan with nature for the protection of our natural resources"—one must be conscious that there is no entity "nature," an old mother with whom one has interviews, but the word is only a useful tag for summing up a great variety of natural processes: the hydrologic cycle, soil formation, wind and storm, plant life, animal life, and so on.[1]

In this statement, however, Mr. Chase, as he frequently does, indulges in a practice which he himself severely condemns, namely, that of talking in circles: there is no old mother "nature," but only an aggregate of "natural" processes which account for our "natural" resources. But what are "natural" processes and "natural" resources? And what does Mr. Chase mean by the phrase, "and so on"? That is, what does the "and so on" take in? We understand, of course, that Mr. Chase is writing here of the resources of "nature," as the term is commonly used, namely, to include the resources of the subhuman world— mineral, vegetable, and animal resources. Is man himself, then, not a part of "nature"? Is thought not a "natural" process? One thing is sure—that without human thought the resources of the subhuman world would be of little utility. The word "nature" is, in itself just a tag, of course. But, to speak in Mr. Chase's own semantic terms, it must have a "referent." What is that referent?

The question I raise is this: Where does the "natural" leave off and the "supernatural" begin? Or, is the "super-natural" but the rest of the "natural," the not-yet-understood or even apprehended "natural"? Who can answer these questions with any degree of certainty? Does "nature" include only the sensible, the tangible, the palpable? If so, it cannot include thinking, for the simple reason that no one has ever yet apprehended a thought through the media of his physical senses; and if "nature" does not include all those higher thought processes

1. *The Tyranny of Words*, 82-83.

which are characteristic of man, that is to say, if thinking is a "supernatural" process, then man himself belongs to a "supernatural" order. Again, should someone object that the activity of angels is contrary to human experience, I should reply by asking, Contrary to *whose* experience? Contrary perhaps to the experience of men and women of the present day, or indeed men and women of several immediately past centuries, although the are some of these, no doubt, who would affirm the contrary. But does this fact necessarily prove that the presence of angels is contrary to the experience of all men who have lived upon the earth since the beginning of human history, or, to be specific, contrary to the experiences of those men, those great servants of God, whom God used so mightily in unfolding His Plan of Salvation for man? However we approach these problems, we merely beg the question. The fact remains that no one can successfully refute the proposition that angels may be, after all, just as truly a part of the order of Nature as a whole, as man is. Under this view, Nature embraces all creatures, and angels, let us remember, are created beings. We may therefore properly say that they are *superhuman* beings, but no man has any right dogmatically to assert that they are "supernatural" beings. This business of asserting unproved hypotheses is another prolific source of the confusion that exists in present-day thinking.

Let us suppose, rather, that "Nature" is the proper designation for the total Hierarchy of Being. Then let us believe—and it is undoubtedly the most rational belief possible, far more so indeed than the creed of the materialist—that God, the Eternal Spirit, is all-embracing, in some manner inscrutable to us, and that He evolves everything out of Himself by a timeless process of Thought, at the same time remaining Himself the great, infinite, eternal Other. In Tennyson's memorable words:

> Only That which made us meant us to be mightier by and by,
> Set the sphere of all the boundless heavens within the
>     human eye,
> Sent the shadow of Himself, the boundless, through the
>     human soul;
> Boundless inward in the atom, boundless outward in the
>     Whole.

Under such a view, our world is indeed One World—the World of the Spirit. That is what I prefer to believe that it is.

Again, on the other hand, if the Totality of Being should

be, in fact, not a hierarchy, but a continuum, without any definite breaks—or ledges, let us say—between the inorganic and the organic, between the plant and the animal, between the animal and man, and between man and the angelic order, —well, what of it? After all, such words as "inorganic" and "organic," "material" and "spiritual," "physical" and "mental," "natural" and "supernatural," and the like, may turn out to be dualistic impositions upon Reality—mere verbalizations and no more—by the human intellect itself, prone as it is to categorize and to classifly. Indeed, such distinctions may not exist at all in the total structure of Being. Even so, that is, should this prove to be the case, would our world be any less the One World, any less the World of the Spirit? We firmly believe, however, that the overwhelming testimony of the scholarship of the ages is that Being is a hierarchy, not a continuum, of existents.

Indeed, it must be the World of the Spirit and the spirits, for the simple reason that to anything less than Person it is meaningless. As far as we know, persons and persons alone are capable of experiencing and evaluating, in the fullest sense of these terms, the world in which they have their being. Persons and persons only are capable of seeking the meaning of it all, of pursuing the ageless quest for the Holy Grail of Truth. As Lotze argues, in the ninth book of his great work, *Mikrokosmus*, the universal is everywhere inferior to the particular, the species to the individual, and the contents of the realm of true reality are restricted to the living, personal Spirit of God and the world of personal spirits, whch He has created.[1]

We are now ready to enter upon the second phase of our study—that of Spirit in God.

# ADDENDA: COSMOLOGICAL THEORIES

## (Theories of the Origin and Organization of the Cosmos)

EMANATIONISM: Unity is prior to plurality. Creation is conceived as a process of the "watering down" of perfection, as, for example, light, in moving away from its source and thus becoming diffused, is finally lost in darkness. Darkness is non-being, and non-being is usually identified with gross matter. The most thoroughgoing emanation cults were those of the

1. *Vide* Dr. F. Ueberweg, *A History of Philosophy*, Vol. II, 321. Translated from the Fourth German Edition by George S. Morris.

Gnostics and especially that of Plotinus, which is known as Neoplatonism.

## PLOTINUS (A.D. 205-270).

(The Egyptian Neoplatonist, who derived his system largely from his teacher, Ammonius Saccas. His writings were published by Porphyry in six books, each consisting of nine sections, hence entitled the *Enneads*.) Origen and Augustine both were greatly influenced by Neoplatonism. The following should be read downward:

The One

|  |  |
|---|---|
| Nous | one: world unity, prior to the possibility of plurality |
|  | many: "ideas" or "forms" of all possible existents: (1) universals, (2) particulars |
| Soul | one: world soul, undivided |
|  | many: individual souls, (1) unconscious, (2) conscious of ideas |
| Body | one: world body, as a whole |
|  | many: particular bodies (1) as wholes (2) decomposed |

The Void

Gross matter: non-being

Gnosticism, in its various cults, postulated a series of emanations from the Absolute Being or Unity in the forms of psychic intermediaries, known as *aeons*. According to this early Christian heresy, Christ Himself was just such an emanation or aeon. It is interesting to note, in this connection, that the Deists of a later age were prone to regard the "laws of nature" as emanations, hence as having a kind of independent existence.

## PHILOSOPHICAL HINDUISM

(or Hindu Mysticism. Very old, as set forth in the *Upanishads*)

Again, read downward:

Brahman (perfect unity)

Atman ( unity that pervades plurality)

   Souls (plurality that is really unity)

   Bodies (plurality that is mistaken for reality)

     Castes (levels of social classes)

     Animals (levels of animal life)

     Plants (levels of plant life)

      Matter (levels of decomposition)

*Illusion (Maya)*

It will be noted that emanationist systems all tend toward pantheism, the doctrine that identifies God with what we commonly call His Creation. The fallacies of pantheism are clearly pointed out in the following terse statements by C. H. Toy, *Introduction to the History of Religions,* p. 476: "Pantheism has never commended itself to the masses of men . . . The demand for a deity with whom one may enter into personal relations—the simple concept of a God who dwells apart satisfies the religious instincts of the majority of men. The ethical questions arising from pantheism seem to them perplexing: how can man be morally responsible when it is the deity who thinks and acts in him? and how can he have any sense of loyalty to a deity whom he cannot distinguish from himself? . . . Man demands a method of worship, and pantheism does not permit organized worship." Moreover, pantheism, by distributing the Divine essence through all cosmic existents, inanimate or animate, amoral or moral, makes God to be the author of evil as well as of good; to this fact the only alternative would be *that evil is illusion,* and this is the corner in which Absolutists are uniformly forced to take refuge. May I remind the student that an illusion is necessarily an illusion of something: an illusion of nothing or nothingness is inconceivable.

## PLATO'S COSMOLOGY

(Plato lived 427-347 B.C. See his "likely story" of the Creation, in the *Timaeus.*)

253

Being: The Forms (Ideas): The Form of the Good, Unity

Forms of all classes of existents

The Demiourgos (Craftsman, Architect)

The World: World-Soul

Becoming: Rational Souls
Irrational Souls
Inanimate Bodies

Non-being: Indeterminate matter

Plato can hardly be classified as an emanationist: in fact it is difficult to put his cosmology in any definite category. In the *Timaeus,* he pictures the Creation as having been actualized by the Demiourgos (Master Craftsman, Great Architect), as the World-Soul, according to the archetypal Forms, out of what he calls the Receptacle. This last term seems to have been the word he used to designate the Void (empty space). It will be recalled that the Greek word *chaos* denoted, not disorder, but empty space; hence this was the Greek term generally used for non-being which was conceived to be what we call "matter." (Cf. Plotinus, above). The Forms, in Plato's thought, were the Principles of classification, *e.g.,* the "mustardness" of a mustard seed, the "horseness" of a horse; that is, that which specifies the individuals of each particular kind of things. Had he put these Forms in the Mind of "The Divine"—The Form of the Good, that is, Unity—his system would have to be regarded as theistic; however, there seems to be no evidence in his writings that he took this step; he apparently gave the Forms an eternally separate existence in themselves. Hence, we must conclude that on the whole Plato favored a view of the Deity as immanent, and that his system was weighted in the direction of a "higher pantheism." This is evident from the fact that the World-Soul (as the "Prime Mover") is presented as spreading out throughout the cosmos and as directing its processes and changes from within. As a matter of fact, Plato obviously belonged to the Greek philosophical tradition (Aristotelianism alone excepted) in which the Divine Principle ("God") is conceived pantheistically as That Which Is, in striking contrast to the Hebrew voluntarism in which God is revealed as He Who Is (Exo. 3:14), in a word, as pure personality.

# ARISTOTLE'S HIERARCHY OF BEING

God
(defined as Pure Thought Thinking Itself: cf. John 4:24)

rational psyche ("soul")
(physiochemical processes, cellular processes, sensitivity, locomotion, *plus* reason)

animal psyche
(physiochemical processes and cellular processes *plus* sensitivity and locomotion)

vegetable psyche
(physiochemical processes, *plus* the cellular processes)

matter-in-motion
(or in modern terms, the physiochemical processes of the inanimate world)

Aristotle, in his *De Anima* ("On the Soul"), pictures the totality of being as a hierarchy, that is, as organized on different levels in an ascending scale of complexity of powers, in which each higher order subsumes the powers of those below it. Analysis of the nature of "movement" (change) convinced Aristotle that in order to account for the complex of contingent causes-and-effects which is the cosmos, there must be a First Cause, a First or Prime Mover, who is self-existent (*sui generis*), that is, non-contingent and without beginning or end, the only alternative being that somewhere, at some time, nothing must have originated the first something—a notion utterly absurd, of course; or, as someone has put it, the "first mover" must himself be unmoved, except from within, and different from the "first moved." This Prime Mover, otherwise described as Pure Thought Thinking Itself, is Aristotle's God, who is presented as affecting the universe without being a part of it. Hence, it will be seen that Aristotle's God is transcendent, and that his system more nearly approximates theism than that of any other Greek philosopher. (Aristotle lived 384-322 B.C., and was a student at Plato's school, the Academy, for some twenty years.)

Why does our world exist instead of any other kind of world? asked the German philosopher, Leibniz (1646-1716).

255

Simply because (Leibniz concluded) God has chosen, not to create any kind of world at random, but to create the best of all possible worlds, that is, the best He found it possible to create for achieving His ends, the actualization of the greatest possible good and the least possible evil. (Evil, Leibniz held, is of three kinds, namely, physical evil (suffering), moral evil (sin), and metaphysical evil: this he defined in terms of the necessary imperfection of finite beings.) Therefore, because our world is the handiwork of this Perfect Being (The Absolute Monad), it must be the actualization of the fulness of created being. In such a world (reasoning *a priori*, of course), all possible beings must be actualized, all possible levels (grades) filled therein: there must be *unbroken continuity in the form of progressive gradation of organisms* from the very lowest living being up to the very highest, God Himself. Thus arose the doctrine of the Great Chain of Being, a doctrine which flourished in early modern times, and which, obviously, is largely in accord with present-day evolutionism. (For a thoroughgoing presentation of this view, see the excellent book by Arthur O. Lovejoy, *The Great Chain of Being,* published by the Harvard University Press, 1950. The concept is also clearly set forth in the poem by Alexander Pope, "An Essay on Man.")

## EMERGENTISM

(This is the view that unity is in the process of emerging out of plurality. The process is, and probably will always be, an unfinished process. The following tables are to be read upward.)

| | God | |
|---|---|---|
| Mind | Mind | Society |
| | Life | Mind |
| Life | | |
| | Matter | Life |
| Matter | Space-Time | Matter |
| C. Lloyd Morgan, in his book, *Emergent Evolution,* 1923. | Samuel Alexander, in his book, *Time and Deity,* 1920. | Roy Wood Sellers, in his book, *Evolutionary Naturalism,* 1922. |

256

*Emergentism,* though at times paying lip service to a *"God,"* is strictly pantheistic in character. In all cases, it rejects the theistic doctrine of God's transcendence. It ignores uniformly the necessity of Efficient Causality in all cosmic processes.

I have presented the foregoing concepts (and diagrams) for the purpose of demonstrating the futility of all efforts to obtain complete knowledge of the origin and organization of the cosmos through unaided human reason. The ultimate mysteries are inscrutable. These various philosophical theories surely prove this to be true; that is, they prove the inherent incapacity of the human mind to explain (as Chesterton has put it) how nothing could turn into something or how something could turn into something else. How refreshing to turn away from the best that human wisdom can afford us, and to accept by faith the Biblical teaching, on these subjects! (Cf. Job 11:7; Isa. 55:6-11; 1 Cor. 1:18-25, 3:18-20; Rom. 11:33-36; Heb. 11:3).

The following tables will serve to point up the correspondences between the empirical (commonsense) and the Biblical accounts of the origin and organization of the created world:

self-consciousness
(the person)

God
(Pure Spirit: John 4:24)

consciousness
(the brute)

Angels
(ethereal beings, "minister-

life
(the cell)

ing spirits": Heb. 1:14)

Souls
(Gen. 2:7)

energy-matter
(non-living)

Bodies

Matter

The EMPIRICAL AC-
COUNT of the Dimensions
of Being, based on observation and experience.

The BIBLICAL AC-
COUNT of Being.

(Read upward)

(Read upward)

257

Day 7—rest

Day 6—man and woman, *bara,* v. 28; Gen. 2: 7
land animals

Day 5—water and air species,
*bara,* v. 21

Day 4—chronology (measurement
of time)

GOD

Day 3—plants,
lands and seas

Day 2—atmosphere ("expanse")

Day 1—energy, light, matter:
*bara,* v. 1

## THE HEBREW COSMOGONY (Gen. 1:1—2:3)
### (read upward)

Some hold that God, the Eternal Spirit, created without the use of pre-existing materials, inserting new increments of power into the Creative Process at successively higher levels. Some hold that God put into Prime (First) Matter all potentialities (Forms) later actualized by His Efficient Causality.

N.B.—For the diagrams presented above as illustrative of the Emanation and Emergent Evolution theories of the origin and organization of the cosmos, I am indebted to Dr. Archie J. Bahm, Professor of Philosophy, University of New Mexico. These diagrams appear in his well-known book, *Philosophy: An Introduction,* published by Wiley and Sons, 1953. It is by his permission that I reproduce them here, and for this privilege I am deeply grateful.—C.C.C.

Dr. A. H. Strong, in his *Systematic* Theology, suggests that the content of the Biblical teaching falls under the category of what is philosophically designated Ethical Monism.

It is my conviction, however, that Dr. Bahm, in the work cited above, presents a philosophical view which approximates rather closely the essence of the Genesis Cosmogony. Dr. Bahm has named his theory Organicism. Should the student wish to pursue the subject further, he can do so by familiarizing himself with the argument presented in Chapter 20 of Bahm's book.

The late Martin Buber, the Jewish theistic existentialist, in his book entitled *The Eclipse of God* develops the thesis that whereas philosophy holds fast to an image of God, or even to a faith in God, religion holds fast to God Himself. This is a true contrast.

Now may I close this volume with a personal confession, namely: I could never substitute for faith in the Biblical Heavenly Father who has revealed Himself to us in His Son Jesus Christ (Heb. 1:1-4, 11:6; John 15:1), any coldly intellectual philosophical theory of the origin and nature of the Mystery of Being. I recall here the striking forcefulness of the questions which Zophar the Naamathite addressed to Job in olden times: "Canst thou by searching find out God? Canst thou find out the Almighty unto perfection?" (Job 11:7). There is but one answer to these questions—an unequivocal negative. Or, as the Apostle Paul puts it: "The wisdom of this world is foolishness with God" (1 Cor. 3:19). Again: "For seeing that in the wisdom of God the world through its wisdom knew not God, it was God's good pleasure through the foolishness of the preaching to save them that believe" (1 Cor. 1:21). Through the foolishness of the preaching of what? The preaching of "Christ crucified, unto Jews a stumblingblock, and unto Gentiles foolishness; but unto them that are called, both Jews and Greeks, Christ the power of God and the wisdom of God" (1 Cor. 1:23-24).

## THE TEILHARDIAN HIERARCHY OF BEING

It will be recalled that Spinoza, the Jewish philosopher (1632-1677), set out in his *Ethica* to deal with the problems of how an immaterial Being (God) could create a material universe, only to "explain away" the problem at the end, simply by identifying God with the world, nature, the universe, etc. (the totality of being). His system was a rigid pantheism which "explained" little or nothing *in re* the basic problem with which he was trying to deal. In like manner, in recent years, the late French priest-scientist-philosopher, Pierre Teilhard de Chardin, in his principal works, *The Divine Milieu* and *The Phenomenon of Man*, created a stir of some proportions in the academic world by undertaking to explain the *modus operandi* of evolution (as did Bergson earlier in his work entitled *Creative Evolution*). Teilhard envisions evolution through a gradation of forms, from atomic particles up to human beings, in ever increasing complexity of structure, and along with it, the development of consciousness (Bergson uses the term "Spirit"). The result is a kind of *pan-psychism*. Man is the focal point in whom all facets of the evolutionary process converge, and in man reflective thought finally emerges. The unique feature of Teilhard's system is his concept that the ultimate reality of this cosmic development is the Incarnate Christ (not the "Superman" of Nietzsche, nor that of Samuel Butler, nor that of Shaw's *Man and Superman* or his *Back to Methuselah*), but the God-Man, who ultimately gathers all things up into Himself and truly becomes *all in all*. "The only universe," says Teilhard, "capable of containing the human person is an irrevocably 'personalizing' universe." Again: "In one manner or the other, it still remains true that, even in the view of the mere biologist, the human epic resembles nothing so much as a way of the Cross" (PM, 290, 311). Like that of Bergson, Teilhard's system was an honest effort to describe the *modus operandi* of the evolutionary process. However, we are safe in saying that both Bergson and Teilhard have failed to explain how a new species emerges—indeed how novelty of any kind enters into the process —just as Spinoza failed to explain how an immaterial God could have created this material world. *Obviously, these are mysteries which lie beyond the scope of human comprehension* (Job 11:7, Isa. 55:8-9). Nevertheless Teilhard's presentation is sufficiently intriguing to merit an analysis of it, in its main outlines, for whatever it may be worth to the student. One thing can be said in its favor: it has received little but scorn, and even sneers, from the materialistic evolutionists. The following diagram and explanatory matter will suffice, perhaps, to place the Teilhardian view before readers of the present text.

---

OMEGA: Creation and Creator Become One
Through Christ
Plerome
Socialization
*Homo sapiens*
N O O G E N E S I S
(from *nous*, "reason," "mind")

---

Hominisation
Threshold of Reflection
Primates
A N T H R O P O G E N E S I S
(from *anthropos*, "man")

---

Mammals, etc.

Animals      (Consciousness)

Plants      Cellular Processes

Monocellulars      Bacteria

B I O G E N E S I S

(from *bios,* "life")

---

Threshold of Life

Minerals

Molecules      Crystals

Atoms

Granules of Energy

C O S M O G E N E S I S

(from *cosmos,* "order"—of the non-living world)

---

A L P H A

(Read upward, according to what Teilhard calls the Axis of Ascending Complexity and Consciousness)

---

EXPLANATORY: Evolution, according to Teilhard, moves along a kind of vertical line which he calls "the axis of ascending complexity and consciousness," each cosmic particle (monad) being composed of a "within" (of psychic or radial energy, also called psychism, which is not amenable to physical sense), and a "without" (physical or "tangential" which is measurable): both form an indivisible "spirit-matter" entity. (Hence this must not be thought of as a dualism.) 1. *Period of "Cosmogenesis."* The more complex the matter becomes, the more consciousness (psyche) it gains. Evolution is simply the continuous intensification of the psychical or radial energy. Cosmogenesis is the process of *becoming,* on an evolutionary line between a past and a future. The point of departure from the axis is designated ALPHA, or the Alpha Point. Through "granulation" of energy the first elementary particles took form, and over an unimaginable stretch of time assumed the status of what present-day science calls atomic nuclei, atoms, or molecules (these are simply tools of explanation in physics). The birth of our planet probably occurred about five million years ago. 2. *Period of "Biogenesis."* When the "corpuscular number" in a particle reached a certain level matter "came alive." This "vitalisation" occurred when matter crossed the threshold of life and marked the beginning of the age of biogenesis. As physical matter became more and more complex, the psychism of the individual monad increased proportionately. 3. *Period of "Anthropogenesis."* At the point when the brain reaches the necessary degree of complexity, the threshold of reflection was crossed and man was born. This power of thought made man a being distinct from all other species. This was "not a matter of change of degree, but of a change of nature, resulting from a change of state" (PM, 166). The hominisation of the species introduced the age of anthropogenesis. This occurred probably at some point within the last million years: Concern-

261

ing *instinct* in animals, Teilhard writes: "We realize better in our minds the fact and the reason for the *diversity* of animal behavior. From the moment we regard evolution as primarily psychical transformation, we see there is not *one* instinct in nature, but a multitude of forms of instincts each corresponding to a particular solution of the problem of life. The 'psychical' make-up of an insect is not and cannot be that of a vertebrate; nor can the instinct of a squirrel be that of a cat or an elephant: this is in virtue of the position of each on the tree of life" (PM, 167). "The individual and instantaneous leap from instinct to thought" marked the beginning of "hominisation," which then advanced by means of "the progressive phyletic spiritualisation in human civilisation of all the forces contained in the animal world" (PM, 180). As Julian Huxley puts it, in his Introduction: "The intensification of mind, the raising of mental potential" is regarded "as being the necessary consequence of complexification" (PM, 11-16). 4. *The Period of Noogenesis.*" (From the Greek *noesis*, from *noein*, "to perceive," from *nous*, "mind": hence, *noesis* in English, which, in philosophy, means purely intellectual apprehension.) This phase began as a result of the gradual evolution of mental powers, with the appearance of the first *homo sapiens*, (There are different races, Teilhard emphasizes, but only *one* *homo sapiens.*) Evolution has now reached the stage at which major physical development has lost significance. Science holds that man is unique in nature because of his brain processes, not because his brain is the biggest in capacity but because it is more complex. According to Teilhard, "the noosphere (and more generally the world) represents a whole that is not only closed but also *centred*. Because it contains and engenders consciousness, space-time is necessarily *of a convergent nature.* Accordingly, its enormous layers, followed in the right direction, must somewhere ahead become involuted to a point which we might call *Omega*, which fuses and consumes them integrally in itself" (PM, 259). At the present time we are in the period of socialisation in which, according to Teilhard, mankind becomes more and more united and integrated. This will come about as a consensus of mankind will gradually replace the growing capacity of the individual intellect because the human brain will cease to grow. This common consciousness will lift humanity to a higher level. Man inevitably continues to socialize: it is his nature to do so; hence all things will converge at one center, Omega, the point where humanity and the universe is bound to converge in the cosmic Christ.

What roles are played by God and Christ in the Teilhardian system? He puts the totality of being in the hands of the omnipresent God. He places man in the Divine Milieu, yet in such a way that man is not depersonalized in spite of ever increasing socialization. On the contrary, it is this personal link which connects each of us to God, who is the center, and the motor, so to speak, of the evolutionary process. We become God's partner in leading the world forward to the Omega point. For some persons, man is the center, the only point of adoration in the totality of being; for others, man is little or nothing in this grandiose universe—he is lost in it. Neither position is right. Referring to Paul's sermon on the Areopagus, Teilhard writes (DM, 25): "God who has made man in order that he may find him—God whom we try to grasp through the experiment of our lives—this God is as tangible and present as the atmosphere in which we are submerged. He surrounds us from all sides like the world itself." Man cannot escape the Divine Milieu. Each right action brings him into closer communion with Christ. "Whatsoever ye do," writes the Apostle, "do all in the name of the Lord Jesus" (Col. 3:17). This means we should always act in close fellowship with our Lord. The totality of man's life, even in its most "natural" aspects, is sanctifiable. From this point of beginning, the Christian life receives its content and direction, how and where to go. How does man enter upon this path? By purifying his intentions and acting according to the Will of God. As man adheres to the creative power of God, he becomes its instrument, or even more, its living extension. Man is thus united with God and in God on this earth in a common love to create. And in spite of the individual's failures and sins the world as a whole will achieve victory over evil, because God is on man's side. Mankind is assured that the universe, all creation, will rejoin the One when all evolution shall have converged in the point Omega. This will be the mysterious Plerome, where Creator and Creation will be one totality, without, however, adding anything essential to God. The active center of the Plerome in which everything is united, the creative Soul in whom everything is consummated, is Jesus Christ, "Religion and science are the two conjugated faces or phases of one and the same act of complete knowledge—the only one which can embrace the past and the future of evolution so as to contemplate, measure, and fulfill them" (DM. 284, 285). Note well the following concluding statements (PM, 293, 294): "Is the Kingdom of God a big family? Yes, in a sense it is. But in another sense it is a prodigious biological operation—that of the Redeeming Incarnation. As early as in St. Paul and St. John, we read that to create, to fulfill and to purify the world is, for God, to unify it by uniting it organically with himself. How does He unify it? By partially immersing himself in things, by becomng 'element,' and then, from this point of vantage in the heart of the matter, assuming the control and leadership of what we now call evolution. Christ, principle of universal vitality because sprung up as man among men, put himself in the position (maintained ever since) to subdue under himself, to purify, to direct, and superanimate the general ascent of consciousness into which he inserted himself. By a perennial act of communion and sublimation, he aggregates to himself the total psychism of the earth. And when he has gathered everything together and transformed everything, he will close in upon himself and his conquests, thereby rejoining, in a final gesture, the divine focus he has never left. Then, as St. Paul tells us, *God shall be all in all.* . . . The universe fulfilling itself in a synthesis of centres in perfect conformity with the laws of union. God, the Centre of centres. In that final vision the Christian dogma culminates." (Cf. Eph. 1:5-12, I Cor. 15:20-28, Col. 1:9-23, Rev. 1:8, 1:17-18).

It will thus be seen that Teilhard's God is essentially *theistic* rather than pantheistic: He is presented as the Eternal Being, in Himself separate from the creation, and as immersing Himself into all created being as the "center" and "motor" of the evolutionary process. His portrayal of the Omega Point as the ultimate fusion of Creation and Redemption in the Beatific Vision (Union with God) is hardly a variation from the Apostle Peter's description of the "new heavens and a new earth, wherein dwelleth righteousness" (2 Pet. 3:13; cf. Matt. 5:8, 1 Cor. 13:12, 1 John 3:2; Rev. 21:1-8, 22:1-5). It strikes this writer that the most obvious weakness in the Teilhardian exposition is his failure to recognize the juridical aspect of the totalty of being, and his consequent failure to deal adequately with the fact of evil and its consequences, including the Scripture doctrines of judgment, rewards, and punishments. (See Psa. 89:14, John 5:28-29, Matt. 25:31-46, Rom. 2:1-16, 2 Thess. 1:7-10, Acts 17:30-31, Rev. 20:11-15, etc.) This, of course, is a tragic lacuna in all the branches of human knowledge in our day.

*In summary: It will thus be seen that in all these conceptions the creation is pictured in the form of an ascending sequence of levels of being; that is, as essentially hierarchical in character. The notion of an ascending continuum comprehending*

263

*all kinds of being certainly lies beyond all possibility (or even probability) of credible acceptance.* As previously stated, to assume that matter is to be regarded as the sole reality is to attribute to atoms all the facets and powers that theologians attribute to God, including supreme intelligence, creative power, autonomous eternal (timeless) existence. Those who leave God out of their philosophy are under the necessity of showing how (or even that) mindless, non-living matter has been capable of organizing itself, of becoming alive, and of endowing itself with consciousness, reason, and self-consciousness (personality). On these conclusions we rest our intelligent faith upon the fact of the self-existent living and true God of the Bible. *Being is a hierarchy, not a continuum of existents.*

[However, see my essay on "Evolution and Evolutionism" at the end of this volume.]

## QUESTIONS FOR REVIEW OF PART THREE

1. How do we know that man is a creature? What is the significance of this fact?
2. What are the ultimate intrinsic and extrinsic ends of man? What is our basis for these beliefs?
3. What is the necessary means to man's attainment of Perfect Happiness?
4. In what does the life with the Holy Spirit begin?
5. What are are prerequisites, according to Scripture, of betrothal to Christ?
6. What are the essential facts of the Gospel? What is the fundamental truth of the Gospel message?
7. State the three commands and the three great promises of the Gospel.
8. What is the meaning of the title *Messias* or *Christ*?
9. When does the actual marriage of Christ and His Bride take place? Give Scripture proofs.
10. Explain what is meant by the *Hierarchy* of Being. How does this differ from a continuum?
11. Explain Lotze's theory of the breaks in the continuity of Being?
12. What are the obvious gaps in the ascending Continuity of Being?
13. Is *any* theory of Creation possible that would ignore the necessity of a Creative Power?
14. Can Creation ever be accounted for if Efficient Causality is rejected?
15. State LeConte's definition of evolution.
16. Why do we reason that a Creation did take place, whatever may have been the method?
17. Explain the philosophy of Holism, as related to the Hierarchy of Being. Explain "This is a universe of whole-making."
18. State the substance of Montague's discussion of the chances of surviving death.
19. According to Montague's argument what are the four "fields of existence" which make up the Hierarchy of Being.
20. "Heaven is a prepared place for a prepared people." What are the reasons for this affirmation?

21. What, according to Scripture, are the different levels on which the Spirit operates in the Totality of Being? By what designation is His activity described in each of these areas?
22. What are the evidences in the first chapter of Genesis that support our empirical view of the Hierarchy of Being?
23. Distinguish between *primary* creation and *secondary* creation. How does this distinction harmonize with the distinction of *general* and *special* Providence?
24. What three stages of Creation are clearly marked out in the Biblical narrative?
25. Give the substance of Hesiod's cosmogony.
26. What did *Chaos* mean in Greek thought? How does this accord with the first two verses of Genesis?
27. What were the advances in the Creative Process that were brought about in an ascending order by the Breath of God?
28. What, according to Scripture, did God plan from before "the foundation of the world"?
29. What is the ultimate phase of the Creative Process?
30. In what state of being will the Divine Cosmic Plan be realized in the saints? In what respects will they be "conformed to the image of God's Son"?
31. What two classes will appear in the Judgment and what will be the destiny of each?
32. Why do we say that Redemption will be the second—and the last—phase of the whole Creative Process?
33. What are the three integral parts, or events, of the Divine Plan of the Universe?
34. What is the highest level in the total Hierarchy of Being?
35. Explain: Being is a *hierarchy*, not a *continuum*.
36. Explain spiritual progression from the Kingdom of Nature, through the Kingdom of Grace into the Kingdom of Glory.
37. Distinguish between *evolution* and *evolutionism*.
38. What error is involved in presenting *evolution* as a *fact*.
39. What do we mean by saying that the theory is built on *inference?*
40. Is the inference *necessary* inference? Explain your answer.
41. What is Jauncey's explanation of the misguided zeal of evolutionists? What is his evaluation of the current state of the hypothesis?
42. What fallacy is involved in the title, "Can Science Produce Life?"
43. What is one unfortunate "pragmatic" effect of evolutionism?
44. Explain why there is no adequate explanation of the cosmos without Efficient Causality.
45. Why is the angelic host essential to any adequate presentation of the Hierarchy of Being?
46. What does the Bible teach regarding the origin of the angelic host?
47. How are angels differentiated from men with respect to origin? With respect to their essential nature?
48. What seems to be the outstanding attribute of the angelic nature?
49. Is angelic power and intelligence limited? Explain, and give Scriptures to justify your answer.
50. What do we mean by saying that angels are "ethereal" beings? Can you think of any other adjective that would properly describe them?
51. What, according to Heb. 1:14, is the work of the angelic host? How prominently are angels presented in Scripture? Cite cases of their activities as reported in Scripture.
52. Are we logical in affirming that the angelic host occupies properly the intermediate position between man and God?

53. What statement of Jesus justifies our conclusion that angels are without sex distinctions?
54. How is the angelic host represented in Scripture (1) as to number, (2) as to organization.
55. What is pictured to be the activity of the good angels?
56. In what ways do the angels minister God's providence?
57. Give instances of the ministration of angels to individual believers.
58. In what ways do the angels execute God's will in *nature* and *in history?*
59. Summarize the doctrine of fallen angels as presented in the Bible.
60. What will be the ultimate destiny of the good angels?
61. What will be the ultimate destiny of the evil angels?
62. Who was Satan originally? Summarize what is stated about him and his activities as revealed in Scripture.
63. Summarize the role of angels in the Drama of Redemption.
64. What position do the angels hold in the Hierarchy of Being?
65. Are angels presented in Scripture as "supernatural" or as "superhuman"? Explain your answer.
66. What is meant by *nature* and *natural* processes, as distinguished from *human* and *superhuman?*
67. What is meant by *dualistic (dichotomic)* "impositions of the human mind upon reality"?
68. Certainly "nature" is a term which includes all *created* beings. But, is there any justification for assuming that God is a part of nature, or the whole of nature Himself?
69. Explain what is meant by *emanationism.*
70. Diagram the hierarchical interpretation of the cosmos as suggested by the Neoplatonists.
71. What general theory of emanation did the Gnostics hold?
72. Explain the hierarchical view of the cosmos as put forward by the various cults of Hinduism.
73. Why, according to Toy, has pantheism never "commended itself to the masses of men"?
74. Diagram Plato's concept of the Hierarchy of Being.
75. Diagram Aristotle's description of the Hierarchy of Being.
76. Note the hierarchical implications of self-styled Emergentism.
77. What is the empirical account of the Dimensions of Being?
78. Diagram the Biblical account of the Hierarchy of Being. Show the correspondence between the Biblical and empirical accounts.
79. Diagram the hierarchical picture that is given us in the Genesis account of the Creation.
80. Diagram the Teilhardian account of the Hierarchy of Being.
81. What significant features are added in the Teilhardian presentation that are not to be found in preceding philosophical descriptions?
82. Explain the theory of the Great Chain of Being.
82. What is our "conclusion of the whole matter"?

# PART FOUR

# SPIRIT IN GOD

## 1. Man the Image of God

In the Biblical account of the Creation, we read the following words with which every Bible student is familiar:

> And God said, Let us make man in our image, after our likeness: and let them have dominion over the fish of the sea, and over the birds of the heavens, and over the cattle, and over all the earth, and over every creeping thing that creepeth upon the earth. And God created man in his own image, in the image of God created he him; male and female created he them (Gen. 1:26-27).

One would be right in affirming, I think, that no other idea in all literature has so profoundly affected almost every phase of our Western culture as the idea embodied in this Scripture, the idea that every human being is the image or likeness of the Divine Being. This, in fact, is the concept which underlies the doctrine of the natural equality of men, and consequently the democratic form of the state; if the concept does not represent an objective fact, then human equality is only a myth and democracy a great delusion. Moreover, the truth itself is the foundation of the whole judicial order, that is, the order of human rights and duties; otherwise, such an order does not exist, and the alternative view—that Might makes Right—must be accepted as the true one.

*Man is the image of God*: so affirm the Scriptures. That is to say, as God is essentially Spirit, so man is essentially spirit, though in his present state clothed in a physical "tabernacle." Or, in equivalent terms, as God is a Person, so man is a person. In either sense, man is the image, the reflection, although no doubt a very feeble and imperfect one, of the Being of God. It will be remembered, in this connection, that Jesus was Scripturally declared to be "the very image of God's substance" (Heb. 1:3); that is, whereas the natural man is only the *personal* image, Jesus, Himself the God-Man, was both the personal *and moral*, image or likenes of God.

Now is this affirmation—that man is the image of God— a Divine revelation of an eternal truth? or is it a mere anthropomorphism? That is, did God actually create man in His own image, or did man create God in his own imagination?

The old Greek iconoclast, Xenophanes of Kolophon, the earliest rebel, in so far as our knowledge goes, against the anthropomorphic mythological deities of his time, is often quoted as having said: "Mortals seem to have begotten Gods to have their own garb and voice and form"; also, "Now if horses or oxen or lions had hands or power to paint and make the works of art that men make, then would horses give their Gods horse-like forms in painting or sculpture, and oxen ox-like forms, even each after its own kind"; and again: "The Aethiop saith that his Gods are snub-nosed and black, the Thracian that his have blue eyes and red hair," etc.[1] Now we must not infer from these statements that Xenophanes was an atheist. Obviously he was not, for among other sayings attributed to him are the following, which clearly indicate that he was thinking in monotheistic, or perhaps it would be nearer the truth to say pantheistic, terms: "There's one God greatest among Gods and men, who is like to mortals neither in form nor mind",[2] the divine, a living thing, "is all eye, all mind, all ear,"[3] "without toil it perceiveth and agitateth all things with its mind";[4] "it ever abideth in one place, and never moveth, nor doth it beseem it to go now this way and now that," etc.[5] It is evident from these fragments that Xenophanes was only repudiating the anthropomorphic polytheisms of Homer and Hesiod (who, said he, "have ascribed unto the gods all that is reproach and blame in the world of men, stealing and adultery and deceit"[6]) for a more rational conception of the Deity, just as did Socrates, and his pupil Plato, some two centuries afterward. Even so, this critique of anthropomorphism by Xenophanes, which has been parroted by so-called "free-thinkers" in almost every age, embraces at least two glaring fallacies. In the first place, his introductory *if* is an insurmountable barrier to the truthfulness of his statement. IF, said the old Greek thinker, horses or oxen or lions had power to conceive of Deity, or hands to represent Him in painting or sculpture, they would picture Him in a horse-like, or an ox-like, or a lion-like form, etc. But, as Shakespeare would say, "Aye, there's the rub!" Horses, oxen, or lions give no evidence whatever of any capacity to conceive of God; brutes are utterly incapable of receiving or entertaining the idea. A man might try to "explain" God to his old dog Rover, but Rover would be utterly unable to comprehend; Rover, in fact, could do nothing but wag his tail and lick his master's hand. Man alone,

1. *Elegy and Iambus*, Loeb Classical Library, 201, 203. J. M. Edmonds, translator. Fragments from *Miscellanies* of Clement of Alexandria.
2. *Elegy and Iambus*, Loeb Classical Library, 207. J. M. Edmonds, translator. From Clement of Alexandria, *Miscellanies*.
3. *Ibid.*, 207. From Sextus Empiricus, *Against the Mathematicians*.
4. *Ibid.*, 207. From Simplicius on Aristotle, *Physics* (on the All).
5. *Ibid.*, 207. From Simplicius on Aristotle, *Physics* (on the All).
6. *Ibid.*, 201. From Sextus Empiricus, *Against the Mathematicians*.

of all creatures of earth, is capable of apprehending the fact of God, capable of receiving a revelation from God, hence capable of religious belief and activity. Thus at most the statement of Xenophanes is only a half-truth and can never be anything more. In the second place, even man himself is compelled to think of God primarily in terms of his own experience; he can hardly do otherwise. This is no doubt the reason why so many of the presentations of the thoughts and acts of God, especially in the Old Testament, are put in anthropomorphic form; this form was in adaptation to man's finite intelligence; God was under the necessity of revealing Himself in terms of man's very limited experience. And particularly is this true of revelations that were communicated in the infancy of the race. In fact the entire Old Testament revelation gives evidence of having been constructed on what might properly be called principles of kindergarten pedagogy; the New Testament revelation, on the other hand, couched as it is in spiritual terms, is obviously adapted to a race that is supposed to have put away childish things. All this hue and cry of anthropomorphism, in so far as the content of the Old Testament is concerned, gives evidence of shallowness rather than of profundity of thought; in most cases it is but the outpouring of a profane spirit. As a matter of fact, these anthropomorphisms make our God more intelligible to us; they bring Him nearer to us; they make Him more "human," if indeed the use of this adjective with reference to the Deity is pardonable. The God of the Bible is far more lovable, far more attractive to mankind, than the God fabricated by human reason, the cold, intellectually-constructed Demiourgos of Plato, for example, or the Substance of Spinoza, or John Dewey's "humanistic" non-entity.[1] Besides, the anthropomorphic portrayals of God in the Old Testament are not to be taken in strict literalness; obviously they were not even intended to be so taken; undoubtedly many of them were consciously metaphorical. I quote here from Dr. Knudson:

> What we are, however, here concerned about is not to determine the extent of the literal and the metaphorical in the Old Testament use of anthropomorphisms, but to point out the fact that the great purpose actually served by these anthropomorphisms is to emphasize the personality of God. He is a living, acting Being, a Being touched with the feeling of our infirmities. He does not stand apart from men but enters in the most intimate way into their experiences. He counsels them, commands them, blesses them, punishes them. In a word, He is the great outstanding fact of their lives. This truth it is that lies

1. *Vide* Plato, *Timaeus;* Spinoza, *Ethics;* John Dewey, *A Common Faith.*

back of the biblical use of anthropomorphisms and is enforced by them. In no other way could the personality of God at that time have been adequately and effectively expressed. Concrete conceptions and concrete modes of speech, such as we find in the anthropomorphisms of the Old Testament, were the only ones that could then be fully understood.[1]

Man was created in the image of God; so the Scriptures declare. Every human being is a likeness of God. Certainly this likeness is not in any sense physical; there is nothing in Scripture that can be construed to support such an interpretation. This likeness is comprehended, rather, in the terms of Person and Spirit. Man is the likeness of the Divine in his possession of the attributes and powers of Person, of Spirit. Of course this does not mean that God is a Person in precisely the same modes, or in precisely the same degree, with respect to the intensity of His powers, that man is a person; hence, some writers have chosen to write of God as "super-" or "suprapersonal." Granting, however, that due allowance must be made for the difference in rank and power between deity and humanity, nevertheless, again as Knudson puts it,

personality is the highest category of which we know anything. "Superpersonal existence" is a phrase without any concrete content, an unknown quantity that means no more to us than an algebraic *xy*. If we are, therefore, to think of God, it must be either under the personal or some subpersonal form. There is no third alternative.[2]

C. E. M. Joad writes, *God and Evil*, 250-251: "Now it may be true that God permits Himself to be conceived as a personality, but if so, His personality can be at most only one aspect of the whole that He is." But, because Person is the highest category of which we have knowledge, reason forbids our conceiving God as being less than Person, for in that case He would be less than man—an unthinkable conclusion with respect to the Deity. Hence we must conclude that God belongs in the category of Person, but necessarily of Person in the fullest and most intense degree of those powers characteristic of the personal order of being. In a word, . must be Person or Spirit in perfection, eternal in His being, infinite in His inexhaustibleness.

"The spiritual, *as we know it*," writes Rufus Jones

is always superposed on the physical, the biological, the natural. It does not come down from above by a Jacob's ladder as a purely heavenly "emergent." It comes rather as a new and subtle elevation,

1. Albert C. Knudson, *The Religious Teaching of the Old Testament*, 61.
2. *Op. cit.*, 58.

a sublimation, of what was here before. The spiritual, in some way not yet known, "breaks through" the natural as its organ of expression, somewhat as electricity "breaks through" into manifestation as soon as the dynamo is sufficiently perfected, though the analogy is very lame and halting. . . . In some unexplainable way, which remains as mysterious as the functions of Aladdin's lamp is the Arabian story, refined forms of matter—like that for example which composes our brain cortexes—allows consciousness, mind, intelligent purpose, to break forth. There comes a stage in the unfolding of life when a type of consciousness emerges which may quite properly be called *spirit*. It is characterized first of all by the truly amazing fact that it knows itself. It would seem to be mystery enough to be able to know an object in space. How that is done is and remains a fundamental mystery. But mind of what I am calling the spirit type not only knows an object but knows that it knows it, and knows itself as knowing it. The Jacob's ladder is now within, and mind can climb up and overspan as from a watchtower both subject and object, both self and others, and can know *that* it knows as well as *what* it knows. . . . The mind of man, throughout its experience of knowing, transcends the act of knowing an object, and in the same pulse of experience in which it knows the object knows itself as knowing it. This unique peculiarity of self-identity and the inner grasp of itself in all its intelligent processes belongs inherently to mind at this stage of spirit. We shall get nowhere with our theories of knowledge until we stop talking of the mind as though it were merely a receptacle—a bird-cage to be filled from the outside—and learn to think of it as a living active system of experience, unified and controlled from within. What Kant called "the transcendental unity of consciousness" is one of the most majestic of all our interior marvels. We need not be unduly bothered by his beloved word "transcendental." It does not imply something which comes from a mystical beyond, some vague addendum to our inherent structural organ of consciousness. It is native to us as men. It means here only that the *unity* of consciousness under consideration is presupposed in all our experience. This unity is an essential condition of knowledge. It is constitutive of knowledge, and cannot be a product of it. It is what gives our type of experience its *universal* and *necessary* character. It means that at every sane moment of our lives we look out upon each new fact of knowledge from a unified comprehensive self, which binds the new fact, with proper linkages of thought-forms, in with a larger background and persistent self-center, with slowly formed dispositional traits, and with the added mark and brand that *this is I that think and know this fact*. All knowledge that can be called "knowledge" involves something new confronted and apprehended by a larger apperceiving self which fuses the new with the old, gives it its place in the comprehending system, and weaves the new fact, with this mysterious inner shuttle of "I know it," into the web of persistent knowledge. There are certain well-known phrases, such as "psychological climate" or "apperception's mass," or "dispositional traits" or "meaning-mass" or "mnemonic mass," for the assimilation of the new experience with the old; but the current phrases are often used too loosely and with too little stress upon *the operating dominion of an identical self* which does the apperceiving, the assimilating of the new with the old. The structural unity of which I am speaking and the self-identity of our knowing self need to have signal emphasis if we are ever to arrive at the true significance of the life of the spirit. The dominion of meaning from within, all the time, dominates our perceptions.[1]

1. *Spirit in Man*, 6-10.

## Dr. Jones then goes on to say:

Mind, when it reaches the stage of spirit in beings like us—the only beings in whom we see it manifested—is no longer completely dependent on objects perceived, objects "given" in space. It can now attend to objects of its own order, to that which is mental, spiritual, ideal. It can produce and attend to what are well called "free ideas." Free ideas become detached from the experiences and the settings and the occasions in which they arose. Free ideas are explicit thoughts which are independent of what is given at the time in sense. They are our universals, our working concepts, our ideas of connection and relationship. These free ideas are the basic unities, the linkages, and the forms through which we interpret all our experiences. They are the patterns and forms for our experiences of beauty and goodness. They are the controlling ideals in our forecasts of life. . . . These "free ideas" become the instruments of new ranges of thought, and they enable us to anticipate and handle situations not yet experienced. The mind rolls up and accumulates a body of experience which not only conserves the past but which outruns its stocks of income and creates values of its own. It can perceive with an inward eye—"an eye made quiet by the power of harmony"—and can behold what never was before on sea or land. It can, through its accumulated powers, deal with those intangibles and impalpables, which crude senses are bound to miss, as they also miss the vibrations which apparently make sensations possible. It is thus that we become *creative* beings.[1]

This power, Dr. Janes continues, "to save the past by memory and to anticipate the future by creative imagination makes ideal forecasts possible and gives us a prophetic faith that the gates of the future are open to us."[2] It creates "a beyond within us."

The characteristic of a beyond within us belongs essentially to spirit in man, and is one of our most momentous characteristics. An *immanent* ideal, operating in all our life aims, is essential to our nature as persons. There is always a "more yet" which carries our minds over and beyond the margins of any given situation. . . . This feature of a beyond within us, this capacity of before and after, this power to see our deed in the light of an ideal forecast, furnishes us with a fundamental form of distinction between what was, or is, and what might have been—between a good and a possible better. Then we slowly roll up and accumulate through life-experience with others a concrete or dispositional conscience which becomes, or may become, a perennial nucleus of inward moral wisdom and guidance. This becomes, or may become, to us the deep self which we really *are*, the self we propose to *be*, the self which we would even die to preserve. This deep-lying nuclear moral guardian in us is one of the most amazing features of a rightly fashioned life, but one must have it in order to appreciate it.[3]

## Finally, in this connection:

First, last, and all the time, *i.e.*, in our sanity, we possess an integral, self-identical self, which knows what it knows and does what

1. Rufus M. Jones, *op. cit.*, 10-11.
2. *Ibid.*, 11-12.
3. *Ibid.*, 12-13.

it does. It is, or at least can become, a highly complex spiritual reality, with a sphere and range of its own. We are in large measure the makers of ourselves; but fortunately we start with a precious impartation, of birth-gift, which is big with its potentiality of spirit— otherwise we might have ended as a hop-toad,

> A creature predestined to move
> In a well-defined groove,

with no power to build a self from within, such as we now possess. And that self of ours, whatever its ultimate destiny may be, is utterly *unique*.[1]

It is only by the cultivation of the "nuclear moral guardian" within him, Dr. Jones points out, that a man attains ultimately to the status of a *real person;* by failing to to cultivate it, he simply drops back to the biological level. Where there is life, there is growth, in the moral as in the biological realm; the only alternative to growth, to advancement, is atavism. One is reminded here of the words of Jesus: "Enter ye in by the narrow gate: for wide is the gate, and broad is the way, that leadeth to destruction, and many are they that enter in thereby. For narrow is the gate, and straitened the way, that leadeth unto life, and few are they that find it" (Matt. 7:13-14). The attainment of the status of a *real person,* moreover, is contingent upon a man's cultivation of the Mind of Christ within himself, upon his living the life with the Holy Spirit. Obviously, then, in the light of both reason and Scripture teaching, this attainment of the status of a real person *can* be realized only by the saints of God, and *will* be realized by them only in their ultimate union with God in knowledge and love. And the necessary concomitant of this union, as we have already seen, will be the putting on of immortality—the saint's exchange of his physical for his spiritual body. This spiritual life, moreover, emerges from within a person only as a result of the fructifying of spiritual seed, the Word of God, implanted from without. For it is a law of the moral as well as of the biological realm that each living thing shall reproduce after its own kind; hence "that which is born of the flesh is flesh; and that which is born of the Spirit is spirit" (John 3:6). There is no reversing of the orderly processes of Nature.

I quote again:

We are so wedded by habit to the forms and moulds which the substantial matter of our bodies supplies here in this sphere of mutability that we are helpless to imagine a realm of real and actual life in which the enswathement of personality is of wholly different and far more subtle stuff. But a "spiritual body" is by no means an impossi-

1. Jones, *op. cit.*, 21-22.

bility, and it would be no more of a mutation than that of the butter-fly that emerges from the chrysalis. What we really care for and must have, if immortality is to be a desirable gain, is real *conserva-tion of personality* and the possibility of progressive personal life— of going on. . . . And, furthermore, it is not just "going on" that we are thinking about. It is not enough to attain the status of an infinitely extended Methuselah-type of life, with the mere dimension of length. What we mean when we talk of eternal life is life that opens expansively into the Life of God—the Over-World of Spirit—that takes on amplitude and that shares with God in the spiritual tasks of His expanding creation.[1]

I trust that I shall be pardoned for quoting at such length from Dr. Jones' excellent—and stylistically exquisite—little book, *Spirit in Man.* I have done so because I consider it the clearest presentation of the subject that can be found anywhere in secular literature, and because, too, the presentation parallels so closely the argument I am trying to present here, namely, that *spirit in man is the sole ground for the attainment of real personality, through the life with the Holy Spirit here and ulti-mate perfect union with God hereafter.* There is a spirit in man; spirit in man is, in its attributes and powers, a likeness of Spirit in God; and in this likeness lies the potentiality of final union with God, Beatitude, Everlasting Life.

I think, therefore, that I may be permitted one more ex cerpt, in this connection. Dr. Jones writes:

There is a stage in this upward climb of our strange Jacob's ladder of spirit when we can see and can enjoy realities which to a certain degree are spiritual in their own sovereign right. I mean of course the intrinsic values of Beauty, Truth, Goodness, and Love . . . . A mind which can see and appreciate those realities has already trans-cended the realm of time and space and matter and *sensa* and the bio-logical order, and belongs already to an intrinsic, that is, eternal order. These ideal values are the unmoved movers which shape our destiny; and in the realm of the spirit they are eternal, *i.e.*, they are time-transcending realities[2]

This "eternal order" is, of course, what we mean here by the order of sainthood.

The power of the mind to transcend the realm of space and time and sense and biological life, and consequently (1) to generate "free ideas," and (2) to apprehend values, evinces unmistakably the *metaphysical* likeness of the human spirit to the Divine Spirit. By metaphysical likeness is meant of course similarity of attributes and powers, that is, beyond the merely physical and biological. What is yet necessary for man, that is, for him to attain his natural and proper end as a

1. *Op. cit.,* 69-70.
2. *Ibid.,* 14.

spiritual being, is for this metaphysical likeness to grow into a genuine moral likeness as well, through man's own voluntary choice of, and devotion to, the life of the Spirit; *in a word, for the human spirit to become possessed, guided, filled and moulded by the Spirit of God.* Such moral likeness existed as it has been pointed out already, in the person of Christ, our perfect Exemplar; He possessed the Holy Spirit without measure (John 3:34); whereas ordinary mortal man is the personal image of God, Christ the Son is the *very* image, that is, *moral as well as personal*, of the Divine Substance (Heb. 1:3). His supreme interest in life was to do the Will of the Father in all things; He is "Christ the power of God, and the wisdom of God" (1 Cor. 1:24). He could say in all truth, "I and the Father are one" (John 10:30), and, "He that hath seen me hath seen the Father" (John 14:9); and in all truth He could pray to the Father, with reference to all believers, "that they may all be one; even as thou, Father, are in me, and I in thee, that they also may be in us: that the world may believe that thou didst send me" (John 17:21). And, although the saint cannot ever, either in this world or in the world to come, attain to the ontological status of deity—any more than a rock can transform itself into a living thing, or a plant into an animal, or a brute into a man—he can, nevertheless, become more and more like Christ morally, and the more he attains "unto the measure of the stature of the fulness of Christ" (Eph. 4:13), the more he becomes like God or godlike, and in this manner comes to be in truth a partaker (sharer) of the Divine Nature morally and spiritually (2 Pet. 1:4). This attainment of moral perfection is the attainment of Wholeness or Holiness. In our use of the terms "spirit" and "spiritual," however, we must always be careful to distinguish between their metaphysical and their moral content. Every man is now, in his present state, the *metaphysical* likeness of God, that is, *personally* spiritual (in the sense that God is the "Father of our spirits" by creation, Heb. 12:9); only through the power of the Gospel of Christ and the life of the Spirit, however, can he hope to become the *moral* likeness of God, that is truly or *fully* spiritual. And to be fully spiritual is to be *whole* or holy.

Again, one readily sees the benevolence of God in His endowment of the human spirit with free will, that is, the power of self-determination and self-direction. That *conation*—purposive striving toward a goal, striving that is not itself reducible to mechanism—is characteristic of man, can hardly be denied. Man's activity always has directionality. This fact was clearly brought out by the investigations of Dr. C. Buhler and her associates.

In their study of approximately two hundred life histories, the most definite conclusion was that each life seemed definitely ordered and steered toward some selected goal; each person had something quite special to live for. Each had a characteristic *Bestimmung* and *intention*. The style, of course, varied; some staked everything one single great objective; others varied their goals from time to time, but goals there always were. A supplementary study of would-be suicides showed that life becomes intolerable to those who can find nothing to aim at, no goal to seek.[1]

Human nature is purposive; God constituted it so, as an indispensable condition of man's attainment of holiness. In order to attain God as his natural and proper ultimate end, man must deliberately choose to attain God, out of the pure love in his heart for God. He must purposively direct his life in the path of *right*—the path that leads to ultimate union with God. Although God has indeed provided him with the indispensable means to his attainment of union with the Divine as his ultimate end, nevertheless, it is man's part to willingly and purposefully utilize those necessary means; otherwise, he will fall short of attainment. Man cannot travel in two directions at the same time; he cannot serve both God and Mammon. God has graciously provided the means whereby man may preserve himself in existence physically, and the means also whereby he may be reconciled to his heavenly Father, enter into covenant relationship with Him, and grow thereafter in the grace and knowledge of Christ (2 Pet. 3:18)—the means whereby he may become a partaker of the Divine Nature by living the life of the Spirit. But man must, in turn, accept those gracious provisions and utilize them to his own growth in holiness and ultimate attainment of the Life Everlasting. Thus God and man, grace and faith, working together in covenant relationship, in holy fellowship, effect the latter's redemption from the guilt, and ultimately from the consequences, of sin, that is, from mortality itself (2 Cor. 5:4). Hence the Apostle admonishes us as follows: "Work out your own salvation with fear and trembling; for it is God who worketh in you both to will and to work, for his good pleasure" (Phil. 2:12-13). "God so loved the world, that he gave his only begotten Son, that whosoever believeth on him should not perish, but have eternal life" (John 3:16). But of what value is this priceless Gift to man, if man refuses to accept

1. G. W. Allport, *Personality: A Psychological Interpretation*, 219. *Vide* C. Buhler, *Der menschliche Lebenslauf als psychologisches Problem*, 1933.

Him? Not even Omnipotence can compel men to love Him; that must come freely from their own hearts. As Lecomte du Nouy says:

It is clear that God abdicated a portion of his omnipotence when he gave man liberty of choice. Man—according to the second chapter of Genesis, and to our hypothesis—possesses a real independence, willed by God, and which becomes, in the human species, the tool of selection. It is no longer the strongest, the most agile, the fittest physically who must survive, but the best, the most evolved morally. The new supremacy can only manifest itself in man if man is free to choose his path. This is, therefore, an apparent limitation of the omnipotence of the Creator, consented to by Him in order to bestow freedom upon the chosen species, so as to impose a final test. Having been endowed with conscience, man has acquired an independence of which he must show himself to be worthy, under pain of regressing toward the beast.[1]

As we shall see later, this self-determination, self-direction, purposiveness, characteristic of spirit in man, is also characteristic of Spirit in God.

Finally, the power of the human spirit, evident in every people in every age of human history, to apprehend and to enjoy such intrinsic realities as Truth, Beauty, Goodness and Love, points unmistakably to the Spirit of God, in whom such realities, such values, if they exist at all—and they surely do, otherwise the human race would have destroyed itself long ago—must have their source and being. The Eternal Spirit Himself is in the fullest sense of all these terms Truth, Beauty, Goodness and Love. Our God is Himself Love, and He is Spirit.

John 4:24 [the words of Jesus]: God is a Spirit, and they that worship him must worship in spirit and truth. John 14:6 [again the words of Jesus]: I am the way, and the truth, and the life: no one cometh unto the Father, but by me. 1 John 4:8—He that loveth not knoweth not God; for God is love.

In this manner do we reason from the human spirit, the image of God, to the Divine Spirit, very God. The attributes and powers of the human spirit become clear intimations to us of the attributes and powers of the Divine Spirit. And the Divine Spirit becomes knowable to us in terms of the potencies of the human spirit. Then, turning to the Scriptures, we find the voice of reason and experience corroborated, as is always the case, by the testimony of revelation. Nature and revelation are never contradictory.

## 2. The Triune Personality of God

Our approach to the study of Spirit in God, as that subject

1. *Human Destiny*, 197.

is revealed in Scripture, is necessarily by way of the doctrine of the triune personality of God. Hence it becomes necessary at this time to summarize the teaching of the Scriptures on this latter subject—by correlating the various passages in which the doctrine is set forth—in as brief a manner as possible.

This doctrine is commonly designated the doctrine of the "Trinity." The word "Trinity," however, does not occur in the Bible.

The doctrine may be stated summarily as follows: Our God, as to essence, is one and unique; this unity of essence, however, embraces a "trinity" of Persons. That is to say, speaking by way of analogy from human experience, this "trinity" is—I take it—to be conceived as an "organic" rather than as mathematical unity. Nor is this statement to be dismissed as an absurdity, for, as Leonard Hodgson says:

> We have no actual experience of any existing unity in this world of space and time which is not of the organic type. . . . If either of the two types of unity is to be called a figment of the human imagination, the absolutely simple and undifferentiated unity of the mathematician has the greater claim to that status.[1]

And again·

> The difference between the two ideas of unity is this. The mathematical is so simple that one instance is enough to establish the fact that it cannot exist in mutually differing varieties of itself, as triangularity can exist in three and only three. In contrast with both these mathematical ideas, the idea of internally constitutive unity is so complex that we have to be continually revising our opinion of what content it will admit of in different instances of itself. Only by studying the empirical evidence in various instances can we determine the possible range of contents of an atom, a crystal, an animal, a man, a nation or a work of art.[2]

The same author concludes:

> This world is the world wherein the ultimate unities of reality are made known to us not in their unity but in their multiplicity. Why, then, should we be surprised that in His revelation of Himself to man on earth God makes Himself known in His multiplicity, that He should be revealed to us as Father, as Son, and as Spirit, but that clear understanding of His unity should be beyond our ken?[3]

As Professor James B. Green has written:

> When we say that there are three persons in the Godhead, we mean to deny Unitarianism. Unitarianism is the belief that God is one essence or being without distinction in the mode of His being; that He is a monad in every sense—a unit and not a unity. Again, when

1. *The Doctrine of the Trinity*, 94.
2. Hodgson, *op. cit.*, 108.      z
3. *Ibid.*, 108.

we affirm that there are three persons in the Godhead we mean to deny Sabellianism. Sabellianism is the doctrine that Father, Son and Spirit are names not of three persons, but of three relations or functions of one and the same person. We are not tritheists, as the Unitarians affirm and the Sabellians fear. We are monontheists. We are as monotheistic as the Unitarians or the Sabellians. We believe in one God, but in a God whose mode of being is such that He can say with reference to Himself, "I," "Thou," "He." The Father can say, "I will send Him, the Spirit, through Thee, the Son." This is the catholic or commonly accepted Christian doctrine of God. No man, as Denney says, means all that a Christian means by "God," unless he puts into "God" all that is meant by the separate terms "Fathers," "Son," "Spirit."[1]

In this connection, one might cite the triune liturgical ascription before the Throne of God in Heaven: "Holy, holy, holy, is Jehovah of hosts; the whole earth is full of his glory" (Isa. 6:3). Again, "Holy, holy, holy, is the Lord God, the Almighty, who was and who is and who is to come" (Rev. 4:8).

In Old Testament times God sought constantly to impress upon the minds of His chosen people the fact of His *uniqueness*. "Hear, O Israel: Jehovah our God is one Jehovah: and thou shalt love Jehovah thy God with all thy heart, and with all thy soul, and with all thy might" (Deut. 6:4-5). There is nothing, however, in this affirmation of monotheism to exclude the fact of God's triune personality. Obviously this Old Testament pronouncement, that our God is one God is essentially the affirmation of His uniqueness as the one living and true God. Cf. *Jerusalem Bible* on Deut. 6:4—

Another translation sometimes adopted, "Listen, Israel: Yahweh is our God, Yahweh alone," but it is more likely that we have here a declaration of monotheistic faith. This verse was later to be used as the opening words of the *Shema*, a prayer still central to Jewish piety.

This idea of uniqueness (that is, "I am Yahweh, and there is none else," etc.) is emphasized through both the Old and New Testament Scriptures.

Cf. Deut. 4:35—Unto thee it was showed, that thou mightest know that Jehovah he is God; there is none else besides him. Deut. 4:39 —Know therefore this day, and lay it to thy heart that Jehovah he is God in heaven above and upon the earth beneath; there is none else. Isa. 43:10—Before me there was no God formed, neither shall there be after me. Isa. 45:5-6: I am Jehovah, and there is none else; besides me there is no God. I will gird thee, though thou hast not known me; that they may know from the rising of the sun, and from the west, that there is none besides me; I am Jehovah, and there is none else. Isa. 46:9-11: I am God, and there is none else; I am God, and there is none like me; declaring the end from the beginning, and from ancient times things that are not yet done. . . . yea, I have spoken, I will also bring it to pass; I have purposed, I will also do it.

1. *Studies in the Holy Spirit*, 35-36.

And in the New Testament, we read that when one of the scribes on occasion questioned Jesus as to the greatest commandment in the Law, Jesus answered: "The first is, Hear, O Israel; the Lord our God, the Lord is one: and thou shalt love the Lord thy God with all thy heart, and with all thy soul, and with all thy mind, and with all thy strength." Whereupon the scribe answered: "Of a truth, Teacher, thou hast well said that he is one; and there is none other but he" (Mark 12:28-34). Language could hardly be more explicit. Hence the significance of such phrases as the "true God," the "living God," found throughout the Bible:

Jer. 10:10—Jehovah is the true God; he is the living God. John 17:3—This is life eternal, that they should know thee, the only true God, and him whom thou didst send, even Jesus Christ [the words of Jesus]. 1 Thess. 1:9—how ye turned unto God from idols, to serve a living and true God. Josh. 3:10—Hereby ye shall know that the living God is among you, etc. Psa. 84:2—My heart and my flesh cry out unto the living God. Matt. 16:16 [the Good Confession required of all who become Christians]: Thou art the Christ, the Son of the living God. Acts 14:15—that ye should turn from these vain things unto a living God, who made the heaven and the earth and the sea, and all that in them is. 2 Cor. 3:3—the Spirit of the living God.

These are just a few of the many pasages in which these phrases are used in Scripture. Their significance is obvious, Our God, the living and true God, is the *only* God; there is no other.

The fact remains, however, that the triune personality of the Divine Being was not clearly revealed in Old Testament times; it was only intimated. In the Old Testament, we have God, the Spirit of God, and the Word (or Wisdom) of God, as, *e.g.*, in the first chapter of *Genesis;* but nowhere in the Hebrew Scriptures are they revealed as distinct subsistences. The reason is evident: God's elect were not yet prepared for such a disclosure. Had the revelation been made to the children of Israel, surrounded on all sides as they were by heathen polytheisms, undoubtedly they would have prostituted their religion into a tritheism, that is, a worship of three Gods. Hence it is not until we come into the clear light of the New Testament revelation that God, the Word of God, and the Spirit of God of the Old Testament, become the Father, Son, and Holy Spirit. It is significant, too, that it was Jesus Himself who first revealed this truth in its fulness. In giving the Great Commission, He said to His Apostles: "All authority hath been given unto me in heaven and on earth. Go ye therefore, and make disciples of all the nations, baptizing them into the name of the Father and of the Son and the Holy Spirit," etc. (Matt.

281

28:18-20). In other words, one immersion brings the penitent believer into the name, *i.e.*, into or under the *authority*, of the Father, Son, and Holy Spirit. Why the singular—"name"? Obviously, because the Three are in essence One; they have but one name, one rule, one authority. Incidentally, this very fact— the use of the singular "name," rather than "names"—invalidates so-called "trine immersion" or three dippings, which is erroneously practiced by certain sects of Christendom.

The Scripture doctrine of the triune personality of God may be summarized in the following propositions:

1. *In the Scriptures there are Three, each of whom is recognized as God.*

(1) The Father is recognized as God. For example:

John 6:27—for him the Father, even God, hath sealed. Matt. 6:9— After this manner therefore pray ye: Our Father who art in heaven, etc. Eph. 1:3—Blessed be the God and Father of our Lord Jesus Christ. 1 Pet. 1:2—according to the foreknowledge of God the Father. [Scripture passages in which the Father is recognized as God are numerous.]

(2) The Son, whose eternal name is the Word (Logos), is also recognized as God.

(a) John 1:1, 2, 14—In the beginning was the Word, and the Word was with God, and the Word was God. The same was in the beginning with God. . . . And the Word became flesh, and dwelt among us (and we beheld his glory, glory as of the only begotten from the Father), full of grace and truth. [Here the inspired writer is explicit: In the beginning, he says, the Word was *with* God, that is, there were *two;* then, lest anyone get the notion that the Word was inferior to God, he adds, *and the Word was God.*] [That is, as to essence, the Word is deity as truly as God is deity. Note also the omission of the article here: the Word was not *a* God, but God, for there is only one God.] Now the Word of God, the inspired writer goes on to tell us, became the Son of God through the mystery of the Incarnation: *The Word became flesh, and dwelt among us.* [This doctrine of the Logos is fully treated in a subsequent section.] (b) John 1:18—No man hath seen God at any time; the only begotten Son, who is in the bosom of the Father, he hath declared him, [that is, declared His will, revealed Him to mankind; this was the specific mission of Logos who Himself said]: *He that hath seen me hath seen the Father* (John 14:9). [In the foregoing passage, many ancient authorities read], "God only begotten," instead of "the only begotten Son." [Cf. the words of Jesus in His great intercessory prayer]: "And now, Father, glorify thou me with thine own self with the glory which I had with thee before the world was (John 17:5). (c) John 20:28—Thomas answered and said unto him, My Lord and my God. [The fact that Thomas accepted this ascription of deity to Himself, without a word of reproof, is *prima facie* evidence of His inherent right to it.] (d) Rom. 9:5—whose are the fathers, and of whom is Christ as concerning the flesh, who is over all, God blessed for ever. [That is, although Jesus received His human nature from the seed of Abraham through Mary, who was the passive instrumentality of His incarnation; yet in His eternal nature He is *God blessed for ever.*] (e) Heb. 1:8-9: But of the Son he saith, Thy throne,

282

O God, is for ever and ever; And the sceptre of thy uprightness is the sceptre of thy kingdom. Thou hast loved righteousness, and hated iniquity; Therefore God, thy God, hath anointed thee With the oil of gladness above thy fellows. [In this passage the inspired writer quotes Psalm 45:6-7 as referring expressly to the Son of God. This is a clear declaration of the deity of Jesus which can hardly be challenged from any point of view] (f) John 8:58—Jesus said unto them, Verily, verily, I say unto you, Before Abraham was born, I am. [Here Jesus is represented as taking unto Himself the great and incommunicable Name of the Deity, cf. Exo. 3:13-15. No wonder His Jewish contemporaries charged Him with blasphemy! Jesus was either everything He claimed to be, or He was the greatest impostor who ever appeared before the world!]

Again, there are many Scriptures in which the attributes of Deity are ascribed to the Son, such as, for example:

[(a) *Infinite Life.*] John 1:4—In him was life, and the life was the light of men. John 14:6—I am the way, and the truth, and the life; no one cometh unto the Father, but by me. John 5:26—For as the Father hath life in himself, even so gave he to the Son also to have life in himself. John 11:25—Jesus said unto her, I am the resurrection and the life. Rev. 1:17-18: I am the first and the last, and the Living One. [(b) *Eternity.*]John 17:5—Father, glorify thou me with thine own self with the glory which I had with thee before the world was. Col. 1:17—and he is before all things, and in him all things consist. Rev. 21:6—I am the Alpha and the Omega, the beginning and the end. [(c) *Self-Existence.*] John 8:58—Before Abraham was born, I am." John 5:26—For as the Father hath life in himself, even so gave he to the Son also to have life in himself. John 10:17-18; Therefore doth the Father love me, because I lay down my life, that I may take it again. No one taketh it away from me, but I lay it down of myself. I have power to lay it down, and I have power to take it again. Heb. 7:16—[here we are told that after the likeness of Melchizedek there ariseth another priest, who hath been made, not after the law of a carnal commandment, but after the power of an endless life. The reference is to the priesthood of Christ.] [(d) *Immutability.*] Heb. 13:8—Jesus Christ is the same yesterday and today, yea and for ever. [(e) *Omnipresence.*] Matt. 28:20—Lo, I am with you always, even unto the end of the world. Eph. 1:23—the church, which is his body, the fulness of him that filleth all in all. [(f) *Omnipotence.*] Matt. 28:18—All authority hath been given unto me in heaven and on earth. Rev. 1:8—I am the Alpha and the Omega . . . who is and who was and who is to come, the Almighty. [The context shows that it was the sovereign Christ who was speaking here to John.] [(g) *Omniscience.*] John 2:25—for he himself knew what was in man. Acts 1:24—And they prayed, and said, Thou, Lord, who knowest the hearts of all men, etc. [(h) *Infinite truth.*] John 14:6—I am the way, and the truth, and the life. John 6:63—The words that I have spoken unto you are spirit, and are life. Matt. 24:35—Heaven and earth shall pass away, but my words shall not pass away. John 18:37—To this end have I been born, and to this end am I come into the world, that I should bear witness unto the truth. Every one that is of the truth heareth my voice. [(i) *Infinite love.*] John 15:13—Greater love hath no man than this, that a man lay down his life for his friends. 1 John 3:16—Hereby know we love, because he laid down his life for us. [(j) *Infinite holiness.*] Luke 1:35—Wherefore also the holy thing which is begotten shall be called the Son of God. John 6:69—And we have believed and know that thou art the Holy One of God. Acts 2:27—Neither wilt thou give thy Holy

One to see corruption" [a quotation of Psa. 16:10]. Heb. 7:26—For such a high priest became us, holy, guileless, undefiled, separated from sinners, and made higher than the heavens.

In the third place, the Scriptures ascribe to the Son the works of Deity, such as the following:

[(a) *Creation.*] John 1:13—All things were made through him; and without him was not anything made that hath been made. Col. 1:16-17: For in him were all things created, in the heavens and upon the earth, things visible and things invisible, whether thrones or dominions or principalities or powers; all things have been created through him, and unto him; and he is before all things, and in him all things consist. 1 Cor. 8:6—Yet to us there is one God, the Father, of whom are all things, and we unto him; and one Lord, Jesus Christ, through whom are all things, and we through him. Heb. 1:8-10—But of the Son he saith . . . Thou, Lord, in the beginning didst lay the foundation of the earth, And the heavens are works of thy hands. [(b) *Conservation of the physical creation.*] Col. 1:17—in him all things consist, [*i.e.,* are constituted, or hold together.] Heb. 1:3—upholding all things by the word of his power. [(c) *Raising the dead to life, and* (d) *Judging the world.*] John 5:25-27: Verily, verily, I say unto you, The hour cometh, and now is, when the dead shall hear the voice of the Son of God; and they that hear shall live. For as the Father hath life in himself, even so gave he to the Son also to have life in himself; and he gave him authority to execute judgment, because he is a son of man. John 11:26—Whosoever liveth and believeth on me shall never die. Matt. 25:31 ff.—But when the Son of man shall come in his glory, and all the angels with him, then shall he sit on the throne of his glory; and before him shall be gathered all the nations: and he shall separate them one from another, as the shepherd separateth the sheep from the goats. 2 Thess. 1:7-8: at the revelation of the Lord Jesus from heaven with the angels of his power in flaming fire, rendering vengeance to them that know not God, and to them that obey not the gospel of our Lord Jesus.

In the fourth place, there are Scriptures which represent the Son as receiving honor and worship which should be given only to the Deity. For example:

John 5:22-23: For neither doth the Father judge any man, but he hath given all judgment unto the Son; that all may honor the Son, even as they honor the Father. Phil. 2:9-11: Wherefore also God highly exalted him, and gave unto him the name which is above every name; that in the name of Jesus every knee should bow, of things in heaven and things on earth and things under the earth, and that every tongue should confess that Jesus Christ is Lord, to the glory of God the Father. Eph. 1:22-23: God put all things in subjection under his feet, and gave him to be head over all things to the church, which is his body, the fulness of him that filleth all in all. 1 Pet. 3:22—Jesus Christ, who is on the right hand of God, having gone into heaven; angels and authorities and powers being made subject unto him. Rev. 5:12-13: . . . saying with a great voice, Worthy is the Lamb that hath been slain to receive the power, and riches, and wisdom, and might, and honor, and glory, and blessing. And every created thing which is in the heaven, and on the earth, and under the earth, and on the sea, and all things that are in them, heard I saying, Unto him that sitteth on the throne, and unto the Lamb, be the blessing, and the honor, and the

284

glory, and the dominion, for ever and ever. [Many passages of like character may be found throughout the New Testament.]

In the fifth place, there are Scriptures in which the Son's equality with the Father is explicitly declared. Jesus declared it Himself.

John 5:17-18: But Jesus answered them, My Father worketh even until now, and I work. For this cause therefore the Jews sought the more to kill him, because he not only brake the sabbath, but also called God his own Father, making himself equal with God.

And the Apostle Paul testifies, by inspiration of the Spirit:

Phil. 2:5-8: Have this mind in you, which was also in Christ Jesus: who, existing in the form of God, counted not the being on an equality with God a thing to be grasped, but emptied himself, taking the form of a servant, being made in the likeness of men; and being found in fashion as a man, he humbled himself; becoming obedient even unto death, yea, the death of the cross.

That is to say, the Logos, the Son of God, did not count His "being on an equality with God a thing to be grasped, "*i.e.*, to be taken hold of and clung to—simply because it was His by nature and by right. For He was not only *with* God "in the beginning," but He *was* God. He "emptied himself," we are told, "taking the form of a servant, being made in the likeness of man; and being found in fashion as a man, he humbled himself, becoming obedient even unto death, yea, the death of the cross." Perhaps it should be explained at this point that the doctrine of the Kenosis or Humiliation of the pre-incarnate Logos during the period of His incarnation clarifies certain other Scriptures which might seem to militate against the fact of His equality with the Father. The passages in question indicate that He was subject to certain limitations throughout His public ministry. It should be understood, however, that these limitations were not concomitants of His original and eternal nature; nor were they forced upon Him, but rather were self-imposed in adaptation to His incarnate nature. For instance, He limited Himself with the frailties of the flesh, such as hunger, fatigue, exhaustion and the like, *E.g.*, John 4:6—"Jesus, therefore, being wearied with his journey, sat thus by the well." There are numerous Scriptures of like import. He also limited Himself with our human emotions, thus making Himself subject to the mental depression and anguish such as He experienced in Gethsemane, when he prayed, "My Father, if it be possible, let this cup pass away from me" (Matt. 26.39). Of like import was His great mental anguish, occasioned by an overwhelming sense of alone-ness, when He hung on the Cross: "My God, my God, why hast thou

285

forsaken me?" (Matt. 27:46). His mental anguish, however, was not sin. Sin is transgression of the law of God (1 John 3:4), and at no time during those terrible hours in the Garden and on the Cross did Jesus manifest the slightest inclination to disobey the Will of the Father. His prayers invariably ended on the note of complete submission: "Nevertheless, not as I will, but as thou wilt" (Matt. 26:39). Again, He limited Himself in certain items of knowledge. For instance, He said on one occasion, concerning His second advent: "But of that day or that hour knoweth no one, not even the angels in heaven, neither the Son, but the Father" (Mark 13:32). It should be understood of course that any manifestation of ignorance on Jesus' part did not involve error; while at times His teaching may have been incomplete, it was never false. He never stated an untruth. Moreover, He always answered His opponents with finality and His answers admitted of no further controversy. The whole stage of human history was before His mind constantly like a vast panorama; He could look back to the dawn of Creation, or forward to the events connected with His second coming and the end of our age. And He could discern infallibly the thoughts and intents of the hearts of all those with whom He conversed. Finally, He limited Himself *officially*, during His three years in the flesh, subordinating Himself to both the Father and the Holy Spirit:

> John 14:28—the Father is greater than I. John 5:43—I am come in my Father's name. John 6:38—For I am come down from heaven, not to do mine own will, but the will of him that sent me. Acts 1:2— after that he had given commandment through the Holy Spirit, unto the apostles whom he had chosen. Heb. 9:14—Christ, who through the eternal Spirit offered himself without blemish unto God.

All these self-imposed limitations were in adaptation to His earthly mission as the God-Man; it was essential that He identify Himself with us mortals in order that He might qualify Himself for the High Priesthood which He was to assume after His resurrection from the dead. He became a partaker of our fleshly nature in order to enable us to become partakers of the Divine Nature, through the efficacy of the Atonement which He provided for us. And while we are on the subject of the Humiliation of the Logos, let us not overlook the fact that there is a like Humiliation of the Holy Spirit in each instance that He condescends to indwell a penitent believer. In fact, the Spirit's indwelling of the Body of Christ is a universal Condescension which should move our hearts to profound thankfulness and cause us to keep our bodies pure, that they may serve as fit receptacles for His abiding presence.

Know ye not, says Paul, that your body is a temple of the Holy Spirit which is in you, which ye have from God? and ye are not your own; for ye were bought with a price: glorify God therefore in your body (1 Cor. 6:19-20). Cf. 1 Cor. 3:16-17: Know ve not that ye are a temple of God, and that the Spirit of God dwelleth in you? If any man destroyeth the temple of God, him shall God destroy; for the temple of God is holy, and such are ye. Cf. also 1 Pet. 2:5— ye also, as living stones, are built up a spiritual house, to be a holy priesthood, to offer up spiritual sacrifices, acceptable to God through Jesus Christ. [And finally], Eph. 2:19-22: So then ye are no more strangers and sojourners, but ye are fellow-citizens with the saints, and of the household of God, being built upon the foundation of the apostles and prophets, Christ Jesus himself being the chief corner stone; in whom each several building, fitly framed together, groweth into a holy temple in the Lord; in whom ye also are builded together for a habitation of God in the Spirit. [The fact must not be overlooked that *these promises are addressed only to God's saints.*]

(3) In the New Testament, the Holy Spirit is also recognized as God. (This phase of the subject is fully treated in a subsequent section.)

2. *These Three—Father, Son, and Spirit—are so presented in Scripture that we are compelled to think of them as three distinct Persons.*

(1) The Son distinguishes the Father from Himself. John 5:37—"And the Father that sent me, he hath borne witness of me." The New Testament abounds in passages of like import.

(2) The Son prays to the Father. The entire seventeenth chapter of the Fourth Gospel is the "intercessory" prayer of the Son addressed to the Father.

(3) The Son is distinguished from the Father as the Begotten and the Begetter. John 1:14—"and we beheld his glory, glory as of the only begotten from the Father." John 3:16—"For God so loved the world, that he gave his only begotten Son," etc. Heb. 1:5—"Thou art my Son, This day have I begotten thee"; a quotation of Psa. 2:7, applied explicitly to Jesus Christ.

(4) The Father is distinguished from the Son as the Sender from the One Sent.

John 10:36 [the words of Jesus]: Say ye of him, whom the Father sanctified and sent into the world, Thou blasphemest; because I said, I am the Son of God? John 5:30—I seek not mine own will, but the will of him that sent me. John 20:21—[Jesus speaking to the Apostles]: As the Father hath sent me, even so send I you. Gal. 4:4—But when the fulness of the time came, God sent forth his Son, born of a woman, born under the law.

(5) The Son distinguishes the Spirit both from the Father and from Himself.

John 14:16-17: And I will pray the Father, and he shall give you another Comforter, that he may be with you for ever, even the Spirit of truth, etc. John 15:26—But when the Comforter is come, whom I will send unto you from the Father, even the Spirit of truth, which proceedeth from the Father, he shall bear witness of me. John 16:7, 13—It is expedient for you that I go away; for if I go not away, the Comforter will not come unto you; but if I go, I will send him unto you. . . . Howbeit when he, the Spirit of truth, is come, he shall guide you into all the truth.

(6) The Spirit is said to proceed from the Father.

John 15:26—But when the Comforter is come, whom I will send unto you from the Father, even the Spirit of truth, which proceedeth from the Father, he shall bear witness of me.

(7) The Spirit is said to be sent both by the Father and by the Son.

John 15:26—But when the Comforter is come, whom I will send unto you from the Father, even the Spirit of truth, etc. John 14:26—But the Comforter, even the Holy Spirit, whom the Father will send in my name, etc. [And in Acts 1:4, we read that the risen Christ, being assembled together with His Apostles], charged them not to depart from Jerusalem, but to wait for the promise of the Father. [The *promise of the Father* was the promise that Holy Spirit should be sent to them to guide them into all the truth.] Cf. Gal. 4:6—And because ye are sons, God sent forth the Spirit of his Son into our hearts, etc. [Now is the Holy Spirit is a Person, as we shall see later that He is, then He must be a Person in some sense distinct from either the Father or the Son.]

Thus in the conversation between Jesus and the Eleven in the Upper Room, after the Last Supper, as recorded in the fourteenth, fifteenth and sixteenth chapters of *John*, the Son, one Person, is represented as praying to the Father, another Person, to send the Holy Spirit, a third Person, upon the Apostles to guide them into all the truth, that is, to qualify them with authority and infallibility as ambassadors of Christ.

(8) The same differentiation is made by the Spirit Himself, speaking through the Apostle Peter, on the Day of Pentecost.

Acts 2:32-33: This Jesus did God raise up, whereof we all are witnesses. Being therefore by the right hand of God exalted, and having received of the Father the promise of the Holy Spirit, he hath poured forth this, which ye see and hear.

That is, the Father raised the Son, and the Son, having been exalted, poured forth the Spirit; the Three exist simultaneously, and each sustains His own peculiar relation to man.

(9) The distinctness of the three Persons appears also in the account of the Annunciation to Mary.

Luke 1:30-35: And the angel said unto her, Fear not, Mary: for thou hast found favor with God. And behold, thou shalt conceive in thy womb, and bring forth a son, and shalt call his name Jesus. He shall be great, and shall be called the Son of the Most High: and the Lord God shall give unto him the throne of his father David. . . . And Mary said unto the angel, How shall this be, seeing I know not a man? And the angel answered and said unto her, The Holy Spirit shall come upon thee, and the power of the Most High shall overshadow thee: wherefore also the holy thing which is begotten shall be called the Son of God.

The same distinctions appear also in the account of Christ's conversation with Nicodemus:

John 3:1-15: Now there was a man of the Pharisees, named Nicodemus, a ruler of the Jews: the same came unto him by night, and said to him, Rabbi, we know that thou art a teacher come from God; for no one can do these signs that thou doest, except God be with him. Jesus answered and said unto him, Verily, verily, I say unto thee, Except one be born anew, he cannot see the kingdom of God. Nicodemus saith unto him, How can a man be born when he is old? can he enter a second time into his mother's womb, and be born? Jesus answered, Verily, verily, I say unto thee, Except one be born of water and the Spirit, he cannot enter into the kingdom of God. That which is born of the flesh is flesh; and that which is born of the Spirit is spirit. . . . And no one hath ascended into heaven, but he that descended out of heaven, even the Son of man, who is in heaven, etc.

(10) Finally, these Three—Father, Son, and Holy Spirit— are represented as capable of dissociating themselves in such a way as to be in separate places at one and the same time. Following the baptism of Jesus, for example, the Son is pictured as standing on the bank of the Jordan River, while at the same time the Spirit is descending through the air "as a dove, and coming upon him," and the Father is speaking from heaven to say, "This is my beloved Son, in whom I am well pleased" (Matt. 3:16-17).

Despite these obvious distinctions of person, however, the fact should not be lost sight of that this doctrine of the triune personality of God is not a tritheism. There are not three Gods: there is but one God as to essence, but this essence comprises, in some inscrutable manner, three Persons. The Father is not God as such, because God is also Son and Holy Spirit. The Son is not God as such, because God is also Father and Holy Spirit. The Spirit is not God as such, because God is also Father and Son. That is to say, there are three Persons, each of whom as to essence is God, but no one of whom is the fulness of the Godhead without the other Two. "No man means all that a Christian means by 'God,' unless he puts into 'God' all that is meant by the separate terms 'Father,' 'Son,' 'Spirit'."

3. *The Three Persons—Father, Son, and Spirit—must be re-*

*garded as equal.* They are associated on a footing of equality in Scripture:

(1) [In the baptismal formula, the words of Jesus Himself], Matt. 29:19—baptizing them into the name of the Father and of the Son and of the Holy Spirit. (2) [In the apostolic benediction], 2 Cor. 13:14—The grace of the Lord Jesus Christ, and the love of God, and the Communion of the Holy Spirit, be with you all. (3) [In the address and salutatory of *First Peter*, 1:2]—according to the foreknowledge of God the Father, in sanctification of the Spirit, unto obedience and sprinkling of the blood of Jesus Christ. (4) [In other passages in the apostolic writings.] 1 Cor. 12:4-6: Now there are diversities of gifts, but the same Spirit. And there are diversities of ministrations, and the same Lord. And there are diversities of workings, but the same God, who worketh all things in all. Eph. 4:4-6: There is one body, and one Spirit, even as also ye were called in one hope of your calling; one Lord, one faith, one baptism, one God and Father of all. Rev. 1:4-5: John to the seven churches that are in Asia: Grace to you and peace, from him who is and who was and who is to come; and from the seven Spirits that are before his throne; and from Jesus Christ, who is the faithful witness, the firstborn of the dead, and the ruler of the kings of the earth.

Again, the three Persons are represented as being distinct in their subsistences to such an extent that distinct operations are ascribed to each in relation to the others. For example:

(1) The Father is said to know and to love the Son, and the Son is said to "see," to know, and to love the Father.

Matt. 11:27—no one knoweth the Son, save the Father; neither doth any know the Father, save the Son, and he to whomsoever the Son willeth to reveal him. John 3:35—The Father loveth the Son, and hath given all things into his hand. John 5:20—For the Father loveth the Son, and showeth him all things that himself doeth. John 6:46—Not that any man hath seen the Father, save he that is from God, he hath seen the Father. John 7:28-29 [the words of Jesus again]: I am not come of myself, but he that sent me is true, whom ye know not. I know him; because I am from him, and he sent me. John 14:31—that the world may know that I love the Father, and as the Father gave me commandment, even so I do. John 1:18—No man hath seen God at any time; the only begotten Son, who is in the bosom of the Father, he hath declared him.

(2) The Spirit is said to search and to reveal the "deep things of God."

1 Cor. 2:10-13: For the Spirit searcheth all things, yea, the deep things of God. For who among men knoweth the things of a man, save the spirit of the man, which is in him? even so the things of God none knoweth, save the Spirit of God. But we received, not the spirit of the world, but the spirit which is from God: that we might know the things that were freely given to us of God. Which things also we speak, not in words which man's wisdom teacheth, but which the Spirit teacheth; combining spiritual things with spiritual words.

(3) The Father is said to give, to send, and to command the Son in the latter's capacity as Redemer and Mediator.

John 3:16-17; For God so loved the world that he gave his only begotten Son . . . for God sent not his Son into the world to judge the world, etc. John 3:34—For he whom God hath sent speaketh the words of God. John 3:35—The Father loveth the Son, and hath given all things into his hand. John 5:37—And the Father that sent me, he hath borne witness of me. John 5:36—for the works which the Father hath given me to accomplish, the very works that I do, bear witness of me, that the Father hath sent me. John 8:28-29: When ye have lifted up the Son of man, then shall ye know that I am he, and that I do nothing of myself, but as the Father taught me, I speak these things. And he that sent me is with me; he hath not left me alone; for I do always the things that are pleasing unto him. John 15:10— If ye keep my commandments, ye shall abide in my love; even as I have kept my Father's commandments, and abide in his love. Gal. 4:4—but when the fulness of the time came, God sent forth his Son, born of a woman, born under the law. 1 John 4:9—Herein was the love of God manifested in us, that God hath sent his only begotten Son into the world that we might live through him.

(4) And both the Father and the Son are said to have actuated the Spirit's activities as Organizer, Administrator, and Sanctifier of the Body of Christ.

John 14:16-17: And I will pray the Father, and he shall give you another Comforter, that he may be with you for ever, even the Spirit of truth. John 14:26—But the Comforter, even the Holy Spirit, whom the Father will send in my name, he shall teach you all things, and bring to your remembrance all that I said unto you. John 15:26— But when the Comforter is come, whom I will send unto you from the Father, even the Spirit of truth, which proceedeth from the Father, he shall bear witness of me. John 16:7, 13, 14—It is expedient for you that I go away; for if I go not away, the Comforter will not come unto you; but if I go, I will send him unto you. . . . when he, the Spirit of truth, is come, he shall guide you into all the truth; for he shall not speak from himself; but what things so ever he shall hear, these shall he speak; and he shall declare unto you the things that are to come. He shall glorify me: for he shall take of mine, and shall declare it unto you. John 20:22-23: And when he had said this, he breathed on them [the Eleven], and saith unto them, Receive ye the Holy Spirit: whose soever sins ye forgive, they are forgiven unto them; whose soever sins ye retain, they are retained. Acts 1:4-5: and being assembled together with them [the Eleven], he charged them not to depart from Jerusalem, that he was to wait for the promise of the Father, which, said he, ye heard from me: for John indeed baptized with water; but ye shall be baptized in the Holy Spirit not many days hence. [Cf. the fulfilment of all this, in Acts 2: 32-33]: This Jesus did God raise up, whereof we all are witnesses. Being therefore by the right hand of God exalted, and having received of the Father the promise of the Holy Spirit, he hath poured forth this, which ye see and hear. [The Holy Spirit entered upon His official duties, with the incorporation of the Church or Body of Christ on the Day of Pentecost. The present Dispensation is that of the Spirit.]

In these numerous Scriptures an inter-relation and inter-communion of the three Persons of the Godhead is clearly indicated. Furthermore, the Holy Spirit in His capacity of Administrator of the Christian Church is said to have called certain

291

persons to do each a certain work, to have furnished them with the proper credentials for their task, and to have sent them to perform it.

*E.g.*, Acts 13:1-4: Now there were at Antioch, in the church that was there, prophets and teachers . . . and as they ministered to the Lord, and fasted, the Holy Spirit said, Separate me Barnabas and Saul for the work whereunto I have called them. Then, when they had fasted and prayed and laid their hands on them, they sent them away. So they, being sent forth by the Holy Spirit, went down to Seleucia, etc. Acts 8:29—And the Spirit said unto Philip, Go near, and join thyself to this chariot. Acts 10:19-20; And while Peter thought on the vision, the Spirit said unto him, Behold, three men seek thee. Arise, and get thee down, and go with them, nothing doubting: for I have sent them.

This fact alone is conclusive evidence of the Spirit's own personal nature.

Finally, if each of the three Persons is, as to essence, God, it follows that they must be equal; from our human viewpoint at least, there can be no degrees in deity.

4. *This tripersonality of God is inherent and eternal,* even though it was not fully revealed in Old Testament times. This is evident from the following Scriptures:

(1) Those Old Testament passages in which the plural form *Elohim* is used, with a singular verb, for the Deity.

Gen. 1:1—In the beginning *Elohim* created the heavens and the earth. Gen. 1:3—And *Elohim* said, Let there be light. Gen. 1:27—And *Elohim* created man in his own image. [And so on, in many, many passages throughout the entire Old Testament.]

(2) Those Old Testament passages in which inter-communion within the Godhead is intimated.

Gen. 1:26—And God said, Let *us* make man in *our* image, after *our* likeness. Gen. 3:22—And Jehovah God said, Behold, the man is become as one of *us*, to know good and evil, etc. Gen. 11:6-7: And Jehovah said . . . Come, let *us* go down, and there confound their language. Isa. 6:8—And I heard the voice of the Lord, saying, Whom shall I send, and who will go for *us?*

(3) Those passages which assert the eternal pre-existence of the Word (or Wisdom) of God, the Word who became flesh and dwelt among us.

Prov. 1:20—Wisdom crieth aloud in the street. Prov. 8:1—Doth not wisdom cry, and Understanding put forth her voice? [So throughout the book of *Proverbs*.] John 1:1-3, 14—In the beginning was the Word, and the Word was with God, and the Word was God. The same was in the beginning with God. All things were made through him; and without him was not anything made that hath been made. . . . And the Word became flesh and dwelt among us (and we beheld his glory, glory as of the only begotten from the Father), full of grace and truth. John 1:18—No man hath seen God at any time; the only be-gotten Son, who is in the bosom of the Father, he hath declared him. John 8:58—Jesus said unto them, Verily, verily, I say unto you, Before Abraham was born, I am. 1 Cor. 1:24—Christ the power of God, and the wisdom of God. Gal. 4:4—But when the fulness of the time came, God sent forth his Son, born of a woman, born under the law, etc. John 17:5 [the words of Jesus Himself]: And now, Father, glorify thou me with thine own self *with the glory which I had with thee before the world was.* Col. 1:16-17—In him were all things created, in the heavens and upon the earth . . . all things have been created through him, and unto him; and he is before all things, and in him all things consist. Phil. 2:6-8: Christ Jesus, who, existing in the form of God, counted not the being on an equality with God a thing to be grasped, but emptied himself, taking the form of a servant, being made in the likeness of men; and being found in fashion as a man, he humbled himself, becoming obedient even unto death, yea, the death of the cross. [Here we have the *fact* of the Word's *Kenosis* clearly affirmed.] Heb. 2:14-15; Since then the children are sharers in flesh and blood, he also himself in like manner partook of the same: that through death he might bring to nought him that had the power of death, that is, the devil; and might deliver all them who through fear of death were all their lifetime subject to bondage. [In this pas-sage the function or *purpose* of our Lord's *Kenosis* is stated.] Heb. 1:1-3: God, having of old time spoken unto the fathers in the prophets by divers portions and in divers manners, hath at the end of these days, spoken unto us in his Son, whom he appointed heir of all things, through whom also he made the worlds; who being the effulgence of his glory, and the very image of his substance, and upholding all things by the word of his power, when he had made purification of sins, sat down on the right hand of the Majesty on high. 1 Tim. 3:16— And without controversy great is the mystery of godliness: He who was manifested in the flesh, Justified in the spirit, Seen of angels, Preached among the nations, Believed on in the world, Received up in glory. [The Mystery of Godliness is, of course, the God-Man, Im-manuel, the Eternal Logos who became flesh and dwelt among men.]

(4) Those passages which identify the Spirit of God of the Old Testament with the Holy Spirit of the New Testament.

2 Sam. 23:1-2: Now these are the last words of David. David the son of Jesse saith . . . The Spirit of Jehovah spake by me, And his word was upon my tongue. [Cf. Matt. 22:43-44]: He saith unto them, How then doth David in the Spirit call him Lord, saying, The Lord said unto my Lord, Sit thou on my right hand, Till I put thine enemies underneath thy feet? [a quotation of David's Psalm 110:1]. Acts 1:16, 17, 20—"Brethren, it was needful that the scripture should be fulfilled,—which the Holy Spirit spake before by the mouth of David concerning Judas, who was guide to them that took Jesus. For he was numbered among us, and received his portion in this ministry. . . . For it is written in the book of Psalms, Let his habitation be made desolate, And let no man dwell therein, and, His office let another take [quotations of Psalm 69:25 and Psalm 109:8.] Heb. 3:7 ff. —Wherefore, as the Holy Spirit saith, Today if ye shall hear his voice, Harden not your hearts, as in the provocation, Like as in the days of the trial in the wilderness, Where your fathers tried me by proving me, And saw my works forty years, etc. [This is a quotation, in substance, of Psalm 95:7-11.] 1 Sam. 16:13—and the Spirit of Jehovah came mightily upon David from that day forward.

[Again] Heb. 9:14—the eternal Spirit. 2 Pet. 1:21—For no prophecy ever came by the will of man; but men spake from God, being moved by the Holy Spirit. 1 Pet. 1:10-12: Concerning which salvation the prophets sought and searched diligently, who prophesied of the grace that should come unto you: searching what time or what manner of time the Spirit of Christ which was in them did point unto, when it testified beforehand the sufferings of Christ, and the glories that should follow them. To whom it was revealed, that not unto themselves, but unto you, did they minister these things, which now have been announced unto you through them that preached the gospel unto you by the Holy Spirit sent forth from heaven; which things angels desire to look into.

These various passages show conclusively that the Spirit of God, Spirit of Jehovah, Spirit of Christ, and Holy Spirit are all one and the same Eternal Spirit. The Spirit of God who inspired the Old Testament prophets, beginning with Enoch, "the seventh from Adam" (Jude 14), and terminating with Malachi, is the Holy Spirit who inspired the apostles and prophets of the New Testament revelation. There is but one Spirit (Eph. 4:4).

5. *This triune personality of God is inscrutable.* Numerous suggestions of "trinities" in nature have been made by churchmen in all ages. And while it is apparent that these analogies are inadequate, and often far-fetched, yet it has to be admitted that the triune principle does prevail quite generally. In logic, for example, we have thesis, antithesis, and synthesis; in metaphysics we have a trinity of subject, object, and subject-object; in the family we have the social trinity of father, mother, and child. As Raymond Calkins writes:

> All through the fabric of the world and of human life there has been a threeness. In the physical world there are three dimensions; in human life, three functions—mind, will, and feeling. Just so in the Godhead, the sum of all existence, Christian thinking has found permanent place for Father, Son, and Holy Spirit.[1]

Tripersonality in God, however, is to a large extent inscrutable to human reason; the doctrine is, and must continue to be, essentially an article of faith, that is to say, a product of Divine revelation. Such a conception of the Deity could hardly have arisen in finite mind *per se.*

6. *The fact of the triune personality of God underlies both Divine revelation and human redemption.*

It is essential to a correct understanding of God. The God who loves must make common cause with the object of His love. It has been rightly said that "love is an impossible exercise in a solitary being." We need not only a God who is eternal

1. *The Holy Spirit,* 125.

and sovereign, but a God as well who "so loved the world, that He gave his only begotten Son, that whosoever believeth on him should not perish, but have eternal life" (John 3:16). The fundamental fact of the Old Testament revelation is that God created man in His own likeness; the fundamental fact of the New Testament revelation is that God Himself, in the person of the Son, entered into human flesh and became the likeness of man, that "God was in Christ reconciling the world unto himself" (2 Cor. 5:19).

It is essential to a proper revelation of God. If there are not three Persons, then there is no Son who can adequately reveal the Father. Herein lies the emptiness of Unitarianism: it has no perfect revelation of God. Certainly no mere man could ever say, in truth: "He that hath seen me hath seen the Father" (John 14:9). And if there is no Holy Spirit, the self-communication of the Divine Being to a human being is impossible. (Cf. again Gen. 2:7 and 1 Cor. 2:6-15).

The doctrine of the triune personality of God is essential to the Scheme of Redemption. If God is one, solitary and alone, then there can be no mediation, no atonement, no intercession, no redemption. The gulf between God and man is not one of degree, but one of kind; it is infinite. Only One who is God can bridge that gulf and effect a reconciliation (1) by the vicarious sacrifice of Himself (for only a Divine offering can satisfy the claims of Eternal Justice upon the Divine Government, thus sustaining the majesty of the Divine law which was violated by man, and thus providing an atonement for man's sins); and (2) by the vicarious sacrifice of Himself as a demonstration of God's immeasurable love for man, an offering of love sufficient to overcome the rebellion in man's heart and to woo him back into covenant relationship with his Creator. This is precisely what the Son of God has done for us by His voluntary offering of Himself upon the Cross. He "humbled himself, becoming obedient even unto death, yea, the death of the cross" (Phil. 2:8). "His own self bare our sins in his body upon the tree, that we, having died unto sins, might live unto righteousness" (1 Pet. 2:24). Without a Redeemer, redemption and reconciliation are meaningless terms, and religion is a vain exercise.

The doctrine of the triune personality of God is essential to all true worship of God. Worship, says Jesus, is the communion of the human spirit with the Divine Spirit, on the terms and conditions as revealed by the Spirit in the Word

(John 4:24). Therefore, without both Spirit and Word there can be no true worship.

The doctrine is also essential to any adequate Christology. Rejection of this doctrine suffices to explain the inadequacy of all Unitarian and so-called "modernistic" views of Jesus. If Jesus was just a man, and not the Word who became flesh and dwelt among us, not Immanuel, the God-Man, then He cannot be the Savior of mankind. If He was just a teacher, a "divinely illumined" philosopher and ethical teacher, and no more, then His teaching, like all philosophy, is just another guess at the riddle of the universe, and the world is back where it was two thousand years ago, floundering in the muck and mire of pagan superstition.

The doctrine of the tripersonality of God is essential to any perfect pattern of human life and conduct. We believe that Jesus was truly "God with us" (Matt. 1:23). Therefore His teaching and conduct are the perfect norms for us to follow if we would be like God or godlike. Without the Son to reveal and to live the perfect life, the life that God would live and have us live, then we are without an Exemplar; there is no Way, no Truth, no Life.

In fact, every fundamental doctrine of the Christian System is rooted deeply in the fact of the triune personality of God.

Moreover, to speak of so-called heathen "trinities" in the same breath with the Biblical triune God is to manifest a mind blinded by prejudice and a perverted will. In the first place, what are commonly called "trinities" in heathen mythologies are not trinities at all; that is, not *three in one,* but *three separate ones* for whom no unity of essence was ever conceived or claimed. In the second place, these so-called "trinities" of paganism are, in most cases, vague and unidentifiable; they are invariably surrounded by other "gods" regarded as equally powerful. In the Vedas, there were Dyaus, Indra, and Agni. In Brahmanism, there were Brahma, Vishnu, and Siva, the last-named being the principle of evil and destruction. These, among the oldest of the deities of "natural religion," more nearly approximated a trinity than any similar groups; yet in either case the three were regarded as separate deities. In Egyptian mythology, there were Osiris, Isis his consort, and Horus their son. But there were many other great gods in Egypt, in addition to these three, who were a comparatively late development in Egyptian history. Nor is there any well-defined triad in Greek mythology. Was it Zeus, Poseidon, and Hades, who were reputed to have divided the Cosmos among them, the first-named taking the earth, the second the sea, and the third the underworld? Or was it Zeus, Hera, and Athene? Or Zeus, Athene, and Apollo? Instead of a triad, the ancient Greeks generally referred to their twelve great gods. The same is generally true of the Romans. The Romans had gods for everything: the making of gods, as Augustine pointed out so eloquently, was the chief business of the superstitious Roman people. According to a witticism of Petronius: "Indeed, our land is so full of divine presences that it is easier to meet a god than a man."[1] Then, in addition to all this, the gods of heathen mythologies were crude, grossly anthropomorphic, and downright immoral. Every great god had his female consort—in the case of Zeus, Hera was his sister-wife—and as many mistresses, including even ordinary women, as his passions might impel him to appropriate. Zeus was perhaps the most assiduous philanderer of the lot; he stopped at nothing, including incest, rape, kidnaping, and treachery of every kind. There is absolutely nothing of this character in the Biblical presentation of the triune personality of God of the Judean-Christian revelation. It is entirely void of anthropomorphism. The inter-relations among Father, Son, and Holy Spirit are wholly incorporeal and spiritual. It is significant, moreover, that there is no word for goddess in the Hebrew Scriptures. In fact, the only relations sustained by the three Persons of the Biblical Godhead, of a semi-earthly character, are those sustained with men spiritually and for man's redemption. These relations are signified by the two terms, the "begetting" of the Son and the "procession" of the Spirit. The term "begetting" in reference to the Son, describes an event—the Incarnation—which took place *in time,* and through the passive instrumentality of the Virgin Mary. Prior to His incarnation, His name was The Word. By the miracle of the Incarnation He became the Only Begotten Son of God (Luke 1:35, John 3:16), the Mystery of Godliness (1 Tim. 3:16). The same is true of the "procession" of the Spirit. That, too, is an event which, whenever it occurs, occurs *in time* (time being, of course, coetaneous with the Creative Process), and for specific divine ends, as, for example, the coming of the Spirit on the Apostles on the Day of Pentecost (Acts 2:1-4). To speak of the inter-relations among the three Persons of the Biblical Godhead in corporeal, or even in anthropomorphic, terms is a gross perversion of the truth. And by no stretch of

1. Petronius, *Satyricon,* 17, 5.

the imagination can any resemblance be found between the variously associated deities of heathen myth and legend and the triune personality of the God of the Bible. For our God is a Spirit, and "they that worship him must worship in spirit and truth" (John 4:24). This means, of course, that in their eternal and unoriginated being, all three Persons—Father, Son, and Holy Spirit—are essentially spiritual: that is, no corporeal relations are sustained among the Three. In the words of an old Catechism: "We call God a Spirit because He has understanding and free will, but no body."

## 3. The Personality of the Holy Spirit

The only proper method of ascertaining the essential nature of the Holy Spirit is to find out from the teaching of the Bible, and of the New Testament in particular, what the Holy Spirit does. The man who presides in a classroom is a schoolteacher; one who practices law is a lawyer; one who tills the soil is a farmer; and so on. We can ascertain what a man is by what he does. And so, although the analogy is far from precise, we can ascertain the nature of the Holy Spirit by finding out what the Holy Spirit does. On looking through the Scriptures we find that the Holy Spirit is represented as doing certain things, as follows:

1. [He *hears*.] John 16:13—Howbeit when he, the Spirit of truth, is come, he shall guide you into all the truth; for he shall not speak from himself; but what things soever he shall hear, these shall he speak.

2. [He *speaks*, i.e., communicates thought by words.] 1 Tim. 4:1—But the Spirit saith expressly, that in later times some shall fall away from the faith, etc. [Here the Spirit is said to speak through the inspired writer, the Apostle Paul.] Acts 8:29—And the Spirit said unto Philip, Go near, and join thyself to this chariot. Acts 10:19-20: And while Peter thought on the vision, the Spirit said unto him, Behold, three men seek thee. But arise, and get thee down, and go with them, nothing doubting: for I have sent them. [I take it that in these two instances the Spirit spoke in audible tones, or at least in words addressed to the subconsciousness of the recipient. Now a speaker, one who uses language intelligibly, must be a person. No mere personification or impersonal influence can speak.]

3. [He *teaches*.] Luke 12:12—For the Holy Spirit shall teach you in that very hour what ye ought to say. 1 Cor. 2:13—which things also we speak, not in words which man's wisdom teacheth, but which the Spirit teacheth.

4. [He *quickens the memory*.] John 14:26—But the Comforter, even the Holy Spirit, whom the Father will send in my name, he shall teach you all things, and bring to your remembrance all that I said unto you.

5. [He *bears witness, testifies*.] John 15:26—But when the Com-

298

forter is come, whom I will send unto you from the Father, even the Spirit of truth . . . he shall bear witness of me.

6. [He *reveals*.] 1 Cor. 2:9-10: Whatsoever things God prepared for them that love him . . . unto us God revealed them through the Spirit. John 16:13-14; Howbeit when he, the Spirit of truth, is come, he shall guide you into all the truth . . . and he shall declare unto you the things that are to come. He shall glorify me, for he shall take of mine, and shall declare it unto you.

7. [He *leads* and *forbids*.] Matt. 4:1—Then was Jesus led up of the Spirit into the wilderness to be tempted of the devil. Acts 16:6-7: And they [Paul and Timothy] went through the region of Phrygia and Galatia, having been forbidden of the Holy Spirit to speak the word in Asia; and when they were come over against Mysia, they assayed to go into Bithynia; and the Spirit of Jesus suffered them not.

8. [He *comforts*.] Acts 9:31—So the church throughout all Judea and Galilee and Samaria had peace, being edified; and, walking in the fear of the Lord and in the comfort of the Holy Spirit, was multi-. plied.

9. [He *searches*.] 1 Cor. 2:10—the Spirit searcheth all things, yea, the deep things of God.

10. [He *strives* with men.] Gen. 6:3—And Jehovah said, My Spirit shall not strive with man for ever. John 16:7-8: It is expedient for you that I go away; for if I go not away, the Comforter will not come unto you; but if I go, I will send him unto you. And he, when he is come, will convict the world in respect of sin, and of righteousness, and of judgment.

In these passages the Holy Spirit is said to hear, to speak, to testify, to quicken the memory, to reveal, to guide, to lead, to forbid, to comfort, to search the mind and heart, to strive with men, etc. These are things that can be done only by a person.

Having ascertained what the Holy Spirit does, let us now seek out the attributes, powers, or faculties, which the Holy Spirit has. In this connection, He is said to have the following:

1. [*Mind*.] Rom. 8:27—He that searcheth the hearts knoweth what is the mind of the Spirit.

2. [*Knowledge*.] 1 Cor. 2:11—even so the things of God none knoweth, save the Spirit of God.

3. [*Affection*.] Rom. 15:30—Now I beseech you, brethren, by our Lord Jesus Christ, and by the love of the Spirit, that ye strive together with me in your prayers to God for me.

4. [*Will*.] 1 Cor. 12:11—but all these worketh the one and the same Spirit, dividing to each one severally as he will.

5. [*Goodness*.] Neh. 9:20—Thou gavest also thy good Spirit to instruct them.

6. [*Holiness*.] Psa. 51:11—Take not thy holy Spirit from me. Isa. 63:10—But they rebelled, and grieved his holy Spirit. Luke 11:13— How much more shall your heavenly Father give the Holy Spirit to them that ask him? Eph. 4:30—And grieve not the Holy Spirit of God, in whom ye were sealed unto the day of redemption.

These several endowments—mind, knowledge, affection, will, and goodness or holiness—all are essential attributes of personality. By no stretch of the imagination can they be ascribed to a mere impersonal energy or influence. Someone has rightly

299

said that "these five characteristics form the fingers of the hand of certainty by which we grasp the fact of the personality of the Holy Spirit."

Again, we find that the Holy Spirit is said to suffer slights and injuries such as can be suffered only by a person:

1. [He can be *grieved*.] Isa. 63:10—But they rebelled, and grieved his holy Spirit; therefore he was turned to be their enemy and himself fought against them. Here the prophet describes the sins of ancient Israel against the Spirit of God. [Eph. 4:30 again]: And grieve not the Holy Spirit of God, in whom ye were sealed unto the day of redemption.

2. [He can be *despited*.] Heb. 10:29—of how much sorer punishment, think ye, shall he be judged worthy, who has trodden under foot the Son of God, and hath counted the blood of the covenant wherewith he was sanctified an unholy thing, and hath done despite unto the Spirit of grace? [To do despite is to act with malice, contempt, or scorn.]

3. [He can be *blasphemed*.] Matt. 12:31—Every sin and blasphemy shall be forgiven unto men; but the blasphemy against the Spirit shall not be forgiven. [To blaspheme, as the word is used in this context, is to ascribe an exercise of the Spirit's power to the agency of Satan, thus manifested spiritual blindness that can arise only from a hopelessly perverted will; hence to treat the Holy Spirit in an impious and irreverent manner.]

4. [He can be *lied to*.] Acts 5:3-4: But Peter said, Ananias, why hath Satan filled thy heart to lie to the Holy Spirit, and to keep back part of the price of the land? . . . Thou hast not lied unto men, but unto God. [To lie to an inspired man, who is a man of the Spirit (as Peter was in this instance), is made equivalent here to lying to the Holy Spirit.]

5. [He can be *resisted*.] Acts 7:51—Ye stiffnecked and uncircumcised in heart and ears, ye do always resist the Holy Spirit.

6. [Men can *speak against* the Spirit, *sin against* Him, and *rebel against* Him.] Matt. 12:32—whosoever shall speak against the Holy Spirit, it shall not be forgiven him, neither in this world, nor in that which is to come. Mark 3:29—whosoever shall blaspheme against the Holy Spirit hath never forgiveness, but is guilty of an eternal sin. Isa. 63:10—But they rebelled, and grieved his holy Spirit.

Obviously it is impossible to lie to a mere personification. It is impossible to grieve or vex, or to wound in any way, an impersonal energy or influence. These are slights that can be experienced only by a person.

Again, the various offices and works ascribed to the Holy Spirit in Scripture clearly indicate His personality. He is presented as acting in the following capacities:

1. [As *Revealer*.] John 14:26—But the Comforter, even the Holy Spirit . . . he shall teach you all things, and bring to your remembrance all that I said unto you. John 16:13-14 again: Howbeit when he, the Spirit of truth, is come, he shall guide you into all the truth . . . and he shall declare unto you the things that are to come. He shall glorify me: for he shall take of mine, and shall declare it unto you. Luke 12:12—for the Holy Spirit shall teach you in that very hour what ye ought to say. [These are all sayings addressed by Jesus Himself to the men who were to become His Apostles.] I Pet. 1:10-12:

Concerning which salvation the prophets sought and searched diligently, who prophesied of the grace that should come unto you; searching what time or what manner of time the Spirit of Christ which was in them did point unto, when it testified beforehand the sufferings of Christ and the glories that should follow them. To whom it was revealed, that not unto themselves, but unto you, did they minister these things, which now have been announced unto you through them that preached the gospel unto you by the Holy Spirit sent forth from heaven. 2 Pet. 1:21—For no prophecy ever came by the will of man; but men spake from God, being moved by the Holy Spirit. 1 Cor. 2:10-12: But unto us God revealed them [*i.e.*, the things God prepared for them that love him] through the Spirit: for the Spirit searcheth all things, yea, the deep things of God. For who among men knoweth the things of a man, save the spirit of the man, which is in him? even so the things of God none knoweth, save the Spirit of God. But we received, not the spirit of the world, but the spirit which is from God; that we might know the things that were freely given to us of God." [The "we" in this passage has reference, of course, to the Apostles.]

2. [As *Teacher*.] Luke 12:12—for the Holy Spirit shall teach you in that very hour what ye ought to say. John 14:26—But the Comforter, even the Holy Spirit, whom the Father will send in my name, he shall teach you all things, etc. 1 Cor. 2:13. Which things also we speak, not in words which man's wisdom teacheth, but which the Spirit teacheth, combining spiritual things with spiritual words.

3. [As *Witness*.] John 15:26-27: But when the Comforter is come . . . even the Spirit of truth, which proceedeth from the Father, he shall bear witness of me. John 16:14—He shall glorify me; for he shall take of mine, and shall declare it unto you. Rom. 8:16—The Spirit himself beareth witness with our spirit, that we are children of God, etc. 1 Pet. 1:11—searching what time or what manner of time the Spirit of Christ which was in them did point unto, when it testified beforehand the sufferings of Christ and the glories that should follow them.

4. [As *Guide*.] John 16:13—when he, the Spirit of truth, is come, he shall guide you into all the truth.

5. [As *Comforter*, literally, *Paraclete*. This is the New Testament name for the Spirit, which signifies in a special sense His relations with the Apostles. It is a name that is difficult to translate; it seems to connote such meanings as Advocate, Counselor, Helper, etc.] John 14:16-17: I will pray the Father, and he shall give you another Comforter . . . even the Spirit of truth. John 14:26—But the Comforter, even the Holy Spirit, whom the Father will send in my name, he shall teach you all things, etc. John 15:26—But when the Comforter is come, whom I will send unto you from the Father, even the Spirit of truth, etc. John 16:7—for if I go not away, the Comforter will not come unto you, etc. [It must be always kept in mind that these promises incorporated in the fourteenth, fifteenth and sixteenth chapters of the Fourth Gospel, were promises made by our Lord to the Eleven only, that is, to the men who were to become His Apostles. Recognition of this fact by Bible exegetes in the past would have prevented a great deal of the confusion which exists today in regard to the office and work of the Holy Spirit.]

6. [As *Intercessor*.] Rom. 8:26-27: And in like manner the Spirit also helpeth our infirmity: for we know not how to pray as we ought; but the Spirit himself maketh intercession for us with groanings which cannot be uttered; and he that searcheth the hearts knoweth what is the mind of the Spirit, because he maketh intercession for the saints

301

according to the will of God. Eph. 6:18—with all prayer and supplication praying at all seasons in the Spirit, etc.

7. [As *Demonstrator*, or Worker of Miracles.] [The Father is primarily the Source of *faith;* the Son, of *doctrine;* the Spirit, of *evidence.* Revelation has always been attested by *demonstration* or miracles.] Matt. 12:28—But if I by the Spirit of God cast out demons, then is the kingdom of God come upon you. 1 Cor. 12:4-11: Now there are diversities of gifts, but the same Spirit. And there are diversities of ministrations, and the same Lord. And there are diversities of workings, but the same God, who worketh all things in all. But to each one is given the manifestation of the Spirit to profit withal. For to one is given through the Spirit the word of wisdom; and to another the word of knowledge, according to the same Spirit: to another faith, in the same Spirit; and to another gifts of healings, in one Spirit; and to another workings of miracles; and to another prophecy; and to another discernings of spirits; to another divers kinds of tongues; and to another the interpretation of tongues: but all these worketh the one and the same Spirit, dividing to each one severally even as he will. Heb. 2:4—God also bearing witness with them, both by signs and wonders, and by manifold powers, and by gifts of the Holy Spirit, according to his own will. [The reference here is, primarily, to the miracle-working powers of the Apostles.] [Cf. 1 Cor. 2:4-5, the words of Paul]: And my speech and my preaching were not in persuasive words of wisdom, but in demonstration of the Spirit and of power: that your faith should not stand in the wisdom of men, but in the power of God.

8. [As *Administrator* of the Church.] The Holy Spirit came on the day of Pentecost, to act as the Vicegerent of Christ, to abide with the Church throughout the present Dispensation. His activity is paramount throughout the history of the Church in apostolic times as recorded in the book of *Acts.* So many instances of His direct leadership are given that it would protract this section to undue length to record all of them here. A few examples, therefore, will suffice.] Acts 8:29— And the Spirit said unto Philip, Go near, and join thyself to this chariot. Acts 8:39—the Spirit of the Lord caught away Philip. Acts 10:19-20: And while Peter thought on the vision, the Spirit said unto him, Behold, three men seek thee. But arise, and get thee down, and go with them, nothing doubting; for I have sent them. Acts 13:1-4: Now there were at Antioch, in the church that was there, prophets and teachers. . . . And as they ministered to the Lord, and fasted, the Holy Spirit said, Separate me Barnabas and Saul for the work whereunto I have called them. Then, when they had fasted and prayed, and laid their hands on them, they sent them away. So they, being sent forth by the Holy Spirit, went down to Seleucia, etc. Acts 15:28—[the decisions of the first general church council of apostles and elders held at Jerusalem, as set forth in a letter dispatched to the surrounding congregations]: For it seemed good to the Holy Spirit, and to us, to lay upon you no greater burden than these necessary things, etc. [Note that the authority of the Holy Spirit was claimed for these decisions.] Acts 16:6-7: [here we are told that Paul and Timothy] went through the region of Phrygia and Galatia, having been forbidden of the Holy Spirit to speak the word in Asia; and when they were come over against Mysia, they assayed to go into Bithynia; and the Spirit of Jesus suffered them not, etc. Acts 20:28—[the words of Paul to the elders of the church at Ephesus]: Take heed unto yourselves, and to all the flock, in which the Holy Spirit hath made you overseers, to feed the church of the Lord which he purchased with his own blood. Acts 21:4—And having found the disciples we tarried there seven days: and these said to Paul through the Spirit, that he

should not set foot in Jerusalem [cf. vv. 10-11]. (Cf. also Acts 1:8, 2:1-4, 4:8, 4:31, 5:3, 5:9, 5:32, 6:3, 6:5, 6:10, 8:14-24, 9:17, 9:31, 10:44-47, 11:12-18, 11:24, 11:28, 13:9-10, 13:52, 15:6-9, 19:1-7, 20:22-23, etc.).

Thus it will be seen that, in His capacity as Administrator of the Church, the Spirit is said to have called certain persons to perform certain tasks, to have qualified them with proper credentials for their respective tasks, and to have sent them forth to accomplish the tasks which He had commissioned them to perform, and even to have accompanied them personally and in many instances to have given them the added powers necessary to accomplish the tasks which He had assigned them. All these offices and works clearly indicate His personality.

Dr. Strong summarizes clearly as follows:

> That which searches, knows, speaks, testifies, reveals, convinces, commands, strives, moves, helps, guides, creates, recreates, sanctifies, inspires, makes intercession, orders the affairs of the church, performs miracles, raises the dead—cannot be a mere power, influence, efflux, or attribute of God, but must be a person.

Again:

> That which can be resisted, grieved, vexed, blasphemed, must be a person; for only a person can perceive insult and be offended The blasphemy against the Holy Ghost cannot be merely blasphemy against a power or attribute of God, since in that case blasphemy against God would be a less crime than blasphemy against his power. That against which the unpardonable sin can be committed must be a person.[1]

Again, the Holy Spirit is invariably presented in Scripture in association with some other person or persons in such a way as to imply His own personality.

[*E.g.,* Acts 15:28 again]: For it seemed good to the Holy Spirit, and to us, to say lay upon you no greater burden than these necessary things, etc. [As already pointed out, these words occurred in the letter dispatched to the churches following the council of apostles and elders at Jerusalem.] [Acts 8:29 again]: And the Spirit said unto Philip, Go near, and join thyself to this chariot. [In this case Philip was one of the seven "deacons" of the Jerusalem congregation (Acts 6:1-6) who had now turned evangelist (Acts 21:8).] Acts 10:19—And while Peter thought on the vision, the Spirit said unto him, Behold, three men seek thee, etc. [Passages in the book of *Acts* in which the Holy Spirit is described as having been a companion and guide to the leaders of the early church are numerous, as we have already seen. The Holy Spirit is presented as having been in a special sense a Companion and Guide to the Apostles. This special relationship, moreover, is indicated by a special name, Paraclate, translated—imperfectly—Comforter.] [See again Luke 24:44-49; John 14:16-17, 14:26, 15:26, 16:7-14, 20:21-23; Acts 1:1-8, 2:1-4, etc.]

1. A. H. Strong, *Systematic Theology*, One-Volume Edition, 324.

303

The Spirit is also presented as being in association with the Father and the Son, and on a footing of equality with them.

2 Cor. 13:14—The grace of the Lord Jesus Christ, and the love of God, and the communion of the Holy Spirit, be with you all. 1 Pet. 1:2—according to the foreknowledge of God the Father, in sanctification of the Spirit, unto obedience and sprinkling of the blood of Jesus Christ. Jude 20-21: But ye, beloved, building up yourselves on your most holy faith, praying in the Holy Spirit, keep yourselves in the love of God, looking for the mercy of our Lord Jesus Christ unto eternal life. [And especially the baptismal formula], Matt. 28:19— baptizing them into the name of the Father and of the Son and of the Holy Spirit.

According to the Great Commission, as given by our Lord Himself "through the Holy Spirit" (Acts 1:2), we are, first, to make disciples (i.e., learners, believers, followers) from among all nations; then we are to baptize these believers (i.e., those who have been made disciples) "into the name of the Father and of the Son and of the Holy Spirit." Baptism is transitional: by means of it, as a Divine appointment, a change of state is effected: the believing penitent is translated out of the kingdom of darkness (John 8:44, Acts 26:18) into the kingdom of God's son (Col. 1:13). This change of state is essentially a change of relationship. Baptism is the ordinance Divinely appointed as the means wherein the penitent believer formally yields himself in body, soul, and spirit, to the authority of the Father, Son, and Holy Spirit. Now it is admitted by all Bible students that the Father and Son are distinct persons. True it is, of course, that some will deny the deity of Jesus, but no intelligent person would think of questioning His personality. It follows, therefore, that if the Father and the Son are distinct Persons, this baptismal formula clearly indicates that the Holy Spirit is also a Person distinct from both the Father and the Son. If the Holy Spirit be merely a force, virtue, attribute, or impersonal emanation of some sort, these words are meaningless. Moreover, "name," in this text as elsewhere in the Scriptures, signifies authority: hence to be baptized into the name of the Father and of the Son and of the Holy Spirit, is to own the authority of all three Persons, the fulness of the Godhead. If in baptism we yield to the authority of the Father and of the Son as Persons—and authority inheres only in personality; an impersonal power or influence could not possibly have or exercise authority—it follows that in the same act of faith we also yield to the authority of the Holy Spirit as a Person. Apart from the fact of the tripersonality of God the baptismal formula is unintelligible.

304

Moreover, the Holy Spirit is said to have been sent, according to promise, by the Father and by the Son (cf. again Luke 24:45-49; John 14:26; 15:26; 16:7; Acts 1:1-5). To think that either the Father or the Son sent Himself, in fulfilling this Promise, is simply out of the question. The Holy Spirit is said to have *proceeded, i.e.,* gone forth in time, from God (John 15:26). And Jesus told the Eleven explicitly that the Father would give them *another* Paraclete (John 14:16-17), that is, one distinct from Jesus Himself (John 16:7). Again, in Romans 8:26-27, as we have seen, the Spirit is said to make intercession for the saints: certainly this cannot mean that the Spirit intercedes with Himself. Finally, the pronouns used in reference to the Holy Spirit clearly indicate His personality. *E.g.,* John 14:17—"ye know *him,* for *he* abideth with you." John 14:26— "*he* shall teach you all things." John 15:26—"*he* shall bear witness of me." John 16:8—"and *he,* when *he is* come," etc. As a matter of fact, the evidence respecting the Spirit's personality is piled so high in Scripture that "wayfaring men, yea fools, shall not err therein" (Isa. 35:8). It is doubtful that the doctrine could have been set forth more clearly than it is in the teaching of Jesus and the Apostles.

We can only conclude that the Holy Spirit is presented in the Scriptures, not as an impersonal force, influence, efflux, or emanation, but as a Person. He is said to do things that only a person can do. He is said to possess faculties and endowments that only a person can possess. He is presented as suffering slights and injuries such as only a person can suffer. Men are described as sustaining attitudes and relations toward Him such as are possible only toward a person. He is given only such designations as imply personality, and He is represented as being associated with other persons in such terms as to indicate His own personality. Therefore the Holy Spirit must be a Person.

This conclusion is further corroborated by Scripture teaching regarding the Spirit's work in connection with the Church of Christ. He is represented as being the Agent of Christ in administering the affairs of the Church, that is, of the true Church, which takes in all of God's elect in the present Dispensation. As such He is said to indwell the Church and to govern it. As John Owen has written:

If a wise and honest man should come and tell you, that in a certain country where he has been, there is an excellent governor who wisely discharges the duties of his office; who hears causes, discerns right, distributes justice, relieves the poor, and comforts the distressed;

305

would you not believe that he intended by this description, a righteous, wise, diligent, intelligent person? What else could any living man imagine? But now suppose that a stranger, a person of suspicious character and credit, should come and say that the former information which you had received was indeed true, but that no man or person was intended, but merely the sun, or the wind, which by their benign influences, rendered the country fruitful and temperate, and disposed the inhabitants to mutual kindness and benignity; and therefore that the whole description of a governor and his actions, was merely figurative, though no such intimation had been given you. Must you not conclude, either that the first person was a notorious trifler, and designed your ruin, if your affairs depended on his report; or that your latter informer, whose veracity you had reason to suspect, had endeavored to abuse both him and you? It is exactly thus in the case before us. The Scriptures tell us that the Holy Ghost governs the church, appoints overseers of it; discerns and judges all things; comforts the faint; strengthens the weak; is grieved and provoked by sin; and that in these and many other affairs, he works, orders, and disposes all things, according to the counsel of his will. Can any man discredit this testimony, and conceive otherwise of the Spirit, than as a holy, wise, and intelligent person?[1]

In conclusion, the personality of the Holy Spirit is a truth which must of necessity be apprehended by faith. Because of this fact, men have found it difficult not to hold the idea in question; or possibly more convenient, let us say, to substitute therefore more materialistic notions of the Spirit as an impersonal efflux, influence, or energy. The doctrine itself is so profoundly spiritual that the human intellect experiences difficulty in taking hold of it. We do not find it difficult to conceive of the Son of God as a Person, for the simple reason that we are able to view Him objectively, so to speak, that is, as a historical personage, Jesus of Nazareth, the Word who became flesh and dwelt among men. Nor do we find it such a strain on the imagination to conceive of our Heavenly Father in terms of personality, as One who thinks and feels and wills, in some manner even as we do these things; as One whom we approach in our petitions with the familiar words. "Our Father who art in heaven" (Matt. 6:9). *Indeed the notion of the brotherhood of man is predicated upon the fact of the Fatherhood of God, and the Fatherhood of God, in turn, upon the personailty of God.* How could there be Fatherhood apart from Personality? But to grasp the idea of the Holy Spirit's personality necessitates a mode of thinking so far transcending ordinary processes of thought that many have been inclined to reject the doctrine altogether. As H. Wheeler Robinson has written:

We have no single historical figure with which to identify the

1. *A Discourse Concerning the Holy Spirit*, abridged by George Burder, 43-44.

Holy Spirit, no complete and perfect example (apart from Jesus Christ) of what He is in Himself. But, instead, we have a wealth of revelation that overwhelms us by its immensity. Through the centuries, from countless lives of the most varied type, He has been reflecting Himself, as if in the myriad flashing jewels on the wavelets of a sunlit sea. . . . God Who is present with men is present as Spirit, and the Holy Spirit Who is God's presence active with the fulness of Christ's personality cannot Himself be less than personal.[1]

Let us be content, therefore, to accept the fact of the Spirit's personality as a matter of faith and a sublime reality; as one of those "things that were freely given to us of God." For in the final analysis of the case, God the Eternal is Spirit, and they that worship Him must worship in spirit and truth.

God Who is present with men as Spirit, and the Holy Spirit Who is God's presence active with the fulness of Christ's personality cannot Himself be less than personal. Our metaphors of a quasi-personal energy break down utterly when we try to conceive an "ether" itself endowed with the love whose expression it serves to transmit. If the Spirit were but a means of transmission, or a mediating "energy," then the cardinal assumption or conviction of the real presence of God with us would be denied, and we should be left with a distant and inaccessible God.[2]

How profoundly encouraging, then, to the faith of the saints is this conviction of the Spirit's personality! How thrilling becomes Paul's declaration that the Christian's body is a temple for the Spirit's indwelling (1 Cor. 6:19)! How vital this to the growth of the saints in righteousness and holiness! In the light of this sublime truth, the life with the Holy Spirit becomes truly a life of fellowship with God and with Christ, through the abiding presence in the souls of the redeemed, of this Divine Counselor, Companion, Guide, and Advocate. In Tennyson's well-known words,

> Speak to Him thou, for He hears, and Spirit with
> Spirit can meet —
> Closer is He than breathing, and nearer than hands
> and feet.[3]

## 4. The Deity of the Holy Spirit

It will be agreed by all Bible students, I think, that in so far as we are informed by revelation and by experience, there are three, and only three, orders of persons, namely: (1) those Persons who constitute the Godhead, to whom alone the term

1. *The Christian Experience of the Holy Spirit*, 277-278.
2. *Ibid.*, 278-279.
3. "The Higher Pantheism."

"deity" is applicable; (2) the angels, who are described in Scripture as "ministering spirits" (Heb. 1:14), an order of ethereal creatures; and (3) human beings—each a body-spirit unity—who are described as "living souls" (Gen. 2:7).

Now, if the Holy Spirit is a Person, as indeed we have learned that He is, the question that arises in this connection is this: To what *rank* or *order* of persons does He belong?

This question has already been answered inferentially. We have already learned that our God is a Unity of three Persons—Father, Son, and Holy Spirit. God is one as to essence; but this oneness embraces a triple personality. The Holy Spirit is one of the three Persons of the Godhead.

Hence, the term "deity" in reference to the Spirit, is preferable to "divinity." Divinity may be a matter of quality or of degree: in fact the word is often used equivocally, as, for example, of Christ, in describing Him, as the Unitarian does, as a "divinely illumined man," but a man withal. But deity is a matter of rank: it signifies a distinct order of being. Hence, this *is a word that can be used only univocally. There are no degrees in deity.*

The following facts are offered as additional evidence of the deity of the Holy Spirit:

1. *In Scripture, the Holy Spirit is explicitly recognized as God.* By correlating various Scriptures we find that what is spoken of God absolutely in one place, is elsewhere ascribed to the Holy Spirit.

(1) E.g., in Isaiah 6:8 [the prophet says], I heard the voice of the Lord, saying, etc. [By comparing v. 3 of the same chapter we find that the *Lord* here is *Jehovah of hosts.*] [In Acts 28:25-27, the Apostle Paul, quoting this passage from Isaiah, writes] Well spake the Holy Spirit through Isaiah the prophet unto your fathers, saying, etc. [Again, in Jeremiah 31:31, it is written], Behold, the days come, saith Jehovah, that I will make a new covenant with the house of Israel, and with the house of Judah, etc. Heb. 10:15ff. [it is written], And the Holy Spirit also beareth witness to us, for after he hath said, etc., [and the actual words of the passage from Jeremiah are then quoted]. Lev. 26:11-12: And I will set my tabernacle among you. . . . And I will walk among you, and will be your God, and ye shall be my people. 1 Cor. 3:16-17: Know ye not that ye are a temple of God, and that the Spirit of God dwelleth in you? If any man destroyeth the temple of God, him shall God destroy; for the temple of God is holy, and such are ye. 1 Cor. 6:19—Know ye not that your body is a temple of the Holy Spirit which is in you, which ye have from God? Deut. 32:12, Jehovah alone did lead him [*i.e.*, the children of Israel]. Isa. 63:11, 14— Where is he that put his holy Spirit in the midst of them? . . . As

the cattle that go down into the valley, the Spirit of Jehovah caused them to rest. [Here we have a positive identification, even in Old Testament times, of the Holy Spirit with the Spirit of Jehovah]. [Also, in this connection, Psa. 78:17-19]: Yet they went on still to sin against him, To rebel against the Most High in the desert. And they tempted God in their heart, By asking food according to their desire; Yea, they spake against God, etc.

(2) Acts 5:3, 4—[Here the Apostle is represented as saying to Ananias], Why hath Satan filled thy heart to lie to the Holy Spirit? [To this he adds in the very next breath], Thou hast not lied unto men, but unto God. [To lie to a Spirit-filled man is to lie to the Holy Spirit, and to lie to the Holy Spirit is to lie to God.] [Cf. again 1 Cor. 3:16-17 and 1 Cor. 6:19: Here the words are addressed to Christians. If they mean anything, they surely mean that the Holy Spirit indwells the body of every true saint. If our bodies are *temples of God* because the Spirit of God indwells them, it follows that the Holy Spirit, must be, in essence, God.]

(3) Eph. 6:21, 22—Christ Jesus, in whom each several building, fitly framed together, groweth into a holy temple in the Lord; in whom ye also are builded together for a habitation of God in the Spirit. [Here the Apostle is writing of the church as a whole, the church catholic, consisting of all the elect of God under the New Covenant. This body, or church, he says, is *the habitation of God in the Spirit.*] 1 Pet. 2:5— ye also as living stones, are built up a spiritual house, to be a holy priesthood, to offer up spiritual sacrifices, acceptable to God through Jesus Christ. [Now if God indwells the whole Church of Christ in the person of His Spirit, again it follows that the Holy Spirit, as to essence and rank, is God.]

(4) John 4:24—God is a Spirit, and they that worship him must worship in spirit and truth. [These are the words of Jesus Himself.] Heb. 9:14—*the eternal Spirit*: [God is a Spirit, the eternal Spirit; it follows, therefore, that the Holy Spirit is God.]

## 2. In Scripture, the attributes and perfections of God are ascribed to the Holy Spirit.

[(1) *Eternity* or *Self-Existence.*] Heb. 9:14—the eternal Spirit. [(2) *Omniscience.*] 1 Cor. 2:9-11: But as it is written, Things which eye saw not, and ear heard not, and which entered not into the heart of man, Whatsoever things God prepared for them that love him. But unto us God revealed them through the Spirit; for the Spirit searcheth all things, yea, the deep things of God. Isa. 40:13—Who hath directed the Spirit of Jehovah, or being his counsellor hath taught him?

[(3) *Omnipotence.*] Micah 3:8—I am full of power by the Spirit of Jehovah, and of judgment, and of might. 1 Cor. 2:4—in demonstration of the Spirit and of power. 1 Cor. 12:11—but all these worketh the one and the same Spirit, dividing to each one severally even as he will.

[(4) *Omnipresence.*] Psa. 139:7-10: Whither shall I go from thy Spirit? Or whither shall I flee from thy presence? If I ascend up into heaven, thou art there; if I make my bed in Sheol, behold, thou art there. If I take the wings of the morning, And dwell in the uttermost parts of the sea, Even there shall thy hand lead me, And thy right hand shall hold me. Jer. 23:23-24: Am I a God at hand, saith Jehovah, and not a God afar off? Can any hide himself in secret places so that I shall not see him? saith Jehovah. Do not I fill heaven and earth? saith Jehovah.

309

[(5) *Prescience.*] Acts 1:16—Brethren, it was needful that the scripture should be fulfilled, which the Holy Spirit spake before by the mouth of David concerning Judas, etc. Matt. 22:43—How then doth David in the Spirit call him Lord? etc. [All prophecy is evidence of the prescience of the Spirit.]

[(6) *Infinite Life.*] Rom. 8:2—the Spirit of life.

[(7) *Infinite Love.*] Rom. 5:5—the love of God hath been shed abroad in our hearts through the Holy Spirit which was given unto us. Rom. 15:30—by the love of the Spirit.

[(8) *Infinite Holiness.*] Neh. 9:20—thy good Spirit. Isa. 63:11—his holy Spirit. Matt. 28:19—the Holy Spirit [and so in many instances in the New Testament].

### 3. In Scripture, the Holy Spirit is represented as having shared in, or Himself performed, the works of Deity.

[(1) *Creation.*] Gen. 1:1-3: In the beginning God created the heavens and the earth. And the earth was waste and void; and darkness was upon the face of the deep: and the Spirit of God moved upon the face of the waters. And God said, "Let there be light; and there was light. Job 26:13—By his Spirit the heavens are garnished. Job 33:4—The Spirit of God hath made me, And the breath of the Almighty giveth me life. Psa. 33:6—By the word of Jehovah were the heavens made, And all the host of them by the breath of his mouth. [Cf. Gen. 2:7].

[(2) *Preservation.*] Psa. 104:30—Thou sendest forth thy Spirit, they are created; And thou renewest the face of the ground.

[(3) *Inspiration* and *Revelation.*] Acts 2:4—[Here we read that the Apostles were all filled with the Holy Spirit, and began to speak with other tongues, as the Spirit gave them utterance. [Inspiration and revelation are, in a special sense, works of the Spirit of God. See again 2 Pet. 1:21, 1 Pet. 1:10-12, 1 Cor. 2:9-16, etc.].

[(4) *Demonstration* or *Miracles.*] [This again is distinctively a work of the Spirit. The Father is primarily the Source of *faith;* the Son, of *doctrine;* the Spirit, of *evidence* or *proof.*] Matt. 12:28—But if I by the Spirit of God cast out demons, then is the kingdom of God come upon you. Also 1 Cor. 2:4—in demonstration of the Spirit and of power; and Heb. 2:4, 1 Cor. 12:4-11, etc.

[(5) *Regeneration.*] John 3:5—Except one be born of water and the Spirit, he cannot enter into the kingdom of God. Titus 3:5—according to his mercy he saved us, through the washing of regeneration and renewing of the Holy Spirit.

[(6) *Resurrection* and *Immortalization.*] Rom. 8:11—But if the Spirit of him that raised up Jesus from the dead dwelleth in you, he that raised up Christ Jesus from the dead shall give life also to your mortal bodies through his Spirit that dwelleth in you.

### 4. In Scripture, the Holy Spirit is represented as receiving obedience and worship that is due only to the Deity.

(1) Matt. 28:19—[According to the Great Commission, all believers are to be baptized into the name of the Father and of the Son and of the Holy Spirit. It should be noted, in this connection, that baptism is the only act recorded in Scripture as having *the name of the Father and of the Son and of the Holy Spirit* connected with it. The modern church is inclined to make too little of baptism rather than too much. Baptism is—cannot be, if real baptism—a mere form or ceremony;

310

it is not a mere ceremonial *putting away of the filth of the flesh,* but *the appeal of a good conscience toward God* (1 Pet. 3:21); to be baptism, it must be an act of faith, a profoundly spiritual, heart act.] [As Paul puts it, writing of baptism], Rom. 6:17—But thanks be to God that, whereas ye were servants of sin, ye became obedient *from the heart* to that pattern of teaching whereunto ye were delivered, etc. [Now the teaching was the Gospel which consisted of three facts, namely, the death, burial, and resurrection of Christ (1 Cor. 15:1-4); the pattern of that teaching is baptism, which pictorializes the death, burial, and resurrection of Christ. To the pattern of that teaching, *i.e.,* baptism, the Roman Christians, says Paul, had been obedient *from the heart.* Baptism is a heart act, a spiritual act, an act of faith, and cannot be anything else.]

(2) 2 Cor. 13:14—the communion of the Holy Spirit be with you all. [Here *the communion of the Holy Spirit* is invoked for all the sants, along with *the grace of the Lord Jesus Christ* and *the love of God.*]

(3) Rev. 1:4—the seven Spirits that are before his throne. [The *seven Spirits* here stand for the Holy Spirit; in Scripture the number seven is indicative of completeness, perfection.] Cf. Isa. 11:2—and the Spirit of Jehovah shall rest upon him, the spirit of wisdom and understanding, the spirit of counsel and might, the spirit of knowledge and of the fear of Jehovah.

(4) Matt. 12:31-32: Every sin and blasphemy shall be forgiven unto men; but the blasphemy against the Spirit shall not be forgiven. And whosoever shall speak a word against the Son of man, it shall be forgiven him; but whosoever shall speak against the Holy Spirit, it shall not be forgiven him, neither in this world, nor in that which is to come. [Here Jesus tells us that the only *remediless* sin is the sin against the Holy Spirit. In view of this statement, the deity of the Holy Spirit must be accepted as a necessary inference.]

**5. *Finally, the Holy Spirit is represented in Scripture as being associated on a footing of equality with both the Father and the Son.***

(1) [In the baptismal formula], Matt. 28:19—baptizing them into the name of the Father and of the Son and of the Holy Spirit.

(2) [In the apostolic benediction], 2 Cor. 13:14—The grace of the Lord Jesus Christ, the love of God, and the communion of the Holy Spirit, be with you all.

(3) [In 1 Pet. 1:2]—according to the foreknowledge of God the Father, in sanctification of the Spirit, unto obedience and sprinkling of the blood of Jesus Christ.

(4) [In Jude 20-21]: praying in the Holy Spirit, keep yourselves in the love of God, looking for the mercy of our Lord Jesus Christ unto eternal life.

(5) [In 1 Cor. 12:4-6]: Now there are diversities of gifts, but the same Spirit. And there are diversities of ministrations, and the same Lord. And there are diversities of workings, but the same God, who worketh all things in all.

(6) [In Eph. 2:19-22]: ye are fellow-citizens with the saints, and of the household of God, being built upon the foundation of the apostles and prophets, Christ Jesus himself being the chief corner stone; in whom each several building, fitly framed together, groweth into a holy temple in the Lord; in whom ye also are builded together for a habitation of God in the Spirit.

311

(7) [In Eph. 4:4-6]: There is one body, and *one Spirit*, even as also ye were called in one hope of your calling; *one Lord*, one faith, one baptism, *one God and Father* of all, who is over all, and through all, and in all.

In view of this array of evidence, we must accept the deity of the Holy Spirit as a divinely-revealed truth, as one of the fundamentals of our Christian faith. As a matter of fact, the fundamental truths of the deity of the Spirit (Heb. 9:14—"the eternal Spirit") and the Spirithood of the Deity (John 4:24— "God is a Spirit") are in a sense identical.

But what is the practical significance of these truths? Of what value are they to Christians? What use are we to make of them in our everyday thinking and living?

"Know ye not," exclaims the Apostle, writing to Christians, "that ye are a temple of God, and that the Spirit of God dwelleth in you?" (1 Cor. 3:16). Beloved, we are, *individually,* temples of the Holy Spirit "which is in us and which we have from God" (1 Cor. 6:19). We are, *collectively,* that is, as the Church or Body of Christ, "living stones, built up a spiritual house" (1 Pet. 2:5), "builded together for a sanctuary of God in the Spirit" (Eph. 2:22). As Andrew Murray has written:

> There is a Presence in the Church of Christ as Omnipotent and Divine as was Christ Himself when on earth; yea, rather, as He is now on the Throne of Power. As the Church wakes up to believe this, and rises out of the dust to put on her beautiful garments . . . her witness for Christ will be in living power. She will prove that her Almighty Lord is in her.[1]

If we as Christians could in some way come to believe and to realize this truth of the God's personal indwelling of us through the agency of His Holy Spirit, to such an extent that we should actually *live* the conviction in all that we say and think and do, what would be the result? Our attitudes would be changed, our hearts would be warmed with new spiritual fires, our unused powers would be utilized, and our lives would be transformed "into the same image from glory to glory" (2 Cor. 3:18). Cares, anxieties, fears, and countless accompanying physical afflictions would be cast out of our lives, and a spiritual revival would be generated that would sweep Satan from his throne as god of this world! This is the kind of revival that the modern church needs, and must have, if she is to do the work of Christ in this

1. *The Spirit of Christ*, 143.

present world, if she is to be in deed and in truth His Bride, His Counterpart, His Spouse.

May I close this section, therefore, with Andrew Murray's eloquent prayer:

> Most Holy God! In adoring wonder I bow before Thee in presence of this wondrous mystery of grace; my spirit, soul, and body Thy temple.
>
> In deep silence and worship I accept the blessed revelation, that in me too there is a Holiest of all, and that there Thy hidden Glory has its abode.
>
> O my God, forgive me that I have so little known it.
>
> I do now tremblingly accept the blessed truth: God the Spirit, the Holy Spirit, who is God Almighty, dwells in me.
>
> O my Father, reveal within what it means, lest I sin against Thee by saying it and not living it.
>
> Blessed Jesus! to Thee, who sittest upon the throne, I yield my whole being. In Thee I trust to rise up in power and have dominion within me.
>
> In Thee I believe for the full streaming forth of the living waters.
>
> Blessed Spirit! Holy Teacher! Mighty Sanctifier! Thou art within me. On Thee do I wait all the day. I belong to Thee. Take entire possession of me for the Father and the Son. Amen.[1]

In the words of the old hymn,

> Holy Spirit, all divine,
> Dwell within this heart of mine;
> Cast down every idol throne,
> Reign supreme, and reign alone.

## 5. Spirit in the Godhead

"There is a spirit in man," said Elihu to Job, "and the breath of the Almighty giveth them understanding" (Job 32:8). This "spirit" in man is, as we have learned, personal life with all its potentialities. But man is the image or likeness of God: so there is Spirit in God. Spirit in God, however, is personal life in all its actuality, in all its metaphysical and moral *wholeness*, that is, Holy Spirit. "God is a Spirit" (John 4:24), and the Spirit of God is the Eternal Spirit (Heb. 9:14).

Speaking in strictly metaphysical terms, of course, the Father is also, as to essence, Spirit; hence He is said to be the "Father of spirits" (Heb. 12:9). And the Son likewise is, in His eternal nature, as to essence, Spirit: "the Lord is the Spirit" (2 Cor. 3:17). That is to say, they are both incorporeal and of the same metaphysical essence as the Holy Spirit, who is Himself the Eternal Spirit. We must keep in mind always that

1. *Op. cit.*, 240-241.

313

it takes Father, Son, and Spirit, to make up the Being of our God who is essentially Spirit. The term "Spirit" with reference to the Godhead in general ("God is a Spirit," John 4:24) seems to mean simply that no physical or corporeal—but exclusively psychical and moral—relations are sustained among the three Persons who constitute our God.

Certainly our God, if He is to meet the deepest aspirations of the human heart, must be a holy Spirit. Human outreaching could hardly be satisfied with anything less in deity. Indeed, it was the prophet Isaiah, writing several centuries before the advent of the Messiah, harking back to the rebelliousness of God's ancient people under Moses, gave expression to the following exquisite bit of literature:

> But they rebelled, and grieved his holy Spirit: therefore he [Jehovah] was turned to be their enemy, and himself fought against them. Then he remembered the days of old, Moses and his people, saying, Where is he that brought them up out of the sea with the shepherds of his flock? where is he that put his holy Spirit in the midst of them? that caused his glorious arm to go at the right hand of Moses? that divided the waters before them, to make himself an everlasting name? that led them through the depths, as a horse in the wilderness, so that they stumbled not? As the cattle that go down into the valley, the Spirit of Jehovah caused them to rest: so didst thou lead thy people, to make thyself a glorious name (Isa. 63:10:14).

And it was Isaiah who, at least seven centuries before Christ, was privileged to behold, in a wondrous Vision, "the Lord sitting upon a throne, high and lifted up, and his train filled the temple"; and to hear the words of the heavenly anthem to which John the Beloved was also privileged to listen, some eight hundred years afterward, on the barren isle of Patmos: "Holy, holy, holy, is Jehovah of hosts" (Isa. 6:3, Rev. 4:8). In similar vein, the Psalmist cried out unto God saying, "Teach me to do thy will; For thou art my God: Thy Spirit is good; Lead me in the land of uprightness" (Psa. 143:10), and again, "Cast me not away from thy presence, and take not thy holy Spirit from me" (Psa. 51:11). And in the great day of national rejuvenation under Nehemiah the prince and Ezra the priest-scribe, the intercessory prayer of the Levites for the people, contained these words with reference to the experience of their fathers under Moses: "Thou gavest also thy good Spirit to instruct them, and withheldest not thy manna from their mouth, and gavest them water for their thirst" (Neh. 9:20). Indeed, I am convinced that God's saints, from the earliest dawn of human history, have known full well that God is essentially holy Spirit.

According to Scripture, the relation of the Spirit to the

Godhead may be stated in three basic propositions, as follows: 1. *God IS Spirit, or a Spirit* (John 4:24). That is to say, God is, as to essence, Spirit or spiritual (pure thought, will, love, being); hence, *not* physical or corporeal. This is equally true of all three Persons of the Godhead in their eternal and unoriginated nature. Ordinarily we describe God, therefore, as Pure Spirit, that is, "without body or parts, but having intelligence and free will." I might point out, however, that this designation does not necessarily exclude the idea of His existing in some form of what has been called "psychical ether," far subtler than matter. Comprehension of the essence of God is, of course, completely beyond our ken. As Knudson writes:

> The word "spirituality" as applied to God has at least three distinct meanings. It means that God is a spirit as distinguished from material or physical existence. It means that he is free from the weakness of flesh, and is a supramundane power, superior to the forces of nature. It means also that there is an inner side to his personality, a rational and ethical side, and that it is here that his essential nature is to be found. He is not primarily substance or force, but a rational and ethical Being, who seeks to control men not by the sheer exercise of power but by appeal to their reason and intelligence, and who consequently, when worshiped, must be worshiped in spirit and in truth.[1]

Since our God is a Spirit, any move to conceive Him, to represent Him, or to worship Him, in the form of a material object, or even in the form of a natural object—such as a tree, river, plant, or animal, or the sun, moon, earth, or any other heavenly body, or even Nature as a whole—is manifestly unspiritual and false. Hence, the Second Commandment of the Decalogue: "Thou shalt not make unto thee a graven image, nor any likeness of any thing that is in heaven above, or that is in the earth beneath, or that is in the water under the earth; thou shalt not bow down thyself unto them, nor serve them: for I Jehovah thy God am a jealous God," etc., and there follows here the Biblical statement of the *law of heredity* (Exo. 20:4-6). Idolatry, animism, or nature-worship of any kind— all are derogatory of our God. There is but one Eternal Being—God—and He is a Spirit, or, to put it conversely, the Spirit who is Eternal is God.

2. *God HAS Spirit.* To have Spirit, of course, is to have the attributes and powers of Spirit. (In studying the nature and work of the Holy Spirit, one must always be careful to distinguish between the Spirit Himself, a Person, on the one hand, and His attributes, powers, gifts, influences, etc., on the other hand. Failure to make such a distinction has been a prolofic source of

1. A. C. Knudson, *The Religious Teaching of the Old Testament*, 93.

confusion in the past.) Such designations as "My Spirit" ("The Spirit of Me"), "Thy Spirit" ("The Spirit of Thee"), "His Spirit" ("The Spirit of Him"), "The Spirit of God," "The Spirit of Jehovah," etc.—all imply the same thing, namely, the Spirit *belonging to* God, the Spirit *belonging to* Jehovah, etc. As man has spirit "in him," so God has Spirit in Him. Job 32:8—"There is a spirit in man." 1 Cor. 2:11-12: "For who among men knoweth the things of a man, save the spirit of the man, which is in him? even so the things of God none knoweth, save the Spirit of God. But we received, not the spirit of the world, but the spirit which is from God; that we might know the things that were freely given to us of God."

3. *God GIVES Spirit.* That is to say, God gives to men the gifts (influences, powers, endowments) that ensue from the procession, presence, and power of the Spirit.

Matt. 7:11—If ye then, being evil, know how to give good gifts unto your children, how much more shall your Father who is in heaven give good things to them that ask him? Luke 11:13—How much more shall your heavenly Father give the Holy Spirit to them that ask him? Eph. 4:8—When he [Christ] ascended on high, he led captivity *captive*, And gave gifts unto men [cf. Psa. 68:18; Neh. 9:20; Acts 5:32, 15:8; Rom. 5:5; 2 Cor. 1:22, 5:5; 1 Thess. 4:8; 1 John 3:24, 4:13.]

Obviously, no man knows, indeed no man is capable of knowing, all that Spirit in God comprehends. In this present life at least, this knowledge is beyond the range of the human intellect. The most we can do, therefore, in this connection, is to summarize the teaching of the Scriptures on this phase of our subject, keeping in mind at all times that the Bible is the Book of the Spirit. This we shall now undertake to do, as follows:

1. *Spirit in God means Power.*

Indeed one of the Scriptural names of the Spirit is "The Power of the Most High." From the words of the Annunciating Angel to the virgin Mary we read the following: "The Holy Spirit shall come upon thee, and the power of the Most High shall overshadow thee: wherefore also the holy thing which is begotten shall be called the Son of God" (Luke 1:35).

Spirit is the *dynamis* ("power"), the *energeia* ("activity") of God. Spirit-power is the ultimate source of both "physical" and "psychical" energy; and, as we have already noted, the line separating these two kinds of energy has been drawn so fine in recent years, in scientific thought, as to become almost nonexistent. Hence, the activity of the Spirit is said, in Scripture, to result in the heightening, in some instances of the physical, in others of the psychical, powers of men. Such activity is always exerted, of course, for the realization of some Divine purpose. Thus the Spirit of Jehovah "came mightily upon" Samson, to endow him with extraordinary physical strength for the deliverance of his people from their enemies (Judg. 14:6, 15:14). And thus their infilling by the Spirit qualified Bezalel and Oholiab with extraordinary artistic talent to construct and to adorn the furnishings of the Tabernacle (Exo. 31:1-11, 35:30-35); and thus the coming of the Spirit upon them qualified other divinely-chosen leaders of God's ancient people with special abilities for civil and military direction (e.g., Othniel, Judg. 3:10; Gideon, Judg. 6:34; Jephthah, Judg. 11:29; Saul, 1 Sam. 10:10; David, 1 Sam. 16:13, 2 Sam. 23:1-2). Again, David, we are told, received from the Spirit the plans and specifications for the Temple (1 Chron. 28:12), which plans he handed down to his son Solomon for execution. And thus the inspiration of the Spirit endowed men of God, from beginning to end of the unfolding of the Plan of Redemption, with foreknowledge of subsequent events, especially of the circumstances of the life and work of the Messiah and of the future trials and triumphs of the Church. (Cf. 2 Sam. 23:2, 2 Pet. 1:21, 1 Pet. 1:10-11; Rev. 1:10.) Needless to say, too, that the presence of the Spirit in a human individual is the source of great moral power. No wonder then that the Apostles, filled as they were with the Spirit of God, "with great power . . . gave their witness of the resurrection of the Lord Jesus" (Acts 4:33). Had not Jesus told them, before His return to the Father: "Behold, I send forth the promise of my Father upon you: but tarry ye in the city, until ye be clothed with power from on high" (Luke 24:49)? And again: "Ye shall receive power, when the Holy Spirit is come upon you: and ye shall be my witnesses both in Jerusalem, and in all Judea and Samaria, and unto the uttermost part of the earth" (Acts 1:8)? Whether in these various cases additional physical, psychical or moral power was imparted to those persons who were being utilized as special instruments of the Spirit's activity, or whether that Divine activity only heightened the powers already inherent in those persons, we have no means of knowing; in any case, the results were the same. Where the Spirit is, God is; and where God is, there is Power—inexhaustible Power—physical, psychical and moral. There is no such thing as "entropy" in the Spirit of our God.

As a matter of fact, the Scriptures clearly teach that Spirit-power is the ultimate Source of the energy which, by self-transmutation into gross matter, goes to make up our physical universe and all its parts. Gen. 1:1-2: "In the beginning God created the heavens and the earth. And the earth was waste and void; and darkness was upon the face of the deep; and the Spirit of God moved upon the face of the waters." Atomic power itself, of which we hear so much in these days, is but the manifestation of the power of God; the same is true of all forms of electromagnetic radiation. All forms of so-called "physical" energy have their primary source in the activity of the Divine Spirit, who is Pure Being, Pure Actuality. They are His "creations" or "projections"—which, we do not know, nor does it make a great deal of difference whether or not we do know. As H. Wheeler Robinson writes:

> Analogies are perilous, but perhaps we should get near to the shifting lights and colors of the *New Testament* use of "Spirit" and "spirit" if we thought of it as the "spiritual" counterpart of an encompassing and penetrating psychical ether, far subtler than "matter," yet quasi-material, and nucleated, as it were, into specialized centres of *energy*, both in men, angels and God, to all of whom in such varying degrees belong those qualities we call "spiritual." In many ways modern theories of physics approximate to ancient theories of "spirit" though this does not justify us in the unguarded use of physical analogies for the formation of a modern theory of Spirit.[1]

In a word, all individuals and individual objects are but media of the Divine Energy which created and which sustains our *one* world. So-called "material" objects are, as centers of this energy, but evanescent indeed, ever-changing symbols whereby spirits or persons—who constitute that aspect of the Cosmos which alone may properly be designated *reality*—preserve themselves in being and communicate with one another, to the achievement of their natural and proper ultimate ends. Our one world is, at its roots, so to speak, that is, stripped of its externality or sensible aspects, the World of the Spirit. Truly, in the Eternal Spirit of God—in His activity, in His actualization of all being, we, as persons, and indeed all sub-personal things as well, "live, and move, and have our being" (Acts 17:28); that is, in a purely *natural* sense. In a *moral* sense, of course, persons—and persons only—can and do live in neglect of God and in open rebellion against His Will. Hence, but in a *moral* sense only, persons and persons alone are capable of living outside God, that is, outside covenant relationship, outside fellowship with Him. Moreover, to live in God morally, which is to live the life of the Spirit, is to live *naturally*, to live as God orders us to live in order to attain our natural and

1. *Op. cit.*, 229.

proper ultimate ends as human beings. For the Will of God is the constitution—that which constitutes—all Nature. On the other hand, to live outside God morally, outside covenant relationship or fellowship with Him, is to live *unnaturally*. Sin is acting and living contrary to God's Will; all sin, therefore, is *unnatural*. The whole kingdom of darkness, in its every aspect, is unnatural; it lies wholly outside Nature, the Realm of the Good. It is the kingdom which has been thrust into the natural order of things by Satanic and human rebellion. We read that at the conclusion of the physical creation, "God saw everything that he had made, and, behold, it was very good" (Gen. 1:31). It became bad subsequently, only when sin entered into the moral order, when man allowed himself to be seduced by Satan. Satan's throne is the throne of the arch-rebel, the prince of darkness; and all his duped satellites from among angels and men, all of whom seek to prostitute liberty into license, make up the constituency of his rebel rule. This rebel kingdom will ultimately, and quite naturally, gravitate to its proper place, the place of its eternal segregation—to Hell, the penitentiary of the moral universe. And, as the Scriptures assure us, the Kingdom of Heaven under the reign of the Anointed, will, in the finality of temporal events, become co-extensive with the New Heavens and New Earth wherein dwelleth righteousness.

Cf. Matt. 28:18 [the words of the risen Christ]: All authority hath been given unto me in heaven and on earth. 1 Cor. 15:25-26: For he must reign, till he hath put all his enemies under his feet. The last enemy that shall be abolished is death. [Cf. Isa. 65:17, 66:2; 2 Pet. 3:13; Rev. 21:1-3.]

*Note the marvelous unity of Bible teaching that is presented in these Scripture. Hence, the only perfectly natural life for a human individual to live is not the life of gratification of animal impulses and desires, but the life with the Holy Spirit, which is the life of righteousness, joy and peace.* "For the kingdom of God is not eating and drinking, but righteousness and peace and joy in the Holy Spirit" (Rom. 14:17). "Man," Jesus tells us, "shall not live by bread alone, but by every word that proceedeth out of the mouth of God" (Matt. 4:4, cf. Deut. 8:3). It follows, therefore, since the Son was the incarnate Logos, that "he that hath the Son hath the life; he that hath not the Son of God hath not the life" (1 John 5:12). True life is the life of the Spirit in the human heart, the life of fellowship "with the Father and with his Son Jesus Christ" (1 John 1:3).

Spirit-power, again, is the power which actuates and sus-

319

tains all the processes of nature. It is the unchanging Reality which persists through all outward appearance and change. The problem of change is one of the most profound problems confronting human experience and thought. That, in order to make change possible, there must be something that persists throughout the continuous, never-ending flux of this world of time and space and place, is obvious. To repeat an illustration used previously: A log, for example, is thrown into the fireplace; in a short time it has "changed" into ashes and gases. But there must be something that remains itself throughout this process of change; otherwise, there is not change at all, but an annihilation followed by a creation. So it is with respect to all change. If something does not persist *as the same* throughout all change, then our world is simply a sequence of annihilations and creations. But such an interpretation violates our reason: it implies a continuous process, if indeed it could be called a process, of passing into nothing and becoming out of nothing; instead of an original creation commonly described as *ex nihilo,* we have an infinitely repeated creation *ex nihilo.* The only reasonable conclusion we can reach, therefore, is that there is an abiding, timeless, never-changing Something which is the source and cause of all things, the Principle of Unity and of Generation, and which persists throughout all their changing appearances. That Something, moreover, must be dynamic; it would be utterly absurd to conceive it as static. That Something, we Christians contend, is the Activity, the *Energeia* of God— Spirit-power, which actualizes every form of energy in the Totality of Being. In the words of the old hymn:

> Swift to its close ebbs out life's little day;
> Earth's joys grow dim, its glories pass away;
> Change and decay in all around I see;
> O Thou who changest not, Abide with me!

Spirit-power is the power which effectuates, *i.e.,* makes operative, all natural physical and moral law. "The law," said Aristotle, "is reason unaffected by desire." Said Abraham Lincoln: "Law is the expression of the will of the lawgiver." Thomas Aquinas defined moral law as "an ordination of reason for the common good, by him who has the care of the community, and promulgated." The essential elements of law are (1) a lawgiver, or authoritative will (authority being the moral right to use force); (2) a prior exercise of reason, for law is essentially purposive; (3) subjects, or beings toward whom the authoritative will is directed; (4) a general command or edict, the expression of the authoritative will; (5) the power of enforcing the command; and (6) a penalty for the violation of the law, for law would not be law, but merely counsel or wish, without a penalty for its violation. Law, because it is without exception an expression of reason and will, presupposes an intelligent lawgiver, one who has the power not only to promulgate the law but to enforce it as well. (That is, *just* law is the expression of reason and will. Law that is the expression of arbitrary will alone, is apt to be unjust. Law that is the expression essentially of reason, uninfluenced by ambition, prejudice, or emotion, is most apt to be constructive and just.) This is as equally true of physical as of moral law. Force of any kind, in fact, that operates in a uniform manner, presupposes an authoritative intelligence and will. Now our world, in its general framework at least, is not a Chaos, but a Cosmos. *Kosmos,* in Greek, means "order." It signifies that ours is a world of order, hence that it is an *ordered* world, that is, a world ordered by a Supreme Intelligence and Will. If our world were not a Cosmos, there never could have been, nor could there ever be, a *science,* for science is simply man's knowledge—or interpretation, to be precise—of the order that prevails in the various departments of Nature. In fact, if our world were not a world of order, human beings—or any other living creature, for that matter—could not live in it. If men were not reasonably sure that day and night, seedtime and harvest, summer and winter, would come and go in orderly sequence, tomorrow as in the manner of yesterday, they could not plan to live or even live at all. Life would be utterly impossible in a chaotic, unpredictable world. Hence, in its very use of such terms as "cosmos," "cosmology," "laws of nature," "natural laws," "science," and the like, human science, consciously or unconsciously (it makes no difference with respect to the fact itself) recognizes the existence and operation of a Sovereign Intelligence and Will,— God. As Strong has put it: "Physical science, in her very use of the word 'law' implicitly confesses that a supreme Will has set general rules which control the processes of the universe."[1] To use a simple illustration: According to the law of chemical affinity, two atoms—and two only— of hydrogen invariably unite with one atom—and one only—of oxygen, to form a molecule of water. Obviously, this "law," expressed in the formula $H_2O$, merely describes *how*, or in what proportions, these atoms unite to form water; any variation from this formula, in the

1. A. H. Strong, *op. cit.*, 533.

number of the respective kinds of atoms uniting, would result not in water but in some other substance. But the significant question is, *Why* do they so unite without exception? What *causes* the atoms to unite in such fixed proportions? To assume the positivistic position and blithely assert that they *do* so act and that ends the matter in so far as our knowledge extends or can extend, is simply burying one's head, ostrich-like, in the sands of ignorance. It is simply to ignore efficient causality altogether. The assumption of such an attitude is nothing but a will-act whereby a canon is set up arbitrarily to restrict any further attempt to know the answer to the *why*. Had science always followed this technique, throwing away altogether "the music and the dream" of life, we should still be living in the environment of the Stone Age; for science, as truly as art, is the product of man's creative imagination. Not even science can afford to imprison itself by such a method; in so doing it would destroy itself. In the final analysis of the case, positivism is sheer *wilful* ignorance, ignorance that is stifling—and nothing more can be made of it. Besides, the human spirit will never be content to remain imprisoned in a positivistic cage; its natural habitat is the great intellectual out-of-doors. We are all Columbuses, and the pull of the horizon beckoning us into the mysteries of uncharted seas, is a force which human nature has ever found to be irresistible; indeed this instinct for penetrating the secrets of the "more beyond" is of the very essence of progress. And so the human mind will go on asking, *why?*— nor will all the self-styled "positivists" under the sun ever be able to change it. Indeed most psychologists will agree, I think, that the *exploratory* tendency in man is instinctive, *i.e.*, innate. *Why*, then, do two atoms of hydrogen invariably unite with one atom of oxygen to form a molecule of water? What *causes* Nature, in her various aspects as known to science, always to act thus, uniformly? What causes Nature to operate according to well-defined "laws"? What is the Power back of all the operations of Nature? What activates these operations? The answer is clear: The *ultimate* Cause is the intelligently self-determined Will of God; the *proximate* Cause is Spirit-power. No other intelligent answer to the question of the WHY of things is conceivable. And to attribute such uniformity to mere chance—whatever that term may signify—is about the most unintelligent answer imaginable.

*To ignore efficient causality with reference to the Cosmos is to be blinded by wilful ignorance—the worst form of ignorance conceivable. That there has to be a Creative Power sufficient to account for the natural world and all its parts and creatures is too obvious to be open to question. And both Reason and Revelation agree in affirming that Creative Power or Efficient Cause to be the Spirit-power of God.*

Now Spirit-power being the Power which sustains the processes of Nature, it follows quite logically that Spirit-power is the only Power which can, in a particular time and place and for a special Divine purpose, supersede the ordinary processes of Nature in the specific instance, and thus effect what is described in Scripture as a *miracle.* And, inasmuch as right human reason and Divine revelation are always in accord, the Bible, throughout, witnesses to the truth of this statement.

Luke 1:35, 37—[the words of the angel Gabriel to Mary]: The Holy Spirit shall come upon thee, and the power of the Most High shall overshadow thee: wherefore also the holy thing which is begotten shall be called the Son of God. . . . For no word from God shall be void of power. Matt. 12:28—[the words of Jesus]: But if I by the Spirit of God cast out demons, then is the kingdom of God come upon you. Luke 24:49 [here the risen Jesus says to the Eleven]; And behold, I send forth the promise of my Father upon you: but tarry ye in the city, until ye be clothed with power from on high. Acts 1:8—[the risen Christ again speaking to the Eleven]: Ye shall receive power, when the Holy Spirit is come upon you, etc. Acts 2.22—[from Peter's sermon on the Day of Pentecost]: Jesus of Nazareth, a man approved of God unto you by mighty works and wonders and signs which God did by him in the midst of you, even as ye yourselves know. [That is, mighty works—miracles—which God, by the agency of the Spirit, wrought in and through the Son, Jesus Christ, who possessed the Spirit without measure [John 3:34]; indeed the personal spirit of Jesus was so possessed by the Holy Spirit that, in Scripture, *Spirit of Christ* (1 Pet. 1:11), *Spirit of Jesus* (Acts 16:7), *and Holy Spirit* are interchangeable terms.] Acts 10:38—Jesus of Nazareth, how God anointed him with the Holy Spirit and with power. Acts 8:18-19: Now when Simon saw that through the laying on the apostles' hands the Holy Spirit was given, he offered them money, saying, Give me also this power, that on whomsoever I lay my hands, he may receive the Holy Spirit. [The allusion here is to the miracle-working power by which the early church was strengthened in the faith; cf. 1 Cor. 12:4-11.] Rom. 15:18-19 [Paul writing]:For I will not dare to speak of any things save those which Christ wrought through me, for the obedience of the Gentiles, by word and deed, in the power of signs and wonders, in the power of the Holy Spirit. 1 Cor. 2:4-5, [Paul again]: And my speech and my preaching were not in persuasive words of wisdom, but in demonstration of the Spirit and of power: that your faith should not stand in the wisdom of men, but in the power of God. Heb. 2:3-4: How shall we escape, if we neglect so great a salvation? which having at first been spoken through the Lord, was confirmed unto us by them that heard; God also bearing witness with them, both by signs and wonders, and by manifold powers, and by gifts of the Holy Spirit, according to his own will. 1 Cor. 12:11—but all these [miracles] worketh the one and the same Spirit, dividing to each one severally even as he will.

Thus it will be seen that Spirit-power is, according to Scripture, the power that necessarily enters into the working of a miracle, an event which is Scripturally designated, as to rank, a "mighty work"; as to its effect upon spectators, a "wonder"; and as to its purpose in the economy of God, a "sign" (Acts 2:22). Miracles cease to be a problem once it is realized that the Will of God is the constitution of the universe and that Spirit-power is the Efficient Cause of every form of being.

A fundamental truth needs to be stated, in this connection, as follows: *Spirit-power cannot be dissociated from either Thought-power or Word-power in God. Thought-power is the expression of Spirit-power, and Spirit-power is the actuation or realization of Thought-power.* Descartes' celebrated dictum, "I think, therefore I am," the beginning-point of all philosophy, is equally true stated conversely, "I am, therefore I think." Being and thought cannot be dissociated in a person. *Word-power, moreover, is equivalent either to Spirit-power or to Thought-power. The power of the Spirit is in the Word, and both Spirit and Word actuate the Divine Thought and Will with respect to created things.* Hence, Christ the Incarnate Logos is said to be "the power of God and the wisdom of God" (1 Cor. 1:24). *God's Spirit and His Word go together. All of which adds up to the mighty truth that, in God, Spirit-power, Thought-power, Word-power, and Will-power are essentially one. For this reason, we often find the terms used interchangeably in Scripture: what is said to be effected by one is said also to be effected by the others, and so on.* In studying the nature and work of the Spirit, and especially the relationship between the Spirit and the Word, it is exceedingly important to keep these facts in mind.

2. *Spirit in God means Vitality.* Where the Spirit is, there is life, for He is the Spirit of Life. This is the great truth made crystal clear in Ezekiel's Vision of the Valley of Dry Bones (Ezek. 37:1-14): whatever else the coming of the Spirit of God into this charnel-house meant, it certainly meant the difference between death and life. Spirit-power it is that actuates every form of life in the total Hierarchy of Being. Thus the Spirit of God, at the beginning, brooded like a great Mother-Bird over the "deep" of infinite Space, generating the primal forms of energy, actuating and cherishing incipient life, and the universe with its myriads of species of living things marched into being (Gen. 1:2). Thus the Spirit brooded over the first corporeal human form and implanted therein the attributes and

324

powers of a person, and the first creature Divinely fore-determined to be a likeness of God was constituted, by the Breath of God, "a living soul" (Gen. 2:7). Thus the Holy Spirit, the Power of the Most High, "came upon" and "overshadowed"— brooded over again, as at the Creation—the pure Virgin Mary, and the holy thing that was begotten in her womb was the Son of God, Divine Life Incarnate (Luke 1:26-38). As the Son Himself said, later: "I am the Way, and the Truth, and the Life" (John 14:6), and again, "I am the resurrection and the life . . . whosoever liveth and believeth on me shall never die" (John 11:25-26). In like manner, the Hily Spirit superposes the richness of His Divine Life upon the mental processes of the receptive human individual in regeneration—upon the "honest and good heart" (Luke 8:15),—and literally begets in him a new life, a new spiritual life (John 3:3-6), the life that "is hid with Christ in God" (Col. 3:3); literally recreates him, makes him over, into a new creature in Christ Jesus. "Wherefore if any man is in Christ, he is a new creature: the old things are passed away; behold, they are become new" (2 Cor. 5:17). "For we are his workmenship, created in Christ Jesus for good works, which God afore prepared that we should walk in them" (Eph. 2:10). Thus does the Spirit transform the one-time alien to God's commonwealth and covenant, into a fellow-citizen with the saints and a member of the household of God (Eph. 2:19); thus does He transform the old *natural* personal life, into the new *spiritual* personal life of unhindered access to, and fellowship with, God.

1 John 1:3—our fellowship is with the Father, and with his Son Jesus Christ. 1 John 4:12-13—If we love one another, God abideth in us, and his love is perfected in us: hereby we know that we abide in him, and he in us, because he hath given us of his Spirit. 1 John 3:24—hereby we know that he abideth in us, by the Spirit which he gave us. 1 John 5:12—He that hath the Son hath the life; he that hath not the Son of God hath not the life.

Regeneration, however, is only the beginning of the Spirit's activity in relationship with the saints: He takes up His abode in their hearts, and continues His work of sanctification throughout their earthly lives, thus fitting them for their proper inheritance of which His very indwelling is the earnest or pledge— the inheritance "incorruptible and undefiled, and that fadeth not away, reserved in heaven" for them (1 Pet. 1:4). (Cf. Eph. 1:13-14, also 2 Cor. 1:21-22.) And not only does the Spirit thus make the saints "meet"—in holy habits, disposition and character—"to be partakers of the inheritance of the saints in light"

(Col. 1:12), but at the end of their earthly lives He actually leads them into the possession of this eternal inheritance, into glory and honor and immortality—the Life Everlasting. "But if the Spirit of him that raised up Jesus from the dead dwelleth in you, he that raised up Christ Jesus from the dead shall give life also to your mortal bodies through his Spirit that dwelleth in you" (Rom. 8:11). And so in this manner, line upon line, precept upon precept, here a little, there a little—for the Christion life is a process of continuous growth in the grace and knowledge of our Lord and Savior Jesus Christ (2 Pet. 3:18)— the Holy Spirit transforms the spiritual personal lives of the saints on earth into their eternal personal lives in the Bosom of God—the Life Everlasting. The *natural* progression for human beings (persons), under the aegis of the Spirit, is from natural to spiritual to eternal life; from the Kingdom of Nature, through the Kingdom of Grace, into the Kingdom of Glory, there to be conformed to the immortalized image of God's Son (Rom. 8:29).

Life is activity, and activity presupposes an *actor* and the *power* to act. The Spirit-power of God is God in action, and the ultimate source of the Life Force which preserves and perpetuates the race in its present or "natural" mode of being. As the Seer of the Apocalypse puts it: "And he showed me a river of water of life, bright as crystal, proceeding out of the throne of God and of the Lamb" (Rev. 22:1).

Every form of life in the total Hierarchy of Being—from the lowest to the highest, from that of the lowly cell to that of the immortalized saint—is actualized by the Spirit-power of God, and hence is a Divine gift. The Holy Spirit of God is the Spirit of Life, because He is the Spirit of the *living* God. 2 Cor. 3:3—"ye are an epistle of Christ, ministered by us, written not with ink, but with *the Spirit of the living God.*" Our God is not a thing carved out of wood, stone or marble. He is not any of the things of the Nature which surrounds us— not sun, moon, earth, star, plant, tree, bird or beast. Nor is He identical with the whole of Nature, as the pantheist would have it; on the contrary, Nature is His handiwork. And even though His Spirit-power is back of, and pervades and sustains, all Nature, yet He Himself is the Almighty Other than Nature and all her creatures including man. He is the living and true God, the eternal Spirit who is the Source and Cause of all things, in whom, *i.e.*, through whose power and activity, we live and move and have our being. (Cf. Acts 17:24-31, 14:15-17.)

The Second Commandment of the Decalogue is specifically a prohibition of all forms of idolatry and nature-worship. "Thou shalt not make unto thee a graven image, nor any likeness of any thing that is in heaven above, or that is in the earth beneath, or that is in the water under the earth; thou shalt not bow down thyself unto them, nor serve them" (Exo. 20:4-5). This prohibition was designed to preserve the knowledge of the *living* God in the world, as distinguished from the dead gods of so-called "natural religion," gods worshiped in the form of images or as personifications of the forces of Nature. The same fundamental truth is made explicit in the Christian creedal formula: "Thou art the Christ, the Son of the *living* God" (Matt. 16:16). Our God is alive, vitally active; *He gets things done;* He accomplishes whatever He purposes to do (Isa. 46:9-11). He is the true and *living* God; hence Jesus Christ, His Son, is the Son of the *living* God; and the Holy Spirit, the Spirit of Life, is the Spirit of the *living* God.

Where the Spirit of God is, there is Vitality, Life. And Vitality is activity, actuality, creativity. Every kind of life in the universe is the gift of the Spirit of God.

3. *Spirit in God means Personality.*

The great and incommunicable Name of our God the eternal Spirit is The I AM, HE WHO IS.

Exo. 3:13-15: And Moses said unto God, Behold, when I come unto the children of Israel, and shall say unto them, The God of your fathers hath sent me unto you; and they shall say to me, What is his name? what shall I say unto them? And God said unto Moses, I AM THAT I AM: and he said, Thus shalt thou say unto the children of Israel, I AM hath sent me unto you. And God said moreover unto Moses, Thus shalt thou say unto the children of Israel, Jehovah, the God of your fathers, the God of Abraham, the God of Isaac, and the God of Jacob, hath sent me unto you: this is my name for ever, and this is my memorial unto all generations.

Let us compare, in this connection, the words of Jesus to the unbelieving Jews: "Verily, verily, I say unto you, Before Abraham was born, I am" (John 8:58). Thus did Jesus appropriate unto Himself the great and incommunicable Name of the Deity. No wonder the Jews, regarding Him to be a blasphemer, took up stones and cast them at Him. Obviously, He was either all that He claimed to be, or else He *was* a blasphemer, and not only that, but the greatest impostor who ever appeared in the world. But this latter conclusion is impossible, in the light of His unimpeachable life and character.

"I AM THAT I AM . . . Thus shalt thou say unto the children of Israel, I AM hath sent me unto you." The Name of our God—the God of Abraham, Isaac, and Jacob, and the God and Father of our Lord Jesus Christ (Eph. 1:3, 1 Pet. 1:3, etc.) —is I AM, HE WHO IS. I AM THAT I AM signifies I AM, BECAUSE I AM; that is, *self-existence*, a Being whose ground of subsistence is within Himself, a Being unoriginated and eternal, without beginning or end. I AM signifies *timeless* Being: with our God, it is always NOW: "Behold, now is the acceptable time; behold, now is the day of salvation" (2 Cor. 6:2). I AM THAT I AM signifies I AM WHO I AM, that is, *self-conscious* Being. I AM THAT I AM signifies I WILL BE THAT I WILL BE, that is, *self-determining, self-directing Being*. To sum up: The Name I AM signifies all the attributes and powers of a person, of a unique, eternal, solitary Divine Person. (Cf. Deut. 4:35, 39; Isa. 43:10-11, 45; 5-6, 46:9-11.)

It is utterly inconceivable that such a profoundly spiritual conception of deity, or such as exclusively spiritual Name for the Deity, could have arisen spontaneously in the mind of a people or an individual, living at such an early age of human history and surrounded on all sides by the grossest forms of idolatry, polytheism, and nature-worship, as the Jews were throughout their entire national existence from the time of Moses to that of Ezra or even to that of John the Baptizer. Human reason itself proclaims that this great and incommunicable Name could never have sprung from the unaided human intelligence or imagination alone; that indeed it must have been a direct revelation from God Himself to His great servant and lawgiver, Moses, as the Scriptures affirm. This very Name, in and of itself, accounts for the preservation by the Hebrew People of the concepts of the uniqueness, personality and spirituality of God throughout their entire national history, although the Name was never given its full signification until Jesus Himself interpreted it in these meaningful words: "God is a Spirit; and they that worship him must worship in spirit and truth" (John 4:24).

Herein, too, lies the fundamental superiority of the God of the Judaeo-Christian revelation over the God of Greek philosophy and indeed of all philosophical thought. Whereas the latter, the God of human philosophical speculation, is usually conceived in pantheistic terms, as That Which Is, the God of the Bible is Pure Spirit or Person, I AM, HE WHO IS. Our God is not a *scientific probability*,—He is indeed a *metaphysical necessity*.

Now Person is the highest category of being of which we

have knowledge; certainly, then, it would be the height of unreason to assign God to a category inferior to that of Person. This does not mean, of course, that He is Person in the limited sense that human beings are persons, or, as Gilson puts it, that He is an anthropomorphic God; on the contrary, it is to be taken for granted that Person in God embraces infinitely greater attributes and powers than it embraces in man. But if God were less than Person, less than what that term signifies to us, then certainly He would be inferior to man in attributes and powers. And this is unthinkable, in Deity. Hence revelation, which invariably supplements the voice of reason, presents our God to us as a Spirit, as the eternal Spirit, as The I AM, HE WHO IS. Spirit implies personality in some form; therefore our God is a personal God. And because our God is a Spirit or Person, He can enter into fellowship with us, and we with Him, because we too are persons created in His image. 1 John 1:3—"Our fellowship is with the Father, and with his Son Jesus Christ." Whatever more Person may be in God than in us, and surely it is infinitely more, the fact remains that if God were less than Person, our fellowship with Him would be impossible. "For my thoughts are not your thoughts, neither are your ways my ways, saith Jehovah. For as the heavens are higher than the earth, so are my ways higher than your ways, and my thoughts than your thoughts" (Isa. 55:8-9). Therefore we come to Him in faith, the only avenue indeed by which we can approach God; we "believe that he is, and that he is a rewarder of them that seek after him" (Heb. 11:6).

4. *Spirit in God means Everywhereness.*

As vital force permeates every part of a living organism, so Spirit-power permeates and pervades the Cosmos and its parts and creatures.

Psa. 139:7-10: Whither shall I go from thy Spirit? Or whither shall I flee from thy presence? If I ascend up into heaven, thou art there; If I make my bed in Sheol, behold, thou are there. If I take the wings of the morning, And dwell in the uttermost parts of the sea, Even there shall thy hand lead me, And thy right hand shall hold me. Jer. 23:23-24: Am I a God at hand, saith Jehovah, and not a God afar off? Can any hide himself in secret places so that I shall not see him? saith Jehovah. Do not I fill heaven and earth? saith Jehovah. Acts 17:27-28: that they should seek God, if haply they might feel after him and find him, though he is not far from each one of us; for in him we live, and move, and have our being. Rom. 11:36—For of him, and through him, and unto him, are all things. Eph. 4:6—one God and Father of all, who is over all, and through all, and in all.

Perhaps this doctrine of the immanence of God can best be presented by resort to Aristotle's well-known Four Causes. According to Aristotle, every entity in the universe has four causes or grounds of "explanation," namely: (1) a *material* cause—the matter or stuff of which the thing is made; (2) a *formal* cause—that which gives to the matter the specific form it assumes in the object; (3) an *efficient* cause—that which unites the form and the matter, thus giving the object concrete existence; and (4) a *final* cause—the function or end the object is designed to serve in the scheme of nature. For example, the *material* cause of a given desk is the wood of which it is made; the *formal* cause is the idea of the desk in the mind of the builder, the idea (pattern) which gives to the matter the precise form (a desk) which it has; the *efficient* cause is the cabinetmaker who joins the form to the matter, thus giving the desk concrete existence as a desk; and the *final* cause is the purpose which the desk serves, in an office, store, classroom, etc., the use to which it is put. Now when we say that Spirit-power (God) is everywhere, actualizing all things that exist, we do not mean that Spirit-power (God) is either the formal or material cause of the Cosmos: that would be pantheism, in that it would identify God with either matter or form (idea), or both, as indeed Spinoza does in his pantheistic doctrine of Substance. We mean, rather, that God is the *efficient*, hence *extrinsic*, cause of all things. Many modern philosophers have striven desperately to eliminate efficient causality from the universe (scientists ignore it)—but in vain. Without it there is no adequate explanation of anything. It is regrettable indeed that with most of these "thinkers" the wish seems to have been father to the thought.) Although Himself extrinsic to, other than, all things and the world as a whole, nevertheless His Spirit-power actualizes all things. As Thomas Aquinas has put it: "Created being is the proper effect of God, just as to ignite is the proper effect of fire." "The reason is," writes Garrigou-LaGrange, elucidating Thomas' arguments on this point.

that God is essentially being. Thus He is the cause of participated being. For the proper effect is that which necessarily and immediately depends on its proper cause. The proper effect is like a property manifested *ad extra*, for it is related to its proper cause, as a property is related to its essence; but it is external to its cause. Thus the killer kills (for there can be no one killed without a killer); so also the builder builds, the painter paints, the singer sings. Thus God brings things into existence and preserves them in being. Indeed, as St. Thomas says more explicitly, the more universal effects must be reduced to the more universal and prior causes. But among all effects the most universal is being itself. Hence it must be the effect of the first and most universal cause, and that is God.[1]

To quote Aquinas again: "God is in all things, neither as part of their essence (matter or form) nor as accident, but as an agent is present to that upon which it works."[2] These statements remind us of the words of the Psalmist: "O Jehovah, how manifold are thy works! In wisdom hast thou made them all; The earth is full of thy riches. . . . Thou sendest forth thy Spirit, they are created; And thou renewest the face of the ground" (Psa. 104:24, 30). The Spirit-power which proceeds from the Being of God is the ultimate cause of every form of energy and life which permeates the structure of our universe. Hence Spirit-power is everywhere, actualizing, supporting, renewing every created thing. (What better proof of this statement could be offered than science's own laws of the conservation of energy and of matter?)

The Spirit is everywhere, too, in the sense of being wholly unrestricted by time or space. Even lesser spirits, including men, as we have already seen, are not themselves necessarily limited to any locale; their thought soars out beyond all the limits of distance, space or time, both in their dreams and in their waking hours; and subconscious communication—telepathy —is wholly independent of the distance separating the communicator and the recipient. Persons *as such*, that is, as *spirits*, are capable of roaming the universe, so to speak, even though their bodies are confined to a definite location. And if this attribute of "everywhereness" is characteristic of created persons, how much more so of the Persons of the Godhead.

Cf. Matt. 4:5, 8—[in the account of the Temptation of Jesus]: Then the devil taketh him into the holy city; and he set him on the pinnacle of the temple, . . . Again, the devil taketh him unto an exceeding high mountain, and showeth him all the kingdoms of the world, and the glory of them. [In like manner, the Spirit of God is frequently represented in Scripture as transporting God's servants from one place to another, seemingly without regard to the distance involved.] 1 Kings 18:12—[here Obadiah, meeting Elijah, says to him]: It will come to pass, as soon as I am gone from thee, that the Spirit of Jehovah will carry thee whither I know not. [Also 2 Kings 2:16; Ezek. 3:12, 3:14-15, 8:3, 11:1, 37:1, 43.5; 2 Cor. 12:2-4 (Cf. Acts 14:19); Acts 8:39-40 8:29, 0:19-20, 16:6-7.] The passages in Ezekiel, however, obviously imply a great deal more: they imply movement of persons independently of corporeal relations or relations of time and space. They imply that the Spirit of God can, at any one time, be at any place, or in all

1. Reginald Garrigou-LaGrange, O.P., *The One God*, trans. by Dom. Bede Rose, 255-256. Cf. St. Thomas Aquinas, *Summa theologica*, I a, q 45, art. 5.
2. Quoted by Garrigou-LaGrange, *ibid.*, 254.

places, where He may will to be. It should be noted, however, that here again, in attempting to expound the doctrine of His everywhereness, we are greatly handicapped by the inadequacy of human language.

Finally, the fact of the everywhereness of the Divine Spirit is implicit in the oft-repeated solemn affirmations of Scripture that the Thought-power of God constantly penetrates the most secret places of the individual human heart. (Cf. 1 Sam. 16:7; Luke 16:15; Heb. 4:12-13; Tim 5:24; 2 Cor. 5:10; Rev. 20:12-13.) No man can possibly escape the everywhereness of the Spirit of God.

5. *Spirit in God means Inexhaustibleness.*

This attribute is closely related to that of the Spirit's everywhereness. Spirit-power not only operates at will *everywhere* throughout the Cosmos, but also operates everywhere *in whatever measure* may be necessary to the accomplishment of the Divine purposes. Whereas in the realm of Matter, the whole is equal to the sum of its parts, in the realm of Spirit quite the reverse is true; in Spirit any "part"—to speak by way of analogy —is equivalent qualitatively to the "whole." The life, for example, that pervades my organism is present in equal measure in every part of it; there is as much of total organic life in my little finger as in my stomach or in my big toe or in any other part of my body. Similarly, life is present, in whatever qualitative measure each species may require for its own specific mode of being, in the myriads of organisms which go to make up the totality of the animate creation. And what is true in the realm of "natural" life is equally true in that of spiritual life. The Scriptures inform us—and every sincere Christian knows it to be true—that the Church, the Body of Christ, is the habitation of God in the Spirit (Eph. 2:22). That is to say, God in the Person of His Holy Spirit indwells every obedient believer in Christ, every member of the Body; and thus by indwelling and infilling the individual members, the Spirit indwells, unifies and vitalizes the whole "organism."

> The love of God hath been shed abroad in our hearts through the Holy Spirit which was given unto us (Rom. 5:5). Know ye not that your body is a temple of the Holy Spirit which is in you, which ye have from God? (1 Cor. 6:19). Know ye not that ye are a temple of God, and that the Spirit of God dwelleth in you? (1 Cor. 3:16). Eph. 1:22-23: He gave him to be head over all things to the church, which is his body, the fulness of him that filleth all in all. Eph. 4:4—There is one body, and one Spirit, even as also ye were called in one hope of your calling.

Individual saints are, so to speak, the cells who go to make up the Mystic Person, of which they constitute the Body, and of which Christ Himself is the Head, the whole mystic organism being unified and vitalized by the Holy Spirit-Life of God. And the wonder of it all is that this universal and timeless expenditure of Spirit-power in so many different forms of energy and life never results in the decrease, much less in the depletion, of the original total supply. The Reservoir which is the source of this Power remains undisturbed by any or all expenditures of it in any form. The River of the Water of Life which proceeds "out of the throne of God and the Lamb" (Rev. 22:1) never runs dry; quite the contrary, it is always at flood tide. This River proceeds from a bottomless Spring—the Being of God.

Cf. John 4:14 [the words of Jesus to the Woman of Samaria, at Jacob's well]: Whosoever drinketh of the water that I shall give him shall never thirst: but the water that I shall give him shall become in him a well of water springing up unto eternal life. John 7:37-39: Now on the last day, the great day of the feast, Jesus stood and cried, saying, If any man thirst, let him come unto me and drink. He that believeth on me, as the scripture hath said, from within him shall flow rivers of living water. But this spake he of the Spirit, which they that believed on him were to receive: for the Spirit was not yet given; because Jesus was not yet glorified. [Also Psa. 42:1-2, 63:1; Isa. 55:1; Rev. 22:17.]

Whatever else our God may be, whatever else Infinity may be, one thing He is, we may be sure: *inexhaustibleness,* richness of power, of spiritual nourishment and refreshment.

6. *Spirit in God means Creativity.*

Whether creativity is simply the re-combination of elements which constitute the Cosmos a *plenum,* in which case the "new" is simply the offspring, so to speak, of the potencies of "seeds" pre-existing or already *given,* or whether it is the oft-repeated addition, or emergence, of new elements in a dynamic and rapidly expanding Cosmic Process, is purely an academic question, a question indeed which philosophers have argued pro and con from time immemorial. To speak truthfully, this is just another one of those circular arguments which have harassed philosophic thought from the time of its inception. The fact of the matter is that insofar as the Spirit of God is involved the solution is irrelevant. That is to say, whether Spirit-power created *ex nihilo,* or effected re-combinations of potencies already given, the point to be remembered is that it was the Spirit-power of God which engendered the original potencies and which effected the ultimate results, namely, the creation and preservation of the Cosmos and its creatures.

In the present treatise, the entire Cosmic Process is viewed as a progressive development, with new increments of power

333

coming in from the Creator at the different stages which mark off the various levels in the Hierarchy of Being. (This is true, whatever *yom* may mean in the Creation Narrative.) The coming in of these new increments of power, each progressively higher in qualitative characteristics than its predecessor, resulting first in successive forms of energy and matter, then in plant life, animal life, and personal life, in the order named, was, in each case, the result of the procession of Spirit-power from the Being of God. This general view of the Creative Process is, as we shall see later, fully corroborated by the Scriptural account of the physical or natural Creation as given in the first and second chapters of the book of Genesis.

Dr. Louis Berman, a distinguished physician as well as an author, writes of the universe as a "psychocontinuum," in certain respects an apt phrase. Calling attention to the fact that the purely inanimate part of the Cosmos is characterized, apparently at least, by a process of entropy, he advances the thesis that the Life Process itself is, however, the anti-entropic phase of the total structure.

> Energy is like an electric bulb slowly dimming its light, because it is discharging its power without replenishment. In fact light is the very prototype of all energy and of its fate. All cosmic energy moves at the same speed as light and has the same vibratory constitution. Radiation is a form of energy and the melodic rhythms of the different wave lengths, or frequencies, of radioactivity are its spectrum. There is a great continuous range of radiating frequencies comprising all its known forms. . . . Energy, whether liberated from the embrace of matter, radiating as light waves, heat waves, electrical waves, or as chained in the bonds of repulsion and attraction which are organized as the ultimate units of the atoms and molecules of matter, is the primeval essence of the cosmos, out of which all things are made and to which all things return. It appears in all the manifestations and transformations of the universe. It may appear as solid or liquid particles, as the incandescent gas of the stars and nebulae, as beams of light, as a consuming fire, as the purposeful mind of man, or as the profoundly brooding psychoactivity of the universe. But for all and equally alike the inexorable law is the law of entropy. It can be predicted that the time will come when there will be no more energy to waste. All energy will then exist at the same level, so to speak, from which nothing can be lifted and nothing can fall. Such will be the end of the world: a universe in which nothing will happen because there will be no energy left for happenings. After its eons of stormy activities, the cosmos will be for a long while viscous and slow, like a tired old man, and then there will come an eternal stillness, the rest of death.[1]

Is this what will happen eventually? Probably so, according to the physicists—unless there is some sort of a counter-process.

1. *Behind the Universe*, 219-221.

Dr. Berman believes that there is such a process, namely the Life Process itself. He writes:

A universal cosmic consciousness begetting a continuing life-personality is embedded in the roots of the universe. It is growing and driving through the eons of time toward some apparently entirely ineffable and incomprehensible goal. And it embraces within itself all the vast extent and range of time and space, matter and energy.[1]

This is all reminiscent, of course, of Bergson's *Elan Vital.*

What is this "universal cosmic consciousness," after all, but the living God, the eternal Spirit? And what is this force, which grows and drives through the eons of time toward some "ineffable and incomprehensible goal," but the Spirit-power of God? (Why are scientists so afraid of the word, "God"?—for their writings prove that, in spite of their reluctance to use the designation, they do have a "God.") All this points clearly to the fact that the Life Force is creative, that it is constantly ushering in new and higher forms of being. There seems to be a side of the Divine Being which is never satisfied short of reaching outside Him, short of the constant expenditure of Spirit-power in creative effort; otherwise there would be no accounting for the universe and its myriad forms of life. Creativity is of the very essence of the Spirit of God. Therefore, we may conclude that the Life Process is driving "toward some apparently entirely ineffable and incomprehensible goal."

That the Life Process is driving toward an ineffable goal, we heartily agree. But with Dr. Berman's assertion that the goal is entirely incomprehensible, we cannot agree. That it is incomprehensible to unaided human reason, of course, may be admitted. But revelation, in this as in every like instance, supplies what reason, because of its natural limitations, lacks of ascertainment. "The only goal of man," says LeComte Du Nouy, "should be the attainment of human dignity with all its implications."[2] This goal, according to the Scriptures, is ultimate Wholeness or Holiness: the creation of a holy, redeemed race to inhabit a wholly renovated or, so to speak, redeemed Cosmos— an environment purged both of the guilt and of the consequences of sin, an environment that is all Good. Nothing short of this could effectuate fully the attainment of human dignity, that of a creature created in the image of God.

Rev. 21:1-4: And I saw a new heaven and a new earth: for the first heaven and the first earth are passed away; and the sea is no more.

1. *Op. cit.*, 226-227.
2. *Human Destiny*, 244.

And I saw the holy city, new Jerusalem, coming down out of heaven from God, made ready as a bride adorned for her husband. And I heard a great voice out of the throne saying, Behold, the tabernacle of God is with men, and he shall dwell with them, and they shall be his peoples, and God himself shall be with them, and be their God; and he shall wipe away every tear from their eyes; and death shall be no more; neither shall there be mourning, nor crying, nor pain, any more; the first things are passed away. [Also Matt. 5:8; Rev. 3:5; 7:14-17, 22:1-5.]

Thus it will be seen that a new creation has taken place, as a result of the procession of Spirit-power from God, at every forward step in the onward and upward surge of the Life Process. At every forward step new increments of power have come in from the Being of God. The final advance, in so far as this earth is concerned, occurs in the creation of the Body of Christ, consisting of redeemed—recreated—persons, new creatures in Jesus Christ.

Rom. 8:1 2: There is therefore now no condemnation to them that are in Christ Jesus. For the law of the Spirit of life in Christ Jesus made me free from the law of sin and death. Eph. 2:10—For we are his workmanship, created in Christ Jesus for good works, which God afore prepared that we should walk in them. 2 Cor. 5:17—Wherefore if any man is in Christ, he is a new creature: the old things are passed away; behold, they are become new. [(Also John 3:3, Gal. 6:15, Rom. 6:4, Col. 3:9-10, Eph. 4:23-24, Tit. 3:5.]

The final phase of the Creative Process occurs in the creation, by the Spirit-power of God, of spiritual bodies for the redeemed saints, bodies adapted to their celestial environment in the ultimately renovated Cosmos.

John 14:2-3: In my Father's house are many abiding-places; if it were not so, I would have told you; for I go to prepare a place for you. And if I go and prepare a place for you, I come again, and will receive you unto myself; that where I am, there ye may be also. [Undoubtedly the "many abiding-places" alluded to here are those spiritual bodies which await the saints at the moment of their resurrection.] Rom. 8:23 —Ourselves also, who have the first-fruits of the Spirit, even we ourselves groan within ourselves, waiting for our adoption, to wit, the redemption of our body. [Also Phil. 3:20-21; 2 Cor. 5:1-4, not that we would hope to become disembodied spirits, but rather become "clothed upon" with spiritual (ethereal?) bodies. Cf. esp. Rom. 8:11, 1 Cor. 15:20 ff.]

How important, in view af all these considerations, is the Christian doctrine of immortality—that of the resurrection and glorification of the bodies of God's saints that "they may be conformed to the image of his Son" (Rom. 8:29)! How essential the doctrine is, to a proper understanding of the Plan of the Universe! Regeneration, sanctification, and immortalization are the supreme manifestations of that creativity which is of the essence of the Spirit-power of our God.

**7. *Spirit in God means Sociality, Fellowship, Service.***
This truth becomes clear especially in the light of the New Testament revelation.

"Spirit" surely signifies sociality in man. Although psychologists, for the most part, reject the view that gregariousness is an instinct in man, the fact remains, nevertheless, that normal persons do constantly seek the fellowship of their kind. Experience teaches them early in life, though perhaps unconsciously, that they cannot satisfy even their basic organic drives, much less their intellectual outreachings, in a word, that they cannot realize their potentialities and thus attain fulness of being, *as* persons, short of association with kindred spirits in the various fields of human endeavor. Otherwise, how account for the vast number of clubs, lodges, guilds, unions, societies and associations which characterize the history of man upon earth? Professor Goldhamer of Stanford University, for example, who has collected voluminous statistics on voluntary associations in the United States, estimated that there are some 15,000 such different associations in Chicago alone. Think what a vast number there must be, then in the world at large! Associations there are of every kind and description—athletic, recreational, educational, literary, professional, occupational, social, political, agricultural, military, youth, ethical, missionary, religious, and so on, almost *ad infinitum.* And besides all these more or less casual or impermanent groupings, there are also the basic social *institutions* of human history to be taken into account, those which have been defined as "organized, established ways of satisfying certain basic human needs,"[1] and which, therefore, are found in some form or other practically among all peoples in all ages. These are the family (biological), the state (political), the corporation (economic), and the church (religious) or its equivalent With the development of private property, of course, and the increase of abundance of material goods generally, the business corporation, with all its ramifications, has superseded the older family and feudal economic organizations, and has become the paramount economic institution of modern commerce and finance. Economic organization there has been, however, of one kind or another, from the very dawn of human history, and even extending back into prehistory.

From these facts it is evident that sociality in man is a part of the natural order of things, an ordination of Nature's God for man's general well-being. This is true whether or not

1. Ogburn and Nimkoff, *Sociology*, 555.

gregariousness is an instinct in man. Sociality must be regarded as a necessary and natural fact of the order of personal beings, for persons (or spirits) alone are capable of proper personality integration and development only through association with other persons. There is no getting around the fact that spirit in man includes the attribute of sociality. Therefore, since man is the image of God, we may reasonably conclude that Spirit includes sociality in God also. Perhaps this attribute of Spirit in God accounts for the Creative Process itself; perhaps that process is the inevitable outlet for that side of the Divine Nature which craves holy fellowship with kindred creature-spirits, that side of the Divine Nature which is Love. As a matter of fact, it is difficult for us to see how Divine Love could have found adequate expression except in fellowship with creatures made in His own image, and more particularly in such acts as atoning for, redeeming, forgiving, and sanctifying one-time lost sinners. And it is equally difficult to see how Divine Love could have wooed and won rebellious man back into covenant fellowship with Himself by any means other than a supreme sacrifice—the Supreme Sacrifice, in fact—intelligible to man in terms of human experience; in a word, by dying as an innocent man would die, willingly and freely, for the salvation of the guilty. "Greater love that no man than this, that a man lay down his life for his friends" (John 15:13), but the love of God for man is greater than the love of man for man ever could be, for God willingly gave His Son, and the Son willingly gave His life, not only for His friends, but for His enemies as well. And Jesus, dying on the Cross, prayed for those who were putting Him to death: "Father, forgive them; for they know not what they do" (Luke 23:34). Be that as it may, vicarious sacrifice is still the noblest manifestation of love within the scope of human experience. That the accomplishment of such an end as reconciliation required in turn that Divine Love condescend to share our human nature with its frailties, temptations, and needs, is obvious. Thus it will be seen that the mysteries of the Trinity, the Incarnation, the Atonement, and the Resurrection—the fundamental doctrines of Christianity—are all closely bound up with the activity of the Holy Spirit in the regeneration, sanctification, and immortalization of the saints. Not one of these doctrines can be omitted without destroying the whole Christian System. Moreover, under the view presented here, the Christian System is the final phase of the Plan of the Universe, that is, of the whole Creative Process itself. Under this view, too, the physical

338

world becomes God's medium for the shaping of human souls to be meet for the inheritance of the saints in light, an end that can be achieved only by the superposition of the life of the Spirit upon the natural personal life of man. As the writer of the *Epistle to the Hebrews* puts is so clearly:

But we behold him who hath been made a little lower than the angels, even Jesus, because of the suffering of death crowned with glory and honor, that by the grace of God he should taste death for every man. For it became him, for whom are all things, and through whom are all things, in bringing many sons unto glory, to make the author of their salvation perfect through sufferings. For both he that sanctifieth and they that are sanctified are all of one: for which cause he is not ashamed to call them brethren, saying, I will declare thy name unto my brethren, In the midst of the congregation will I sing thy praise (Heb. 2:9-12).

Human redemption, effected by the death and resurrection of our Christ, is realized and applied by the work of the Holy Spirit.

Throughout the Old Testament Dispensations, the Patriarchal and the Jewish—the period of preparation— the activity of the Spirit was exerted exclusively through *indivduals,* men chosen by God to be special instruments for the execution of His eternal purpose. These holy men of old, men of great faith, enjoyed conscious fellowship with God through the immediacy of Spirit-power in them and exerted through them. Such a man especially was Enoch, "the seventh from Adam" (Jude 14), who "walked with God; and he was not; for God took him" (Gen. 5:24). Such also were Noah, "a preacher of righteousness" to his generation (1 Pet. 3:18-22, 2 Pet. 2:5); Abraham, called "the friend of God" (Jas. 2:23, 2 Chron. 20:7, Isa. 41:8); Isaac, Jacob, and Joseph; Moses, the mediator of the Old Covenant, and his successor, Joshua (Heb. 3:1-6, Num. 11:16-17, Num. 27:18-25, Deut. 34:9-12); and the Judges, civil and military dictators, chosen and used by God for the leadership of His people, at successive intervals throughout the long chaotic period of the Conquest (Judg. 3:10, 4:4, 6:34, 11:29, 13:25, 14:6, 15:14, 1 Sam. 3:19-21, 1 Sam. 9:6, etc.). Of the kings, David especially, the sweet singer of Israel, enjoyed intimacy of personal communion with God (1 Sam. 16:13); among David's last words were these: "The Spirit of Jehovah spake by me, And his word was upon my tongue" (2 Sam. 23:2). And the Hebrew Prophets—that illustrious line which began with Samuel and terminated with John the Baptizer—were in a very special sense "men of that Spirit," men who walked with God and who spoke for Him (1 Ki. 20:28; 2 Kings 4:25, 5:14; Isa. 6:1-5; Ezek. 2:2, 3:12;

Luke 1:15; 2 Pet. 1:21, 1 Pet. 1:10-12, etc.). To all these great men of faith, the immediacy of the Spirit meant personal fellowship, sweet and holy fellowship, with God.

Under the present Dispensation, the Church or Body of Christ is in a special mystical sense a holy *fellowship* with God the Father and with his Son Jesus Christ (1 John 1:3), through the mutual sharing by its members of the presence, gifts and powers of the Holy Spirit. No longer is the immediacy of Spirit-power confined exclusively to chosen leaders; it is shared, in various measures corresponding to respective ends, by all members of the Body. The Church is "the communion of the Holy Spirit" (2 Cor. 13:14). Hence, each member's physical body is described in Scripture as a temple that is indwelt by the Spirit (1 Cor. 3:16, 6:19), and all members of the Body collectively are said to be "as living stones, built up a spiritual house, to be a holy priesthood, to offer up spiritual sacrifices, acceptable to God through Jesus Christ" (1 Pet. 2:5), "builded together for a habitation of God in the Spirit" (Eph. 2:22), that is, in the Person of the Spirit who indwells them. The Christian Church is described as "the elect . . . according to the foreknowledge of God the Father, in sanctification of the Spirit, unto obedience and sprinkling of the blood of Jesus Christ" (1 Pet. 1:2). It is the one Body vitalized and unified by the one Spirit (Eph. 4:4); hence its members are bound together in Christ by the communion—the mutual sharing—of the Spirit (2 Cor. 13:14). Both the love of God and the efficacy of Christ's Atonement are mediated to the members of the Body through the Holy Spirit which is given unto them, Rom. 5:5). In the one Spirit are they all baptized (*i.e.*, incorporated) into one body, and are all made to drink of one Spirit (1 Cor. 12:13). They are sealed by the Spirit, the Holy Spirit of promise, which is the earnest of their final inheritance, Life Everlasting (Eph. 1:13-14, 2 Cor. 1:22). By the help of the Spirit they put to death the deeds of the body, and live spiritually (Rom. 8:13). They are led by the Spirit, they walk by the Spirit, they live by the Spirit, and they bring forth the fruit of the Spirit which is "love, joy, peace, long-suffering, kindness, goodness, faithfulness, meekness, self-control" (Gal. 5:16-25). The Spirit in them is the ever-present agent of their sanctification, and, at the end of their pilgrimage through this present world, because the Spirit of Him that raised up Jesus from the dead dwelleth in them, He that raised Christ Jesus from the dead shall give life also to their mortal bodies through His Spirit that dwelleth in them (Rom. 8:11). And in

340

this manner their fellowship with God the Father and with the Lord Jesus Christ and with one another, mediated in this life through the Holy Spirit dwelling in them, will become full and complete— an ineffable fellowship—around the very Throne of God and of the Lamb. George MacDonald's exquisite lines might well serve as the prayer of God's saints from day to day:

> Leave me not, God, until; nay, until when?
> Not till I am with Thee, one heart, one mind,
> Not till Thy life is light in me, and then
> Leaving is left behind.

The consciousness of a new and joyous fellowship, a oneness with the Father and with the Son and with one another, through their mutual sharing of the Divine Presence in the Person of the Holy Spirit, was certainly most intense in the hearts of those men and women who constituted the first Christian *ekklesia* at Jerusalem, on and immediately following the Day of Pentecost. At the heart and center of that fellowship were, of course, the Apostles themselves, who had received the Holy Spirit in baptismal (overwhelming) measure. To them were added on that first day of Gospel preaching, by the Lord Himself as the Head of the Body (Acts 2:41, 47), some three thousand souls (Acts 2:41), who too were vitalized by the regenerative measure of the Holy Spirit's power. Thus the Body of Christ was created, incorporated, and vitalized by the Presence who had come down from heaven, as the Agent of both the Father and the Son, for the very purpose of incorporating the Body and taking up His abode therein. To those first Christians, this Presence brought the realization of a rich and joyous fellowship. And anyone who reads the early history of the Church as recorded in the book of *Acts* cannot fail to realize that this sense of the Divine Presence with them and in them was especially characteristic of the saints throughout the apostolic age. As H. Wheeler Robinson writes:

To the men whom Jesus had trained in the ways of the Spirit there came at Pentecost a new discovery, the discovery of a *fellowship* with one another and with Him, that made Him still present with power in their midst. They spoke of the Presence in their fellowship as an unquestioned reality: It seemed good to the Holy Spirit and to us (Acts 15:28). Their discovery (which was God's revelation) created an epoch. The new fellowship had the distinctive marks of its new creation, for it was marked by reverence, mutual helpfulness, joy, and a graciousness that won men by its life more than by its speech. Thus to the love of God that had issued in the grace of Christ there was added the fellowship created by the Holy Spirit.[1]

1. *The Christian Experience of the Holy Spirit*, 7.

That this early Christian fellowship expressed itself characteristically in joyous service is evident from Luke's account of it in the book of *Acts*. The inspired historian tells us, for example, that on the Day of Pentecost, following Peter's sermon and exhortation, "they then that received his word were baptized; and there were added unto them" (literally "put together" or "added together") "in that day about three thousand souls." "And," he goes on to say, "they continued steadfastly in the apostles' teaching and fellowship, in the breaking of bread and the prayers" (Acts 2:41-42). It is interesting to note that the Greek word *koinonia*, here rendered "fellowship," in certain other New Testament passages is translated "contribution." (E.g., Rom. 15:26, 2 Cor. 9:12-13, 2 Cor. 8:4.) Obviously, in these various passages the word has reference specifically to the contributions of tithes and offerings for the relief of poor and distressed brethren. That this is one of the primary connotations of the word in the second chapter of *Acts* also, is clear from the verses that immediately follow verse 42, in which it is first used with reference to the Jerusalem *ekklesia*. Vv. 43-47 read as follows:

And fear came upon every soul: and many wonders and signs were done through the apostles. And all that believed were together, and had all things common; and they sold their possessions and goods, and parted them to all, according as any man had need. And day by day, continuing stedfastly with one accord in the temple, and breaking bread at home, they took their food with gladness and singleness of heart, praising God, and having favor with all the people. And the Lord added together day by day those that were saved.

In a word, this first Christian fellowship manifested itself primarily in unity and in liberality: it was essentially a *fellowship of joyous service*. And so we read in Acts 4:32-35;

And the multitude of them that believed were of one heart and soul; and not one them said that aught of the things which he possessed was his own; but they had all things common. And with great power gave the apostles their witness of the resurrection of the Lord Jesus: and great grace was upon them all. For neither was there among them any that lacked: for as many as were possessors of lands or houses sold them, and brought the prices of the things that were sold, and laid them at the apostles' feet: and distribution was made unto each, according as any one had need.

Thus it becomes quite clear that this first Christian fellowship, that of the Church of Christ in Jerusalem, manifested itself in a voluntary, spontaneous outpouring of love (there is not one iota of evidence that it was done in obedience to any command of the Apostles or of anyone else), a spontaneous outpouring of love in the form of joyful *service*. We have been told repeatedly in recent years, by self-styled "forward-looking breathren," that we must look to the future for the ideal church, never to the past. It strikes me, however, that it would be difficult for any congregation of Christians to excel the standard set by that first *ekklesia* in Jerusalem, in unity, in liberality, and in service. As a matter of fact, I am convinced that if any local church, as large numerically as was that Jerusalem church, could be found anywhere in the world today, of which it could be reported truthfully, as it was of that church, that the multitude of them that believe are of one heart and soul, and that not one of the members considers aught that he possesses as his own, but they have all things common; and of which it could be reported further that the members have actually sold their possessions and goods and made distribution unto each, according as every man had need—I am quite sure, I repeat, that if such a church could be found today, it would make the front page, and in bold headlines, of every metropolitan daily in the world. I am equally sure that I myself would go a long way to visit such a church in order to share its fellowship, if only temporarily, if indeed such a church could be found. That Jerusalem church stood at the very fountain-head of Christianity. By its spontaneous manifestations, in joyful service, of the fellowship which it enjoyed as a result of its consciousness of the Divine Presence in its midst, that church, I contend—a thesis I stand ready to defend at any time, anywhere—made itself a *pattern*—a *norm*, if you please—of Christian ecclesiastical fellowship for all time to come.

Moreover, judging from the record given us in the book of *Acts*, we must conclude that *joyful service* continued to be the outstanding characteristic of Christian fellowship throughout the entire apostolic age. Those early Christians were never content short of sharing their spiritual joy with others. In many instances, as in those indicated in the foregoing paragraph, this service took the form of voluntary contribution of tithes and offerings for the relief of the poor and distressed saints. In others, it took the form of personal evangelism. For example, when the members of the Jerusalem church "were all scattered abroad throughout the regions of Judea and Samaria," by persecutions instigated by Saul of Tarsus, "they therefore that were scattered abroad," we are told, "went about preaching the word." Now it must be remembered that these very first Christians were all Jews: thus did love, engendered by the Divine Presence in their hearts, break down the age-old "middle wall of partition" between Jew and Samaritan. And so we find Philip, who had previously been set apart as a "deacon" of the Jerusalem church (Acts 6:1-6), down in the city of Samaria proclaiming unto the once-despised Samaritans, the Christ. And when the people of that city, we are told, "believed Philip preaching good tidings concerning the kingdom of God and the name of Jesus Christ, they were baptized, both men and women" (Acts 8:1-12). "And there was much joy in that city" (v. 8). The fact is that whatever form this joyous service of the *Koinonia* took in apostolic times, it was invariably a service of *love*. Hence, in later years, when the saints at Corinth began to give too much weight to religious excitement and enthusiasm, in the form of public displays of "spiritual gifts" (tongues, prophesies, superhuman knowledge, healings, etc.), it became necessary for the Apostle Paul to reprove them and to set them back on the right track. This he did his first *Epistle to the Corinthians*. Although he does not disparage spiritual gifts, and indeed urges them to "desire earnestly the greater gifts" (1 Cor. 12:31), yet he goes on to say:

> And moreover a most excellent way show I unto you. If I speak with the tongues of men and of angels, but have not love, I am become sounding brass, or a clanging cymbal. And if I have the gift of prophecy, and know all mysteries and all knowledge; and I have all faith, so as to remove mountains, but have not love, I am nothing.

And he concludes with the well-known words, "But now abideth faith, hope, love, these three; and the greatest of these is love" (1 Cor. 12:31, 13:1-13). The most excellent way of life, the Christian way, is the way of love. Thus did the Apostle rebuke them for their spiritual exclusiveness, for their narrow horizon and littleness of spirit, in their exploitation of their miraculous powers as evidence of their high standing with God. Thus did he call their attention sharply to the fact that those gifts of the Spirit are superior which issue in *Service,* that the way of the Spirit is essentially the way of loving service, not only to those of the household of the faith but to all mankind. "To Paul it was given to know and preach the nobler realities of spiritual experience, and to call men from the debauch of religious emotion to the inspiration of duty."[1]

In like manner, the fellowship of the saints in all ages, with God the Father and with his Son Jesus Christ and with one another, mediated by the consciousness of the Divine Presence— the Holy Spirit—in their hearts, issues forth in pure worship,

1. H. W. Robinson, *op. cit.,* 8.

344

in Spirit and truth, including the proper observance of the Christian ordinances; and in joyous service, the service of love. Thus, through the avenues of pure worship and loving service, do God's people always find within themselves reservoirs of spiritual power upon which they can draw constantly for moral, spiritual, and even physical strength; and thus are they "strengthened with power through his Spirit in the inward man" (Eph. 3:16).

For, to the saints in all ages the Communion of the Spirit has always meant strength—moral, psychical, and even physical. As a result of their sense of the Spirit's indwelling, they have ever found within themselves reservoirs of power, of hitherto unused power, wells of living water. They have discovered themselves to be but channels through which the Divine Energy courses, and issues forth in joyful service. These facts are evident from their many recorded testimonies (Zech. 4:6; Psa. 23:1-2; Isa. 30:15, 35:4-10; John 14:1, 16:33; Phil. 4:13; Eph. 6:10; 1 Pet. 1:5, 8; Rom. 14:17; 1 John 1:4, 5:4). The Communion of the Spirit is the life of joyous service, which is joy unspeakable and full of glory.

The impulsion of Spirit-power does not send great spiritual leaders into seclusion behind monastic walls, but rather urges them out into the highways and byways of pulsating everyday life, there to seek and to save the lost. This was the lesson which our God sought to impress upon the minds of the Apostles Peter, James, and John in the course of the Transfiguration of Christ. It will be remembered that frail impulsive Simon Peter, moved to rapture by the sublimity of that mountain-top experience, burst forth into speech, saying to Jesus: "Lord, it is good for us to be here: if thou wilt, I will make here three tabernacles; one for thee, and one for Moses, and one for Elijah." We read, however, that "while he was yet speaking, behold, a bright cloud overshadowed them: and behold, a voice out of the cloud, saying, This is my beloved Son, in whom I am well pleased; *hear ye him*" (Matt. 17:1-6). What was this but a kindly rebuke to Peter, a patient reminder that this work of Jesus and His disciples was not to be done on the mountain-top but down in the valley where dwelt the hungering and thirsting —and lost—souls of men? And so we read (v. 9) that "as they were coming down from the mountain, Jesus commanded them, saying, Tell the vision to no man, until the Son of man be risen from the dead." Yes, *they came down from the mountain*, down to the fields that were white unto the harvest, into the regions inhabited by the toiling sons of men whom Jesus came to seek and to save. In a word, the fellowship of the Spirit means superabundant energy, activity, loving service, all tempered with profoundly practical rationality.

8. *Spirit in God means Holiness.*

This sublime truth was apprehended by individual saints in olden times. Psa. 51:11, "Take not thy holy Spirit from me." Isa. 63:10-11: "his holy Spirit." Neh. 9:20—"thy good Spirit." It is in a special sense, however, a New Testament revelation.

Holiness means *Wholeness, i.e.,* completeness, perfection, of being. Negatively, it is the absence of lack; there is no power, virtue or excellence lacking to the Being of our God. He is infinite (inexhaustible) Truth, Beauty, Goodness, Love, and Justice. Moreover, because Wholeness embraces the orderly relationship of all parts or powers, Holiness means *Order,* and the *love of Order.* In God there is perfect order, perfect equilibrium of all powers, perfect ordering of all things to their proper ends. In Him there is no conflict, but only perfect harmony, of intellect and will, of thought and purpose, of love and justice, of goodness and power. In God "mercy and truth are met together; righteousness and peace have kissed each other" (Psa. 85:10). "Holy, holy, holy, is Jehovah of hosts: the whole earth is full of his glory" (Isa. 6:3). "Holy, holy, holy, is the Lord God, the Almighty, who was and who is and who is to come" (Rev. 4:8): this is the celestial anthem which is continuously lifted up by voices of praise before the Throne of God.

The New Testament Scriptures especially make it very clear that Spirit-power is the dynamic which effects miracles, including miracles of healing of the physical body. This power of God was manifested through holy men of old (*e.g.,* Elisha and the Shunammite woman's son, 2 Kings 4:32-37); and through Jesus especially, who possessed the Holy Spirit without measure, *i.e.,* in the fulness of His powers and influences (John 3:34); and finally through the Apostles, who possessed the Spirit's power in baptismal measure (Acts 1:4, 5, 8; 2:1-4): that is to say, the power to make men and women *whole* physically. (*Vide* Matt. 9:12, 9:20-22; Luke 7:2-10; John 5:6, 14, John 7:23; Acts 4:8-10; 9:34, 20; 7-12, 28:1-6, etc.).

The fact should be kept in mind, of course, that the Spirit-power which effected these miracles of healing was essentially *psychical.* If subconscious thought (suggestion) in man has control over the bodily functions, as we have seen that it does, who can successfully gainsay the fact that this power in the

346

Divine Spirit has *absolute* power over corporeal things and functions?

Again, the Spirit makes men whole *personally* by writing in their inward parts, by inscribing in their hearts, the Word of Christ, which is the expression of the Mind and Thought of Christ. (*Vide* Jer. 31:33, Heb. 8:6-13; 2 Cor. 3:2-3, Phil. 2:5, 1 Cor. 2:16; Col. 3:16; Rom. 8:2, note that the Word of Christ is designated here, "the law of the Spirit of life in Christ Jesus." God's people have "the mind of Christ" as mediated by the Spirit.

Commenting on the phrase, "the mind of Christ," Cruden says:

> We who are endued with the Spirit, have an experimental knowledge of God's will, and of spiritual divine things, revealed to us by the Spirit, who is our teacher, and knows the mind of Christ, and reveals it to us.[1]

Jesus Himself says: "The words that I have spoken unto you are spirit, and are life" (John 6:63). And it will be remembered that Jesus said to the men who were to become His Apostles: "But the Comforter, even the Holy Spirit, whom the Father will send in my name, he shall teach you all things, and bring to your remembrance all that I said unto you" (John 14:26). Again: "When he, the Spirit of truth, is come, he shall guide you into all the truth; for he shall not speak from himself; but what things soever he shall hear, these shall he speak: and he shall declare unto you the things that are to come. He shall glorify me: for *he shall take of mine, and shall declare it unto you*" (John 16:13-14). And Paul testifies: "But we [the Apostles] received, not the spirit of the world, but the spirit which is from God: that we might know the things that were freely given to us of God. Which things also we speak, not in words which man's wisdom teacheth, but which the Spirit teacheth; combining spiritual things with spiritual words" (1 Cor. 2:12-13); that is, communicating or revealing spiritual realities in spiritual terms. Thus the Word of Christ is that Word which is revealed in the New Testament by the Spirit, and to receive that Word into the heart, to digest it and assimilate it, to turn it into one's spiritual blood, so to speak, is to acquire the Mind of Christ. *And so by implanting within the saints the Mind of Christ, the Spirit integrates their personalities around the Person of Christ, and makes them whole personally.*

1. A. Cruden, *Concordance, s.v.*

Eph. 4:11-16: And he [Christ] gave some to be apostles; and some, prophets; and some, evangelists; and some, pastors and teachers; for the perfecting of the saints, unto the work of ministering, unto the building up of the body of Christ: till we all attain unto the unity of faith, and of the knowledge of the Son of God, unto a fullgrown man, unto the measure of the stature of the fulness of Christ: that we may be no longer children, tossed to and fro and carried about with every wind of doctrine, by the sleight of men, in craftiness, after the wiles of error; but speaking truth in love, may grow up in all things into him, who is the head, even Christ; from whom all the body fitly framed and knit together through that which every joint supplieth, according to the working in due measure of each several part, maketh the increase of the body unto the building up of itself in love.

The Apostle is envisioning, in this passage, the integration, not only of the individual personality, but also of the entire Mystic Personality (the Church), around and into the Person of Christ.

Cf. Heb. 12:1-2: Let us . . . lay aside every weight, and the sin which doth so easily beset us, and let us run with patience the race that is set before us, looking unto Jesus the author and perfecter of our faith. 2 Pet. 3:18—But grow in the grace and knowledge of our Lord and Savior Jesus Christ.

Jesus Christ is the focal point or object around whom the spiritual life is integrated.

The vast majority of psychologists will agree, I think, that the unfailing criterion of a mature personality is a unifying philosophy of life. Dr. Gordon W. Allport, for example, writes as follows:

Religion is the search for a value underlying *all* things, and as such is the most comprehensive of all the possible philosophies of life. A deeply moving religious experience is not readily forgotten, but is likely to remain as a focus of thought and desire. Many lives have no such focus; for them religion is an indifferent matter, or less a purely formal and compartmental interest. But the authentically religious personality unites the tangible present with some comprehensive view of the world that makes this tangible present intelligible and acceptable to him. Psychotherapy recognizes this integrative function of religion in personality, soundness of mind being aided by the possession of a completely embracing theory of life.[1]

Or, to put the same fundamental truth in another form: Biological science of recent years has had a great deal to say about "adaptation to environment." But what does it mean by "environment"? What does "environment" include? Just the immediate family in which one grows up? Or the immediate family *plus* the community in which one is reared? Or does "environment" take in both these factors, and, in addition, the national state of which one is a citizen and for the preservation of which he may be called upon to give his life? As a matter of fact, it

1. *Personality: A Psychological Interpretation*, 226.

takes in all of these—family, community, and state—and infinitely more. The total environment in which a personality is integrated is the whole wide world: every human being is an inhabitant of the Cosmos itself. And no man is fully adapted to his environment until he has satisfied himself with respect to the whence and whither of his own being; that is to say, with respect to his relations to the Totality of Being of which he is himself an integral part. In the sense that every person is the center of his own world, that world which he constructs for himself by his formulation of a unifying philosophy of life, the world may rightly be said to be anthropocentric. Furthermore, any unifying philosophy of life must be, in the nature of the case, essentially a Faith. Even though it may, and indeed should, be based on necessary inferences drawn from rational observation and experience, still it remains a Faith, for it is bound to embrace elements which lie beyond all possibility of experimental proof or disproof. Such a unifying philosophy of life is, however, the principal criterion of a mature personality.

I am reminded here of the concluding paragraph of H. A. Overstreet's excellent little book, *The Mature Mind*. The paragraph reads as follows:

Where there is no vision, we are told, the people perish. Where there is no maturity, there is no vision. We now begin to know this. We realize that the evils of our life come not from deep evil within us but from ungrown-up responses to life. Our obligation, then, is to grow up. This is what our time requires of us. This is what may yet be the saving of us.[1]

There is a world of truth in these lines. Truly we need to grow up! But most of all do we need to grow up, to integrate our personalities, around the proper Object, the proper Focus. Now the Focus of the Christian life—the life of the Spirit—is a Person, Jesus Christ of Nazareth, the Incarnate Word, the Son of the living God, and The One Altogether Lovely (Song of Sol. 5:16). Christ is Christianity, and Christianity is Christ. And the true Unifier of the human personality, around Christ as the Focus, is the Spirit of God. The specific mission of the Spirit on earth, in the present Dispensation, is to bear witness of Christ, His life, death, resurrection, glorification, and sovereignty. Said Jesus Himself with respect to the Spirit's mission: "He shall glorify me; for he shall take of mine, and shall declare it unto you" (John 16:14). Now the testimony concerning Christ, the testimony necessary to beget faith in Christ—for "belief cometh of

1. *Op. cit.*, 292.

hearing, and hearing by the word of Christ" (Rom. 10:17) —
and to effect the integration of the human personality in Christ,
is presented by the Spirit, through the prophets, apostles, and
other inspired writers, in the Scriptures—and nowhere else, I
might add—and particularly in the New Testament which is the
Word of Christ—His Last Will and Testament—communicated to
men by the agency of the Spirit. (See again John 15:26-27,
16:7-14; 1 Cor. 2:6-13; 2 Pet. 1:21; 1 Pet. 1:10-12; 1 Thess. 2:13,
etc.). This testimony was begun through holy men of old, who
were moved by the Spirit; it was continued through the Hebrew
Prophets, who were in a special sense "men of the Spirit"; it
was brought to completeness through Jesus, who possessed the
Holy Spirit without measure (John 3:34), and through His
Apostles, who were guided into all the truth by the same Spirit
(John 16:13). This testimony of the Spirit was at the first communicated orally to men, in the present Dispensation, by the
Apostles and early evangelists; before the death of the latter,
however, it was embodied by them in permanent form in the
New Testament canon. The New Testament canon, revealed by
the Spirit through the inspired Apostles and evangelists, is in
a special sense the Word of Christ. By means of this written
Word, the Apostles are themselves witnessing for Christ "unto
the uttermost part of the earth" (Acts 1:8), just as Jesus told
them that they would do while He was yet with them in person.
Moreover, to the extent that this Word is presented to men
"through the foolishness of preaching"—by means of which it
is God's good pleasure to save them that believe (1 Cor. 1:21) —
and accepted into their hearts and assimilated into their thoughts
and lives, they, too acquire the Mind of Christ; and to the extent that they acquire the Mind of Christ, their personalities become integrated around Him and in Him, and they become *personally whole*. This consummation is said to be realized, of
course, by the agency of the Spirit, for the Spirit is in the Word
and exercises His powers of regeneration and sanctification
through the Word. God's Spirit-power and Word-power always
go together.

*The temporal mission of the Holy Spirit in all ages has
been, and is, to glorify Christ (John 16:14).*

Again, through this same process of integrating the personalities of men around and in Christ, and making them whole
personally, the activity of the Spirit effects also their *moral*
wholeness, that is, their oneness with God. Regeneration and
sanctification are in a special sense works of the Holy Spirit,

works by which He actualizes the efficacy of the love of God and the grace of the Lord Jesus Christ in the lives of the saints. In regeneration, the Spirit begets in them—through the instrumentality of the Word—a new life, a new moral and spiritual life of covenant relationship with God. As Jesus said to Nicodemus: "Verily, verily, I say unto thee, Except one be born of water and the Spirit, he cannot enter into the kingdom of God. That which is born of the flesh is flesh; and that which is born of the Spirit is spirit. Marvel not that I said unto thee, Ye must be born anew" (John 3:5-7). Again, in progressive sanctification, the Spirit nurtures this new moral and spiritual life in the saints—again through the instrumentality of the Word—and thus effects their moral and spiritual growth, growth in the grace and knowledge of our Lord and Savior Jesus Christ (2 Pet. 3:18). Now to grow in the grace and knowledge of Christ is to grow like God or godlike; for it was an important part of the mission of Christ to reveal God the Father to mankind. "No man hath seen God at any time; the only begotten Son, who is in the bosom of the Father, he hath declared him" (John 1:18). And Jesus Himself said: "He that hath seen me hath seen the Father" (John 14:9). And the writer of *Hebrews* tells us that Christ the Son is the effulgence of the Father's glory and the very image of the Father's substance (Heb. 1:3). In this manner, that is, by this continuous process of nurture on the Divine side and growth on the human side, the Spirit brings the minds of the saints into oneness with the Mind of God in knowledge and their wills into oneness with the Will of God in love. The ultimate result is their complete oneness with the Divine. The man whose mind and will are one with the Mind and Will of God is *morally* whole or holy. He is fully prepared for the inheritance of the saints in light; prepared to see God "face to face," to enter into Everlasting Life.

There is yet one work, however, for the Spirit to do as the vicegerent of Christ, in order to make complete His activity in behalf of the saint, in order to make the latter perfectly *whole*. That work is to make him *spiritually* (*metaphysically?*) whole, by clothing him in his spiritual body (1 Cor. 15:35-58); by fashioning anew this body of our humiliation, that it may be conformed to the glorified body of Christ—the body, for example, in which our Lord appeared in the Transfiguration scene (Matt. 17:2), and in which He appeared later to Saul of Tarsus on the Damascus road, Acts 9:1-9, 26:12-15). For God, we are told expressly, will thus give life to our mortal bodies *through His Spirit that dwelleth in us* (Rom. 8:11). Redemption begins in the redemption of the spirit from the guilt of sin; it becomes complete in the ultimate redemption of the body from the consequences of sin (Rom. 8:20-23). When the redeemed saint shall appear in the Judgment purified in spirit and clothed in glory and honor and immortality, he will then be spiritually, metaphysically, *absolutely whole*. He will lack nothing of wholeness, nothing of perfection, in body, soul, and spirit. As the Apostle puts it: "And the God of peace himself sanctify you *wholly;* and may your spirit and soul and body be preserved entire, without blame at the coming of our Lord Jesus Christ" (1 Thess. 5:23).

The Spirit-power of God makes men whole—physically, personally, morally and spiritually. Spirit in God means Holiness, Where the Spirit of God is, there is order, unity, wholeness, perfection. Where the Spirit of God is not, there is disorder, disunity, disintegration, and imperfection or lack.

"The grace of the Lord Jesus Christ, and the love of God, and the communion of the Holy Spirit, be with you all."

## 6. Personality in God

On the subject of personality in God and in man, Dr. Edgar Sheffield Brightman summarizes as follows:

> God and man both enjoy complex self-experience, *qualia* (including ideal norms) which low grade selves are not conscious of, a wide range of temporal and spatial consciousness, time-transcendence and space-transcendence, free purposive self-control, rational awareness of meaning, free response to environment, and privacy of consciousness. All these traits belong to the essence of personality.[1]

The essentials of personality enumerated here may—it seems to me—be reduced to the four traditionally given, namely, (1) self-consciousness, (2) self-determination (purposiveness), (3) individuality (uniqueness, otherness, "privacy," *i.e.*, separate and distinct existence), and (4) transcendence (of time and space). Personality in God embraces all these characteristics.

1. *Personality in God, as in man, includes self-consciousness.* Self-consciousness is the ability to become subject and object, knower and known, at one and the same time. It is the ability to say, I am, with rational awareness of the meaning of the saying. Personality, therefore, is explicit in the very Name of our God, I AM. "And God said unto Moses, I AM THAT I AM; and he said, Thus shalt thou say unto the children of Israel,

---

1. *A Philosophy of Religion,* 363.

I AM hath sent me unto you" (Exo. 3:14). Only a person can say, meaningfully to himself, I am.

2. *Personality in God, as in man, includes self-determination, self-direction, purposiveness.* Our God is Pure Act. He acts, moreover, toward specific ends. And he accomplishes His purposes: *He gets things done.* As He Himself has said, through the prophet Isaiah:

> I am God, and there is none else; I am God, and there is none like me; declaring the end from the beginning, and from ancient times things that are not yet done; saying, My counsel shall stand, and I will do all my pleasure . . . Yea, I have spoken, I will also bring it to pass; I have purposed, I will also do it. (Isa. 46:9-11).

Because our God is purposive, we have in Scripture what is designated "the eternal purpose" of God, the "mystery of his will," etc. That eternal purpose was, *proximately,* to send Jesus Christ, His Son, in the fulness of the time, to make atonement for sin and to conquer death, thereupon to publish the Gospel, establish the Church, and unite both Jews and Gentiles in the one Body of Christ. That eternal purpose is, *ultimately,* to create a holy redeemed race of saints, conformed to the image of His Son in both spirit and body; to present this race in the Judgment, clothed in glory and honor and immortality: and thus to vindicate Himself in the minds of all intelligent creatures of the false charges hurled against Him by Satan and his rebel host before the foundation of the world. (We suggest the following Scriptures, in this connection, to be read in the order given here.)

> (1) Rom. 16:25-26: Now to him that is able to establish you according to my gospel and the preaching of Jesus Christ, according to the revelation of the mystery which hath been kept in silence through times eternal, but now is manifested, and by the scriptures of the prophets, according to the commandment of the eternal God, is made known unto all the nations unto obedience of faith, etc.
> (2) Eph. 1:3-12: Blessed be the God and Father of our Lord Jesus Christ, who hath blessed us with every spiritual blessing in the heavenly places in Christ: even as he chose us in him before the foundation of the world, that we should be holy and without blemish before him in love; having foreordained us unto adoption as sons through Jesus Christ unto himself, according to the good pleasure of his will, to the praise of the glory of his grace, which he freely bestowed on us in the Beloved: in whom we have our redemption through his blood, the forgiveness of our trespasses, according to the riches of his grace, which he made to abound toward us in all wisdom and prudence; making known unto us *the mystery of his will, according to his good pleasure which he purposed in him unto a dispensation of the fulness of the times, to sum up all things in Christ, the things in the heavens, and the things upon the earth; in him, I say, in whom also we were made a heritage, having been foreordained according to the purpose of him who worketh all things after the counsel of his will;* to the end that we should be unto the praise of his glory, we who had before hoped in Christ.

(3) Eph. 3:1-12: For this cause I Paul, the prisoner of Christ Jesus in behalf of you Gentiles,—if so be that ye have heard of the dispensation of that grace of God which was given me to you-ward; *how that by revelation was made known unto me the mystery*, as I wrote before in few words, whereby, when ye read, ye can perceive *my understanding in the mystery of Christ;* which in other generations was not made known unto the sons of men, as it hath now been revealed unto his holy apostles and prophets in the Spirit; *to wit, that the Gentiles are fellow-heirs, and fellow-members of the body, and fellow-partakers of the promise in Christ Jesus through the gospel*, whereof I was made a minister, according to the gift of that grace of God which was given me according to the working of his power. Unto me, who am less than the least of all saints, was this grace given, to preach unto the Gentiles the unsearchable riches of Christ; and *to make all men see what is the dispensation of the mystery which for ages hath been hid in God who created all things; to the intent that now unto the principalities and the powers in the heavenly places might be made known through the church the manifold wisdom of God, according to the eternal purpose which he purposed in Christ Jesus our Lord;* in whom we have boldness and access in confidence through our faith in him.

(4) 1 Pet. 1:10-12: Concerning which salvation the prophets sought and searched diligently, who prophesied of the grace that should come unto you: searching what time or what manner of time the Spirit of Christ which was in them did point unto, when it testified beforehand the sufferings of Christ, and the glories that should follow them. To whom it was revealed that not unto themselves, but unto you, did they minister these things, which now have been announced unto you through them that preached the gospel unto you by the Holy Spirit sent forth from heaven; which things angels desire to look into.

(5) Gal. 4:4-5: But when the fulness of the time came, God sent forth his Son, born of a woman, born under the law, that he might redeem them that were under the law, that we might receive the adoption of sons.

(6) Rom. 8:28-30: And we know that to them that love God all things work together for good, *even to them that are called according to his purpose. For whom he foreknew* [i.e., in His eternal purpose] *he also foreordained to be conformed to the image of his Son*, that he might be the first born among many brethren: and whom he fore-ordained, them he also called [i.e., in His eternal purpose]; and whom he called, them he also justified [i.e., in His eternal purpose] and whom he justified, them he also glorified [i.e., in His eternal purpose]. This eternal purpose will be fully realized in the immortalization of the saints, in which process they will be conformed to the image of the glorified Christ. [Also Phil. 3:20-21; Rom. 8:18-25; 1 Cor. 6:2-3, 15:24-28; 2 Pet. 3:10-13; Rev. 20:10-15, 21:1-8, 22:1-5; Rom. 2:7; 1 Tim. 1:17, 6:13-16; 2 Tim. 1:10.]

"That God may be all in all"—such will be the glorious Consummation. Thus it will be seen that the Bible teaches clearly that our world is, after all, neither geocentric nor anthropocentric, but *theocentric*. All things begin and end with God.

3. *Personality in God, as in man, includes individuality, uniqueness, otherness.* Dr. Berman writes:

The discontinuity of the personal self with all other selves is the essential fact of every human existence. The human individual continually perceives himself as a concentrated entity, a consciousness bounded by the limitations of his own personality, segregated from every other human being. Even in the most intimate fellowship there is a consciousness of those invisible and intangible barriers which permanently divide one individuality from another. Because he lives alone in his consciousness, every man lives alone in the cosmos. This ultimate solitude of every human being is the central fact of all his experience and all his knowledge.[1]

To quote Dr. Rufus Jones:

First, last, and all the time, i.e., in our sanity, we possess an integral, self-identical self, which knows what it knows and does what it does. It is, or at least can become, a highly complex spiritual reality, with a sphere and range of its own. We are in large measure the makers of ourselves; but fortunately we start with a precious impartation, or birth-gift, which is big with the potentiality of spirit—otherwise we might have ended as a hop-toad,

A creature predestined to move
In a well-defined groove,

with no power to build a self from within, such as we possess now. And that self of ours, whatever its ultimate destiny may be, is utterly unique.[2]

A person is a unique being, a being with thoughts, images, memories, experiences, all of which are, in the very nature of the case, exclusively his own. He is inevitably characterized by what Brightman calls "privacy of consciousness." Hence he is never duplicated. To quote Emerson again: "Nature never rhymes her children nor makes two men alike."

Personality, therefore, in relation to all other persons, is *otherness*: a person is an *other* to all other persons, and all other persons are *other* to one another and to him. To some extent every person is indeed, in Leibniz's phrase, a "windowless monad." Hence Karl Barth's emphasis on the *otherness* of God is in perfect harmony with the fact of the personality of God.

H. Wheeler Robinson writes:

In both man and God there is a principle of self-consciousness, unshared by any other, that exclusive principle of individual personality which gives the peculiar quality to "my" experience, as distinct from another's. The name "Spirit" is given to this principle in God, just as "spirit" denotes it in man. The gift of the Spirit of God means that this exclusive consciousness of his is exceptionally shared with man, or, as a Hebrew prophet would have put it, that man is admitted into the council of Yahweh, to think His thoughts (Jer. 23:18, 22). At present, however, we have no more than the "earnest" of the condition of full knowledge (1 Cor. 8:2; 13:12; Gal. 4:9), the condition itself being full transformation by the Spirit (2 Cor. 3:18).[3]

1. Louis Berman, *Behind the Universe*, 13.
2. *Spirit in Man*, 21-22.
3. *The Christian Experience of the Holy Spirit*, 227-228.

Personality in God means, then, that the Mind of God is not the totality of human minds, as the pantheist would have it. Pantheism has always found the problem of evil difficult to handle, for the simple reason that in the pantheistic view, God, as the totality of intelligences in the Cosmos, would necessarily embrace the evil as well as the good in human thinking. The only alternative, of course, is to treat evil as non-existent, as an "illusion of mortal mind." This is precisely what most pantheists —and Absolutists—do. But personality in God, I repeat, does not mean that the Mind of God is identical with the totality of creaturely minds. It means, in fact, just the opposite—that the Mind of God is the Absolute Other to any or all human minds. I thank God that such is the case, for it means that we frail human beings can pray to God and enter into communion with God, as person in relation to Person.

4. *Personality in God, as in man, includes transcendence of time and space.* God is *absolutely* free from all temporal and spatial limitations. "But forget not this one thing, beloved, that one day is with the Lord as a thousand years, and a thousand years as one day" (2 Pet. 3:8). This is, of course, but a poetic way of saying that time means nothing to God. The same is true of space.

As the Psalmist cries out:

> Whither shall I go from thy Spirit?
> Or whither shall I flee from thy presence?
> If I ascend up into heaven, thou art there;
> If I make my bed in Sheol, behold, thou art there.
> If I take the wings of the morning,
> And dwell in the uttermost parts of the sea,
> Even there shall thy hand lead me,
> And thy right hand shall hold me.

This great truth of God's transcendence of time and space relations, however, has been fully presented in a foregoing section and needs not to be elaborated here.

Finally, should we be speaking more correctly if we were to designate God a "Superperson"? Some philosophers have thought so, on the ground that to call God personal is to make Him finite, or speaking more precisely perhaps, anthropomorphic. On this point I quote again from Brightman:

> If God be a person, it is self-evident that his experience is incomparably vaster than man's. It is certain that he has powers unknown to man, and goodness utterly transcending man's. It is highly probable that he has indefinitely many types of experience unknown to us, which are barely hinted at by such facts as the ultraviolet and infrared rays, invisible to man. But it is one thing to say that per-

sonality which is in part known includes kinds of experience of which we do not yet know; and it is quite another thing to say that there is an entity of some sort which is lacking in all consciousness and experience and rational personal identity, and yet is higher than personality. In the former sense we may say that God is superpersonal, meaning superhumanly personal. In the latter sense, since we cannot define our hypothesis except wishfully, we cannot know whether an unconscious "superpersonality" would be better or worse than personality, and we cannot use the concept to explain any aspect of actual conscious entities such as ourselves. As far as we can know, the unconscious and impersonal, if such there be in the universe, is below and not above the level of conscious personality. At best the unconscious superpersonal is but a label for the unknown, and not a definable hypothesis.[1]

Let us conclude, therefore, with Dr. Brightman, that it would be legitimate, undoubtedly, to speak of God as a superhuman Person, for *that* He is indeed, especially in the fact that, in the light of His own revelation of Himself, His personality embraces, in some inscrutable manner, a triplicity of Persons— Father, Son, and Holy Spirit—each of whom is a Personality in His own right, so to speak. But to describe God as a "Superperson" means nothing, in the light of our human experience. Moreover, in response to the hue and cry of "anthropomorphism," we are on solid ground in affirming that man can hardly think of God as less than a Person, because Person is the highest category of being of which man has knowledge. And since man is a person, and knows that he is a person, he cannot properly think of God as less than, or inferior to, himself. Therefore, we are content to accept the revealed Name of our God, with all its implications—I AM THAT I AM, HE WHO IS. *The Person of God thus authenticates our love for Him, the prayers we lift up to Him, and the fellowship we enjoy with Him. None of these privileges would be possible, if God is less than person!*

## QUESTIONS ON REVIEW OF PART FOUR

1. In what sense is a human being "the image of God"?
2. What fallacies are involved in the writing of Xenophanes about anthropomorphism? Why is anthropomorphic representation apparently necessary to make God congenial to us?
3. Why do we say that much of the Old Testament is constructed on principles of "kindergarten pedagogy"?
4. Explain what is meant by the cold, intellectually-constructed concepts of God. Cite examples.
5. Explain what is implied in the word *person* as descriptive of God.
6. What does Dr. Jones mean by "mind when it reaches the stage of spirit in beings like us"?
7. How does a man ultimately attain the stature of a *real person*, according to New Testament teaching?

1. E. S. Brightman, *op. cit.*, 237.

357

8. Explain what is meant by the power of the mind to generate "free ideas." What bearing does this have on the teaching that every man is God's "image"?
9. What follows from the possession of the human spirit by the Divine Spirit?
10. In what special sense, according to Heb. 1:3, was Christ the image of God?
11. How is the benevolence of God manifested in the constitution of man?
12. Explain what is meant by self-determination in man. What power in a special sense enables him to attain his own divinely determined ends?
13. How are means and ends related in the constitution of the human being?
14. How do these reflect the similar powers characteristic of Spirit in God?
15. What is clearly intimated by the attributes and powers of the human spirit?
16. Discuss: "Nature and revelation are never contradictory."
17. Why do we not make use of the word "Trinity" with reference to God?
18. Explain as best you can what is meant by the tripersonality of God?
19. Distinguish the "unitarian" from the "trinitarian" concept of God.
20. What is the uniqueness of the Old Testament revelation of God? How is this corroborated in the New Testament?
21. How is the tripersonality of God intimated in the Old Testament?
22. Why, in all likelihood, was this not fully revealed in Old Testament times?
23. How is it fully revealed in the New Testament?
24. Cite Scriptures in which the Father is fully recognized as God.
25. Cite Scriptures in which the Son is fully recognized as God.
26. Cite Scriptures in which the attributes of deity are ascribed to the Son. List these attributes.
27. What works of deity are ascribed to the Son? Cite Scriptures.
28. Cite Scriptures which represent the Son as receiving honor and worship which should be given only to the Deity.
29. Cite Scriptures in which the equality of the Father and the Son are declared.
30. Explain what is meant by the Kenosis ("Humiliation") of the Son. What did this include?
31. Explain what is meant by the Condescension ("Humiliation") of the Holy Spirit.
32. Cite Scriptures in which the Three are so presented that we must think of them as distinct personalities.
33. Cite Scriptures in which the Son distinguishes the Father from Himself.
34. Cite Scriptures in which the Son distinguishes the Spirit from both the Father and the Son.
35. How is the Spirit said to come from the Father?
36. Cite Scriptures in which the Spirit is said to be sent by both the Father and the Son.
37. Show how the distinction between the Three appears in the Annunciation.
38. Show how the same distinctions appear in the Son's conversation with Nicodemus.
39. Show how these distinctions are specifically revealed in the scene following the baptism of Jesus.
40. Summarize this revealed doctrine of the triune personality of our God.

41. Cite evidences to support the doctrine that the Three must be regarded as co-equal.
42. Cite Scriptures which indicate the affective relations among the Three.
43. Cite Scriptures which show that the Spirit searches and reveals the "deep things of God."
44. Cite Scriptures in which the Father is said to command the Son in the latter's capacity as Mediator and Redeemer.
45. Cite Scriptures affirming that both the Father and the Son actuate the Spirit's activities with respect to the Body of Christ.
46. What are these fundamental activities of the Spirit with respect to the Church?
47. What does the Bible tell us about the work of the Spirit in His capacity of Administrator of the church of the apostolic age?
48. Cite Old Testament passages in which inter-communion among the Three is intimated.
49. Cite Scriptures in which the plural form *Elohim* is used, with a singular verb, to designate the Deity. What does this teach us?
50. Cite passages which assert the eternal pre-existence of the Word (Logos). What is the special significance of the words of Jesus in John 17:5 and in John 8:58.
51. Cite passages in which the Spirit of God of the Old Testament is identified with the Holy Spirit of the New Testament.
52. Why do we say that this triune personality of God is inscrutable? Therefore, on what basis do we accept it?
53. How may this doctrine be said to underlie divine inspiration?
54. How is it essential to the Scheme of Redemption?
55. In what respect is it essential to the true worship of the living and true God?
56. How is it essential to any adequate Christology?
57. How is it essential to any perfect pattern of human life and conduct?
58. How is it related to the Christian doctrine of the Atonement?
59. List some of the so-called pagan "trinities." Distinguish between "trinities" and "tritheisms" or "triads."
60. How do the inter-relationships among the Father, Son, and Holy Spirit, of the Bible differ from the inter-relationships among the heathen gods?
61. What does the term "begetting" of the Son, and that of the "procession" of the Spirit, signify especially?
62. How shall we approach the question of the personality of the Spirit?
63. What activities are attributed to the Spirit which indicate His personality?
64. What attributes and powers are attributed to the Spirit that indicate His personality?
65. What slights and injuries are said to be suffered by the Spirit which indicate His personality?
66. What various offices and works are attributed to the Spirit which indicate His personality?
67. Cite Scriptures in which the Holy Spirit is invariably pictured in association with other persons in such a way as to imply His personality.
68. How are the Three associated in the Great Commission (cf. Matt. 28:19 and Acts 1:2).
69. What must be our conclusion, in view of this array of evidence, about the nature or being of the Holy Spirit?
70. Cite Scripture passages in which the Holy Spirit is explicitly recognized as God.

71. Cite Scriptures in which the perfections of God are ascribed to the Holy Spirit.
72. Cite Scriptures in which the works of deity are ascribed to the Holy Spirit. List these works.
73. Cite Scriptures in which the Spirit is represented as receiving obedience and worship that is due only to Deity.
74. Cite Scriptures in which the Holy Spirit is represented as being associated on a footing of equality with the Father and the Son.
75. What is the practical significance of all these truths? Of what value are they to Christians? What use are we to make of them in our everyday thinking and living?
76. What does "Spirit" mean with reference to the Godhead in general?
77. In what ways does the God of the Bible satisfy the aspirations of the human heart?
78. How does Jesus describe God in John 4:24?
79. Cite Old Testament passages in which God is designated *holy* Spirit.
80. What three meanings does "spirituality" have as applied to God?
81. What de we mean by saying that God *has* Spirit?
82. What do we mean by saying that God *gives* Spirit?
83. What is included in the affirmation that Spirit in God means Power? What *kinds* of power (energy) are attributed to Him?
84. Explain as clearly as possible what Acts 17:28 means.
85. What is meant by the phrase "living *naturally*"?
86. What sustains all the processes we discover in nature?
87. Explain the statement: *only that which is permanent can change.*
88. To what fact do such terms as "law," "order," "cosmos," etc., apply?
89. What is meant by *material, formal, efficient,* and *final* causes?
90. Who, according to Bible teaching, is the Efficient Cause of all aspects of the Cosmos? (cf. Psa. 3:6, 9; also Psa. 148:5-6.)
91. How are the Spirit-power, Thought-power, and Word-power of God inter-related?
92. What is the *constitution* of all cosmic order? What must the fact of cosmic order presuppose?
93. Explain the relation of Spirit-power to all forms of *life.*
94. Relate Spirit in God to the Incarnation.
95. Relate Spirit in God to regeneration, sanctification, and immortalization.
96. What is the significance of the divine prohibition of idolatry?
97. What is implicit in the Biblical revelation of God as the *living* God?
98. What is the significance of the Biblical NAME of God (Exo. 3:14)?
99. What is the significance of the Old Testament teaching, "The Lord our God is *one* Lord"?
100. Explain Aristotle's Four Causes. How related to the Biblical revelation of God?
101. Is is possible to eliminate Efficient Causality from any study of the origin and preservation of the Cosmos? Explain your answer.
102. What according to Aquinas, is the "proper effect" of God? Explain.
103. Explain what is meant by the "everywhereness" of the Spirit. Cite Scriptures which affirm it.
104. In what sense is *everywhereness* a characteristic of personality?
105. In what sense does the Thought-power of the Spirit evince His everywhereness?
106. Explain how Spirit in God includes His *inexhaustibleness.* Relate John 7:37-39 to this truth.
107. In what respect does Spirit in God signify *creativity?* How is this truth related to regeneration, sanctification and immortalization?

108. Explain how Spirit in God is related to the natural sociality of man, and especially to the fellowship of the redeemed.
109. How did the early Christian *fellowship* of the saints find expression?
110. What is the full significance of the phrase, "the communion of the Spirit"?
111. Explain how Spirit in God signifies *holiness*. What does this word mean?
112. Around whom does the Spirit of God integrate the personality of each of His saints?
113. In what final change does the Christian personality become a *whole?*
114. What powers does *personality* in God, as well as in man, include?
115. What is revealed to be God's Eternal Purpose for the redeemed? Cite Scriptures.
116. In what sense does personality in God mean *uniqueness?*
117. In what sense does it mean *otherness?* What significance does this truth have for the prayer life and personal worship of the Christian?
118. Is there any point in regarding God as "superpersonal"? Explain.
119. Can the notion of *impersonality* as related to God have any meaning for us?
120. Summarize all that Spirit in God in God includes.

# PART FIVE

# THE
# NOMENCLATURE
# OF THE SPIRIT

# 1. Names and Titles of the Spirit

There are some eighty-eight passages in the Old Testament, and two hundred and sixty-two in the New, in which the Spirit is directly mentioned. (*Vide* James Elder Cumming, *Through the Eternal Spirit*, 36, 44. A few of these passages are doubtful, but the doubtful ones are of no great consequence.) It would be well to note at this point the names and titles which the Spirit, the Author of Scripture, applies to Himself in these various passages, bearing in mind of course that all Biblical names are especially meaningful.

In the Old Testament, the Spirit designates Himself (1) "The Spirit of God" (Gen. 1:2, 41:38; Exo. 31:3, 35; 31; Num. 24:2; 1 Sam. 10:10, 19:20, 25; 2 Chron. 15:1, 24:20; Job 33:4; Ezek. 11:24). (2) "The Spirit of Jehovah" (Judg. 3:10; 6:34, 11·29, 13:25; 14:6, 19; 15:14; 1 Sam. 10:6, 16:13, 14; 2 Sam. 23:2; 1 Ki. 18:12, 22:24; 2 Ki. 11:16; 2 Chron. 18:23, 20:14; Isa. 11:2, 63:14; Ezek. 11:5; 37:1; Micah 2:7, 3:8). (3) "The Spirit of the Lord Jehovah" (Isa. 61:1). (4) "Good Spirit" (Neh. 9:20). (5) "Holy Spirit" (Psa. 51:11; Isa. 63:10, 11). (6) "Spirit of wisdom" (Exo. 28:3, Deut. 34:9). Cf. Isa. 11:2—"The Spirit of Jehovah . . . the spirit of wisdom and understanding, the spirit of counsel and might, the spirit of knowledge and of the fear of Jehovah" (the *sevenfold* or perfect Spirit).

The designations given by the Spirit to Himself in the New Testament are classified by Cumming as follows:[1]

1. Those which express His relationship to the Father: (1) "The Spirit of God" (Matt. 3:16). (2) "The Spirit of the Lord" (Luke 4:18; here evidently of the Father. Acts 5:9, 8:39; in these passages the term "Lord" probably has reference to Christ). (3) "The Spirit of our God" (1 Cor. 6:11). (4) "The Spirit of the living God" (2 Cor. 3:3). (5) "The Spirit of your Father" (Matt. 10:20). (6) "The Spirit of Glory and the Spirit of God" (1 Pet. 4:14). (7) "The Promise of the Father" (Acts 1:4).

2. Those which express His relationship to the Son: (1) "The Spirit of Christ" (Rom. 8:9, 1 Pet. 1:11). (2) "The Spirit of Jesus Christ" (Phil. 1:19). (3) "The Spirit of Jesus" (Acts 16:7). (4) "The Spirit of His [God's] Son" (Gal. 4:6). (5) "Paraclete" or "Comforter" (John 14:16). This last designation describes the special relationship of the Holy Spirit to the Apostles of Christ.

3. Those signifying His own essential deity: (1) "One Spirit"

---

1. Cumming, *op. cit.*, 48-50.

(Eph. 4:4). (2) "Seven Spirits" (the Perfect Spirit, Rev. 1:4; 3:1). (3) "The Lord the Spirit" (2 Cor. 3:18). (4) "The Eternal Spirit" (Heb. 9:14).

4. Those which express His spiritual attributes: (1) "Holy Spirit" (Matt. 1:18, 28:19, etc.). (2) "The Holy One" (1 John 2:20).

5. Those which express the gifts that He bestows: (1) "The Spirit of Life" (Rom. 8:2). (2) "The Spirit of Holiness" (Rom. 1:4). (3) "Spirit of Wisdom" (Eph. 1:4). (Cf. Isa. 11:2.) (4) "The Spirit of Faith" (2 Cor. 4:13). (5) "The Spirit of Truth" (John 14:17, 16:13). (6) "The Spirit of Grace" (Heb. 10:29; cf. Zech. 12:10: "the Spirit of Grace and of Supplication"). (7) "The Spirit of Adoption" (Rom. 8:15). (8) "Spirit of Glory" (1 Pet. 4:14).

There are numerous Scriptures which identify the Holy Spirit of the New Testament with the Spirit of God of the Old. For instance, in Luke 4:18-19, Jesus is represented as quoting a prominent Old Testament prophecy as follows: "The Spirit of the Lord is upon me, because he anointed me to preach good tidings to the poor: He hath sent me to proclaim release to the captives, and recovering of sight to the blind, to set at liberty them that are bruised, to proclaim the acceptable year of the Lord." This is the passage from Isa. 61:1-2, in which practically the same words are attributed to "the Spirit of the Lord Jehovah." Again, by correlating Acts 2:17-21 and the second chapter of Joel, we find that the Spirit who inspired Joel's prophecy and the Spirit who inspired Peter's sermon on the day of Pentecost were one and the same Spirit. Again, in Matt. 22:43, Jesus says, "How then doth David in the Spirit call him Lord, saying, The Lord said unto my Lord," etc., quoting from Psalm 110:1, where David, under the inspiration of the Spirit, said: "Jehovah saith unto my Lord, Sit thou at my right hand until I make thine enemies thy footstool." Also, in Acts 4:25, we read (the words of the apostolic "company" in Jerusalem uttered in prayer) . . . who by the Holy Spirit, by the mouth of our father David thy servant, didst say," etc., and the quotation that immediately follows is from Psalm 2:1-2. Again, in Acts 1:16, the Apostle Peter is represented as saying, "Brethren, it was needful that the scripture should be fulfilled, which the Holy Spirit spake before by the mouth of David concerning Judas," etc. The passages immediately quoted are from the Psalms of David 69:25 and 109:8). And in Heb. 3:7 ff., we read: "Wherefore, even as the Holy Spirit saith, Today if ye shall hear his voice, harden not your hearts," etc. The passage quoted here is from Psalm 95: 7 ff. Referring back to the Old Testament regarding David's inspiration, we read in 1 Sam. 16: 13: "Then Samuel took the horn of oil, and anointed him in the midst of his brethren; and the Spirit of Jehovah came mightily upon David from that day forward." And we find David himself saying, 2 Sam. 23: 2, "The Spirit of Jehovah spake by me, and his word was upon my tongue." *These various passages definitely identify the Holy Spirit of the New Testament with the Spirit of Jehovah of the Old.* Finally, in this connection, we read, 2 Pet. 1: 21, "For no prophecy ever came by the will of man; but men spake from God, being moved by the Holy Spirit." But in 1 Pet. 1: 10-11, we are told that the Spirit who inspired the Hebrew prophets was the Spirit of Christ: "Concerning which salvation the prophets sought and searched diligently, who prophesied of the grace that should come unto you: searching what time or what manner of time the Spirit of Christ which was in them did point unto, when it testified beforehand the sufferings of Christ, and the glories that should follow them." Thus by the correlation of pertinent Scriptures we have positive proof that the Spirit of Jehovah, the Spirit of Christ, and the Holy Spirit, are designations of one and the same Spirit, the Eternal Spirit (Heb. 9: 14).

## 2. Significance of Certain Names of the Spirit

Undoubtedly the Holy Spirit, as the Author of Revelation, encountered difficulties in making His ways, and the ways of the Godhead in general, intelligible to men. We may reasonably suppose, it seems to me, that this revelation necssitated (1) that spiritual concepts, concepts denoting spiritual realities, be communicated in spiritual terms (cf. 1 Cor. 2:13—"combining spiritual things with spiritual words"); and (2) that they be communicated in the language or languages extant at the time the revelation was given. Now the paucity of ancient languages as vehicles of such spiritual communication must have been a formidable barrier to the Spirit's accomplishment of His task. A word was needed, for example, to signify the metaphysical aspect of the Spirit. But there was none. Today of course we have the terms "person" and "personality." Another word was needed to signify the ethical aspect of the Spirit's being and activity. But again, no such word was available, at least no such word that was clean of the taint of ceremonial connotation. Is it to be wondered at, then, that the Spirit resorted to symbol, metaphor, poetic imagery, and even anthropomorphism, to embody His revelation in terms of human comprehension?

Despite these facts, however, the nomenclature employed by the Spirit in the Bible to describe His being and His operations, and the operations of the Godhead in general, is both interesting and revealing. A brief survey of this nomenclature, at this point in our study, will be helpful to our understanding of the Biblical doctrine of the Spirit as a whole. Such a survey begins logically with an examination of the import of the names and titles which the Holy Spirit gives to Himself, as follows:

1. *"The Spirit."* The Hebrew word *ruach* occurs 400 times in the Old Testament, and is rendered "spirit" 240 times, "breath" 28 times, "wind" 95 times, "mind" 6 times, and in eighteen different ways in the remaining instances of its occurrence. The Greek word *pneuma* is used by the inspired writers of the New Testament as the equivalent in meaning of the Hebrew *ruach*. *Pneuma* occurs 385 times in the New Testament, and is the only word rendered "spirit." (These figures are given by Benjamin Wilson, in Alphabetical Index to *The Emphatic Diaglott,* under "Spirit.") (*Anemos* is the word commonly used for "wind" in the New Testament; *pnoē* is used in Acts 2:2—"the rushing of a mighty wind.") Both *ruach* and *pneuma* signify wind (air in motion) or breath; that is, something that moves (energizes, vitalizes) and is not seen. Because air is a most powerful, though subtle and invisible agent, it is used in Scripture, metaphorically, for a variety of things which cannot be sense-perceived. *Ruach* rendered "spirit," is also used (but rather loosely) to indicate (1) the life principle—"animal soul"—of a brute, referring of course to a brute's conscious life (Eccl. 3:21); (2) any incorporeal (but probably ethereal) substance, as opposed to flesh or corporeal substance (Isa. 31:3, 1 Ki. 22:21-23); (3) most frequently the life principle—"rational soul"—in man (Psa. 31:5, Job 32:8, etc.); (4) a passion, or motion, of the inner man (Mal. 2:15-16, Isa. 19:14). The metaphorical significance of wind and breath in relation to the essence, nature and operations of the Spirit of God will be fully discussed in the succeeding section.

The name "Spirit" is peculiarly and constantly ascribed in Scripture to the Third Person of the Trinity. As Dr. John Owen writes:

> It declares his special Manner and Order of existence, so that wherever the Holy Spirit is mentioned, his relation to the Father and Son is included; for he is the Spirit of God. And herein is an allusion to the breath of man; for as the vital breath of man has a continual

emanation from him, and yet is never so utterly separated from his person as to forsake him; so the Spirit of the Father and the Son proceedeth from them by a continual divine emanation, still abiding one with them. Hence our Savior signified the communication of the Spirit to his disciples by breathing on them (John 20:22).[1]

## 2. *"The Spirit of God," "The Spirit of Jehovah." Ruach Elohim*: Spirit of God.

Spirit of Jehovah: literally, Spirit of Yahweh. These two names are characteristic of the Old Testament especially, although their equivalent occurs in the New (*e.g.,* Matt. 3:16, *to pneuma tou theou, theos* being the Greek equivalent for "God"; also 1 Cor. 6:11, 2 Cor. 3:3, 1 Pet. 4:14). *Elohim* is the plural form in Hebrew; hence, this name is probably used, as, for example, in designating the God of the Creation (Gen. 1:1), to intimate the triune personality of God. As Delitzsch puts it: "The *Trinitas* is the plurality of Elohim which becomes manifest in the New Testament."[2] The name *Jehovah* (*Yahweh*), on the other hand, would seem to designate God in His unity or uniqueness. In fact, the name *Elohim* seems to be used generally throughout the Old Testament to designate God as the Creator and Sovereign of the universe, whereas *Jehovah* is the name employed to indicate His Uniqueness, Personality, Benevolence, Saviorhood. Commenting on this use of the two Divine Names in the Old Testament, on the basis of which some very fantastic critical theories of the Old Testament text have been evolved, J. P. Lange says:

Although there is much in Genesis in favor of the distinction of Elohistic and Jehovistic records, yet the fact made prominent by Hengstenberg and others cannot be denied, viz., that the names Elohim and Jehovah are throughout so distinguished, that the one prevails in those passages which speak of the general relation of God to the world, the other in those in which the theocratic relation of God to his people and kingdom rises into prominence. This contrast, embraced by the unity of the consciousness of faith in revelation, not only runs through the Pentateuch, but appears in a marked form in the opposition between the general doctrine of wisdom as viewed by Solomon, and the Davidic theocratic doctrine of the Messiah. It pervades the Old Testament Apocrypha, in the New Testament celebrates its transfiguration in the contrast between the Gospel of John, his doctrine of the Logos on the one side, and the synoptical and Petrino-Pauline view on the other; and finally, in the opposition between the Christian and ecclesiastical dogmatism, and the Christian and social humanitarianism, runs through the history of the church, manifesting itself in the Reformation through the twin forms, Luther and Melanchthon, Calvin and Zwingli.[3]

1. John Owen, *A Discourse Concerning the Holy Spirit*, abridged by George Burder, 34-35.
2. *Vide* Delitzsch, *Genesis*, 66 ff.
3. John Peter Lange, Introduction to the Old Testament, *Genesis*, 33. Translated by Lewis and Gosman. *Critical, Doctrinal and Homiletical Commentary on the Holy Scriptures*, Vol. 1 of the Old Testament. Fifth Edition Revised.

## Again:

We assume that Elohim relates to the circumferential revelation of God in the world and its powers (Isa. 40:28), as Jehovah relates to the central revelation of God in Christ. . . . We repeat it: The pure and harmonious contrast of Elohim and Jehovah will be recognized only in the contrast of the universalistic and the theocratic revelation of God and idea of religion,—only in the combination of Melchisedek and Abraham, of human culture and theocracy, civilization and church-dom (not civilization and Christianity, because Christianity embraces both, just as the religious consciousness of faith in the Old Covenant.)[1]

### On the same point, Delitzsch comments:

The creation is the beginning and the completion of everything created, according to its idea, is the end. The kingdom of power is to become the kingdom of glory. In the midst lies the kingdom of grace, whose essential content is the redemption. Jehovah is the God who mediates between middle and end in the course of this history, in one word, the Redeemer.[2]

Thus the name *Jehovah* is commonly employed by the inspired writers in those passages in which God is represented as dealing with His creatures in acts of goodness, mercy or judgment; indeed some scholars are inclined to think that the name signifies in particular the Second Person of the Trinity. In some Old Testament passages the two names are combined, as *Yahweh Elohim,* (as in Gen. 2:7, the more detailed account of the creation of man); the combined name probably signifies the joint exercise of omnipotence and benevolence. In any case, however, that is, regardless of the name used for the Deity, the Spirit is the Spirit of the living God (2 Cor. 3:3). Moreover, as we have seen already, the Scriptures explicitly identify the Spirit of God of the Old Testament with the Holy Spirit of the New.

3. *The "Good Spirit" of God.* Neh. 9:20—"Thou gavest also thy good Spirit to instruct them." Psa. 143:10—"Teach me to do thy will; For thou art my God: Thy Spirit is good" (marginal rendering: "Let thy good Spirit lead me"). The Spirit is so called because He is essentially good, and because His operations are all good as to design and productive only of good effects in believers.

4. *"The Spirit of God's Son," "The Spirit of Christ," "The Spirit of Jesus," "The Spirit of Jesus Christ."* By correlating such passages as Gal. 4:6, Rom. 8:9-11, 1 Pet. 1:10-12, Acts 16:6-8, Phil. 1:19, etc., we find that the Holy Spirit and the Spirit of Christ are one and the same Spirit. (1) He is not

1. *Op. cit.,* 112.
2. Delitzsch, *Genesis,* 66 ff.

369

called the Spirit of Christ, however, because God the Father anointed Jesus of Nazareth "with the Holy Spirit and with power" (Acts 10:38) on the occasion of the baptismal scene at the Jordan River (Matt. 3:16-17, Luke 3:21-22). On the contrary, He was antecedently, in fact from all eternity, the Spirit of Christ. In 1 Pet. 1:10-12, we are told that it was the Spirit of Christ who inspired the Hebrew Prophets to utter their Messianic predictions. But Christ's human nature did not yet exist, i.e., in the time of the Prophets. We must conclude, therefore, that it was only the human nature of Christ which received the Divine anointing with the Holy Spirit at the Jordan River. The Holy Spirit is *eternally* the Spirit of the Son (Logos) as well as of the Father. (2) He is called the Spirit of Christ because, since the return of the Son to the Father, He, the Spirit, proceeds from the Son also.

John 14:16, 17—I will pray the Father, and he shall give you another Comforter . . . even the Spirit of truth, etc. John 14:26—But the Comforter, even the Holy Spirit, whom the Father will send in my name, etc. John 15:26—But when the Comforter is come, whom I will send unto you from the Father, even the Spirit of truth, which proceedeth from the Father, etc. Luke 24:49—Behold, I send the promise of my Father upon you.

These statements were all addressed by Jesus to those men who were to be qualified for the apostleship. Hence we read in John 20:22, that just before His ascension to the Father, "he breathed on them, and saith unto them, Receive ye the Holy Spirit,"—a symbolic act which received its fulfilment on the Day of Pentecost following (Acts 2:1-4). This breathing upon them by Jesus certainly signified that the Spirit, in coming upon them to clothe them with infallibility and authority, was to proceed from the Son as well as from the Father. The Promise of the Father was of course the Holy Spirit Himself. (3) He is called the Spirit of Christ, because He was sent by the Son to effectuate, in the hearts and lives of the saints, the latter's work of mediation.

John 16:14—He shall glorify me; for he shall take of mine, and shall declare it unto you. Acts 1:8—Ye shall receive power, when the Holy Spirit is come upon you; and ye shall be my witnesses both in Jerusalem, and in all Judea and Samaria, and unto the uttermost part of the earth. John 16:7, 8—It is expedient for you that I go away; for if I go not away, the Comforter will not come unto you; but if I go, I will send him unto you. And he, when he is come, will convict the world of sin, and of righteousness, and of judgment. 1 Cor. 6:11— But ye were washed, but ye were sanctified, but ye were justified in the name of the Lord Jesus Christ, and in the Spirit of our God. 2 Cor. 3:17, 18—Now the Lord is the Spirit: and where the Spirit of the

Lord is, there is liberty. But we all, with unveiled face beholding as in a mirror the glory of the Lord, are transformed into the same image from glory to glory, even as from the Lord the Spirit. 2 Thess. 2:13—God chose you from the beginning unto salvation, in sanctification of the Spirit and belief of the truth. 1 Pet. 1:2—elect . . . according to the foreknowledge of God the Father, in sanctification of the Spirit, unto obedience and sprinkling of the blood of Jesus Christ. [Cf. the words of Jesus] John 6:63—the words that I have spoken unto you are spirit, and are life.

(4) He is called the Spirit of Christ, because He acts as the Agent of Christ, the Head of the Church, throughout the present dispensation. This is the Dispensation of the Spirit. God dwells in the Church, His sanctuary, in the Person of the Spirit (Eph. 2:22); and Christ, as Head of the Church, administers its affairs through the agency of the Spirit. The Communion of the Spirit (2 Cor. 13:14) is the bond of our fellowship with both the Father and the Son (1 John 1:3). The Spirit who indwells every member of the Body is the Holy Spirit (1 Cor. 6:19), the Spirit of Christ (Rom. 8:9).

5. *"The Power of the Most High."* The Spirit is so called to denote His efficacy as the Agent of the Godhead; He exerts the power of the Most High as His own power; He is the Spirit of Power.

Luke 1:35 [the words of the Angel Gabriel to the Virgin]: The Holy Spirit shall come upon thee, and the power of the Most High shall overshadow thee; wherefore also the holy thing which is begotten shall be called the Son of God. [This power is exerted, however, through means, and the means is the Word. Hence the Angel's closing statement]: For no word from God shall be void of power. Cf. Rom. 15:13, 18— Now the God of hope fill you with all joy and peace in believing, that ye may abound in hope, in the power of the Holy Spirit . . . For I will not dare to speak of any things save those which Christ wrought through me, for the obedience of the Gentiles, by word and deed, in the power of signs and wonders, in the power of the Holy Spirit.

6. *"Paraclete."* This name is used only four times in the New Testament (never in the Old), and all four times to designate the Holy Spirit; and it is used all four times by Jesus Himself in His discourses to the Eleven as recorded in the fourteenth, fifteenth and sixteenth chapters of John's Gospel. The name designates—and describes—only the relationships sustained by the Spirit to the Apostles. To the Apostles He was Advocate, Companion, Comforter, Monitor, Guide, etc.; the term Paraclete seems to embrace all these meanings.

7. *"The Holy Spirit."* This designation, occurring rarely in the Old Testament, prevails throughout the New Testament. (1) There are some actions wrought upon men, by God's sufferance, by evil spirits whose personalities and acts are opposed

371

to the Spirit of God. 1 Samuel 16:14, 15—"Now the Spirit of Jehovah departed from Saul, and an evil spirit from Jehovah troubled him. And Saul's servants said unto him, Behold now, an evil spirit from God troubleth thee," etc. (cf. 1 Sam. 16:23, 18:10, 19:9, etc.). This does not mean that the evil spirit emanated from God, but that it was commissioned by Him to punish and terrify Saul, and thus perchance to lead him to repentance. The Spirit of Jehovah having withdrawn from him those influences whereby he was commissioned for his kingly office, and as a result of which he had been temporarily a changed man (cf. 1 Sam. 10:6-9), the evil spirit came upon him out of his own melancholy and out of his distempered mind and body, to excite discontent, a sense of guilt, and terrifying apprehension. This, however, was but an execution of the righteous judgment of God; it was an example of the manner in which God can make use of evil agents to His own glory. In similar manner, a Watcher and a Holy One from heaven smote King Nebuchadnezzar with madness (Dan. 4:13-18, 28-33). (2) The Spirit of God is the antithesis of every unclean or unholy spirit. Mark 3:29, 30—Jesus, to the scribes: "But whosoever shall blaspheme against the Holy Spirit hath never forgiveness, but is guilty of an eternal sin: because they [the scribes] said, He hath an unclean spirit." (3) God is described, in virtue of the glorious perfection or wholeness of His nature, as "The Holy One" (Isa. 40:25, 43:15); "The Holy One of Israel" (2 Ki. 19:22); "Glorious in Holiness" (Exo. 15:11); "Holy, Holy, Holy" (Isa. 6:3); "The High and Lofty One that inhabiteth eternity, whose name is Holy" (Isa. 57:15). Cf. Lev. 19:2—"I Jehovah your God am holy." In like manner, the Spirit is called Holy, to describe the eternal glorious Holiness of His nature. (4) The Spirit is so designated also with reference to His operations, all of which are holy (that is, directed toward the perfection and wholeness of the creature), and especially with reference to His works of regeneration, sanctification, and immortalization. The designation points directly to the purifying and sanctifying powers of the Spirit. He is the Holy Spirit (Psa. 51:11, Isa. 63:10-11, and in many passages in the New Testament); the Spirit of Holiness (Rom. 1:4); The Holy One (1 John 2:20). And the Way of the Spirit is called The Way of Holiness (Isa. 35:8).

The name Holy Spirit is used by way of eminence. No higher revelation, no nobler conception, of God is possible. This designation occurs chiefly, therefore, in the fulness of the light of divinely revealed truth, that is, in the New Testament Scriptures. Moreover, it embraces all the other names by which the Spirit is designated in relation to His various gifts and enduements, viz., "The Spirit of Truth," "The Spirit of Wisdom," "The Spirit of Faith," "The Spirit of Grace," "The Spirit of Life," "The Spirit of Adoption," "The Spirit of Power," and "The Spirit of Glory." These various names and titles will be elaborated, in their proper contexts, in our subsequent work. They designate the activities of the Spirit in connection with the New, rather than with the Old, Creation.

### 3. Symbols and Metaphors of the Spirit

Scripture types, symbols, and metaphors of the Spirit are especially meaningful. They give us deeper insight into His nature and operations than mere language alone could possibly convey. Moreover, we must remember that these symbols and metaphors were selected by the Spirit Himself, largely because of the inadequacy of words, to make as intelligible to us as possible the nature of the Divine Being and the modes of His activities. Among the more significant of these symbols and metaphors of the Spirit, descriptive of His nature and operations, are the following:

1. *Breath.* (1) The metaphor of *breath* suggests primarily the Spirit's mode of subsistence. He is the Breath of God in the sense that, as the breath has a continual emanation from man yet is never organically separated from him, so the Spirit proceeds from God by a continual Divine emanation and yet still abides one with God. (2) This metaphor also designates the Spirit as the Author and Source of Life. Among the ancients, breath denoted the life principle in man; as long as a man breathes, he is alive; when he ceases to breathe, he dies. In like manner, the entrance of the Spirit, as the Breath of God, signifies life or union with God, and the departure of the Spirit signifies death or loss of God. Cf. Gen. 7:22—"all in whose nostrils was the breath [i.e., *neshamah*, the bodily breath] of the spirit [*ruach*] of life, of all that was on the dry land, died." Also Isa. 42:5—"Thus saith God Jehovah, he that created the heavens, and stretched them forth; he that spread abroad the earth and that which cometh out of it; he that giveth breath [*neshamah*] unto the people upon it, and spirit [*ruach*] to them that walk therein." In these passages, the bodily breath is explicitly connected with the "spirit of life," and the "spirit of life" is the Spirit of the *living* God, or at least an emanation

from the Spirit of the living God. (3) Thus it will be seen that this metaphor of *breath* suggests also the effects of the Spirit's operations, in His giving of life and breath to all creatures (Acts 17:25); every form of life is, as we have seen, a gift of the Divine Spirit. Thus the original impartation of all the potentialities of personal life to man is described in Scripture as a Divine inbreathing. Gen. 2:7—"And Jehovah God formed man of the dust of the ground, and breathed into his nostrils the breath of life; and man became a *living soul.*" Here we have a graphic picture of the Almighty stooping down and placing His lips and nostrils upon the lips and nostrils of the lifeless body He had just created, and expelling into it *life*—personal life—from His own Being. Anthropomorphic, of course. But where in all ancient literature can be found such an exalted conception,—indeed it must have been a *revelation*, namely, that the River of Life, of the personal life which we ourselves enjoy, has its source in the Being of our God, from whom and by whose Spirit first life was breathed into man at his creation?

Cf. Rev. 22:1—And he showed me a river of water of life, bright as crystal, proceeding out of the throne of God and of the Lamb. Gen. 1:27—And God created man in his own image, in the image of God created he him; male and female created he them. Job 27:3—For my life is yet whole in me, and the spirit of God is in my nostrils. Job 32:8—But there is a spirit in man, and the breath of the Almighty giveth them understanding. [As the entrance of the Spirit brings life, so the departure of the Spirit means death.] Gen. 6:3—My Spirit shall not strive with man for ever, for that he also is flesh. 1 Sam. 16:14—Now the Spirit of Jehovah departed from Saul, and an evil spirit from Jehovah troubled him. [The departure of the Spirit marked the beginning of Saul's downward plunge, ending in suicide.] (4) John 20:21-23: The disciples therefore were glad when they saw the Lord. Jesus therefore said to them again, Peace be unto you; as the Father hath sent me, even so send I you. And when he had said this, he breathed on them, and saith unto them, Receive ye the Holy Spirit: whose soever sins ye forgive, they are forgiven unto them; whose soever sins ye retain, they are retained.

In this manner, Jesus, just before His ascension to the Father, *symbolically* indicated the coming of the Holy Spirit upon the Apostles to qualify them with His own infallibility and authority. The actual advent of the Spirit took place of course a few days later, on the Day of Pentecost (Acts 2:1-4). Moreover, this advent of the Spirit upon the Apostles on the Day of Pentecost marked the beginning of the New Creation, the new spiritual life in Christ enjoyed by all the saints of God. The Church, the Body of Christ, vitalized by the indwelling Spirit, is God's sanctuary throughout the present dispensation (Eph. 2:22). And finally, the communion or "sharing together"

374

of the enduements of the Spirit, by the saints, is the bond of their union with God through Christ, hence the earnest of their enjoyment of spiritual life.

1 John 5:12—He that hath the Son hath the life; he that hath not the Son of God hath not the life. Rom. 8:2—For the law of the Spirit of life in Christ Jesus made me free from the law of sin and of death. Eph. 1:20-22: Christ Jesus Himself being the chief corner stone, in whom each several building, fitly framed together, groweth into a holy temple in the Lord; in whom ye also are builded together for a habitation of God in the Spirit. 2 Cor. 1:22—God, who also sealed us, and gave us the earnest of the Spirit in our hearts. 2 Cor. 5:5—Now he that wrought us for this very thing [immortality] is God, who gave us the earnest of the Spirit. Eph. 1:13, 14—in whom [Christ], having also believed, ye were sealed with the Holy Spirit of promise, which is an earnest of our inheritance, unto the redemption of God's own possession, unto the praise of his glory.

*The Breath of God is the source of every form of life in the universe—corporeal, personal, spiritual, eternal.* (5) Finally, this metaphor of *breath* suggests the intimate union existing between the activity of the Spirit and that of the Word: as words accompany the breath from the mouth of man, so the Word accompanies the Spirit from the Being of God. His Spirit and His Word go together; or, to speak more precisely, the Spirit operates through the instrumentality of the Word.

Acts 9:1—Saul, yet breathing threatening and slaughter against the disciples of the Lord, went unto the high priest, etc. [How did Saul *breathe* threatening and slaughter against the disciples? Through words, of course. Thought is communicated by persons through the medium of words.] Psa. 33:6, 9—By the word of Jehovah were the heavens made, and all the host of them by the breath of his mouth. . . . For he spake, and it was done; he commanded, and it stood fast. Heb. 11:3—By faith we understand that the worlds have been framed by the word of God, so that what is seen hath not been made out of things which appear.

Spirit-power of God is in the Word. The expulsion of the Divine Word, revealing the Divine Will, resulted in the physical creation. Thoughts are indeed things. Moreover, as it was with respect to the Old or Physical Creation, so it is with respect to the New Spiritual Creation: the Spirit operates (breathes) through the Word in the begetting of spiritual life. The Gospel is "the power of God unto salvation to every one that believeth" (Rom. 1:16), because the Spirit is in it and operates through it.

Luke 8:11—The seed [of the Kingdom] is the word of God. 1 Pet. 1:23—having been begotten again, not of corruptible seed, but of incorruptible, through the word of God, which liveth and abideth. Jas. 1:18—Of his own will he brought us forth by the word of truth. Cf. the words of Jesus, John 6:63—It is the spirit that giveth life; the flesh profiteth nothing: the words that I have spoken unto you are spirit, and are life. Jas. 1:21—receive with meekness the implanted word, which is able to save your souls.

Finally, *the* communication by the Spirit of Divine thoughts and words to chosen instrumentalities, and through them to all mankind, is described under the same general metaphor. Inspired literature is *God-breathed* literature. Inspiration and consequent revelation are primarily works of the Spirit of God (cf. 1 Cor. 2:9-15).

2. *Wind.* (1) This metaphor of wind or air in motion is descriptive primarily of the Spirit's nature or essence as a pure spiritual or immaterial being. So it is said of God, John 4:24, that He is a Spirit, *i.e.*, of a pure spiritual or immaterial nature, not confined to place, nor regarding any one person or people more than another in His worship, the truth which Jesus especially designs to evince to us in this particular text. (2) This metaphor is also descriptive of the operations of the Spirit which in so many respects resemble those of the wind in the physical world. Wind may come in an onrush, with the impact of a tornado, or it may come in a gentle breeze; so the activity of the Spirit may take the form of an invasive energy (as in Ezek. 37:1-10, Acts 2:1-4), or it may take the form of a gentle vivifying and purifying influence. This general idea may be what Jesus designs to teach in John 3:8 (granting of course that the passage is correctly translated in the recognized versions, which I doubt very much): "The wind bloweth where it will, and thou hearest the voice thereof, but knowest not whence it cometh, and whither it goeth: so is every one that is born of the Spirit." Here we have a parallelism, if this rendering be correct, between the unknown ways of the wind and the unknown points of application to the human spirit of the mighty energy of the living God. The sound of wind in the trees or against barriers, and other effects that the rapid motions of the air produces, provides a lively metaphor of the mysterious working, breathing of the Divine Spirit, whose "voice" or "word" may be heard, whose effects are present to our sense and consciousness, but the beginnings and endings of which are always lost in God. That is to say, the mode of the Spirit's operation in the spiritual world— upon the minds and hearts of men—is best represented by that of the air or wind in the physical world, the principal point of resemblance being that both operations are manifest primarily, not in *themselves* (that is, not in the coming and going of either Spirit or wind), but in their *effects*. (3) The Spirit's advent on the Day of Pentecost was manifested outwardly by "a sound

as of the rushing of a mighty wind" and by "tongues parting asunder, like as of fire" (Acts 2:1-4). These were evidential manifestations which could be *seen* and *heard* by the people of Jerusalem, as Peter explicitly stated in his sermon on that occasion (Acts 2:33). This entire divine demonstration was metaphorical, of course, of the coming of the Spirit and the Word— or rather, of the Spirit *with* the Word—upon the Apostles in baptismal or overwhelming measure: they were all "filled with the Holy Spirit" (*i.e.,* completely *overwhelmed,* or to speak by way of analogy, *hypnotized,* by Him), and "began to speak with other tongues, as the Spirit gave them utterance" (Acts 2:4). They were completely under the power of the Spirit, even as a subject is under the mental power of a hypnotist; and they spake only the words *suggested* to them by the Spirit. This coming of the Spirit on Pentecost in invasive power is reminiscent of the coming of the wind in a great onrush into the Valley of Dry Bones, in Ezekiel's Vision (Ezek. 37:1-10). Generally speaking, however, the Spirit operates, as in regeneration and in sanctification, with the quietness, yet all-pervasiveness of the atmosphere by which we are surrounded all the time, and which we inbreathe as essential to our physical life. Cf. Zech. 4:6—"Not by might, nor by power, but by my Spirit, saith Jehovah of hosts." Cf. also the experience of Elijah, 1 Ki. 19:9-14: Jehovah was neither in the strong wind nor in the earthquake nor in the fire, but in "a still small voice." (4) To carry on the metaphor, As the air around us is necessary to our physical life, so the Spirit is necessary to our life spiritually. We cannot grow physically without air, nor can we grow spiritually without the Spirit. When we cease to breathe, we die; and when we yield up the (natural) spirit within us, the body dies (cf. Luke 23:46, John 19:30). And when we quench the Spirit, our spirits die; we separate ourselves from God; this is the second death (1 Thess. 5:19, Rev. 21:8). Nicodemus was inclined to look upon spiritual birth as something unexplainable, even inconceivable. Not so, said Jesus in substance; the Spirit's workings are no more mysterious than the operations of the wind in the world of nature around us. The wind of course is not under our direction nor at our disposal; neither is the Spirit. *There is scarcely any limit to the application of this remarkable metaphor.* In the light of these truths, what infinite wisdom the Spirit Himself manifested in representing Himself and His operations to us under the Hebrew and Greek words, *ruach* and *pneuma* respectively! (See special note on John 3:8 at the end of this part)

3. *The Dove.* (1) Matt. 3:16, 17—"And Jesus, when he was baptized, went up straightway from the water: and lo, the heavens were opened unto him, and he saw the Spirit of God descending as a dove, and coming upon him; and lo, a voice out of the heavens, saying, This is my beloved Son, in whom I am well pleased." The language here (and in Mark's account also, Mark 1:10-11, which parallels that of Matthew) is somewhat ambiguous. The phrase, "the Spirit of God descending as a dove and coming upon him" (Mark 1:10—"the Spirit as a dove descending upon him") may have reference to the *form* in which the Spirit made His appearance, or it may have reference to the *manner* of the Spirit's descending, that is, as a dove descends gently upon her nest. Fortunately, Luke throws some additional light on this problem in his account of the incident: "The Holy Spirit," he says, "descended in a bodily form, as a dove, upon him." (*Vide* Luke 3:21, 22). Thus, in the light of this additional bit of information, the language of the Synoptic biographers in describing this incident would seem to have a double meaning, namely, (1) that the Spirit descended, not in the form of a real dove, but in a luminous (shall we say *ectoplasmic?*) configuration resembling the form of a dove; and (2) that He descended not only in this dove-like form but also in the gentle manner in which a dove descends upon her nest. Moreover, in the Fourth Gospel, we have the further testimony of John the Baptizer, that the Spirit not only descended upon Jesus, but also *abode* upon Him. John 1:32-34: "And John bare witness, saying, I have beheld the Spirit descending as a dove out of heaven; and it abode upon him. And I knew him not: but he that sent me to baptize in water, he said unto me, Upon whomsoever thou shalt see the Spirit descending, and abiding upon him, the same is he that baptizeth in the Holy Spirit. And I have seen, and have borne witness that this is the Son of God." (Cf. Luke 3:2—"In the high priesthood of Annas and Caiaphas, the word of God came unto John the son of Zacharias in the wilderness.") In any case, this radiant glorious Form both Jesus and John saw descending out of heaven, then, bird-like, sinking, hovering, brooding over the Head of the Sinless One, and then alighting, as it were, upon Him and *abiding* there. In all probability, in likening to a dove this cloud of glory descending through the clear heaven and abiding upon the head of the baptized Jesus, John was recalling the rabbinical comment (in the Talmud) on Gen. 1:2, "The Spirit of God like a dove brooded over the waters." "It was not a real

dove," writes John Owen, "that appeared, but some ethereal substance, something of a fiery nature, I conceive, in the form of a dove; and this rendered the appearance more visible, heavenly and glorious."[1] Moreover, the motions of a dove—those of whirling, hovering, fluttering, settling down—make the symbolism of this incident all the more vivid.

(2) It should be noted, too, that the New Testament writers are unanimous in affirming expressly that the heavens were opened to make way for the descent of this dove-like Form, the visible symbol of the procession of the Spirit from the Being of God. Cf. John 15:26—"But when the Comforter is come, whom I will send unto you from the Father, even the Spirit of truth, which proceedeth from the Father," etc.

(3) This manifestation of the Spirit, under the emblem of a dove or dove-like form, was the anointing of Jesus to His holy offices of Prophet, Priest, and King. (Only His human nature was thus anointed, however.) This was an official act of the government of Heaven: it was God Himself who thus anointed His Son "with the Holy Spirit and with power" (Acts 10:38). Hence, we read that, immediately following the Baptism and Temptation, Jesus inaugurated His earthly ministry in Galilee.

And Jesus returned in the power of the Spirit into Galilee; and a fame went out concerning him through all the region round about. And he taught in their synagogues, being glorified of all. And he came to Nazareth, where he had been brought up; and he entered, as his custom was, into the synagogue on the sabbath day, and stood up to read. And there was delivered unto him the book of the prophet Isaiah. And he opened the book, and found the place where it was written, The Spirit of the Lord is upon me, Because he anointed me to preach good tidings to the poor; He hath sent me to proclaim release to the captives, And recovering of sight to the blind, To set at liberty them that are bruised, To proclaim the acceptable year of the Lord. And he closed the book, and gave it back to the attendant, and sat down: and the eyes of all in the synagogue were fastened on him. And he began to say unto them, To-day hath this scripture been fulfilled in your ears. [Luke 4:14-21; cf. Isa. 61:1 ff.].

Thus it will be seen that Jesus explicitly interpreted the language of Isaiah as having reference to Himself, the Messiah.

(4) This descent of the Spirit in a dove-like form upon Jesus at His baptism points back (a) to the Spirit's "overshadowing" of the Virgin at His Incarnation (Luke 1:35), and (2) to the Spirit's brooding over the primordial Chaos at the beginning of the Creation. Cf. Gen. 1:2—"And the earth was waste and void; and darkness was upon the face of the deep;

1. John Owen, *op. cit.*, 46.

379

and the Spirit of God was brooding upon the face of the waters."
As Milton has put it so vividly:

> And chiefly Thou, O Spirit, that dost prefer
> Before all temples the upright heart and pure,
> Instruct me, for Thou knowest; Thou from the first
> Wast present, and with mighty wings outspread,
> Dove-like, sat'st brooding on the vast abyss,
> And mad'st it pregnant.[1]

"As at the beginning of the old creation," writes John Owen,
"the Spirit of God moved on the waters, cherishing and communicating a prolific, vivifying quality to the whole, as a dove
gently moves upon its eggs, communicating vital heat; so at
the new creation, he comes as a dove upon him who was the
immediate author of it."[2]

(5) In the descent of the Holy Spirit in a dove-like form
upon Jesus at His baptism, there may be an allusion also to
Noah's dove. Two times the patriarch sent forth the dove from
the Ark, and two times she returned, thus signifying that the
earth was not yet fully renovated for the habitation of the
righteous (Gen. 8:8-11). But the third time the dove was
sent forth, she did not return. Gen. 8:12—"And he [Noah]
stayed yet other seven days, and sent forth the dove; and she
returned not again unto him any more." Does not this incident
teach us that as the dove, the emblem of purity, found her
proper habitat only in the renovated earth, an earth purged of
all vice and sin, so the Holy Spirit can find His proper habitat
only in the pure in heart? Matt. 5:8—"Blessed are the pure in
heart; for they shall see God."

The dove is a messenger, especially the homing pigeon. In fact,
the ability of the dove to return as a messenger to his home from
far distant places is one of the marvels of nature. Thus the dove
symbolizes to us the Spirit of God as His messenger, bringing first
to our hearts the message of eternal peace. The second time Noah
loosed the dove from the window of the ark, it returned with an olive
leaf in its beak. The olive leaf is the symbol of peace; and Noah knew
by this that the waters of judgment had abated and the dry land had
appeared. It was only after the waters of baptism had fallen from the
body of Jesus as He rose from the watery grave that the Spirit
descended as the messenger upon Him who is the Prince of Peace.
In Him, as it is symbolized by His coming forth from the waters in
Jordan, the waters of judgment have abated for all who will believe.[3]

[Again] As John describes the descent of the Spirit in the form of
a dove, he distinctly says that the Spirit is to remain as an abiding

1. John Milton, *Paradise Lost*, I.
2. John Owen, *op. cit.*, 46.
3. C. Gordon Brownville, *Symbols of the Holy Spirit*, 22, 23.

presence in Him. Referring back to the experience of Noah, we remember that when the window of the ark was opened for the third time and the dove sent forth, it did not return but went to its abiding place on the cleansed earth. Thus the Holy Spirit did not go back into heaven, but abode in Jesus in all His fulness. This fulness of the Spirit was His not only at all times in the Incarnation, but eternally; we cannot divide the Trinity or the Godhead. But here it is manifest, that we might believe and understand.[1]

Again, on Noah's dove as an emblem of the Holy Spirit, F. E. Marsh writes as follows:

Noah's dove came forth from the ark. God's Dove came from heaven. There are two thoughts suggested by this. As the dove came forth from the ark, the ark being a type of Christ, so the Holy Spirit, because of what Christ is, and has done, comes forth to the earth of man's iniquity; and to tell him of the only ark of salvation, where he can find safety and peace. The lighting of the Holy Spirit on Christ as the Dove proclaims two things, first, He could come as the Dove on the Lamb of God, for there was a correspondence between the spotlessness of God's Lamb and the gentleness of God's Dove. Second, He came upon Christ as the Dove to qualify Him for His ministry, and to act through Him in blessing to others. . . . The dove which came from the ark came to the earth to find a resting place. The Spirit came upon Christ as the Son of Man, for He Himself, in speaking of Himself as the Son of Man says: 'Him hath God the Father sealed' (John 6:27). It is not without significance that the manhood of Christ is specially mentioned when reference is made to the Spirit's coming upon Him. Earth has no sorrow that Heaven cannot cure, because Heaven has come down in the Person of Christ and the Holy Spirit to cure the sorrows of earth. The fact that the Son of God and the Holy Spirit have come into the world, proves beyond all demonstration that the Lord alone can meet the deep necessity of man. Man cannot meet the need of his fellow. Mere morality cannot satisfy the human heart. Ritualism with its gaudy trappings does not remove the ache from the heart, nor the sting from the conscience. . . . The Spirit of God comes to reveal the Christ of God, Who makes known the love of God, Who secures by His blood the forgiveness of love, the peace of Heaven and the joy unspeakable. God's Dove imparts His nature to the believer in Christ, infuses the life which ennobles and the love which inspires. None but Jesus can do helpless sinners good, and none but the Spirit can enable the sinner to trust the Christ Who can meet this need. It is His work to do this, and He delights to do it. [Again]: What were the results from the sending forth of the dove from the ark, and the coming of the Spirit upon Christ? There were three sendings forth of the dove from the ark. The first time it found no rest for the sole of its foot, and returned to the ark. Josephus says that 'the dove came back to Noah with her wings and feet all wet and muddy.' May we not take this as illustrative of the fact that in all the missions of the Spirit, from the Fall to the coming of Christ, He always had to bear testimony to man's sin and iniquity? . . . The second time the dove came back to the ark it came with an olive leaf in its mouth, which is significantly said to be 'pluckt off.' The word means, to be freshly torn from the tree. The Hebrew word *taraph* comes from a root which means to tear in pieces, and is generally used to describe the action of wild beasts in rending their prey to pieces. It is rendered 'rent in pieces' in Gen. 37:33, where Jacob takes it for granted that

1. *Op. cit.*, 23.

Joseph has been killed by a wild beast when he sees the blood-stained garments of Joseph. The same root is given 'ravening' in Psalms 22:13, where Christ speaks of the wicked who were surrounding Him like a lot of wild beasts. Rotherham translates the verse: 'They have opened wide their mouth, a lion *rending* and roaring.' Putting these Scriptures together, do they not suggest to us the thought, that as the olive leaf was torn off, and the dove bore in its mouth this emblem of peace, so the Holy Spirit bears testimony to the death of Christ, Who was 'cut off' out of the land of the living for our transgressions, and now proclaims that Christ has made peace by the blood of His cross? The third time the dove came forth from the ark it did not return. It had found a resting place. So with the Holy Spirit. He had gone to and fro from the presence of the Lord, in Old Testament times, finding no resting place, but when He beheld the One in Whom God delighted, then He rested upon Him. The first three gospels mention that the Spirit descended or lighted upon Christ; but John adds, the Spirit 'abode' upon Him. The Greek word *meno* means to dwell, and is so rendered again and again. God rested after His creative work; Christ in figure having accomplished His redemptive work, rests in the satisfaction of God (Heb. 4:10); and now the Spirit rests upon Christ, henceforth to find His permanent abode in Him. All His mission emanates from Christ, all His blessings are found in Him, all His instructions are from Him, all His ministry is toward Him, all His unfolding are about Him, all His aim is to enhance His glory, and all His working in the believer is to reproduce Him. . . . Why is the Holy Spirit given to believers? For the same reason that the dove came to Noah, and the Spirit came upon Christ. First, to assure us that for us the judgment of sin is past, for the storm has burst upon Christ and has exhausted itself upon Him. Second, to take up His abode in the mystical body of Christ through our union with the Head, and to impart His nature and infuse His grace in every part. Tennyson, in speaking of the change which comes to the dragon-fly when it emerges from its grub state, says:

> "To-day I saw the dragon-fly
> Come from the wells where he did lie.
> An inner impulse rent the veil
> Of his old husk; from head to tail
> Came out clear plates of sapphire mail.
> He dried his wings; like gauze they grew;
> Through crofts and pastures, wet with dew,
> A living flash of light, he flew."

Mark how Tennyson makes 'the inner impulse' to rend the old husk. It was the life within which brought it into the liberty and sunshine without. The same is true in the Divine life. We can only rise to the dove-like character as we have the fulness of the Dove-like Indweller.[1]

(6) Again, the dove is the symbol of purity above all things else, and in this characteristic it is especially emblematic of the Holy Spirit; for wherever the Holy Spirit operates upon, and abides in, an intelligent being, the result is always uprightness and purity of heart. The one characteristic which, above all others, the Holy Spirit produces in Christ and in all those who are united with Him, is *purity*. Hence the Church, which is made

1. F. E. Marsh, *Emblems of the Holy Spirit*, 9-14.

up of the elect of God under the new covenant, those who have been redeemed by the blood of Christ and sanctified or purified by the Holy Spirit, is frequently described in Scripture as the Bride of Christ (Eph. 5:22-33; John 3:29; Rev. 21:2, 9; Rev. 22:17), a metaphor suggesting affinity, constancy, and in particular, *purity*. And in all likelihood, it was for this very purpose of impressing this truth upon our minds, the sublime truth of the essential purity of the Bride of the Redeemer, that the Spirit inspired the Old Testament poet to speak of Her in such rapturous terms as "My dove, my undefiled!"

Song of Solomon 2:14—O my dove, that art in the clefts of the rock, In the covert of the steep place, Let me see thy countenance, Let me hear thy voice; For sweet is thy voice, and thy countenance is comely. Song of Sol. 5:2—Open to me, my sister, my love, my dove, my undefiled; For my head is filled with dew, My locks with the drops of the night. Son of Sol. 6:8, 9—There are threescore queens, and fourscore concubines, And virgins without number. My dove, my undefiled, is but one; She is the only one of her mother; She is the choice one of her that bare her. The daughters saw her, and called her blessed; Yea, the queens and the concubines, and they praised her.

There is indeed but *one* Bride of Christ, *one* Body of Christ, *one* Temple of God, *one* Household of the Faith. Eph. 4:4— There is one body, and one Spirit, etc. The Church, moreover, is the chaste Bride of Christ, She who has been purified by the indwelling Spirit and thus made ready to meet the Bridegroom at His coming.

[Hence Paul writes to the Christians at Corinth]: I am jealous over you with a godly jealousy; for I espoused you to one husband, that I might present you as a pure virgin to Christ (2 Cor. 11:2). Rev. 21:2—And I saw the holy city, new Jerusalem, coming down out of heaven from God, made ready as a bride adorned for her husband. [Purity, of course, is equivalent to wholeness or holiness.] 1 Pet. 2:5— Ye also, as living stones, are built up a spiritual house, to be a holy priesthood, to offer up spiritual sacrifices, acceptable to God through Jesus Christ. Col. 3:12—Put on therefore, as God's elect, holy and beloved, a heart of compassion, kindness, lowliness, meekness, long-suffering, etc.

(7) There are other characteristics of the dove, in addition to that of purity, which make her a fit emblem of the Holy Spirit. One of these characteristics, for example, is *cleanness*.

The very fact that the dove could be offered in sacrifice is proof that it was a clean bird, Two of the characteristics of a clean bird were that it could fly and that it did not feed upon flesh. All grain feeding birds that did not feed upon flesh were clean. The difference between the raven and the dove is plainly seen in the two which were sent out of the ark. The raven did not come back into the ark; it undoubtedly found carrion upon which to feed outside, therefore was content to remain outside; but the dove was forced by the necessity of hunger to come back to Noah. The Holy Spirit is very particular in the food upon which He feeds. His one aim and ministry is associated with the Word of God. He finds His satisfaction in making known the message God has given Him to reveal. He is the Inditer of the Word, and He is also the Explainer of it.[1]

Another characteristic of the dove is *gentleness* of manner. This is clearly indicated by the words of Christ in commissioning the Twelve. "Behold," He said, "I send you forth as sheep in the midst of wolves: be ye therefore wise as serpents, and harmless as doves" (Matt. 10:16). Matt. 5:3, 5, 9—"Blessed are the poor in spirit: for theirs is the kingdom of heaven. . . . Blessed are the meek: for they shall inherit the earth. . . . Blessed are the peacemakers: for they shall be called sons of God." The Spirit of Christ is that of humility, harmlessness, lack of bitterness, compassion: in a word, gentleness. And we are told in Rom. 8:9, that "if any man hath not the Spirit of Christ, he is none of his."

A third characteristic of the dove is *constancy*: it lives, we are told, in the strictest monogamy. And so it is only by yielding up our hearts completely to the indwelling Spirit that we can hope to be constant in our love for Christ.

Rom. 12:1, 2—I beseech you therefore, brethren, by the mercies of God, to present your bodies a living sacrifice, holy, acceptable to God, which is your spiritual service. And be not fashioned according to this world; but be ye transformed by the renewing of your mind, that ye may prove what is the good and acceptable and perfect will of God. 1 Cor. 15:58—Wherefore, my beloved brethren, be ye stedfast, unmovable, always abounding in the work of the Lord, foreasmuch as ye know that your labor is not vain in the Lord. Rev. 2:7—To him that overcometh, to him will I give to eat of the tree of life, which is in the Paradise of God (Cf. Rev. 2:11, 17; 3:5, 12, 21). [Think (writes Biederwolf) of the many beautiful characteristics of a dove. How lovely was the character of Jesus because of these dove-like traits, sweet-tempered and gentle, yet just like Him may we be. There is gentleness, tenderness, loveliness, innocence, mildness, peace, purity, patience—all this and more for him in whose heart is made a place for the dove-like Spirit to nestle.[1]] [Cf. Gal. 5:22-25]: But the fruit of the Spirit is love, joy, peace, longsuffering, kindness, goodness, faithfulness, meekness, and self-control: against such there is no law. And they that are of Christ Jesus have crucified the flesh with the passions and the lusts thereof. If we live by the Spirit, by the Spirit let us also walk.

(8) Possessing such qualities as purity, gentleness, harmlessness (lack of guile), the dove appears throughout the Old Testament as a term of affection (Psa. 74:19; Song of Sol. 2:14, 5:2, 6:9). The eyes of the beloved are compared to doves (Song

1. F. E. Marsh, *op. cit.*, 18.
2. W. E. Biederwolf, *A Help to the Study of the Holy Spirit*, 178.

of Sol. 1:15, 4:1, 5:12). Because of its innocence and gentleness, the dove, like the lamb, was frequently offered in sacrifice: in the burnt-offering (Lev. 1:14); in the trespass-offering (Lev. 5:7, 11); in the ceremonial cleansing of the leper (Lev. 14:22, 30); and on other occasions. It was commanded of the mother after childbirth, when the days of her purifying were fulfilled, that she should offer a lamb for a burnt offering, and a young pigeon, or a turtle-dove, for a sin-offering. Lev. 12:6-8, esp. v. 8—"And if her means suffice not for a lamb, then she shall take two turtle-doves, or two young pigeons; the one for a burnt-offering, and the other for a sin-offering; and the priest shall make atonement for her, and she shall be clean." Joseph and Mary took advantage of this provision of the law and offered according to their poverty (Luke 2:22-24). According to the Law of Moses the only birds allowed in sacrifice were the pigeon and the dove. At the Passover these birds were offered for sale in the courts of the Temple; and Jesus drove out those who sold them at the beginning (John 2:14-16) and again the close of His ministry (Matt. 21:12).

(9) J. W. McGarvey writes:

The dove suggests purity, gentleness, peace, etc. In fact the nature of this bird makes it a fit emblem of the Spirit, for it comports well with the fruits of the Spirit (Gal. 5:22-23). The nations of the earth emblazon eagles upon their banners and lions upon their shields, but He who shall gather all nations into his kingdom appeared as a Lamb, and his Spirit appeared under the symbol of a dove. Verily his kingdom is not of this world. It is a kingdom of peace and love, not of bloodshed and ambition. Noah's dove bore the olive branch, the symbol of peace, and the Holy Spirit manifested Jesus, God's olive branch of peace sent into this world (Psa. 72:7, Luke 2:14, John 14:27, Eph. 2:11-18).[1]

4. *The Oil of Anointing.* (1) *To anoint,* in Scripture, means basically *to pour oil upon* a person or thing, *i.e.,* as a religious act. The oil used in anointing was pure olive oil. E.g., Psa. 92:10, 104:15, 141:5; also Gen. 28:18-22:

And Jacob rose up early in the morning, and took the stone that he had put under his head, and set it up for a piller, and poured oil upon the top of it. And he called the name of that place Beth-el: but the name of the city was Luz at the first. And Jacob vowed a vow, saying, If God will be with me, and will keep me in this way that I go, and will give me bread to eat and raiment to put on, so that I come again to my Father's house in peace, and Jehovah will be my God, then this stone which I have set up for a pillar, shall be God's house; and of all that thou shalt give me I will surely give the tenth unto thee. [Cf. Gen. 31:13—the words of the Angel of God (probably the Second Person of the Trinity) to Jacob in a dream, as reported by the latter]:

1. J. W. McGarvey and P. Y. Pendleton, *The Fourfold Gospel,* 86.

I am the God of Beth-el, where thou anointed a pillar, where thou vowedst a vow unto me, etc. *Oil throughout both the Old and the New Testament symbolizes the richness and perfections of the gifts and graces of the Holy Spirit.*

(2) Anointing was a Jewish ceremony employed for various purposes, as follows: (a) Anointing of the guest, as a part of the ritual of hospitality (Psa. 23:5, 92:10; Prov. 27:9; Eccl. 7:1, 9:8; Luke 7:46); (b) Anointing in connection with mourning and fasting (2 Sam. 12:20, 14:2; Dan. 10:3; Matt. 6:17); (c) Anointing for burial (Matt. 26:6-13; John 12:1-8, 19:39-40); (d) Anointing for healing (Isa. 1:6, Jer. 8:22, Luke 10:33-34, Mark 6:13, Jas. 5:14-15). It is apparent, however, as indicated by the Scriptures cited, that in some of these types of anointing precious ointments, rather than oil, were used; and in cases of anointing for healing purposes, oil seems to have been used primarily for its medicinal value. Thus the passage from the Epistle of James certainly authorizes the use of medicine by Christians along with "the prayer of faith."

(3) The principal Jewish ceremony of anointing, however, that in which olive oil was invariably used, and that which has special religious significance, was the ceremony by which persons and things under the Mosaic Institution were consecrated or set apart for the service of God. The significance of the use of pure olive oil in this connection is apparent. The rich medicinal qualities of pure olive oil are well known even to this day; hence, olive oil was a most fitting symbol of the healing efficacy of the Divine Spirit and of the richness of the new spiritual life which He engenders in the human heart.

(4) The Holy Anointing Oil of the Old Institution was compounded of five ingredients, namely, flowing myrrh, sweet cinnamon, sweet calamus, and cassia (all of which contributed richness and fragrance), with pure olive oil as the base of the compound (Exo. 30:22-25). At Sinai, the Tabernacle proper and all its separate furnishings and vessels were consecrated to God, and Aaron and his sons were consecrated to the priesthood, with the Holy Anointing Oil (Exo. 29:4-9, 19-21, 29; 30:26-33; 40:9-16; Lev. 8:10-12, 30). Moreover, according to Divine command, the Holy Anointing Oil was to be used thereafter in the ceremony of consecration to the priesthood (Exo. 30:31: the phrase, "throughout your generations," means here, as it invariably means wherever used in the Old Testament, throughout the Jewish dispensation, or as long as that dispensation lasted; cf. Exo. 40:15). This Holy Anointing Oil, compounded as it was of

386

fragrant spices and pure olive oil, is especially significant as a symbol of the fragrant richness of the life of the Spirit.

(5) The Divine restrictions placed upon the composition and use of the Holy Anointing Oil are likewise significant. *In the first place, it was not to be poured upon man's flesh, but only upon the person qualified to be so anointed* (Exo. 30:32).

Is not this a very definite warning that an unregenerate nature cannot be reformed? . . . Man's nature is sinful. Paul said: 'I know that in me, that is, in my flesh, dwelleth no good thing' (Rom. 7:18). God does not try to reform, nor to pour the oil of His Spirit upon the old nature. He creates anew. 'If any man be in Christ, he is a new creature; old things have passed away' (2 Cor. 5:17). And we know that this new creation is possible only by the regenerating work of the Holy Spirit. Let us be guarded, then, lest we attempt to apply the Spirit's ministry to those who have not been born again.[1]

Cf. John 14:16, 17—"And I will pray the Father, and he shall give you another Comforter, that he may be with you for ever, even the Spirit of truth: *whom the world cannot receive; for it beholdeth him not, neither knoweth him.*" 1 Cor. 2:14— "Now the natural man receiveth not the things of the Spirit of God; for they are foolishness unto him; and he cannot know them, because they are spiritually judged." *In the second place, no imitations of the Holy Anointing Oil were to be made* (Exo. 30:32-33).

So many today are following substitutes and imitations, but are getting none of the Spirit Himself. Oh, that men would see that only that which qualifies itself within the formula of God can be the genuine! As in all days, people today are suffering under false delusions and seem not to be able to discern the mind or Person of the Spirit. . . . It was impossible for the formula to be fulfilled, and the oil given, which was its main ingredient, until the olive had been crushed. So also there cannot be a transformation of nature, without co-crucifixion by faith with and in Jesus Christ. [Again]: The last ingredient [of the Holy Anointing Oil], and the one which was the foundation for the others, was olive oil. This, we know, is obtained by crushing the fleshly part of the olive. How symbolical this is of the giving of the Holy Spirit through the crushing or bruising of the Heavenly One. Not until Jesus Christ had been glorified—and He could not be glorified until He was crucified—could the oil of the Holy Spirit be given. Thus the oil of the Spirit has become the base or foundation for all of our blessings in Christ. Surely, when God gave the divine formula, naming the ingredients, He chose them not only because of their costliness and fragrance and purifying powers; but also because they would be so symbolical and typical and emblematical of Himself in the Person and ministry of His Holy Spirit.[2]

Substitutes for the Holy Anointing Oil were expressly prohibited by Divine command. In like manner, because the Bible

1. C. Gordon Brownville, *op. cit.*, 26-27.
2. C. Gordon Brownville, *op. cit.*, 27, 32.

is the Book, and the only Book, of the Holy Spirit; because the Gospel is the message, and the only message, of the Holy Spirit; because the Church is the dwelling-place, and the only dwelling-place, of the Holy Spirit: *there can be no substitutes for the Bible, the Gospel, or the Church.* The pattern for religious faith, worship and practice is laid down in the Word of God revealed and delivered unto men by the Holy Spirit. The Spirit of God and the Word of God go together. And there is no evidence anywhere in Scripture that regenerating and sanctifying enduements of the Spirit are ever to be enjoyed by men outside the pale of conformity to the Divine pattern laid down in the Word (cf. Exo. 25:40; Acts 1:1-3, 7:38; Rom. 3:1-2; 1 Pet. 4:11; 2 Pet. 1:3; Jude 5).

(6) *The theocratic ceremony of anointing* (that is, theocratic in the sense of having been authorized by God Himself, and hence an official act of the Divine government) was for a twofold purpose: (a) To signify that the person so anointed was divinely set apart to a certain high and holy calling; (b) To signify that this person was endued with the gifts and graces of the Spirit necessary to the proper execution of the specific ministry to which he had been called. This *official* ceremony of anointing was closely related to all the important offices of the servants of Jehovah under the Old Covenant. Three classes of ministers were officially set apart to their respective offices by this ceremony, namely, *prophets, priests,* and *kings. Priests were thus anointed that the people might know that they were holy unto Jehovah* (Exo. 28:36) *to minister unto Him in the priest's office.*

*Vide* Exo. 28:41, 30:30, 40:15; Lev. 8:10-12; Lev. 8:30, 16:32; also Lev. 4:3 [the anointed priest]; Lev. 6:20 [the oblation of Aaron and his sons, to be offered in the day when he is anointed]; Lev. 8:12, 30 [the anointing of Aaron and his sons, by Moses]; Lev. 7:35-36 [the anointing portions of the prescribed offerings were the priests' portions]; Lev. 10:7 [the words of Moses to Aaron and his two sons, Eleazar and Ithamar: the anointing oil of Jehovah is upon you]; Lev. 21:10 [he that is the high priest among his brethren, upon whose head the anointing oil is poured]; Num. 3:1-3 [the names of Aaron's sons, Nadab, Abihu, Eleazar, and Ithamar, the priests that were anointed, whom he (Moses, by the authority of Jehovah) consecrated to minister in the priest's office]; Num. 4:16 [Eleazar appointed to have charge of the anointing oil]. Scripture makes it clear that this ceremony of Consecration to the priesthood by official anointing was to continue throughout the Jewish Dispensation. Exo. 30:31, 40:15: throughout your generations.

*Kings were also anointed under the Old Institution.*

[The ceremony of the anointing of a king signified (a) that he

388

had been divinely selected for the office, and (b) that the Spirit of Jehovah was upon him. Judg. 9:8, the fable of Jotham]: The trees went forth on a time to anoint a king over them; and they said unto the olive-tree, Reign thou over us. [Cf. the anointing of Saul, by Samuel, as the first king of Israel]: 1 Sam. 9:16-17, 10:1-13, 15:1, 17; 1 Sam. 12:1-5 [here Saul is referred to as Jehovah's *anointed*]. [Cf. also the anointing of David: 1 Sam. 16:3, 11-13 (the anointing by Samuel); 2 Sam. 2:4, 7 (anointed by the men of Judah as king over their house); 2 Sam. 5:3, 17 (anointed by the elders as king over Israel, at Hebron); 2 Sam. 12:7 (the words of Nathan the prophet: Thus saith Jehovah, the God of Israel, I anointed thee king over Israel); 2 Sam. 23:1, 2: Now these are the last words of David . . . the anointed of the God of Jacob, And the sweet psalmist of Israel: The Spirit of Jehovah spake by me, And his word was upon my tongue; Psa. 89:20, I have found David my servant, With my holy oil have I anointed him]. [Cf. also the anointing of Solomon: 1 Kings 1:28-40. Cf. also Solomon's prayer at the dedication of the Temple, 2 Chron. 6:42—O Jehovah God, turn not away the face of thine anointed, etc.] [Again, 1 Ki. 19:15, 16: the words of Jehovah to Elijah]: Go, return on thy way to the wilderness of Damascus; and when thou comest, thou shalt anoint Hazael to be king over Syria; and Jehu the son of Nimshi shalt thou anoint to be king over Israel. [The actual anointing of Jehu is narrated in 2 Ki. 9:1-13; Elijah had evidently delegated the task to Elisha, who in turn delegated it to one of the sons of the prophets. The allusions to each of the three great kings of Israel—Saul, David, and Solomon, respectively—as Jehovah's *anointed* are too numerous to be listed here. (E.g., 1 Sam. 24:6, 10; 2 Sam. 23:1, etc.)]

*Prophets were also anointed under the Old Institution, to signify that they were set apart as oracles of God to the people*

[Cf. 1 Ki. 19:16, the words of Jehovah to Elijah]: And Elisha the son of Shaphat of Abel-meholah shalt thou anoint to be prophet in thy room. Cf. v. 19—And Elijah departed thence, and found Elisha the son of Shaphat, who was plowing, with twelve yoke of oxen before him, and he with the twelfth; and Elijah passed over unto him, and cast his mantle upon him.

### A. J. Gordon writes:

No servant of Jehovah was deemed qualified for his ministry without this holy sanctifying touch laid upon him. Even in the cleansing of the leper this ceremony was not wanting. The priest was required to dip his right finger in the oil that was in his left hand and to put it upon the tip of the right ear, upon the thumb of the right hand, and upon the great toe of the right foot of him that was to be cleansed, the oil *'upon the blood of the trespass-offering'* (Lev. 14:17). Thus with divine accuracy did even the types foretell the twofold provision for the Christian life, cleansing by the blood and hallowing by the oil—justification in Christ, sanctification in the Spirit.[1]

(7) Throughout the Patriarchal Dispensation, which extended from Adam to Moses, each of the patriarchs in turn combined in his own person the offices of prophet, priest and king, in relation to his own household. As prophet, he communicated the

1. A. J. Jordan, *The Ministry of the Spirit*, 88-89.

will of God to his household; as king, he ruled over it; and as priest, he offered sacrifices and in general acted as mediator between his household and Jehovah. Hence, the patriarch in his threefold capacity of prophet, priest and king was fully qualified to be designated one of God's "anointed ones."

Psa. 105:4-15: Seek ye Jehovah and his strength; Seek his face evermore. Remember his marvelous works that he hath done, His wonders, and the judgments of his mouth. O ye seed of Abraham his servant, Ye children of Jacob, his chosen ones. He is Jehovah our God: His judgments are in all the earth. He hath remembered his covenant for ever, The word which he commanded to a thousand generations. The covenant which he made with Abraham, And his oath unto Isaac, And confirmed the same unto Jacob for a statute, To Israel for an everlasting covenant, Saying, Unto thee will I give the land of Canaan, The lot of your inheritance; When they were but a few men in number, Yea, very few, and sojourners in it. And they went about from nation to nation, From one kingdom to another people. He suffered no man to do them wrong: Yea, he reproved kings for their sakes, Saying, *Touch not mine anointed ones*, And do my prophets no harm (cf. Gen. 12:17; 20:3, 7; 26:11, etc.).

In this passage, as the context clearly shows, the phrase "mine anointed ones" alludes to the patriarchs of old as persons who were consecrated to God through their possession of the enduements of His Spirit. (Cf. 1 Chron. 16:8-22; Heb. 3:7ff.). In a word, then, to be an *anointed one* of God was to be set apart, by Divine authority, and qualified for a high and holy office under the Divine government. Cf. Ezek. 28:14—"Thou wast the anointed cherub that covereth; and I set thee, so that thou wast upon the holy mountain of God," etc. In this passage, the direct reference was to the king of Tyre; the indirect reference, however, was to Satan, as is evident from the reading of the chapter as a whole. That is to say, Satan, prior to his fall, was an *anointed cherub, i.e.,* one of the angels of God who served the Divine government in an official capacity, probably as an archangel. *The fact must not be lost sight of, that anointing, although it usually signified also enduement with the proper gifts and graces of the Spirit, was the official designation of a person, by God Himself, to a specific form of ministry.*

(8) Now there are frequent references in the Old Testament to the ultimate appearance in the world of One who was to be the Servant and the Anointed One of Jehovah in a special sense. It should be explained here that the Hebrew *Messias* and its Greek equivalent *Christos* both mean "The Anointed One." *These are not names, but titles*—a fact which Biblical exegetes have been all too prone to overlook. The title *Christos* derives from the Greek verb *chrio,* which means "I touch gently"

(the surface of a body), hence "I rub over," "I anoint" (with oil). Messias, Christ, The Anointed One (of God) was, in line with Old Testament prediction, *the* expected *king* of Israel, to be appointed by God as His vicegerent. By the New Testament writers these Old Testament prophetic allusions to Jehovah's Anointed are shown to have their fulfilment in Jesus of Nazareth; hence, the burden of the New Testament message, as embodied in the Christian creedal formula (Matt. 16:16), is that Jesus is Messiah long expected by the Jews, Christ, the Son of the living God, Prophet, Priest and King of His people gathered from both Jews and Gentiles,—the King, not of an earthly kingdom, but of the heavenly kingdom whose locale is in the hearts of men (John 18:36). Cf. Acts 2:36—the words of the Apostle Peter, in concluding the first Gospel sermon: "Let all the house of Israel therefore know assuredly that God hath made him both Lord and Christ, this Jesus whom ye crucified." These truths are all made explicit in the following correlations of Scripture passages from the Old and New Testaments respectively:

(a) Psa. 2:1, 2—Why do the nations rage, And the peoples meditate a vain thing? The kings of the earth set themselves, And the rulers take counsel together, Against Jehovah, and against his anointed, etc. [Turning to the New Testament, we find these words repeated verbatim by the apostolic company in Jerusalem, in their prayer to God for boldness to proclaim the Word of truth in the face of persecution, Acts 4:23-28.] [As a matter of fact, this entire second Psalm is Messianic, and is so interpreted in the New Testament, cf. v. 6 and Heb. 1:5, 5:5; also v. 7 and Acts 13:32-33] (b) Isa. 11:1, 2—And there shall come forth a shoot out of the stock of Jesse, and a branch out of his roots shall bear fruit. And the Spirit of Jehovah shall rest upon him, the spirit of wisdom and understanding, the spirit of counsel and might, the spirit of knowledge and of the fear of Jehovah. Isa. 42:1—Behold, my servant, whom I uphold; my chosen, in whom my soul delighteth: I have put my Spirit upon him; he will bring forth justice to the Gentiles. Isa. 52:13—Behold, my servant shall deal wisely, he shall be exalted and lifted up, and shall be very high. [Cf. also the entire fifty-third chapter of Isaiah, the vivid picture of the Suffering Servant of Jehovah; also Isa. 48:12, 13, 16; Matt. 12:15-18. These verses definitely *identify the Servant with Jesus Christ.* Cf. Rev. 1:17-18, 22:13, also Psa. 102:25-27 and Heb. 1:8, 10-12, with John 1:1-3, Col. 1:15-17, Rom. 11:36, 1 Cor. 8:6, etc. These verses *identify the Servant of Jehovah with God*: indeed, there is very good reason for thinking that the Servant of Jehovah of the Old Testament is the Second Person of the Trinity (Isa. 41:4, 44:6, 48:12; 1 Cor. 10:1-4, Heb. 11:26, etc.) See also Isa. 61:1-2, Luke 4:16-21. These various Scriptures leave no room for doubt: the New Testament expressly affirms Jesus of Nazareth to be the Suffering Servant and the Anointed One of God, that is to say, God's Christ.]

(9) These prophetic references to the Anointed One were

391

all fulfilled in the Divine Anointing of Jesus immediately following His baptism in the Jordan.

Luke 3:21, 22—Now it came to pass, when all the people were baptized, that, Jesus also having been baptized, and praying, the heaven was opened, and the Holy Spirit descended in a bodily form, as a dove, upon him, and a voice came out of heaven, Thou art my beloved Son; in thee I am well pleased (cf. Matt. 3:16, 17; Mark 1:9-11; John 1:29-34).

As in the theocratic ceremony of anointing in olden times, oil was poured upon those servants of God who were divinely ordained to be His prophets, priests and kings—oil being typical of the Holy Spirit, that is, of the anointed person's enduement with the gifts and graces of the Spirit—so the Holy Spirit descended out of heaven, in a dove-like form, upon Jesus at His baptism. Thus did God anoint His only begotten Son—that is, His human nature specifically—"with the Holy Spirit and with power" (Acts 10:38); thus did He avouch His Son's qualification with the gifts and graces of the Spirit without measure (John 3:34, 35); and thus did He signify to the world His Son's official ordination to His threefold office of Prophet, Priest and King under the New Covenant. Acts 4:27 again: "For a truth in this city against thy holy Servant Jesus, whom thou didst anoint, both Herod and Pontius Pilate, with the Gentiles and the peoples of Israel, were gathered together," etc. In this connection, it should be noted well that all four Gospel writers are careful to inform us that it was not an actual dove that descended upon Jesus at His anointing; that, on the contrary, the Holy Spirit descended *as a dove* upon Him. Luke is the most explicit of all: he tells us that the Holy Spirit descended upon Him "in a bodily form, as a dove." It has been suggested, with plausibility, that the Spirit descended from Heaven thus—in a visible configuration—that He might make a *sensible* demonstration to men of His own proper place in the Trinity, that is to say, that He might reveal to the world His true being as a *personal substance* and not a mere operation of the Godhead. Certainly we do have here a specific instance in which the Three Persons of the Godhead were, at one and the same time, completely dissociated: the Son was standing on the bank of the Jordan, while at the same time the Spirit was descending through the air in a dove-like form and the Father was speaking from Heaven to say, "This is my beloved Son, in whom I am well pleased." It should be noted, too, that we have in this incident the two elements of the Good Confession, the creedal formula of the Church of Christ (Matt. 16:16), clearly set forth by Divine authority: (1) Our Lord's anointing with the Spirit ("Thou art the Christ"); (2) His avouching by the Father ("the Son of the living God"). As J. Ritchie Smith writes: "The baptism designates Jesus as a man, made under the law; the anointing of the Spirit proclaims him the Messiah; the voice from heaven declares him to be the Son of God."[1] It would seem, moreover, that the anointing of our Lord's human nature on this occasion was not His enduement with the Spirit at this particular time, for the Simple reason that the Spirit of God and the Spirit of Christ, as it has been pointed out previously, are eternally one and the same Spirit; the anointing, rather, was an act of an *official* character; it was to signify to the world that the Anointed One was God's Prophet, Priest and King, who, as such, actually possessed the fulness of powers of the Divine Spirit and who was now, by this act, authorized to utilize those powers henceforth in the execution of His mission upon earth . *Vide* again, in this connection, Luke 4:16-21.) We must never lose sight of the fact, in studying the Spirit of God, that the essential property of His Being is inexhaustibleness.

(10) One more Scripture remains to be investigated, in this connection, viz., Psa. 45:6, 7—"Thy throne, O God, is for ever and ever; A sceptre of equity is the sceptre of thy kingdom. Thou hast loved righteousness, and hated wickedness: Therefore God, thy God, hath anointed thee With the oil of gladness above thy fellows." The question arises here: Does the Oil of Gladness specified in this text have any metaphorical reference to the Holy Spirit? Some commentators have maintained that no such reference is intended, on the ground that "Oil of Gladness" is a figurative expression deriving its significance solely from the well-known Jewish custom of festive anointings at entertainments and on occasions of great rejoicing (cf. Psa. 23:5, 104:15; Prov. 27:9; Luke 7:46, etc.). It is difficult to see, however, how this position can be maintained legitimately, in view of the fact that the writer of the Epistle to the Hebrews quotes this passage, Psa. 45:6-7, verbatim, with the express declaration that it is Messianic in import and has reference to the Son of God Himself. Heb. 1:8, 9—"*But of the Son he saith, Thy throne, O God, is for ever and ever; And the sceptre of uprightness is the sceptre of thy kingdom. Thou hast loved righteousness, and hated iniquity; Therefore God, thy God, hath anointed thee With the oil of gladness above thy fellows.*"

1. J. Ritchie Smith, *The Holy Spirit in the Gospels*, 156-157.

Language could not be more explicit; the words of the Psalmist definitely do have reference to the Messiah. But—do they have reference to the Anointing of the Messiah with the Holy Spirit?

Cruden suggests alternative interpretations as follows: either, "God hath raised and advanced thee far above all men and angels, to a state of joy and endless glory at his right hand; thus anointing signifies the designation or inauguration of a person to some high dignity or employment (Ezek. 28:14)," or, "God hath endowed thee with all the gifts and graces of the Holy Spirit in an eminent and peculiar manner, to the comfort and refreshment of thine own, and all thy people's hearts; and hath solemnly called thee to be the Priest, Prophet, and King of his church.[1]

It is impossible to determine which of these interpretations is the correct one. Cf. Isa. 61:1, 3—"The Spirit of the Lord Jehovah is upon me; because Jehovah hath anointed me . . . to appoint unto them that mourn in Zion, to give unto them a garland for ashes, *the oil of joy* for mourning, the garment of praise for the spirit of heaviness." This passage is certainly Messianic and is expressly interpreted by Jesus as having reference to Himself and His ministry on earth (Luke 4:16-21). Obviously it indicates that it is a part of the ministry of Jesus to bring joy to sin-cursed human beings through their obedience to the Gospel and consequent enduement with the sanctifying measure (it is called a "gift," Acts 2:38) of the Spirit's power.

In a word, the passage is descriptive of the transforming power of the Gospel of Christ. 2 Cor. 3:18—But we all, with unveiled face beholding as in a mirror the glory of the Lord, are transformed into the same image from glory to glory, even as from the Lord the Spirit. [Moreover, the New Testament teaches that the Holy Spirit is the Spirit of joy.] Gal. 5:22—The fruit of the Spirit is love, joy, peace, etc. Eph. 5:18, 19—Be not drunken with wine, wherein is riot, but be filled with the Spirit: speaking one to another in psalms and hymns and spiritual songs, singing and making melody with your heart to the Lord. 1 Thess. 1:6—And ye became imitators of us and of the Lord, having received the word in much affliction, with joy of the Holy Spirit. [And the Christian life is pre-eminently the life of joy; there is no joy, as saints in all ages have testified, comparable to the joy of conscious fellowship with God the Father and with the Lord Jesus Christ in the Spirit.] 1 Pet. 1:8—Jesus Christ, whom not having seen ye love; on whom, though now ye see him not, yet believing, ye rejoice greatly with joy upspeakable and full of glory. 1 John 1:4— and these things we write, that our joy may be made full. [The Holy Spirit is the Author and Realizer of all spiritual gladness in the human heart, and no more appropriate metaphor could be found of the delectable effect of His sanctifying influence than the *Oil of Gladness*.]

(11) Finally, in this connection, the New Testament teaches

1. A. Cruden, *Concordance*, under "Oil."

394

clearly that all obedient believers in Christ, all the saints of God, have received an anointing with the Holy Spirit.

2 Cor. 1:21, 22—Now he that establisheth us with you in Christ, and anointed us, is God; who also sealed us, and gave us the earnest of the Spirit in our hearts. 1 John 2:20, 27—And ye have an anointing from the Holy One, and ye know all things. . . . And as for you, the anointing which ye received of him abideth in you, and ye need not that any one teach you; but as his anointing teacheth you concerning all things, and is true, and is no lie, and even as it taught you, ye abide in him. Rom. 5:5—the love of God hath been shed abroad in our hearts through the Holy Spirit which was given unto us. 1 Cor. 3:16— Know ye not that ye are a temple of God, and that the Spirit of God dwelleth in you? 1 Cor. 6:19-20: Know ye not that your body is a temple of the Holy Spirit which is in you, which ye have from God? and ye are not your own; for ye were bought with a price: glorify God therefore in your body.

As we shall see later, there are many passages of like import in the apostolic writings. Now it will be recalled that the anointing of Jesus with the Holy Spirit immediately followed His baptism by John in the Jordan. In like manner, the anointing of the obedient believer with the sanctifying presence and influence of the Spirit is directly connected with his baptism into Christ. This is the Spirit's own testimony, as enunciated through the Apostle Peter, at the conclusion of the first Gospel sermon on the Day of Pentecost. We read that some three thousand persons cried out unto Peter and the rest of the apostles, saying, What shall we do? *i.e.*, What shall we do to be saved? Acts 2:38, 39—"And Peter [who was speaking as the Spirit gave him utterance, Acts 2:4] said unto them, Repent ye, and be baptized every one of you in the name of Jesus Christ unto the remission of your sins; and ye shall receive the gift of the Holy Spirit. For to you is the promise, and to your children, and to all that are afar off, even as many as the Lord our God shall call unto him." As will be made clear later in our study, the "gift" of the Holy Spirit promised in this text, on the conditions of prior repentance and baptism, is undoubtedly the permanent sanctifying measure of the Spirit's influence which results from His taking up His abode in the regenerated human heart. The reception of this measure of the Spirit accompanies Christian baptism, that is, the baptism of the penitent believer in water for the remission of his sins. Cf. Gal. 3:1, 2—"O foolish Galatians . . . This only would I learn from you, Received ye the Spirit by the works of the law [*i.e.*, the Law of Moses] or by the hearing of faith?" This entrance of the Spirit into a human heart effects *spiritual circumcision*, which is the cutting off of the body of the guilt of sin from the soul and the subsequent

395

sealing of it by the Holy Spirit. The Apostle Paul makes it crystal clear that such spiritual circumcision takes place in connection with baptism and accompanying remission of sins, the specific grace or blessing connected by Divine authority with that particular ordinance. That is to say, baptism is *not* itself spiritual circumcision (and hence has *not* taken the place of fleshly circumcision of the Old Covenant, as it has often been erroneously contended); on the contrary, spiritual circumcision is that act of the Spirit Himself which is performed by Him at His entrance into the obedient believer's heart in connection with the latter's baptism. *It is the cutting off of the body of the guilt of sin, effected by the entrance of the Spirit into the obedient believer's heart* (Rom. 6:6).

Col. 2:11-14: in whom [Christ] ye were also circumcised with a circumcision not made with hands, in the putting off of the body of the flesh, in the circumcision of Christ; having been buried with him in baptism, wherein ye were also raised with him through faith in the working of God, who raised him from the dead. And you, being dead through your trespasses and the uncircumcision of your flesh, you, I say, did he make alive together with him, having forgiven us all our trespasses; having blotted out the bond written in ordinances that was against us, which was contrary to us: and he hath taken it out of the way, nailing it to the cross. Gal. 3:27—For as many of you as were baptized into Christ did put on Christ. Rom. 6:2-7: We who died to sin, how shall we any longer live therein? Or are ye ignorant that all we who were baptized into Christ Jesus were baptized into his death? We were buried therefore with him through baptism into death: that like as Christ was raised from the dead through the glory of the Father, so we also might walk in newness of life. For if we have become united with him in the likeness of his death, we shall be also in the likeness of his resurrection; knowing this, that our old man was crucified with him, that the body of sin might be done away, that so we should no longer be in bondage to sin; for he that hath died is justified from sin. [Cf. again Acts 2:38, Gal. 3:1-2.] Rom. 8:2—For the law of the Spirit of life in Christ Jesus made me free from the low af sin and of death.

This entrance of the Holy Spirit into the regenerated heart in connection with baptism is God's *anointing* of the obedient believer with the Holy Spirit; from that moment, the saint, unless of course he should grieve, despite, and eventually quench the Spirit, is sealed with "the Holy Spirit of promise" (Eph. 1:13). *Moreover, this entire process is typified in the procedure by which priests were consecrated under the Old Covenant.* The following points of resemblance between the *washing of consecration* of priests under the Old Institution and the *washing of regeneration* (Tit. 3:5) of saints under the New Institution, are indeed significant: (a) In the former, the whole body was washed with water (Exo. 29:4, Lev. 8:6), and in the latter the whole body is immersed in water (Acts 8:36-39, Rom. 6:3-4, Col. 2:12). (b) The former was to be performed but once; so also is the latter. (c) The former was a part of the ceremony of consecration to the priest's office, and the latter is for a similar purpose. All baptized believers are made kings and priests unto God (Isa. 61:6; Rom. 12:1; 1 Pet. 2:5, 9; Rev. 1:6, 5:10, 20:6; cf. Exo. 19:6). (d) The former was followed by the donning of priestly garments by, and by the sprinkling of sacrificial blood and of the holy anointing oil upon, the persons so washed and purified (Exo. 29:5-9, Exo. 29:21; Lev. 8:6-9, Lev. 8:30). And it is in and through the latter that believers are brought under the efficacy of the atoning blood of Christ, receive the anointing with the Holy Spirit, and thus put on their priestly garment, the fine linen of righteousness.

Tit. 3:5—Not by works done in righteousness, which we did ourselves, but according to his mercy he saved us, through the washing of regeneration and renewing of the Holy Spirit. Eph. 5:25, 26—As Christ also loved the church, and gave himself for it; that he might sanctify it, having cleansed it by the washing of water with the word. Heb. 10:21, 22—Having a great priest [Christ] over the house of God, let us draw near with a true heart in fulness of faith, having our hearts sprinkled [by the application of the blood of Christ] from an evil conscience, and having our body washed with pure water [in baptism]. Rev. 7:9-14: After these things I saw, and behold, a great multitude, which no man could number, out of every nation and of all tribes and peoples and tongues, standing before the throne and before the Lamb, arrayed in white robes, and palms in their hands . . . And one of the elders answered, saying unto me, These that are arrayed in the white robes, who are they, and whence came they? And I say unto him, My lord, thou knowest. And he said unto me, These are they that come out of the great tribulation, and they washed their robes, and made them white in the blood of the Lamb, etc. Rev. 19:8—And it was given unto her [the Lamb's wife] that she should array herself in fine linen, bright and pure: for the fine linen is the righteous acts of the saints. (Cf. Rev. 3:5, 4:4, 15:4, 19:14, etc.)

*For all the saints of God, the life which begins with their anointing with the indwelling Spirit in baptism is the life with the Spirit, the continuously enlarging, intensifying and enriching life which leads ultimately to the Beatific Vision.* They are themselves (as anointed ones) kings and priests unto God (1 Pet. 2:5, Rev. 1:6, 5:9), and their great High Priest is the Lord Jesus Christ Himself, "named of God a high priest after the order of Molchizedek" (Heb. 4:14, 5:10), who "now once at the end of the ages hath been manifested to put away sin by the sacrifice of himself" (Heb. 9:27). "Wherefore also he is able to save to the uttermost them that draw near unto God through him, seeing he ever liveth to make intercession for them" (Heb. 7:25).

5. *Oil as the Source of Light.* (1) There are numerous passages in the Old Testament in which oil is described as the source of light. The majority of these are statements concerning oil for the Golden Candlestick by which the Holy Place of the Tabernacle (and later, the Temple) was illumined.

Lev. 24:1-4: And Jehovah spake unto Moses, saying, Command the children of Israel, that they bring unto thee pure olive oil beaten for the light, to cause a lamp to burn continually. Without the veil of the testimony, in the tent of meeting, shall Aaron keep it in order from evening to morning before Jehovah continually; it shall be a statute for ever throughout your generations. He shall keep in order the lamps upon the pure candlestick before Jehovah continually. (Cf. also Exo. 25:6, 27:20-21, 35:8, 14; Exo. 39:37; Num. 4:9, 16.). Cf. Exo. 35:28—And the spice, and the oil: for the light, and for the anointing oil, and for the sweet incense [here the oil for tha light is clearly distinguished from the holy anointing oil (as also in Exo. 39:37-38 and in Num. 4:16].

The Candelabrum stood on the south side of the Holy Place of the Tabernacle, over against the Table of Showbread (literally, *Presence-bread*) on the north side (Exo. 25:23-30, 37:10-16). It was wrought or beaten out of a talent of pure gold, and consisted of one upright shaft and six branches, all ornamented with "cups," "knops," and "flowers" (Exo. 25:31-40, 37:17-24). In these lamps pure olive oil burned "continually" (Exo. 27:20-21, Lev. 24:1-4). The Candelabrum was, of course, a dispenser of light, and was therefore a type or symbol of the Word of God by which the Church of Christ, the antitype of the Holy Place, is illumined. This living Word, moreover, shines out into the dark places of earth, and into unregenerated human hearts, through the testimony and the lives of all the saints. The twofold mission of the Church is to preserve this eternal Word and to spread it abroad throughout the earth "for a testimony unto all the nations" (Matt. 24:14), for this Word of God, this Word of Christ alone is the Truth that makes men free.

John 8:31, 32—[the words of Jesus]: If ye abide in my word, then are ye truly my disciples; and ye shall know the truth, and the truth shall make you free. Psalm 119:105—Thy word is a lamp unto my feet, And light unto my path. Psa. 119:130—The opening of thy words giveth light. 2 Pet. 1:19—And we have the word of prophecy made more sure; whereunto ye do well that ye take heed, as unto a lamp shining in a dark place, until the day dawn, and the day-star arise in your hearts [cf. Rev. 22:16]. John 6:63 [Jesus speaking]: The words that I have spoken unto you are spirit, and are life. Matt. 24:35—[Jesus speaking again]—Heaven and earth shall pass away, but my words shall not pass away. [Hence, Jesus as the incarnate Logos is the Light of the World, the fountain and author of all knowledge both natural and spiritual. He Himself declared]: I am the light of the world; he that followeth me shall not walk in the darkness, but shall have the light of life. (Isa. 42:6, 49:6; Luke 2:32; John 1:7-9; Acts

13:47, 26:23; 1 John 2:8, etc.). [And as Christ was the incarnation of God, so the Church (both as a whole, and every true Christian individually as well) is the incarnation of Christ.] Matt. 5:14-16: Ye are the light of the world. A city set on a hill cannot be hid. Neither do men light a lamp, and put it under the bushel, but on the stand; and it shineth unto all that are in the house. Even so let your light shine before men; that they may see your good works, and glorify your Father who is in heaven.

*It should be observed, however, that the Candelabrum of the Tabernacle was only a dispenser of light; it was the oil in the lamps that produced the light. And, as we have already seen, oil, throughout the whole Bible, is used as a common and appropriate symbol of the Holy Spirit. In like manner, the spiritual light which is dispensed through the Word of God, is produced by the Spirit of God, who is invariably the Author and Revealer of Divine Truth, the Truth that makes men free* (1 Cor. 2:6-15, 1 Pet. 1:10-12, 2 Pet. 1:21). Hence, Jesus, the Incarnate Word, the Light of the World, possessed the Holy Spirit without measure (John 3:34); that is, He always spoke and acted under the guidance of the Spirit. The whole Church of Christ, moreover, the Temple of God under the New Covenant (Eph. 2:19-22), is illumined by the light of the Word as revealed by the Holy Spirit. And, carrying the analogy to its proper conclusion, the saints themselves are said to be epistles of Christ "known and read of all men . . . written not with ink but with the Spirit of the living God; not in tables of stone, but in tables that are hearts of flesh" (2 Cor. 3:2-4). All true Christians are called "sons of the light" (Luke 16:8), "children of the light" (Eph. 5:8). Cf. Phil. 2:15, 16—"That ye may become blameless and harmless, children of God without blemish in the midst of a crooked and perverse generation, among whom ye are seen as lights in the world, holding forth the word of life." And in Rev. 21:10-11, we are told that the light of "the holy city Jerusalem [the Bride, the wife of the Lamb] coming down out of heaven from God, having the glory of God" was "like unto a stone most precious, as it were a jasper stone, clear as crystal." That is to say, all true Christians having been brought to the saving knowledge of God and of Jesus Christ (that knowledge which is life eternal, John 17:3) and being enlightened by the Holy Spirit, their lives reflect the fruit of the Spirit—the living Truth—as exemplified in the incarnate life of their Divine Exemplar and Elder Brother, Jesus Christ. The Holy Spirit as the Spirit of Truth (John 14:17, 16:13) is at the same time the Spirit of Light. Finally, it is well worth noting also that *the*

399

*seven lamps of the Candelabrum of the Tabernacle symbolized perfect light, the number seven being the Biblical symbol of completeness or perfection.*

Cf. Rev. 1:4—the seven Spirits that are before his throne; Rev. 3:1— he that hath the seven Spirits of God; Rev. 4:5—And there were seven lamps of fire burning before the throne, which are the seven Spirits of God; Rev. 5:6—And I saw in the midst of the throne and of the four living creatures, and in the midst of the elders, a Lamb standing, as though it had been slain, having seven horns, and seven eyes, which are the seven Spirits of God, sent forth into all the earth.

When we correlate these passages with the description of the sevenfold Spirit of Jehovah in Isa. 11:1-2 (here described as "resting upon" Jehovah's Anointed), their meaning becomes obvious, viz., that Jesus, Messiah, should possess the fulness of the powers of the Holy Spirit.

And there shall come forth a shoot out of the stock of Jesse, and a branch out of his roots shall bear fruit. And the Spirit of Jehovah shall rest upon him, the spirit of wisdom and understanding, the spirit of counsel and might, the spirit of knowledge and of the fear of Jehovah. Isa. 9:6-9: For unto us a child is born, unto us a son is given; and the government shall be upon his shoulder; and his name shall be called Wonderful, Counsellor, Mighty God, Everlasting Father, Prince of Peace. Of the increase of his government and of peace there shall be no end, upon the throne of David, and upon his kingdom, to establish it, and to uphold it with justice and with righteousness from henceforth even for ever. The zeal of Jehovah of hosts will perform this.

*Where the Spirit dwells in the fulness of His powers, there is Wholeness or Holiness. In a word, Being is Truth; that is to say, that which is, to the extent that it is, is Truth. The Divine Spirit is wholeness of Being; hence He is properly named Holy Spirit. And as wholeness of Being, He is wholeness of Truth, Beauty, and Goodness; and this wholeness He contributes to God's moral creatures who open their hearts to receive His Divine presence and power.* (2) Oil is again portrayed as the source of light in Zechariah's Vision of the Golden Candlestick (Zech. 4:1-12). The prophet's vision was that of a Golden Candlestick fed by two inexhaustible streams of oil supplied by two living olive-trees growing on either side of the bowl of the Candelabrum. The import of the vision was for Zerubbabel; it was to signify to him that the work of rebuilding the Temple and thus preparing the way for the Church of spiritual Israel, was to be accomplished by relying, not on human resources, however potent, but on Divine grace and power, that is, on the power of the Spirit of Jehovah. Zech. 4:6—"This is the word of Jehovah to Zerubbabel, saying, Not by might, nor by power, but by my Spirit, saith Jehovah of hosts." The symbolic import of Zechariah's vision is very clear. In like manner, the Church, as the preserver and proclaimer of the Word of God, the function of which is spiritual illumination, for the accomplishment of her twofold divine task must depend wholly upon her supply of oil from God, which is the Holy Spirit. When the Church neglects this Divine Source of supply of spiritual illumination and power, and thus vexes, grieves or perhaps quenches the Holy Spirit, she becomes impotent, as indeed the Church has become in many parts of the world today. When she resorts to the wisdom of men, which is mere foolishness with God, and substitutes human philosophy, tradition and ritual for the Truth revealed by the Spirit; when she becomes presumptuous or indifferent to the plain teaching of the Word of God, the Spirit's Word which is the sole dispenser of spiritual light; then she loses her candlestick, even as the Spirit Himself forewarned the church in Ephesus: "But I have this against thee, that thou didst leave thy first love. Remember therefore whence thou art fallen, and repent and do the first works; or else I come to thee, and will remove thy candlestick out of its place, except thou repent." Returning again for a moment to Zechariah's Vision, we read, Zech. 4:11-14:

Then answered I, and said unto him [the Angel], What are these two olive-trees upon the right side of the candlestick and upon the left side thereof? And I answered the second time, and said unto him, What are these two olive-branches, which are beside the two golden spouts, that empty the golden oil out of themselves? And he answered me and said, Knowest thou not what these are? And I said, No, my lord. Then said he, These are the two anointed ones, that stand by the Lord of the whole earth.

The following exposition, by the W. J. Deane, of this remarkable passage is clear and to the point:

The oil that supplies the lamps is the grace of God, the influence of the Holy Spirit, which alone enables the Church to shine and to accomplish its appointed work. The two olive trees are the two authorities [the two anointed ones], viz., the civil and the sacerdotal [the former represented by Zerubbabel, the latter by Joshua the high priest], through which God communicates his grace to the Church; these stand by the Lord because, instituted by him, they carry out his will in the ordering, guiding, extending, and purifying the kingdom among men. The two olive branches remit their oil into one receptacle, because the two authorities, the regal and priestly, are intimately connected and united, and their action tends to one end, the promotion of God's glory in the salvation of men. In Messiah these offices are united; he is the channel of Divine grace, the source of light to the whole world.[1]

1. W. J. Deane, *The Pulpit Commentary* (The Book of Zechariah), Vol. 32, p. 42. New Edition.

It should be noted, in this connection, that our Lord Jesus Christ was declared to be a high priest after the order of Melchizedek; that is, as the Lord's Anointed, He combines in His own Person, as Melchizedek did, the offices of both King and High Priest (Gen. 14:18; Psa. 110:4; Heb. 6:20, 7:1-28). (3) In the New Testament, oil is presented as the source of light (symbolic of the Spirit as the Source of spiritual light), in our Lord's Parable of the Wise and Foolish Virgins, Matt. 25:1-13:

> Then shall the kingdom of heaven be likened unto ten virgins, who took their lamps, and went forth to meet the bridegroom. And five of them were foolish, and five were wise. For the foolish, when they took their lamps, took no oil with them; but the wise took oil in their vessels with their lamps. Now while the bridegroom tarried, they all slumbered and slept. But at midnight there is a cry, Behold, the bridegroom! Come ye forth to meet him! Then all those virgins arose, and trimmed their lamps. And the foolish said unto the wise, Give us of your oil; for our lamps are going out. But the wise answered, saying, Peradventure there will not be enough for us and you: go ye rather to them that sell, and buy for yourselves. And while they went away to buy, the bridegroom came; and they that were ready went in with him to the marriage feast; and the door was shut. Afterward came also the other virgins, saying, Lord, Lord, open to us. But he answered and said, Verily, I say unto you, I know you not. Watch therefore, for ye know not the day nor the hour.

Surely the import of this parable is clear: The necessary prerequisite of a man's attainment of his natural and proper end, which is union with God (The Vision of God, Beatitude, Life Everlasting, described here as the Marriage Feast of the Lamb) is his living, in this world, the life with the Holy Spirit (in the language of the parable, his keeping oil in the lamp of his life), the life whereby he acquires the Mind of Christ, which is the Will of God and the Living Word as revealed to him by the Spirit. Just as it is, in the very nature of the case, utterly impossible for one to appreciate a great symphony who has never cultivated music appreciation in his own soul; just as it is utterly impossible for one to stand entranced before a great painting who has never personally cultivated the appreciation of art; just as it is utterly impossible for one to enjoy a great poem who has never cultivated within himself the understanding and appreciation of poetry; so it is equally impossible for one who never reads or feeds upon the Word of God, one who has never received the indwelling Spirit through his union with Christ, who consequently has never experienced the joy of the Spirit's presence and companionship, never cultivated in his own soul love for God and for the things of the Spirit, never brought forth in his life the fruit of the Spirit (Gal. 5:22-23)—it is equally impossible, I repeat, for such a one to experience union with God, to se God "face to face," at the end of his earthly pilgrimage. Paul's affirmation that "the natural man receiveth not the things of the Spirit of God" (1 Cor. 2:14), is just as true today as it was when the Apostle indited these words on parchment. Only that person who receives into his heart the Word of God revealed by the Spirit, who feels upon that Word, assimilates it into his own being, and thus grows in the grace and knowledge of our Lord and Savior Jesus Christ (2 Pet. 3:18), one whose personality is integrated around Christ the Living Word and whose life is spiritually illumined (enlightened) thereby, and who in this manner prepares himself to experience Beatitude at the end of his life on earth, can hope to enter into the Marriage Feast when the Bridegroom shall appear. This is true for the simple reason that only such a person will be found to have made the necessary preparation for the Vision of God by his cultivation, in the present life, of his own mind and will in appreciation of, and in response to, spiritual realities. In a word, only that person who comes to the Marriage Feast with a sufficient supply of oil in his lamp—that is, of the enlightening and sanctifying gifts of the Spirit in his soul—can expect to enjoy union of his mind with the mind of God in knowledge and union of his will with the will of God in love. This is the long of it, the short of it, and the all of it. As Jesus Himself puts it: "By their fruits ye shall know them. Do men gather grapes of thorns, or figs of thistles? Even so every good tree bringeth forth good fruit; but the corrupt tree bringeth forth evil fruit. A good tree cannot bring forth evil fruit, neither can a corrupt tree bring forth good fruit. Every tree that bringeth not forth good fruit is hewn down, and cast into the fire. Therefore, by their fruits ye shall know them" (Matt. 7:16-20). The Divine law, each after its kind (Gen. 1:11, 21, 25), prevails in the moral just as truly as in the biological realm. Those who come to the Marriage Feast without oil in their lamps will find themselves, by their very lack of spiritual discernment, excluded therefrom. And when once such persons stand in the presence of Infinite Holiness and thus fully realize what they have lost by failing to live the life with the Holy Spirit, they will indeed, in their overwhelming remorse and despair, cry out "to the mountains and to the rocks, Fall on us, and hide us from the face of him that sitteth on the throne, and from the wrath of the Lamb: for the great day of their wrath is come; and who is able to stand?" (Rev. 6:16-17). There is but one natural progression in the Creative Process, and that is from the Kingdom of Nature through the Kingdom of Grace into the Kingdom of Glory, "the eternal kingdom of our Lord and Savior Jesus Christ" (2 Pet. 1:11). Gal. 6:8—"For he that soweth unto his own flesh shall of the flesh reap corruption; but he that soweth unto the Spirit shall of the Spirit reap eternal life."

Another fundamental truth, which deserves attention here, stands out in this Parable of the Virgins. It should be noted that the wise virgins did not share their supply of oil with the foolish ones. Why not? For the obvious reason that, if the symbolism of the parable is to remain logically sound, they *could not* do so. Oil is symbolic of the Holy Spirit, and the holiness which the enlightening and sanctifying influences of the Spirit engenders in the individual human heart is not something that can be transferred willy-nilly from one person to another. Holiness is an *individual* attainment. There is no such thing in Christianity as justification, regeneration or sanctification by proxy. *Holiness is a qualitative excellence which can be acquired only by the individual as such, by his opening of his own heart to the Spirit's presence and guidance.* No person can attain holiness for another person, nor can any one person transfer his holiness to one of his fellows. Hence, we are told that in the final Judgment, every man will be judged according to *his own* deeds (Matt. 16:27; Rom. 2:6, 14:12; 2 Cor. 5:10; Eph. 6:8; Col. 3:25; Rev. 2:23, 20:12; cf. 1 Cor. 3:13). The Kingdom of Grace is basically as individualistic as the Kingdom of Nature.

We may now sum up the import of this entire section on oil as the source of light, in a single statement, as follows: *As oil was the source of artificially-produced physical illumination, so the Holy Spirit is the Source of divinely-produced spiritual illumination (knowledge) with respect to the things of both Spirit in God and spirit in man; moreover, this spiritual knowledge of which the Holy Spirit is the Source, is dispensed throughout the Church, and by the Church, through her apostles, prophets and evangelists, throughout the world, through the living Word of God, personal (Christ), oral, written or printed.* To the extent that the Word of God is spread abroad in the hearts of men, there is always freedom—freedom from error, from superstition, from anxiety, from lust, from fear; because the living Word of God, the Word revealed by the Spirit, *is* the Truth that makes men free.

6. *Water.* In several instances in Scripture, water is made symbolic of the graces and comforts of the Holy Spirit. (1) John 7:37-39: "Now on the last day, the great day of the feast, Jesus stood and cried, saying, If any man thirst, let him come unto me and drink. He that believeth on me, as the scripture hath said, from within him shall flow rivers of living water." "But this," the inspired writer himself goes on to say, "spake he of the Spirit, which they that believed on him were to receive; for the Spirit was not yet given, because Jesus was not yet glorified." That is, prior to the Messiah's coronation and assumption of universal sovereignty at the right hand of God— in a word, under the Old Covenant—the gifts and comforts of the Holy Spirit were not bestowed upon believers generally, but only certain special gifts were bestowed, and these only upon chosen individuals to qualify them for various types of service in the unfolding of the divine Plan of Redemption. Cf. John 17:7, the words of Jesus to the Eleven: "It is expedient for you that I go away; for if I go not away, the Comforter will not come unto you; but if I go, I will send him unto you." Now "living water" is water that engenders life, that is necessary to the generation and sustenance of life; as such it is a fitting emblem of the life-giving and life-sustaining graces and powers of the Holy Spirit. Hence, says John the Revelator, in concluding the account of his vision of the Holy City, New Jerusalem: "And he showed me a river of water of life, bright as crystal, proceeding out of the throne of God and of the Lamb, in the midst of the street thereof. And on this side of the river and on that was the tree of life, bearing twelve manner of fruits, yielding its fruit every month; and the leaves of the tree were for the healing of the nations" (Rev. 22:1-2). Obviously, we have described here in poetic imagery, under the symbol of the River of Water of Life, the continuous procession of the Spirit as life-giving Power from the Being of God, that is, of the one Holy Spirit who is the ultimate Source of every form of life in the universe. Undoubtedly, too, the Tree of Life is Christ Himself, the Living and Sovereign Word of God, the bond of union between creature and Creator. Hence, as the Tree of Life, in John's vision, was fed by life-giving streams from the River of Life upon whose banks it grew, so the Living Word was generated and fed by the inner presence and power of the Eternal Spirit. Indeed the Spirit of Christ is, as we have

405

already shown, the Holy Spirit of God. Moreover, as the leaves of the Tree were, in John's vision, for the healing of the nations, so the sin-cursed human soul is healed, that is, restored to fellowship with God, by receiving into itself the living Word, by feeding upon it, and, so to speak, by digesting and assimilating it into its very being. For the reception of the Word into the human heart is the reception also of the transforming and life-giving powers and comforts of the Spirit. God's Word and God's Spirit go together. Hence, we hear Jesus Himself saying to the woman of Samaria at Jacob's well: "Every one that drinketh of this water shall thirst again; but whosoever drinketh of the water that I shall give him shall never thirst; but the water that I shall give him shall become in him a well of water springing up unto eternal life" (John 4:13-14). Language could hardly be more explicit. (2) Hence, exclaimed Isaiah, alluding undoubtedly to the graces and comforts of the Spirit mediated to man through the Gospel: "Ho, every one that thirsteth, come ye to the waters" (Isa. 55:1). Again, picturing Zion's happy future, the joys of fellowship with God under the New Covenant, he says:

Then the eyes of the blind shall be opened, and the ears of the deaf shall be unstopped. Then shall the lame man leap as a hart, and the tongue of the dumb shall sing; for in the wilderness shall waters break out, and streams in the desert. And the glowing sand shall become a pool, and the thirsty ground springs of water; in the habitation of jackals, where they lay, shall be grass with reeds and rushes. And a highway shall be there, and a way, and it shall be called, The way of holiness; the unclean shall not pass over it; but it shall be for the redeemed; the wayfaring men, yea fools, shall not err therein. No lion shall be there, nor shall any ravenous beast go up thereon; they shall not be found there: but the redeemed shall walk there; and the ransomed of Jehovah shall return, and come with singing unto Zion; and everlasting joy shall be upon their heads: they shall obtain gladness and joy, and sorrow and singing shall flee away (Isa. 35:5-10). Again: Behold, God is my salvation; I will trust, and will not be afraid; for Jehovah, even Jehovah, is my strength and song; and he is become my salvation. Therefore with joy shall ye draw water out of the wells of salvation. And in that day shall ye say, Give thanks unto Jehovah, call upon his name, declare his doings among the peoples, make mention that his name is exalted. Sing unto Jehovah; for he hath done excellent things; let this be known in all the earth (Isa. 12:1-5).

These exquisite passages are all in harmony with the prophecy of Joel: "And it shall come to pass afterward, that I will pour out my Spirit upon all flesh; and your sons and your daughters shall prophesy, your old men shall dream dreams, your young men shall see visions; and also upon the servants and upon the handmaids in those days will I pour out my Spirit"

(Joel 2:28-29; cf. Acts 2:16-21). And the New Testament comes to a close sounding out the Lord's precious invitation: "And the Spirit and the bride say, Come. And he that heareth, let him say, Come. And he that is athirst, let him come; he that will, let him take the water of life freely" (Rev. 22:17). In all these passages, water is emblematic of the graces, satisfactions and joys bestowed upon men by the Holy Spirit. (3) In Exo. 17:6, we see Moses, at the command of Jehovah, smiting (with his rod) a rock in the wilderness. And out of the rock flowed a stream of water pure and fresh, of which the children of Israel drank and were satisfied. That rock, says the Apostle Paul, was Christ: "For I would not, brethren, have you ignorant, that our fathers were all under the cloud, and all passed through the sea, and were all baptized unto Moses in the cloud and in the sea; and did all eat the same spiritual food; and did all drink the same spiritual drink; for they drank of a spiritual rock that followed them; and the rock was Christ" (1 Cor. 10:1-4). That is, the rock smitten by Moses was a symbol of Christ, who was smitten for us (Isa. 53:4-5). Hence the water which flowed from the rock, life-giving and refreshing, becomes a symbol of the graces and comforts bestowed by the Holy Spirit. And so the Apostle, writing to Christians, goes on to say, in a subsequent chapter: "For in one Spirit were we all baptized into one body, whether Jews or Greeks, whether bond or free; *and were all made to drink of one Spirit*" (1 Cor. 12:13). (4) In the forty-seventh chapter of Ezekiel, the prophet describes his Vision of Healing Waters flowing out from the Temple on Mount Moriah, swelling into a great river as they flow, carrying life and healing wherever they spread, and finally pouring their healing properties into the waters of the Dead Sea itself. "And he brought me back unto the door of the house; and, behold, waters issued out from under the threshold of the house eastward (for the forefront of the house was toward the east); and the waters came down from under, from the right side of the house, on the south of the altar. Then he brought me out by the way of the gate northward, and led me round by the way without unto the outer gate, by the way of the gate that looketh toward the east; and, behold, there ran out waters on the right side" (vv. 1-2). This vision is prophetic of course. No river ever flowed from the actual Temple on Mount Moriah. Obviously, the Temple of Ezekiel's vision is the spiritual temple of God, the Church of redeemed Israel, which was set up in Jerusalem on the Day of Pentecost, A.D. 30 (cf. Isa. 2:2-4).

Hence the healing waters flowing forth from the Temple symbolize the spreading abroad of spiritual light and influence throughout the world, through the world-wide proclamation of the Gospel; the stream of spiritual healing that flowed first in Jerusalem, then in all Judea and Samaria, and finally unto the uttermost parts of the earth (Acts 1:8), causing the wilderness and the solitary parts of the Earth to be made glad and the very desert to rejoice and blossom as the rose. *It should be noted, in the first place, that these healing waters, greatly increasing both in depth and in breadth as they flowed eastward, swelled into a veritable River of Water of Life.*

When the man went forth eastward with the line in his hand, he measured a thousand cubits, and he caused me to pass through the waters, waters that were to the ankles. Again he measured a thousand, and caused me to pass through the waters, waters that were to the knees. Again he measured a thousand, and caused me to pass through the waters, waters that were to the loins. Afterward he measured a thousand; and it was a river that I could not pass through; for the waters were risen, waters to swim in, a river that could not be passed through (vv. 3-5).

In like manner, the stream of spiritual (the Holy Spirit's) influence and life was small at first, but it has become wider and wider, and deeper and deeper, throughout the centuries, and eventually it shall fill the world, and the knowledge of the Lord shall cover the earth as the waters cover the sea. The Scriptures leave no room for doubt that the Gospel of Christ will eventually prevail throughout the earth, if not in the present Dispensation then certainly in that which shall follow the Second Advent. *In the second place, the healing virtues of the waters of Ezekiel's vision are described as very remarkable.*

And he said unto me, Son of man, hast thou seen this? Then he brought me, and caused me to return to the bank of the river. Now when I had returned, behold, upon the bank of the river were very many trees on the one side and on the other. Then said he unto me, These waters issue forth toward the eastern region, and shall go down into the Arabah [desert]; and they shall go toward the sea [the Dead Sea]; into the sea shall the waters go which were made to issue forth; and the waters shall be healed. And it shall come to pass, that every living creature which swarmeth, in every place whither the rivers come, shall live; and there shall be a very great multitude of fish; for these waters are come thither, and the waters of the sea shall be healed, and everything shall live whithersoever the river cometh. And it shall come to pass, that fishers shall stand by it; from En-gedi even unto Eneglaim shall be a place for the spreading of nets; their fish shalt be after their kinds, as the fish of the great sea [the Mediterranean], exceeding many (vv. 6-10).

This [writes Milligan] is a beautiful illustration of the sanctifying and soul-redeeming influences of the Gospel. The world is a sea— *a Dead Sea.* Mankind are all dead in trespasses and in sins. But a fountain has been opened in the house of David; a living stream has gone forth from the side of our Redeemer. It has purified the Sanctuary; it has cleansed the temple of God. But it can not be confined within the narrow limits of any one town, city, or continent. It is the remedy which God has provided to supply the wants of a fallen world, and hence he has made it as free as the air or the sunlight of heaven.[1]

Only the enlightening, regenerating and sanctifying activities of the Holy Spirit can transform the Dead Sea of this present evil world into a garden blossoming with flowers; and this transformation can become universal only when the knowledge of the Lord, brought to men everywhere by the Spirit through the Word, shall cover the whole earth as the waters cover the sea. It cannot be emphasized too strongly that the chief characteristic of these waters of Ezekiel's vision was their power *to give life;* and in this respect especially are they symbolic of the Holy Spirit. *In the third place, lest in our optimism we become unrealistic, Ezekiel's Vision forewarns us that the life of the Spirit, mediated through the Gospel, will not be accepted and enjoyed by all men: on the contrary, many will reject it.* "But the miry places thereof, and the marshes thereof, shall not be healed; they shall be given up to salt" (v. 11).

The meaning of these words is very obvious from the context. The influence of the Gospel will be felt and enjoyed under the whole heavens; it will cover the whole Earth as the waters cover the sea. But all parts of the Earth will not enjoy it equally. In some places the water will be so shallow and so mixed with clay that they will only produce mire. These localities will still, like the banks of the Dead Sea, remain unproductive. That is, some persons, and probably even some communities, will not receive the Gospel in the love of it. Like the ancient Pharisees and some modern professors of Christianity, they will still continue to make void the law of God by their traditions and their own inventions. . . . And while the world will be a temple filled with sweet incense from a thousand altars, the moral miasma of the sin-polluted Earth will ever continue to rise from a few remaining bogs and quagmires. The saint and the sinner will, therefore, live together during even the Golden Age of Christianity. The tares and the wheat will grow together in the same field till the time of the world's great harvest.[2] (cf. Luke 8:4-15, Matt. 13:24-30).

*Finally, according to Ezekiel's vision, many perennial and fruitful trees, whose fruit shall be for food and whose leaves shall be for healing, will line the banks of this River of Life.* "And by the river upon the bank thereof, on this side and on that side, shall grow every tree for food, whose leaf shall not wither, neither shall the fruit thereof fail; it shall bring forth new fruit every month, because the waters thereof issue out of the sanctuary; and the fruit thereof shall be for food, and the

1. R. Milligan, *Scheme of Redemption,* 563.
2. R. Milligan, *op. cit.,* 564-565.

leaf thereof for healing" (v. 12). The figure harks back of course to the Tree of Life in Eden (symbolic of the Word), which was watered by the river of Eden (symbolic of the Spirit), the fruit of which was designed to counteract man's natural mortality and thus to preserve his physical youth and vigor; that Tree was for a time Heaven's antidote for physical decay, and those who ate of it had no need of any other panacea (cf. Gen. 2:8-10, 3:22-24). That is to say, in the account of the Tree of Life given in Genesis, the symbolism has reference to the operation of the Spirit and the Word in the Kingdom of Nature. This symbolism is repeated on the *metaphysical* level (that is, having reference to the operation of the Spirit and the Word in the Kingdom of Glory) in John's vision of the Tree of Life growing along the banks of the River of Water of life, and fed by life-giving streams from that celestial river, in the New Jerusalem (Rev. 22:1 2). Evidently, in Ezekiel's vision we have the same symbolism, but with reference to the operation of the Spirit and the Word in the Kingdom of Grace; that is, as pertaining to the spiritual life engendered and nourished in God's saints in this present world or prior to their assumption of glory and honor and immortality. As the Trees which lined the banks of the River of Life in Ezekiel's vision were fed by waters issuing out of the Sanctuary, so the means and appointments by which the life of the Spirit is generated and nurtured in men derive their life-giving properties from the Divine Spirit Himself. The food provided by these trees is spiritual food, the Bread of Life provided by the living Word of God; and the leaves of these trees which are for spiritual healing are the gifts and graces and consolations of the Spirit. Hence the fruit of these trees never fail—they are described as bringing forth new fruit every month—because the life-giving resources of the Spirit of God are inexhaustible. The symbolism is exceedingly vivid, spiritual, and fruitful: indeed it "combines spiritual things with spiritual words" (1 Cor. 2:13); it is difficult to express in human language. Suffice it to say, in summing up, that we have here, in Ezekiel's Vision of the Healing Waters, a symbolic representation of the gifts and graces of the Spirit, mediated primarily through the Word and secondarily through the appointments of that Word, viz., the ordinances of the Christian faith, the exercises of Christian worship, and acts of Christian love and service to those of the Household of Faith and to our fellow-men generally. The entire vision is a graphic portrayal of the universal spread—through the proclamation and acceptance of the Gospel—of the enlightening and sanctifying gifts and influences of the Spirit of God. (5) There are a few Scripture passages in which water, although not itself made a symbol of the gifts and graces of the Spirit, is nevertheless, *as a symbol of cleansing,* directly associated with the reception of the regenerating and sanctifying operations of the Spirit. The first of these passages occurs in Ezek. 36:24-28:

> For I will take you from among the nations, and gather you out of all the countries, and will bring you into your own land. And I will sprinkle clean water upon you, and ye shall be clean; from all your filthiness, and from all your idols will I cleanse you. A new heart also will I give you, and a new spirit will I put within you; and I will take away the stony heart out of your flesh, and I will give you a heart of flesh. And I will put my Spirit within you, and cause you to walk in my statutes, and ye shall keep mine ordinances, and do them. And ye shall dwell in the land that I gave to your fathers; and ye shall be my people, and I will be your God. [Cf. Jeremiah's promise of the New Covenant, Jer. 31:31-34; also Ezekiel's Vision of the Valley of Dry Bones, Ezek. 37:1-14, especially vv. 12-14]. Thus saith the Lord Jehovah: Behold, I will open your graves and cause you to come up out of your graves, O my people; and I will bring you into the land of Israel. . . . And I will put my Spirit in you, and ye shall live; and I will place you in your own land; and ye shall know that I, Jehovah, have spoken it, saith Jehovah.

Undoubtedly the cleansing alluded to in the first of the texts cited, as is evident from the context, in which cleansing from the pollution of idolatry is clearly indicated, had reference to the *ceremonial cleansing,* and the term "clean water" to the water of Purification, prescribed by the Law of Moses in Num. 19:17-19. This water was compounded by mixing the ashes of the sin offering (a red or earth-colored heifer "without spot, wherein is no blemish, and upon which never came yoke," Num. 19:3) in running or spring water (v. 17). The preparation was to be sprinkled upon polluted persons or things, with a bunch of hyssop (v. 18), by a clean person, on the third day and again on the seventh day following the occurrence of the pollution, after which the one who sprinkled the water was himself thereby made unclean, and was required to wash his clothes and remain outside the camp until evening (vv. 19, 21). It should be noted that this mixture is specifically named "the water for impurity" (vv. 13, 21), that is, for symbolic pollution of any kind. Cf. Psa. 51:7—"Purify me with hyssop, and I shall be clean: Wash me, and I shall be whiter than snow. And it was further specified that any person who wilfully neglected this ordinance, and thus by his presence defiled the Sanctuary, was to be cut off from the congregation as a presumptuous sinner (Num. 19:13, 19:20-

22; cf. Num. 15: 22-31, also 1 Cor. 3: 17, 2 Cor. 3: 7). Now the significant point in the passage from Ezekiel is that this general ceremonial cleansing of the nation, whenever it was to occur, was to be accompanied by a general outpouring of the Spirit upon all the people, the "putting" of the Spirit within them. This makes it difficult for us to interpret the passage (and the Vision of the Valley of Dry Bones as well) as having reference to the restoration of the Theocracy some half-century and more later, under Ezra and Zerubbabel. For the Scriptures certainly make it clear that there was no general outpouring of the Spirit (*i.e.*, upon all obedient believers) under the Old Covenant or prior to the advent of the Spirit on the Day of Pentecost to incorporate, indwell and vitalize the Church (cf. Joel 2: 28-32; John 7: 37-39, 20: 21-23; Acts 1: 6-8, 2: 1-33, 19: 1-2, etc.). Do these two passages from Ezekiel, then, in harmony with Jeremiah's promise of the New Covenant, point forward to the establishment of the Church of Christ, spiritual Israel, and the reception of the Jews into the New and spiritual covenant of faith? If so, the Water of Purification of the Old Covenant must be interpreted as having been a type of Christian Baptism of the New. It is difficult to accept such an interpretation, however, for the following reasons: (a) The water of baptism is simply *water* in its natural form—not "clean water" or the Water of Purification at all. As a matter of fact, there is no specification in the New Testament even that baptism shall be performed in running water. All that is required for baptism is a sufficient quantity of water for an immersion (John 3: 23, Acts 8: 36-38). (b) Baptism has no ceremonial or ritualistic import whatever. This truth is made crystal clear in 1 Pet. 3: 20-21. Here the Apostle expressly declares that baptism is "not the putting away of the filth of the flesh" (*i.e.*, not a ceremonial cleansing, not a mere ritualistic observance), "but the interrogation of a good conscience toward God, through the resurrection of Jesus Christ" (that is to say, *an act of faith*). In other words, by his dying with Christ in the likeness of Christ's death, in the water of baptism, and then being raised with Christ in the likeness of His resurrection (Rom. 6: 3-11), the penitent believer declares to the world his belief in the death, burial and resurrection of Christ—the facts of the Gospel (1 Cor. 15: 1-4)—and his belief as well in his own ultimate resurrection. Baptism is essentially an act of faith; otherwise, it is not a baptism at all, but a mere dipping in water. If a candidate does not submit to baptism solely out of his love for

God and for the Lord Jesus Christ who died for him, and out of his desire to submit his own will and life to the Divine Will, he goes down into the water a dry sinner and comes up a wet one. The Apostle Paul corroborates this fundamental truth explicitly, in Rom. 6:17-18. "But thanks be to God," he says, "that, whereas ye were servants of sin, ye became obedient *from the heart* to that form [pattern or mould] of teaching whereunto ye were delivered; and being made free from sin, ye became servants of righteousness." Here, the teaching alluded to is, of course, the Gospel with its three facts, viz., the death, burial and resurrection of Christ (1 Cor. 15:1-4), and the pattern or mould of the teaching is baptism (the subject under discussion throughout the chapter), the ordinance in which the death, burial and resurrection of Christ are set forth pictorially to the world. The Apostle is simply expressing his gratitude at knowing that those to whom he is addressing the Epistle have been obedient *from the heart* to the divine ordinance of baptism. Obedience to baptism, as to any ordinance of the Lord, to be genuine must flow out of a heart motivated by faith, hope and love. Hence, throughout the apostolic writings it is made very clear that the necessary pre-conditions of baptism are individual faith and repentance (Acts 2:38, 8:34-39, 16:14-15, 16:31-34; Rom. 10:9-10, etc.). It is a sign of spiritual ignorance to speak of Christian baptism as a "mere rite," "mere outward act," "mere external performance," etc. It is a perversion of Scripture to speak of it even as a *rite;* it is a sacred, solemn, spiritual *act of faith,* or it is nothing. I am convinced that instead of too much having been made of baptism throughout the centuries, by the Church and her Ministry, not enough has been made of it, that is, as an essentially *spiritual* heart act. (c) Again, the *sprinkling* of the Water of Purification under the Old Covenant can hardly typify the *act* of baptizing under the New, for the simple reason that the act of baptizing, in apostolic times, was that of dipping or *immersing* the believer in, and then lifting him out of, the water as the element. I know of no practice in connection with the faith and worship of the early Church that is more generally authenticated, by both the apostolic and the post-apostolic writings, than this fact. (Cf. Matt. 3:13-17; Mark 1:9-11; Acts 8:36-39; Rom. 6:3-4; Col. 2:12, etc.) Therefore, in view of all these considerations, I find it difficult to accept the interpretation of the passages quoted from Ezekiel as pointing forward to spiritual Israel, the Church of the New Covenant. Obviously, *it is a national restoration*

413

*that is prophetically indicated in both of these texts, a national restoration to a national homeland.* If the particular national restoration indicated was that which occurred under Ezra and Zerubbabel, then the promise, "I will put my Spirit within you," can mean only, "I will put my Spirit in your midst," that is, in the heart of your nation, in your civil and ecclesiastical leaders, to give them wisdom and strength to lead the nation in the paths of righteousness. I am very much inclined, however, to think that the third interpretation of these texts from Ezekiel is the correct one, namely, that they constitute a prophecy, couched in general terms, of a *yet future restoration of the nation of Israel to the Holy Land, a restoration to be consummated with appropriate ceremonial cleansings of a national character, and to be followed, it would seem, by the conversion of the nation as a whole to Christ,* and their reception—as individuals—of the Holy Spirit, on the terms of the New Covenant of course, viz., faith, repentance, confession, and baptism. (Cf. Deut., ch. 28; Ezek., chs. 38, 39; Dan., ch. 12; Luke 21:24; Rom., ch. 11; Rev. 16:12-21, etc.)

In the New Testament, however, the water of baptism is clearly indicated to be the visible symbol of the *real cleansing* of the penitent believer's soul from the guilt of sin, and as such is directly connected with the regenerating and sanctifying operation of the Spirit through the Word John 3:3-5, in the conversation between Nicodemus and Jesus: "Jesus answered and said unto him, Verily, verily, I say unto thee, Except one be born anew, he cannot see the kingdom of God. Nicodemus saith unto him, How can a man be born when he is old? can he enter a second time into his mother's womb, and be born? Jesus answered, Verily, verily, I say unto thee, Except one be born of water and the Spirit, he cannot enter into the kingdom of God." The subject of conversation here is the *new birth,* which, says Jesus explicitly, is one birth, *a birth of water and the Spirit* at one and the same time. Now, since the only point at which a believer comes into contact with water, in the process of becoming a Christian, is in the ordinance of Christian baptism, it seems too evident to admit of any question that "water," in this great affirmation of Jesus, has reference to baptism. The text itself teaches clearly that the new birth, which is accomplished in the human heart by the agency of the Spirit (by means of the Word, of course, the spiritual and incorruptible Seed of the Kingdom, Matt. 13:23, Luke 8:11-15, 1 Pet. 1:23, Rom. 10:17, etc.) actually takes place in baptism, in which the

414

penitent believer actually dies to the old life of sin and rises to walk in the new life of righteousness (Rom. 6:4-11). Water is the element in which the birth takes place; however, because the Spirit is the active Agent of both the Father and the Son in the whole transaction (Scripturally designated *regeneration*, that is, the begetting and bringing forth of a *new creature* in Jesus Christ, 2 Cor. 5:17, Eph. 2:10, Eph. 4:24, Col. 3:10, etc.), the new birth is described as *a birth of water and the Spirit*. All this is in exact harmony with the first public statement of the terms of pardon ("the keys of the kingdom," Matt. 16:19) under the New Covenant, in Acts 2:38. Here we find the Spirit Himself (Acts 2:4), speaking through the Apostle Peter in answer to some three thousand persons who, convicted of their sins, were asking what to do to be saved, and saying: "Repent ye, and be baptized every one of you in the name of Jesus Christ unto the remission of your sins; and ye shall receive the gift of the Holy Spirit." These words teach clearly that the gifts of God specifically connected by Divine authority with the baptism of the penitent believer, are remission of sin and the indwelling of the Spirit of God. Now remission is cancellation, full pardon; it is complete removel of the burden of sin's guilt. This pardon, moreover, takes place, not in the penitent believer's mind or heart, but in Heaven itself, at the seat of the Divine government; in a word, the pardon takes place in the Mind of God; He forgives us our trespasses, and when He forgives them, we are told, He forgets them—O wondrous thought! Moreover, this pardon, this removal of the burden of guilt from the penitent's heart, opens the way for the entrance of the Spirit in sanctifying measure into that heart which is purified by faith. Hence, we find Ananias saying to the penitent Saul of Tarsus, "Arise, and be baptized, and wash away thy sins, calling on His name" (Acts 22:16), that is, on the name of Christ. Not that water itself washes away sin; obviously it does not; there is no magical efficacy in any material element to rid the soul of the burden of the guilt of sin. But that when the Word of God connects, by promise, a certain Divine blessing with obedience on man's part to a specific Divine ordinance, then the man who takes God at His Word and joyfully obeys the ordinance is certain, and *knows* that he is certain, to receive the blessing which the Divine promise has attached to that act of loving obedience. And in this manner Divine grace, by specific appointment, meets human faith. Now, as we have seen, remission of sin and the indwelling Spirit

415

are the Divine promises specifically attached to the ordinance of baptism. That settles the matter—for the man of faith. Therefore says Paul: "For as many of you as were baptized into Christ did put on Christ" (Gal. 3:27). Again: "There is therefore now no condemnation to them that are in Christ Jesus" (Rom. 8:1). And on the same grounds Christian baptism is designated "the washing of regeneration" and is specifically connected, in the same passage, with the "renewing of the Holy Spirit" (Tit. 3:5). All this adds up to the fundamental truth, that the water of baptism, as the visible symbol of the actual cleansing of the soul from the guilt of sin, is invariably connected with the regenerating and sanctifying operation of the Holy Spirit in the human heart.

To sum up, under this caption: *Water is life-giving, growth-producing, cleansing, refreshing, reviving,* and *satisfying; so also is the Holy Spirit whenever and wherever He operates in the human heart and life.*

7. *The Seal.* A seal (*sphragis*), in Scripture, is either (1) an *instrument* (signet, signet-ring) for sealing, *i.e.,* for imprinting a design upon something; or (2) the *impression* made by such an instrument. The ancient Hebrews, like many other more advanced early peoples, wore their seals or signets in rings on their fingers or in bracelets on their arms. *E.g.,* Judah, Jacob's son, left his seal, his bracelet and his staff, as a pledge with Tamar, whom he did not know (Gen. 38:18, 25). Sealing, Scripturally speaking, may be for any one or more of various purposes: (1) It may be the setting of a mark upon letters, books, and other things for purposes of secrecy and security. Deut. 32:34—"Is not this laid up in store with me, Sealed up among my treasures?" Job 14:17—"My transgression is sealed up in a bag, And thou fastenest up mine iniquity." Isa. 8:16—"Bind thou up the testimony, seal the law among my disciples." Dan. 12:4—"But thou, O Daniel, shut up the words, and seal the book, even to the time of the end." Cf. also Rev. 5:1ff., the Book sealed with seven seals. This was the Book of God's decrees respecting the remarkable things that would happen to His Church throughout the present Dispensation, that is, to the end of the present age; its being sealed signified that the matter contained it was locked up and hence unknown to His creatures. Cf. also Rev. 20:1-3: Here we have John's vision of an angel binding the Old Serpent, the Devil, casting him into the bottomless pit, and then closing and sealing the pit, "that he [Satan] should deceive the nations no more, until the thousand

years should be finished." This teaches us that the time is coming when the Divine Government will impose a restraint upon Satan, segregate him, and make him absolutely incapable of doing any considerable amount of mischief to the Church throughout the period of one thousand years described in the context. (2) Sealing may also be for the purpose of signifying ownership. Job 9:7—"Him that commandeth the sun, and it riseth not, and sealeth up the stars." That is, God has put the stars under His seal, as their owner and governor, and allows them to appear whenever he deems it proper. (3) Again, sealing may be for the purpose of authenticating the genuineness of a person or thing, as, e.g., the Divine sealing of the Messiah Himself (John 6:27). (4) A seal may also have the character of a pledge. Fleshly circumcision, for instance, is described by Paul as "a seal of the righteousness of the faith which he [Abraham] had while he was in uncircumcision" (Rom. 4:11); that is, it was a pledge on God's part, both to Abraham and to his spiritual seed (Gal. 3:29), that He would give them Messias, the Promised Seed, out of the loins of Abraham, and in Him (Christ) accept them as His own people, pardon their sins on the ground of their faith and obedience, cleanse them from their natural corruption, etc., all of which was signified by their cutting off of their foreskins; in a word, fleshly circumcision was a pledge of the Covenant of Grace. (5) A seal may also be the evidence of a contract that has been entered into. Jeremiah, for instance, bought a field in his own country of Anathoth, of a man named Hanamel; he wrote the deed of purchase in duplicate, called witnesses to attest it, sealed one copy of the deed and left the other unsealed; then he put both copies in the hands of his disciple Baruch, and said to him, after invoking the authority of Jehovah in support of the transaction: "Take these deeds, this deed of the purchase which is sealed, and this deed which is open, and put them in an earthen vessel; that they may continue many days" (Jer. 32:6-15). (6) Sealing may also be confirmatory in character. For example, the Apostle Paul, writing to the Christians at Corinth, says: "The seal of mine apostleship are ye in the Lord" (1 Cor. 9:2). That is, Ye are yourselves the evidence of my divine call to the apostleship; my apostolic office has confirmation in you who are the effect of my preaching, as the writing is confirmed by the seal; for how could anyone think that the blessing of God should accompany the Gospel preached by me, to such an extent as to turn you from your pagan idolatry and lewd manner of life,

417

to the true Christian religion, and to a holy life and conversation, if God had not sent me and been with me? (7) An official seal, such as every government has, signifies that the sealing, and the seal as well, has back of it the authority and power of the particular government. Thus Jezebel wrote letters to the elders of Israel authorizing them to bring about the death of Naboth, and sealed the letters with King Ahab's seal (1 Ki. 21:8-10). And Haman sealed the decrees of King Ahasuerus against the Jews with the king's seal (Esth. 3:12). A state seal impressed upon a contract or other legal document is an official guarantee that the authority and power of government will be invoked to make sure that the provisions of the contract shall be carried out by the contracting parties. In a word, an official seal signifies *authority* (the moral right to use force) and *power* (the actual use of force) to render inviolate contracts, agreements, edicts, etc., officially decreed or sanctioned (8) In some cases, sealing is for a combination of two or more of these purposes. Thus Nebuchadnezzar sealed the stone placed across the opening to the den of lions into which Daniel had been cast, "that nothing might be changed concerning Daniel" (Dan. 6:17). And in like manner the stone rolled across the entrance to the sepulchre of Christ, at the instigation of the Jewish leaders, was sealed with a Roman seal, in order that the disciples might not be able to steal the corpse, as the rabbis feared they would attempt to do (Matt. 27:62-66). In both of these cases, the sealing was not only for purposes of security, but was also a pledge that the authority and power of government supported the act and would be invoked to punish anyone who might dare to tamper with the official seal. Moreover, the Divine sealing of the Messiah, and the Divine sealing of all the saints of God, with the Holy Spirit of promise, combines, as we shall now see, practically all these various significations.

Now the universe in which we live is a moral government under the sovereign rule of God the Creator and Preserver of all things. Hence, just as every human government has its seal of state (for, because of the divinely-implanted power of reason in man, all human things of value are patterned after the Divine), so God the Sovereign of the universe and Head of the Divine government has His official act of sealing and His official or royal seal. Rev. 7:2—"And I saw another angel ascend from the sunrising, having the seal of the living God" (cf. Rev. 9:4). This Divine seal, moreover, has the authority and power of the Divine government back of it. And even though heaven and earth should pass away, "the firm foundation of God standeth, having this seal, The Lord knoweth them that are his; and, Let every one that nameth the name of the Lord depart from unrighteousness" (2 Tim. 2:19).

*It should be made unequivocally clear at this point that Divine sealing is not some mysterious emotion or ecstasy or experience in the heart of the believer. On the contrary, it is an official act of the government of Heaven. The Scriptures state expressly that Christ Himself was sealed; and that all obedient believers in Christ are likewise sealed, with the Seal of God. In the case of the saints, God's official act of sealing accompanies such other Divine acts as pardon, justification, remission of sin, etc. It must be understood of course that, because God is a Spirit, these acts are, speaking by analogy from human experience, mental; that is, they occur in the Mind or Thought of God.*

The Divine Sealer in every case is God the Father. This is our Lord's explicit testimony with regard to His own sealing, John 6:27: "Work not for the food which perisheth, but for the food which abideth unto eternal life, which the Son of man shall give unto you: for him the Father, even God, hath sealed." The saints also are said to be sealed by God the Father. In Ephesians 1:3-14, the Apostle Paul enumerates the Father's loving acts toward all obedient believers in Christ, as follows: He has blessed them with all spiritual blessings in the heavenly places in Christ (v. 3); He has chosen them in Christ before the foundation of the world, that they "should be holy and without blemish before him in love" (v. 4); in His good pleasure He predestinated them to the position of His children (v. 5); He has bestowed His grace freely upon them, in His Beloved Son (v. 6); in the name of His Son, He has enriched them with abundant spiritual endowments (vv. 7-8); He has redeemed them through the blood of Christ and freely forgiven their trespasses (v. 7); He has revealed to them the mystery of His will, His eternal purpose "to sum up all things in Christ" (vv. 9-10); He has displayed His glory in them, through these acts of His love (vv. 11, 12); and *He has marked them for His own possession (as His own property) by sealing them "with the Holy Spirit of promise"* (v. 13). All these acts are clearly set forth as acts of the Heavenly Father. It is well for us to remember, at this point, that the Father is the Source, the Son the Channel, and the Spirit the Power, of every Divine blessing. Father originates, the Son executes, the Spirit applies and realizes.

419

God is the Divine Sealer. The Sealed, as it has been stated already, are Christ Himself, and all obedient believers in Christ. Christ was sealed in virtue of what He was in Himself, and obedient believers in Christ are sealed in virtue of what they are in Him. 2 Cor. 1:21, 22—"Now he that establisheth us with you in Christ, and anointed us, is God; who also sealed us, and gave us the earnest of the Spirit in our hearts."

The Sealing of Christ evidently occurred in connection with His baptism in the Jordan (Matt. 3:13-17, Mark 1:9-11, Luke 3:21-22, John 1:29-34). We hear Jesus Himself saying, to the multitude who were thronging Him for the loaves and fishes with which He was supplying them: "Work not for the food which perisheth, but for the food which abideth unto the eternal life, which the Son of man shall give unto you: for him the Father, even God, hath sealed" (John 6:27). Obviously the sealing of Christ alluded to here was connected with the descent of the Holy Spirit upon Him "in a bodily form, as a dove" (Luke 3:22) immediately following His baptism.

One of the most instructive writers on the Hebrew worship and ritual tells us that it was the custom for the priest to whom the service pertained, having selected a lamb from the flock, to inspect it with the most minute scrutiny, in order to discover if it was without physical defect, and then to seal it with the temple seal, thus certifying that it was fit for sacrifice and for food. Behold the Lamb of God presenting Himself for inspection at the Jordan! Under the Father's omniscient scrutiny he is found to be "a lamb without blemish and without spot." From the opening heaven God gives witness to the fact in the words: "This is my beloved Son, in whom I am well pleased," and then he puts the Holy Ghost upon him, the testimony to his sonship, the seal of his separation unto sacrifice and service.[1]

The Sealing of Christ (1) authenticated Him as the true Anointed One of Jehovah; (2) marked Him as possessing the fulness of the Spirit's presence and power (John 3:34); (3) marked Him as God's own possession (1 Cor. 3:20-23: "For all things are yours . . . and ye are Christ's; and Christ's is God's"); (4) marked His separation unto His divine task of obtaining eternal redemption for His people, through the shedding of His own precious blood (Eph. 1:6, 7); and (5) was the Father's pledge or earnest that He would raise Him from the dead (Rom. 1:4) and set Him at His own right hand in the heavenly places, "far above all rule, and authority, and power, and dominion, and every name that is named, not only in this world, but also in that which is to come" (Eph. 1:20-21).

As in the sealing of Christ Himself, so also the Divine seal-

1. A. J. Gordan, *The Ministry of the Spirit*, 77.

ing of all believers in Christ occurs in connection with their baptism. Gal. 3:27—"For as many of you as were baptized into Christ did put on Christ." Having been baptized *into Christ* and having thereby *put on Christ*, they are sealed in virtue of their being *in Christ*. Their formal translation, by the Father, "out of the power of darkness . . . into the kingdom of the Son of his love" (Col. 1:12-13) occurs in connection with their baptism; in baptism they literally die to the old life of sin, and arise, as new creatures in Christ Jesus (2 Cor. 5:17), to walk in the new life of righteousness (Rom. 6:3-11). Rom. 8:1— "There is therefore now no condemnation to them that are in Christ Jesus." The fact must be kept in mind also that this formal translation or transfer, along with pardon, justification, remission of sin, etc., takes place in the Mind or Thought of God.

The Sealing, on the other hand, although indeed it takes place *officially* in the Thought of God, takes place *actually* in the mind and heart of the obedient believer. In this connection, the following observations may help to clarify this rather difficult subject: (1) All true Christians are Scripturally described as living epistles of Christ, known and read of all men (2 Cor. 3:2), and as vessels or cabinets filled with spiritual treasure (2 Cor. 4:7). (2) Hence, the *wax,* so to speak, upon which the Divine inscription is stamped, in the Divine process of sealing, is the impressionable human heart, which is apt to take any impression. Psa. 22:14—"My heart is like wax; It is melted within me." Cf. 2 Cor. 3:3—"written not with ink, but with the Spirit of the living God; not in tables of stone, but in tables that are hearts of flesh." Heb. 10:16—"This is the covenant that I will make with them after those days, saith the Lord: I will put my laws on their heart, and upon their mind also will I write them" (cf. Jer. 31:31-34). (3) The *design* which is stamped upon the wax is the Mind of Christ, the living Thought and Word of God; this living Word is impressed upon the mind and heart of the believer by the Spirit of God Himself, but invariably through the preaching and acceptance of the facts, commands and promises of the Gospel. There is no more thoroughly established fact in the history of Christianity than the fact that where there is no preaching of the Gospel, no dissemination of the Word written or spoken, there is no operation of the Spirit and no conversion to Christ. The whole missionary enterprise of the Church is predicated upon this basic fact.

Jas. 1:21—Receive with meekness the implanted word, which is able to save your souls. John 16:13, 14—Howbeit, when he, the Spirit

421

of truth, is come . . . He shall glorify me; for he shall take of mine, and shall declare it unto you [the words of Jesus]. Phil. 2:5—Have this mind in you, which was also in Christ Jesus, etc. 1 Cor. 2:16—But we have the mind of Christ. 1 Cor. 1:21—it was God's good pleasure through the foolishness of the preaching to save them that believe. Rom. 10:17—So belief cometh of hearing, and hearing by the word of Christ.

As there can be no harvest in the natural world without the sowing of seed, so there can be no harvest in the spiritual world without the sowing of the Seed of the Kingdom, which is the Word of God (Luke 8:11). The Word of God is "living, and active, and sharper than any two-edged sword" (Heb. 4:12), because the power of the Holy Spirit is embodied in it. The Gospel is not *a* power, nor *one of* the powers, but *"the* power of God unto salvation to every one that believeth" (Rom. 1:16), because the Holy Spirit is in it and His power is exercised through it upon the human heart. (4) Hence, the design being the Living Word of God, the Divine *Seal* which carries the design is the Holy Spirit Himself. Eph. 1:13—"in whom [Christ], having also believed, ye were sealed with the Holy Spirit of promise." Eph. 4:30—"And grieve not the Holy Spirit of God, in whom ye were sealed unto the day of redemption." Now the Holy Spirit, as we have learned, is a Person. Obviously, one person can dwell in or inhabit another person only by means of influences that are essentially psychical; that is to say, primarily by means of thought. Hence, because Christ was in Himself the Thought and Word of God (the Logos), the Divine Seal in His case was the presence of the Spirit in all the fulness of His power. In the sealing of believers, however, the Divine Seal is the presence of the Spirit—*in the living Word, accepted by faith*—in regenerating and sanctifying power. Therefore, to say that the Divine Seal is the presence of the Holy Spirit in regenerating and sanctifying power (as Cruden calls it, "the grace of sanctification wrought in the soul by the Holy Ghost"), and to say that the Divine Seal is the Spirit Himself, is practically to say one and the same thing. For the Spirit of God is the Power of the Most High, and, the Spirit being a Person, the Power must be essentially *psychical*. Hence, in whatever measure, or for whatever purpose, the Spirit indwells the human heart, He does so as the Power of Divine Thought and Divine Love.

Now, as in the ordinary process of sealing, the wax receives the image, impressed upon it, of the design which is carried by

1. A. Cruden, *Concordance*, under "Seal."

the stamp or seal, so in the Divine sealing of the saints, they receive in their hearts the Living Word, Christ (who is the very image of the Divine substance, Heb. 1:3), which is the design carried and impressed upon them by the Holy Spirit, the Divine Seal. That is to say, *by faith* they receive in their hearts the mind of Christ, in the process of regeneration, and in so doing, become like Christ, Christlike and hence Godlike. This spiritual resemblance of the believer to Christ, realized by the agency of the Spirit through the Gospel, is the sign of the believer's sanctification. Moreover, the visible evidence of this sanctification is the fruit of the Spirit with which the everyday life of the true Christian abounds. Cf. Matt. 7:20, 21—"By their fruits ye shall know them. Not every one that saith unto me, Lord, Lord, shall enter into the kingdom of heaven; but he that doeth the will of my Father who is in heaven." And undoubtedly to do the will of the Heavenly Father is to bring forth the fruit of the Spirit in one's life. Gal. 5:22—"But the fruit of the Spirit is love, joy, peace, longsuffering, kindness, goodness, faithfulness, meekness, self-control; against such there is no law." Now there is a somewhat mysterious passage in 2 Tim. 2:19 which, despite its obscurity, certainly corroborates this teaching. Here the Apostle affirms that, despite the detection and unbelief of some one-time professing Christians of his day, "howbeit, the firm foundation of God standeth, having this seal, The Lord knoweth them that are his; and, Let every one that nameth the name of the Lord depart from unrighteousness." Whatever else this passage implies, it certainly teaches us that Divine Sealing, which has for its sure foundation the authority and power of the Almighty, signifies two facts: (1) ownership, on God's part—"The Lord knoweth them that are his"; and (2) holiness, on man's part—"Let every one that nameth the name of the Lord depart from unrighteousness." These two facts are here set forth symbolically as *inscriptions* included in the design impressed upon the human heart by the Divine Seal. That is, the two inscriptions, taken together, show forth the two sides of the saint's standing with his God. Those who are sealed are themselves holy, *i.e.*, in the sense that it is their disposition to depart from unrighteousness; and, being holy, God marks them as His own possession. The Sealing is, therefore, a ratification of the covenant relationship existing between God and His people. Let us now examine the *inscriptions* themselves in some detail: (1) "The Lord knoweth them that are his." (This sentence is taken *verbatim* from the LXX.

of Num. 16:5). That is, the Lord marks the true saints as belonging in thought, motive and disposition to Him, marks them for His own possession, as His very own property. As a matter of fact, only God Himself can know those who are really His, for the simple reason that He alone is capable of discerning the thoughts and intents of the human heart. He and He alone is capable of knowing whether or not the person who presents himself to the Christian evangelist for baptism is truly a penitent believer coming to the baptismal pool from pure motives. Hence only the Lord Christ Himself has the proper knowledge, and hence the proper authority, to add believers to His own Body, the Church, and to excommunicate persons therefrom (Acts 2:47, 5:14).

John 10:14—[the words of Jesus]: I am the good shepherd; and I know mine own, and mine own know me. John 10:27 [again the words of Jesus]: My sheep hear my voice, and I know them, and they follow me. 1 Cor. 6:19, 20—Or know ye not that your body is a temple of the Holy Spirit which is in you, which ye have from God? and ye are not your own; for ye were bought with a price: glorify God therefore in your body. 1 Pet. 2:9—But ye are an elect race, a royal priesthood, a holy nation, a people for God's own possession, etc. Tit. 2:14—the great God and our Savior Jesus Christ, who gave himself for us, that he might redeem us from all iniquity, and purify unto himself a people for his own possession, zealous of good works. 1 Cor. 3:9—Ye are God's husbandry, God's building. 1 Cor. 3:20, 23— For all things are yours. . . . And ye are Christ's, and Christ is God's.

"When we receive the gift of the Holy Spirit," writes A. J. Gordon,

it is that we may count ourselves henceforth and altogether Christ's. If any shrink from this devotement, how can he have the fullness of the Spirit? God cannot put His signature upon what is not his? Hence, if under the sway of a wordly spirit we withhold ourselves from God and insist on self-ownership, we need not count it strange if God withholds himself from us and denies us the seal of divine ownership. God is very jealous of his signet. He graciously bestows it upon those who are ready to devote themselves utterly and irrevocably to his service, but he strenuously withholds it from those who, while professing his name, are yet "serving divers lusts and pleasures." There is a suggestive passage in the Gospel of John which, translated so as to bring out the antitheses which it contains, reads thus: "Many trusted in his name, beholding the signs which he did; but Jesus did not trust himself to them" (John 2:23, 24). Here is the great essential to our having the seal of the Spirit. Can the Lord trust us? Nay; the question is more serious. Can he trust himself to us? The Holy Spirit, which is his signet ring, can he commit it to our use for signing our prayers and for certifying ourselves, and his honor not be compromised?[1]

(2) The other inscription is: "Let every one that nameth

1. A. J. Gordon, *op. cit.*, 79.

424

the name of the Lord depart from unrighteousness." It should be noted that this is substantially the same as that upon the mitre of the Jewish High Priest: "HOLY TO JEHOVAH" (Exo. 39:30). The possession of the Spirit commits the possessor irrevocably to a life of separation from sin. Holiness, therefore, the life of the Spirit which is manifested in the fruit of the Spirit, is both the badge of sanctification and the ground on which the sanctified are officially marked as God's own possession. 1 John 1:6—"If we say that we have fellowship with him [God] and walk in the darkness, we lie, and do not the truth." 1 John 3:7, 8—"He that doeth righteousness is righteous, even as he is righteous: he that doeth sin is of the devil, for the devil sinneth from the beginning."

The great office of the Spirit in the present economy is to communicate Christ to his church which is his body. And what is so truly essential of Christ as holiness? "In him is no sin; whosoever abideth in him sinneth not." The body can only be sinless by uninterrupted communion with the Head; the Head will not maintain communion with the body except it be holy.[1]

As sinners, men are quickened by the Holy Spirit; as saints, they receive His grace of sanctification.

Finally, the Seal of God in the saints is not only the attestation of His ownership of them, and not only the badge of their own sanctification or separation unto a life of holiness, but also a *pledge* or *earnest* on the part of the Heavenly Father that He will lead them into their eternal inheritance "incorruptible, and undefiled, and that fadeth not away, reserved in heaven" for them (1 Pet. 1:4). It is the earnest of their ultimate attainment of heavenly glory and honor and immortality (Rom. 2:7). 2 Cor. 1:22—"God, who also sealed us, and gave us the earnest of the Spirit in our hearts." Eph. 1:13, 14—"in whom [Christ], having also believed, ye were sealed with the Holy Spirit of promise, which is an earnest of our inheritance, unto the redemption of God's own possession, unto the praise of his glory." Cf. also Eph. 4:30—"Grieve not the Holy Spirit of God, in whom ye were sealed unto the day of redemption." The "day of redemption" alluded to here, the day "of the redemption of God's own possession," is obviously the day of the Lord's return in glory with his holy angels (Matt. 25:31), when He shall raise the dead and translate the living (1 Cor. 15:51-54). For the present, however, His own people, those whom He has purchased with His own precious blood (Acts 20:28) are in this

1. A. J. Gordon, *op. cit.*, 80.

world, and, although the world knows them not (John 1:10, 15:19; 1 John 3:1), He has put His mark upon them, the mark whereby they shall be recognized at His coming.

Cf. Rev. 7:3—Hurt not the earth, neither the sea, nor the trees, till we shall have sealed the servants of our God on their forehead. Rev. 14:1—And I saw, and behold, the Lamb standing on the mount Zion, and with him a hundred and forty and four thousand, having his name, and the name of his Father, written on their foreheads. Rev. 22:3, 4—And there shall be no curse any more; and the throne of God and of the Lamb shall be therein; and his servants shall serve him; and they shall see his face; and his name shall be on their foreheads.

(Is not this poetic imagery designed to signify the Mind of Christ, the impression stamped upon the believer's heart by the Divine Seal, the Holy Spirit of promise, whose special mission it is, in the present Dispensation, to communicate Christ the Word to His Church)? And in that great quickening, at the Redeemer's Second Advent, the indwelling Spirit (the presence of the Spirit in sanctifying power, whereby the saints are little by little transformed into the image of Christ from glory to glory, 2 Cor. 3:18) will be the Seal by which Christ's own will be recognized, and not only that, but the Power also by which they shall be taken up to meet the Bridegroom (1 Thess. 4:13-17). This—the personal life with the Spirit—is the essential condition of final quickening, which shall include the redemption of the body, that great change for which God's people now wait in hope (Rom. 8:22-25). Rom. 8:11—"But if the Spirit of him that raised up Jesus from the dead dwelleth in you, he that raised up Christ Jesus from the dead shall give life also to your mortal bodies through his Spirit that dwelleth in you." "As the magnet attracts the particles of iron and attaches them to itself by first imparting its own magnetism to them, so Christ, having given his Spirit to his own, will draw them to himself through the Spirit."[1] How vitally important it is, then, that all Christians take heed lest they grieve the Holy Spirit of God in whom they are sealed, lest they mar the Seal by which they have been stamped as God's own possession, lest they deface or obscure the signature by which they are to be recognized in the Day of Redemption. For they certainly can, if they will to do so, turn aside into unbelief, worldliness, and genuine irreligiousness, as the dog turns again to his own vomit (Prov. 26:11, 2 Pet. 2:22), and thereby obliterate the Divine Seal once within them; in which case, the Righteous

1. A. J. Gordon, op. cit., 81.

Judge will be compelled to say to them in the Day of Reckoning, according to the dispensation of Divine Justice: "I never knew you: depart from me, ye that work iniquity" (Matt. 7:23; cf. Matt. 25:41).

To sum up: The Divine Sealing of the saints of God with the Holy Spirit of promise (1) confirms the covenant relationship existing between God and His own people, (2) signifies God's ownership of them, (3) signifies their own separation unto a life of holiness, and (4) is God's pledge that He will bring them into heavenly glory and honor and incorruption, eternal life (Rom. 2:5-7).

8. *The Finger of God.* This metaphor occurs occasionally in Scripture and signifies an operation of the Spirit-power of God. Pharaoh's magicians, for example, discerned the power of God in the miracles which Moses wrought at the Egyptian court, and exclaimed, "This is the finger of God" (Exo. 8:7). In affirming such a judgment, these superstitious pagans no doubt gave expression to a truth more profound than they themselves realized. For demonstration, the work of miracles for evidential purposes, is essentially a work of the Spirit of God. Again, the Decalogue delivered by Moses to the children of Israel is said to have been indited by the finger of God upon "the two tables of the testimony, tables of stone" (Exo. 31:18; cf. Exo. 32:16, Deut. 9:10). This means, obviously, that the Decalogue was communicated to Moses by inspiration of the Spirit. This must be true, for the simple reason that the Spirit is invariably the Revealer of Divine truth, for it is He alone, we are told, who searches and knows "the deep things of God" (1 Cor. 2:10-13). Moreover, since an operation of this kind, that is, one of the character of a revelation, is customarily wrought by the Spirit through the instrumentality of an inspired man, we may reasonably conclude that, whereas the Spirit did the inspiring and the revealing, it was Moses himself who actually did the work of inditing or engraving the words of the Decalogue upon the stone tablets, although he—just as the Apostles on the Day of Pentecost hardly realized, if indeed they realized at all, what they were saying (Acts 2:4)—probably at the time of performing the task was unaware that he was doing so. This conclusion is in harmony with Exo. 34:27-28, which reads as follows: "And Jehovah said unto Moses, Write thou these words: for after the tenor of these words I have made a covenant with thee and with Israel. And he was there with Jehovah forty days and forty nights; he did neither eat

bread, nor drink water. And he wrote upon the tables the words of the covenant, the ten commandments." Again, Jesus Himself, according to Luke, made use of this metaphor in connection with His exorcism of demons. Said He to the Pharisees: "If I by the finger of God cast out demons, then is the kingdom of God come upon you" (Luke 11:20). Matthew, however, quotes Him as saying: "But if I by the Spirit of God cast out demons, then is the kingdom of God come upon you" (Matt. 12:28) Thus it is evident that here again the finger of God is a metaphor of the operation of the Spirit-power of God exercised for the purpose of demonstration. That is to say, when God points His finger at a demon, and says, "Go," it must go. The metaphor is indeed expressive.

9. *The Laying on of Hands.* This act, throughout the Scriptures, is a visible symbol (1) of the communication by the Spirit of special gifts and powers for special Divine purposes, or (2) of the approval by the Spirit of the appointment of a person to some form of ministry in the Church, which is under the administration of the Spirit, or (3) of both enduement of a person with special powers and his ordination to a ministry at one and the same time. The outward sign indicated the transfer of inward spiritual power or authority or both. (1) Num. 27:18-23:

And Jehovah said unto Moses, Take thee Joshua the son of Nun, a man in whom is the Spirit, and lay thy hand upon him; and set him before Eleazar the priest, and before all the congregation; and give him a charge in their sight. And thou shalt put of thine honor upon him, that all the congregation of the children of Israel may obey. And he shall stand before Eleazar the priest, who shall inquire for him by the judgment of the Urim before Jehovah: at his word shall they go out, and at his word shall they come in, both he, and all the children of Israel with him, even all the congregation. And Moses did as Jehovah commanded him; and he took Joshua, and set him before Eleazar the priest, and before all the congregation: and he laid his hands upon him, and gave him a charge, as Jehovah spake by Moses.

Here, evidently, the imposition of hands upon Joshua was for a twofold purpose: to ratify outwardly, in the eyes of all the people, his Divine call to be the successor to Moses; and to signify the Spirit's communication to him of such special inward gifts as might be needed by him in discharging the duties of the office to which he was divinely called (cf. Deut. 34:9). (Cf. Jehovah's "taking of the Spirit that was upon Moses" and "putting it upon" the seventy elders, Num. 11:16-30.) (2) Acts 6:1-6. Here we are told that there arose within the church in Jerusalem, not long after its establishment, a "murmuring" of the Hellenistic Jews against the Palestinian or native Jews, that the widows of the former were being neglected in the daily ministration of charity. Whereupon the Twelve (Apostles) "called the multitude of the disciples unto them, and said, It is not fit that we should forsake the word of God, and serve tables. Look ye out therefore, brethren, from among you seven men of good report, full of the Spirit and of wisdom, whom we may appoint over this business. But we will continue stedfastly in prayer, and in the ministry of the word." This apostolic counsel, we are told, pleased the congregation, and forthwith they selected seven men, "whom they set before the apostles; and when they had prayed, they [the apostles] laid their hands upon them." It is worthy of note that the seven "deacons" in this case were first selected (no doubt *elected*) by the members of the congregation themselves; *then the* Apostles laid their hands upon them. It has been contended by some that the imposition of hands here was merely a part of the ceremony of ordination, a symbol of the Spirit's authorization of their appointment as special servants of the local church. That the act had this symbolic import is no doubt true. But, in my opinion, it signified a great deal more, namely, the communication to these seven men of the *charismatic* measure of the Spirit's power, the measure responsible for the extraordinary (commonly called *miraculous*) gifts of the Spirit which characterized the Church generally throughout the apostolic age. That one of these seven men, namely, Philip, who came to be known as Philip the evangelist (Acts 21:8), possessed these *charismata*, the Scriptures leave no room for doubt. For, in Acts 8:5-8, we find this same man down in Samaria preaching the Gospel to the people of that city. "And Philip went down to the city of Samaria, and proclaimed unto them the Christ. And the multitudes gave heed with one accord unto the things that were spoken by Philip, when they heard, and saw the signs which he did. For from many of those that had unclean spirits, they came out, crying with a loud voice; and many that were lame, were healed. And there was much joy in that city." Now, as the inspired historian goes on to inform us, there was a certain magician or sorcerer in that city by the name of Simon, who had acquired a considerable reputation with the superstitious populace for his apparently extraordinary powers. we read that when the people "believed Philip preaching good tidings concerning the kingdom of God and the name of Jesus

429

Christ, they were baptized, both men and women. And Simon also himself believed, and being baptized, he continued with Philip; and beholding signs and great miracles wrought, he was amazed" (Acts 8:12-13). The question that arises here is this: Whence had Philip, who was *not* an apostle, obtained this charismatic measure, these extraordinary gifts, of the Spirit? There can be but one answer: *At the time the Apostles laid their hands upon him,* when he was ordained a deacon of the Jerusalem congregation; the imposition of apostolic hands at that time was the visible symbol of the Spirit's communication of these special gifts to those upon whom hands were laid. *That this charismatic measure of the Spirit could be conferred only by an apostle* (the Twelve having themselves first received the *baptismal* or *overwhelming* measure of the Spirit on the Day of Pentecost, Acts 2:1-4) is evident from the remainder of the narrative in the eighth chapter of Acts. Here we read, vv. 14-20, as follows:

> Now when the apostles that were at Jerusalem heard that Samaria had received the word of God, they sent unto them Peter and John: who, when they were come down, prayed for them, that they might receive the Holy Spirit: for as yet it was fallen upon none of them; only they had been baptized into the name of the Lord Jesus Christ. Then laid they their hands on them, and they received the Holy Spirit [that is, the *charismatic measure* of the Spirit]. *Now when Simon saw that through the laying on of the apostles' hands the Holy Spirit was given,* he offered them money, saying, Give me also this power, that on whomsoever I lay my hands, he may receive the Holy Spirit. But Peter said unto him, Thy silver perish with thee, because thou hast thought to obtain the gift of God with money, etc.

In this account, the facts regarding the bestowal of the charismatic measure of Spirit-power are made so plain that misunderstanding is impossible. These facts are (a) that this measure of the Spirit could be conferred upon another person only by an apostle, and (b) that the outward sign of the conferring of it was the laying on of an apostle's hand. This explains why Philip, who had received this measure of the Spirit from the Apostles themselves in Jerusalem, as signified outwardly by their laying of their hands upon him, could not himself impart the gift to those converted under his preaching—*Philip was not an apostle.* Hence it was necessary for the Apostles Peter and John to come down to Samaria from Jerusalem, and lay their hands upon Philip's converts, that the latter might, in common with the saints generally throughout the apostolic age, be endued with this measure of the Spirit, for evidential purposes in relation to the unconverted world and for their

430

own strengthening in the most holy faith. The same facts are brought out in the account of Paul's meeting with certain disciples at Ephesus several years later.

Acts 19:1-7: Paul having passed through the upper country came to Ephesus, and found certain disciples: and he said unto them, Did ye receive the Holy Spirit when ye believed? And they said unto him, Nay, we did not so much as hear whether the Holy Spirit was given. And he said, Into what then were ye baptized? And they said, Into John's baptism. And Paul said, John baptized with the baptism of repentance, saying unto the people that they should believe on him that should come after him, that is, on Jesus. And when they heard this, they were baptized into the name of the Lord Jesus. And *when Paul had laid his hands upon them, the Holy Spirit came on them; and they spake with tongues, and prophesied.* And they were in all about twelve men.

Here again it was the charismatic measure of the Spirit which was imparted to new converts, and the outward sign of the communication of the spiritual gift was the laying on of an apostle's hand. That the actual presence of an apostle was necessary to the communication of this gift goes without saying, for only by being present in person could he lay his hands upon another person; the gift was not communicable *in absentia.* Hence says Paul, writing to the Christians in Rome: "For I long to see you, that I may impart unto you some spiritual gift, to the end that ye may be established," that is, confirmed in the faith (Rom. 1:11). All this adds up to one basic incontrovertible fact, namely, that the imposition of an apostle's hand signified at times, whatever secondary import the act may have had, the inward communication of the charismatic measure of Spirit-power. (3) There are instances in the New Testament, however, in which the imposition of hands, accompanied by fasting and prayer, seems to have signified only the Spirit's authorization, as Administrator of the Church of Christ, of the appointment of some person or persons to a special ministry in the Church. A notable instance of this occurs in Acts 13:1-4. Here was read as follows:

Now there were at Antioch, in the church that was there, prophets and teachers, Barnabas, and Symeon that was called Niger, and Lucius of Cyrene, and Manaen the foster-brother of Herod the tetrarch, and Saul. And as they ministered to the Lord, and fasted, the Holy Spirit said, Separate me Barnabas and Saul for the work whereunto I have called them. Then, when they had fasted and prayed and laid their hands on them, they sent them away. So they, being sent forth by the Holy Spirit, went down to Seleucia; and from thence they sailed to Cyprus.

It should be observed that in this entire passage not one word is said about charismatic gifts, and that there is absolutely

431

nothing in the context to warrant the conclusion that any such gifts were imparted. On the contrary, the command of the Holy Spirit in this case, to the prophets and teachers in the Antioch church, was not that they should qualify Paul and Barnabas for the work to which they were being called, but simply that they should formally set them apart to this work. Moreover, since the impartation of such extraordinary gifts of the Spirit was one of the peculiar functions of the Apostolic office, it goes without saying that these prophets and teachers lacked both the authority and the power to impart such gifts. Moreover, even if it could be proved, which it cannot, that these prophets and teachers did have the power to confer on others this special gift of working miracles, it would, nevertheless, be sufficient for our present purpose to point to the fact that Paul at least stood in need of no such gifts. He was not dependent on these gifts, nor on ordination by any group of men, for his divine commission and attendant qualifications to preach the Gospel and to exercise the prerogatives and powers of an apostle (cf. Galatians, chs. 1 and 2). We are therefore compelled to conclude that the imposition of hands, by the prophets and teachers of the Antioch church, was simply the Spirit's outward and formal authorization of these two evangelists, Paul and Barnabas, to the assumption of the special task to which He, the Spirit, had called them. (4) One other passage needs to be considered in this connection, viz., the words of the Apostle Paul to the young preacher, Timothy, 1 Tim. 4:14—"Neglect not the gift that is in thee, which was given thee by prophecy, with the laying on of the hands of the presbytery." The "presbytery," in this passage, is literally the *eldership,* and should be so translated; there is no excuse for using the *transliterated* word here, in this one isolated case in the entire New Testament. Correlating this passage with Acts 16:1-3, it becomes evident that the elders at Lystra had laid their hands on this young preacher for some purpose. It is also clear that Timothy received the same or some other gift by the laying on of Paul's hands. In 2 Tim. 1:6, the Apostle himself says to his protege: "For which cause I put thee in remembrance that thou stir up the gift of God, which is in thee through the laying on of my hands." We may safely conclude, therefore, that whatever the miraculous gift was that Timothy received, he received it from Paul, and that from the elders at Lystra he received the gift of his office as an evangelist. There is no evidence in the New Testament that prophets, teachers or elders had the authority or power to impart to another the charismatic measure of the Spirit; that was a function only of the Apostolic office. Thus the laying on of hands may be the outward symbol of the Spirit's communication of special spiritual gifts, or it may be the outward symbol of His commission to a special ministry in the Church of Christ.

*Fire* is regarded by some commentators as a symbol of the Holy Spirit. This view is based almost exclusively on the correlation of John the Baptizer's statement regarding the mission of Jesus, "He shall baptize you in the Holy Spirit and in fire" (Matt. 3:11), with the description in the second chapter of Acts of the external signs which accompanied the advent of the Spirit on the Day of Pentecost. These signs were "a sound as of the rushing of a mighty wind" and "tongues, parting asunder, like as of fire" (Acts 2:1-4). I am convinced, however, that the Scriptures generally speaking do not support this interpretation. Fire, in Scripture, is a symbol of the Word rather than of the Spirit. Hence the sound as of a rushing mighty wind and the tongues parting asunder resembling fire, on the Day of Pentecost, symbolized the joint operation of the Spirit and the Word, namely, the advent of the Spirit to incorporate and indwell the Church of Christ and the first proclamation of the facts, commands and promises of the Gospel as revealed by the Spirit (Acts 2:1-47). God's Spirit and God's Word go together. Isa. 59:21—"This is my covenant with them, saith Jehovah, my Spirit that is upon thee, and my words which I have put in thy mouth, shall not depart out of thy mouth," etc. Hence, as the Word of God is a savor from life unto life to the saved, being the Divine standard by which they are purified and acquitted, and a savor from death unto death to the lost, being the standard by which they are condemned (2 Cor. 2:16-17, 1 Cor. 3:13), so Fire, which destroys dross, and purges only by destroying, is quite properly a symbol of the moral judgment executed by the Word upon sin and upon the unforgiven sinner (Matt. 25:41, Rev. 20:10, 14). (Matt. 3:11-12, 25:41; 2 Thess. 1:7-10; Rev. 20:10, 14).

## 4. The Holy Spirit as Distinguished from His Gifts

*It is absolutely necessary for anyone who desires to obtain anything like a clear understanding of the Holy Spirit and His work, to keep in mind always the distinction existing between the Spirit Himself on the one hand, and His powers, influences, and gifts, on the other.* As we have already seen, the Scriptures make it clear that the Holy Spirit is Himself, that is, as to essence or being, a Person. He is not a mere impersonal energy or force, something like electricity, for example; nor is He a mere personification of some physical or mental force; He is essentially a Person. As such He is not ontologically one with the powers and influences which He exerts in the physical and moral worlds, but the Source of those powers and influences. As a matter of fact, before there can be activity of any kind, there must of necessity be *a being capable of acting.* Before there can be thought, there must of necessity be a thinker; before there can be love, there must be a lover; before there can be a sin, there must be a sinner. Metaphysically speaking, *being* is the first of all categories, upon which all activity, either physical or mental, is necessarily predicated. The failure to recognize this fundamental truth, or perhaps it would be more correct to say, the deliberate will to ignore it, on the part of a great many thinkers of modern times, has been the cause of much of the confusion which has prevailed in philosophical thought since the time of Descartes. And if we are going to avoid confusion, in our attempt to understand, even partially, the nature and activities of the Spirit of God, we must never lose sight of this ontological distinction between the Spirit Himself and the gifts of the Spirit.

To illustrate, although the illustrations are perforce inadequate: Jennie Lind, for instance, was a person. But she had a gift of song, which we call an art, which enabled her to hold her audience enraptured when she sang "Home, Sweet Home" in Madison Square Garden. But the person, Jennie Lind, was one thing, and the gift or art was another. Leonardo De Vinci was one of the great painters of all time. His talent enabled him to produce the immortal masterpiece, "The Last Supper," a painting which will bless and adorn humanity as long as time lasts. But the person was one thing, and the painting—the person's gift to humanity—was another thing. Thomas A. Edison was a person. But his gifts to humanity were the electric light, the phonograph, and others of like character. Marconi was a person, but his gift to humanity was wireless telegraphy. Similarly, St. Augustine was a great theologian and philosopher. His books have influenced Christian thought and doctrine for centuries. But the man himself, the author, was one thing; his books, and the influences he exerted through them, were another thing. Harriet Beecher Stowe wrote a great novel entitled

*Uncle Tom's Cabin.* The influence of this book was far-reaching; in fact it was one of the direct causes of the American Civil War. By no stretch of the imagination, however, can we regard the book and its author as having been ontologically identical. The same reasoning may be applied to Tom Paine and his *Age of Reason*: Paine himself was a person, one thing; his book, which has influenced thousands of uninformed persons into infidelity, is quite another thing. The author himself has died, but his book and its influence lives on; as a matter of fact, the influence of the book itself will live forever, and in its disastrous effects upon the souls of men will be felt throughout eternity. *Every person exerts individual energies and influences of various kinds; however, the person and his influences are distinct things. So it is with the Holy Spirit: His Person is one thing ontologically, but His powers, influences, and gifts are another thing.*

Moreover, the Holy Spirit being a Person, and incorporeal (that is, in the physical sense of the term), we may reasonably conclude that His powers, influences and gifts are essentially *psychical.* Perhaps some would say that they are "superpsychical." Obviously, however, in the light of our human experience, the adjective "superpsychical," like "superpersonal," is meaningless. The most we can say, with any degree of comprehension, is that the powers of the Spirit are essentially psychical. As such, of course, they may transmute themselves into physical manifestations; for thoughts, as we have learned, may indeed become things. Now, because both the *being* and the *activity* of the Spirit are characteristically psychical (and incorporeal), it is practically impossible for the human intellect, unless it is trained acutely in logical and in ontological discernment, to be able to differentiate between these two aspects of existence. As a matter of fact, with respect to man himself *as a person,* it is very difficult to grasp the distinction between a human being *as a being* (person), on the one hand, and that person's *thought* or characteristic activity as a person, on the other hand. What indeed is the ontological difference between a human being and his own thought? About all we can say is that, logically, *thinking presupposes being,* that is, a *thinker.* Beyond this we cannot go, because science has no instruments, no means of any kind whatsoever, for ascertaining experimentally the real nature of either being or thinking, or of the difference ontologically between being and thinking, in man. If this be true with respect to *being* and *activity* in man, and we know that it is, how infinitely more true it is with respect to the Being and Activity of the

Holy Spirit. Hence, in the nomenclature of the Spirit Himself, as found in Scripture, no such distinction is explicitly asserted: the Bible, it must be remembered, is not a text on metaphysics. The Spirit reveals Himself to us in Scripture in terms adapted to our comprehension, that is, as possessing the faculties or powers that only a person is known by us to possess, as doing the things that only a person is known by us to do, and as experiencing the slights that only a person is known by us to experience. By the revelation of these truths in the simplest form possible, the Spirit impresses upon our minds the fact that He is, in Himself, in His essential being, a Person. On the other hand, because the Holy Spirit, is made known to us (imparted to us, it may be truly said) only through His psychical powers and influences, the nomenclature of the Spirit, for all practical purposes and in adaptation especially to the limitations of the human intellect, treats the *being* of the Spirit as fundamentally identical with His psychical *activity*. However, in order that we may not become confused, we must never lose sight of the fact that the Spirit Himself is a Person, and that *as a Person* He Himself is to be kept distinct from His activity, in our thinking about Him.

For example, we are told by Jesus Himself (John 4:24) that God IS *a* Spirit (or Spirit). That is to say, He is a spiritual or incorporeal Being: in the words of one of the older catechisms, a Being "without body or parts, yet possessing understanding and free will." Then again the Scriptures make it clear that God HAS Spirit (1 Cor. 2:10-14). That is to say, God HAS Spirit in that He includes in the totality of His Being the being of the Spirit and therefore the powers and influences of the being of the Spirit. In the third place, it is frequently asserted in Scripture that God GIVES Spirit, or *the* Spirit, to human individuals under certain conditions and for specific purposes (Neh. 9:20, John 3:34, John 7:39, Acts 5:32, Acts 15:8, Rom. 5:5, 1 Thess. 4:8, 1 John 3:24, etc.). How, then, does God give the Spirit, Himself a Person, to another person? Obviously, it is only by giving to men—imparting to them—the psychical powers and influences of the Spirit, that God can impart to them in any sense the being of the Spirit. Strictly speaking, one person as such could hardly give himself, or be given by someone else, to another person, because every person is a distinct individual and therefore an absolute *other* to all other persons; rather, it is only the psychical powers and influences of one person that can be given or imparted to another person. Hence, when God is said to *give* the Spirit to men, it is really the psychical powers and influences which are given; it is only in this sense that the Spirit Himself can be said to be given. It is worthy of note, too, as confirmed by human experience, that psychical powers and influences can in a very real sense be transferred from one person to another; as a matter of fact, practically all human learning is of the character of such a transfer. And it can be said also that in such a transfer the being of one person is, in a certain sense, communicated to the other; that is, in the sense that the communicated influences become an integral part of the personality receiving them. This indeed is the perfectly natural and inevitable result of living the life with the Holy Spirit. Hence, men are said in Scripture, that is, in the nomenclature of the Spirit Himself, to *receive* the Spirit (Acts 8:15, 17, 19; Acts 10:47, 19:2; Gal. 3:2), to *have* the Spirit (Rom. 8:9, 1 Cor. 7:40, Jude 19), to be *filled with* the Spirit (Exo. 31:3, 35:31; Luke 1:15, 41, 67; Acts 2:4, 4:8, 4:31, 9:17, 13:9, 13:52; Eph. 5:18), to be *full of* the Spirit, etc. (cf. especially Luke 4:1—here it is said that "Jesus, full of the Holy Spirit, returned from the Jordan"; cf. also Deut. 34:9; Acts 6:3, 5; Acts 7:55, 11:24, etc.); that is to say, they receive, they have, they are filled with, or full of, the powers and graces of the Spirit (in various measures, of course, for various ends, as we shall see later). And, conversely, the Spirit is said to be— through His various powers and influences—*upon* men (Isa. 42:1, 59:21; Isa. 61:1; Luke 2:25, 4:18, etc.), *in* men (Gen. 41:38; Num. 27:18; Psa. 51:11; Ezek. 36:26; Rom. 8:11; 1 Cor. 6:19; Jas. 4:5; cf. Jer. 3:14, Hos. 2:19 ff., with marginal rendering of Jas. 4:5: "That Spirit which he made to dwell in us yearneth for us even unto jealous envy"); to *come upon* men (Num. 24:2; Judg. 3:10, 11:29; 1 Sam. 19:20, 23; 2 Chron. 15:1; Luke 1:35; Acts 1:8); to *come mightily upon* them (Judg. 14:6; 14:19, 15:14; 1 Sam. 10:6, 10:10, 11:6, 16:13); to *come unto* them (John 16:7, 8, 13); to *fall upon* them (Ezek. 11:5; Acts 10:44, 11:15); to *rest upon* them (Num. 11:25, 26; Isa. 11:2); to *enter into* them (Ezek. 2:2, 3:24); to *clothe Himself with* them (Judg. 6:34, 1 Chron. 12:18, 2 Chron. 24:20); to *dwell in* them (Rom. 8:9, 11; 1 Cor. 3:16, 6:19; Jas. 4:5); to *abide in, upon or among* them (John 1:33; Isa. 63:11; 2 Chron. 20:14; Hag. 2:5); and to *depart from* them (Psa. 51:11, 1 Sam. 16:14, 1 Ki. 22:24). The Spirit accomplishes all these operations through the media of His powers, influences and graces. With the same signification, God Himself is said to *give* the Spirit to men, as we have seen already; to *put His Spirit* upon them (Num. 11:17, 25, 29; Isa. 42:1; Matt. 12:18); to *put His Spirit within* them (Ezek. 11:19, 36:26, 37:14); to *pour out His Spirit upon* them (Prov. 1:23; Isa. 32:15, 44:3; Ezek. 39:29; Joel 2:28-29; Zech. 12:10; Acts 2:17, 18, 33; Acts 10:45); to *fill them with* His Spirit (Exo. 28:3, 31:3, 35:31; Acts 2:4); and to *take His Spirit from* them (Psa. 51:11). Obviously, the reference in all these passages is to the powers, influences and graces of the Spirit. To give these powers and influences to men is equivalent to giving the Spirit to them; to pour out these powers and influences upon men is equivalent to pouring out the Spirit upon them; to put these powers and influences upon or in men is equivalent to putting the Spirit upon or in them; to fill men with these powers and influences of the Spirit is equivalent to filling them with the Spirit; and to take these powers and influences from men is equivalent to taking the Spirit from them. However, as previously stated, in studying the Holy Spirit and His activity, it is exceedingly important, if we would avoid confusion in our thinking, to keep in mind at all times the distinction that exists ontologically between the Spirit Himself and the gifts and graces which He bestows upon men.

It seems to me that the key to a proper understanding of this whole subject of the enduements of the Spirit is to be found in the testimony of John the Baptizer respecting Jesus the Messiah, in John 3:27-36. Among other things, the Baptizer says, v. 34: "For he whom God hath sent speaketh the words of God: for he giveth not the Spirit by measure" (the rendering of the American Revised Version). There is a textual difficulty here, however; namely, as to whether the *ho theos*, which appears in some ancient sources as the subject of *didōsin* ("giveth"), in the second sentence, is genuine. Those who do not regard it as genuine (it is marked doubtful by Lachmann, and is deleted by Tischendorf (8th edition), Westcott and Hort, and others) usually give some such rendering as that of the American Revised Version: "for he giveth not the Spirit by measure." Obviously this rendering tends to obscure the meaning of the passage; it makes it impossible to determine whether it is God, Christ ("he whom God hath sent"), or even the Spirit Himself, "who giveth the Spirit without measure." As a matter of fact, three interpretations have been suggested, viz., (1) *For God giveth not the Spirit by measure*, (2) *For he, i.e., the Messiah, giveth not the Spirit by measure* (preferred by Westcott, and those who see in the entire passage the reflections of the author of the Gospel, rather than the testimony of the Baptizer), and (3) *For the Spirit giveth not by measure,* the object to be supplied being "the words of God." Granting that the *ho theos* is genuine, the passage would read, of course: "For God giveth not the Spirit by measure." It is so translated in the Authorized Version, the King James translators having added the phrase "unto him," to complete the meaning, rendering the entire passage as follows: "For he whom God hath sent speaketh the words of God; for God giveth not the Spirit by measure unto him." This seems to me to be the correct rendering of the passage. For, regardless of the difficulties of text, its meaning is made crystal clear by the context. Throughout this entire passage (namely, vv. 27-36), the Baptizer is testifying regarding the Messiah: "he that cometh from above," "he that cometh from heaven" (v. 31), "he whom God hath sent" (v. 34). And even though John is speaking here in general terms, the reference in v. 34 is plainly to Jesus, the Son of God, the One whom God hath sent,—He who alone was capable of receiving the fulness of the Spirit, and upon whom alone, as the Scriptures expressly assert, the fulness of the Spirit was bestowed. "The Spirit of God, even in the inspired prophets, was but a partial and intermittent gift (1 Cor. 7:25, 13:9; 1 Pet. 1:11; Heb. 1.1, etc.), but in Jesus, the Messiah and the Son of God, the Spirit of God dwelt fully and uninterruptedly."[1] "The God-man, in his servant-form, knew and taught and performed only what the Spirit permitted and directed."[2]

Cf. Col. 1:19—For it was the good pleasure of the Father that in him should all the fulness dwell. Heb. 1:1-3: God . . . hath at the end of these days spoken unto us in his Son . . . who being the effulgence of his glory, and the very image of his substance, etc. 2 Cor. 3:17—Now the Lord is the Spirit. Heb. 9:14: How much more shall the blood of Christ, who through the eternal Spirit offered himself without blemish unto God, etc. Matt. 4:1—Then was Jesus led up of the Spirit into the wilderness to be tempted of the devil. Luke 4:1— And Jesus, full of the Holy Spirit, returned from the Jordan, and was led in the Spirit in the wilderness, etc. Matt. 12:28—[the words of Jesus Himself]: But if I by the Spirit of God cast out demons, then is the kingdom of God come upon you. From these Scriptures, and many others of like import, it is evident that Jesus, the Messiah, the One whom God sent into the world to speak the words of God, *always* spoke and acted under the inspiration and guidance of the Holy Spirit. Hence, the Baptizer, who was himself inspired by the Spirit, was right in declaring that Jesus, God's Son, *possessed the Holy Spirit without measure.* And that this is precisely what John did declare in the text in question, John 3:34, is crystal clear. In the first place, it is the

1. J. W. McGarvey and Philip Y. Pendleton, *The Fourfold Gospel,* 137.

2. A. H. Strong, *Systematic Theology,* One-volume Edition, 696.

only interpretation that is in harmony with the context, both with the verses which immediately precede it, as we have already seen, and also those which immediately follow, in which John concludes his testimony with these words: The Father loveth the Son, and hath given all things into his hand. He that believeth on the Son hath eternal life; but he that obeyeth not the Son shall not see life, but the wrath of God abideth on him (vv. 35-36). In the second place, it is the only interpretation that is in harmony with Scripture teaching as a whole. Hence Dr. Goodspeed's excellent rendering of the passage: "For he whom God has sent speaks God's words, for God gives him his Spirit without measure.[1] It was a common observation among the Jews that the Holy Spirit was given only in certain measures to the prophets, some writing only one book, some two, and so on. But Jesus, the perfect Teacher, possessed the Holy Spirit without measure, not for any particular time, purpose, or people, but for all time and from all eternity. Moreover, it should be noted that the present tense, "giveth," in this text, points to a continuous communication (or possession) of the Spirit; in other words, if Christ had received the Spirit "by measure," then His gift of the Spirit might conceivably have been exhausted. And of course we know that this did not happen, for we read that at the end of His earthly ministry He through the eternal Spirit offered himself without blemish unto God (Heb. 9:14).

The significance of this text, however, for our present purpose is in the truth which it asserts implicitly. Explicitly it affirms that Jesus, the God-man, possessed the Holy Spirit *without measure*. Implicitly it asserts, therefore, that human beings can possess the Spirit only *by measure;* that is to say, they possess various measures of the Spirit—actually of the Spirit's powers and influences—for various Divine ends, the measure bestowed being in adaptation to the Divine purpose to be accomplished in the bestowing of it. This is a truth of the utmost importance. It is my conviction that the failure of churchmen to differentiate between these different measures of Spirit-power, and the corresponding purposes respectively for which they were conferred, has been the source of much of the confusion which has always prevailed in Christian doctrine regarding the operations of the Holy Spirit in general. This subject will be dealt with later, in some detail, in separate chapters on these various measures of Spirit-power and the respective ends served by the conferring of them. For the present purpose, however, it will suffice to present the bare facts, with the Scripture references to support them, as follows:

1. God gives the Spirit *by measure* unto men, as clearly implied in the words of John the Baptizer, in John 3:34. Jesus Christ alone possessed the powers and influences of the Spirit *without measure, i.e.,* in their fulness (Col. 1:19, 2:9).

1. Edgar J. Goodspeed, *The New Testament: An American Translation,* 179.

2. The *baptismal* or *overwhelming* measure of Spirit-power (designated in Scripture *the baptism of the Holy Spirit*), the greatest measure of the Spirit ever conferred upon men, was administered by Christ Himself, and was conferred directly from Heaven in fulfilment of Divine promise (Luke 24:45-49; John 14:16-17, 14:26, 15:26, 16:7; Acts 1:1-8). In so far as the facts are revealed in the book of Acts, in which the history of the Church in apostolic times is given, this measure of Spirit-power was conferred only twice: it was conferred *first* upon the Apostles in Jerusalem on the Day of Pentecost (Acts 1:26— 2:4, 2:32-33), and the *second* time upon Cornelius and his household at Caesarea some years afterward (Acts 10:44-48, 11:15-18, 15:7-9).

[Note Peter's words], Acts 11:15-17—And as I began to speak, the Holy Spirit fell on them [Cornelius and his house], even as on us at the beginning [*i.e.*, on the Apostles, on the Day of Pentecost, the day of the beginning of the New Institution, the Church of Christ]. . . . And I remembered the word of the Lord, how he said, John indeed baptized with water, but ye shall be baptized in the Holy Spirit. If then God gave unto them [Gentiles] the like gift as he did also unto us [Jews], when we believed on the Lord Jesus Christ, who was I, that I could withstand God? [Note also Peter's words in Acts 15:8, 9— referring again to the conversion of Cornelius]: And God, who knoweth the heart, bare them [Gentiles] witness, giving them the Holy Spirit, even as he did unto us [Jews]; and he made no distinction between us and them, cleansing their hearts by faith.

The Apostle's language in both of these passages makes it very clear that no similar outpouring of Spirit-power in baptismal measure had taken place in the interim between the Day of Pentecost and the conversion of the first Gentiles in the persons of Cornelius and the members of his household. Nor is there the slightest intimation in the book of Acts that any similar outpouring occurred after this first admission of Gentiles into the Body of Christ. Moreover, in both of these instances Holy Spirit baptism was a special miracle for a special Divine purpose. This baptismal measure of the Spirit's powers and influences was conferred upon the Apostles on Pentecost (1) to clothe them with infallibility in presenting the Christian System —the Gospel, with its facts, commands and promises—to men, thus bringing to completion the progressive revelation of God to His moral creatures (cf. again Luke 24:45-49; John 14:26, 15:26-27, 16:7-14, 20:21-23; Acts 1:8, 2:32-36, 10:39; 1 Cor. 2:10-13, etc.), and (2) to endue them with the power to work miracles to demonstrate the divine origin and authority of this message which they were to give to the world (1 Cor. 2:1-5,

Heb. 2:3-4, etc.). The same measure of the Spirit conferred upon Cornelius and his household at Caesarea some years later, for the purpose of breaking down "the middle wall of partition" between Jews and Gentiles (Eph. 2:11-18); in a word, it was to signify to the Jews in unmistakable terms that the Gentiles were to be admitted to the blessings of the New Covenant along with them and on the same conditions (cf. again Acts 10:44-48, 11:15-18, 15:7-9; 1 Cor. 12:13). Finally, it should be noted, for our present purpose, that *to receive the baptismal measure of the Spirit's powers and influences was, in the words of the inspired Apostle himself, to receive the Holy Spirit.* Cf. again the two passages having reference to Holy Spirit baptism, viz., Acts 10:46, 47—"Then answered Peter, Can any man forbid the water, that these should not be baptized, who have received the Holy Spirit as well as we?" And Acts 15:8—"And God, who knoweth the heart, bare them witness, giving them the Holy Spirit, even as he did unto us."

3. The *evidential* or *confirmatory* measure of Spirit-power was conferred only by the Apostles themselves and only upon obedient believers, that is, upon Christians. This measure of the Spirit was conferred upon the saints generally, and upon Christian prophets and teachers in particular, throughout the apostolic age and prior to the writing and formation of the Canon. The visible symbol of the communication of this measure of spiritual power was the laying on of an Apostle's hands (Acts 6:3-6, 8:14-29, 19:1-7; Rom. 1:11-12; 2 Tim. 1:6, etc.), and the saints who received this transfer of spiritual power were qualified with certain abnormal (usually called *miraculous*) endowments which are Scripturally designated "spiritual gifts" (1 Cor. 12:1, 4, 31; 14:1). The Greek word for such a "gift" is *charisma* (plural, *charismata*); hence this measure of Spirit-power may properly be called the *charismatic* measure. This measure of the Spirit was conferred upon the early Christians for a twofold purpose: (1) to evince to the outside world the Divine origin and authority of the Gospel message, and (2) to confirm the saints themselves in the most holy faith (Mark 16:19-20; Acts 8:4-8; Rom. 1:11, 12; 1 Cor. 2:1-5; Rom. 1:11-12; Heb. 2:2-4). In view of the fact that the presence of an Apostle was necessary to the communication of this measure of Spirit-power, the transfer of it obviously terminated with the death of the last of the Apostles. Hence there is no evidence that these *charismata* extended beyond the apostolic age; as a matter of fact, Paul himself clearly asserts that they were to be "done

away" (1 Cor. 13:8-13) and to be superseded by "the most excellent way" of Love (1 Cor. 12:31, 13:1 ff.). "In the primitive churches," writes Moses E. Lard,

these gifts took the place, and answered the purpose of the present written word. By them the churches were built up and kept in order. In a word, every thing was done by them—the gospel was preached, the disciples instructed, and the churches ruled. They were then indispensable; but now they are not, the New Testament supplying their place.[1]

Finally, it should be noted again that, as in the receiving of Holy Spirit baptism, *the receiving of the charismatic measure of Spirit-power is described, in the nomenclature of the Spirit Himself, as the receiving of the Spirit.* We read, for example, in Acts 8:14-19, that

when the apostles that were at Jerusalem heard that Samaria had received the word of God [from Philip the evangelist], they sent unto them [*i.e.*, Philip's converts] Peter and John: who, when they were come down [to Samaria], prayed for them, that they might receive the Holy Spirit: for as yet it was fallen upon none of them: only they had been baptized into the name of the Lord Jesus. Then laid they [*i.e.*, Peter and John] their hands upon them, and *they received the Holy Spirit.* [We go on to read that when Simon the sorcerer, himself a baptized believer] saw that through the laying on of the apostles' hands the Holy Spirit was given, he offered them money, saying, Give me also this power, *that on whomsoever I lay my hands, he may receive the Holy Spirit,* etc.

In other words, to receive the charismatic measure of Spirit-power was to receive the Holy Spirit. The same truth is clearly set forth in Acts 19:1-7.

[Here we read that] Paul having passed through the upper country came to Ephesus, and found certain disciples: and he said unto them, *Did ye receive the Holy Spirit when ye believed?* And they said unto him, Nay, we did not so much as hear whether the Holy Spirit was given. And he said, Into what then were ye baptized? And they said, Into John's baptism. And Paul said, John baptized with the baptism of repentance, saying unto the people that they should believe on him that should come after him, that is, on Jesus. And when they heard this, they were baptized into the name of the Lord Jesus. And when Paul had laid his hands upon them, the Holy Spirit came on them; and they spake with tongues, and prophesied. And they were in all about twelve men.

In this instance again it is quite clear that in receiving the charismatic measure of Spirit-power, these baptized believers are said to have received the Holy Spirit, and, conversely, *they are said to have received the Spirit in the sense that, through the laying on of the Apostle's hands, they received the charismatic measure of the Spirit's powers and influences. The point to*

1. Moses E. Lard, *Commentary on Romans*, 384.

be remembered, however, is that proper distinction must be made in our thinking between the Spirit Himself and the various measures of His powers and influences which were, and are, bestowed upon the saints.

4. Finally, there is the *regenerating* and *sanctifying* measure of Spirit-power which is given to every baptized believer in Christ. This measure of the Spirit is received "by the hearing of faith" (Gal. 3:2); that is, by the reception of the living Word into one's heart and the assimilation of that Word into one's life.

Rom. 10:6-10: But the righteousness which is of faith saith thus, Say not in thy heart, Who shall ascend into heaven? (that is, to bring Christ down:) or, Who shall descend into the abyss? (that is, to bring Christ up from the dead.) But what saith it? The word is nigh thee, in thy mouth, and in thy heart: that is, the word of faith, which we preach: because if thou shalt confess with thy mouth Jesus as Lord, and shalt believe in thy heart that God raised him from the dead, thou shalt be saved: for with the heart man believeth unto righteousness; and with the mouth confession is made unto salvation.

This measure of Spirit-power is received, then, to the degree that one walks in the light of the Word (which is to walk by the Spirit, Gal. 5:16, 25), lives by the Word, and triumphs by means of the Word over all the obstacles of this present world which would hinder his growth in holiness. 1 John 5:4—"This is the victory that hath overcome the world, even our faith." This is the measure of the Spirit which is promised to men on the conditions of their repentance and baptism (in water) into Christ (Gal. 3:26-27). Both the promise itself and the necessary conditions to its fulfilment are clearly stated at the conclusion of the first Gospel sermon ever preached to men, Acts 2:38— "Repent ye, and be baptized every one of you in the name of Jesus Christ unto the remission of your sins; and ye shall receive the gift of the Holy Spirit." The phrase, "the gift of the Holy Spirit," here, is equivalent to "the Holy Spirit as a gift." The passage means simply that the Holy Spirit comes to take up His abode in the heart of every obedient believer at the time of his baptism into Christ, and continues to dwell in him thereafter according to the measure of his faith, which in turn is determined by the degree of his own yielding of his mind and affection and will to the revealed Mind (the Word) of Christ. Rom. 10:17—"So belief cometh of hearing, and hearing by the word of Christ." Hence the Church, the Body of Christ, constituted of all the elect of God under the New Covenant, is said to be the "habitation of God in the Spirit" (Eph. 2:22), because all individual members of the Body are indwelt by the one and the same Spirit (Rom. 5:5; 1 Cor. 3:16, 6:19; 2 Cor. 1:22; Eph. 1:13; Gal. 4:6, etc.). Now one can be filled with the sanctifying measure of the Spirit only by being filled with the Thought and Love of the Spirit, which are the Thought and Love of God. And one can be filled with the Spirit's Thought and Love only by feeding upon, digesting, and assimilating the Word, *i.e.*, into the structure of his personality and life; for it is in the Word that the Thought and Love of the Spirit are embodied, and it is by the Word that the Thought and Love of the Spirit are mediated to men. To possess the Word in great measure is, therefore, to possess the sanctifying power of the Spirit in great measure. Not that the Spirit is the Word, but that the power of the Spirit is in the Word and is exercised through the Word in the regeneration and sanctification of sinners. Certainly where there is no hearing, no reading, of the Gospel, no contact whatever of the alien sinner with the facts, commands and promises of the Gospel, there is no conversion to Christ, no subsequent growth in the grace and knowledge of Christ; that is to say, no growth in holiness. The whole missionary enterprise of the Church is predicated upon this fundamental fact. *God's Spirit and God's Word go together* (Isa. 59:21). Hence the implanted Word (Jas. 1:21) is the mode of the Spirit's indwelling, and the evidence of this Divine indwelling is the fruit of the Spirit manifested in the indivdual Christian life (Gal. 5:22-25). And finally, as with the baptismal and charismatic measures of Spirit-power, *baptized believers are said in Scripture to receive the Spirit in the sense that they receive, through the obedience of faith on their part, the regenerating and sanctifying measure of the Spirit's powers and influences.* But once more this word of caution: *We must keep in mind the ontological distinction between the Spirit Himself and the various measures of Spirit-power dispensed by the Spirit.*

Again, it is significant, I think, that each of these measures of the Spirit's powers and influences, viz., the baptismal, charismatic, and sanctifying measures, respectively, is described in Scripture as a *gift*. And it is equally significant that the Greek word for "gift," as signifying a bestowal of any one of these three general measures of Spirit-power, is the word *dōrea*, as distinguished from the word *charisma*, which is used generally to signify the abnormal endowments which ensued, in apostolic times, from the reception of the *evidential* measure of the Spirit. For example, in Acts 10:45, the baptismal measure of the Spirit is designated a *gift*. Here we read as follows, with reference to

445

the coming of the Spirit in baptismal measure upon Cornelius and his household: "And they of the circumcision that believed were amazed, as many as came with Peter, because that on the Gentiles also was poured out the gift of the Holy Spirit." And Peter himself, later, defending his action in preaching the Gospel to Gentiles, said with reference to the same event: "If then God gave unto them [Gentiles] the like gift as he did also unto us [Jews], when we believed on the Lord Jesus Christ, who was I, that I could withstand God?" (Acts 11:17). Again, in Acts 8:20, in the reply of the Apostle Peter to Simon the sorcerer, the charismatic measure of the Spirit is designated "the gift of God": "Peter said unto him, Thy silver perish with thee, because thou hast thought to obtain the gift of God with money." And in Acts 2:38, the text in which Peter first stated the terms of pardon under the New Covenant, that sanctifying measure of the Spirit is also designated a gift: "And Peter said unto them, Repent ye, and be baptized every one of you in the name of Jesus Christ unto the remission of your sins; and ye shall receive the gift of the Holy Spirit." Now in all of these texts the Greek word *dōrea* is used for "gift"; and in two of them, Acts 10:45 and Acts 2:38, *dōrea* is used with the genitive of that of which the gift consists, namely, the Holy Spirit, that is to say, His indwelling presence and power. Thus in the nomenclature of the Spirit Himself, a clear distinction is made between those general gifts from above, on the one hand, which were in the form of various *measures* of Spirit-power, and the special *distributions* of Spirit-power, on the other hand, which were granted to the saints generally throughout the apostolic age (*i.e.*, the *charismata*), which took the form of special abnormal endowments for evidential purposes.

A word or two becomes necessary at this point regarding the *charismata* themselves.

[In Mark 16:15-18, we read that Jesus, just before His ascension to the Father, said to the Eleven] Go ye into all the world, and preach the gospel to the whole creation. He that believeth and is baptized shall be saved; but he that disbelieveth shall be condemned. And these signs shall accompany them that believe: in my name shall they cast out demons; they shall speak with new tongues; they shall take up serpents, and if they drink any deadly thing, it shall in no wise hurt them; they shall lay hands on the sick, and they shall recover. [To these statements the writer of the Gospel himself adds these words]: So then the Lord Jesus, after he had spoken unto them, was received up into heaven, and sat down at the right hand of God. And they went forth, and preached everywhere, the Lord working with them, and confirming the word by the signs that followed (vv. 19-20).

446

I realize of course that this entire section, Mark 16:9-20, does not appear in the two oldest Greek manuscripts, and that its genuineness is therefore in question. Be that as it may, however, the fact remains that the content of the entire passage is in strict harmony with what follows in Luke's account of the early Church, in Acts, and in the various New Testament Epistles. Thus, in Heb. 2:2-4, we read the following:

> For if the word spoken through angels proved stedfast, and every transgression and disobedience received a just recompense of reward; how shall we escape, if we neglect so great a salvation? which having at the first been spoken through the Lord, was confirmed unto us by them that heard; God also bearing witness with them, both by signs and wonders, and by manifold powers, and by gifts of the Holy Spirit, according to his own will.

Now the word in this text which is translated "gifts" in the American Revised Version (Greek, *merismos;* dative plural, *merismois*), literally rendered is "distributions"; hence the entire phrase should be given, "distributions of the Holy Spirit." Thus the meaning of the passage is clear: These special distributions of Spirit-power, or rather the miracles performed as a result of them, were the means by which God Himself attested the Gospel message as proclaimed by the Apostles, Prophets, Teachers and Evangelists of the early Church. These extraordinary powers are designated, in this text and elsewhere in the New Testament, (1) *signs*, with reference to their design; (2) *wonders*, with respect to their nature as abnormal manifestations calculated to excite amazement in the minds of those who witnessed them; (3) *manifold powers*, with respect to their origin from the being of God; and finally, in their specifically Christian aspect, *gifts* or *distributions of the Holy Spirit*, imparted to the original witnesses and proclaimers of the truth, according to the will of God. These abnormal powers are designated elsewhere in the New Testament, in the Greek, *charismata*, which, rendered in English, is "gracious gifts." The general New Testament name for them is "spiritual gifts." Paul enumerates these *charismata* in 1 Cor. 12:4-11:

> Now there are diversities of gifts [*charismaton*] [he writes] but the same Spirit. And there are diversities of ministrations, and the same Lord. And there are diversities of workings, but the same God who worketh all things in all. But to each one is given the manifestation of the Spirit to profit withal. For to one is given through the Spirit the word of wisdom; and to another the word of knowledge, according to the same Spirit; to another faith, in the same Spirit; and to another gifts of healings, in the one Spirit; and to another workings of miracles; and to another prophecy; and to another discernings of spirits; to another divers kinds of tongues; and to another the inter-

pretation of tongues. [Then the Apostle concludes by saying]: But all these worketh the one and the same Spirit, dividing to each one severally even as he will.

These various "manisfestations" of the Spirit ensued from the reception of the charismatic measure of Spirit-power. And this measure, as it has already been made clear, (1) was conferred upon the early Christians generally, prior to the inditing of the Word, and (2) was conferred for a twofold purpose, viz., to attest the Divine origin and content of the Gospel message, and to confirm the saints in "the faith which was once for all delivered" (Jude 6). (*Revelation* is thus, as always, attested by *demonstration*.) Moreover, the outward symbol of the communication of this inward spiritual power was, as has also been shown, the laying on of an Apostle's hands. I cannot emphasize the fact too strongly that failure to recognize the purpose served by the *charismata*, and hence their temporary significance only, has always been a prime source of error regarding the operations of the Spirit in general.

To sum up: "There is one body, and one Spirit" (Eph. 4:4). "There are diversities of gifts[*charismata*], but the same Spirit" (1 Cor. 12:4). Again: "But all these [*charismata*] worketh the one and the same Spirit, dividing to each one severally even as he will" (1 Cor. 12:11). In a word, there is but one Spirit; the distributions of His powers and influences, however, are many and varied. These distributions—all of which are called *gifts*, in Scripture—are distributions both according to *measure* and according to *kind*; in the former category, the gift is designated a *dōrea*; in the latter, a *charisma*. There is but one Spirit, and He Himself must be kept distinct in our thinking, both (1) from the general gifts (singular, *dōrea*), in the form of distinct measures of Spirit-power conferred upon various classes of persons for as many different ends; and (2) from the *charismata*, those special gifts, varying as to kind, conferred upon the early Christians in general as a result of their enduement with the charismatic measure of Spirit-power, and conferred upon them for the twofold purpose as explained in the foregoing paragraphs. The Holy Spirit is one, His gifts are something else, ontologically.

## 5. Modes of Dispensing the Spirit

By this caption, "modes of dispensing the Spirit," is meant, of course, modes of dispensing the powers, graces and gifts of the Spirit. On the basis of the nomenclature of the Spirit, these various modes may be classified in two categories, namely, (1) the modes by which God disposes the powers and influences of the Spirit to the three great works of Creation, Providence and Redemption — those three Divine works which embrace all other activities of Deity; and (2) the modes by which the Spirit Himself voluntarily applies His powers and influences to the works which He condescends to perform.

In the nomenclature of the Spirit, as found in Scripture, God is said to do the following:

1. To *give* the Spirit, *i.e.*, the powers, gifts and graces of the Spirit. Thus, as we have already noted, God gave the Spirit without measure to His Only Begotten Son, Messiah (John 3:34); He gave the Spirit, in the capacity of Comforter (Revealer, Strengthener, Advocate, Guide), in baptismal measure to the Apostles (John 14:16-17, 14:26, 15:26; Acts 1:1-5, 2:1-4); He gave the Spirit in evidential measure to the saints generally throughout the apostolic age (Acts 8:14-20, 19:1-7; 1 Cor. 12:4-11; Heb. 2:3-4); and He gives the Spirit in sanctifying measure to all obedient believers in all ages (Luke 11:13; John 7:39; Acts 2:38, 5:32; Rom. 5:5; 1 Cor. 3:16, 6:19; 1 Thess. 4:8; 1 John 3:24, etc.). Hence, throughout Scripture, the Holy Spirit is graciously and significantly designated the *gift* of God (*e.g.*, Acts 2:38, 8:20); and those different classes upon whom the various powers and influences of the Spirit were bestowed are said to have *received* the Spirit as a Divine gift. Only chosen leaders received Him in Old Testament times, and that not for the salvation of their souls, but for the working of various needful works in the unfolding of God's Plan of Redemption for man. Under the present Dispensation, all true members of the New Covenant receive Him, in various measures adapted to corresponding Divine ends (Joel 2:28-29, John 7:37-39; Acts 2:15-21, etc.). The Apostles received Him in *overwhelming* measure, to vest them with authority to act as ambassadors of Christ to men (John 20:21-23; Luke 24:45-49; Acts 1:8; 2 Cor. 5:20; Eph. 6:20), and to clothe them with infallibility to reveal all truth pertaining to the Kingdom of God (John 14:26, 16:13-15; 1 Cor. 2:9-13; Eph. 3:3-12; 1 Pet. 1:10-12) and to embody this final revelation in permanent form in the New Testament canon (2 Pet. 1:3). And Cornelius and his household, the first converts to Christianity from among the Gentiles, also received Holy Spirit baptism, to establish the fact once for all that the blessings of the Gospel are for both Gentiles and Jews and on the same conditions (Acts 10:47, 11:17, 15:7-9). Moreover,

Christians generally throughout the apostolic age received the Spirit's powers and influences in *extraordinary* measure, and for evidential purposes; that is, to evince to the outside world, by these *signs,* the divine origin of the Gospel message and to confirm the saints themselves in the most holy faith (1 Cor. 12:4-11, Rom. 1:11-12, Heb. 2:3-4). And all true Christians in all ages receive His indwelling presence—the *sanctifying* measure of His power—by opening their hearts to Him through the obedience of faith (Gal. 3:2, Acts 2:38, etc.). As to the question whether the giving and receiving of the regenerating and sanctifying measure of Spirit-power involves some sort of a mystical communication from the Spirit Himself to the converted person, as a result of the latter's faith, obedience and pardon, I am prepared to say only that I find no intimation, in Scripture, of such an impartation. However, I certainly am not so presumptuous as to attempt myself to impose limitations upon the Spirit's power or activity. Moreover, this question is not one of *power,* but of *fact;* that is, of the facts revealed *in the Scriptures* regarding the Divine mode of dispensing this measure of the Spirit. And to my way of thinking the Scriptures make it very clear that, in so far as the generality of Christians is concerned, God gives the Spirit to them in regenerating and sanctifying measure through the Word which they receive into their hearts (Jas. 1:21, 1 Pet. 1:22-25, Eph. 1:13), and upon which they feed thereafter as spiritual bread (1 Pet. 2:2, 1 Cor. 3:2, Heb. 5:11-14) and by feeding upon which they become partakers of the divine nature (2 Pet. 1:4, Eph. 4:13-24, Heb. 12:10, 1 John 3:2) and thus "meet to be partakers of the inheritance of the saints in light" (Col. 1:12).

2. To *send* the Spirit. John 14:26—"But the Comforter, even the Holy Spirit, whom the Father will send in my name," etc. "In the name of Christ" is a phrase that is used in Scripture to signify *by the authority of Christ* (cf. Matt. 28:18). Hence to be sent by the Father *in the name of Christ* is equivalent to being sent by Christ Himself, for the Father and the Son are one (John 10:30).

Cf. Luke 24:49—Behold, I send the promise of my Father upon you; but tarry ye in the city, until ye be clothed with power from on high. John 15:26—But when the Comforter is come, whom I will send unto you from the Father, even the Spirit of truth, which proceedeth from the Father, etc. John 16:7—It is expedient for you that I go away; for if I go not away, the Comforter will not come unto you; but if I go, I will send him unto you. [All these statements were made by Jesus Himself, to the men who were to be qualified subsequently for the apostleship.]

450

This term, *send,* or *send forth,* implies a local motion; a person who is sent usually moves from one place to another. But we are told in Scripture that the Spirit is omnipresent (Psa. 139:7-10); hence this expression must be a metaphor signifying special manifestations of the Spirit's grace and power to those to whom He is said to be sent. It implies, of course, that the Spirit was not previously in or with that person, or those persons; it indicates a communication of the Spirit's presence and power to be in, and to guide, the recipient. Cf. Gal. 4:4-6: "But when the fulness of the time came, God sent forth his Son, born of a woman, born under the law, that he might redeem them that were under the law, that we might receive the adoption of sons. And because ye are his sons, God sent forth the Spirit of his Son into our hearts, crying, Abba, Father." The reference here, of course, is to all the saints of God under the New Covenant, to whom the indwelling Spirit is the Spirit of adoption (cf. Rom. 8:14-17). Cf. also Psa. 104:30, here the Psalmist says, with reference to the things of the physical creation: "Thou sendest forth thy Spirit, they are created; And thou renewest the face of the ground." This is an affirmation of the fact of the creative and conservative operations of the Divine Spirit in the Kingdom of Nature.

3. To *put His Spirit upon* men. Thus God is said to have taken of the Spirit that was upon Moses and to have put it upon the seventy elders of Israel (Num. 11:17, 25). And concerning His Anointed, God said through the prophet Isaiah: "Behold, my servant, whom I uphold; my chosen, in whom my soul delighteth; I have put my Spirit upon him; he will bring forth justice to the Gentiles." Cf. Isa. 61:1—"The Spirit of the Lord Jehovah is upon me, because Jehovah hath anointed me to preach good tidings to the meek," etc. Cf. Matt. 12:15ff. and Luke 4:17ff.: in these passages Jesus quotes the two passages from Isaiah as having their fulfilment in Himself and in His ministry. This expression signifies primarily the Divine investiture of those upon whom the Spirit is put, with the proper authority, together with the credentials necessary to support that authority, for the execution of some divine task of special significance.

4. To *pour out* or *pour forth* His Spirit. Inasmuch as it would be impossible to pour out or pour forth one person upon another person, this expression again obviously has reference, not to the Person, but to the powers, gifts and graces of the Spirit. It signifies an eminent act of Divine bounty, a pouring

451

out of the powers and graces of the Spirit *in abundance.* The expression refers directly, wherever used, to Gospel times. Although God did give His Spirit in some measure to His chosen leaders in Old Testament times, there was no general pouring forth of the Spirit's gifts and graces prior to the ratification of the New Covenant and the inauguration of the New Institution— the Christian System. Cf. Joel's prophecy, quoted verbatim by the Apostle Peter as having the beginning of its fulfilment with the advent of the Spirit on the Day of Pentecost: "And it shall come to pass afterward, that I will pour out my Spirit upon all flesh; and your sons and your daughters shall prophesy, your old men shall dream dreams, your young men shall see visions; and also upon the servants and upon the handmaids in those days will I pour out my Spirit" (Joel 2:28-29; cf. Acts 2:16-21). This prophecy has reference primarily of course to the two outpourings of the Spirit in baptismal measure, upon Jews and Gentiles respectively, that is, upon the Apostles on the Day of Pentecost in Jerusalem, and upon Cornelius and his household some years later at Caesarea, both of which were attended by extraordinary outward manifestations, namely, "a sound as of the rushing of a mighty wind" and "tongues parting asunder, like as of fire" (Acts 2:2-3). With reference to the first of these two instances of Holy Spirit baptism, that which introduced the events of that memorable first Pentecost after the Resurrection, Peter himself said, in the course of his sermon on that occasion: "This Jesus did God raise up, whereof we all are witnesses. Being therefore by the right hand of God exalted, and having received of the Father the promise of the Holy Spirit, *he hath poured forth this, which ye see and hear*" (Acts 2:32-33). And with reference to the second instance of Holy Spirit baptism, that which marked the first reception of Gentiles into the Church of Christ, Luke, the inspired historian, says: "And they of the circumcision that believed were amazed, as many as came with Peter, *because that on the Gentiles also was poured out the gift of the Holy Spirit*" (Acts 10:45). That these outpourings were of the same general character, that is, attended by the same outward signs, on both occasions, is evident from Peter's own statement later to the brethren of the Jerusalem church. "As I began to speak," he said, "the Holy Spirit fell upon them," that is, upon the Gentile Cornelius and his household, "even as on us at the beginning," that is to say, in the same manner that he fell upon us Jews (in the person of the Apostles themselves) on the Day of Pentecost,

452

the day of the beginning of the Gospel Dispensation. To this, the Apostle adds: "And I remembered the word of the Lord, how he said, John indeed baptized with water, but ye shall be baptized in the Holy Spirit. If then God gave unto them [Gentiles] the like gift as he did also unto us [Jews], when we believed on the Lord Jesus Christ, who was I, that I could withstand God?" (Acts 11:15-17). This phrase, the *pouring out* or *pouring forth* of the Spirit, has reference, however, not only to the conferring of Holy Spirit baptism and to that of the *charismata* as well, but also relates to the Spirit's purifying and sanctifying powers and influences; in fact, it is a general expression taking in all the gifts and graces of the Spirit bestowed by God upon His elect throughout the entire Gospel Dispensation. The present Dispensation is, in fact, the Dispensation of the Holy Spirit. It is the age of the outpouring of His own gracious gifts through His indwelling of all the saints of God. For He came on the Day of Pentecost to take up His abode in the Body of Christ and to dwell therein until the end of the age. Hence, in Scripture the effects of the presence and power of the Spirit in the hearts of all true believers are often compared to the effects of the outpouring of water.

Isa. 32:1 2: "Behold, a king shall reign in righteousness, and princes shall rule in justice. And a man shall be as a hiding-place from the wind, and a covert from the tempest, as streams of water in a dry place, etc. Isa. 44:3, 4—For I will pour water upon him that is thirsty, and streams upon the dry ground; I will pour my Spirit upon thy seed, and my blessing upon thine offspring. John 4:14 [the words of Jesus to the woman of Samaria]: But whosoever drinketh of the water that I shall give him shall never thirst; but the water that I shall give him shall become in him a well of water springing up unto eternal life. John 7:37-39: Now on the last day, the great day of the feast, Jesus stood and cried, saying, If any man thirst, let him come unto me and drink. He that believeth on me, as the scripture has said, from within him shall flow rivers of living water. But this spake he of the Spirit, which they that believed on him were to receive; for the Spirit was not yet given; because Jesus was not yet glorified.

When the fountains of the great deep are opened, the rain is poured down in *abundance;* hence, "through the washing of regeneration and renewing of the Holy Spirit" (in regeneration and in sanctification), God is said in Scripture to "pour out upon us *richly,* through Jesus Christ our Savior" the gifts and graces of His Spirit (Tit. 3:4-6).

He [the Spirit] comes on the dry, barren, parched ground of men's hearts, causing them to spring, and produce fruits of holiness and righteousness, Heb. 6:7. And thus Christ, by His Spirit, 'comes down

453

like rain upon the sown grass; as showers that water the earth,'
Psalm 72:6.[1]

5. To *supply* the Spirit. Gal. 3:5—"He therefore that supplieth to you the Spirit, and worketh miracles among you [or, *powers in you*], doeth he it by the works of the law, or by the hearing of faith?" This text clearly indicates that the measure of Spirit-power within a Christian is in proportion to his faith. Cf. Phil. 1:19—"For I know that this shall turn out to my salvation, through your supplication and the supply of the Spirit of Jesus Christ." The Greek verb, *epichorēgeō*, (noun, *epichorēgia*), means literally to "supply further," "furnish besides," etc. It signifies the adding of one thing to another, and hence indicates the further conferring and renewing of the Spirit's powers and graces from day to day. The essential property of Spirit-power, as we have already learned, is inexhaustibleness.

6. To *fill men with His Spirit*. Exo. 31:1 ff. "And Jehovah spake unto Moses, saying, See, I have called by name Bezalel the son of Uri, the son of Hur, of the tribe of Judah: and I have filled him with the Spirit of God, in Wisdom, and in understanding, and in knowledge, and in all manner of workmanship," etc. (cf. Exo. 35:31). The reference here is to an endowment with special artistic ability to construct and adorn the furnishings of the Tabernacle. Cf. Acts 2:4—"And they [the Apostles] were all filled withe the Holy Spirit, and began to speak with other [unacquired] tongues, as the Spirit gave them utterance." Here again the reference is to an infilling with Divine knowledge and wisdom (revelation), for the proclamation of the Truth that makes men free, the communication of Divine thought having been attended no doubt by the heightening of the natural psychical powers of the men who were thus qualified to go into all the world as ambassadors of the Lord Jesus Christ.

Again, in the nomenclature of the Spirit, the Spirit Himself is said to do the following:

1. To *proceed* from the Father.

John 15:26—But when the Comforter is come, whom I will send unto you from the Father, even the Spirit of truth, which proceedeth from the Father, he shall bear witness of me. [The Spirit proceeds from the Father; however, in view of the fact that He acts as the Vicegerent of Christ throughout the present Dispensation, He is said to be sent by the Father *in the name of* (i.e., *by the authority of*) the Son; and in this sense He is said to be sent by the Son also.] John 14:16—I will pray the Father, and he shall give you another Comforter . . . even the Spirit of truth, etc. John 14:26—But the Comforter, even the Holy Spirit, whom the Father will send in my name, etc. Luke 24:49—

1. John Owen, *A Discourse Concerning the Holy Spirit*, 63.

And behold, I send for the promise of my Father upon you, etc. Acts 2:32, 33—This Jesus did God raise up, whereof we all are witnesses. Being therefore by the right hand of God exalted, and have received of the Father the promise of the Holy Spirit, he hath poured forth this which ye see and hear.

(1) There is a procession of the Spirit which is *natural* or *personal*. This term expresses the eternal relation between the Spirit and both the Father and the Word; the Spirit is of both by eternal procession, *i.e., emanation*. Evidently the mode of this procession is essentially psychical; over-speculation regarding this matter, however, is both foolish and hurtful. (2) There is also a procession of the Spirit which is *dispensatory* or *administrative*. This term has reference to the egress of the Spirit from the Godhead in His own voluntary application of His powers and influences to the work which He has undertaken to perform in the realization of God's general Plan for His Creation. Thus, under the old Dispensations, the Spirit condescended to act as God's agent in qualifying certain leaders—men of great faith—for the divers special works which they were divinely elected to perform in the course of the unfolding of the Eternal Purpose (Eph. 3:1-13, Heb. 1:1-2, 1 Pet. 1:10-12, 2 Pet. 1:21). These great Old Covenant leaders are all designated "prophets" in Scripture. It must be remembered that the primary function of a prophet, in the Biblical sense of that term, is to reveal— through the Spirit— the will and word of God to men, and that only secondarily he is a foreteller of future events. Under the present Dispensation, however, the Holy Spirit acts as the agent both of the Father, and in a special sense of the Son, the Head of the Church, in administering the affairs of the Body of Christ and in perfecting and realizing the work of salvation in the saints (Eph. 2:22; John 16:12-15). In this latter sense, then, the procession of the Spirit has reference to, and results in, the enduement of believers with various measures of His powers and influences as adapted to corresponding divine ends. In some cases, the end is revelation; in others, demonstration; in still others, regeneration and sanctification. "There are diversities of gifts, but the same Spirit" (1 Cor. 12:4).

2. To *come unto* or *upon* men. God *sends* the Spirit; hence the Spirit Himself *comes*, voluntarily of course. This term signifies motion, action; that is, motion or action of a psychical kind. In other words, the Holy Spirit, by His own will and consent, begins to work where He has not worked before, always of course to effectuate the purposes of the Heavenly Father. Thus

455

the Spirit is said to have come upon Balaam (Num. 24:2), Othniel (Judg. 3:10), Jephthah (Judg. 11:29), the messengers of Saul (1 Sam. 19:20), Saul himself (1 Sam. 19:23), Azariah (2 Chron. 15:1), Jahaziel (2 Chron. 20:14). Again, He is said to have come upon, in the sense of having "clothed himself with," Gideon (Judg. 6:34), Amasai (1 Chron. 12:18), and Zechariah (2 Chron. 24:20).

Cf. Luke 1:35 [the words of Annunciating Angel to Mary]: The Holy Spirit shall come upon thee, and the power of the Most High shall overshadow thee. [Cf. also the following statements of Jesus to the men who were to become His Apostles]: John 15:26—But when the Comforter is come, whom I will send unto you from the Father, etc. John 16:7, 8, 13—For if I go not away, the Comforter will not come unto you . . . and he, when he is come, will convict the world in respect of sin, and of righteousness, and of judgment . . . when he, the Spirit of truth is come, he shall guide you into all the truth, etc. Acts 1:8—But ye shall receive power, when the Holy Spirit is come upon you, etc. [And concerning the disciples whom Paul found at Ephesus, we read]: And when Paul had laid his hands upon them, the Holy Spirit came on them; and they spake with tongues, and prophesied (Acts 19:6).

Again, the Spirit is said to have *come mightily upon* certain persons, that is, in extraordinary measure producing some outward manifestation of an unusual kind. Thus He is said to have come mightily upon Samson( Judg. 14:6, 14:19, 15:14), and upon King Saul (1 Sam. 10:6, 10; 11:6), and upon King David (1 Sam. 16:13). These expressions, wherever used, mean apparently that the Spirit began to operate where He had not operated before.

3. *To fall on men.* (1) That which makes Heaven to be Heaven is the presence of God, and where God is, if course, is the eternal "home" of the Spirit. Hence this phrase, *to fall on men,* expresses the idea of the Spirit's *descending* from above, from Heaven, His natural habitat; as, *e.g.,* He is said to have *descended* out of the opened "heaven"—"in a bodily form, as a dove"—to anoint Jesus of Nazareth as the Messiah, our Prophet, Priest, and King (Matt. 3:16, Mark 1:10, Luke 3:21-22, John 1:32). (2) The phrase expresses also the idea of a sudden and unexpected operation, and one that produced visible effects which startled and amazed spectators, even as, for example, the fire of Jehovah fell suddenly upon Elijah's offering on Mount Carmel, and the spectators were amazed and cried out, "Jehovah, he is God" (1 Ki. 18:38-39). Cf. Acts 10:44-46, the narrative of the conversion of Cornelius, as told by Luke: "While Peter yet spake these words, the Holy Spirit fell on all them

456

that heard the word. And they of the circumcision that believed were amazed, as many as came with Peter, because that on the Gentiles also was poured out the gift of the Holy Spirit. For they heard them speak with tongues, and magnify God." Cf. also Peter's account, of the same occurrence, Acts 11:15: "And as I began to speak, the Holy Spirit fell on them, even as on us at the beginning." This is to say, the Holy Spirit fell on Cornelius and his house, Gentiles, in the same manner that He fell on the Apostles, Jews, at the beginning of the Gospel Dispensation. This points back to the advent of the Spirit on the Day of Pentecost. Although Luke, in his narrative (Acts 2:1-13), does not state explicitly that the Spirit *fell on* the Apostles, on that occasion, he makes it very clear that His advent was precisely of that character. His coming was sudden ("suddenly there came from heaven," v. 2), and as to its character quite unexpected. It was attended, moreover, by outward manifestations ("a sound as of the rushing of a mighty wind" and "tongues parting asunder, like as of fire," vv. 2, 3) and evinced by visible effects upon and in the Apostles, the recipients (they "were all filled with the Holy Spirit, and began to speak with other tongues, as the Spirit gave them utterance," v. 4), all of which startled and amazed the entire populace of Jerusalem. Cf. vv. 6-8, 12—"And when this sound was heard, the multitude came together, and were confounded, because that every man heard them [the Apostles] speaking in his own language. And they were all amazed and marvelled, saying, Behold, are not all these that speak Galileans? And how hear we, every man in our language wherein we were born? . . . And they were all amazed, and were perplexed, saying one to another What meaneth this?" Thus it will be seen that the Holy Spirit fell on the recipients, in these two instances, in the sense of having conferred upon them the *baptismal* measure of His powers and influences. (3) This expression is used also, in Acts 8:16, to indicate the communication of the *evidential* measure of the Spirit. Here we read with reference to the Samaritans who had been converted by the preaching of Philip the evangelist, Acts 8:14-17: "Now when the apostles that were at Jerusalem heard that Samaria had received the word of God, they sent unto them Peter and John: who, when they were come down, prayed for them, that they might receive the Holy Spirit; for as yet it was fallen upon none of them: only they had been baptized into the name of the Lord Jesus. Then laid they their hands upon them, and they received the Holy Spirit." In this instance, the reception of the Spirit by baptized believers resulted in their enduement with the *charismata* characteristic of the Church generally throughout the apostolic age. (4) This phrase, *to fall upon men*, however, *is never used in Scripture to describe the communication of the sanctifying measure of the Spirit's powers and influences.* On the contrary it is used only to describe those operations of the Spirit which were for the special purpose of establishing some divine truth or purpose; that is to say, for purposes of revelation and demonstration only. This is a fact of the utmost significance. (5) The expression is used only once in the Old Testament. The prophet Ezekiel says, ch. 11, v. 5— "And the Spirit of Jehovah fell upon me, and he said unto me, Speak, Thus saith Jehovah," etc. Cf. Ezek. 8:1, 3—"And it came to pass in the sixth year, in the sixth month, in the fifth day of the month, as I sat in my house, and the elders of Judah sat before me, that the hand of the Lord Jehovah fell there upon me. . . . And he put forth the form of a hand, and took me by a lock of my head; and the Spirit lifted me up between earth and heaven, and brought me in the visions of God to Jerusalem," etc. Here again the phrase is used to describe the beginning of an operation of the Spirit for purposes of revelation only. The series of visions thus vouchsafed Ezekiel are written down in his great book for all men to read and to profit withal.

4. To *rest upon* men, that is, upon persons to whom He is given or sent.

Num. 11:25, 26—And Jehovah came down in the cloud, and spake unto him [Moses], and took of the Spirit that was upon him, and put it upon the seventy elders: and it came to pass that, when the Spirit rested upon them, they prophesied, but they did so no more. But there remained two men in the camp, the name of the one was Eldad, and the name of the other Medad: and the Spirit rested upon them; and they were of them that were written, but had not gone out unto the Tent; and they prophesied in the camp. [We continue to read that when this latter incident was reported to Moses, he exclaimed]: Would that all Jehovah's people were prophets, that Jehovah would put his Spirit upon them! (v. 29).

Thus whereas and when God is said to *put His Spirit upon men*, the Spirit Himself is said to *rest upon* them. The idea suggested by these terms is that of a continued brooding over, or overshadowing, which in turn implies an abiding interest in, oversight of, and communication of spiritual powers to, the person or persons who are thus objects of the Divine solicitude and instrumentalities for the realization of Divine ends. Cf. John 1:32, 33—the testimony of John the Baptizer respecting the anointing of Jesus with the Holy Spirit: "I have beheld the

458

Spirit descending as a dove out of heaven; and it *abode upon* him. And I knew him not; but he that sent me to baptize in water, he said unto me, Upon whomsoever thou shalt see the Spirit descending, and *abiding upon* him, the same is he that baptized in the Holy Spirit." From the moment of His conception in the womb of the Virgin, by the overshadowing of the Holy Spirit (Luke 1:35), to the time when, "through the eternal Spirit," He "offered himself without blemish unto God" (Heb. 9:14), as an all-sufficient Atonement for the sins of the world, Jesus, Messiah, received the fulness of the abiding presence and power of the Spirit, both upon Him and in Him (John 3:34). In like manner, the Spirit is said to rest upon all who are truly saints of God under the New Covenant. 1 Pet. 4:14—"If ye are reproached for the name of Christ, blessed are ye, because the Spirit of glory and the Spirit of God resteth upon you." Where the Spirit rests, in works of sanctification, there He abides in complacence and in delight. And because the ultimate effect of such an abiding will be, for the recipient, the putting on of glory and honor and immortality, through the working of the power of the same Spirit, the Spirit Himself is designated the Spirit of Glory.

5. To *enter into* men, and to *dwell in* them. Ezek. 2:2— "And the Spirit entered into me when he spake unto me, and set me upon my feet." Ezek. 3:24—"Then the Spirit entered into me, and set me upon my feet, and he spake with me," etc. Here, the phrase, *enter in*, signifies an entrance primarily for the purposes of inspiration and revelation. The phrase, *dwell in*, however, occurs only in the New Testament. It is the expression uniformly used in the New Testament to describe the Holy Spirit's indwelling of the saints in sanctifying measure, and it occurs, either explicitly or implicitly, in many different passages.

Rom. 8:9—But ye are not in the flesh but in the Spirit, if so be that the Spirit of God dwelleth in you. Rom. 8:11—But if the Spirit of him that raised up Jesus from the dead dwelleth in you, etc. 1 Cor. 3:16—Know ye not that ye are a temple of God, and that the Spirit of God dwelleth in you? (cf. Eph. 2:22, 1 Cor. 6:19). Jas. 4:5—That Spirit which he made to dwell in us yearneth for us even unto jealous envy.

The Spirit is said to dwell in the saints as the Spirit of their adoption (Rom. 8:14-17, Gal. 4:4-6), as the seal of their election (Eph. 1:13, 4:30), and as the earnest (pledge) of their eternal inheritance (2 Cor. 1:21-22, 5:5; cf. Rom. 8:18-25). This spiritual indwelling is, of course, by means of, and in proportion to, the continuous reception of the Word into their hearts. For it is only by feeding upon the Word and assimilating it, in the forming of their thoughts and attitudes, and the moulding of their personalities, that Christians can possibly bring forth the fruit of the Spirit in their lives (Gal. 5:22-25).

6. To *depart from* men. Gen. 6:3—"And Jehovah said, My Spirit shall not strive with man for ever." Psa. 51:11—"Take not thy holy Spirit from me." 1 Sam. 16:14—"Now the Spirit of Jehovah departed from Saul," etc. The fact cannot be emphasized too strongly that *any abiding or indwelling of the Spirit in the human heart presupposes our keeping our hearts open to His presence, hence open and receptive to the Word which is the means of His indwelling.* In the very nature of the case, only "they that hunger and thirst after righteousness" can expect to be "filled" (Matt. 5:6). "The natural man receiveth not the things of the Spirit of God: for they are foolishness unto him: and he cannot know them, because they are spiritually examined" (1 Cor. 2:14). In every generation, there are a great many persons who profess their faith in Christ, but thereafter become entangled in temptations, and conquered by their lusts, and turn again into the ways of disobedience and sin. The gifts imparted to them by the Spirit dry up and wither; their light goes out, and darkness settles down upon their minds and obscures their vision. Thus they quench the Spirit (1 Thess. 5:19). And if to this general neglect and indifference, they add positive *despite* unto the Spirit of Grace, their case is, in general, irremediable.

Heb. 6:4-8: "For as touching those who were once enlightened and tasted of the heavenly gift, and were made partakers of the Holy Spirit, and tasted the good word of God, and the powers of the age to come, and then fell away, it is impossible to renew them again unto repentance; seeing they crucify to themselves the Son of God afresh, and put him to an open shame. For the land which hath drunk the rain that cometh oft upon it, and bringeth forth herbs meet for them for whose sake it it also tilled, receiveth blessing from God; but if it beareth thorns and thistles, it is rejected and nigh unto a curse; whose end is to be burned. Heb. 10:26-31: For if we sin wilfully after that we have received the knowledge of the truth, there remaineth no more a sacrifice for sins, but a certain fearful expectation of judgment, and a fierceness of first which shall devour the adversaries. A man that hath set at nought Moses' law dieth without compassion on the word of two or three witnesses: of how much sorer punishment, think ye, shall he be judged worthy, who hath trodden under foot the Son of God, and hath counted the blood of the covenant wherewith he was sanctified an unholy thing, and hath done despite unto the Spirit of grace? For we know him that said, Vengeance belongeth unto me, I will recompense. And again, The Lord shall judge his people. It is a fearful thing to fall into the hands of the living God.

460

I am convinced that Christians generally speaking do not comprehend the enormity of the sin of backsliding.

The abiding attributes of the Spirit are seven in number: "And the Spirit of Jehovah shall rest upon him, the spirit of wisdom and understanding, the spirit of counsel and might, the spirit of knowledge and of the fear of Jehovah" (Isa. 11:2). Jesus possessed these attributes perfectly. And all saints possess them in the measure that they keep their hearts open and receptive to the Spirit's presence and power. Hence, John the Revelator, saluting the seven churches of Asia, prays for grace and peace for them, from the Father and "from the seven Spirits that are before his throne" (Rev. 1:4). In this passage, the term "seven Spirits"—the number *seven* being, in Scripture, the symbol of perfection—has reference to the seven attributes or graces of the one Spirit of God. Therefore, in view of the fact that our Lord Jesus Christ, as the Foundation of the Church (Psa. 118:20-24, Acts 4:10-12), was anointed with all these graces in their perfection, it was said of the Stone, in Zechariah's vision—the Stone which symbolized the Branch, the Suffering Servant of Jehovah—that upon that one Stone should be "seven eyes" (Zech. 3:8-10); that is, the seven graces of the one Spirit of God.

\* \* \*

## SPECIAL NOTE ON JOHN 3:5

I have presented above, in its fullness, the interpretation of John 3:8 which has prevailed generally in the past as a result of the influence of the *Authorized Version*. However, there is another view of this passage which seems to me to have been neglected, and which presents some aspects of the subject that surely need to be given serious consideration. I therefore present this alternative interpretation, as stated by A. J. Gordon, in his excellent book, *The Ministry of the Spirit* (p. 166, fn.) as follows:

(John 3:8): The wind bloweth where it listeth, etc. Without pronouncing dogmatically, it must be said that the translation of Bengel and some others—*The Spirit breatheth where he wills, and thou hearest his voice*—has reasons in its favor which are well-nigh irresistible; *e.g.*, if *to pneuma* here is the wind, it has one meaning in the first part of the sentence and another meaning in the second; and that meaning too, one which it bears in no other instance of the more than two hundred and seventy uses of the word in the New Testament. It is not the word used in Acts 2:2, as might be expected if it signified wind. Then it seems unnatural to ascribe volition to the wind, *thelei*. On the contrary, if the words apply to the Spirit, the saying is in entire harmony with other Scriptures, which affirm the sovereignty of the Holy

Ghost in regeneration (John 1:13), and in the control and direction of those who are the subjects of the new birth (1 Cor. 12:4-11).

With this McGarvey agrees (although Pendleton dissents), as follows:

> In this sentence we have the word *pneuma* translated by the two words "wind" and "spirit." There can be no justification in rendering *pneuma* "wind," when the last clause of the same sentence, and three times in the immediate context, it is rendered "spirit." There can be no doubt that it means the same in both clauses of this verse, and if we render it "wind" in the first clause, we must say "born of the wind" in the last clause. Whatever is the meaning of this verse, it must be extracted from the rendering which the Revisers [American Standard Revision] have strangely placed in the margin, viz., "The Spirit breathes where it will, and thou hearest," etc. It teaches that a man is born of the Spirit by hearing the voice of the Spirit, breathing as He wills through inspired men. It is equivalent to Paul's maxim that faith comes by hearing and hearing by the word of God. [McGarvey and Pendleton, *The Fourfold Gospel*, 128.]

But Pendleton would accept the rendering of the *Authorized Version*:

> From this (Bro. McCarvey's) construction of verse 8 I dissent, and hold that the Revisers have given us the true reading in the text. . . . I take the passage to mean that the process by which a man is regenerated by the Spirit of God is no more mysterious than other operations in the natural world, of which operations the blowing of the wind is taken as an example [*ibid.*, 129, fn.].

It is interesting to note that the Douay (Roman Catholic) Version, following the Vulgate, gives this verse as follows:

> The Spirit breatheth where he will and thou hearest his voice: but thou knowest not whence he cometh and wither he goeth. So is every one that is born of the Spirit. [This is accompanied by the following footnote]: By these words our Savior hath declared the necessity of baptism; and by the word *water* it is evident that the application of it is necessary with the words, Matt. 28:19.) [Here the reference is to the meaning of vv. 1-5.]

"The Spirit breathes where he pleases," etc. So does Rotherham give it (*Emphasized New Testament*, 94). So reads the currently popular *King James II Version*, with a slight change: "The Spirit breathes where He desires, and you hear His voice, but you do not know from where He comes and where He goes," etc. So reads *The Emphatic Diaglott*, with the sole exception of using "it" for "he," with reference to the Spirit.

As a mater of fact, this rendering seems to be more in harmony with the meaning of the text. Whoever heard of the wind (unless personified, of course) "listing" (*i.e.*, voluntarily *pleasing*) to do something? How can the wind be said to *will* to do anything? How could anyone be "born of the wind"

462

in any sense whatever? Then, why translate the word *pneuma* "wind" in the first clause, but render it "Spirit" in the last? To dismiss the whole question with the bland statement, as does the *Revised Standard Version* in a footnote, that "the same Greek word means both *wind* and *spirit*" is simply begging the question. The Greek word used for wind in the New Testament is *anemos; pnoē* is used once, in Acts 2:2, as previously noted. In the first clause of John 3:8, we have the *only* instance in the New Testament in which *pneuma* is rendered "wind." These facts ought surely to settle this controversy—if indeed it *is* a controversial matter *per se.*

\* \* \*

# QUESTIONS FOR REVIEW OF PART FIVE

1. List the names by which the Spirit designates Himself in the Old Testament Scriptures.
2. Explain what is meant by the sevenfold or perfect Spirit. In what Scripture passage is this designation found?
3. List the names by which the Spirit designates His relationship to the Father.
4. List those by which the Spirit designates His relationship to the Son.
5. List the Scripture terms which designate the Spirit's deity.
6. List the names by which the Spirit designates His spiritual attributes.
7. List the names by which the Spirit designates His own spiritual attributes.
8. Correlate the Scriptures which identify the Spirit of Yahweh, the Spirit of Christ, and the Holy Spirit as the one Eternal Spirit.
9. What problem must have been involved in the communication of God's word to man?
10. Through what divine agency was this revelation delivered?
11. What is meant by the nomenclature of the Spirit?
12. What various meanings do the terms *ruach* and *pneuma* convey to us?
13. What does the term "Spirit" signify with reference to God?
14. What distinctive meanings are suggested by the names of God, *Elohim* and *Yahweh?*
15. What is the significance of the name, "The Good Spirit of God"?
16. From what four points of view may we regard the Spirit of Christ as the Holy Spirit?
17. In what sense is the Holy Spirit "The Power of the Most High"? In what Scripture passage de we find this name? What relation to the Word is indicated in this passage?
18. Explain—as best one can—the full significane of the name "Holy Spirit."
19. What is suggested by the term *Breath* as a metaphor of the Spirit?
20. Explain Gen. 2:7 and John 20:21-23.
21. What does the metaphor *Wind* suggest with reference to the Spirit?

22. What outward manifestations of the Spirit took place on Pentecost and what did they signify?
23. What does the *Dove* suggest as a metaphor of the Spirit?
24. What importance is indicated by this term in connection with the baptism of Jesus?
25. For what purposes was anointing used as a Jewish ceremony?
26. What does *anointing* signify, specifically, in Scripture?
27. What were the ingredients of the "holy anointing oil," and what did they signify?
28. What was the theocratic ceremony of anointing and what was its import with reference to the Messiahship?
29. What classes of public leaders were officially inducted into their respective offices by the ceremony of anointing?
30. Where do we find prophetic references in the Old Testament to the advent and ministry of God's Anointed?
31. Explain fully the meaning of the title, *Messiah* or *Christ*.
32. What are the suggested interpretations of the term, "The Oil of Gladness"? What seems to be the interpretation justified by the Scriptures themselves?
33. What is spiritual circumcision and when does it take place? What is the nature of it?
34. How does the Spiritual Life begin and what is the essential nature of it?
35. What is meant by references to oil as the source of light? From what feature of the Tabernacle and Temple does this truth have its origin?
36. What is the correlation between this metaphor and Christ Himself, the Gospel, the Church, and the Spiritual Life?
37. In what sense are the redeemed themselves *epistles of Christ?*
38. What was symbolized by the seven lamps of the Candelabrum of the Tabernacle?
39. What is designated by the terms *wholeness* and *holiness?* How is the designation *Holy Spirit* related to these terms?
40. Explain the significance of Zechariah's Vision.
41. Explain the import of the Parable of the Wise and Foolish Virgins with respect to oil as the source of light.
42. How is the meaning of this parable suggestive of man's ultimate ends and the attainment of them?
43. What do we mean by saying that holiness is a qualitative excellence? How is holiness to be actualized?
44. What is the significance of *Water* as a metaphor of the Holy Spirit?
45. Explain the meaning of "living water," in this connection; also that of the "river of water of life" (Rev. 22:1).
46. How does Isaiah describe the joys of fellowship with God under the New Covenant?
47. Explain the spiritual significance of the Smitten Rock (Exo. 17:6).
48. Explain the significance of the Ezekiel's Vision of the Healing Waters.
49. Cite the Scriptures in which water is described as a symbol of cleansing. How related metaphorically to operations of the Holy Spirit?
50. What was the Water of Purification under the Old Testament Dispensations? What difficulties do we meet in trying to correlate the Water of Purification of the Old Testament with the water of baptism of the New Testament?
51. What is designated in Scripture by the term *Seal?*

464

52. Scripturally speaking, for what purposes was *sealing* employed?
52. Relate the term *sealing* to the divine sealing of Messiah and the divine sealing of the saints.
53. What was the import of the use of the Roman seal impressed on the stone that was rolled across the entrance to the Sepulchre of Christ?
54. In what special sense does *sealing* have an authoritarian character?
55. Where did the *sealing* of Christ take place? What did it imply?
56. Where does the *sealing* of God's saints take place? What does it imply?
57. How does the *sealing* of the saints take place *officially*, and where does it take place *actually*?
58. In the sealing of the saints, what may we understand to be the *wax*, and what the *design*?
59. What is the relation between the Spirit and the Word in this divine sealing?
60. In what sense is the Holy Spirit Himself the divine Seal? Cite Scriptures to prove this.
61. What is the sign of the believer's sanctification?
62. Explain, as best one can, the meaning of 2 Tim. 2:19.
63. In what sense is sealing the ratification of the New Covenant relationship?
64. Explain the statement: "The Holy Spirit is the saint's signet-ring."
65. Explain: "Holiness is the life of the Spirit which is manifested in the fruit of the Spirit." Correlate Gal. 5:22-24.
66. In what sense is the sealing of the saints a *pledge* or *earnest* on God's part?
67. What four facts are signified by the *Divine Sealing* of the saints with "the Holy Spirit of promise"?
68. What is the import of "the Finger of God" as a metaphor of the Spirit? Cf. Luke 11:20 with Matt. 12:28.
69. In what sense in Scripture is the ceremony of "the Laying on of Hands" related to the operations of the Spirit?
70. What instances do we have in the New Testament of the ceremony of the laying on of hands as indicative of ordination to a special ministry in the Church?
71. What was signified by the joint appearing, on the Day of Pentecost, of the sound of "the rushing of a mighty wind" and the "tongues like as of fire"?
72. On what grounds do we take the position that *Fire* was a metaphor of the Word? (Cf. Isa. 59:21).
73. What was the joint symbolism of the *Wind* and the *Fire* as mentioned in this instance?
74. What is the importance of distinguishing between the Holy Spirit Himself and His gifts and powers?
75. Explain what is meant by the doctrines that God IS Spirit, that God HAS Spirit, and that God GIVES Spirit.
76. What are the terms used in Scripture to indicate the various ways in which men receive the Spirit?
77. What terms are used to designate the ways in which the Spirit is said to be *in* men, to come *upon* men, etc.?
78. What terms are used to indicate the ways by which God gives the Spirit to men?
79. What Scripture establishes the truth that God gives the Spirit to men in various measures?

80. In whom did the Spirit of God dwell constantly and fully? Cite Scriptures to support this truth.
81. Upon whom, under what circumstances, and for what purposes, was the *baptismal* measure of Spirit-power conferred, as related in the New Testament?
82. What was the *evidential* measure of Spirit-power, upon whom conferred, and for what purposes, as revealed in the New Testament?
83. To whom is the *regenerating* and *sanctfying* power of the Holy Spirit promised in the New Testament? What determines the measure of Spirit-power that the saints receive?
84. Cite Scriptures in which all three measures of Spirit-power are designated a *gift*.
85. What specifically were the *charismata?* What purpose were they to serve especially?
86. What different words apparently are used to distinguish the "distributions" of the Spirit according to *measure*, from those according to *kind?*
87. Explain, as fully as possible, what is implied in the doctrine that God gives the Spirit.
88. What is generally implied in the teaching that God *sends* Spirit?
89. What is signified in particular by the teaching that God *puts His* Spirit *upon* men?
90. What is signified especially by the teaching that God *pours out* His Spirit on men?
91. What is signified by the doctrine that God *supplies* the Spirit?
92. What is signified by the doctrine that God *fills* men with His Spirit?
93. In what sense is the Spirit said to *proceed from* the Father?
94. In what sense is the Spirit said to *come unto* or *come upon* men?
95. In what sense is the Spirit said to *fall on* men?
96. In what sense is the Spirit said to *rest upon* men?
97. In what sense is the Spirit said to *enter into* and to *dwell in* men?
98. In what sense is the Spirit said to *depart from* men?
99. What is the meaning of the term, "the seven spirits"?
100. How was this truth related to Christ in Zechariah's vision?

# PART SIX

# THE SPIRIT AND
# THE WORD

## 1. The Logos

It becomes necessary at this point to make a brief study of the relations between the Spirit of God and the Word of God in the various operations of the Godhead. Now the Word of God may be considered in two general aspects: (1) as *impersonal* or *stereotyped,* as in the Scriptures, and (2) *personal,* as the Logos.

The impersonal or stereotyped Word, as embodied in Scripture, is of course, a revelation by the Son of God through the agency of the Spirit. Jesus Himself said, with respect to the Spirit's mission: "He shall teach you all things, and bring to your remembrance all that I said unto you" (John 14:26)—words addressed to the men who were to become His Apostles; again, "He shall bear witness of me" (John 15:26); and again: "He shall guide you into all the truth, for he shall not speak from himself, but what things soever he shall hear, these shall he speak; and he shall declare unto you the things that are to come. *He shall glorify me, for he shall take of mine, and shall declare it unto you"* (John 16:13-14). To these words He added the following explicit statement: *"All things whatsoever the Father hath are mine: therefore said I, that he taketh of mine, and shall declare it unto you"* (John 16:15). From the very beginning *the temporal mission of the Holy Spirit has been that of glorifying Christ, God's Son.* It was the Logos who *declared* the Will of God and the Spirit who *communicated* it, through the instrumentality of inspired men. To the Father we look, therefore, for *faith;* to the Son, for *doctrine;* and to the Spirit, for *evidence* or *proof.*

In view of these truths, the proper point of beginning of a study of the relations between the Word of God and the Spirit of God, is with what the Scriptures reveal concerning the being and function of the personal Word, the Word who became flesh and dwelt among us, the Logos.

In one of His numerous brushes with the Pharisees, Jesus put to them the two most important questions—that is, the most far-reaching in their implications—of all questions that ever come before the human mind for consideration. These two questions were: "What think ye of the Christ? whose Son is he?" (Matt. 22:42). Of these two questions, however, the second is the more important; one's answer to the first question is necessarily determined by the answer one gives to the second. If Jesus, Messiah, was only the natural son of Joseph and Mary, conceived and born as all human beings are conceived and born,

THE SPIRIT AND THE WORD

then He was only a man, a great Teacher of course, and perhaps more "divinely illumined" than other teachers who have arisen in the course of human history, but withal a man. Under this view, moreover, the teaching of Jesus, like that of all other philosophers, is just another guess at the riddle of the universe. But, on the other hand, if Jesus was the Son of God, begotten by the overshadowing by the Holy Spirit of the womb of the Virgin; in a word, if He was, as Scripture expressly declares, the Eternal Word who became flesh and dwelt among us; then He was everything that He claimed to be, both Son of God and Son of man; Immanuel, *Theanthropos*, the Divine-Human Person; The Way, the Truth, and the Life; Savior, Redeemer, Prophet, Priest and King of His people, the elect of God of both Covenants. Everything in Christianity hinges upon the answer to the question: "Whose Son is He?"

Let us approach this question from the only viewpoint from which we can approach it to get at the truth as revealed in Scripture. The crux of the problem may be stated thus: Did the Person whom we know *historically* as Jesus of Nazareth have His beginning in the Bethlehem manger? Fortunately for us, both the Old and New Testament writers leave us in no doubt as to the true answer to this question; they uniformly and explicitly assert that the One whom we know historically as Jesus and whom we accept wholeheartedly as Christ and our Savior, is co-eternal and co-equal with the Father, that His goings forth are from of old, from everlasting. The following Scriptures, just as a few of the several texts throughout the Bible all of which assert the same truth, will suffice to establish the point:

Phil. 2:5-7: Christ Jesus, who, *existing in the form of God, counted not the being on an equality with God a thing to be grasped, but emptied himself, taking the form of a servant, being made in the likeness of men;* and being found in fashion as a man, he humbled himself, becoming obedient even unto death, yea, the death of the cross. [That is to say, the Messiah did not consider His own original equality with God a thing to be striven for, because it was His inherently, as He was Deity by nature and rank; hence He could subordinate His Deity and resume it again as He pleased.] John 10:17-18: Therefore doth the Father love me, because I lay down my life, that I may take it again. No one taketh it away from me, but I lay it down of myself. I have power to lay it down, and I have power to take it again. Heb. 2:14— Since then the children are sharers in flesh and blood, he also himself in like manner partook of the same; that through death he might bring to nought him that had the power of death, that is, the devil. [Whereas in the passage quoted above from *Philippians* the *fact* of the Son's Humiliation is asserted, the *purpose* of that Humiliation is here set forth: it was for the purpose of expelling ultimately from our universe all sin, both its guilt and its consequences, the chief of which is death.] Col. 1:17—He is before all things, and in him all things consist. John

8:58 [the words of Jesus Himself]: Before Abraham was born, *I am.* [Here we find Jesus assuming for Himself the "great and incommunicable" Name of the Deity, and in so doing asserting His own self-existence from eternity.] John 17:5, [from the prayer of Jesus on the night of His betrayal]: Father, glorify thou me with thine own self *with the glory which I had with thee before the world was.* [Language could hardly be more explicit.] Rev. 1:17-18 [the words of the risen and glorified Christ]: Fear not; I am the first and the last, and the Living One. Rev. 21:6—I am the Alpha and the Omega, the beginning and the end [that is, I am without beginning or end.]

[Cf. from the Old Testament]: Isa. 9:6—His name shall be called Wonderful, Counsellor, Mighty God, Everlasting Father, Prince of Peace. [This is clearly in allusion to the Messiah.] Micah 5:2—But thou, Bethlehem Ephrathah, which are little to be among the thousands of Judah, out of thee shall one come forth unto me that is to be ruler in Israel; *whose goings forth are from of old, from everlasting.* [The statements of Jesus to the Apostles]: John 6:62—What then if ye should behold the Son of man *ascending where he was before?* John 14:2—In my Father's house are many mansions; if it were not so, I would have told you; for I go to prepare a place for you. [Also His statements to the Pharisees, John 7:33-34]: Yet a little while am I with you, and I go unto him that sent me. Ye shall seek me, and shall not find me: and where I am, ye cannot come.

These passages and others—too numerous to be quoted here—clearly set forth the fact of the pre-existence of Christ, not to mention of course the numerous other Scriptures in which His work of creating and upholding all things is explicitly affirmed:

E.g., John 1:3—All things were made through him; and without him was not anything made that hath been made. Col. 1:16—for in him were all things created, in the heavens and upon the earth, things visible and things invisible, whether thrones or dominions or principalities or powers; all things have been created through him, and unto him. Col. 1:17—He is before all things, and in him all things consist. 1 Cor. 8:6—There is one God, the Father, of whom are all things, and we unto him; and one Lord, Jesus Christ, through whom are all things, and we through him. Heb. 1:1-3: God, having of old time spoken unto the fathers in the prophets by divers portions and in divers manners, hath at the end of these days spoken unto us in his Son, whom he appointed heir of all things, through whom also he made the worlds; who being the effulgence of his glory, and the very image of his substance, and upholding all things by the word of his power, when he had made purification of sins, sat down on the right hand of the Majesty on high. Heb. 1:10—Thou, Lord, in the beginning didst lay the foundation of the earth, And the heavens are the works of thy hands [this quotation from Psa. 102:25 ff. is explicitly affirmed here to have reference to the Messiah, v. 8—but of *the Son* he saith, etc.] Heb. 11:3—By faith we understand that the worlds have been framed by the word of God, so that what is seen hath not been made out of things which appear.

These and many other Scriptures make it equally clear, too, that His was a *personal,* and not merely an ideal, pre-existence. Take his own words, for example, in John 17:24: "Father . . . thou lovedst me before the foundation of the world." This statement expresses infinitely more than the mere fact of God's foreknowledge of a *man's* appearance in the world. Cf. also Gal. 4:4— "But when the fulness of the time came, God sent forth his Son, born of a woman, born under the law," etc. In the light of all these Scriptures it is impossible to reduce Jesus to the status merely of a "divinely illumined" man.

*What, then, was the nature of the relation that existed between God the Father and the One whom we know as Jesus, the Christ, the Son of the living God, prior to the latter's incarnation in the womb of the Virgin? And by what name does the Holy Spirit designate that relation in Scripture?* In considering these two questions, I suggest the following *postulata* which to me appear to be incontrovertible. [For the position stated here regarding the eternal Name of the Person whom we know historically as Jesus of Nazareth, I am indebted to Alexander Campbell. The substance of the material presented below appeared in an issue of the *Christian Baptist*, May 7, 1827. This journal was edited by Mr. Campbell, and the article on Jesus as the Word of God was written by him. I have never found any clearer presentation of the doctrine of the Logos in our literature. C.C.]

1. No relation existing among human beings can perfectly exhibit the relation which the Savior sustained, anterior to His birth in the flesh, to the God and Father of all. The reason is, that relation is not homogeneous, *i.e.*, not of the same kind, with relations originating from creation and subsequent natural reproduction. All relations of which we have any knowledge have resulted from creation and natural reproduction. Now I object just as much to a created relation as I object to a creature as properly signifying the original relation of God and the One who came to earth to be our Savior and King. *That* was an uncreated and unoriginated relation. And in the nature of the case no relation existing among *created* beings could literally or fully express a relation existing between *unoriginated* or self-existent beings.

2. Hence, this relation between God and the pre-existent Savior being *eternal*, that is, independent of time or the temporal process, obviously it could not have been designated by the term *Son of God*, because, where there are father and son, the father of necessity antedates the son. The relation of father and son is a temporal, creaturely relation, and therefore could not properly express an unoriginated or eternal relation. Such a prophetic affirmation, for example, as that which appears in

Psalm 2:7, "I will tell of the decree: Jehovah said unto me, Thou art my son; This day have I begotten thee" (quoted in Acts 13:33, and in Heb. 1:5 and 5:5, as having reference explicitly to the Messiah) obviously has reference to an *eternal decree*, that is, a decree existing in the *eternal purpose* of God (cf. again Eph. 1:3-4, 3:3-12, etc.) Just as it is said, for instance, in Rom. 8:29-30, that the particular class whom God foreknew *as a class* (*i.e.*, the saints) in His eternal purpose, He foreordained to be called (through the Gospel, 2 Thess. 2:14), to be justified (through their own obedience of faith, Rom. 10:16, 2 Thess. 1:8), and eventually to be glorified (*i.e.*, raised up from the dead and clothed in "glory and honor and incorruption," Rom. 2:7), and thus finally to be conformed to the image of His glorified Son. The calling, justifying and glorifying described here was in the eternal purpose of God; this eternal purpose shall be fully realized when the immortalized saints shall stand in God's presence fully redeemed in spirit and soul and body (1 Thess. 5:23). In like manner, the Savior was from eternity, that is, in God's eternal purpose, the Only Begotten Son of God. The actual begetting, however, took place *in time*, in the womb of the Virgin Mary.

[Similarly, Jesus is said to have been the Lamb slain, that is, in the *purpose* of God, from the foundation of the world (*kosmos*), and the saints are said to have been chosen *in Him*, again in the *purpose* of God, from the foundation of the world.] Acts 2:23—him, being delivered up by the determination counsel and foreknowledge of God, ye by the hand of lawless men did crucify and slay. 1 Pet. 1:18-20— ye were redeemed . . . with precious blood, as of a lamb without blemish and without spot, even the blood of Christ: who was foreknown indeed before the foundation of the world, but was manifested at the end of the times for your sake, etc. Matt. 25:34—Then shall the King say unto them on his right hand, Come, ye blessed of my Father, inherit the kingdom prepared for you from the foundation of the world. Eph. 1:3-4: in Christ, even as he chose us in him before the foundation of the world, that we should be holy and without blemish before him in love. Rev. 13:8—every one whose name hath not been written from the foundation of the world in the book of life of the Lamb that hath been slain. Rev. 17:8—they whose name hath not been written in the book of life, from the foundation of the world, etc.

3. When in the fulness of the time it became necessary in the wisdom of God to exhibit the Savior to the world, it became expedient to present some view of the original and eternal dignity of this Divine Visitant to the human race. And since this view, in the very nature of the case, had to be communicated in human language, we can only conclude that the whole vocabulary of human speech was examined for a suitable term or name.

4. Of all the terms to be found in human language expressive of the eternal relation to be disclosed, the most suitable had to be, and unquestionably was, selected. Moreover, as the relation to be designated was not *carnal*, but spiritual or of the nature of mind or spirit, such terms only were eligible which had respect to purely spiritual relations. Of this category of terms, there was *only one* in all the archives of human knowledge and speech, which *could* be selected. And this precisely was the term which was selected.

5. The Holy Spirit selected the Name *Logos* or *Word*. We may therefore safely assert that this is the best, if not actually the only term in the whole vocabulary of human speech which is at all adapted to express properly the relation which existed "in the beginning," that is, anterior to Time iteself, between God the Father, and the One whom we know as Savior.

[Cf. in this connection Rev. 19:11-16]: And I saw the heaven opened; and behold, a white horse, and he that sat thereon called Faithful and True; and in righteousness he doth judge and make war. And his eyes are a flame of fire, and upon his head are many diadems: and he hath a name written which no one knoweth but he himself. And he is arrayed in a garment sprinkled with blood: and his name is called *The Word of God*. And the armies which are in heaven followed him upon white horses, clothed in fine linen, white and pure. And out of his mouth proceedeth a sharp sword, that with it he should smite the nations: and he shall rule them with a rod of iron: and he treadeth the winepress of the fierceness of the wrath of God, the Almighty. And he hath on his garment and on his thighs a name written, KING OF KINGS, AND LORD OF LORDS.

The foregoing *postulata* having been stated, we now proceed to inquire as follows: What sort of a relation does this term Logos or Word designate? What is included in it? Here we are dealing with matters that are relatively easy of comprehension. The following would, I think, be admitted by all who are capable of intelligent reflection:

1. A word is a sign or symbol of an idea; in a sense it *is* the idea; it is the idea in an audible or visible form. Perhaps it should be made clear at this point that we are accustomed to use the term *word* today in two senses: a fact which, unfortunately, is overlooked by present-day enthusiasts on the subject of semantics. We use the term, first, in its primary or epistemological sense, that is, as embodying *the essence of an idea* that is being communicated. But we use the term also in an exclusively symbolic sense, that is, to describe a given *letter-formation* or combination of letters. Now letter-formations may differ, as indeed they do, in different languages, but the word as em-

bodying the essential meaning of the idea communicated remains the same in all languages. Incidentally, this is precisely what *translation* is, as distinguished from *transliteration*: it is the transfer of the same meaning from the letter-formation which expresses that meaning in one language to the letter-formation which expresses that same meaning in another language (Transliteration is merely the transfer of the letters themselves). Thus, for example, an image of the same object—a man—flashes into the mind of one who is versed in several languages, whether the letter-formation (spoken or written) that is used be "man," *homme,*" "*Mann,*" "*hombre,*" or indeed the letter-formation in any language which conveys the same meaning. W*ord* as an element of language is symbolical, but *word* as meaning conveyed by the symbol is epistemological. Now I am using the term *word* here in its epistemological sense. In this sense it may properly be called the image of the invisible thought which it conveys from one mind to another—that thought which remains a complete secret to all the world until it is expressed in the word.

2. All men think, that is, form ideas, and communicate those ideas, by means of images and words. Whether "imageless thinking" ever takes place in the human mind is, of course, a moot question.

3. Hence it follows that, in this sense, epistemologically, the idea and the word which represents it are coetaneous, that is, of the same age or antiquity. It is true of course that the symbolic word may not be uttered or "born" for years, even ages, after the idea exists; nevertheless, the word, as the essence of the idea, is just as old as the idea itself.

4. The idea and the word are, nevertheless, distinct from each other, even though the relation between them is the most intimate relation that is known on earth. It might be said to be comparable to the relation existing between a being and his own thought.

5. Moreover, the person who is acquainted with—that is, who "understands"—the word, is acquainted also with the idea, for the idea is wholly in the word.

6. Finally, this relation between the word and the idea which it represents is wholly a mental or spiritual relation; it is more closely akin to the spiritual order of being than any other relation of which we have any knowledge. It is a relation of the most sublime order, for which reason no doubt it was selected by the Holy Spirit as the one relation known to man

which most closely approximates an analogy of the eternal relation of the Person whom we know as our Savior to the God and Father of all. Searching the whole vocabulary of human speech, the Spirit could find no Name more appropriate to the designation of this relation than the name *Logos, Word,* of God. And so we read, in one of the most profound passages to be found in Scripture: "In the beginning was the Word [Logos], and the Word was with God, and the Word was God. The same was in the beginning with God. All things were made through him; and without him was not anything made that hath been made" (John 1:1-3).

By putting together the foregoing remarks on the significance, epistemologically, of the term *word,* we have a full view of the truth which the inspired writer designs to communicate in this sublime text. As a word, in its epistemological sense, is an exact image of the idea which it represents, so The Word is an exact image of the invisible God. He is "the effulgence of God's glory and the very image of God's substance" (Heb. 1:3). He Himself said: "He that hath seen me hath seen the Father" (John 14:9). Again, as a word cannot exist without its idea, nor the idea without its word, so God was never without The Word, nor The Word without God. Or, as a word is coetaneous or of equal age with its idea, so The Word and God are co-eternal. And as an idea does not create its word, nor the word its idea, so God did not create The Word nor did The Word create God. "In the beginning," writes the author of the Fourth Gospel (whom I still believe to have been John the Beloved, despite critical attempts to prove the contrary), "was the Logos." That is, anterior to Time, before Time began, The Word was: He existed. "And the Word was *with* God," that is, there were Two—God and The Word. Obviously when I am *with* you, there are two of us present. Then lest anyone—contemporary Greek Stoic or Alexandrian Jew, or later-day Arian, or present-day Unitarian—should get the erroneous notion that The Word is inferior in rank to God, the inspired writer adds: "And the Word *was* God" (John 1:1). That is to say, The Word was just as truly deity as God is deity.Then again, as if to give added emphasis to the facts of the co-eternity and co-equality of God and The Word, he adds: "The same was in the beginning with God" (John 1:2). Whatever the phrase, "in the beginning," means here, it applies equally to The Word and to God. Both participated in the Creation, which marked the beginning of the temporal process. For in the very next verse we are told

475

that The Word was the instrumentality through whom all things were created: "All things were made through him; and without him was not anything made that hath been made" (John 1:3).

Such a general view does the language used here by the inspired writer suggest, and to this view the Scriptures agree throughout. Then in verse 14 of the same chapter, the matter is further clarified: "And the Word became flesh, and dwelt among us (and we beheld his glory, glory as of the only begotten from the Father), full of grace and truth." Hence the final affirmation of this Prologue, in verse 18: "No man hath seen God at any time: the only begotten Son, who is in the bosom of the Father, he hath declared him." Certainly the language here is too plain for misconception. The Word was made flesh, we are told, and dwelt among us, that is, among *men;* and in consequence of His becoming incarnate, He is designated The Son of God, The Only Begotten from the Father. As from eternity God was manifest in and by The Word, so now God is manifest in the flesh—and in Time—by the incarnate Word, His Only Begotten Son. As Paul puts it: "And without controversy great is the mystery of godliness; *He who was manifested in the flesh,* Justified in the Spirit, Seen of angels, Preached among the nations, Believed on in the world, Received up into glory" (1 Tim. 3:16). He who was manifested in the flesh is, of course, the incarnate Word. Again, as God is always with The Word, so when The Word became flesh, He was Immanuel, God with us (Matt. 1:23). As God was never manifest but by the agency of the Spirit in conformity to the edicts (*decrees*) of The Word, so "the heavens and the earth and all the host of them" were brought into existence by the Spirit (Spirit-power) at the *ediction* of The Word. (*decrees,* Psa. 148:6) And as The Word is ever the effulgence of the glory, and the very image of the substance, of the invisible God, so He will ever be known and adored as The Word of God. So will He return in judgment at the last great day, leading the armies of Heaven, Himself arrayed in a garment sprinkled with blood, and having on His garment and on His thigh a name written, King of Kings and Lord of Lords (Rev. 19:11-16). Surely this is the interpretation of the relation—the uncreated and unoriginated relation existing between God and the Person whom we know as our Savior—which the inspired language especially of the Prologue to the Fourth Gospel, and indeed of the Scriptures throughout, inculcates. The substance of this

476

Prologue I should paraphrase thus: From eternity was The Word, and The Word was with God, and The Word was God. He was, I say, from eternity with God. Through Him all things were made, and without Him was nothing made which exists. And He became flesh and dwelt among men; He became a child born and the Son of man. As such He is called Jesus, Immanuel, Son of God, the Only Begotten of the Father.

In a word, the names Jesus, Only Begotten Son, Son of God, Son of Man, and the title Messias or Christ as well, all belong to the Founder of the Christian religion. These names all express, not a relation that existed eternally except, of course, in the purpose of God, but relations which began in time, to be specific, in the reign of Augustus Caesar. When The Word was made incarnate by the overshadowing of the Holy Spirit, and was delivered from the womb of the Virgin, in the Bethlehem manger, then and there He became in fact The Only Begotten Son of God, precisely as the Annunciating Angel had said to Mary previously: "The Holy Spirit shall come upon thee, and the power of the Most High shall overshadow thee: wherefore also the holy thing which is begotten shall be called the Son of God" (Luke 1:35). "Son of God" is the name which designates the relation which began at Bethlehem through the passive instrumentality of the Virgin, from that time on through the New Testament, it is no longer God and The Word, but the Father and the Son. There was no Jesus, no Messias, no Christ, no Only Begotten, no Son of God, I repeat, prior to the reign of Augustus Caesar. The relation that existed between God and the Savior prior to the Christian era was not that of father and son, terms which imply disparity; it was the relation, rather, that is expressed in the Prologue to John's Gospel, by the terms God and the Logos, terms which imply equality. The nomenclature of this Prologue—the nomenclature of the Spirit who inspired it—unfolds a relation quite different from that of father and son—a relation of perfect equality, intimacy, and glory—the relation designated by the name, The Word of God. Hence we find the Son Himself praying, at the close of His earthly ministry, when He had finished the work which the Father had given Him to do: "And now, Father, glorify thou me with thine own self with the glory which I had with thee before the world was" (John 17:5).

In the archives of secular history, the Savior of men is known as Jesus of Nazareth: Jesus is His historical name. Even this name, however, was Divinely authorized: said the

477

angel of the Lord unto Joseph in a dream: "Joseph, thou son of David, fear not to take unto thee Mary thy wife: for that which is conceived in her is of the Holy Spirit. And she shall bring forth a son; and thou shalt call his name JESUS; for it is he that shall save his people from their sins." (Matt. 1:20-21). Luke's account is substantially the same; Luke tells us that the Annunciating Angel said to Mary: "And behold, thou shalt conceive in thy womb, and bring forth a son, and shalt call his name JESUS; He shall be great, and shall be called the Son of the Most High; and the Lord God shall give unto him the throne of his father David" (Luke 1:31-32). According to the Old Testament prophet, His name was to be called Immanuel (Isa. 7:14, Matt. 1:23): this is His incarnate name, God With Us; this designates Him as the Divine-human Person. The designation applies to Him as the Head of the New or Spiritual Creation, the Elect of God.

1 Cor. 15:45-49: So also it is written, The first man Adam became a living soul. The last Adam became a life-giving spirit. Howbeit that is not first which is spiritual, but that which is natural; then that which is spiritual. The first man is of the earth, earthy: the second man is of heaven. As is the earthy, such are they also that are earthy; and as is the heavenly, such are they also that are heavenly. And as we have borne the image of the earthy, we shall also bear the image of the heavenly. Col. 1:18—And he is the head of the body, the church: who is the beginning, the firstborn from the dead: that in all things he might have the pre-eminence. Eph. 1:22-23: God put all things in subjection under his feet, and gave him to be the head over all things to the church, which is his body, the fulness of him that filleth all in all. Eph. 5:23—as Christ also is the head of the church, being himself the savior of the body.

The name Son of God expresses His relation to the Heavenly Father which began in time; as the Son of God He is God's Only Begotten (John 3:16—"God so loved the world that He gave his only begotten Son") by the agency of the Holy Spirit (Matt. 1:20, Luke 1:35). But the risen Christ's affirmation to John on the isle of Patmos, "I am the first and the last" (Rev. 1:17, also v. 8), means, literally, "I am without beginning or end." The name Logos or Word, therefore, designates His eternal or unoriginated relation with God the Creator and Preserver of all things. In the Old Testament, the Holy Three are God, The Word of God, and The Spirit of God; in the New Testament, they are Father, Son, and Holy Spirit.

On the other hand, the term *Messias* (in Hebrew), *Christos* (in Greek) or *Christ* (as transliterated into English), meaning "The Anointed One," as applied to Jesus, is not a name at all, but a title. It is our Savior's official designation as Prophet,

Priest and King of His people, God's elect. Edward King, for example, is the name of a man, but Edward the King is the name of a ruler. In like manner, Jesus is the name of a historical personage, whereas Jesus the Christ is the name *and title* of a sovereign. Cf. in this connection the words of Jesus Himself, after His conquest of death: "All authority hath been given unto me in heaven and on earth" (Matt. 28:18); also the Apostle Peter's great affirmation, in concluding the first Gospel sermon, on the Day of Pentecost: "Let all the house of Israel therefore know assuredly that God hath made him both Lord and Christ, this Jesus whom ye crucified" (Acts 2:36). Jesus was *christed* (*i.e.*, anointed) with the Holy Spirit following His baptism in the Jordan (Matt. 3:16-17); this act signified His formal setting apart to His threefold office of Prophet, Priest and King (Acts 10:38—"even Jesus of Nazareth, how God anointed him with the Holy Spirit and with power"). He was crowned King of kings and Lord of lords (Rev. 19:16) immediately following His conquest of death and subsequent ascension to the Father (Acts 1:9-11). Evidently the coronation ceremonies were taking place in Heaven throughout the period of ten days between His ascension and the advent of the Spirit on the Day of Pentecost.

1 Pet. 3:22—Jesus Christ, who is on the right hand of God, having gone into heaven; angels and authorities and powers being made subject to him. Phil. 2:9-11: God highly exalted him, and gave unto him the name which is above every name; that in the name of Jesus every knee should bow, of things in heaven and things on earth and things under the earth, and that every tongue should confess that Jesus Christ is Lord, to the glory of God the Father. 1 Cor. 15:24-26: Then cometh the end, when he shall deliver up the kingdom to God, even the Father; when he shall have abolished all rule and all authority and power. For he must reign, till he hath put all his enemies under his feet. The last enemy that shall be abolished is death. [In all probability we have a prophetic picture of the antiphonal strains of the coronation ceremonies, in Psalm 24:7-10]: Lift up your heads, O ye gates: And be ye lifted up, ye everlasting doors: And the King of glory will come in. Who is the King of glory? Jehovah strong and mighty, Jehovah mighty in battle. Lift up your heads, O ye gates; Yea, lift them up, ye everlasting doors: and the King of glory will come in. Who is this King of glory? Jehovah of hosts, He is the King of glory.

The Eternal Word, whom we know historically as Jesus of Nazareth, is now seated at the right hand of God, as both Lord and Christ: that is (1) Lord of all things, or Acting Ruler of the universe, and (2) Absolute Monarch of the Kingdom of God. It is worth noting too that the facts of His Sonship, Priesthood and Kingship, and His office as Revealer of God (Prophet) as well, are all embodied in the formula by which the Christian Creed—Christ Himself—is confessed by men unto their salvation: "Thou art the Christ, the Son of the living God" (Matt. 16:16).

[As Paul puts it]: "If thou shalt confess with thy mouth Jesus as Lord, and shalt believe in thy heart that God raised him from the dead, thou shalt be saved; for with the heart man believeth unto righteousness; and with the mouth confession is made unto salvation (Rom. 10:9-10).

Now to confess Jesus as Lord is to confess Him as the Christ, the Son of the living God; and to confess Him as Christ—as God's Anointed—is to confess him as our Prophet, the One to whom we go for the words of eternal life; as our Priest, who intercedeth for us at the right hand of God the Father; and as our King who has all authority over our hearts and lives. To the Jews this confession was especially meaningful; every Jew knew full well that in the times of his fathers, prophets, priests and kings were formally inducted into their respective offices by the ceremony of anointing with pure olive oil. Hence to confess Jesus today as the Christ, the Son of the living God, is to yield to Him in all those relationships which He sustains with the individual members of His Body, the Church.

It is exceedingly important to a proper understanding of the Scriptures, and of the fundamental truths of the Christian religion as a whole, that one differentiate clearly the import of the various names and titles which are applied, in the nomenclature of the Spirit, to the Savior of the world. These names and titles are especially meaningful.

In what sense, then, is our Savior eternally the Word of God? In a twofold sense, I should say. In the first place, He is the Word of God *inwardly*, that is, within the triune personality of the Godhead. "In the beginning was the Word, and the Word was *with God*, and the Word was God. The same was in the beginning with God." (Note the repetition, for emphasis, of the "with.") Note also the present tense of John 1:18, "No man hath seen God at any time; the only begotten Son, *who is in the bosom of the Father*, he hath declared him." The Eternal Word is—always—in the bosom of the Father: without regard to space or time, the Father and He are one. This truth He expressly asserts Himself: "I and the Father are one" (John 10:30). As Jesus Himself prayed, John 17:20-21: "Neither for these [the Apostles] only do I pray, but for them also that believe on me through their word; that they may all be one; even as thou, Father, art in me, and I in thee, that they also may be in us: that the world may believe that thou didst send me." As God is Pure Spirit, and hence Pure Thought, so The Word is the image of Pure Thought, "the very image" of the Divine Substance (Heb. 1:3), personally, morally, and in every way; and as there is nothing quite so close to a thought as the image of that thought—that is to say, its meaning—so there is no more intimate relation than that which exists eternally between God and The Word. As the image, moreover, is in the idea, so the Word is eternally in the bosom of the Father. In the second place, our Savior is The Word of God *outwardly*: He is God's final and perfect revelation of Himself to mankind. "No man hath seen God at any time; the only begotten Son, who is in the bosom of the Father, *he hath declared him.*" God's last and perfect revelation to the human race is a Person, the eternal Person who became flesh and dwelt among us, and in whom "dwelt all the fulness of the Godhead bodily" (Col. 2:9).

In him was life; and the life was the light of men (John 1:4). [He is the Light of the world (John 8:12, 9:5), the Way, the Truth, and the Life (John 14:6)]. [He is] the Word of life . . . the eternal life, *which was with the Father, and was manifested unto us* (1 John 1:2). [He is] "the image of the invisible God" (Col. 1:15), "the effulgence of God's glory" (Heb. 1:3).

[Cf. the words of Jesus Himself] John 14:9—Have I been so long time with you, and dost thou not know me, Philip? he that hath seen me hath seen the Father: how sayest thou, Show us the Father? Again, John 12:44-45: He that believeth on me, believeth not on me, but on him that sent me. And he that beholdeth me beholdeth him that sent me.

While The Word was in the flesh, He lived as God would live, He taught as God would teach, He wrought such mighty works as only God Himself could work, and He died as God would die, out of sheer love giving Himself freely for sinful men, the Divine for the human, the innocent for the guilty. If anyone would receive the wisdom of God, let him listen to Jesus proclaiming in gentle accents the Beatitudes of the Sermon on the Mount. If anyone would look upon the working of the mighty power of God, let him look upon Jesus casting out demons, healing the sick and the blind and the maimed, stilling the winds and waves, feeding a multitude with a few loaves and fishes, and even raising the dead to life, in each case by a spoken word. If anyone would be acquainted with the holiness of God, let him look upon Jesus, not only proclaiming, but living every day and hour the life of complete moral purity before all men, infinitely compassionate toward the weak and helpless, but flashing forth righteous indignation upon every form of self-pride, irreverence, injustice, and hypocrisy. And if anyone would desire a demonstration of the immeasurable love of God, let him gaze upon that awful scene on a lonely hill back of Jerusalem, let him take a look at that Holy Form hanging suspended between earth and sky on the middle cross, let him see the blood dripping from the lacerated head and hands and feet of the Son of God, and let him realize that that blood was being shed for the remission of his sins and the sins of the whole world. Let all men realize that *"God so loved the world,* that He gave his only begotten Son, that whosoever believeth on him should not perish, but have eternal life" (John 3:16). The Mystery of Godliness is a Person: "He who was manifested in the flesh, justified in the spirit, seen of angels, preached among the nations, believed on in the world, received up into glory" (1 Tim. 3:16). The Creed of Christendom is this Person: the Christ, the Son of the living God. We repeat: Christ is Christianity, and Christianity is Christ. The work of the Holy Spirit throughout the present Dispensation is to bear witness of, and to glorify, this Person (John 15:26, 16:14)—the Person, both Son of God and Son of man, the image of the invisible God, the central Figure of all history, and the only Savior of men. Lebreton writes:

In Christian theology, this conception of the Son as the image of God derives a new significance for the fact of the Incarnation; for, by taking flesh and manifesting himself to men, the Son reveals them to the Father. (Again) human speculation flattered itself in vain that it could sound the depths of the life of God, its proud efforts resulted in nothing but barren and deceptive dreams; it is in the humility of the Incarnation that the mystery of God has been revealed: for the Jews, a scandal; a folly to the Greeks; the strength and wisdom of God. for the elect.[1] [Cf. Paul, 1 Cor. 1:22-24: Seeing that Jews ask for signs, and Greeks seek after wisdom; but we preach Christ crucified, unto Jews a stumbling block, and unto Gentiles foolishness; but unto them that are called, both Jews and Greeks, Christ the power of God and the wisdom of God.]

Another question arises in this connection: namely, Are we to understand that the Logos existed *as a Person* prior to His incarnation? A few observations will suffice to answer this question, as follows: Thinking is the act of a person; my thinking, moreover, is my own activity and in the very nature of the case cannot be someone's else's; the meaning of my thought also, being what it *means to me,* cannot be identical with the meaning of another person's thought to him. A person is, as we have learned, an individual; he is unique, he is an *other*

1. Jules Lebreton, S.J., *History of the Dogma of the Trinity,* I, 299, 414. Translated by Algar Thorold from the Eighth Edition.

to all other persons. The mental processes and accummulations of one person are *never* exactly duplicated in any other person. Hence, as God Himself is, in His essential Being, Pure Thought and therefore personal, it follows that The Word as the image of the Divine Mind or Thought is likewise personal. This is true of Him both as the pre-incarnate and as the incarnate Word. His mode of existence, whether He be non-incarnate or temporarily tabernacled in an angelic or in a human form, is essentially psychical, hence personal. This conclusion, moreover, to which even our limited human reason points, is certainly corroborated by the Scriptures as a whole, and by those of the New Testament in particular; it is only in the New Testament of course that the tripersonality of God is fully revealed.

For example, it is most significant that throughout the New Testament, the masculine personal pronoun is invariably used with reference to His pre-incarnate mode of being. "For *in him* were all things created . . . all things have been created through *him* and unto *him;* and *he is before all things,* and *in him* all things consist" (Col. 1:16-17). "Christ Jesus, who, existing in the form of God, counted not the being on an equality with God a thing to be grasped, but *emptied himself,* taking the form of a servant," etc. (Phil. 2:5-7). If the pre-incarnate Logos existed in the form *(morphe)* of God and was on a footing of equality with God, certainly then since God is personal, He too was a Person. "Since then the children are sharers in flesh and blood, *he also himself* in like manner partook of the same," that is, He—obviously as a pre-incarnate Person—voluntarily took upon Himself a human body with its infirmities, "that through death he might bring to nought him that had the power of death, that is, the devil" (Heb. 2:14). Moreover, in the Prologue to the Fourth Gospel, the personal identity so strongly affirmed of the pre-existing Logos and Christ, admits of no doubt whatever as to the personality of the Logos prior to His incarnation.

Verse 3—All things were made through *him;* and without *him* was not anything made that hath been made. Verse 10—*He* was in in the world, and *the world was made through him,* and the world knew *him* not. Verse 11—*He came* unto his own, [that is, to His own people] and they that were *his* own received *him* not. V. 12—But as many as received *him,* to them gave *he* the right to become children of God, even to them that believe on *his* name. V. 14—And the Word became flesh, and dwelt among us, etc. V. 18—No man hath seen God at any time; the only begotten Son, who *is in the bosom of the Father,* he hath declared him. [And Paul gives testimony thus]: Yet to us there is one God, the Father, of whom are all things, and we unto him; and one

Lord, Jesus Christ, *through whom are all things*, and we through him (1 Cor. 8:6). [Language could hardly teach more explicitly that the pre-incarnate Logos was a Person.]

[Cf. again the words of Jesus Himself, in His sublime intercessory prayer to the Father, John 17:3-5]: And this is life eternal, that they should know thee the only true God, and him whom thou didst send, even Jesus Christ. I glorified thee on the earth, having accomplished the work which thou hast given me to do. And now, Father, glorify thou me with thine own self with the glory which I had with thee before the world was. [Certainly if He was a person while in the flesh and uttering this prayer, as we know that He was, then He could not have been less than personal while with the Father in eternal glory, before the foundation of the world.] Again, Verse 16—They [the Apostles] are not of the world, even as I am not of the world [note the personal pronoun here and the time-transcendence indicated by this last clause]. [Again, V. 24]—Father, I desire that they also whom thou hast given me be with me where I am, that they may behold my glory, which thou hast given me: for thou lovedst me before the foundation of the world. [Certainly the fact of the personality of the pre-incarnate Logos is implicit in all these passages.]

[Cf. also in this connection, the well-known passage from the Old Testament, Micah 5:2] But thou, Bethlehem Ephrathah, which art little to be among the thousands of Judah, out of thee shall come forth unto me that is to be ruler in Israel: whose goings forth are from of old, from everlasting. [That this prophecy alludes to a person, and to none other than the One who was born in Bethlehem of Judea—in a word, to the Messiah—is obvious; cf. Matt. 2:4-6. Here the Spirit expressly asserts, through the prophet Micah, that this Person's *goings forth* from the Godhead are from of old, from everlasting.]

That is to say, to quote Adam Clarke:

There is no *time* in which He has not been *going forth*, coming in various ways to save man. And He that *came forth* the moment that time had its birth, was *before that time* in which He began to *come forth* to save the souls which He had *created*. He was *before* all things. As He is the *Creator* of all things, so He is the *Eternal*, and *no part* of what was *created*. All being but God has been *created*. Whatever has *not been created* is God. But Jesus is the *Creator* of all things; therefore, He is God: for He cannot be *a part of His own* work.[1] This text teaches clearly that His birth in the Bethlehem manger as the Only Begotten Son of God was not His first appearance, that it was in fact but one of His many appearances, in the world, to declare and execute God's will toward men. We must conclude that, being of the rank of God who is personal, and Himself a member of the Godhead, the Logos can never be anything less than personal.

We need not be surprised to know, therefore, that even though the fact of the triune personality of the Godhead is not clearly set forth in the Old Testament, still there are many Old Testament passages in which manifestations of the pre-incarnate Logos in the world are clearly implied. These passages may be classified generally in three categories, as follows:

1. *Those describing the appearance and activities of the Angel of Jehovah*:

1. Adam Clarke, *Commentary, in loc.*

[In certain texts, for instance, the Angel of Jehovah identifies Himself with Jehovah.] Gen. 22:11, 15, 16—And the angel of Jehovah called unto him out of heaven, and said, Abraham, Abraham. . . . And the angel of Jehovah called unto Abraham a second time out of heaven, and said, By myself have I sworn, saith Jehovah, etc. [We must remember, in this connection, that the primary meaning of the word *angelos* is "messenger," a "messenger" who conveys news and behests from God to men.] Gen. 31:11-13: And the angel of God said unto me in the dream, Jacob; and I said, Here am I. And he said . . . I am the God of Bethel, where thou anointedst a pillar, etc. Cf. Gen. 18:1-2: And Jehovah appeared unto him [Abraham] by the oaks of Mamre, as he sat in the tent door in the heat of the day. Cf. vv. 13, 17, 20 following: And Jehovah said unto Abraham, etc; also v. 33—And Jehovah went his way, as soon as he had left off communing with Abraham.

[Note that the visitation in this instance was that of three "men"]— and lo, three men stood over against him; and when he saw them, he ran to meet them from the tent door, and bowed himself to the earth, etc. (v. 2). Exo. 14:19—And the angel of God, who went before the camp of Israel, removed and went behind them. [In this instance, the Angel's presence was indicated by the pillar of cloud by day and the pillar of fire by night, symbols of the presence of the Spirit and the Word, who go together (Isa. 59:21).] Cf. Exo. 13:21-22: And Jehovah went before them by day in a pillar of cloud, to lead them the way, and by night in a pillar of fire, to give them light; that they might go by day and by night: the pillar of cloud by day, and the pillar of fire by night, departed not from before the people. [Correlate with these pasages Paul's testimony, 1 Cor. 10:1-4]: For I would not, brethren, have you ignorant, that our fathers were all under the cloud, and all passed through the sea; and were all baptized unto Moses in the cloud and in the sea; and did all eat the same spiritual food; and did all drink the same spiritual drink: for they drank of a spiritual rock that followed them: *and the rock was Christ.* [Hence, in Heb. 11:26-27, Moses, their great leader, is said to have endured as seeing him who is invisible, accounting the reproach of Christ greater riches than the treasures of Egypt.]

[Again, in other Old Testament texts the Angel of Jehovah is represented as having been identified with Jehovah by other persons.] Gen. 16:7, 9, 13—And the angel of Jehovah found her [Hagar] by a fountain of water in the wilderness . . . and the angel of Jehovah said unto her, Return to thy mistress, and submit thyself under her hands. . . . And she called the name of Jehovah that spake unto her, Thou art a God that seeth, etc. Cf. Gen. 32:30—[here we are told that Jacob, after wrestling with the Messenger of God, at the ford of the Jabbok, until break of day] called the name of the place Peniel: for, said he, I have seen God face to face, and my life is preserved. [Cf. Gen. 48:15-16: the words of Israel, with respect to Joseph's two sons]: The God who hath fed me all my life long unto this day, the angel who hath redeemed me from all evil, bless the lads, etc.

[Again, in certain other texts the Angel of Jehovah is represented as accepting worship that is due only to God.] Exo. 3:2, 4-5: And the angel of Jehovah appeared unto him [Moses] in a flame of fire out of the midst of a bush. . . . And when Jehovah saw that he turned aside to see, God called unto him out of the midst of the bush . . . and he said, Draw not nigh hither: put off thy shoes from off thy feet, for the place whereon thou standest is holy ground. Judg. 13:20-22: The angel of Jehovah ascended in the flame of the altar, and Manoah and his wife . . . fell on their faces to the ground. . . . And Manoah said unto his wife, We shall surely die, because we have seen God.

Josh. 5:13-15: And it came to pass, when Joshua was by Jericho, that he lifted up his eyes and looked, and, behold, there stood a man over against him with his sword drawn in his hand: and Joshua went unto him, and said unto him, Art thou for us, or for our adversaries? And he said, Nay; but *as prince of the host of Jehovah* am I now come. And Joshua fell on his face to the earth, and did worship, and said unto him, What saith my lord unto his servant? And the prince of Jehovah's host said unto Joshua, Put off thy shoe from off thy foot; for the place whereon thou standest is holy. And Joshua did so. Dan. 3:25, 28—He [Nebuchadnezzar] answered and said, Lo, I see four men loose, walking in the midst of the fire, and they have no hurt; and the aspect of the fourth is *like a son of the gods.* . . .Nebuchadnezzar spake and said, Blessed be the God of Shadrach, Meshach, and Abednego, *who hath sent his angel,* and delivered his servants that trusted in him, etc. Although the phrase, "angel of the Lord" is used in later Scriptures to denote a created angel (Matt. 1:20, Luke 1:11, Luke 1:26, Acts 8:26, Acts 10:3, Heb. 1:14, etc.), there is every reason for believing that the Angel of Jehovah of the Old Testament revelation was the preincarnate Logos, whose manifestations in angelic or in human form foreshadowed His final advent in the flesh as the Messiah. [Finally who was the King-Priest Melchizedek?]

**2. Those passages in which Wisdom is represented as existing eternally with God, though apparently distinct from God.**

Job 28:20-23: Whence then cometh wisdom? And where is the place of understanding? Seeing it is hid from the eyes of all living, And kept close from the birds of the heavens. . . . God understandeth the way thereof, and he knoweth the place thereof. Prov. 8:1—Doth not wisdom cry, And understanding put forth her voice? Prov. 8:2-6: [here Wisdom is represented as pressing upon men her invitation to matriculate in her school]: On the top of high places by the way, Where the paths meet, she standeth; Beside the gates, at the entry of the city, At the coming in at the doors, she crieth aloud: Unto you, O men, I call; And my voice is to the sons of men. O ye simple, understand prudence; And, ye fools, be of an understanding heart. Hear, for I will speak excellent things; And the opening of my lips shall be right things. Prov. 8:35-36 [Here we are told that the good things that Wisdom promises, including life, are the same things which God gives]: For whoso findeth me findeth life, And shall obtain favor of Jehovah, But he that sinneth against me wrongeth his own soul; All they that hate me love death. Prov. 9:1-5: Wisdom hath builded her house; She hath hewn out her seven pillars: She hath killed her beasts; She hath mingled her wine: She hath also furnished her table: She hath sent forth her maidens; She crieth upon the highest places of the city: Whoso is simple, let him turn in hither: As for him that is void of understanding, she saith to him, Come, eat ye of my bread, etc. Cf. Matt. 11:19—Wisdom is justified by her works (or by her children). Luke 11:49—Therefore also said the wisdom of God, I will send unto them prophets and apostles, etc. Luke 7:35—And wisdom is justified of all her children. Again, Prov. 3:19—Jehovah by wisdom founded the earth; By understanding he established the heavens. Cf. Heb. 1:2—his Son . . . through whom also he made the worlds. Heb. 1:8, 10—but of the Son he saith, . . . Thou, Lord, in the beginning didst lay the foundation of the earth, etc. See especially Prov. 8:22-31: Jehovah possessed me [Wisdom] in the beginning of his way, Before his works of old. I was set up from everlasting, from the begining, Before the earth was. . . . While as yet he had not made the earth, nor the fields, Nor the beginning of the dust of the world. When he established the heavens, I was there: When he set a circle upon the face of the deep. When he made firm the skies above, When the fountains of the deep became strong, When he gave to the sea its bound, That the waters should not transgress his commandment, When he marked out the foundations of the earth; *Then I was by him, as a master workman;* And I was daily his delight, Rejoicing always before him, Rejoicing in his habitable earth; And my delight was with the sons of men. [It is difficult to see in this passage nothing more than personification; in fact, most commentators are in agreement that Wisdom is here presented as distinguished from God, or at least that the tendency in this text is in that direction.]

Again [in the Apocryphal book of *Wisdom,* 7:24-26, Wisdom is described as] a breath of the power of God, a clear effluence of the glory of the Almighty, an effulgence from everlasting light, an unspotted mirror of the working of God, And an image of his goodness. [Heb. 1:3, in which the Son of God is described as] *the effulgence of his glory, and the very image of his substance.* [Also in *Wisdom* 9:9-10, Wisdom is represented as having been present with God when He made the world, and the author of the book prays that Wisdom may be sent to him out of God's holy heavens and from the throne of his glory]. [And in *I Esdras* 4:35-38, Truth in a similar manner is spoken of as personal]: Great is truth, and stronger than all things. All the earth calleth upon truth, and the heaven blesseth her; all works shake and tremble, but with her is no unrighteous thing. . . . But truth abideth, and is strong for ever; she liveth and conquereth for evermore. [Cf. the words of Jesus, John 14:6]—I am . . . the Truth. And John 18:37— To this end have I been born, and to this end am I come into the world, that I should bear witness unto the truth. Every one that is of the truth heareth my voice.

[Again, in the Apocryphal book of *Ecclesiasticus,* 24:1-22, Wisdom is represented as speaking in the assembly of the angels, as declaring her eternal subsistence, and as constantly exercising her ministry in the holy tabernacle of Zion (*i.e.,* in the Temple in Jerusalem). In v. 23 of the same chapter, Wisdom is identified with the Law.] [And in the book of *Wisdom* again, Wisdom is expressly affirmed to be a spirit (1:6—for wisdom is a spirit that loveth man; 9:17—who ever gained knowledge of thy counsel, except thou gavest wisdom, And sentest thy holy spirit from on high?); is said to order all things and to do all things (8:1, 7:27); is said to choose out for him the works of God (8:4); and is described as the guide of men and the leader of the chosen people in particular (cf. 10 ff.). Wisdom is presented here, moreover, as the artificer of things that are (8:6, 7:21); in a word, Wisdom plays precisely the same role as the Logos or Word of God.]

[The significance of these texts becomes clear in the light of New Testament teaching.] 1 Cor. 1:22-24: Seeing that Jews ask for signs, and Greeks seek after wisdom: but we preach Christ crucified, unto Jews a stumblingblock, and unto Gentiles foolishness; but unto them that are called, both Jews and Greeks, *Christ the power of God, and the wisdom of God.* 1 Cor. 1:30—But of him are ye in Christ Jesus, *who was made unto us wisdom from God, etc.* [Cf. also from the Old Testament, Jer. 10:10-12]: Jehovah is the true God; he is the living God, and an everlasting King. . . . He hath made the earth by his power, he hath established the world by his wisdom, and by his understanding hath he stretched out the heavens. Jas. 3:17—But the wisdom that is from above is first pure, then peaceable, gentle, easy to be entreated, full of mercy and good fruits, without variance, without hypocrisy.

3. *Those passages in which the Word, as distinguished from God, is presented as the executor of God's Will from everlasting.*

[Note again the formula, *And God said,* which is used in the first chapter of *Genesis* to introduce the account of what happened on each successive "day" of Creation.] Psa. 33:6, 9—By the word of Jehovah were the heavens made, And all the host of them by the breath of his mouth. . . . For he spake, and it was done; He commanded, and it stood fast. Psa. 148:5-6: For he commanded, and they were created. He hath also established them [all created things] for ever and ever; He hath made a decree which shall not pass away. Psa. 119:89—For ever, O Jehovah, Thy word is settled in heaven. Psa. 147:15, 18-20: He sendeth out his commandment upon earth; His word runneth very swiftly. . . . He sendeth out of his word. . . . He showeth his word unto Jacob, His statutes and his ordinances unto Israel. He hath not dealt so with any nation, etc. Psa. 107:20—He sendeth his word, and healeth them [sinners], And delivereth them from their destructions. Heb. 11:3—By faith we understand that the worlds have been framed by the word of God, so that what is seen hath not been made out of things which appear. 2 Pet. 3:5—For this they wilfully forget, that there were heavens from of old, and an earth compacted out of water and amidst water, by the word of God. Cf. v. 7—but the heavens that now are, and the earth, by the same word have been stored up for fire, being reserved against the day of judgment and destruction of ungodly men.

It must be admitted, of course, that in none of these Old Testament passages descriptive of the Divine Wisdom and Word is the idea of personality clearly developed; nor indeed is that of the personality of the Spirit developed in the Old Testament. These developments came later, in the Christian revelation. As a matter of fact, the doctrine of the triune personality of God is set forth in the Old Testament only by *intimation,*—as we have noted previously—never explicitly. In the Old Testament, we meet God, the Word of God, and the Spirit of God. These Three become, in the fulness of the light of the Christian revelation, Father, Son, and Holy Spirit, respectively. As St. Epiphanius has put it, the Divine unity was first proclaimed by Moses (Deut. 6:4—"Jehovah our God is one Jehovah"); the Divine duality, that is, the distinction between the Father and the Son, as the Messiah, by the prophets (Isa. 9:6—"For unto us a child is born, unto us a son is given . . . and his name shall be called Wonderful, Counsellor, Mighty God, Everlasting Father, Prince of Peace"); but the Divine tripersonality was first clearly set forth in the teaching of Christ and the Apostles (Matt. 29:19—"baptizing them into the name of the Father and of the Son and of the Holy Spirit"). The reason for this progressive revelation is evident: Had such a revelation as that of the triune personality of the Godhead been made in Old Testament times, there is little doubt that it would have been perverted into a tritheism by the children of Israel, surrounded on all sides as they were by pagan polytheistic systems. Hence the fulness of the revelation waited for the appearance of the Logos Himself in human flesh and the inauguration of the Gospel Dispensation.

"In the beginning was the Logos, and the Logos was with God, and the Logos was God. The same was in the beginning with God. All things were made through him; and without him was not anything made that hath been made." (It is interesting to note how closely this is paralleled by the concept which pervaded all Greek philosophical thought, and especially that of Plato and Aristotle, that *psyche* (*soul* or *mind*) is the *archē* or first principle of motion, *i.e.,* of activity or change. This in fact seems to have been the most widespread of all ancient philosophical doctrines. May we not reasonably conclude, therefore, that it had its true source in the fact of the Logos?) Cf. Rev. 3:14—"And to the angel of the church in Laodicea write: These things saith the Amen, the faithful and true witness, *the beginning of the creation of God.*" And Rev. 1:5—"Jesus Christ, who is the faithful witness, the firstborn of the dead, and the ruler of the kings of the earth." He, the eternal Logos, became flesh and dwelt among us as God's Only Begotten Son. Through the Eternal Spirit He offered Himself up for us, as a Lamb without blemish and without spot (Heb. 9:14). Whereupon God the Father, again through the agency of the Spirit (Rom. 8:11), raised Him up from the dead and set Him at His own right hand in the heavenly places (Eph. 1:20). There He shall reign until He hath put all His enemies under His feet, including the last and greatest enemy, death (1 Cor. 15:25-26), for it is the immutable Will of God the Father Almighty that ultimately "in the name of Jesus" every knee shall bow, and every tongue shall confess "that Jesus Christ is Lord, to the glory of God the Father" (Phil. 2:9-11). Men may be assured that if they do not make that Confession here—in this present life—*in faith,* they shall make it in the Judgment to their everlasting remorse and despair.

Finally, not only did the Holy Spirit select the only name in the whole vocabulary of human speech—the name Logos—that adequately describes the relation which exists eternally between the Heavenly Father and our Savior, but *He also selected the most appropriate, most opportune moment in all human history to reveal this name to the world.* Logos doctrines of both Greek and Hebrew origin, and notions of intermediaries of various kinds between God and men, were rife throughout the Roman world at the time the Fourth Gospel was written. Perhaps the oldest and most widespread Logos doctrine extant in the apostolic age was that of the Stoics. It will be recalled that in the *Timaeus*, Plato had pictured the Divine Reason or Demiourgos as creating the world according to archetypal Forms or Ideas which would seem to have subsisted, in Plato's view, in a transcendent, exclusively intelligible world. In the same work, however, Plato, implicitly at least, identifies the Demiourgos with the Soul of the World, which he distinguishes from the World-Body, and thereby seemingly becomes involved in a self-contradiction. Be that as it may, it was inevitable that the Platonic World-Soul should become incorporated by later thinkers into a Logos doctrine. This development was furthered of course by the metaphysics of Aristotle. Throughout his writings Aristotle, in common with Plato, repeatedly affirms that Psyche (Soul or Mind) is the First Principle of motion, but insists, in opposition to the Platonic view, that this First Principle, rather than subsisting in a transcendent intelligible world, exists in the particular things themselves of the present visible world; Psyche was for Aristotle essentially the Principle of Form. Hence, from these sources arose the Stoic doctrine of the Logos as the *material* principle of energy and determination, the immanent force and law of the world which moves everything to the fatefully imposed goal of its destiny, but which moves things nevertheless, in virtue of its immanence, spontaneously and naturally. Soul, for the Stoics, was a sort of burning air (a vestige of the ancient Herakleitean doctrine) which permeates the world and each individual man, a rarefied form of fire which will consume all things in the final conflagration which was envisioned by the Stoics as the predetermined end of the whole temporal process. The fact must not be overlooked that the Stoic Logos was essentially *material* and *immanent;* in the main, the Stoics built their pantheism upon the Aristotelian foundation.

A separate development occurred, however, which was basically Platonic. Again it will be recalled that in his *mythos* of the Creation, in the *Timaeus,* Plato had pictured the Demiourgos as having been thwarted by Necessity in his operations within the Receptacle (Space). This evidently was a doctrine of the recalcitrancy of matter, and savored of dualism. Hence, other thinkers who followed Plato seized upon this doctrine of Necessity and, utilizing it as a basis, tried to work out a solution of the problem of imperfection and evil. The inevitable result was the gross, in some instances fantastic, exaggeration of existing evil, and alongside this development the theoretical removal of God from this evil as far as possible, even to the point of complete inaccessibility. And between such an inaccessible God and such an evil world, religio-philosophical speculation originating with, and developed by, Jewish, Greek, and later nominally Christian Gnostic sects, multiplied intermediary powers to the point of absurdity: the Logos, aeons, powers, angels, demons, and what not. In all these systems the Logos was reduced to the status of a *created* power, inferior to God both in nature and in rank. Philosophically, this view flowered in the third century in Neoplatonism. Theologically, it flowered in the first two centuries in the various forms of so-called Gnosticism which sought a haven under the aegis of the Christian religion; in the fourth century, in Arianism; and in modern times, it expresses itself in the Christology—if such it properly can be called—of Unitarianism. This theosophy presented a great temptation to the early Christians, in the fact that it seemed quite ready and anxious to make room for their Christ. But the Apostles would have none of it. The *Epistle to the Colossians*, for example, was devoted for the most part to dissuading the saints from the worship of angels; and the author, in the first chapter of the epistle, declares unequivocally the facts of the self-existence and creatorhood of the Messiah. The *Epistle to the Hebrews* reminded them insistently of the infinite distance separating Christ, who is the Son of God, from angels, who are merely "ministering spirits" or servants of God. And the pastoral Epistles continued to denounce the superstitions, fables, and interminable genealogies which were extant in the religious world in the first two centuries of the Christian era. The essence of this post-Platonic development was the reduction of the Logos to the status of a created impersonal intermediary between God and man. In some cases, the Logos was conceived as essentially material, in others as quasi-psychical, according to the extent, of course, that Christian teaching had impinged upon the thinking of the protagonists of the doctrine.

The third development of the Logos doctrine occurred at Alexandria, culminating in the writings of the learned Alexandrian Jew, Philo Judaeus. His system might properly be called a Platonized interpretation of the Old Testament doctrines of the Divine Wisdom and Word. Philo seems to have approached recognition at times of the personality of the Logos, but at other times his monotheistic scruples seem to have led him to contradict all such intimations. Hence, throughout his writings the Logos remained essentially impersonal, an intermediary power—either the thought of God or its expression in the world—between the creature and the Creator. Lebreton writes:

> In order better to understand this Philonian conception of the Logos as an intermediary being between God and the world, we may compare it to the belief of Christians in the mediatory Word: the problem to be solved is the same, namely, to bring the infinitely perfect God near to his weak and guilty creatures, but the two solutions are entirely different. The Incarnate Word unites in his person these two extremes, God and the flesh, being at the same time truly God and truly man; on the contrary, Philo's Logos does not unite in himself the two terms, he is half way between them; as Philo makes him say in the [following] passage: being neither without beginning like God, nor created like you, but intermediary between these two extremes, I am, as it were, a hostage for both parties.[1]

(One might well ask: If the Logos was neither unoriginated nor created, just how did He come into existence or exist?) Lebreton concludes thus, rightly:

> The Messianic belief is as foreign as belief in the Incarnation to the Philonian theory of the Logos, and is equally characteristic of Christianity. As the Messias, prepared for by the whole past of Israel, awaited and predicted by the prophets, came upon earth to inaugurate the Kingdom of God and redeem the elect, and due, later on, to return to judge the whole world, Jesus fills the whole of history. The Philonian Logos is foreign to history; he may be the object of the speculation of philosophers, he has no contact with the life of man.[2]

Into this welter of human speculation, at the very time when such speculation was most rife, came the revelation of the true Logos by the Spirit of God. The true Logos, said He, is, in the first place, a Person—*the* Person who became flesh and dwelt among us as God's Only Begotten Son, the Christ. In the second place, this Person was not a mere created power; quite the contrary, anterior to time or before time began, this Person, the true Logos, *was*. From eternity He not only *was*, but He was *with God*: that is, there were Two who were unoriginated and eternal—God and the Logos. In the third place, this Person, the true Logos, was not inferior in nature or rank to God; on the contrary, He was not only *with God* from eternity but He *was God*: that is to say, the Two were not only co-eternal but also co-equal. In the fourth place, this Person, the true Logos, is not a mere intermediary between God and the world; on the contrary, He is infinitely more than that—He is the one and only *Mediator* between God and man. He became our Mediator,

1. *Op. cit.*, 117-178.
2. *Ibid*, 187.

the Mediator of the New Covenant established upon better promises, through the Incarnation, the Atonement, and the Resurrection: by His uniting in His own Person the two natures, Divine and human, He qualified Himself as the Head of the Spiritual Creation, and as Prophet, Priest and King of His people. "For there is one God, one mediator also between God and men, himself man, Christ Jesus" (1 Tim. 2:5). In the fifth place, this Person, the true Logos, is not creature—neither an emanation from God, nor a creation of God—but Creator: "all things were made through him; and without him was not anything made that hath been made" (John 1:3). "In him were all things created, in the heavens and upon the earth, things visible and things invisible, whether thrones or dominions or principalities or powers; all things have been created through him, and unto him; and he is before all things, and in him all things consist" (Col. 1:16-17). In Him, the Incarnate Logos, dwelt "all the fulness of the Godhead bodily" (Col. 2:9); He is "the effulgence of God's glory, and the very image of his substance" (Heb. 1:3); "wherefore also he is able to save to the uttermost them that draw near unto God through him, seeing he ever liveth to make intercession for them" (Heb. 7:25). *The living Creed of the living Church of the living God is the ever-living Christ.* He Himself tells us: "I am the first and the last, and the Living One; and I was dead, and behold, I am alive for evermore, and I have the keys of death and of Hades" (Rev. 1:17-18).

> All hail the power of Jesus' name!
> Let angels prostrate fall!
> Bring forth the royal diadem,
> And crown Him Lord of all!

The foregoing exposition is certainly sufficient to prove that the Christian doctrine of the Logos definitely was *not*, as it has not infrequently been alleged, the point of insertion of Hellenism into Christianity. On the contrary, it was the point at which primitive Christianity began positively to resist and to repudiate the speculations both of Hellenism and of Hellenistic (Alexandrine) Judaism. And whereas, even for us today, Greek speculation and Jewish theology must be considered and evaluated as doctrines, the coming of the Son of God into the world must be considered, and accepted or rejected, as a fact, that is to say, as an *event* that took place in space and time. In Christianity, two things are to be considered, namely, the

Person and the System; and of these the Person is first, for the simple reason that the System depends *in toto* upon the Person. The point of departure for doctrine in the New Testament is the Person rather than a teaching. To his disciples Plato, for example, was master; to the Jews, Moses was lawgiver; but to Christians, Christ is the very Object of their faith, the Power of God and the Wisdom of God. The essential thing in primitive and pure Christianity as it came directly from the Holy Spirit was not an organization, institution or hierarchy; not an elaborate creedal statement; but *the personal* Christ. Jesus said Himself, with respect to the work of the Spirit: "He shall glorify me" (John 16:14). Christianity in its pure form is not a speculation imagined by a philosopher, but the religion born of *a person who actually lived on earth* and finding in Him its only significance for mankind. *Christianity is therefore essentially authoritarian.* Its Founder makes this claim: "All authority hath been given unto me in heaven and on earth" (Matt. 28:18). To this authoritarian aspect, all other aspects of the Christian religion, including even the ethical, must be regarded as subordinate. The whole Christian System stands or falls with the Person—Jesus of Nazareth, the Christ, the Son of the living God. "What think ye of the Christ? whose Son is he?"

## 2. The Spirit and the Word

The Word of God is presented to us in Scripture in two general forms, namely, as *personal* and as *impersonal.*

The personal Word is, of course, the Eternal Logos, the one who became flesh and dwelt among us as The Only Begotten Son of God.

The impersonal Word also exists in two general forms, namely, (1) as oral or spoken, and (2) as stereotyped, *i.e.,* written, printed, etc. Incidentally, in this particular connection, the argument has often been heard that "the Church existed before the Book," thus implying that Scripture is secondary in authority to ecclesiastical leadership or that churchmen are vested with authority to "interpret," and even to supplement, Scripture teaching. Protagonists of this view— to whom the wish is father to the thought—presume to find their norm of Christian faith and practice in the Church, and this means, of course, in Church "officials," rather than in the Scriptures. But a mere babe in Christ should be able to detect the glaring fallacy in this position. True it is that the Church existed for some time prior to the formation of the New Testament *canon*. But the Church certainly did not exist prior to the Word of Christ; indeed it came into existence as a result of the preaching of that Word, the Gospel of our salvation. As Paul wrote to the Thessalonians: "We thank God without ceasing that, when ye received from us the word of the message, even the word of God, ye accepted it not as the word of men, but, as it is in truth, the word of God, which also worketh in you that believe" (1 Thess. 2:13). The Apostles' teaching, which is the Word of Christ communicated to them by the Holy Spirit and by them to the rest of mankind, existed cotemporaneously with the first proclamation of the  facts of the Gospel (the death, burial and resurrection of Christ) and the incorporation of the Church on the great Day of Pentecost. On that day the Spirit descended from Heaven, according to the promise of Christ, and clothed the Apostles with proper infallibility for their message and proper authority for their mission and work (Luke 24: 45-49, John 20: 21-23, Acts 1: 1-8, 2: 1-4, etc.), and on that day the Gospel Dispensation was ushered in. (If there was a Church in existence prior to Pentecost, certainly it lacked the presence and power of the Spirit, because it was on that day that He came to earth to assume His work of incorporating and administering the Body of Christ.) The Apostles' teaching had its inception from that day and hour that the Spirit descended to qualify them as ambassadors of Christ, as infallible witnesses of His death, burial and resurrection.

Cf. Acts 1:8—But ye shall receive power, when the Holy Spirit is come upon you: and ye shall be my witnesses both in Jerusalem, and in all Judea and Samaria, and unto the uttermost part of the earth. Acts 2:32—This Jesus did God raise up, whereof we all are witnesses. Acts 10:40-41: Him God raised up the third day, and gave him to be made manifest, not to all the people, but unto witnesses that were chosen before of God, even to us, who ate and drank with him after he rose from the dead. 1 Pet. 1:12—To whom [the prophets] it was revealed, that not unto themselves, but unto you, did they minister these things, which now have been announced unto you through them that preached the gospel unto you by the Holy Spirit sent forth from heaven. Acts 4:33—And with great power gave the apostles their witness of the resurrection of the Lord Jesus. 2 Cor. 5:20—We are ambassadors therefore on behalf of Christ, as though God were entreating by us: we beseech you on behalf of Christ, be ye reconciled to God.

Hence we read that the members of the newly-formed congregation at Jerusalem, the first Church of Christ in all the world, the first-fruits of the spiritual harvest, *"continued stedfastly in the apostles' teaching* and fellowship, in the breaking of bread and the prayers" (Acts 2:42). Now the Apostles' teaching was, at that time and for about a century following, communicated *orally;* later it was embodied in permanent form in the New Testament canon. And through this stereotyped Word the original (and only) Apostles themselves have witnessed, and to this day continue to witness, for Jesus, "unto the uttermost part of the earth," just as He told them that they should do. Hence it follows that this Word of Christ communicated to the Apostles by the Spirit sent down from Heaven, and delivered by them to the rest of mankind, is the all-sufficient guide in faith and practice for all Christians in all ages and in all parts of the world. It embraces all truth essential to the regeneration of sinners and to the growth of saints in that holiness without which no man shall see the Lord. With this body of truth— the Apostles' teaching—Divine revelation was perfected and consummated. Both revelation and demonstration came to an end with the Apostles; in the truth communicated by them to mankind "all things that pertain unto life and godliness" are given (2 Pet. 1:3); the final revelation made through them constitutes "the faith which was *once for all* delivered unto the saints" (Jude 3). The Apostles' teaching, therefore, the Last Will and Testament of our Lord and Savior Jesus Christ, at first communicated orally, now existing in canonized or stereotyped form, is the all-sufficient authority—the norm of religious faith and practice—for all, anywhere and in any age, who profess to be Christians. As Paul puts it: "Every scripture inspired of God is also profitable for teaching, for reproof, for correction, for instruction which is in righteousness: that the man of God may be complete, furnished completely unto every good work" (2 Tim. 3:16-17). *If the Scriptures "complete" the man of God and furnish him completely unto every good work, what more is needed?* As a matter of fact, nothing that has been written by men, either in the established creeds and "confessions" of Christendom or in ordinarily published literature, since the last of the Apostles and primitive evangelists died, has added one iota of moral and spiritual truth to the body of truth which they themselves delivered to mankind in the New Testament Scriptures.

Now, as previously stated, the Word of God is presented to us in Scripture as existent in two generic forms, namely, as *personal* (The Logos, Son of God, Jesus, Messiah), and as *impersonal* (spoken, and written or stereotyped, as in Scripture). The Scriptures make it clear, moreover, that the impersonal

Word, either spoken or written, invariably emanates from the personal Word, the Logos. He it is who has ever *edicted* or *decreed* the Thought and Will of God *outwardly*, in the form of the spoken or written Word, as communicated in turn by the Spirit "by divers portions and in divers manners" both to inanimate and animate Nature and to men, and as permanently embodied in Scripture. Furthermore, His very life—the Divine Life—energizes this impersonal Word; and His Spirit, who is the Holy Spirit, impregnates, vitalizes, this same impersonal Word. He Himself says: "The words that I have spoken unto you are spirit, and are life" (John 6:63). Again, "Heaven and earth shall pass away, but my words shall not pass away" (Matt. 24:35). Being Himself the embodiment of Divine Truth, it has ever been His work to declare that Truth, for communication in turn by the Spirit to those creatures ordained to receive it. *Ediction, decree, declaration, promulgation*—this has ever been eminently the work of the Logos, He who became flesh and dwelt among us as The Only Begotten Son of God.

Cf. John 14:6—I am the way, and *the truth*, and the life. John 8:31-32: If ye abide in my word, then are ye truly my disciples; and ye shall know the truth, and the truth shall make you free. John 18:37— To this end have I been born, and to this end am I come into the world, that I should bear witness unto the truth. Every one that is of the truth heareth my voice. John 14:23-24: If a man love me, he will keep my word: and the Father will love him, and we will come unto him, and make our abode with him. He that loveth me not keepeth not my words: and the word which ye hear is not mine, but the Father's who sent me. John 3:34—For he whom God hath sent speaketh the words of God: for he giveth not the Spirit by measure unto him. [As in the Authorized Version, the words, "unto him," must be supplied in this passage, to give it meaning, the only meaning it can have in relation to its context; it is Jesus Himself who is referred to here as possessing the Spirit without measure.]

Even in Old Testament times, from the dawn of Creation in fact, the Thought and Will of God was *edicted* or *decreed* by the Logos in the form of words or language, and then effectuated by the Spirit.

Cf. Gen. 1:1-3: In the beginning God created the heavens and the earth . . . and the Spirit of God moved upon the face of the waters. And God said, Let there be light; and there was light. [The formula, *and God said*, occurs at the beginning of each successive epoch of Creation, and, we are told, whatever God *said* or decreed, in each instance, *was so*, that is, it was done.] Psa. 33:6, 9—By the word of Jehovah were the heavens made, and all the host of them by the breath of his mouth. . . . For he spake, and it was done; He commanded, and it stood fast. Psa. 148:5-6: Let them [all created things] praise the name of Jehovah; For he commanded, and they were created. He hath also established them for ever and ever: He hath made a decree which shall not pass away. Cf. Heb. 11:3—By faith we understand

497

that the worlds have been framed by the word of God, so that what is seen hath not been made out of things which appear. Also John 1:3 again: All things were made through him; and without him was not anything made that hath been made. Col. 1:16-17—all things have been created through him, and unto him; and he is before all things, and in him all things consist. Heb. 1:2—his Son . . . through whom he made the worlds, etc. [By correlating these passages, we must conclude that, in the Creation and Preservation of the physical universe and its creatures, it was the *personal* Logos who *edicted* or *decreed*, and that the ediction took the form of the impersonal Word, that is, the Will of God as communicated in the language of men.

[See again 1 Pet. 1:10-12]: Concerning which salvation the prophets sought and searched diligently, who prophesied of the grace which should come unto you: searching what time or what manner of time the Spirit of Christ which was in them did point unto, when it testified beforehand the sufferings of Christ, and the glories that should follow them. To whom it was revealed, that not unto themselves, but unto you, did they minister these things, which now have been announced unto you through them that preached the gospel unto you by the Holy Spirit sent forth from heaven; which things angels desire to look into. [Here it is explicitly stated that the Spirit who inspired the Old Testament prophets was the Spirit of Christ; moreover, in this passage of Scripture, the Spirit of Christ is positively identified with the Holy Spirit: they are one and the same Spirit.] 2 Pet. 1:21—For no prophecy ever came by the will of man; but men spake from God, being moved by the Holy Spirit. [Does not Paul state expressly that the children of Israel, in olden times, drank of a spiritual rock that followed them: and the rock was Christ (1 Cor. 10:4)? From eternity, the Will of God has been edicted eminently by the personal Word, the Logos.]

And the New Testament Scripture, as everyone knows, is the *edicted* Last Will and Testament of our Lord and Savior Jesus Christ, communicated to mankind by the Spirit, in the form of words or human language, as revealed through the instrumentality of the inspired Apostles, prophets and evangelists of the first century.

[To the men who were to be qualified as His Apostles, Jesus, the incarnate Logos, said]: The Holy Spirit, whom the Father will send in my name, he shall teach you all things, and bring to your remembrance all that I said unto you (John 14:26). Again, the Spirit of truth, which proceedeth from the Father, he shall bear witness of me (John 15:26). Still again: When he, the Spirit of truth is come, he shall guide you into all the truth: *for he shall not speak from himself, but what things soever he shall hear, these shall he speak; and he shall declare unto you the things that are to come. He shall glorify me: for he shall take of mine, and shall declare it unto you* (John 16:13-14) [Hence says the Apostle Paul]: But we received, not the Spirit of the world, but the spirit which is from God; that we might know the things that were freely given to us of God. Which things also we speak, not in words which man's wisdom teacheth, but which the Spirit teacheth; combining spiritual things with spiritual words. . . . For who hath known the mind of the Lord, that he should instruct him? But we have the mind of Christ (2 Cor. 2:12-13, 16). [The pronoun "we" in these statements has reference, of course, to the Apostles.] Eph. 3:4-5: the mystery of Christ, which in other generations was not made known unto the sons of men, as it hath now been revealed unto his holy apostles and prophets in the Spirit, etc. 1 Thess. 4:15—For this we say unto you by the word of the Lord, etc. Acts 8:25—They therefore, when they had testified and spoken the word of the Lord, returned to Jerusalem. Col. 3:16—Let the word of Christ dwell in you richly. Rev. 3:8 [the risen Christ, through the Spirit, to the church in Philadelphia]: I know thy works . . . that thou hast a little power, and didst keep my word, and didst not deny my name. [Scriptures of like import can be cited from every book of the New Testament.]

From all these passages of Scripture it becomes evident that *ediction* has ever been eminently the work of the personal Word, the Logos; and that *communication*—that is, inspiration and revelation—has ever been eminently the work of the Spirit.

Now one of the fundamental truths impressed upon us by the Scriptures repeatedly, is that God's Spirit and His Word— both personal and impersonal, for let it not be forgotten that the former indwells, vitalizes and energizes the latter—go together, and act together, in the various Divine operations that are performed in relation to the Cosmos and its creatures. This truth is nowhere more clearly revealed than in one of the familiar passages of the Old Testament:

> And as for me, this is my covenant with them, saith Jehovah: my Spirit that is upon thee, and my words which I have put in thy mouth, shall not depart out of thy mouth, nor out of the mouth of thy seed, nor out of the mouth of thy seed's seed, saith Jehovah, from henceforth and for ever [Isa. 59:21].

In the verse immediately preceding, v. 20, it is said: "And a Redeemer will come to Zion, and unto them that turn from transgression in Jacob, saith Jehovah." Obviously this entire passage is of prophetic import: that is to say, it has reference to the gifts and blessings of the New Covenant. This New Covenant is to be marked by the giving of God's Spirit to His people, the Church; and this Spirit, it is here promised, shall not depart from them, Spiritual Israel, as long as time endures. Moreover, according to the promise here given, the Spirit is to be accompanied with "words" which will be put in His people's (the Church's) mouth; and these words are to remain unchanged, and to be passed on by faithful men from mouth to mouth, from generation to generation, until time shall be no more. What are the "words" alluded to here? Obviously all of God's communications to men—the entire impersonal Word as embodied in the Scriptures—which the Church will maintain as inspired truth through all the ages. The details of this specific promise of the New Covenant are given in the book of *Jeremiah* and agree precisely with this prophetic passage from *Isaiah*:

Behold, the days come, saith Jehovah, that I will make a new covenant with the house of Israel, and with the house of Judah: not according to the covenant that I made with their fathers in the day that I took them by the hand to bring them out of the land of Egypt; which my covenant they brake, although I was a husband unto them, saith Jehovah. But this is the covenant that I will make with the house of Israel after those days, saith Jehovah: *I will put my law in their inward parts, and in their heart will I write it;* and I will be their God, and they shall be my people. And they shall teach no more every man his neighbor, and every man his brother, saying, Know Jehovah; *for they shall all know me, from the least of them unto the greatest of them,* saith Jehovah; for I will forgive their iniquity, and their sin will I remember no more (Jer. 31:31-34).

In view of these prophetic passages from the Old Testament, we are not surprised that the Apostle Paul should designate the Church—in a metaphor of course—"the pillar and ground of the truth" (1 Tim. 3:15), that is, the support of its preservation and of its proclamation throughout the world; or that he should have exhorted his son in the Gospel, the young evangelist Timothy, in these words: "And the things which thou hast heard from me among many witnesses, the same commit thou to *faithful men,* who shall be able to teach others also" (2 Tim. 2:2). Nor are we surprised to read the anathemas which the Apostle pronounces upon any or all who would pervert the Word, the Gospel, of Christ:

But though we, or an angel from heaven, should preach unto you any gospel other than that which we preached unto you, let him be anathema. As we have said before, so say I now again, If any man preacheth unto you any gospel other than that which ye received, let him be anathema (Gal. 1:8-9).

This Gospel of Christ is the Word of Christ, the personal Logos, as revealed by the Spirit. And these and many other Scriptures teach, both explicitly and implicitly, that God's Spirit and His Word—personal and impersonal, the former in the latter, and mediating the Divine Life through it—go together and act together in all the operations of the Godhead.

Now the relation between the Spirit and the personal Logos in the latter's eternal (pre-incarnate) mode of being, is of the nature of that which is sustained among the members of the Godhead themselves, and as such remains essentially inscrutable to our human understanding. The most we can know, it seems, is that—speaking in metaphysical terms—it is a personal (*i.e.,* mental and spiritual) relationship, and one of such intimacy as completely transcends our limited human experience. We can know, too, from Divine revelation alone, that it has ever been the work *eminently* of the eternal Logos to edict or decree what the Father wills, and that of the Spirit *eminently* to communicate and to effecutate outwardly the edicts of the Divine Will as decreed by the Logos. Beyond this we cannot go. As for the relationship, however, between the Holy Spirit and the incarnate Logos, Jesus of Nazareth, the Son of the living God, the essential facts of that relationship are revealed in the Scriptures. In the first place, it is made clear that Jesus, by virtue of His human nature, possessed a human "spirit," in the sense probably of possessing *personal* human life; in some unfathomable manner He was man as well as God, the God-man; and as a man He possessed, naturally, the spirit that is in man.

Luke 2:52—And Jesus advanced in wisdom and stature, and in favor with God and men. [This passage shows that His growth was as that of a normal child.] Mark 8:12—And he sighed deeply in his spirit, etc. John 11:33—When Jesus therefore saw her weeping, and the Jews also weeping who came with her, he groaned in the spirit, and was troubled, etc. Luke 23:46—[the final Word from the Cross]: And Jesus, crying with a loud voice, said, Father, into thy hands I commend my spirit: and having said this, he gave up the ghost. 1 Cor. 15:45— The first man Adam became a living soul. The last Adam became a life-giving spirit.

In the second place, it is made equally clear in Scripture that the human spirit of Jesus was so fully possessed by the Spirit of God as to leave no ground for any distinction of being between them. We are told expressly that God gave not the Spirit *by* measure unto Him (John 3:34); that is to say, Jesus possessed the gifts and powers of the Spirit without measure or in an unlimited manner; in all that He said and did He acted under the guidance and inspiration of the Spirit of God.

Matt. 1:20—Joseph, thou son of David, fear not to take unto thee Mary thy wife: for that which is conceived in her is of the Holy Spirit. Luke 1:35—And the angel answered and said unto her [Mary], the Holy Spirit shall come upon thee, and the power of the Most High shall overshadow thee: wherefore also the holy thing which is begotten shall be called the Son of God. Matt. 1:18—Now the birth of Jesus Christ was on this wise: When his mother Mary had been betrothed to Joseph, before they came together she was found with child of the Holy Spirit. Matt. 3:16-17: And Jesus, when he was baptized, went up straightway from the water: and lo, the heavens were opened unto him, and he saw the Spirit of God descending as a dove, and coming upon him; and lo, a voice out of the heavens, saying, This is my beloved Son, in whom I am well pleased. Matt. 4:1—Then was Jesus led up of the Spirit into the wilderness to be tempted of the devil. Luke 4:1——And Jesus, full of the Holy Spirit, returned from the Jordan, and was led in the Spirit in the wilderness, etc. Luke 4:16 ff.— And he came to Nazareth . . . and he entered into the synagogue on the sabbath day, and stood up to read. And there was delivered unto him the book of the prophet Isaiah. And he opened the book, and found the place where it was written, The Spirit of the Lord is upon me, Because he anointed me to preach good tidings to the poor; He hath sent me to proclaim release to the captives, And recovering of sight to the blind, To set at liberty them that are bruised, To proclaim the acceptable year of the Lord. . . . And he began to say unto them, Today hath this scripture been fulfilled in your ears. [The quotation is from Isa. 61:1 ff.] Matt. 12:28—If I by the Spirit of God cast out demons, then is the kingdom of God come upon you. Luke 10:21—In that same hour he rejoiced in the Holy Spirit, and said, etc. Acts 10:38—Jesus of Nazareth, how God anointed him with the Holy Spirit and with power. Heb. 9:14—how much more shall the blood of Christ, who through the eternal Spirit offered himself without blemish unto God, cleanse your conscience from dead works to serve the living God? Rom. 1:3-4: Concerning his Son . . . who was declared to be the Son of God with power, according to the Spirit of holiness, by the resurrection from the dead. Acts 1:2—until the day in which he was received up, after that he had given commandment through the Holy Spirit unto the apostles whom he had chosen. [The "commandment" alluded to here was the Great Commission (Matt. 28:18-20).] John 3:34—For he whom God hath sent speaketh the words of God: for he giveth not the Spirit by measure unto him.

To sum up: Jesus was begotten by the agency of the Spirit; He was anointed with the Spirit; at all times He was led by the Spirit; He preached by inspiration of the Spirit; He performed miracles by the power of the Spirit; through the eternal Spirit He offered Himself up to God as the Lamb without blemish and without spot; by Spirit-power He was raised up from the dead; and even after His resurrection He gave the Great Commission "through the Holy Spirit unto the apostles whom he had chosen."

These numerous Scriptures clearly indicate the intimacy of the relationship that existed between the Holy Spirit and Jesus of Nazareth, the incarnate Logos. Jesus was so possessed, inspired and guided by the Holy Spirit that what He is said to have done by or in His own spirit may also rightly be said to have been done by or in the Spirit of God. Indeed the relation was so intimate that throughout the Scriptures the terms "Spirit of Jesus," "Spirit of Christ," "Spirit of God," and "Holy Spirit," are all used interchangeably.

[See again 1 Pet. 1:10-12]: Concerning which salvation the prophets sought and searched diligently, who prophesied of the grace that should come unto you: searching what time or what manner of time *the Spirit of Christ which was in them* did point unto, when it testified beforehand the sufferings of Christ, and the glories that should follow them. To whom it was revealed, that not unto themselves, but unto you, did they minister these things, which now have been announced unto you through them that preached the gospel unto you *by the Holy Spirit sent forth from* heaven. 2 Pet. 1:21—For no prophecy ever came by the will of man; but men spake from God, being moved by the Holy Spirit. [These passages clearly teach that the Spirit of Christ who inspired the Old Testament prophets is the Holy Spirit.] Acts 16:6-7: And they went through the region of Phrygia and Galatia, *having been forbidden of the Holy Spirit* to speak the word in Asia; and when they were come over against Mysia, they assayed to go into Bithynia; and *the Spirit of Jesus suffered them not.* [Here again the Holy Spirit and the Spirit of Jesus are identified as the one and the same Spirit.] Rom. 8:9—But ye are not in the flesh but in the Spirit, if so be that the Spirit of God dwelleth in you. But if any man hath not the Spirit of Christ, he is none of his. Rom. 8:2—the law of the Spirit of life in Christ Jesus made me free from the law of sin and death. Gal. 4:6—And because ye are sons, God sent forth the Spirit of his Son into our hearts, crying, Abba, Father. Cf. Rom. 5:5—the love of God hath been shed abroad in our hearts through the Holy Spirit which was given unto us. Rom. 8:14-15:For as many as are led by the Spirit of God, these are the sons of God. For ye received not the Spirit of bondage again unto fear; but ye received the spirit of adoption, whereby we cry, Abba, Father. Phil. 1:19—through your supplication and the supply of the Spirit of Jesus Christ. Eph. 4:30—And grieve not the Holy Spirit of God, in whom ye were sealed unto the day of redemption.

As for the relation between the Spirit and the impersonal Word—that is, the Word spoken or written, which is itself the teaching of the Logos as communicated by the Spirit—again the Scriptures make it clear that they *go together* in the various operations of the Godhead.

The relations existing in God between Thought-power, Will-power, Spirit-power and Word-power, are inscrutable to us, of course, and it would be useless, if not actually presumptuous, for us to speculate regarding them. Suffice it to say that the Word of God—either as Personal or as impersonal—is the revelation or expression of the Thought and Will, and therefore of the Spirit, of God; and conversely the Spirit realizes or effectuates the decrees of the Word. Now the decrees—the statutes, commandments, doctrine or teaching—of God are said in Scripture to be uttered or edicted by the personal Logos. But they are necessarily edicted in the forms of human language, the language of those human individuals through whom they are communicated to men by the inspiration of the Spirit. These decrees (laws, statutes and commandments)—this doctrine or teaching as a whole—constitute the impersonal Word, that is, the Word orally communicated or the Word as embodied in permanent (stereotyped) form in Scripture. Furthermore, the Scriptures make it clear that in practically all operations of the Deity, Spirit-power is exercised either *along with,* or, in most cases, *through the instrumentality* of, the spoken or written (impersonal) Word. I do not mean to affirm by this statement that Spirit-power is in all cases *necessarily* confined to the Word; far be it from me—a mere man—to impose limitations upon the power of the Divine Spirit or upon the extent of His operations. But the operations of the Godhead are orderly: our God is a God of order. "God is not a God of confusion, but of peace"

503

(1 Cor. 14:33). As stated heretofore, and as perfectly obvious to any intelligent being, the whole framework of the physical creation is one of order, otherwise there could never have been a human science. It is perfectly reasonable to conclude, therefore, that the operations of the Deity, both in the kingdom of Nature, and in the Kingdoms of Grace and of Glory, are according to definite arrangement or *ordering* among the three Persons; that is to say, orderly. This conclusion, moreover, is fully corroborated by the Scriptures. Hence, this is not a question of what the Spirit *can do*, in relation to the Word, but of what He actually *does, how* He operates in *fact*. Order is the effect of intelligence and purposiveness. It must be characteristic, therefore, of the operations of the Spirit, because He operates toward specific ends and He adapts means to ends perfectly. Now in the very nature of the case, persons communicate with one another through the media of words or language; hence it is perfectly reasonable to conclude, just as the Scriptures teach, that the Holy Spirit, a Divine Person, communicates with human persons through the same media. As a matter of fact, according to the Scripture, in all operations of the Godhead, God's Spirit and His Word go together in effectuating and realizing the Divine purposes *within* and *for* the whole of the Creation. This is equally true of the impersonal Word as of the personal Word or Logos. This does not mean that the Spirit *is* the spoken or written Word: indeed the Spirit is, as we have seen, a Person. This means simply that the Spirit operates *together with*, or in most cases *through the instrumentality of*, the spoken or written Word.

1. *God's Spirit and His Word acted together in the Creation of the physical universe and its living creatures.* Hence we find that *God said* (ordered, decreed) something, at the beginning of each epoch of the Creation, and that whatever God said, *was done* (Gen. 1:2, 3, 6, 9, 11, 14, 20, 24, 26, 29; Cf. Psa. 33:6, 9; Heb. 11:3, etc.). In the first chapter of the *book* of *Genesis*, of course, we have the Word in its indited or stereotyped form; in the actual Creation, however, the Word was personal, the Logos Himself, and the Spirit operated to effectuate His decrees (Cf. again John 1:1-3, Col. 1:16-17, 1 Cor. 8:6, Heb. 1:1-3, etc.). In Creation, the Spirit and the Word acted together, the Logos as the Executor of the Father's Will and Purpose, and the Spirit as the Realizer or Effectuator of the Word's decrees.

2. *God's Spirit and God's Word act together in sustaining the physical Creation and all commonly designated "natural"*

*processes.* The ultimate Source of every form of life in the universe is the Divine Spirit: He is the Spirit of Life—natural or physical, spiritual, and eternal (Gen. 2:7; Job 27:3, 32:8, 34:14-15; Psa. 104:27-30; John 6:63, 3:3-6; Acts 17:24-25; Rom. 8:2, 8:11, etc.). But again, in general Providence as in Creation, the Spirit effectuates or realizes the decrees of the Word.

> Psa. 33:9—For he spake, and it was done; *He commanded, and it stood fast.* Psa. 148:6-7: He hath also established them [all created things] for ever and ever [*i.e.*, as long as Time lasts]; *He hath made a decree which shall not pass away,* [that is, until He shall rescind it.] Job 38:33—Knowest thou the ordinances of the heavens? Jer. 31:35-36: Thus sayeth Jehovah, who giveth the sun for a light by day, and the ordinances of the moon and of the stars for a light by night, who stirreth up the sea, so that the waves thereof roar; Jehovah of hosts is his name: If these ordinances depart from before me, saith Jehovah, then the seed of Israel also shall cease from being a nation before me for ever. 2 Pet. 3:5-7: there were heavens from of old, and an earth compacted out of water and amidst water, by the word of God; by which means the world that then was, being overflowed with water, perished: but the heavens that now are, and the earth, by the same word have been stored up for fire, being reserved against the day of judgment and destruction of ungodly men.

The Will of God as expressed by the Word is the constitution (that which constitutes) both of the physical and of the moral universe, the authority and power back of all laws of nature and all moral law as well. "He [the Logos] is before all things, and *in him all things consist,*" literally, "hold together" (Col. 1:17). The Son, we are told, is the effulgence of the Father's glory and the very image of His substance, and it is He who *"upholds all things by the word of his power"* (Heb. 1:3). So-called "natural law" is the Word decreed, that is, spoken for all time—the Word as the source of all *secondary causation* in Nature. When the Word acts or is spoken, however, for a special purpose of God, for the working of a unique event in space and time, an event not to be repeated in all its attendant circumstances,—then a miracle or "mighty work" (Acts 2:22) is performed. Natural events (secondary causes) are regular and recurring; miracles (primary causes) are particular events for particular Divine purposes; but all have their constitution in the Will and Word of God. Hence, when in the finality of temporal events, the Word shall be spoken (1 Cor. 15:52—"the trumpet shall sound"), then the earth and the heavens— the whole Cosmos—shall be rolled up as a vesture and "shall be changed" (Psa. 102:25-27, Heb. 1:10-12), and Time shall be no more.

   3. *Both inspiration and revelation, though eminently works*

*of the Spirit of God, are effectuated, nevertheless, through the instrumentality of the Word.*

Both inspiration and revelation are in a special sense works of the Spirit of God; that is, though concurred in by both the Father and the Son, and sometimes ascribed to the Father and sometimes to the Son, they are ascribed eminently to the Holy Spirit. This is, of course, according to the nature of things. For, as Paul puts it, "who among men knoweth the things of a man save the spirit of the man, which is in him? even so the things of God none knoweth, save the Spirit of God." To which he adds, speaking with respect to the *inspiration* of the Apostles:

> But we received, not the spirit of the world, but the spirit which is from God; that we might know the things that were freely given to us of God. Which things also we speak, not in words which man's wisdom teacheth, but which the Spirit teacheth; combining spiritual things with spiritual words (1 Cor. 2:11-13).

What the Apostle has to say here with respect to his own inspiration and that of the Apostles in general, is equally true with respect to the inspiration of the Prophets, holy men of old, from Enoch, "the seventh from Adam" (Jude 14), down to John the Baptizer, the last of that illustrious line. "For no prophecy ever came by the will of man; but men spake from God, being moved by the Holy Spirit" (2 Pet. 1:21). For the purely "natural" man—that is, "natural" in the sense of being uninspired—"receiveth not the things of the Spirit of God: for they are foolishness unto him; and he cannot know them, because they are spiritually examined" (1 Cor. 2:14). Divine Truth is, and in the nature of the case has to be, communicated to man by the Spirit Himself. To the Spirit of God we are indebted for all that is known or knowable of God and of His Plan for the human race. Furthermore, to the Spirit of God we are indebted also for whatever individual capacity we may have for understanding the Truth of God and thus knowing God. For even reason itself was implanted in man at his creation by the Breath of God, that is, by the procession of the Spirit from the Being of God.

Now *revelation* is twofold, as to mode; that is, it is of two kinds. Primarily, revelation is *historical;* that is, it has taken the form of those successive historical events which occurred in the execution of the Plan of Redemption.

[Among those events were the following: (1) the universal application of the penalty of sin, following man's first disobedience (Gen.

3:14-19); (2) the institution of sacrifice, to point forward to the Atonement made once for all "at the end of the ages" (Heb. 9:26); (3) the moral purification of the world by the Deluge, and the preservation of the race through Noah and his sons; (4) the Call of Abraham, the Abrahamic Promise, and the inauguration of the Old Covenant; (5) the formation of the Hebrew Theocracy under Moses at Sinai, with its ordinances, institutions, and rites, all of which were designed to be typical of Christ and the Christian System; (6) the ministry of the Hebrew Prophets, accounting the details of the life and work of the Messiah to come; (7) the special ministry of John the Baptizer to the Jewish nation, heralding the immediate advent of the Messiah; (8) the incarnation, ministry, death, resurrection, and exaltation to universal sovereignty, of the Messiah Himself, the Son of God; (9) the advent of the Holy Spirit on the Day of Pentecost, the incorporation of the Church of Christ, and the institution of the New Covenant; (10) the special ministry of the Apostles as witnesses and ambassadors of Christ; and (11) the subsequent preaching of the Gospel for a testimony unto all the nations.]

All these were historical events; that is, events occurring in time and space. They are presented to us in Scripture as a chain of historical events, all linked together in the Divine Purpose, and all leading eventually to one final and supreme end, namely, the Second Coming of Christ and the Day of the Consummation of all things (Acts 3:20-21).

Revelation is, in the second place, *documentary*. The events came first, after thom, the recording and the interpretation. This was wrought by the agency of the Spirit (1) in the medium of words or language, (2) through the instrumentality of inspired—God-breathed—men. That is, the Spirit moved, impelled, and inspired certain men to set down in permanent form the account of these successive historical events by which the Divine Plan was progressively effectuated on earth, and to record also the correct interpretation of the significance of those events for man. Thus Moses is said to have written a book, at Jehovah's command, containing the account of "the journeys of the children of Israel, when they went forth out of the land of Egypt" (Exo. 17:14, 24:4; Num. 33:1-2, etc.). Sometimes these revelations of Divine Truth were first communicated to the people orally, and were put in written form afterward. This was especially true of the Apostles' teaching. Throughout the first century, the local congregations of Christians were under the personal supervision of the Apostles, and the Spirit's revelation, with accompanying instruction, was communicated to them orally by the Apostles and by the early evangelists who were personally taught by the Apostles themselves. Thus the church in Jerusalem is said to have "continued stedfastly in *the apostles' teaching* and fellowship, in the breaking of bread and

507

the prayers" (Acts 2:42). It is evident that the Apostles' teaching was at that time communicated vocally to the saints. Little by little, however, this teaching was reduced to permanent form in the Gospels, histories, epistles, and prophetic books of the New Testament canon, as indited by inspired or Spirit-taught men. The fact to be remembered is that, whether oral or written, it was the Apostles' teaching, and, because the Apostles were guided into all the truth by the Holy Spirit, the Vicegerent of Christ on earth throughout the Gospel Dispensation, it was, and is, the teaching or Word of Christ. We today have the Apostles' teaching in permanent form in the New Testament Scriptures.

In a word, *revelation* is the term which has reference to the *disclosure* of God's Plan of Redemption for man, both as a historical development, and as the documentary record of that development. *Inspiration*, on the other hand, is the term which has reference to the actual communication, or to be more precise, to the *mode of communication* of this Divine revelation. Inspiration, in Scripture, is invariably connected with the realization of the Divine Plan in the world, or with the communication of Divine Truth respecting that Plan, its origin, execution and ends. For this reason, purely human psychical "inspiration," which may account for the great productions of human genius, is, nevertheless, of an order inferior to Divine inspiration, which invariably has for its end Divine revelation in one or both of its forms, *i.e.*, either as historical or as documentry.

Now both inspiration and revelation (oral or written), though eminently works of the Spirit of God, are wrought, nevertheless, through the instrumentality of words. To *inspire* is, literally, to *breathe into;* and in this connection, it means, literally, to *breathe words into.* Saul the persecutor, we are told, "yet breathing threatening and slaughter against the disciples of the Lord," sought authority from the Jewish high priest at Jerusalem to journey to Damascus and to destroy the church at that place (Acts 9:1). How did Saul "breathe" threatening and slaughter against the Christians? Obviously, *in words.* When a man enounces words, he literally *breathes them out* of his mouth. So when the Holy Spirit enounces Divine Truth, He too, just as literally, breathes that Truth into the mind of the recipient in the form of words. "Man shall not live by bread alone, but *by every word that proceedeth out of the mouth of God*" (Matt. 4:4). The Breath of God is, as we have already learned, a metaphor of the Spirit, particularly of the procession

508

of the Spirit from the Being of God. When God breathes—that is, acts through His Spirit-power—He may move to extraordinary deeds, or He may communicate Truth to them, in which case He does so *in words*. It is well and good to contend, as some churchmen do, that only the Thought of God is communicated by inspiration. But I should like to ask, How can that thought be made intelligible to men, or by them in turn to other men, if it is not communicated in words—that is to say, in language—which they can understand; and which in fact, by translation, can be made intelligible to all men? The fact remains, therefore, that inspiration, especially inspiration which has revelation for its end, the communication of Divine Truth, is effectuated by means of *words*. Moreover, the words so communicated constitute what we mean here by the impersonal Word. As Jesus Himself says: "The words that I have spoken unto are spirit, and are life" (John 6:63). And as Simon Peter said to Jesus: "Lord, to whom shall we go? thou hast the words of eternal life" (John 6:68). Paul gives us "the conclusion of the whole matter" as follows: "But we received, not the spirit of the world, but the spirit which is from God; that we might know the things that were freely given to us of God. Which things also we speak, *not in words which man's wisdom teacheth, but which the Spirit teacheth; combining spiritual things with spiritual words*" (1 Cor. 2:12-13). Thus it will be seen that all of God's revelations by His Spirit have been preserved for us *in words*, in the indited or stereotyped Word, the Scriptures.

4. *God's Spirit and His Word act together in the work of demonstration or miracles.* Inspiration and revelation have ever been attested, in the economy of God, by miracles; moreover, when inspiration and revelation came to an end with the Apostles, demonstration or miracles ceased also.

The Will of God, as expressed by the Word and realized by the Spirit, being the constitution of the physical universe, it follows that the Will of God, again as expressed by the Word and realized by the Spirit, or as effectuated by the Spirit through the instrumentality of the Word, is the Divine factor that must enter into the working of what is known in Scripture as a miracle. Hence we find that in the performing of miracles, as described in the Scriptures, the usual procedure was that *the Word was spoken* (either vocally, or subvocally, *i.e.*, by suggestion) *and the miracle was wrought immediately*. Sometimes, of course, an emblem of the Word, instead of the spoken Word itself, was employed to work miracles; a symbol such as,

509

for example, the rod of Moses or that of Aaron, by the use of which wonders and signs were wrought by these great men of God, in Egypt, at the Red Sea, and in the Wilderness (Exo. 4:1-5, 7:8-13, 14:16; Acts 7:36). However, as the subject of Miracles is to be fully elaborated in a complementary work, I shall not attempt to discuss it here.

5. *God's Spirit and His Word go together in the work of regeneration or recreation.*

Regeneration is ascribed, in Scripture, to God the Father as the *source,* to the Spirit of God as the *agent,* to the Word (spoken or written) as the *means,* and to the preacher as the *instrument.*

1 Pet. 1:3—Blessed be the God and Father of our Lord Jesus Christ, who according to his great mercy begat us again unto a living hope by the resurrection of Jesus Christ from the dead. Jas. 1:17-18· the Father of lights . of his own will he brought us forth by the word of truth, that we should be a kind of firstfruits of his creatures.
John 3:5-7: Jesus answered, Verily, verily, I say unto thee, Except one be born of water and the Spirit, he cannot enter into the kingdom of God. That which is born of the flesh is flesh; that which is born of the Spirit is spirit. Marvel not that I said unto thee, Ye must be born anew. Tit. 3:5—according to his mercy he saved us, through the washing of regeneration and renewing of the Holy Spirit.
Heb. 8:10—For this is the covenant that I will make with the house of Israel, After those days, saith the Lord: I will put my laws into their mind, And on their heart also I will write them: And I will be to them a God, And they shall be to me a people [cf. Jer. 31:31-34]. 2 Cor. 3:2-3: Ye are our epistle . . . known and read of all men; being made manifest that ye are an epistle of Christ, ministered by us, written not with ink, but with the Spirit of the living God; not in tables of stone, but in tables that are hearts of flesh. Rom. 1:16— For I am not ashamed of the gospel of Christ; for it is the power of God unto salvation to every one that believeth: to the Jew first, and also to the Greek. Rom. 10:14-17: How then shall they call on him in whom they have not believed- and how shall they believe in him whom they have not heard? and how shall they hear without a preacher? . . . So belief cometh of hearing, and hearing by the word of Christ. 1 Cor. 1:21—it was God's good pleasure through the foolishness of the preaching to save them that believe. John 1:12-13: But as many as received him, to them gave he the right to become children of God, even to them that believe on his name; who were born, not of blood, nor of the will of the flesh, nor of the will of man, but of God. Luke 8:11—[from the Parable of the Sower]: The [spiritual] seed is the word of God. 1 Pet. 1:23—having been begotten again, not of corruptible seed, but of incorruptible, through the word of God, which liveth and abideth. V. 25, following: And this is the word of good tidings which was preached unto you. 1 Cor. 15:1-4: Now I make known unto you, brethren, *the gospel which I preached unto you,* which also ye received, wherein also ye stand, *by which also ye are saved,* if ye hold fast the word which I preached unto you, except ye believed in vain. For I delivered unto you first of all that which also I received: that Christ died for our sins according to the scriptures; and that he was buried; and that he hath been raised on the third day according to the scriptures, etc. [The whole Christian missionary enterprise is

510

predicated on the fact that where there is no promulgation of the Gospel, there is no operation of the Spirit, no conversion to Christ. The matter is hardly debatable that the Spirit operates through the Word, spoken or written, in the conversion and regeneration of sinners.] [1 Cor. 4:15, here Paul says]: In Christ Jesus I begat you through the gospel. Philemon 10 [Paul to Philemon]: I beseech thee for my child, whom I have begotten in my bonds, Onesimus. 1 Tim. 1:2— Timothy, my true child in faith. Tit. 1:4—to Titus, my true child after a common faith. [In the sense that a man is begotten spiritually by means of the Word as proclaimed by a given evangelist, he is said in Scripture to have been "begotten" by that evangelist.]

**6. God's Spirit and His Word act together in the work of sanctification of the saints.**

1 Cor. 6:11—but ye were washed, but ye were sanctified, but ye were justified in the name of the Lord Jesus Christ, and in the Spirit of our God. Rom. 15:16—that the offering up of the Gentiles might be made acceptable, being sanctified by the Holy Spirit. 2 Thess. 2:13— that God chose you from the beginning unto salvation in sanctification of the Spirit and belief of the truth. 1 Pet. 1:2—according to the foreknowledge of God the Father, in sanctification of the Spirit, unto obedience and sprinkling of the blood of Jesus Christ. Gal. 5:16— Walk by the Spirit, and ye shall not fulfil the lust of the flesh. Gal. 5:25—If we live by the Spirit, by the Spirit let us also walk. Rom. 14:17—for the kingdom of God is not eating and drinking, but righteousness and peace and joy in the Holy Spirit.

Sanctification is not a work wrought instantaneously by the Spirit of God in the human heart. It is, rather, the result of continuous activity of the Spirit, through the instrumentality of the Divine Word and its ordinances; and is equivalent, on the human side, to Christian growth or growth in holiness. All life is growth; the essential property of life is growth; and the new spiritual life begotten in the human heart in regeneration is no exception to this rule; that life indeed is a continuous growth in "the grace and knowledge of our Lord and Savior Jesus Christ" (2 Pet. 3:18). Sanctification, therefore, though wrought by the agency of the Spirit, is effectuated through the instrumentality of the Word. It is only by receiving the Word into their hearts, by feeding upon it as spiritual food, by digesting it, by assimilating it, by turning it, so to speak, into their own spiritual blood, that regenerated persons can live the life of the Spirit, and thus become in fact partakers of the Divine Nature themselves (2 Pet. 1:4), and grow in that holiness "without which no man shall see the Lord" (Heb. 12:14). In sanctification, as in regeneration, the Spirit is the *agent*, and the Word the *means*.

1 Thess. 2:13—And for this cause we also thank God without ceasing, that, when ye received from us the word of the message, even the word of God, ye accepted it not as the word of men, but, as it is in truth, the word of God, *which also worketh in you that believe.*

511

John 8:31—If ye abide in my word, then are ye truly my disciples. John 15:10—If ye keep my commandments, ye shall abide in my love. John 17:17—*Sanctify them in the truth: thy word is truth.* 1 John 3:24—And he that keepeth his commandments abideth in him, and he in him. Matt. 7:24-27: Every one therefore that heareth these words of mine, and doeth them, shall be likened unto a wise man, who built his house upon the rock; and the rain descended, and the floods came, and the winds blew, and beat upon that house; and it fell not: for it was founded upon the rock. And every one that heareth these words of mine, and doeth them not, shall be likened unto a foolish man, who built his house upon the sand: and the rain descended, and the floods came, and the winds blew, and smote upon that house; an it fell; and great was the fall thereof. Col. 3:16—*Let the word of Christ dwell in you richly.* 2 Tim. 2:16-17: Every scripture inspired of God is also profitable for teaching, for reproof, for correction, for instruction which is in righteousness: that the man of God may be complete, furnished completely unto every good work. 1 Pet. 2:2—as newborn babes, long for the spiritual milk which is without guile, that ye may grow thereby unto salvation. Heb. 5:12-14: For when by reason of the time ye ought to be teachers, ye have need again that some one teach you the rudiments of the first principles of the oracles of God; and are become such as have need of milk, and not of solid food. For every one that partaketh of milk is without experience of *the word of righteousness;* for he is a babe. But solid food is for fullgrown men, even those who by reason of use have their senses exercised to discern good and evil. Matt. 28:20—teaching them to observe all things whatsoever I commanded you. Tit. 2:2—Speak thou the things which befit the sound doctrine. 2 Tim. 1:13—Hold the pattern of sound words which thou hast heard from me, in faith and love which is in Christ Jesus.

The life of sanctification is the expanding and deepening life that is lived personally with the Holy Spirit, as mediated by the Word and its appointments; the life which becomes, little by little, as the saint becomes transformed into the image of Christ "from glory to glory" (2 Cor. 3:18), the life of the Spirit Himself within him. The Holy Spirit, through the Word of Truth, instructs, guides, and leads the Christian; and the latter, "hungering and thirsting after righteousness" (Matt. 5:6), responds to this Divine instruction, guidance and leadership, by feeding upon, digesting, and assimilating the Word, by keeping the Divine appointments that are authorized by the Word, and by conforming his life to the standard of righteousness that is ordained by the impersonal Word and that was exemplified in the incarnate life of the personal Word. (Rather than praying to possess the Holy Spirit, should we not ask help to "open our hearts" so that He may possess us?) In this manner are God's children from day to day "strengthened with power through his Spirit in the inward man" (Eph. 3:16); in this manner do they add to their faith, virtue; and to virtue, knowledge; and to knowledge, self-control; and to self-control, patience; and to patience, godliness; and to godliness, brotherly kindness; and to brotherly kindness, love (2 Pet. 1:5-7). And in the end there shall be richly supplied unto them "the entrance into the eternal kingdom of our Lord and Savior Jesus Christ" (2 Pet. 1:11), where they shall be clothed in glory and honor and incorruption, and where they shall see God "face to face." Therefore, my fellow Christians, "be ye stedfast, unmovable, always abounding in the work of the Lord, forasmuch as ye know that your labor is not in vain in the Lord (1 Cor. 15:58).

The late Z. T. Sweeney, in his excellent little treatise entitled *The Spirit and the Word*, points out sixteen different effects which the Holy Spirit might—and indeed does—work by indwelling the saint of God, and shows that the same effects are said in Scripture to be accomplished by the Word, as follows:

[1. *The Spirit might give us faith.* But the Word is said to give faith.] Rom. 10:17—So belief cometh of hearing, and hearing by the word of Christ. Rom. 10:8—The word is nigh thee, in thy mouth, and in thy heart: that is, the word of faith, which we preach. Acts 15:7—Brethren, ye know that a good while ago God made choice among you, that by my mouth the Gentiles should hear the word of the gospel, and believe.

[2. *The Spirit might enable us to enjoy a new birth.* But He does this also through the Word.] 1 Pet. 1:23—having been begotten again, not of corruptible seed, but of incorruptible, through the word of God, which liveth and abideth.

[3. *The Spirit might give us light.* But He does this likewise through the Word.] Psa. 119:130—The opening of thy words giveth light. Psa. 119:105—Thy word is a lamp unto my feet, And light unto my path. Prov. 6:23—For the commandment is a lamp; and the law is light. 2 Cor. 4:4—in whom the god of this world hath blinded the minds of the unbelieving, that the light of the gospel of the glory of Christ, who is the image of God, should not dawn upon them.

[4. *The Spirit might give us wisdom.* But He does it through the Word.] Psa. 19:7—The testimony of Jehovah is sure, making wise the simple. 1 Cor. 1:24—Christ the power of God, and the wisdom of God. 2 Tim. 3:14-15: But abide thou in the things which thou hast learned and hast been assured of, knowing of whom thou hast learned them; and that from a babe thou hast known the sacred writings which are able to make thee wise unto salvation through faith which is in Christ Jesus.

[5. *The Spirit might convert us.* He does it, however, by means of the Word.] Psa. 19:7—The law of Jehovah is perfect, converting the soul. [The Revised Version gives it: *restoring the soul*, which is equivalent of course.] Acts 28:27—For this people's heart is waxed gross, And their ears are dull of hearing, And their eyes they have closed; Lest haply they should perceive with their eyes, And hear with their ears, And understand with their heart, *And should turn again*, And I should heal them [cf. Isa. 6:9-10, Matt. 13:14-15].

[6. *The Spirit might open our eyes.* But this He does also through the Word.] Psa. 19:8—The precepts of Jehovah are right, rejoicing the heart; The commandment of Jehovah is pure, enlightening the eyes. Acts 26:17-18: Delivering thee from the people, and from the Gentiles, unto whom I send thee, *to open their eyes*, that they may turn from

513

darknes to light and from the power of Satan unto God. [Paul opened the eyes of the Gentiles, of course, by preaching the Gospel to them.]

[7. *The Spirit might give us understanding.* But He does it through the Word.] Psa. 119:104—Through thy precepts I get understanding. Acts 28:27 again: lest haply they should perceive with their eyes, and hear with their ears, and understand with their heart, etc.

[8. *The Spirit might quicken us.* But again He does it through the Word.] Psa. 119:50—For thy word hath quickened me. Psa. 119:93 —I will never forget thy precepts; For with them thou hast quickened me. John 6:63—the words that I have spoken unto you are spirit, and are life. Matt. 4:4—Man shall not live by bread alone, but by every word that proceedeth out of the mouth of God (cf. Deut. 8:3).

[9. *The Spirit might save us.* But He does it through the instrumentality of the Word.] Jas. 1:21—receive with meekness the implanted word, which is able to save your souls. Eph. 1:13—in whom ye also, having heard the word of truth, the gospel of your salvation. Rom. 1:16—For I am not ashamed of the gospel of Christ: for it is the power of God unto salvation to every one that believeth.

[10. *The Spirit might sanctify us.* But this He is said to do through the Word.] John 17:17—Sanctify them in the truth: thy word is truth. 2 Thess. 2:13—for that God chose you from the beginning unto salvation in sanctification of the Spirit and belief of the truth.

[11. *The Spirit might purify us.* This He does also through the Word.] 1 Pet. 1:22—Seeing ye have purified your souls in your obedience to the truth unto unfeigned love of the brethren, love one another from the heart fervently.

[12. *The Spirit might cleanse us.* But He does it through the Word.] John 15:3—Already ye are clean because of the word which I have spoken unto you. Acts 15:9—and he made no distinction between us and them, cleansing their hearts by faith.

[13. *The Spirit might make us free from sin.* This freedom, however, is mediated through the Word of Truth.] John 8:31-32: If ye abide in my word, then are ye truly my disciples; and ye shall know the truth, and the truth shall make you free. Rom. 6:17-18: But thanks be to God, that, whereas ye were servants of sin, ye became obedient from the heart to that form of teaching whereunto ye were delivered; and being made free from sin, ye became servants of righteousness.

[14. *The Spirit might impart a divine nature to us.* But He does it through the Word.] 2 Pet. 1:4—whereby he hath granted unto us his precious and exceeding great promises; that through these ye may become partakers of the divine nature, having escaped from the corruption that is in the world by lust.

[15. *The Spirit might fit us for glory and immortality.* But He does it through the Word.] Acts 20:32—And now I commend you to God, and to the word of his grace, which is able to build you up, and to give you the inheritance among all them that are sanctified. Acts 26:18 —that they may receive remission of sins and an inheritance among them that are sanctified by faith in me.

[16. *The Spirit might strengthen us.* But this, too, He does through the Word.] Psa. 119:28—Strengthen thou me according unto thy word.

We have enumerated here about all the conceivable things that the Holy Spirit could do for a Christian by dwelling in him. These works, moreover, undoubtedly the Spirit does effect in the saint, acting in His capacity as the Agent of the Godhead. But the numerous Scriptures quoted above make it evident that the Spirit effects these works of conversion, regeneration, and sanctification, through the instrumentality of the Word spoken or indited. God's Spirit and His Word act together in the New or Spiritual Creation just as in the Old Physical or Natural Creation.

7. *Finally, the Scriptures clearly intimate that God's Spirit and His Word will act together in the immortalization of the saints.*

The same Spirit who seals us, who indwells us, who is in us as the earnest of our inheritance, who transforms us from glory unto glory, who intercedes for us with groanings which cannot be uttered, will never leave us—provided, of course, that we do not quench the Spirit—until He shall have raised our bodies from the dead and transformed them into spiritual bodies, like unto the glorified body of our Redeemer: that is, "conformed" them unto the image of God's Son, in *body* as well as in spirit (Rom. 8:29). This work of the Spirit is known in Scripture as *glorification;* glorification—to speak more precisely —is the final phase of the entire process of immortalization. As we read in Rom. 8:30, those whom God foreordained to be conformed ultimately to the image of His Son (*i.e.,* in His Eternal Purpose), "them he also called; and whom he called, them he also justified; and whom he justified, them he also *glorified*" (all this in His Eternal Purpose, of course). Now this Eternal Purpose will be fully realized when the saints are raised from the dead and clothed in glory and honor and incorruption (Rom. 2:7). This final work of immortalization, furthermore, we are told in Scripture, will be effectuated by the agency of the Spirit of God. "But if the Spirit of him that raised up Jesus from the dead dwelleth in you, he that raised up Christ Jesus from the dead *shall give life also to your mortal bodies through his Spirit that dwelleth in you*" (Rom. 8:11). As the Jewish Dispensation came to an end with the Ascension of the Son of God, so the present or Gospel Dispensation will terminate with the Ascension of the Spirit and the Bride of Christ, the Church.

But again we have clear intimations in Scripture that the Spirit—even in the quickening and immortalization of the bodies of the saints—will act only in conformity to the edictions or decrees of the Word. (In this last operation, the redemption of the body, even mortality itself shall be swallowed up of life, Rom. 8:23, 2 Cor. 5:4.)

1 Thess. 4:15-17: For this we say unto you by the word of the Lord, that we that are alive, that are left unto the coming of the Lord,

515

shall in no wise precede them that are fallen asleep. For the Lord himself shall descend from heaven, with a shout, with the voice of the archangel and with the trump of God: and the dead in Christ shall rise first; then we that are alive, that are left, shall together with them be caught up in the clouds, to meet the Lord in the air: and so shall we ever be with the Lord. 1 Cor. 15:51-54: Behold, I tell you a mystery: We shall not all sleep, but we shall all be changed, in a moment, in the twinkling of an eye, at the last trump; for the trumpet shall sound, and the dead shall be raised incorruptible, and we shall be changed. For this corruptible must put on incorruption, and this mortal must put on immortality. But when this corruptible shall have put on incorruption, and this mortal shall have put on immortality, then shall come to pass the saying that is written, Death is swallowed up in victory.

In these passages such expressions as "the Lord shall descend from heaven with a shout," "the voice of the archangel," "the trump of God," "at the last trump," "the trumpet shall sound," etc., are metaphorical: they teach us simply that the decree of the Logos shall issue forth, that the Word of God will be edicted by the Messiah, the reigning King and Judge, that the time of "the restoration of all things whereof God spake by the mouth of his holy prophets that were from of old" (Acts 3:21) is at hand. He—The Messiah—will speak the Word, proclaiming that the temporal process is at an end, and, by the power of the Spirit, *it will be done,* just as it was done in the physical Creation at the beginning. The Word of God will be spoken and the miracle will be wrought: "in a moment, in the twinkling of an eye," death will be swallowed up in victory. "O death, where is thy victory? O death, where is thy sting?" (1 Cor. 15:55). What profound meditation this teaching should engender in the minds and hearts of all the saints! God's Spirit and His Word will act together—and the Consummation of the Eternal Purpose of God will take place!

God's Spirit and God's Word go together, act together, and together effectuate the Divine purposes in the world of things and in the world of men. This we have seen to be true in the Divine works of Creation, Conservation, Inspiration, Revelation, and Demonstration. It is likewise true in the Divine works of Regeneration, Sanctification, and Immortalization.

Man walks by the Spirit to the extent that he walks in the light provided by the Word spoken or indited; he lives by the Spirit to the extent that he lives by the Word, the oracles of God. Indeed no man can even confess that Jesus is Lord, but in the Holy Spirit (1 Cor. 12:3); that is, by having been convinced by the testimony recorded in Scripture, the Word as revealed by the Spirit, that Jesus is in truth the Christ, the Son of the living God.

[The summarization of the design of the Fourth Gospel applies equally to the entire Bible, and to the New Testament in particular]: Many other signs therefore did Jesus in the presence of the disciples, which are not written in this book: but these are written, that ye may believe that Jesus is the Christ, the Son of God; and that believing ye may have life in his name (John 20:30-31). [Finally, in the Last Judgment, all men will be judged individually according to their fidelity to the light provided by the Word under which they shall have lived]: And books were opened; and another book was opened, which is the book of life: and the dead were judged out of the things which were written in the books, according to their works (Rev. 20:12). [As Jesus himself says]: For whosoever shall be ashamed of me and of my words in this adulterous and sinful generation, the Son of man also shall be ashamed of him, when he cometh in the glory of his Father with the holy angels (Mark 8:38). For the word of God is living, and active, and sharper than any two-edged sword, and piercing even to the dividing of soul and spirit, of both joints and marrow, and quick to discern the thoughts and intents of the heart (Heb. 4:12). [Paul summarizes the whole matter as follows]: For as many as have sinned without the law shall also perish without the law: and as many as have sinned under the law shall be judged by the law. . . . (For when Gentiles that have not the law do by nature the things of the law, these, not having the law, are the law unto themselves: in that they show the work of the law written in their hearts, their conscience bearing witness therewith, and their thoughts one with another accusing or else excusing them); in the day when God shall judge the secrets of men, according to my gospel, by Jesus Christ (Rom. 2:12-16).

In view of all these truths, we must admit that no man is led by the Spirit to reject or to neglect the teaching of the Word. And it becomes equally clear that no man who disregards or disobeys the teaching of the Word can truthfully claim to be led by the Spirit. No man was ever led by the Spirit to act contrary to the Word. God's Spirit and His Word go together, act together, and together effectuate the Divine purposes in every realm of the Totality of Being.

## 3. Operations of the Godhead in General

In the nomenclature of the Spirit, Divine operations are ascribed sometimes to God absolutely, and sometimes to each Person of the Godhead distinctly.

All Divine operations, whether in the Kingdom of Nature or in the Kingdom of Grace, are usually ascribed to God absolutely. As John Owen has written:

All divine operations, whether in nature or in grace, are usually ascribed to God absolutely; because the several persons are undivided

517

in their operations; acting by the same will, the same wisdom, the same power. Each person therefore is the author of every work of God, because each person is God; and the divine nature is the same undivided principle of all divine operations.[1]

However, even though the Divine Persons are one in essence, yet in their manner of subsistence they are Three, and among the Three there is distinction, relation, and order. Hence, in Scripture, every Divine work is assigned *distinctly* to each Person, but at the same time *eminently* to one.

[The work of Creation, for example, is distinctly ascribed to the Father, and again to the Son, and still again to the Holy Spirit.] Acts 4:24—And they . . . lifted up their voice to God with one accord, and said, O Lord, thou that didst make the heaven and the earth and the sea, and all that in them is, etc. Acts 17:24-25: The God that made the world and all things therein, he . . . giveth to all life, and breath, and all things. Heb. 12:9—the Father of spirits. John 1:1-3, 14—In the beginning was the Word, and the Word was with God, and the Word was God. The same was in the beginning with God. All things were made through him; and without him was not anything made that hath been made. . . . And the Word became flesh, and dwelt among us, etc. Col. 1:13, 16—the Son of his love . . . in him were all things created, etc. Psa. 104:30—Thou sendest forth thy Spirit, they are created. Job 33:4—The Spirit of God hath made me, And the breath of the Almighty giveth me life.

[However, the work of Creation is ascribed by way of eminence to the Father; and absolutely to God, who is Father, Son, and Holy Spirit.] Acts 14:15—that ye should turn from these vain things unto a living God, who made the heaven and the earth and the sea, and all that in them is. Acts 17:24—The God that made the world and all things therein, etc. Gen. 1:1-3: In the beginning God created the heavens and the earth. And the earth was waste and void; and darkness was upon the face of the deep; and the Spirit of God was brooding upon the face of the waters. And God said, Let there be light; and there was light. Psa. 33:6, 9—By the word of Jehovah were the heavens made, And all the host of them by the breath of his mouth. . . . For he spake, and it was done; He commanded, and it stood fast.

Again, Divine works are ascribed eminently to one of the three Persons in particular, when the distinguishing attribute of that Person is especially impressed upon the work itself. For example, Creation is ascribed eminently to the Father, because His authority and power especially are impressed upon the old or physical Creation.

Psa. 19:1-2: The heavens declare the glory of God; And the firmament showeth his handiwork. Day unto day uttereth speech, And night unto night showeth knowledge. Psa. 89:5—And the heavens shall praise thy wonders, O Jehovah. Psa. 8:3-4: When I consider thy heavens, the work of thy fingers, The moon and the stars, which thou hast ordained; What is man, that thou art mindful of him? Rom. 1:20—For the invisible things of him [God] since the creation of the world

1. Owen, *A Discourse Concerning the Holy Spirit*, abridged by George Burder, 54, 55.

are clearly seen, being perceived through the things that are made, even his everlasting power and divinity.

In like manner, because the grace and wisdom of the Son, and the love of the Spirit, are especially impressed upon the new or spiritual Creation, *redemption* is ascribed eminently to the former, and *regeneration* and *sanctification* to the latter.

Eph. 1:6-7: the Beloved, in whom we have redemption through his blood, the forgiveness of our trespasses, according to the riches of his grace. Col. 1:13-14: the Son of his love, in whom we have our redemption, the forgiveness of our sins. Heb. 9:11-12: But Christ . . . through his own blood, entered in once for all into the holy place, having obtained eternal redemption. 1 Pet. 1:18-19: knowing that ye were redeemed . . . with precious blood, as of a lamb without blemish and without spot, even the blood of Christ.
John 3:5-7: Verily, verily, I say unto thee, Except one be born of water and the Spirit, he cannot enter into the kingdom of God. That which is born of the flesh is flesh; and that which is born of the Spirit is spirit. Marvel not that I said unto thee, Ye must be born anew. Titus 3:5—according to his mercy he saved us, through the washing of regeneration and renewing of the Holy Spirit. Rom. 5:5—the love of God hath been shed abroad in our hearts through the Holy Spirit which was given unto us. Rom. 15:30—Now I beseech you, brethren, by our Lord Jesus Christ, and by the love of the Spirit, that ye strive together with me in your prayers to God for me. Rom. 15:16—that the offering up of the Gentiles might be made acceptable, being sanctified by the Holy Spirit. 2 Thess. 2:13—for that God chose you from the beginning unto salvation in sanctification of the Spirit and belief of the truth. 1 Pet. 1:2—according to the foreknowledge of God the Father, in sanctification of the Spirit, unto obedience and sprinkling of the blood of Jesus Christ. Rom. 14:17—for the kingdom of God is not eating and drinking, but righteousness and peace and joy in the Holy Spirit.

Again, a Divine work is eminently ascribed to one of the three Persons of the Godhead when the performance of that work involves the peculiar condescension of that Person, and to the doing of which the other Persons give their approval and consent. For example again, redemption is eminently ascribed to the Son because it involved His condescension to assume our human nature, in order to make Atonement for our sins and to qualify Himself to act as our Mediator and High Priest.

Phil. 2:5-8: Have this mind in you, which was also in Christ Jesus: who, existing in the form of God, counted not the being on an equality with God a thing to be grasped, but emptied himself, taking the form of a servant, being made in the likeness of men; and being found in fashion as a man, he humbled himself, becoming obedient even unto death, yea, the death of the cross. Heb. 2:14-15: Since then the children are sharers in flesh and blood, he also himself in like manner partook of the same; that through death he might bring to nought him that had the power of death, that is, the devil; and might deliver all them who through fear of death were all their lifetime subject to bondage. ·

519

[It was a part of the mission of the Son to redeem His people from the bondage of both sin and death.] Heb. 2:17-18:Wherefore it behooved him in all things to be made like unto his brethren, that he might become a merciful and faithful high priest in things pertaining to God, to make propitiation for the sins of the people. For in that he himself hath suffered being tempted, he is able to succor them that are tempted. Heb. 4:15-16: For we have not a high priest that cannot be touched with the feeling of our infirmities; but one that hath been in all points tempted like as we are, yet without sin. Let us therefore draw near with boldness unto the throne of grace, that we may receive mercy, and may find grace to help us in time of need.

Similarly, sanctification is ascribed eminently to the Holy Spirit, because it involves His condescension to His particular office and work in the Body of Christ. The fact must not be overlooked that the Spirit's coming to earth to incorporate and to indwell the Church, to suffer inevitably vexings and grievings at the hands of weak-willed saints and nominal professors of religion, to say nothing of the insults heaped upon Him by reprobate sinners, involved a condescension on the Spirit's part comparable to that involved in the Incarnation and human life and death of the eternal Word, the Son, the Messiah.

Finally, the order of operation among the three Persons of the Godhead seems to depend upon the order of their subsistence in the totality of the Divine Being.

1. *Thus the beginning of Divine operations is assigned, in Scripture, to the Father.*

Gen. 1:26—And God said, Let us make man in our image, after our likeness, etc. Rom. 11:33-36: O the depth of the riches both of the wisdom and the knowledge of God! how unsearchable are his judgments, and his ways past tracing out! For who hath known the mind of the Lord? or who hath been his counsellor? or who hath first given to him, and it shall be recompensed unto him again? For of him, and through him, and unto him, are all things. To him be the glory for ever. Amen. Job 11:7—Canst thou by searching find out God? Canst thou find out the Almighty unto perfection? Matt. 24:36—But of that day and hour knoweth no one, not even the angels of heaven, neither the Son, but the Father only. Acts 1:7—It is not for you to know times or seasons, which the Father hath set within his own authority. Eph. 1:3-4: Blessed be the God and Father of our Lord Jesus Christ, who hath blessed us with every spiritual blessing in the heavenly places in Christ, even as he chose us in him before the foundation of the world, etc. Eph. 3:8-11: Unto me, who am less than the least of all saints, was this grace given, to preach unto the Gentiles the unsearchable riches of Christ: and to make all men see what is the dispensation of the mystery which for ages hath been hid in God who created all things; to the intent that now unto the principalities and the powers in the heavenly places might be made known through the church the manifold wisdom of God, according to the eternal purpose which he purposed in Christ Jesus our Lord.

2. *But whereas the beginning of Divine operations is ascribed*

*in Scripture to the Father, the establishing and upholding of all things is ascribed to the Son.*

Psa. 33:6, 9—By the word of Jehovah were the heavens made, And all the host of them by the breath of his mouth. . . . For he spake, and it was done; He commanded, and it stood fast. Psa. 148:5-6: Let them [all created things] praise the name of Jehovah; For he commanded, and they were created. He hath also established them for ever and ever: He hath made a decree which shall not pass away. [*Decreeing*, or *edicting*, is in a special sense the work of the Logos or Son: to the Father we are indebted primarily for *faith*, to the Son for *doctrine*, and to the Spirit for *evidence* or *proof*.] John 1:3—All things were made through him [the Logos]; and without him was not anything made that hath been made. Col. 1:16-17: For in him were all things created. . . . all things have been created through him, and unto him; and he is before all things, and in him all things consist. Heb. 1:1-3: God, having of old time spoken unto the fathers in the prophets . . . hath at the end of these days spoken unto us in his Son, whom he appointed heir of all things, *through whom also he made the worlds; who being the effulgence of his glory, and the very image of his substance, and upholding all things by the word of his power*, when he had made purification of sins, sat down on the right hand of the Majesty on high. 1 Cor. 15:24-28: Then cometh the end, when he shall deliver up the kingdom to God, even the Father; when he shall have abolished all rule and all authority and power. For he must reign, till he hath put all his enemies under his feet. The last enemy that shall be abolished is death. For, He put all things in subjection under his feet. But when he saith, All things are put in subjection, it is evident that he is excepted who did subject all things unto him. And when all things have been subjected unto him, then shall the Son also himself be subjected to him that did subject all things unto him, that God may be all in all.

*3. Finally, the consummation or realization of all these Divine works is ascribed to the Spirit:*

[Hence the works of the Spirit are, *eminently: Inspiration and revelation; demonstration or miracles; regeneration; sanctification;* and *immortalization*.] 1 Pet. 1:21—For no prophecy ever came by the will of man: but men spake from God, being moved by the Holy Spirit. 2 Sam. 23:1-2: David the son of Jesus saith . . . The Spirit of Jehovah spake by me, And his word was upon my tongue. 1 Pet. 1:10-11: Concerning which salvation the prophets sought and searched diligently, who prophesied of the grace that should come unto you: searching what time or what manner of time the Spirit of Christ which was in them did point unto, when it testified beforehand the sufferings of Christ, and the glories that should follow them. 1 Cor. 2:9-13: Whatsoever things God prepared for them that love him, Unto us God revealed them through the Spirit: for the Spirit searcheth all things, yea, the deep things of God. For who among men knoweth the things of a man, save the spirit of the man, which is in him? even so the things of God none knoweth, save the Spirit of God. But we received, not the spirit of the world, but the spirit which is from God; that we might know the things that were freely given to us of God. Which things also we speak, not in words which man's wisdom teacheth, but which the Spirit teacheth; combining spiritual things with spiritual words. Matt. 12:28—But if I by the Spirit of God cast out demons, then is the kingdom of God come upon you. Luke 24:49—but tarry ye in the city, until ye be clothed with power from on high. Acts 1:8—But ye

521

shall receive power, when the Holy Spirit is come upon you, etc. 1 Cor. 2:4—in demonstration of the Spirit and of power. Heb. 2:4—God bearing witness with them, both by signs and wonders, and by manifold powers, and by gifts of the Holy Spirit, according to his own will. [Thus it will be seen that *evidence* provided by the Spirit, of the workings of the Godhead in the old or physical Creation, has taken the twofold form (1) of recorded *revelation* or Scripture, which is God-breathed literature, and (2) of *demonstration* or miracles designed to attest the revelation.]

[As for the works of regeneration, sanctification, and immortalization, cf. John 3:5 again]: Except one be born of water and the Spirit, he cannot enter into the kingdom of God. Tit. 3:5—according to his mercy he saved us, through the washing of regeneration and renewing of the Holy Spirit. Rom. 15:30—by the love of the Spirit. Rom. 15:16—that the offering up of the Gentiles might be made acceptable, being sanctified by the Holy Spirit. 2 Thess. 2:13—for that God chose you from the beginning unto salvation in sanctification of the Spirit, etc. 1 Pet. 1:2—in sanctification of the Spirit. Gal. 5:25—If we live by the Spirit, by the Spirit let us also walk. Gal. 5:16—Walk by the Spirit, and ye shall not fulfil the lust of the flesh. Rom. 8:11—But if the Spirit of him that raised up Jesus from the dead dwelleth in you, he that raised up Christ Jesus from the dead shall give life also to your mortal bodies through his Spirit that dwelleth in you.

To sum up: The Father is said to be the *originating* Cause of the Plan of the Universe (cf. again Isa. 46:9-11: "I am God, and there is none like me; declaring the end from the beginning, and from ancient times things that are not yet done; saying, My counsel shall stand, and I will do all my pleasure. . . . yea, I have spoken, I will also bring it to pass; I have purposed, I will also do it"), and of all Divine operations pursuant thereto; The Word or Son is said to be the *executing* Cause; and the Holy Spirit the *realizing* or *consummating* Cause; the ultimate end being a holy universe, a universe in which mortality itself shall have been swallowed up of life (2 Cor. 5:4). Hence, whereas the Patriarchal Dispensation was essentially the age of the Father, and the Jewish Dispensation the age of the Son, the present or Christian Dispensation is the age of the Holy Spirit. The Spirit came on the Day of Pentecost to abide with the Church throughout "the times of the Gentiles" (Luke 21:24). When, however, the time shall come for the Gospel Dispensation to be terminated, the Spirit will then return to the Father, even as the Son ascended to the Father at the end of the Jewish Dispensation (Acts 1:9-11), having accomplished the work which the Father had given had given Him to do (John 17:4). But the Spirit will not return to the Father unaccompanied. He will take with Him the Bride of Christ, who shall have been purified and made whole by His presence and power, and He will present her as a chaste virgin unto the Bridegroom, that the two—the Bridegroom and the Bride—may dwell together in sweet converse, in heavenly glory, for ever and ever. (1 Thess. 4:13-18, 2 Cor. 11:2; Rev. 21:1-4, 22:17).

## 4. The First Principle of All Things

In the ancient Pythagorean metaphysic, The One or the Monad, conceived as quasi-material yet essentially dynamic, was regarded as the efficient cause of the cosmogonical process, as the First Principle, the Principle of Unity and Generation, of all things. As such the Monad was thought of as being represented or symbolized, in the numerical process, by the unit or 1. The Monad, moreover, was regarded as embodying within its own nature the elements of Limit and Unlimited, or what were later designated Form and Matter respectively; and by the agency of these elements as diffusing itself throughout, and exhibiting itself in, the number-atoms which were considered to be the ultimate stuff of the whole Cosmos. To quote Alexander Polyhistor again, as describing the Pythagorean theory:

> The first principle of all things is the One. From the One came an Indefinite Two, as matter for the One, which is cause. From the One and the Indefinite Two came numbers, and from numbers, points; from points, lines; from lines, plane figures; from plane figures, solid figures; from solid figures, sensible bodies. The elements of these are four: fire, water, earth, air; these change and are wholly transformed, and out of them comes to be a *cosmos*, animate, intelligent, spherical, embracing the central earth, which is itself spherical and inhabited round about.[1]

Now, as far as we are able to ascertain from ancient sources, this concept of The One as the First Principle of all things originated with the Pythagoreans and in all probability with Pythagoras himself. The concept underwent many developments and ramifications, however, in the thinking of later philosophers. By Plato and his school, who were greatly influenced by Pythagorean concepts, it was developed into the concept of the Form or Idea of the Good, and given a distinctly ethical connotation. Indeed the germ of the notion lingered in Aristotle's Self-thinking Thought, which seems to have been conceived by him as essentially immaterial, like Plato's Form of the Good. But the original concept appears to have been taken over directly by Plotinus and his successors, and amplified into the Neoplatonic One, likewise conceived as the First Principle of all things, and

1. Diogenes Laertius, *Lives and Opinions of Eminent Philosophers*, VIII, 25. Translation by F. M. Cornford, in his *Plato and Parmenides*, 3.

as existing at the farthest remove from the gross matter of our physical universe, just as, conversely, matter was conceived as the most distant emanation from The One. However, the concept had to wait, for its better elaboration, for the appearance of the Italian philosopher, Giordano Bruno, in the sixteenth century; it was he who gave to it much richer content in his celebrated doctrine of the World-Soul. That Bruno, himself originally a Dominican monk, was influenced greatly by the Biblical revelation of God as eternal Spirit, there can be no doubt. Hence said Bruno, from The One, as the World-Soul, as Divine Potency, all being flows. The World-Soul, God, is indeed a Unity, a Whole, but He is a Whole who is present in His completeness in every part. Whereas contingent things are never the same but always in a state of flux, The One, the World-Soul, alone remains eternally the Same. Bruno's doctrine was pantheistic, of course, but it was a pantheism of a more refined type. Incidentally, this concept of The One emerged—with variations —in later years in Spinoza's Substance, and in more recent times in doctrines of The Absolute (*i.e.*, the one all-pervading substance, of which all finite things would be only accidental manifestations), such as those of Spencer, Hegel, Bradley, Royce and others. So much for the history of the concept in philosophic thought.

The question we are especially interested in here is this: What is the attitude of present-day science with regard to such a First Principle? Does modern science hold to the concept of a single Principle of Unity and Generation of all things? It certainly does: it is compelled to do so by the facts in the case. As it has been made clear already, human thought in whatever time or place is logically compelled, in trying to account for the Cosmos, to start with something, that is, with a First Principle. Not only is science compelled to hold to the concept of a First Principle from logical considerations—even if that Principle be nothing more than some form of impersonal energy—but from empirical considerations as well. Everything in science points unmistakably to the existence of some kind of Creative Energy or Life Force as operating in the space-time continuum. I doubt that any scientist would ever question this statement.

In this particular connection, the following story which appeared some years ago in the columns of the metropolitan press becomes most illuminating:

Albert Einstein has developed, after thirty years of arduous labor, a mathematical concept that is expected to lead to new and much deeper insights in the cosmos. The new theory, described by Einstein as a "generalized theory of gravitation," attempts to inter-relate all known physical phenomena into one all-embracing intellectual concept, thus providing one major key to all the multiple phenomena and forces in which the material universe manifests itself to man.

In his special theory, of relativity, published in 1905, Einstein proved by mathematics that space and time, rather than being two separate entities, were actually united in one four-dimensional continuum. Out of this intellectual synthesis emerged the discovery that matter and energy were both interchangeable, matter being "frozen" energy, while energy was matter in a fluid state.

In his general theory of relativity, published in 1916, Einstein proved, again by mathematics, that gravitation and inertia were equivalent, thus bringing space, time, matter, energy, gravitation and inertia into one all-embracing intellectual concept.

However, there still remained one of the great cosmic forces that could not be brought into the unified structure, the all-pervading force of electro-magnetism, which permeates the cosmos at large and the atoms of which the cosmos is constituted. It is this force which Einstein believes he has at last succeeded in bringing into a all-embracing cosmic concept, known among scientists as a "Universal Field Theory." This means that the gravitational field and the electro-magnetic field, the two major "fields" in which the material universe manifests itself, can at last be viewed as being two manifestations of one united cosmic entity. . . .

Einstein's latest work now promises to bridge the gap that now separates the infinite universe of the stars and galaxies and the equally infinite universe of the atom, which are at present widely separated, one being explained by relativity while our knowledge of the other rests on the quantum theory, of which Einstein was also one of the major architects.

He intends to bring the relativity and the quantum theories, the two major pillars on which man's basic understanding of the universe rests, into one all-embracing system. His present work is regarded as a major step in that direction.[1]

Commenting on the latest Einsteinian synthesis, Lincoln Barnett, writing in a later issue of *Life* magazine, says that

the major and immediate triumph of the Unified Field Theory is implicit in the first word of its title. It unifies man's concepts of the universe in which he dwells. Within its vast perspective the distinctions between gravitational and electromagnetic force, matter and energy, electric charge and field, space and time, all fade and dissolve in the light of their revealed relationships; and *the deep underlying unity of the universe is laid bare.*[2]

In a word, the primal energy will have been demonstrated to be *of one kind,* and the cosmos a mathematical construction of that same Primal Unity, the chief property of which, manifestly, is *inexhaustibleness.*

Another very significant Associated Press dispatch appeared

1. From the New York *Times,* issue of December 27, 1949.
2. Art., "The Meaning of Einstein's New Theory," *Life,* issue of Jan. 9, 1950. (Italics mine.)

just a month later, under the date-line, "Princeton, N.J., Feb. 13," which reads in part as follows:

Professor Albert Einstein's new unified field theory—the unity of gravitation and electromagnetism—will be published here within a few days. . . . The new unified theory may have human and spiritual values because it may explain certain mysteries about matter and energy which go to form man and life. Einstein has adopted a new viewpoint differing from the thinking of most physical scientists. He thinks that the forces, gravitation and electro-magnetism, which together govern matter, such as your body, are more important for understanding these mysteries than for understanding merely the material stuff itself. Recently scientific work has concentrated on understanding the material side, by the study of atoms. Biologists have shown that electromagnetic fields of force appear to shape and to guide the formation of living things. These fields are one of the things that make the difference between a man and a mouse. When either a human or an animal is at the start of life, that is, made only of two newly joined tissue cells, an electromagnetic field is present. This field of force comes from the little cells and is part of them. As the embryo forms, this field guides the course. The little personal field is also part of the greater electromagnetic fields which seem to surround everything. Gravitation is part of all these fields.[1]

As stated heretofore, it is a matter of common knowledge that the mystery of life has thus far remained inscrutable to the human mind. What there is in the protoplasm of the living cell which endows it with properties of a higher order than those of the energy of the non-living atom, no one knows. Since the time of Pasteur, it has been universally agreed by scientists that life comes only from antecedent life; spontaneous generation has never been discovered anywhere in Nature. Living things appear to exist and function on a higher level of being than non-living things, with properties and ends that are exclusively their own. If, however, the relation between the energy-principle of the atom and the life-principle of the cell could once be determined, and if both should be found to be functions of the same Primal Energy and Unity, a tremendous step would be taken toward the unification of our understanding of the Cosmos. Truly, despite the potentialities of tragedy which the present atomic age holds for man, it is still the most challenging age in his history on earth!

But even so, that is, even were it possible to prove the energy-principle of the atom and the life-principle of the cell to be manifestations of the same ultimate Principle of Unity, there would still remain even greater mysteries than these to be brought into that Unity, namely, the mysteries of con-

1. This A. P. dispatch appeared in the Albuquerque, N.M. *Journal*, Feb. 13, 1950.

sciousness, memory, the subconscious, and all the thought processes in man; the mysteries of his power of abstract thinking, of his creative imagination, of his sense of values, and the very mystery of *meaning* itself. And above all, there would remain the supreme mystery of *Love*. By no stretch of the imagination can these higher phenomena—the most vital facts of our personal experience and the phenomena by which even matter itself is apprehended and "understood"—be reduced to electromagnetic energy alone or identified with mere concatenations of cells.

This leads me to observe, in conclusion, that the only presentation, in the literature known to man, of the First Principle as *all-comprehensive,* that is, as the Source and Cause of *all* the varied phenomena characteristic of *all* levels of being in the Totality of Being, is the presentation given us, in the Judaeo-Christian Scriptures, of God as the Eternal Spirit. Jesus Himself tells us explicitly: "God is a Spirit; and they that worship him must worship in spirit and truth" (John 4:24). God in His Nature as The Absolute is Spirit. And here I am using the term "Absolute" in its proper sense—as derived from the Latin *absolutum, absolvere, se-luo,* originally from the Greek, *luo,* that is, "self-loosed," "unfettered," or "free from bonds." In this sense, God is the One who is not *necessarily* bound up with anything else, One who is independent, self-sufficing, etc. In His absoluteness, God is a Spirit, even though, as such *essentially,* He is differentiated into three Persons. His absolute Nature, moreover, expresses itself *actively, effectually* (to get things done) through one of these Persons *eminently,* namely, the Spirit of God. In the Old Testament this Person is designated the Spirit of God (*Ruach Elohim*), or, metaphorically, the Breath of God. In the New Testament, He is designated Spirit of God, Spirit of Christ, and in a majority of instances, the Holy Spirit.

The following facts should be noted again, therefore, by way of a final review and summary:

1. The Spirit of God is presented in the Bible as the Source and Cause of energy, matter, motion, and all forms of life. In the opening verses of the Old Testament we read:

> In the beginning God created the heavens and the earth. And the earth was waste and void; and darkness was upon the face of the deep; and the Spirit of God moved upon the face of the waters. And God said, Let there be light; and there was light.

We have here the picture of an illimitable Space or Void filled with, and enshrouded in, impenetrable darkness; the most perfect picture of absolute nothingness in literature. Into this Void came the Spirit of God, brooding, stirring, energizing, creating, that is, bringing into existence, probably projecting from His infinite Being, primal energy which had never before that moment, itself the beginning of Time, been in actuation at least for such a purpose as the creation of a universe in a space-time continuum. Nor is there any reason to doubt any longer that this primal energy was capable of self-transmutation into the various kinds of matter known to us today. The intimation is, moreover, that one of the first forms of energy manifested in this Creative Process was radiant energy or light, again a disclosure that is in harmony with the conclusion of the latest physics. Furthermore, whether this primal energy projected by the agency of the Divine Spirit contained within itself the "seeds" of living things, that is, the potentialities of the vital processes (as indeed many of the early Church Fathers held), or whether vital energy—Life Force—was a *subsequent* projection from the Divine Spirit into the world of matter in motion— this is not a matter of any great significance—or so it seems to me at least. It must be admitted, however, that the original language of the first chapter of *Genesis* seems to point to the latter interpretation as the correct one. Here, as we continue to read, we find, morever, that in the process of physical creation, the brooding of the Spirit did not cease with the bringing into existence of such primary physical phenomena as energy, motion, light, atmosphere—in short, the ingredient of the physio-chemical world; on the contrary the Spirit's brooding was continuous throughout the entire process; indeed it is continuous throughout the entire Time process. There is every reason for thinking that the Creation is still going on; that, in fact, it will be consummated only when the saints stand in the Divine Presence clothed in glory and honor and immortality. In a word, according to the account given in *Genesis*, its was a result of the brooding (energizing and vitalizing) of the Eternal Spirit that the cosmos and its myriads of forms of natural life marched slowly but surely into being. And it is likewise as a result of the Spirit's continuous "brooding" that the Cosmos is preserved (or conserved, to speak in the language of science) from generation to generation, and from age to age, as long as the temporal process shall endure. It is the Divine Spirit who is the actuating Source and Cause of the whole Physical Creation. As Marcus Dods puts it, commenting on Gen. 1:2—

This, then, is the first lesson of the Bible: that at the root and origin of all this vast material universe, before whose laws we are crushed as the moth, there abides a living, conscious Spirit, who wills and knows and fashions all things.[1]

2. The Spirit of God is presented in the Bible as the Source and Cause of personal or rational life in man, with all its characteristic powers: self-consciousness, self-determination, power of abstract thinking, creative imaginations, sense of values, and the powers of the subconscious in man as well. "Yahweh Elohim formed man of the dust of the ground, and breathed into his nostrils the breath of life; and man became a living soul" (Gen. 2:7). This teaches us that the life principle in man derived originally by *the inbreathing of the Divine Spirit* from the very Life of God Himself. That is to say, the life principle in man is essentially spiritual (rather than biological) in nature; or, to put it more precisely, the breath of life in man subsumes the vital principle (previously implanted in the lower orders) *plus* the rational principle; it is by the latter alone that man is specified as man (*homo sapiens*). In other words, God made the human body to live by imparting to it, by causing to be breathed into it, His own mode of life (with all the *moral* implications pursuant thereto); and thus the creature, man, became the image or likeness of his Creator. The body-spirit unity thus effectuated was designated "a living soul." Into the *formed* "dust of the world" (Prov. 8:26) or material elements, God infused something, not of any antecedent matter, but immediately of His own essence. This entrance of the Divine Breath was the entrance of personal or rational life into the human corporeal form, as a result of which man became a living soul. This Divine inbreathing was, of course, an operation of the eternal Spirit. The Spirit of God and the Breath of God are one, the former expression being proper whereas the latter is only metaphorical, describing the procession of the Spirit from the Divine Being.

3. The Spirit of God is presented in the Bible as the Source and Cause of every order of life in the Totality of Being. He is, as we have just seen, the Principle of *natural* life in all created organisms. "The God that made the world and all things therein . . . He himself giveth to all life, and breath, and all things" (Acts 17:24-25). He is, in the second place, the *Source* of *spiritual* life which the saints enjoy in the Kingdom of Grace. As Jesus Himself said to Nicodemus: "Verily, verily, I say unto thee, Except one be born of water and the Spirit, he can-

1. *The Expositor's Bible; Genesis, in loco.*

not enter into the kingdom of God. That which is born of the flesh is flesh; that which is born of the Spirit is spirit. Marvel not that I said unto thee, Ye must be born anew" (John 3:5-7). The Spirit is, in the third place, the effectuating Source of *eternal* life which the redeemed shall enjoy in the Kingdom of Glory. As it has been made abundantly clear on preceding pages of this treatise, the one essential condition of the attainment of ultimate complete Union with God, Beatitude, Life Everlasting, is the submergence of the human spirit in the Life of the Divine Spirit, in the here and now; hence the Holy Spirit is said to be the Source and Agent of wholeness or holiness. As Jesus Himself said: "Blessed are the pure in heart; for they shall see [*i.e.*, apprehend, understand, *know*] God" (Matt. 5:8). And finally, because immortality is an essential property of the Life Everlasting, the Holy Spirit is declared to be the Agent of the Godhead in the immortalization of the saints. "But if the Spirit of him that raised up Jesus from the dead dwelleth in you, he that raised up Christ Jesus from the dead shall give life also to your mortal bodies through his Spirit that dwelleth in you" (Rom. 8:11).

When the saints shall stand before God in the Final Day,— the Day of the Consummation of All Things,—clothed in glory and honor and immortality, their minds united with the Mind of God in knowledge and their wills united with the Will of God in love, then, but not until then, will the Creative Process— the Divine Plan of the Ages—be fully realized. And this entire Process is described in Scripture as having been planned and ordained by the Father, executed by the Son, but effectuated by the Divine Spirit. The Spirit is the effectuating Agent of every form of life characteristic of the different levels of being which make up the Totality of Being—of natural life, in the Kingdom of Nature; of spiritual life, in the Kingdom of Grace; and of eternal life, in the Kingdom of Glory.

"If materialism is true,, writes W. P. Montague,

then, as William James declared, 'the things we cherish most are at the mercy of the things we cherish least.' I do not think this is true. Chaos and Old Night could hardly have been lucky enough to have a world like ours. Yet if we turn from Chaos to Zeus the chances against his reign are just as great. Sweat and blood and tears are not confined to Churchill's land. Nature is stained throughout with ugly, cruel failure. If any god who had omnipotence to draw upon had made this world with all its woe, he would be a god deserving anything but love. Not only far more probable, but far more congenial to our better nature, would be a god who, like Prometheus of old, will not yield right to might, no matter what the pain imposed by the tyrant Zeus.

What we want is such a god as that, a *truly holy spirit*, omnipresent but not omnipotent, pervading the chaos of nature and slowly leavening it with higher beings and higher goods. May faith in Him be justified! [From art., "Philosophy in a World at War," *Fortune*, March, 1942. Italics mine—C.C. The concept expressed here by Montague is implicit in the doctrine of the Incarnation, as stated in Scripture: 'though he was a Son, yet learned obedience by the things which he suffered,' etc., Heb. 5:8.]

Surely, Dr. Montague exaggerates nature's "cruelty" unduly, like many modern writers since Tennyson, from whom they seem to have taken their cue (Tennyson, "In Memoriam," 56: "Nature, red in tooth and claw with ravine," etc.). Some truths we must recall in this connection are these: (1) God is Love, that is, He is the God of Love; (2) Love is unfailingly creative and must constantly be shared with all creatures; (3) Creation was, and is the outpouring and sharing of divine Love; (4) but Love is not to be coerced, because that would not be love; love must be given willingly; (5) man was predestined to be free; (6) the price that he must pay for this freedom is the possibility of evil; (7) God will do whatever He wills to do *that is consistent with His nature as God;* (He could not tell a lie, and be our God); (8) He has already made full provision for the spiritual recovery of all men who will come to Him in faith and obedience; (9) hell is prepared for the devil and his angels; if men go there it will be the consequence of their following their own way instead of God's way. There is a measure of truth in the saying that *in every Paradise there lurks a snake.*

Thus it will be seen that the Pythagorean Monad, the Neoplatonic One, Bruno's World-Soul, indeed every purely philosophical concept of the First Principle of all things, falls short of the Spirit of God of the Bible. Indeed the fundamental difference between the Greek concept of Deity and the Hebrew-Christian presentation of God is that in the former God is implicitly That Which Is, whereas in the latter He is explicitly HE WHO IS; that is, He includes within His own nature not only energy-principle and life-principle, but mind-principle as well. He is essentially Intelligence and Will,—*The* Intelligence and Will that is the First Cause of all created things. "And God said unto Moses, I AM THAT I AM. . . . Thus shalt thou say unto the children of Israel, I AM hath sent me unto you" (Exo. 3:14). "God is a Spirit; and they that worship him must worship in spirit and truth" (John 4:24). As the philosopher, W. S. Hocking, writes:

For the author of *Genesis*, mentality is original. It does not enter a physical world already running on its own. On the contrary, it is

531

the physical world which enters the realm of mind. It is the Eternal Mind who in the beginning created the raw materials of the world, and whose word evoked order from chaos.[1]

It should be re-emphasized here, of course, that in all the operations of the Eternal Spirit, He is represented in Scripture as acting in conjunction with, or through the instrumentality of, the Eternal Word.

We must, however, recognize Professor Montague's general conclusion, namely, that our God, if He is to meet the deepest aspirations of the human heart, must indeed be Holy Spirit. Human outreaching could hardly be satisfied with anything less in the Deity. But I should like to point out, too, that the distinguished professor of philosophy who wrote these lines is many, many centuries behind times. For it was well known to the saints of the Old Testament dispensations, literally hundreds of years before Christ, that the living and true God is essentially Holy Spirit. The prophet Isaiah, writing several centuries before the advent of the Messiah, harking back to the rebelliousness of God's ancient people under Moses, gave expression to the following exquisite bit of literature:

> But they rebelled, and grieved his holy Spirit: therefore he [Jehovah] was turned to be their enemy, and himself fought against them. Then he remembered the days of old, Moses and his people, saying, Where is he that brought them up out of the sea with the shepherds of his flock? where is he that put his holy Spirit in the midst of them? that caused his glorious arm to go at the right hand of Moses? that divided the waters before them, to make himself an everlasting name? that led them through the depths, as a horse in the wilderness, so that they stumbled not? As the cattle that go down into the valley, the Spirit of Jehovah caused them to rest: so didst thou lead thy people, to make thyself a glorious name [Isa. 63:10-14].

And it was the prophet Isaiah who, at least seven centuries before Christ, was privileged to behold, in a wondrous Vision, "the Lord sitting upon a throne, high and lifted up, and his train filled the temple"; and to hear the words of the heavenly anthem to which John the Beloved was also privileged to listen, some eight hundred years afterward, on the barren isle of Patmos: "Holy, holy, holy, is Jehovah of hosts" (Isa. 6:3, Rev. 4:8). In similar vein the Psalmist cried out unto God saying, "Teach me to do thy will; For thou art my God: Thy Spirit is good; Lead me in the land of uprightness" (Psa. 143:10), and again, "Cast me not away from thy presence, and take not thy holy Spirit from me" (Psa. 51:11). And in the great day of

1. Art., "A World-View," in *Preface to Philosophy: A Textbook,* by Hocking, Blanshard, Hendel, and Randall, 436.

national rejuvenation under Nehemiah the prince and Ezra the priest-scribe, the intercessory prayer of the Levites for the people, contained these words with reference to the experience of their fathers under Moses: "Thou gavest also thy good Spirit to instruct them, and withheldest not thy manna from their mouth, and gavest them water for their thirst" (Neh. 9:20). Indeed, I am convinced that God's elect, from the earliest times, have known full well that their God is essentially Holy Spirit.

Let us recall, in this connection, the following statements from the pen of Lincoln Barnett:

> Man's inescapable impasse is that he himself is part of the world he seeks to explore; his body and proud brain are mosaics of the same elemental particles that compose the dark, drifting dust clouds of interstellar space; he is, in the final analysis, merely an ephemeral conformation of the primordial space-time field. Standing midway between macrocosm and microcosm he finds barriers on every side and can perhaps but marvel, as St. Paul did nineteen hundred years ago, that the world was created by the word of God so that what is seen was made out of things which do not appear.[1]

that is to say, out of the Will-power, Thought-power, Spirit-power, Word-power of God.

But let it never be forgotten that saving hope—the "hope both sure and stedfast" which is "an anchor of the soul" (Heb. 6:19)—is held out to man by that same Word of God, the Bible, in which the truth is revealed to him that he is not "merely an ephemeral conformation of the primordial space-time field," but an imperishable person, one who is made in the image and likeness of God and who is therefore the object of God's infinite love and compassion; and that he may become, through the life of the Spirit of God within him, a son of the Almighty (2 Cor. 6:18), an heir of God and joint-heir with Christ of all things (Rom. 8:17, Heb. 1:2). This is the hope that gives meaning to human life, meaning which no system of philosophy ever gave to it. But man, in order to enjoy the fruition of this hope, must yield himself in body, soul, and spirit, to the Spirit of God. The Fountain of Life must spring up, and the Stream flow, within him; silence, unresponsiveness, brutishness, on his part can mean only death: not just the death of the body, which is a Divine appointment to which every man must yield (Heb. 9:27), but the second death (Rev. 21:8), spiritual death, which is total death, "even eternal destruction from the face of the Lord and from the glory of his might" (2 Thess. 1:9).

1. Barnett, *The Universe and Dr. Einstein*, 114.

May I therefore bring this treatise to a proper end with another of Andrew Murray's exquisite prayers?—

Blessed Father! I thank Thee that the Holy Spirit is to us the bearer of the Fulness of Jesus, and that in being filled with the Spirit we are made full with that Fulness. I thank thee that there have been men on earth since Pentecost, not a few, of whom Thou hast seen that they were full of the Holy Ghost. O my God! make me full. Let the Holy Spirit take and keep possession of my deepest, inmost life. Let Thy Spirit fill my spirit. Let thence the fountain flow through all the soul's affections and powers. Let it flow over and flow out through my lips, speaking Thy praise and love. Let the very body, by the quickening and sanctifying energy of the Spirit, be Thy temple, full of the Life Divine. Lord my God! I believe Thou hearest me. Thou hast given it me; I accept it as mine.

Oh, grant that throughout Thy Church the Fulness of the Spirit may be sought and found, may be known and proved. Lord Jesus! our glorified King, oh, let Thy Church be full of the Holy Ghost. Amen.[1]

## QUESTIONS FOR REVIEW OF PART SIX

1. In what two aspects may we consider the Word of God?
2. What has always been the temporal mission of the Holy Spirit?
3. What is the basic issue with respect to the Person of Jesus? How is this related to the doctrine of the Virgin Birth?
4. What is meant by the Humiliation of Jesus (the doctrine of *Kenosis*)?
5. Cite important Scriptures which affirm the pre-existence of Jesus.
6. Cite Scriptures in which Jesus Himself affirmed His pre-existence.
7. How best describe the nature of the pre-existent Savior's relationship with the Heavenly Father?
8. What *Name* best describes this relationship?
9. Why could not the term "Son of God" fully designate this relationship?
10. What is specifically implied in the Apostle John's statement that in the beginning *the Word was with God?*
11. What is specifically implied in his accompanying statement that *the Word was God?*
12. What does the phrase "in the beginning" signify in John 1:1?
13. What, according to Rom. 8:29-30, is God's Eternal Purpose with respect to His saints?
14. What is implied in the risen Lord's declaration that He is *The First and the Last* (Rev. 1:17)?
15. Differentiate the historical, eternal, and incarnate Names of the Messiah.
16. What is the full significance of the name, *The Logos?*
17. Summarize Alexander Campbell's presentation of the doctrine of the Logos.
18. What does the Apostle Paul mean by the Phrase, "The Mystery of Godliness"?
19. Explain what is meant by the *decrees* of God.
20. What were the relations between the Father and Messiah that began in time? What is the Name that signifies these relations?
21. What is the full significance of the title *Messiah* or *Christ?* How is this related to the *Good Confession?*

1. *The Spirit of Christ*, 310-311.

22. How is the word *christen* misapplied in what is called "infant baptism"?
23. When was Jesus *christed?* How may we know this?
24. Why is this referred to as His *anointing?* By whom was He anointed, and for what purpose?
25. When did the coronation ceremonies take place in Heaven? Explain, in this connection, Psalm 24:7-10.
26. What is included under the present Sovereignty of Christ?
27. In what twofold sense is the Savior eternally the Word of God?
28. By what various means did our Christ reveal to us the Heavenly Father?
29. Explain fully the truths expressed in 1 Cor. 1:22-24.
30. On what grounds do we insist that the Logos existed *as a Person* prior to His incarnation?
31. List the categories of Scripture evidences in the Old Testament in which manifestations of the pre-incarnate Logos are implied.
32. List and explain those passages which describe the activities of the "Angel of Yahweh."
33. List the important passages in which Wisdom is represented as existing eternally with God, even though apparently distinct from Him.
34. List important passages in which the Word, as distinguished from God is presented as the Executor of God's will from everlasting.
35. List passages in which our Christ is presented as the Creator of the world.
36. When was the triune personality of God fully revealed? Why, in all likelihood, was this revelation not given to God's elect in the Old Testament dispensations?
37. Explain fully the import of Phil. 2:9-11.
38. What is the probable significance of the following Scriptures: Gen. 14:17-20 and Heb. 7:1-3; also Josh. 5:14, Dan. 3:25? Correlate these passages with Micah 5:2.
39. What facts show that the Spirit selected the most appropriate and most opportune moments in history to reveal the true Logos to the world?
40. What parallels, though imperfect ones, do we find in the Platonic Logos, the Stoic Logos, and the Philonian Logos?
41. In the light of these parallels, what significance was there in the fact that John gave us the doctrine of the true Logos?
42. What facts did John emphasize with regard to the true Logos that sets Him high above the pagan concepts?
43. Why must we conclude that the Christian doctrine of the Logos was *not* the point at which "Hellenism" was inserted into Christian doctrine?
44. In what two forms does the impersonal Word exist?
45. What fallacy is involved in the claim that "the church existed before the Book," and that, therefore, Scripture is secondary in authority to churchly ecclesiasticism? What is the error involved in the quoted cliche?
46. When and under what circumstances was the Gospel Dispensation ushered in? Explain why this was the birthday of the Church? What part did the Spirit play in the events of that great day?
47. Who has always edicted the Will and Thought of God *outwardly,* and who has always served as the infallible Communicator of this Thought to mankind?
48. What evidence have we that God's Spirit and God's Word always "go together"?
49. Explain the significant truths revealed in Jeremiah's prediction of the nature and terms of the New Covenant.

50. What was the relationship between the personal Logos and the Spirit of God?
51. What evidence have we that Jesus had a human "spirit"? What, then, was the relation between this human spirit and the divine Spirit?
52. What is the general relationship sustaining to each other by the Spirit and the Word?
53. Explain how God's Spirit and His Word acted together in the Creation.
54. How do God's Spirit and His Word act together in preserving the physical Creation?
55. How does the Spirit and the Word operate in inspiration and revelation?
56. In what respect was revelation primarily *historical?* State what was progressively revealed.
57. Explain the relation between the Spirit and the Word in the production of the *documentary* revelation.
58. Distinguish between *inspiration* and *revelation.* Distinguish between the products of human inspiration and those of Divine inspiration? What makes the difference?
59. Explain the operation of the Spirit and the Word in the working of miracles.
60. By what agency did Jesus perform miracles? Cite instances.
61. Explain the operation of the Spirit and the Word in regeneration.
62. Explain the operation of the Spirit and the Word in sanctification.
63. According to Sweeney, what sixteen works are said in Scripture to be effected by the Spirit that are said also in Scripture to be effected by the Word?
64. What is said in Scripture of the operation of the Spirit and the Word in the immortalization of the saints?
65. What will be the glorious result of this final operation of the Spirit and the Word in the Plan of Redemption?
66. Recapitulate the teaching of Scripture regarding the relationship between the Spirit and the Word in the totality of God's Cosmic Plan.
67. What works of the Godhead are assigned *eminently* to the Father?
68. What works of the Godhead are ascribed *eminently* to the Son?
69. What works of the Godhead are ascribed *eminently* to the Spirit?
70. What are the norms by which ascription *eminently* is distinguished from ascription *distinctly?*
71. On what do the operations among the Three Persons seem to depend? Explain.
72. To which of the Three is the *planning (origination)* of the operations of the Godhead ascribed? Cite Scriptures.
73. To which of the Three is the *establishing* and *upholding* of all things ascribed? Cite Scriptures.
74. To which of the Three is the *actualizing* of all operations of the Godhead ascribed? Cite Scriptures.
75. How are these distinctions explained in terms of *Causes?*
76. What is meant by *The First Principle* of all things?
77. State some of the philosophical conceptions of the First Principle.
78. What is meant by Barnett's phrase, "the deep underlying unity of the universe"?
79. Why do we claim that the only presentation in literature of the First Principle as *all-comprehensive* is that given us, in the Bible, of the Eternal Spirit?
80. What mean we when we say that God, as the Absolute, is Spirit? What do we mean by the *Absolute?*

81. Of what various phenomena of the Totality of Being is the Eternal Spirit presented in Scripture as the actualizing Cause?
82. Does not the view that matter is the actualizing cause of all things seem utterly incredible?
83. State the substance of the excerpt from the writing of Marcus Dods.
84. State the substance of the excerpt from the writing of Dr. Montague.
85. State the substance of the excerpt from the writing of W. S. Hocking.
86. Comment on the final "word" from the pen of Lincoln Barnett.

# ADDENDUM: ON EVOLUTION AND EVOLUTIONISM

1. The first fact to be recognized, in this connection, is that *evolution* must not be confused with *evolutionism*. The word "evolution" designates only the alleged process itself, the process defined as *continuous progressive change; the word* "evolutionism," however, designates the theory which purports to explain how the process "proceeds," that is, the phenomena that are said to actualize it.

2. A second fact that must be recognized, by way of introduction, is the distinction between *science* and *scientism*. While I have all the respect possible for pure science, I have none whatever for what has come to be called "scientism." By "scientism" we mean the deification of science, and, naturally, of man himself as the author of science. (Devotees of science are prone to forget that their science is purely descriptive of what lies "out there"; of that truth which is written into the structure of the universe; and that all they can do is to *discover* it, and state it in terms of what they designate "hypotheses," "theories," and "laws." "H-2-O," for example, is simply a description (formula) of how hydrogen and oxygen unite to form a molecule of water. As far as human knowledge goes, there has never been an exception to this "law," but no one is qualified to say that there *never will be an exception;* for any man to make such an assertion would be for him to claim *omniscience*, and omniscience is a power that man does not have. Hence, what science calls a "law" is simply a statement of *very, very great probability.* Science has changed its interpretations of the cosmos, both physical and moral, too frequently to justify the ascription of infallibility to the human intellect. Whether they will admit it or not, men live for the most part by *faith*, not by a knowledge which has the quality of absoluteness. In a word, just as true *religion* is not to be identified with *religiosity*, nor true *piety* with *piosity*, so true *science* is not *scientism*.

D. Elton Trueblood's statements are certainly in order here, as follows:

> Scientism is so naive as to be almost unbelievable. . . . God is a fiction because He cannot be discovered by laboratory technique. Prayer is futile because it cannot be proved by scientific method. Religion is unworthy of serious attention because it arose in the prescientific age. What we have here, of course, is not merely *science*, but a particularly unsophisticated philosophy of science, which deserves the epithet *scientism.*[1]

Scientism is, of course, the product of a closed mind, or, in the

1. Trueblood, *Philosophy of Religion,* 168

final analysis, a form of willful ignorance. It feeds on assumptions (as premises) which cannot be proved to be valid.

3. Evolutionism has been blown up into a dogma in recent years. (A dogma is a proposition to be accepted on the ground that it has been proclaimed by the proper authority; in this case, of course, that "proper authority" is human science.) Evolution is presented in many high school and college textbooks as an *established fact;* and in others, the inference that it is factual is expressed by innuendo, with the accompanying inference that persons who refuse to accept it as such are childish or just plain ignoramuses. It seems to be assumed by the devotees of this cult that they have a monopoly on the knowledge of this particular subject. The fact is that the material appearing in these textbooks is simply parroted by instructors who are so ignorant of Biblical teaching that they are not even remotely qualified to pass judgment on the issue involved. Unfortunately, too, persons of eminence in highly specified fields are prone to break into print on various aspects of Biblical doctrine, not realizing that by their own statements they prove themselves to be ignorant of the subjects on which they choose to expatiate. Pernicious fallacies, based on the authority of a great name, thus have a way of persisting from generation to generation even though they have been shown to be fallacious—or at least questionable—many times. It is the prestige of the "great" name or names with which they are associated that gives them a kind of deathlessness. It is the conviction of this writer that the evidence brought forward to justify evolutionism is based all too frequently, not on established fact—that is, by the testimony of eye-witnesses—but on *inference* alone. The important question, therefore, is this: Is the inference drawn from alleged phenomena in this field *necessary* inference, that is, inference the opposite of which is inconceivable? or does much of it savor of little more than *conjecture?* Dr. James Jauncey states the case clearly in these words:

> Of course you will often hear from some enthusiastic evolutionists that evolution is now indisputable, that it has been proved beyond all doubt, and that anyone who disputes this is an ignoramus or a fanatic. This is jumping the gun, to say the least. The vehemence of such statements makes one suspect that the speakers are trying to convince themselves. When a scientific theory crystallizes into law, such as that of relativity, it speaks for itself. All we can say at the moment is that evolution is generally accepted, possibly because of the lack of any scientific alternative, but with serious misgivings on the adequacy of some aspects of it. As for the kind of rigorous proof that science gen-

erally demands, it still isn't there. Indeed, some say that because of the philosophical aspects of the theory, proof will never be possible."[1]

It has been rightly said that a *hypothesis* in science is to be accepted simply as "a fairly good guess."

A clear example of blind spots that occur in the presentation of the theory of evolution—either in published accounts or in the original manuscripts—is the title of an article which appeared in *Reader's Digest* not so long ago, "Can Science Produce Life?" Any honest person can see that this title is misleading, to say the least: life was *never* produced by human agency. (*No man ever created a seed.*) This fact, the author of the article in question, seems to realize. Toward the end he writes, with reference to *microspheres* (proteinoids formed by the fusion of amino acids):

> "Although these spheres are not true cells— they have no DNA genes and they are simpler than any contemporary life— they do possess many cellular properties. They have stability; they keep their shapes indefinitely. They stain in the same way as the present-day protein in cells, an important chemical test. But the real significance of these microspheres is that scientists do not *synthesize* them piece by piece; they simply set up the right *conditions*—and microspheres produce themselves.

Thus it will be noted that the eminent scientist-author of this article flatly contradicts the import of the title, by stating that man can only set up the conditions necessary to the production of microspheres but cannot himself do the producing. (The title is an excellent example of the manner in which confusion can be spread by the careless use of language.) Man indeed sets the stage, but only the God of nature (there is no such thing as nature *per se,* an entity), as the cosmic Efficient Causality, can actualize the life process.

4. While one "school" of scientists will resort to the acceptance of evolutionism because *there is no other scientifically acceptable accounting for the existence of the totality of being;* that is to say, no other explanation that would not involve the *supernatural,* or at least the *superhuman,* and in their thinking this indeed would compel them to range beyond the canons of the scientific method; still and all, there are many so-called scientists who at heart reject *in toto* the basic concepts of religion in general, and especially those which are presented in the Scriptures, simply because *it is their will to do this and therefore they set out deliberately to oppose, and if possible to destroy, every religious belief known to man.* These are the

1. Jauncey, *Science Returns to God,* 57.

541

materialists, the self-styled naturalists, the humanists, the Marxists, the Leninists, and all their ilk. They seek to destroy religious conviction because they *hate* it. "Religion" is to them "the opium of the people." Hence they look upon it as a bounden duty to eliminate it from this world if there can be found any way of doing it. Unfortunately for them, however, it still seems to be true, as was affirmed early in human thinking, that "man is incurably religious," in the sense that he recognizes the existence of the higher Powers and seeks in whatever way possible to be reconciled to them or at least to receive their approbation. Among all nihilists it is a case in which the wish is father to the thought.

5. On the other hand, there are many eminent scientists who either accept reluctantly (and provisionally, let us say) or reject altogether the claims of the evolutionists. For a concrete example, we can cite the Preface to the latest issue of Everyman's Library Edition of Darwin's *Origin of Species*, from the mind and hand of W. R. Thompson, F.R.S., Director of the Commonwealth Institute of Biological Control, Ottawa, Canada. Thompson states expressly in his Preface that the content thereof will not follow the tenor of previous Introductions to Darwin's work, those written by other scientists, in particular that by Sir Arthur Keith. Thompson writes:

> I could not content myself with mere variations on the hymn to Darwin and Darwinism that introduce so many textbooks on biology and evolution. . . . I am of course well aware that my views will be regarded by biologists as heretical and reactionary. However, I happen to believe that in science heresy is a virtue and reaction often a necessity, and that in no field of science are heresy and reaction more desirable than in evolutionary theory.[1]

After stating in no uncertain terms what he considers to be weaknesses of the Darwinian theory (which he describes as a theory of the "origin of living forms by descent with modification"), Thompson goes on to point out the fallacies involved in the argumentation used by the evolutionists. This, he declares, "makes the discussion of their ideas extremely difficult." In what way? Because "personal convictions, simple possibilities, are presented as if they were proofs, or at least valid arguments in favor of the theory" (repeating an evaluation made by De Quatrefages). Thompson adds:

> As an example De Quatrefages cited Darwin's explanation of the manner in which the titmouse might become transformed into the nut-

1. *Op. cit.,* viii.

cracker, by the accumulation of small changes in structure and instinct owing to the effect of natural selection; and then proceeded to show that is is just as easy to transform the nutcracker into the titmouse. The demonstration can be modified without difficulty to fit any conceivable case. It is without scientific value since it cannot be verified, but since the imagination has free rein, it is easy to convey the impression that a concrete example of real transmutation has been given. This is the more appealing because of the extreme fundamental simplicity of the Darwinian explanation. . . . This was certainly a major reason for the success of the *Origin*. Another is the elusive character of the Darwinian argument. Every characteristic of organisms is maintained in existence because it has survival value. But this value relates to the struggle for existence. Therefore we are not obliged to commit ourselves in regard to the meaning of differences between individuals or species since the possessor of a particular modification may be, in the race for life, moving up or falling behind. On the other hand, we can commit ourselves if we like, since it is impossible to disprove our statement. The plausibility of the argument eliminates the need for proof and its very nature gives it a kind of immunity to disproof. Darwin did not show in the *Origin* that species had originated by natural selection; he merely showed, on the basis of certain facts and assumptions, how this might have happened, and as he convinced himself he was able to convince others.[1]

One is reminded, in this connection, of a similar begging of the question, namely, as paleontologists use the alleged ascending levels of the geological map of earth to validate their theory of tho alleged ascending levels of fossil remains, so the geologists profess to establish their alleged ascending levels, as given in the geological map, by the time clock provided by the paleontologists. Surely this is a case of backscratching *par excellence!* One is reminded of Mark Twain's whimsical remark that "there is something so fascinating about science: one gets such wholesale returns of conjecture out of such trifling investments of fact."

6. On the subject of mutations, Thompson writes as follows: "As Emile Guyenot has said, mutations are powerless to explain the general adaptation which is the basis of organization. 'It is impossible to produce the world of life where the dominant note is functional organization, correlated variation and progression, from a series of random events.' "[2]

I should like to interpolate here a few personal statements as follows: An outstanding example of the downright fanatical zeal with which early exponents seized upon Darwin's theory and blowed it up to such fanatastic extremes (notably, by means of the intellectual vacillations of the erratic T. H. Huxley, the semantic pomposity of the agnostic Herbert Spencer, etc.) is the "tree of life" as hypothesized by the arrogant German,

1. *Op. Cit.*, xi.
2. *Ibid.*, xiii.

543

Haeckel). Haeckel presumed to arrange existing forms in an ascending scale from the simple to the complex, by arbitrarily inserting imaginary names to identify all the necessarily numerous "missing links." Today, Haeckel's famous "tree" is largely famous, even in the scientific world, for its absurdities.

7. Dr. Thompson concludes his Preface with what is obviously the most telling of all criticisms of the theory of evolution, as follows:

A long-enduring and regrettable effect of the *Origin* was the addiction of biologists to unverifiable speculation [the net result of which was that] the success of Darwinism was accompanied by *a decline in scientific integrity.* This is already evident in the reckless statements of Haeckel, and in the shifting, devious, and histrionic argumentaton of T. H. Huxley. A striking example, which has only recently come to light, is the alteration of the Piltdown skull so that it could be used as evidence of the descent of man from the apes; but even before this a similar instance of tinkering with the evidence was finally revealed by the discoverer of Pithecanthropus, who admitted many years after his sensational report, that he had found in the same deposits bones that are definitely human. Though these facts are now well known, a work published in 1943 still accepts the diagnosis of Pithecanthropus given by Dubois, as a creature with a femur of human form permitting an erect posture. Not long ago (1947), an exhibit in London, designed for public instruction, presented human development in such a way as to insinuate the truth of the "biogenetic law"; and in the same exhibit were problematic reconstructions indicating the descent of man and including the Piltdown type.[1]

Finally, Dr. Thompson's conclusions, as follows:

It may be said, and the most orthodox theologians indeed hold, that God controls and guides even the events due to chance; but this proposition the Darwinians emphatically reject, and it is clear that in the *Origin* evolution is presented as an essentially undirected process. For the majority of readers, therefore, the *Origin* effectively dissipated the evidence of providential control. It might be said that this was their own fault. Nevertheless, the failure of Darwin and his successors to attempt an equitable assessment of the religious issues at stake indicates a regrettable obtuseness and lack of responsibility. Furthermore, on the purely philosophical plane, the Darwinian doctrine of evolution involves some difficulties which Darwin and Huxley were unable to appreciate. [I might well add that their devoted disciples in our day seem to have closed minds on the same matters.] *Between the organism that simply lives, the organism that lives and feels, and the organism that lives, feels, and reasons, there are, in the opinion of respectable philosophers, abrupt transitions corresponding to an ascent in the scale of being, and they hold that the agencies of the material world cannot produce transitions of this kind.* . . . Biologists still agree on the separation of plants and animals, but the idea that man and animals differ only in degree is now so general among them, that even psychologists no longer attempt to use words like "reason" or "intelligence" in an exact sense. This tendency to eliminate, by means of unverifiable speculations, the

1. *Op. cit.,* xii.

limits of the categories Nature presents to us, is an inheritance of biology from the *Origin of Species*.[1]

One is reminded here of the argument put forward (by Huxley, I think it was) in earlier days, when evolutionism was filling the mental and spiritual atmosphere of our world with paeans to Darwin and Darwinism, that if six monkeys were set to strum at random on typewriters for millions of millions of years they would be bound in time to write all the books in the British Museum.[2] Surely it requires a greater exercise of faith to give credence to this supposition, than is required for belief in God. Of similar grandiose character is Herbert Spencer's definition of evolution as "an integration of matter and concomitant dissipation of motion; during which the matter passes from an indefinite, incoherent, homogeneity to a definite, coherent, heterogeneity; and during which the retained motion undergoes a parallel transformation." (One is reminded of Oliver Goldsmith's statement to the eminent Dr. Johnson, "You make your fishes talk like whales.")

8. There are scientists, as we have noted above, who, even though adhering to the concept of what they call "pure science," according to which "supernatural creation is the denial of scientific intelligibility," still reject, or at least hold questionable, the claims of evolutionism. However, *there are many scientists who reject evolutionism outright for the Biblical doctrine of creation*, commonly known as *creationism*. Many of these men are active in the work of the Creation Research Society (Ann Arbor, Michigan), others in the Bible-Science Association (Caldwell, Idaho). (One of the outstanding publications of the latter is the book (320 pages) by Dr. A. E. Wilder Smith, *Man's Origin, Man's Destiny*.) Those who would try to underscore the impression that all the brains of mankind are on the side of the evolutionists are simply begging the question: that is to say, the burden of proof is on them, not on those who oppose them.

9. The words "evolution" and "evolutionism" are two of the most ambiguous words in our language. "Evolution" means literally "unrolling," "unfolding," etc. As used originally, the term had reference only to the *origin of species*: its use was confined to biological science. Since Darwin's time, however, it has become a yardstick for analyzing and tracing chronologically every cosmical, biological, sociological, and even theological,

1. *Op. cit.*, xxiii, xxiv.
2. Sir James Jeans, *The Mysterious Universe*, 4.

development in the history of humankind. As G. T. W. Patrick
puts it—

> The fact is that evolution is a very much overworked word. At the
> close of the last century and in the beginning of this one, the idea of
> evolution held almost undisputed sway. It was extended far beyond its
> original application and applied quite universally. We began to hear of
> inorganic, cosmic, astral, geologic and atomic evolution. Even the "de-
> lirious electrons" evolved into atoms, and matter itself was a process
> of development. Social evolution had already made its appearance, and
> we learned that the new law applied also to the development of language,
> ideas, beliefs, the family, the church and the state, and to social and
> political institutions. In fact, in those days of first enthusiasms it oc-
> curred to no one that there is any realm of reality at all excluded from
> the field of evolution. Nothing is fixed or final; nothing is created;
> everything just grew and is growing.[1]

Hence, in recent years we have books with such titles as *Stellar
Evolution, From Atoms to Stars, Biography of the Earth,* and
numerous published articles of the same general trend of thought.
Nowhere, perhaps, is this attempted universalization of the term
made more obvious than in the title of the book recently published (and made a required textbook in biology in various
public school systems), *From Molecules to Man.* In all such
evolution is presented *as a fact,* and *dogmatically* presented as
a fact.

In this connection, we recall Herbert Spencer's "cultural
evolution" theory, namely, that all cultures have moved "forward" or "upward" from *savagery* through *barbarism* to *civilization.* This idea has long been abandoned by anthropologists
and sociologists alike. Hegel came forward with his theory of the
course of history, namely, that it is not just the process by which
man comes to a consciousness of God and of the world around
him, but that it is the process as well by which Spirit (Universal
Reason, God) the Absolute comes to a consciousness of Himself;
all this by means of *reported sequences of thesis, antithesis, and
synthesis, each synthesis becoming in turn a sort of progressive
thesis.* This means, in short, that the space-time continuum is
God in the process of fully realizing Himself; and as this process
of Self-realization becomes incorporated into rational human
experience, it becomes known in the physical world as Nature
and in the moral world as History. Again, the evolution yardstick has been, for a long time, applied to the history of religion.
It was contended that *animism* (the belief that everything is
"ensouled," that is, characterized by an inherent vitalizing power,
generally known as "spirit") was the first form of "religion";

1. Patrick, *Introduction to Philosophy,* Revised Edition, 144.

that, in time, animism gave way generally to *polytheism* (characterized by pantheons of anthropomorphic gods and goddesses, essentially personifications of natural forces); that polytheism was succeeded by *henotheism* (a pantheon with a single sovereign deity), which in turn gave way to *monotheism* (belief in one God who alone is deity). In other words, rather than God having created man in His own image, man has really created his gods or God in his own imagination. It is held further that monotheism will ultimately give way to *pantheism*, in which God is identified with Nature, the World, the Universe, the Cosmos, the Totality of Being. Thus any distinction between Creator and what is designated the Creation is eliminated. Pantheism is conceived to be, and presented as, a sophisticated "religion," hence the only system acceptable to the "intelligentsia" (whoever they may be). However, it is doubtful that this general theory is widely entertained in our day: there is too much evidence that monotheism has existed along with these other views, somewhere and in some form, from earliest times. Moreover, a dry-as-dust intellectualized cult, such as pure pantheism, or any other cult which ignores the personal "living" God, will never appeal generally to the aspirations, or satisfy the deeper needs, of the human spirit. (Some wag has remarked that if he were a pantheist, his first act of worship, on awaking from sleep each morning, would be that of turning to his pillow and kissing it fervently. We see here the folly of talking about worshiping "nature," when as a matter of fact nature as an entity does not even exist. We do not worship nature; rather, we worship the God of nature, for the fact remains that "the heavens declare the glory of God, and the firmament showeth his handiwork" (Ps. 19:1, cf. Rom. 1:20).

10. Implicit in the meaning of the word "evolution" as generally used is the idea of progression or "progressive development." The basis of this idea is the *a priori* concept that the historical order must coincide with a certain logical order in each case; that is to say, as applied by evolutionists, all change necessarily takes place from the simple to the more complex. In logic textbooks, this idea is now designated "the genetic fallacy." As stated in one such textbook:

> Our previous discussions ought to make it clear now that the facts of history cannot be deduced from logic alone, that factual data are needed to confirm or verify any speculation as to the past. This truth condemns all attempts current in the eighteenth century, and still widely popular, to reconstruct the history of mankind prior to any reliable records, on the basis of nothing but speculations as to what must have

been. The theories as to the origin of language or religion, or the original social contract by which government was instituted, which were based on empirically unsupported assumptions as to what "the first" or "primitive" man must have done, are all historically untenable. It is clearly a logical error or fallacy to assume that actual history can be so constructed or discovered. Not much different, however, are those speculative *a priori* histories which under the name of social evolution attempt to deduce the stages which all human institutions must go through and therefore actually have gone through. In all of these attempts to trace the history of the family, industry, the state, and the like, the earlier stages are assumed to have been simpler, and the later stages more complex.[1]

What better examples of this genetic fallacy could be offered than those which have prevailed for a century or more in the field of Biblical criticism? What better example *par excellence* could be suggested than the well-known—and archaeologically disproved —Documentary (Graf-Wellhausen) Theory of the Pentateuch? The *a priori* assumed correlation, chronologically, between the cultural background of the Abrahamic era and that of the Exilic and Post-Exilic periods has certainly been exploded by evidence from the diggings at Mari, Nuzi, Ugarit, etc. These diggings establish fully the fact that the cultural background that is portrayed in the book of Genesis is historically accurate.

Quoting again from the source immediately cited above, we read as follows:

It is an inexcusable error to identify the temporal order in which events have actually occurred with the logical order in which elements may be put together to constitute existing institutions. Actual recorded history shows growth in simplicity as well as in complexity. Modern English, for instance, is simpler as regards inflection than Old English, and our legal procedure became less complicated when the old forms of action were abolished. *A priori* evolutionists had no doubt that the matriarchal family must precede the patriarchal form, and that the nomad state of society must precede the agricultural form. This, however, cannot prevent an actual Indian tribe from changing from the patriarchal to the matriarchal form. Nor can it prevent the Peruvians from skipping the nomad stage because the western slopes of the Andes could not provide them with sufficient cattle to serve as a basis of social organization. Indeed, the supposed law of development from the simple to the complex is too vague to induce us to deduce any specific historical events from it. That which seems simple in one state of knowledge or ignorance is seen to be more complex after increased knowledge or on closer examination. And many things bewilderingly complex at first become simpler to us after systematic study. Genetic accounts or theories which attract us by their *a priori* plausibility thus cease to do so when we discriminate between the intelligible and the temporal order, when we subject theories of what actually happened to the test of verifiability. The converse error is the supposition that an actual history of any science, art, or social institution can take the place of a logical analysis of its structure. When anything grows by additions

1. Cohen and Nagel, *An Introduction to Logic and Scientific Method*, 389.

or accretions, a knowledge of the order of such successive additions is a clue to the constitution of the final result. But not all growth is of that form. Science, for instance, as well as art and certain social organizations, is sometimes deliberately changed according to some idea or pattern to which previous existence is not relevant.[1]

11. Again, evolutionists—and scientists generally—are prone to commit the fallacy of *over-simplification*. This is a fallacy which usually attends the inductive (scientific) method. It is also known as the "nothing but" fallacy. For example, "Thought is nothing but the activity of brain cells." "Thinking is nothing but sub-vocal conditioning" (according to John B. Watson). "Man is nothing but a biological entity." Evolutionists commit this fallacy in making no effort to account for the *modus operandi* of the many leaps occurring in the alleged evolutionary process (as Thompson states it, leaps from "the organism that simply lives" to "the organism that lives and feels" to "the organism that lives and feels and reasons"). They simply take for granted that these are matters of degree, although they have no evidence beyond the realm of inference to prove it. These gaps which serve to put in bold outlines the ascending levels in the total hierarchy of being, at which, according to some philosophers, new increments of power are infused into the ongoing (upward-moving) total process. D. Elton Trueblood speaks of this hierarchical character, which Aristotle envisioned in his *De Anima*, as that of "radical discontinuity." This characteristic is surely emphasized in the Genesis narrative of the Creation. (We have taken note of this hierarchical character of the totality of being already, in Part Three above.)

12. Evolutionists, we repeat for the sake of emphasis, simply take it for granted that these "radical discontinuities" in the ascending scale of being are matters of *degree*, and not matters of *kind*. (The notion of the totality of being as a continuum was put forward in early modern times in the famous doctrine of the Great Chain of Being. According to this view our world being the handiwork of a perfect Creator must be "the best of all possible worlds"; hence, again reasoning *a priori*, all possible entities must be actualized, all possible places filled, therein: there must be an unbroken continuity—a progressive gradation —of organisms, from the very lowest living being up to the very highest, God Himself. As stated by Alexander Pope ("Essay on Man"):

Of systems possible if 'tis confest
That wisdom infinite must form the best,

1. *Op Cit.*, 389, 390.

then

> ... all must full or not coherent be,
> And all that rises, rise in due degree.

The complete picture is as follows:

> Vast chain of being! which from God began,
> Natures aethereal, human, angel, man,
> Beast, bird, fish, insect, what no eye can see,
> No glass can reach; from Infinite to thee,
> From thee to nothing.—On superior pow'rs
> Were we to press, inferior might on ours;
> Or in the full creation leave a void,
> Where, one step broken, the great scale's destroyed;
> For Nature's chain whatever link you strike,
> Tenth, or ten thousandth, breaks the chain alike.

Thus it will be seen that this imaginative, poetic portrayal of the Weltanschauung parallels the evolutionary picture, but in so doing points up the utter futility of any human effort to search out and specify the almost innumerable links in the so-called "Great Chain." Far more sensible it is to accept the hierarchical picture which, obviously, is in accord with Scripture, experience the fact.)

In simple truth, evolutionists have no explanation of the leap from an existing species to a new species, except—to a certain extent, possibly—by mutations, and these, of course, themselves need to be explained. As Chesterton writes:

Far away in some strange constellation, in skies infinitely remote, there is a small star, which astronomers may some day discover. . . . It is a star which brings forth out of itself very strange plants and very strange animals and none stranger than the men of science. . . . Most modern histories of mankind begin with the word evolution, and with a rather wordy exposition of evolution. . . . There is something slow and soothing and gradual about the word and even about the idea. As a matter of fact, it is not, touching primary things, a very practical word or a very profitable idea. Nobody can imagine how nothing could turn into something else. It is really far more logical to start by saying, "In the beginning God created heaven and earth" even if you only mean "In the beginning some unthinkable power began some unthinkable process." For God is by s nature a name of mystery, and nobody ever supposed that a man cou. imagine how a world was created any more than he could create one. But evolution really is mistaken for explanation. It has the fatal quality of leaving on many minds the impression that they do understand it and everything else; just as many of them live under a sort of illusion that they have read the *Origin of Species*. But this notion of something smooth and slow, like the ascent of a slope, is a great part of the illusion. It is illogicality as well as an illusion; for slowness has nothing to do with the question. An event is not any more intrinsically intelligible or unintelligible because of the pace at which it moves. For a man who does not believe in a miracle, a slow miracle would be just as incredible as a swift one. The Greek witch may have turned sailors to swine with a stroke of the wand. But to see a naval gentleman of our acquaintance looking a little more like a pig every day, till he ended with four trotters and a curly tail, would not be any more soothing. It might be rather more creepy and uncanny. The medieval wizard may have flown through the air from the top of a tower, but to see an old gentleman walking through the air, in a leisurely and lounging manner, would still seem to call for some explanation. Yet there runs through all the rationalistic treatment of history this curious and confused idea that difficulty is avoided, or even mystery eliminated, by dwelling on mere delay or on something dilatory in the processes of things. . . . the question here is the false atmosphere of facility and ease given by the mere suggestion of going slow; the sort of comfort that might be given to a nervous old woman traveling for the first time in a motor car. . . . What we know, in a sense which we know nothing else, is that the trees and grass [of our world] did grow and that a number of extraordinary things do in fact happen; that queer creatures support themselves in the empty air by beating it with fans of various fantastic shapes; that other queer creatures steer themselves about alive under a load of mighty waters; that other queer creatures walk about on four legs, and that the queerest creature of all walks about on two. These are things and not theories; and compared with them evolution and the atom and even the solar system are merely theories. The matter here is one of history and not of philosophy; so that it need only be noted that no philosopher denies that a mystery still attaches to the two great transitions: the origin of the universe itself and the origin of the principle of life itself. Most philosophers have the enlightenment to add that a third mystery attaches to the origin of man himself. In other words a third bridge was built across a third abyss of the unthinkable when there came into the world what we call reason and what we call will. *Man is not merely an evolution but rather a revolution.* That he has a backbone or other parts upon a similar pattern to birds and fishes is an obvious fact, whatever be the meaning of the fact. But if we attempt to regard him, as it were, as a quadruped standing on his hind legs, we shall find what follows far more fantastic and subversive than if he were standing on his head. . . . Above all, this illustrates what I mean by saying that the more we really look at man as an animal, the less he will look like one.[1]

13. The foregoing excerpt brings out in bold relief another common fallacy of "the scientific method," namely, the *sub rosa* assumption that *to name something is to explain it.* Take *mutations,* for example: what are they? Etymologically, the word, from the Latin, *muto, mutare,* means simply *to change,* i.e., in form, characteristics, powers, etc. In evolutionism, mutations are sudden variations, "long jumps" in the alleged life process, from species to species. Still and all, the name does not give us any thorough explanation of the process itself. Dr. Tsanoff writes: "The theory of mutations, as developed and interpreted by careful geneticists, has reached specific conclusions regarding the evolutionary results of changes in the germ plasm. But the larger pattern of evolutionary cosmology can scarcely be regarded as ascertained."[2] Take the term *protoplasm;* what is

1. Chesterton, *The Everlasting Man,* 21-25.
2. Tsanoff, *The Great Philosophers,* 567.

protoplasm? *First living substance*, of course. But what is this *first living substance*, literally, first matter to be *moulded*? Who knows? Has protoplasm ever been "broken down" in the laboratory? And what is *protoplasmic irritability*? In all these cases one is reminded of John Locke's definition of matter as "something-I-know-not-what." All these words are names which serve for identification, but as for explanation they certainly fall short. *A great need of scientists in our day and age are the disciplines of logic and metaphysics.*

14. Evolutionism requires *an almost unlimited stretch of time to account for all the developments envisioned by the theory.* Apparently, its advocates expect us to accept without question the necessity of such an extent of time to any adequate explanation of the process, and at the same time they arbitrarily use this hypothetical extent of time to support their theory of the process. Is not this a form of begging the question, another case of theoretical backscratching? Is it not true that the stretch of time required by the theory puts it beyond any likelihood of clear proof—and even disproof—*empirically*, that is, by the testimony of eye-witnesses? One is reminded here of Hilaire Belloc's "Ode to a Microbe"—

> The Microbe is so very small
> You cannot make him out at all,
> But many sanguine people hope
> To see him through a microscope,
> His jointed tongue that lies beneath
> A hundred curious rows of teeth;
> His seven tufted tails with lots
> Of lovely pink and purple spots,
> On each of which a pattern stands,
> Composed of forty separate bands;
> His eyebrows of a tender green;
> All these have never yet been seen—
> But Scientists, who ought to know,
> Assure us that they must be so . . .
> Oh! let us never, never doubt
> What nobody is sure about![1]

*It must be realized, in this connection, that Time is not a Creator. In evolutionism, time becomes a factotum to be used in whatever way possible to give substance to the general hypothesis.*

15. As stated heretofore, the term "evolution" in common parlance means simply development, progression, etc., in terms of a sequence. Progression, however, is not always easy to define. I might line up a wheelbarrow, a gig, a buggy, a wagon, an

1. Belloc, *More Beasts for Worse Children*, in *Cautionary Verses.* (Knopf, 1951).

automobile, and even an airplane, in a single row side by side. There would be some structural resemblance, of course. But we know, in this case, that one of these vehicles is not the outgrowth ("emergent") of that type which preceded it; we know, rather, that all of them were products alike of human technology, inventions of the human intelligence. We know also that as a sequence they spell progression; this progression, obviously, is distinct from that kind of progression which is brought about by the operation of *resident* forces characteristic of the different levels of being. However, "evolution" is often used to signify a going forward, a development, a progression, that is not "emergent" in any sense of the term. Hence, we speak of the evolution of political systems, of social organization, of the science of medicine, of technology, of ethics and law, etc. But the evolution that has been in vogue from the beginning in biological science is that which is defined by LeConte as *"continuous progressive change, according to fixed laws, by means of resident forces."* This is the evolution which we are considering here. (Note the full import here of the word, "resident.") As a matter of fact the "time" element works against "progressiveism," that is to say, "increased time spans in biological systems will merely increase the probability of equilibrium being set up and not the probability of improbable reaction products being formed." "As infinite time is approached, infinite randomness will be achieved, namely, complete lack of order." In a word, time does not provide the possibility for the occurrence of the highly improbable. (*Vide* Harold F. Blum, *Time's Arrows and Evolution*, 178A).

16. Obviously, theories of this type, that is, as related to the traditional LeContian definition, are based on the assumption that all so-called progressive change (by means of *resident forces*) is fortuitous, that is occurring by "accident" or by "chance" (purposelessness); hence, they are commonly designated "materialistic" or "mechanistic" theories. This writer finds it difficult to accept the notion that a movement can be repeatedly "progressive" and at the same time "fortuitous." Surely, we have here a semantic paradox, to say the least! (The same is true of the phrase "natural selection." Selectivity surely connotes, presupposes, deliberation and choice; how, then, can impersonal "nature" rightly be said to "select" anything?) However, it is a characteristic of the devotees of evolutionism to indulge "double talk," perhaps unwittingly at times, in their use of terminology. (Again, we call attention to the great need for

the disciplines of logic and metaphysics in the formulation of scientific theory.)

17. Theories of what is called "emergent evolution" tend to the *organismic,* rather than the *mechanistic,* explanation of the various facets of the life process. (We have presented the claims of *emergentism, holism,* etc., in preceding sections of this work; however, we shall briefly restate a few of the facts about this view.) Emergentism is the theory that, in general, evolution is a naturalistic process proceeding from the operation of resident, yet essentially vitalistic, force or forces; that each "emergent" has a different structure with additional properties, and its own behavior patterns; that each "emergent" not only has subsistence *per se* (that is, after "emerging"), but also acts as a causal agency, a transmitter of effects. Moreover, it is said to be beyond the ability of human intelligence to know how many levels of "emergence" there may be or may yet come to be. If one should ask what it is that causes these "emergents" to "emerge," the answer is that a *nisus* or pull does it. The theory of some members of this school is that the pull is exerted by "whatever lies ahead." But it is difficult to understand just how "whatever lies ahead" actually exists in order to exert a pull, when according to the theory it is in the process of being actualized (or should we say, of actualizing itself?). If "God" is envisioned as the Ultimate "Emergent"—the Goal of the Process—as seems to be implicit in the Hegelian theory of the Absolute—then God is, in terms of the theory, in the indeterminable and indeed interminable process of becoming God. Hence, other advocates of the theory indentify the nisus with a push—an impulsion—from within. Be that as it may, in either case, God is presented to us as engaged in the age-long cosmic business of Becoming, not Himself, but Itself. Emergentism is pantheistic: its "God" is either "nature" as a whole, or an impersonal process operating in "nature." (Cf. the philosophical system known as "Holism." According to this system, the Creative Process—that is, Evolution—stabilizes being in successively more complex *wholes* (the atom, the cell, etc.,), of which the most advanced and most complex is the person or personality.[1] Holism is a form of Emergentism.)

On the basis of the inclusion of human intelligence in evolution, as playing, perhaps, the most important role in the process, advocates of the theory in our day take the position generally

1. J. C. Smuts, *Holism and Evolution,* 261-262.

that *societal* (or psychological) evolution has superseded in large measure what has heretofore been known as organic (biological) evolution. (For a clear presentation of this view, see the book, *Human Destiny*, by Lecomte du Nouy; also the concluding chapters of the Mentor books, *The Meaning of Evolution*, by George G. Simpson, and *Evolution in Action*, by Julian Huxley; and especially the books by Pierre Teilhard de Chardin, *The Phenomenon of Man* and *The Future of Man*. See Bibliography *infra*.) Teilhard envisions evolution through a gradation of forms from atomic particles to human beings, in ever increasing complexity of structure, and along with it, development of consciousness (a kind of *panpsychism*). Man is the focal point in whom all facets of the evolutionary process converge, and in man reflective thought finally emerges. The unique idea in Teilhard's system is his view that the ultimate reality of this cosmic development (that is, of evolution) is the incarnate Christ (not the "superman" of Nietzche, nor that of Samuel Butler, nor that of G. B. Shaw's *Man and Superman* or his *Back to Methuselah*, but the God-Man.) Two quotations from this writer are pertinent: "The only universe capable of containing the human person is an irrevocably 'personalizing' universe." Again, "In one manner or the other, it still remains true that, even in the view of the mere biologist, the human epic resembles nothing so much as a way of the Cross."[1] This, to be sure, is another—and more profound—theory of emergentism. Like that of Bergson's *creative evolution* (described below), this is an honest effort to describe the *modus operandi* of the alleged evolutionary process, which in the last analysis becomes an effort to describe the indescribable —the ineffable. *The mystery of the life movement itself is too profound to yield its secrets to the mere human intellect.*

18. *The Mystery of the Life Movement.* Evolution is desribed as *continuous progressive change, according to fixed laws, by means of resident forces.* The word "evolution" designates the *process*; "evolutionism," however, designates *how the process proceeds,* that is, the phenomena that are said to *actualize* it, in Aristotelian terms, the *efficient causality* of it. These are usually listed as follows: (1) Lamarck (1744-1829): the *transmission of characteristics (modifications) acquired through the interaction of the organism and its environment.* This theory is now generally rejected, except by the Russian biologist, Lysenko, who has been all but canonized by the Kremlin oligarchy for his

1. Teilhard de Chardin, *The Phenomenon of Man*, 290-311.

revival of it. (2) Charles Darwin (1809-1882), getting his cue from Malthus's *Essay on Population* (the thesis of which was that because population increases in geometrical proportion, whereas the earth's resources multiply only in arithmetical proportion, the time will come when the earth will not be able to provide food for its population, unless some selective process removes the surplus), proposed the theory of evolution by *natural selection*. The process of struggle for existence, Darwin held, selects out and preserves only those organisms which prove to be the most capable of adapting to environment (the doctrine of *the survival of the fittest*, that is, the fittest to demonstrate survival quality by adaptation). Incidentally, Darwin's contemporary, Alfred Russel Wallace (1823-1913) had arrived at the natural selection theory even before Darwin, but Darwin happened to beat him into print. (They were always good friends, however.) Wallace pointed out the fact to Darwin that while natural selection might account for the survival of an existing species, *it did not account for the arrival of new species.* (3) August Weismann (1844-1914) contended that the explanation of evolution lies in *the continuity of the germ-plasm.* It seems obvious, however, that only process and form (the form being, e.g., in man's case, that which specifies man as man) can be transmitted from generation to generation through the germ-plasm; Germ-cells are affected, it seems, only by variations of mutations in themselves, and not by what goes on in the life of the parent. (Still and all, it seems incontrovertible that any modification in the parent organism is transmissible only through the chromosomes and genes. Moreover, genes are but hypothetical "determiners" of heredity operating beyond the world of sense-perception. (4) Mutations, discovered by the Dutch botanist De Vries (1848-1935) are sudden big leaps to new species which are said to breed true *per se*. It is commonly held that evolution might have proceeded by these abrupt and relatively permanent germinal changes rather than by slight variations. (There are some, however, who contend that mutations might have come about through slowly accumulating changes in the genes. To this writer's thinking mutations are indispensable to any possible validation of the evolution theory. Moreover, mutations have all the appearance of special creations. (This brings us back to the discussion of the "radical discontinuities" which make themselves manifest in the *hierarchical* interpretation of the totality of being, and the view that at different stages in the Creative Process, God infused into it new increments of force, that is, new and distinct powers, by direct action, thus bringing into existence the successively higher levels characterized by energy-matter, life, consciousness, and self-consciousness, in the order named. According to this view, Creation involved *new increments of power plus continuity of plan.* (See again material presented in Part Three of the present work. Cf. also the title of the well-known book by Hoernle, *Matter, Life, Mind and God.*) (5) The "laws" of heredity as first formulated by the Austrian monk and botanist, Gregor Mendel (1824-1884) are believed to play a significant role also in the alleged evolutionary process. (6) Protagonists of the theory in our day are inclined to agree that evolution may have proceeded in all these ways, with the sole exception of the Lamarckian notion of the inheritance of acquired characteristics. However, *the phenomena characterizing this life movement leave the very essence of the movement, the power that produces it and causes it to surge forward, as the theory demands, still unaccounted for.*

19. Under the evolution hypothesis there are two rather significant views of the movement of the process, as follows: (1) What is called *orthogenesis,* that is, "straight line" evolution (of which the poetic version is that of the "Great Chain of Being"). This is the view that variation in successive generations of a succession of parents and offspring follows a specific line of development, finally undeviatingly evolving a new type. The classic example is that of the very ancient and small "eohippus" which by gradual, step-by-step change is said to have evolved in the horse that we know today. This is also known as the theory of "determinate variation." (2) There is also the view of what might properly be called *fountainlike evolution.* This is the doctrine of the late French philosopher, Henri Bergson (1859-1941). Bergson's thesis is that the phenomena envisoned by evolutionism do not explain evolution, that is, the life movement itself; that this surge upward of the what might be called the core of the Creative Process is explainable only as the Elan Vital (Life Force). In Bergson's thought the Elan Vital is the primordial cosmic principle, the ground of all being, that is at the very root of evolution, a vital push or impulsion "pervading matter, insinuating itself into it, overcoming its inertia and resistance, determining the direction of evolution as well as evolution itself."[1] This never-ceasing free activity is Life itself. Indeed Bergson speaks of it as "Spirit," as a directing Consciousness as

1. Bergson, *Creative Evolution.*

557

well as an actualizing Power. The unique aspect of this view is Bergson's picture of Life Force operating like a fountain, so to speak, with a center "from which worlds shoot out like rockets in a fireworks display," "as a series of jets gushing out from the immense reservoir of life." We must be careful, however, not to think of this center as a "thing"—we must think of it only as a process. Moreover, as the core-movement pushes upward, according to Bergson's theory, the push encounters resistance by the matter on which it works; hence, there is a falling back toward gross matter by the residue that is left behind by the progressive push of Life toward fulness of being. According to this theory, the Elan Vital manifests itself in the lower animals in the form of *instinct;* it manifests itself in man in the form of *intelligence* (intellection), the power that enables him to surge upward through learning by trial-and-error; it will ultimately push on to what Bergson calls *intuition* in man, which will be immediacy in man's apprehension of truth, corresponding in a way, but on a much higher level, to the immediacy of the brute's response to sensory stimuli. Bergson envisions nothing beyond this power of intuition. (It would seem indeed that what we have learned in recent years about the phenomena of the subconscious in man constitutes a genuine prognosis of Bergson's theory of human intuition. See *supra,* Part Two, Section 6.) Of course this fountainlike description of the movement of evolution, allowing for both progression and retrogression, is another theory of emergentism. (One of my science professors remarked to me once that to him evolution simply meant variation, and variation either upward or downward. This is approximately Bergson's view.)

20. *Alleged Evidence for Evolutionism.* The evidence generally cited by evolutionists to support their theory may be summarized as follows: (1) *Comparative anatomy,* or structural resemblance among species. (But to what extent does structural resemblance necessarily prove emergence? Could it not be interpreted as supporting the view that a Creative Intelligence simply used the same general pattern in creating living species?) (1) *Embryology:* the embryos of different animal species tend to similar development in early stages. Those of lower animals are said to cease developing at certain points; those of higher animals move upward through additional stages of development. Ontogeny is said to recapitulate phylogeny; that is, each individual organism of a certain phylum tends to recapitulate stages through which its ancestors have passed in their racial history.

(The idea is seriously questioned today by many biologists.) (3) *Serology*: the blood composition of higher animals is the same. Samples of blood from closely related higher animals can be mixed, whereas an antagonistic reaction sets in if there is wide separation between the species. (4) *Vestigial remains*: the presence of unused organs. Usually cited in this category are the appendix in man, degenerate eyes in cave animals, wings of the female gypsy moth, etc. (5) *Geographical distribution of animals*: arrested development of flora and fauna in areas cut off in prehistoric times from continental land masses. The classic example of this are the marsupials of Australia. (Yet the opossum, whose only natural habitat is America, is a marsupial.) (6) *Paleontology*: correlation of the ascending scale of the simple to the more complex of fossil forms with successively earlier to later geological strata. (Thus geologists rely on the evidence of paleontology to support historical geology, and the paleontologists cite the evidence of geology to support their chronology of fossil remains. This, some wag has remarked, borrowing from the comic strips of the nineteen-twenties, is a kind of Alphonse-and-Gaston stunt.) (7) *Artificial selection.* That is, changes brought about by selective breeding, by the application of human intelligence; for example, by Mendel, Burbank, and others. This, it is claimed, adds momentum to the whole process. (8) *Classification of animals* in phyla, classes, genera, species, orders, families, etc., in ascending order of complexity, from unicellular organisms up to man.

21. *Materialistic Evolutionism.* This is the world-view that all things have "evolved" by accident or chance (that is, *purposelessness*). Devotees of this cult simply refuse to recognize Efficient Causality of any kind in the origin and preservation of the cosmos (with the sole exception of some form or forms of primal physical energy); they rest their case on the eternity of matter-in-motion. (Obviously, then, this primal physical energy is their "god.") With disarming simplicity they proceed to describe all phenomena of the cosmos, including those of the life processes and of the thought processes, in terms of a "fortuitous concourse of atoms" (or sub-atomic forces). The *credo* of the materialistic evolutionists is bluntly stated in what rightly may be designated their "Bible," namely, the book by George Gaylord Simpson, *The Meaning of Evolution.* Simpson writes:

In preceding pages evidence was given, thoroughly conclusive, as I believe, that organic evolution is a process entirely materialistic in its origin and operation. . . . It has also been shown that purpose and plan are not characteristic of organic evolution and are not a key to any of its operations. . . . Man was certainly not the goal of evolution, which had no goal. [He goes on to say, however, that with the entrance of the human mind into the process, purpose and plan did come into operation: this he designates "the new evolution"]

[He continues]: But purpose and plan are characteristic in the new evolution, because man has purposes, and he makes plans. Here purpose and plan do definitely enter into evolution, as a result and not as a cause of the processes seen in the long history of life. The purposes and plans are ours, not those of the universe, which displays convincing evidence of their absence.[1]

It is difficult to see how an intelligent man could make such a fatuous statement, especially in view of the *fact* of the *mathematical preciseness* that characterizes the processes of that which we call "nature," and *without which no science could ever be formulated. Any man who denies efficient causality destroys science, and even the possibility of science.* We are reminded here of a statement by the late British philosopher, C. D. Broad, to the effect that the theory of determinism (denial of any freedom of choice) is so absurd that only a very learned man could ever have cojured it up. (Small wonder that materialists prefer to be known by a more felicitous name, such as "naturalist" or "humanist"!)

As stated heretofore, materialistic evolution is usually described as "mechanistic." The word "mechanism," however, has a question-begging aspect. Machines are contrivances, but as far as human experience goes, they are contrivances of some intelligent agent to serve some function, to gain some end. Moreover, anyone who insists that the cosmos is just a great machine, is simply reading into his understanding of it the properties and powers *that he himself sees in a machine.* (Is not this another case of anthropomorphism?) Now it seems obvious that in an organization of any kind an organizing agency is required: some power by which elements are organized into wholes of being; some power to marshal them into a cosmos or world order. This, moreover, would have to be some kind of power that is entirely different from mechanical forces, and the opposite of gravitational force; gravitational force tends to drag the physical world down to a "heat-death," which is technically defined as a state of "maximum entropy." (The physicists tell us that the cosmic clock, so to speak, is running down as matter continues to dissolve into radiation and energy continues to be dissipated into empty space.) However, the basic thesis of evolutionism is progression or progressive development; and

1. Simpson, *op cit.*, 143.

progression is precisely the aspect that is of importance to it. But progression implies a goal to which the movement is directed, toward which someone or something is striving, and thus the idea of progression belies the concept of mechanism. Obviously, "mechanism" and "evolution" are irreconcilable terms. As Bishop Butler has written, in his famous *Analogy*:

> The only distinct meaning of the word "natural" is *stated, fixed,* or *settled*: since what is natural as much requires and presupposes an intelligent agent to render it so, *i.e.*, to effect it continually or at stated times, as what is supernatural or miraculous does to effect it for once.[1]

In a word, with respect to what are called "the laws of nature," we should not say, "the more law, the less God," but we should say, "the more law, the more God." LaPlace once declared that he had swept the heavens with his telescope and could not find a God anywhere. One of his contemporaries remarked that "he might just as well have swept his kitchen with a broom." Because God is not corporeal in any sense (Exo. 3:14, John 4:24); He is not to be apprehended by any physical or corporeal means (John 1:18). Hence the stupidity of the Russian astronaut who is reported to have said that in all his travels throughout the celestial realm he had seearched the stratosphere in every direction to find God but had failed to do so. Of course he failed— the humblest, most secularly-uneducated student of the Bible knows why.

Of course, the Christian cannot possibly accept materialistic evolutionism, because it directly contradicts the Biblical doctrines of the eternal purpose and sovereignty of God. (Cf. Isa. 46:-11; Acts 15:8, 17:30-31; 1 Cor. 15:20-28; Eph. 3:8-12). Nor is there any good reason why any Christian, or any other intelligent person, should accept it, for several reasons. In the first place, any unbiased person can readily see that the phenomena of personality (perception, consciousness, and especially *meaning*) are not entirely reducible, if reducible at all, to "matter-in-motion" (brain cell activity). As the noted physicist, Sir Arthur Eddington, has written:

> Force, energy, dimensions belong to the world of symbols: it is out of such conceptions that we have built up the external world of physics. . . . We have to build the spiritual world out of symbols taken from our own personality, as we build the scientific world out of the symbols of the mathematician.[2]

1. Butler, (Bishop) Joseph, *The Analogy of Religion Natural and Revealed*, Everyman's edition, 20-21.
2. Eddington, *Science and the Unseen World*, 82.

We recall here also the words of Professor Claude Tresmontant, who teaches the Philosophy of Science at the Sorbonne:

> The discoveries of modern science have made it easier to prove the existence of God than it used to be. Those who find no place for God in their philosophy must be prepared to affirm that mindless, inanimate matter has been able to organize itself, to become animated, and to endow itself with consciousness and thought. . . . If the material universe is to be regarded as the only reality, matter must be credited with all the attributes that theologians specify as belonging to God, including supreme intelligence, creative power, and eternal, autonomous existence.

When asked if the emergence of life could not be attributed purely to the laws of chance over a very long period of time, he replied:

> It may be theoretically possible, but mathematically it is so extremely improbable that only a few scientists now seriously think that pure chance can be put forward as an explanation of the emergence of even the simplest living organism.[1]

As Fred Emerson Brooks has written in his poem "The Grave Digger"—

> "If chance could fashion but one little flower
> With perfume for each tiny leaf,
> And furnish it with sunshine and with shower—
> Then chance would be Creator with the power
> To build a world for unbelief."

*Materialistic evolution simply cannot be harmonized with the empirical fact of cosmic order.* This order is clearly evident (1) from the mathematical relations characteristic of the processes of the physical world and the mathematical formulae by which they are amenable to precise description; (2) from the manifold interrelationships of ends and means, as empirically discerned, prevailing throughout the totality of being; (3) from the predetermined (planned) life cycles of all living species, and (4) from the over-all adaptation of nature to human life and its needs. Old Pythagoras was right when he declared that "things are numbers," that is to say, mathematical preciseness is the prime reality of the cosmos. When an astronomer, for instance, predicts the time of an eclipse and it fails to come off as predicted, he does not charge the failure to the movements of the heavenly bodies; no, indeed, he immediately turns to his figures to see where he has made a mistake in his calculations. Again, the atoms of one element are differentiated from those of the other elements by the *number* of protons in the nucleus

1. From "So You Are an Agnostic," Sar Shalom Publications, 236 W. 72nd St., New York, N. Y. 10023

and the corresponding number of electrons in the orbit (from one and one in the hydrogen atom up to 92 and 92 in the uranium atom). Similarly, the differentiation of living species is determined by the number of chromosomes in the reproductive male and female cells. Even the physical phenomenon of color is now found to be reducible to numerical terms, and that of sound as well, and the result is television video and audio. As stated often herein, the word *cosmos* means *order;* lacking this order, human science would be impossible, for the simple reason that science is man's discovery and description of the order prevailing in the various segments of the physical world. Surely this architectonic order presupposes a Supreme Orderer, a directing Mind and Will. *It is inconceivable that sheer chance could have produced the order we find all around us.* (The student is urged to read the little book (107 pages) by the eminent scientist, A. Cressy Morrison, *Man Does Not Stand Alone.*) The Morrison book, according to its author, is written to "challenge the conclusion of Julian Huxley in his book, *Man Stands Alone.*" Contrary to the usual and much over-worked theme of man's adaptation to nature, Morrison's thesis is that of *the amazing adaptation of nature to man.* His conclusions are as follows:

My purpose in this discussion of chance is to bring forcibly to the attention of the reader the fact that the purpose of this book is to point out clearly and scientifically the narrow limits within which any life can exist on earth, and prove by real evidence that all the nearly exact requirements of life could not be brought about on one planet at one time by chance. The size of the earth, the distance from the sun, the temperature and the life-giving rays of the sun, the thickness of the earth's crust, the quantity of water, the amount of carbon dioxide, the volume of nitrogen, the emergence of man and his survival—all point to order out of chaos, to design and purpose, and to the fact that, acording to the inexorable laws of mathematics, all these could not occur by chance simultaneously on one planet once in a billion times. It *could* so occur but it *did not so occur.* When the facts are so overwhelming, and when we recognize, as we must, the attributes of our minds which are not material, is it possible to flaunt the evidence and take the one chance in a billion that we and all else are the result of chance? We have found that there are 999,999,999 chances to one against a belief that all things happen by chance. Science will not deny the facts as stated; the mathematicians will agree that the figures are correct. Now we encounter the stubborn resistance of the human mind, which is reluctant to give up fixed ideas. The early Greeks knew the earth was a sphere, but it took two thousand years to convince men that this fact is true. New ideas encounter opposition, ridicule, and abuse, but truth survives and is verified.[1]

To be sure, in our day, evolutionists admit the introduction of purpose now that—as they contend—psychological evolution

1. *Op. cit.,* 99, 100.

has taken over from the biological. (We have noted this in the excerpt quoted above from Simpson's book.) Purpose entered the cosmic picture, we are told, along with the human intellect and its power of purposeful selection and striving. It strikes us, however, that by correlating purpose with *human mental activity*, by analogy we are bound to conclude that the design which prevails throughout the subhuman world points irrefutably to *another and superior kind of mental activity, that of the Creative intelligence and Will.* Man, obviously, does not create; he simply uses the material which he finds at hand to be used for his own purposes.

This is precisely the argument presented by the distinguished Professor of Philosophy at Earlham College, D. Elton Trueblood, who writes as follows, after first pointing up the fact of the kinship between mind and nature, and showing that this fact lies at the root of the very success of scientific achievement. He writes as follows:

Whatever our explanation of this correspondence, and it may be said in passing that the hypothesis of the existence of God, who is at once the Creator of the natural order and the Creator of man's mind, is a fully adequate explanation, there is no avoiding the fact that the kinship between mind and nature exists. This kinship is the chief basis of whatever success science achieves. *It is what we mean when we affirm the existence of an intelligible world.* The world, of course, is not now fully intelligible, and it may, for all we know, involve fundamentally irrational elements, but the history of science has been the elimination of many supposed irrationalities, which have finally been understood. The meaning of these observations becomes more apparent when we consider the significance of *explanation.*

Trueblood goes on to discuss the role of *purpose* in explanation:

A situation is never understood until we have some intimation of why it has occurred, and we never have an intimation of "why" until we come into contact with purpose. Purpose, in turn, is meaningless apart from a mind which entertains the purpose. Not only is purpose a self-explanatory principle; there is, so far as we are aware, no other. All other types of explanation leave fundamental questions unanswered. We go on asking "Why?" *in exactly the same way as before....* If a nail is being driven, we discover a set of secondary causes reaching all the way from the purpose of the carpenter to the completed process. The nail goes in *because* the hammer hits it. The hammer head moves *because* it is moved by the muscles of a man's arm. The arm muscles move *because* they are directed by nerve impulses. But the whole enterprise takes place *because* a man has a reason for driving a nail in a board. Perhaps he wants to build a house for his friend. Our language obscures the true situation in that we use the same word "because" in each case, but reflection shows that the word in its fourth use means something very different from what it means in the first three uses. The first three do not really explain, but the fourth *does* explain. This remains true even when we ask why the man wants to build the house.

We, then, have solved our first problem and have turned to another. When we try to explain a purpose we find that our only recourse is to refer to other and more inclusive purposes. Thus, Purpose is really an ultimate principle of explanation, and the only adequate explanation of the world would be the Purpose which includes the whole process. If the world is understandable, such a Purpose must exist. But the belief in the existence of such a Purpose is *theism*. Because science shows the world to be intelligible, at least to a considerable degree, science becomes a witness to intelligent Purpose in nature and consequently it bears testimony to the credibility of theism.[1]

At this point Dr. Trueblood quotes from Baron von Hugel as follows:

Already Mathematics and Mechanics absolutely depend, for the success of their applications to actual Nature, upon a spontaneous correspondence between the human reason and the Rationality of Nature. The immensity of this success is an unanswerable proof that this rationality is not imposed but found there by man. But Thought without a Thinker is an absurd proposition. Thus faith in Science is faith in God.[2]

Incidentally, this final statement supports the firm conviction of the present writer, that Biblical students need not fear science. In a word, God has written two books: one is the Book of Nature (Psa. 19:1, Rom. 1:20-21, Heb. 11:3), in which He reveals His everlasting power and divinity; the other is the Book of Scripture (2 Tim. 3:16), in which He reveals His Plan of Redemption for mankind. Science is, of course, man's attempt to interpret the former of these Books, and what is called Systematic Theology is man's attempt to interpret the latter. Obviously there may be apparent discrepancies between these interpretations, for the simple reason that man is liable to error. But, in the very nature of the case, there can be no discrepancies between the content of the two books, because both are from God from whom all Truth comes to man, and Truth does not contradict itself. (Cf. John 8:31-32, 14:6, 17:17, 18:37.) In this connection, we quote again from Trueblood:

When we are told that gas pressure is explained by movement of molecules, we ask why the molecules move, and we are asking precisely the same kind of question again. When we trace an occurrence to the purpose of an intelligent being, however, the situation is completely altered. We may, indeed, ask why such a purpose is entertained, but when we do so we are asking a question of a different order. We have come to the end of one road and are starting on another. The causes which *produce* a purpose are entirely different from the set of secondary causes which *result* from a purpose.[3]

1. Trueblood, *Philosophy of Religion*, 96, 97.
2. Baron Friedrich von Hugel, *Essays and Addresses on the Philosophy of Religion*, 71.
3. Trueblood, *op cit.*, 97.

The process of explaining may come somewhere to an end, and it comes to an end only when we reach "principles deducible from nothing prior to themselves." In explanation we seek a connection between what is to be explained and what we already understand, at least in some measure. "The business of philosophy is not so much to explain things as to find the things that explain themselves."[1]

Due to the correlation of the mind and the natural order which it apprehends, Trueblood contends, ours is the kind of a world in which science is possible. Hence, he affirms, the very existence of science supports what he calls the "fact" of evolution. (He is, of course, like A. Cressy Morrison, what is designated a *theistic evolutionist.*) He finds a conclusive support for this kind of evolutionism in the rationality of the objective order and its discovery by the human mind. Note the following statements:

"Thinking is grounded in the process of adjustment between organism and environment" [quoted from Temple, *op. cit.*, 128]. . . . The highest point in creation, so far as we know, is the capacity to comprehend the world, but this capacity has arisen by degrees in the natural order. At one end of the evolutionary series is unconscious life, and at the other is self-conscious life, but *it is all one series.* . . . The fact that a process is rational does not mean that the ground of that rationality is necessarily revealed in the beginning. In fact the ground of the rationality need not appear until the end of the series of events, but when it appears it illuminates the entire process. This is well illustrated in dramatic poetry and in the lives of good men. Seen in retrospect, such lives are thoroughly rationalized wholes because of what, all along, they were *becoming.* . . . If the general evolutionary theory is true and if man's life be included in the theory, we cannot escape the conclusion, once more, that mind and nature are akin. . . . The relation "akin to" is a symmetrical relation. If mind is akin to nature, nature likewise is akin to mind. . . . "The more completely we include Mind within Nature, the more inexplicable must Nature become except by reference to Mind" [again quoted from Temple, *op cit.*, 133]. A boldly accepted naturalism leads directly to supernaturalism! How can nature include mind as an *integral* part unless it is grounded in mind? If mind were seen as something alien or accidental, the case would be different, but the further we go in modern science, the clearer it becomes that mental experience is no strange offshoot. Rather it is something which is deeply rooted in the entire structure. *Science knows nothing of the entirely fortuitous.*[2]

Dr. Trueblood cites the Second Law of Thermodynamics as additional evidence for what he calls the "fact" of evolution. The Second Law must, of course, be understood in connection with the First Law, that of the conservation of energy.

The Second Law holds that the amount of energy in the world is constant though it changes in form. The fact that the amount of energy is constant does not mean that energy is always available. In so far as we can see, the time will come when energy is not available for work.

1. Quote is from William Temple, *Nature, Man and God,* 129.
2. Trueblood, *op cit.,* 100, 101.

Because there is constant diffusion and because there is no addition to the total energy, we must contemplate a final condition of absolute stagnation. And it is precisely this to which the Second Law points. In all physical systems we note a leveling process. A stone thrown into a pool raises waves, but these slowly dissipate until they are no longer observable. The hot stove radiates its heat into the closed room until a uniform temperature is reached. Just as nature may be said figuratively to abhor a vacuum, so nature abhors differentiation and concentration of energy. Thus, the stars radiate their energy, and this energy, so far as we know, *never makes a return trip.* It is a one-way process. This increase of leveling is called the "increase of entropy."[1]

The following very clear definition of this phenomenon is quoted by Trueblood as follows:

"As the useless energy increases, the useful decreases by the same amount. The ratio of useless to useful energy is called *entropy.* The law of entropy states that the ratio is constantly increasing. This means that the amount of energy available for the energizing process of the world is ever growing less."[2]

Dr. Trueblood goes on to say:

It is always possible for some new force, now unknown, to enter, but, on the basis of present observations, there seems to be no rational escape from the prospect of an ultimate dissipation of all energy. This means not only the "death" of our particular solar system, but of any physical system. The paradox is that the Second Law, depressing as it seems to be, actually supports the theistic claim in a remarkable way. We are driven to the conclusion that the physical world is something which not only will have an end, but also something which had a beginning. "If the universe is running down like a clock," says Dr. Inge, "the clock must have been wound up at a date which we could name if we knew it. The world, if it is to have an ending in time, must have had a beginning in time."[3] The chief metaphysical significance of the law of entropy consists not in the evidence of a beginning in time, important as that is, but rather *in the evidence that the natural world is not self-explanatory.* According to natural law, energy loses its efficacy. But without the operation of a totally different principle there would be no energy to lose its efficacy. *Nature points beyond nature for an explanation of nature.* The Second Law of Thermodynamics thus points directly to theism as an explanation of the world, and the reasoning based upon it provides a modern counterpart to the cosmological argument. . . . The chief strength of atheistic naturalism has lain in the notion that the material world needs no explanation *external to itself,* that it is, indeed, a perpetual motion machine, which had no beginning and will have no end. But when we take the Second Law of Thermodynamics seriously we can no longer hold to this doctrine. The universe as we know it, by the aid of modern science, could not have originated without the action of a creative Source of energy outside itself, and it cannot be maintained without it. The more we delve, by the aid of natural science, into the secrets of nature the more it becomes clear that nature cannot account for itself in any of its parts or in its entirety. The stone which the builders rejected has become the head

1. *Op. cit.,* 102, 103
2. J. A. McWilliams, *Cosmology,* 42.
3. W. R. Inge, *God and the Astronomers,* 10.

of the corner. Science, instead of undermining belief in God, today becomes the first witness. Science means knowledge, and what we have to explain about the world is that knowledge has appeared. How, in a nontheistic world, would knowledge of its nontheism be possible? A. E. Taylor is extremely disturbing when he says we must ask of every theory about the world, "Would the truth of the theory be compatible with knowing the theory to be true?" That is a question on which a person may meditate profitably for a long time.[1]

To recapitulate: Trueblood bases his acceptance of *theistic evolution* on three grounds, namely, (1) that of the very fact of the existence of science as the obvious product of the kinship of nature and mind; (2) that of the evident truth that *progressive* creation necessarily presupposes direction by Creative Intelligence and Power; and (3) that of the evidence provided by the Second Law of Thermodynamics, to the effect that the universe could not have originated, and indeed cannot be maintained, without the action of a Creative Source of energy. (Cf. Psa. 148:1-6) As a matter of fact, *if our universe were the product of sheer chance, it could not be a universe* (a word which means literally "turned into one whole"), *nor could there be such a thing as a science.* "*Science knows nothing of the wholly fortuitous.*"

The credo, or perhaps it would be more in accord with fact to say, the *creedlessness,* of "materialistic evolution" with its doctrine of "chance-creationism," is fairly well expressed, and literally so, in the following lines (author unknown to this writer):

> Once nothing arrived on this earth out of space;
> It rode in on nothing; it came from no place;
> It landed on nothing—the earth was not here—
> It worked hard on nothing for year after year;
> It sweat over nothing with mighty resolve—
> But just about then things began to evolve:
> The heavens appeared, and the sea and the sod;
> This Almighty Nothing worked much like a god.
> It started unwinding without any plan,
> It made every creature and ended with man.
> No god here was needed—there was no creation;
> Man grew like a mushroom and needs no salvation.
> Some savants say this should be called evolution
> And that ignorance only rejects that solution.

Another wag, has contributed a few lines on the subject before us, which read as follows:

1. Trueblood, *op cit.,* 103-105.

Oh, the rising generation
Has lost its veneration
    For the fables and the fantasies of old
In the science of geology
And the study of biology
    Their hearts and heads alike are growing cold.
Since this terrible evolution
Has caused this revolution
    And geology has given us such shocks,
We shall have our legislature
Now repeal the laws of nature,
    And pass a law abolishing the rocks.
        (identity likewise unknown)

It surely is profitable for "instruction in righteousness" (*i.e.*, God's way of doing things) to consider the language of the Spirit as recorded in Peter's second epistle, chapter 3, verses 1-13, and note carefully its intimations with respect to the subject:

This is now, beloved, the second epistle that I write unto you; and in both of them I stir up your sincere mind by putting you in remembrance; that ye should remember the words which were spoken before by the holy prophets, and the commandment of the Lord and Savior through your apostles; knowing this first, that *in the last days mockers shall come with mockery, walking after their own lusts, and saying, Where is the promise of his coming? for, from the day that the fathers fell asleep, all things continue as they were from the beginning of the creation.* For this they willfully forget, that there were heavens from of old, and an earth compacted out of water and amidst water, by the word of God; by which means the world that then was, being overflowed with water, perished; but the heavens that now are, and the earth, by the same word have been stored up for fire, being reserved against the day of judgment and destruction of ungodly men. But forget not this one thing, beloved, that *one day is with the Lord as a thousand years, and a thousand years as one day.* The Lord is not slack concerning his promise, as some count slackness; but is longsuffering to you-ward, not wishing that any should perish, but that all should come to repentance. But the day of the Lord will come as a thief; in the which the heavens shall pass away with a great noise, and the elements shall be dissolved with fervent heat, and the earth and the works that are therein shall be burned up. Seeing that these things are thus all to be dissolved, what manner of persons ought ye to be in all holy living and godliness, looking for and earnestly desiring the coming of the day of God, by reason of which the heavens being on fire shall be dissolved, and the elements shall melt with fervent heat? *But according to his promise, we look for a new heavens and a new earth, wherein dwelleth righteousness.* (Italics mine—C.C.)

We are surrounded on all sides by the *Mystery of Being.* Certainly that which impresses itself upon our consciousness all the time requires some accounting for, some explanation. There can be only two views: neither logic nor experience allows for a third. *Either there is a Power in this universe, the Creator and Preserver of it, who is without beginning or end, whose ground of existence is within Himself; or the only alternative is that the Something which we experience constantly, originally came from nothing. There is no middle ground; no way out of the horns of this dilemma.* To ask, Where did God come from? is to state the question improperly. Our God, the living and true God, has always been and will always be; He is without beginning or end (cf. Rev. 1:17-18, Isa. 46:8-11, etc.). Just this timeless sovereign Power is what we mean when we use the word "God." The real questions for consideration should be: Why is there Something instead of nothing? What is this Something? Whence came it into existence, and for what purpose? The three most far-reaching questions faced by every human being are these: What am I? Whence came I? Whither am I bound? One's answer to these questions, if he ever gives them any great measure of thought, will be his *Weltanschauung.* It follows, of course, that a man's World-View will determine the course and character of his life.

22. The tragically ill effects of the spread of materialistic evolution, with its creed of *chance—purposeless—creation* are to be seen everywhere today, and probably most of all in the world-wide deterioration of *morale* and *morality.* Relativity is the norm which man has blown up into an Absolute. Authority, if indeed there is such a thing, is vested, not in the church, nor in the state (civil society), but in the autonomous reason. Everything is relative to the individual. Truth, beauty, and goodness—again, if these words have any meaning—are what each person thinks them to be. There is no authority (i.e., moral power) beyond that of the individual human being and the social milieu which he, with others of his kind, sets up for himself in the form of custom or "law." There is no Absolute. (It is passing strange that the man who makes such a statement does not have sense enough to see that he is himself affirming an Absolute.) "Glory to man in the highest," shouts Swinburne, "for man is the master of things." And Henley, in true Walt Whitman style, thumps his chest as he cries out,

> It matters not how strait the gate,
> How charged with punishments the scroll,
> I am the master of my fate,
> I am the captain of my soul!

Even Shakespeare is moved to protest this humanistic arrogance:

> But man, proud man,
> Drest in a little brief authority,
> Most ignorant of what he's most assured,

His glassy essence, like an angry ape,
Plays such fantastic tricks before high heaven
As make the angels weep.

Or, in the words of Alexander Pope:

Some are bewilder'd in the maze of schools,
And some made coxcombs Nature meant but fools.

The creedlessness of materialistic evolution is largely responsible for the theme of the sheer futility of living which has dominated both fiction and drama for many decades. Undoubtedly it accounts for the fact that contemporary literature has very little humor in it. Both writers and their writings are so ponderously earthy, so deadly serious (shall we admit, "realistic"?) Beginning with Ibsen, we find the Cult of Futility—of the meaninglessness of life—either explicit or implicit in the dramas of Eugene O'Neill, Arthur Miller, Edw. Albee, Tennessee Williams, and other lesser lights, the playwrights who have dominated Broadway for over half a century. (Williams has done as good a job of outFreuding Freud as Euripides did twenty-four hundred years ago.) Saturated with the same motif are the novels of Thomas Hardy, Dreiser, Maugham, Lewis, Steinbeck, Faulkner, Hemingway, Caldwell, Farrell, James Jones, Salinger, Mailer, and others of like outlook: these are the men who have produced most of the fiction with which the literary markets of the world have been deluged in recent years. (It will be recalled that Cronshaw's carpet, in Maugham's *Of Human Bondage*, is offered as an explicit analogy of the purposelessness of life.) I suppose, however, that the last word in pessimism has been spoken by the self-proclaimed atheistic existentialist, Jean Paul Sartre, in his terrible confession that life is only a vacuum with not exit signs. What a really terrible world this would be if this view were to prevail everywhere! (Cf. O'Neill's *Long Day's Journey into Night*.) No wonder that the faith and moral outlook of thousands of young men and women have been stultified, if not actually destroyed by the literary output to which they have been subjected in our secondary schools and higher institutions of learning!

This cult of chance-creationism has insisted on our treating man as a kind of glorified brute, an aggregate of protons and electrons, a creature of earth only, destined to pass through this "vale of tears" robbed entirely of what was once called "the music and the dream" of living. It would identify mind with perishable brain and so rob mankind of any hope of a

571

better "beyond." It would make death mean only the absorption of the whole person into the "ocean of undifferentiated energy" from which all things emerge and to which they return, according to pre-determined life cycles. For faith, hope and love, it substitutes their opposites, fear and despair and hate, as already evidenced by a whole world at war within itself, a world that is beginning to actualize Thomas Hobbes' notion of man's *first* state as "a warfare of all against all."

The effects of chance-creationism, with its inseparable corollary of the utter meaninglessness of life, become evident in many areas of human culture today, as, for example, in the supersedure of permissiveness for discipline in the home, of sociological statistics for legal precedent in the juridical order, of gross hedonism for the self-discipline of the moral life, of all kinds of cultism for true Biblical faith, of anarchy for the reign of order and law throughout the world, of universal chaos in man's interrelationships with his fellows and with his God. It is one of the main factors in filling our streets and highways with herdes of young men and women who, in trying to experience fully the "Playboy" philosophy of life, have been seduced by the appeal of pseudo-values into rebellion against society in general, becoming even violent revolutionaries, and into a life of parasitism on what they, in their gross ignorance, superciliously call the "Establishment." How many thousands of these pitifully tragic figures are wasting precious time and destroying themselves by doing little or nothing more than what Satan told God he was doing, just "going to and fro in the earth, and walking up and down in it" (Job 1: 7). Insatiable restlessness is an unfailing characteristic of diabolism.

My good friend and ministerial colleague, Curtis Dickinson, has so well stated what we are trying to say here that I feel justified in excerpting his remarks from his excellent little periodical, *The Witness* (*March,* 1972, Lubbock, Texas), as follows:

> Why do some have so little regard for life? Why are the rebels so careless with their own lives and the lives of others? Why do some think so little of their lives as to ruin their health in dissipation and drugs? One reason is faith in evolution. To the evolutionist life is no more than a tiny step in a long process of happenstance. There is no purpose for it and no plan, since there is no planner. One simply exists under prevailing conditions, and has no obligation to the past or hope for the future. His life is an accident, an interval, and with no intrinsic meaning. After millions of years perhaps a better breed and better condition might happen, but then that is of no value to our present generation. No wonder that so many young people, under this depressing

conviction, space out on drugs, cop out and foul up their lives in sin. They do not love life! They may love pleasure, but have no love for living, and the things they may do in this frame of mind tend to destroy chances for a good life.

Live for the pleasure of the moment, for the indulgence of the lusts of the flesh, "eat and drink and be merry, for tomorrow ye die," has been the cry of sinful man even from the ages before the Deluge. The truth lies in the parody, "Eat, drink, and be merry, and tomorrow you will have locomotor ataxia, cirrhosis of the liver, or delirium tremens." The overpowering sin of the antediluvian age was preoccupation with the things of this world, sheer secularism, and it is the universal sin of our age and time. (Cf. Mat. 24: 37-39; Gen. 6: 3-7, 11-12.)

Materialistic evolution, if put into practice universally in daily living, will eventually pressure man, through his insatiable thirst for power, into slavery to one or more of the lusts of the flesh (Gal. 5: 19-21) and into ultimate eternal separation "from the face of the Lord and from the glory of his might" (2 Thess. 1: 7-10).

23. Let us now take a brief look at some of the inadequacies of the theory of evolution, as follows:

(1) *Evolutionism has no adequate explanation of the process by which a variation in the parent organism becomes embodied in the parental reproductive cells* (as in the fertilized ovum of the human male-female), obviously a change necessary to the transmission of the "acquired characteristic" to the offspring.

(2) *Evolutionism does not give us any satisfactory account of the origin of the life process.* Spontaneous generation (abiogenesis) is now *theoretically* considered to have been a possibility, but as yet no direct evidence of its actual occurrence in nature has been brought to light. As Wilder Smith puts it:

> We have no evidence to date that the simple molecules postulated (that is, the first molecules alleged to have been formed by chance) could autoduplicate themselves. To propose this is to pose a problem as difficult as that of life itself. . . . For energy would be needed to operate such a duplicative process, which the heat or light of the sun could not supply without mediation of a complex metabolic motor. A complex association of matter would be indispensable to arrive at autoduplication, yet Dr. Cedrangolo is postulating simple molecules as carrying on this process. We have no evidence for such an hypothesis. Viruses, in duplicating themselves, use the metabolic support of their complex host cells but the host cells are lacking under the conditions on earth before biogenesis. [This author goes on to say that some

scientists are convinced that proteins did not arise spontaneously from non-living matter.] If one cannot explain the spontaneous formation of proteins, a large percentage of scientists would believe that the origin of life was not explicable either.[1]

The truth seems to be that it is not likely that a molecule can increase in complexity spontaneously and suddenly "like a man falling in one fell swoop up a ladder from bottom to top"! Up to the present time, credit must go to Louis Pasteur for demonstrating, as Spallanzani put it, that "even microbes have parents."

(3) *Evolutionism does not afford any explanation of the life process itself,* that is, of the mysterious movement of life; rather, it starts with this movement as an accepted fact, apparently indifferent to the importance of the *how* and *why* of it. One may watch the division of a single cell into two cells (as, again, in the fertilized ovum), but no one understands why the cell divides and the process continues in geometrical proportion (one into two, two into four, four into eight, etc.), or how the daughter cell inherits the particular forms and functions of the parent cell. Why does this movement of life push upward, by differentiation of structure and specialization of function, into vastly more and more complex forms and finally into the most complex form of all,—man? *There is no evidence that a potency can actualize itself*: it must have some help from outside itself. What, then, is the Efficient Causality which actualizes all these changes that are supposed to become stabilized into the multifarious forms that make up the living world? Is it "protoplasmic irritability"? But what is "protoplasmic irritability"? Who knows? Perhaps little more than a factotum brought in to support the unprovable hypotheses of the evolutionist.

(3) As stated heretofore, *evolutionism requires an almost unlimited extent of time to make room for all the changes envisioned by its advocates.* Apparently, they expect us to accept without question the indispensability of such an extent of time to any adequate explanation of the process, and at the same time they arbitrarily use this hypothetical stretch of time to *support* their theory. Is not this question-begging *par excellence?* In substance the argument is as follows: *A fossil is dated by the age of the rock in which it is found but the age of the rock is determined by the fossil it contains.* "Yet the geologic column (obtained by dating fossils on the assumption of evolution) is

1. A. E. Wilder Smith, *Man's Origin, Man's Destiny,* 17ff.

used as the chief evidence for evolution." Surely this supports our view that many scientists of our day and age need the discipline of courses in logic and metaphysics!

(4) *Evolutionism cannot account satisfactorily for the gap that exists between the intelligence potential of man and that of of any known animal species existent or extinct.* That this gap is inconceivably vast is conceded by the evolutionists of our time. Indeed, there are eminent men in biological science who are prone to accept the view that man's appearance on the scene is explainable only in terms of a mutation, or series of mutations. Incidentally, it should be stated here that evolutionists do not take the view that man is "nothing but" an animal. On the contrary, they hold that he has "evolved" beyond the brute stage; that, in a word, he is animal *plus.* However, they insist that the difference is only one of *degree,* not one of *kind.* We hold, however, that such powers inherent in man as (a) *abstract thinking,* that is, in terms of symbols, (b) *creative imagination,* (c) the *sense of values,* and the *sense of humor,* accompanied as often it is by the *power of laughter,* set man apart from the brute creation as *far different in kind.* Hence, man alone has been vested with those powers which qualify him for his God-given responsibilities as lord tenant of the earth (Gen. 1:26-31, Psa. 8:3-9).

(5) The theory of mutations is that new forms come into being as wholes, as the result of sudden jumps in the process, and continue to "breed true" from the time of their "emergence." Do biologists have any explanation of the mysterious process by which a mutation is brought about? Obviously, they do not. They take it for granted, it seems, that resident forces of some kind, or of different kinds, either singly or collectively, work effectively in the genes to produce the mutation. Why this process occurs, or just how it occurs, no one knows. (Cosmic rays, we are told, have been kown to produce mutations in fruit flies.) Yet it is inconceivable that evolution could ever have taken place unless the fact of mutations is granted. Many biologists, however, frown on the theory of mutations because they find it difficult to harmonize this theory with the mechanics of natural selection which they seek to establish. It it obvious that mutations have all the appearance of *special creations.*

The theory of mutations is treated very clearly, under the heading, "Neutral Observation of the Modern Basis for Evolution," printed in the *Bible-Science Newsletter,* May, 1972. The

575

author is Marinus W. Verbrugge of San, Jose, California, and he writes as follows:

The search for gen-.ic change throughout the 19th century failed to produce any concrete results, Lamarck's idea that acquired characteristics are passed on to the next generation is wrong. *Somatic cells do not produce sex cells.* Darwin observed that domestic plants and animals have variable descendants and implied this is evidence of genetic change. He was wrong. This was only a re-combination of previously existing genes in hybrid plants. DeVries mistook the phases of a heterozygous species for genetic change. "Sports" in hybrid plants, which are observed occasionally by commercial growers, are generally caused by the weakening of a precariously dominant gene, resulting in the switch of dominance to the opposite gene in the affected pair. The demand for positive proof of genetic change became strong after DeVries' observation of mutations in *Oeonothera* (evening primrose) appeared to be unfounded. Leading evolutionists prodded the Rockefeller Foundation to dig into its coffers. Morgan received the go-ahead and began breeding *Drosophila* (the genus containing the common fruit fly). This would settle once and for all the truth about mutations. After millions of normal flies, a different one was finally discovered which bred true. Hallelujah! Evolution was a fact. The happy news made headlines in the world press. But the pampered little mutant was not very healthy and homozygotes were lethal. It was the same story with later discoveries of mutants in *Drosophila.* Radiation experiments greatly increased the frequency of mutations, but the results were the same: sickly, unbalanced, weak, unproductive individuals which never could become a new species. Sequence photography with the recently developed electron microscope revealed the cause: broken chromosomes. There was a definite relationship between the severity of the damage to the chromosomes and the resulting individual. Some mildly affected individuals did not show visible damage to the chromosomes. Individual genes are so small that they cannot be detected with the most powerful magnification available to science. If all other mutants in the same culture are caused by chromosome damage, it is a logical conclusion that a minor mutation is caused by the same factor. This is a very important point in this discussion as will be explained. Later evolution is a process of change in stages. From a brand new heterozygous mutant to a homozygote, to a new species, genera, family, etc., etc. The goal of all laboratory experiments with fruitflies, molds, mice, etc., has been to detect the start of this process, to demonstrate a true first-generation mutant. This goal has been reached by Morgan, resulting in exuberant rejoicing in certain circles. But the second phase, *continuation,* did not materialize. On the contrary, all abnormalities in the first discovered mutants which have only one affected chromosome, are very much increased if both chromosomes are so affected. Those with more serious damage are unable to reproduce at all if paired with an identical mate. The very few which had the ability to reach the homozygote stage (with much loving care) were at best a degenerated form of an old type, *not* a healthy *new type.*

Even the prominent evolutionist, Prof. Theodosius Dobzhansky of Columbia University, states in his book, *Evolution, Genetics, and Man;* "All positively demonstrated genetic changes up to this day have only led to races within prevailing existing species."

Seven decades of extensive experiments in laboratories have confirmed what was known for a long time. Variations observed in species, are in degree only, not in kind. This type of variation does not lead to new types ever!!!

## ADDENDUM: ON EVOLUTION AND EVOLUTIONISM

Only *different genes* can cause the emergence of a new species. Geneticists are well aware of this. And the changing of genes has *not* been demonstrated. All claims of *gene* changes are unpoven assumptions. Modern evolutionists want to *see* gene changes; many changes are caused by something else. The new version of evolution is: (1) changing genes, (2) recombination of genes, (3) increased volume of genes by polyploidy. Technology in its present state is unable to resolve whether this is happening. The *results* of demonstrated facts are the only thing to go by. Plans, drawings and calculations of an airplane may seem perfect. The final test comes when it zooms up into the blue yonder. If its prototypes continue to crash, something is amiss. The persistent failure of all known mutants to perform according to expectation is the best proof of the type of change which has taken place. All evidence points in one direction: recombination of old material and loss of genetic material. "There is nothing new under the sun," said Solomon. That is still true today.

We recall that in the first chapter of Genesis it is revealed that God created both plants and animals according to "kinds": note the phrase, "after their kind," in verses 11, 12, 21, 24, 25. What particular categories of biological science, then, are to be identified with this Biblical speciation as to "kind"? *Speciation* in biology designates the process by which species are formed, "the process by which variations become fixed." Classification (in biology) is usually described as proceeding according to the following sequence: phyla, classes, genera, species, orders, families. On this subject Simpson writes as follows:

Most zoologists classify animals into about twenty major groups, called phyla (singular, phylum), each representing a fundamental anatomical plan. Some students recognize more than twenty phyla and some fewer, but the differences of opinion relate almost entirely to a small number of peculiar, soft-bodied living animals of uncertain origin, of no real importance in the modern fauna and practically without fossil remains. *Animals of real importance today or in the history of life may all be referred to only fifteen basic phyla.* Five of these are collectively called "worms" and have poor fossil records. The other ten have, by and large, good fossil records and their histories since the Cambrian or Ordovician can be followed satisfactorily in broad outline, *although it hardly needs saying that innumerable details need to be filled in.* [Italics mine—C]. [Again]: Several striking facts fundamental for the history of life appear. . . . First, all the phyla are of great antiquity. All date from the Cambrian or Ordovician. . . . Since sometime in the Ordovician, around 400,000,000 years ago, no new *major* type of animal has appeared on earth. It would appear that the fundamental possibilities of animal structure had then all been developed, although truly profound changes and progressive developments were yet to occur within each type. [Note well this phrase, *within each type.*] Note, second, that none of the basic types has become extinct. . . . The third major generalization is that on the whole life has tended to increase in variety. The usual pattern for any phylum, or for life as a whole, is to appear in relatively few forms and later to become vastly more diversified. [How account for this diversification?] [Simpson writes]: The same sorts of events have occurred within each class, and here may be seen still more clearly how a new type, once it was

577

originated, tends to spread and to become diversified in adaptation to a variety of environmental conditions and of ways of life. This process is known as "adaptive radiation."[1]

It would seem entirely reasonable to identify the biological phyla with the Biblical "kinds." At any rate, *science thus admits the persistence of original basic categories of animal life, from which (as biology would have it) diversification followed, probably, in genera and species.* Of course science attempts to fathom the *modus operandi* of this diversification, not with any great degree of success; that is, with nothing better, it would seem, than suggestions based solely on inference, and inference that lacks the quality of strictness considered necessary to proof. And even this leaves the problem of all problems still up in the air, namely, the problem of the origin of the basic "kinds" from which the diversification takes place. On this subject, Simpson writes as follows:

How did life arise? Again, the honest answer is that we do not know but that we have some good clues. This ultimate mystery is more and more nearly approached by recent studies on the chemical activity of living particles, of viruses and of genes, the submicroscopic determiners of heredity and growth. The most fundamental properties of life are reproduction and change (or mutation). Particles with these properties would be, in essence, alive, and from them all more and more complex forms of life could really arise. [This would mean, of course, as stated heretofore, that these "submicroscopic" particles must be credited with all the attributes that theologians specify as belonging to God, including (at least the potentiality of) supreme intelligence, creative power, and eternal, autonomous existence. On the metaphysical principle that *being exists either potentially or actually,* these primitive particles of "First Matter" would have in them all the potentialities of the actualized cosmos and its manifoldness. But we are still in the dark as to the origin of these "particles." If they are unoriginated, then they must be regarded as timeless (*i.e.,* eternal), without beginning or ending. This of course would require more faith than is required to believe in the God of the Bible.]

We again quote Simpson:

Current studies suggest that it would be no miracle, not even a great statistical improbability, if living molecules appeared spontaneously under special conditions of surface waters rich in the carbon compounds that are the food and substance of life. And the occurrence of such waters at early stages of the planet's evolution is more probable than not. [Now we are back, first, to surface waters, then to carbon compounds, and finally to the planet itself. Just where is this regress going to reach an end? Or will it? Are we faced with infinite regress? Would this be any logical solution of the Mystery of being?][2]

Note well Simpson's conclusion:

1. Simpson, *op cit.,* 13-21. (My comments in brackets—C.)
2. *Ibid.,* 13, 14.

This is not to say that the origin of life was by chance or by supernatural intervention, but that it was in accordance with the grand, eternal physical laws of the universe. It need not have been miraculous, except as the existence of the physical universe may be considered a miracle.[1]

What sophistry! Did man create himself or was he brought into existence by Power that antedated him? Obviously, if he created himself, he existed before he existed. But this is nonsence. Did the physical universe create itself or was it created by a Power that antedated it? If it created itself, then it, too, existed before it existed. This is arrant nonsense. We base our case on the Power who was before all things, and is in all things. The God of the Bible who is transcendent in His being (as opposed to pantheism) and who is immanent through His power (as opposed to deism) is our all-sufficient answer for these ultimate questions. There is no satisfactory answer but that of theism! (We refer the student here to the great Preservation Hymn, (Psa. 104; cf. Psa. 33:6, 9; Heb. 11:3, Col. 1:16-17, Psa. 148:1-6, 2 Pet. :1-7.)

22. Despite positive assertions to the contrary, in which, as a rule, the theory to be proved is taken for granted, *the simple truth is that as yet no one knows just how a new species emerges or could emerge.* As Alfred Russel Wallace is reported to have said to Darwin: "Your theory may account for the *survival* of a species, but it cannot account for the *arrival* of a new species." This statement is just as true today as when it was first made.

23. *Evolutionism is unable as yet to give us a satisfactory account of the origin of sex differences.* It is interesting to note here that the Genesis cosmogony is silent about the origin of females among subhuman orders, with the sole exception of the implication in Gen. 1:22. It is the human female, Woman, to whom our attention is especially directed in Scripture: Gen. 1:27-31.

24. *Evolutionism has no adequate explanation of the fact of instinct,* of the almost inconceivable manifoldness of instinctive responses among subhuman creatures. Instinct has rightly been called "The Great Sphinx of Nature." If complexity of instinct were to be made the criterion of the classification of living forms in ascending order, it is obvious that the lowly Insecta would stand at the head of the list and man, poor man, *homo sapiens,* would be somewhere near the bottom. Are not

1. *Op. cit.,* 13, 14.

instinctive responses the media by which Divine Intelligence ensures the preservation of non-intelligent species?

25. *It is doubtful that evolutionism could ever account adequately for the great variety of special organs in different species* (characteristic of the entire complex of nature's adaptation to the needs of living creatures); organs such as wings, feathers, eyes, ears, fins and electric organs of fishes, poison glands and fangs of snakes, migratory powers of homing pigeons, and many others too numerous to mention. Perhaps the most amazing phenomenon of the subhuman world is the "radar" system of bats, which, whether it is instinct or not, certainly points up the mathematical precision which characterizes all nature. For example, the following facts about this phenomenon, as given in the Bible-Science *Daily Reading Magazine,* May-June, 1972:

A 1951 Moody Bible Institute filmstrip titled *Flying Wonder* describes the remarkable radar of the bat. This radar enables the bat to feed at night without eyesight. Tests were made in an area with bars placed at intervals closer than a wingspread, yet their wings never touched the bars. The sound frequency of the bat's direction system is about 50,000 cycles, more effective than any man-made radar systems. Of the 1000 species of bats, 39 are found in the United States. The bat's wide gaping mouth enables it to catch flying insects. Bats hibernate in winter and may live up to 20 years. Bats are designated as unclean in the Bible. Few mammals are more odorous than the bat. They sleep while in a hanging position and like to roost in caves, old buildings, and hollow trees. They quickly build up large deposits of highly smelly guano which is often used as manure. Their unusual appearance and habits have long made them the subject of strange beliefs, sometimes with evil association, says G. S. Cansdale. Bats are an example of the wonders of God's creation. Bats are not necessarily harmful pests, and there is much we can learn from them to aid in scientific research. That Scripture considers them unclean is another example of a sin-contaminated nature. Only in the life to come will nature be free from this influence of sin and we will enjoy perfection forever.

For one of the most thoroughgoing treatments of the characteristics and varieties of instinctive behavior in subhuman orders, the reader is referred to the book by Ruth Crosby Noble, titled *The Nature of the Beast.* Mrs. Noble was the widow of the late Dr. G. Kingsley Noble, noted biologist of the American Museum of Natural History, and her book, published in 1945, is said to be based largely on his scientific publications and lecture notes. Mrs. Noble shared in her husband's work, we are told, and was herself an expert in the natural sciences. (See Bibliography.) This book develops the theme that animals are creatures of instinct in a world of sensations. She presents the following significant conclusions: (1) What often appears to us to be reasoned behavior in animals with insight as to the outcome, is really a long line of instinctive behavior. In this connection, she writes as follows:

> In 1824, Emerson at the age of twenty wrote in his *Journal*, "Man is an animal that looks before and after." We have noted the limited capacity of most animals for recalling past experiences. Planning for the future is even more difficult. Foresight, like insight, is largely restricted to humans, though we find in animals much that resembles it—usually falsely. It is doubtful that the squirrel hoarding nuts is able to picture the coming winter with its blanket of snow. Burying objects and hiding them in cracks are activities so natural to these animals than even pets in captivity will try to hide nuts and small articles about the house or in the folds of a bedcover. Even the mother squirrel building her nest probably has no conception of the family soon to arrive. Both hoarding and nesting are primarily instinctive. . . . Though there are many highly talented artisans even among insects and lower invertebrates it is in general only the most intelligent vertebrates who are capable of using *tools* in their trade. The very few who *invent* tools are prodigies indeed. . . . While man shares insight and ability to use tools with the apes, he alone communicates with his fellows by means of language. No other living creature has learned to use words as symbols of objects, situations, or acts. By means of these symbols he projects his ideas into the minds of others. Through them he is able to profit from the experience of others, both in the past and in the present. With the aid of language, written as well as spoken, he has entered into the realm of ideas, a realm probably closed to most animals . . . animals communicate with one another to some extent by means of expressive gestures and sounds, but this is quite different from having a language. . . . So we see that man has a priceless treasure in his highly developed thinking cap."[1]

(2) The sense impressions of animals are quite different from those of man. The bat, for example, flies by sound instead of sight. The wood tick uses its skin to "see" with. Few animals have color vision. But the bee can detect ultraviolet colors and the ant senses infrared. How do we know these things? Over the space of years science has devised many ways to discover the secrets of animal behavior. (The author takes us behind one ingenious test after another: mazes, colored doors, ringing bells, etc.) The variability, selectivity, and specialization of instincts in the subhuman orders is too vast for any adequate explanation in terms of inheritance of acquired characters, natural selection, continuity of germ plasm, mutations, or all of these acting together. It defies human imagination and at the same time proves the universal adaptability of nature to the needs of all her creatures. We do well to recall here Pope's famous lines:

> "Slave to no sect, who takes no private road,
> But looks through Nature up to Nature's God."

1. *Op. cit.*, 53-64.

26. *Structural resemblance does not necessarily prove emergence of the higher form from the lower.* It could well be the product of the activity of the Divine Mind creating according to an archetypal pattern (as in the instance of man's invention of the wheelbarrow, buggy, chariot, wagon, automobile, airplane, all of which manifest a basic structural resemblance).

27. Ordinarily, *nature, when left to inherent resources alone, seems to deteriorate rather than to advance.* Any gardener knows that tomatoes produced by properly cultivated plants are always superior to those which are produced by seed or plant in what is called "volunteer" fashion.

28. *The apparent non-fertility of hybrids would seem to militate against the evolution theory.*

29. *Apparently useless organs are not necessarily reduced or rudimentary,* in many instances. Ignorance of the use or purpose of an organ is not in itself a proof that the organ has no necessary function at all.

30. *Neither similarity nor gradation (nor both together) can prove emergence,* that is, "continuous progressive change, according to fixed laws, by means of resident forces" (LeConte).

31. *Man has no known existing animal ancestors:* those alleged humanoidal forms which are supposed to have existed prehistorically are now extinct, hence hypothetically identifiable only by isolated sparse skeletal remains which have been found in different parts of the world. These remains of prehistoric man—prior to Cro-Magnon—are too fragmentary to allow for any reliable reconstruction of man's ancestry from the so-called *hominidae.* Nor do these widely scattered skeletal remains necessarily indicate that there were "centers" of the origin of *homo sapiens.* What Dr. Broom has said about such finds in Southern Africa is equally applicable to all other such discoveries: "When we speak of Plesianthropus as a found 'missing link,' this does not mean that man came from even that species. We mean only that we have a member of the family from one of whom man arose."[1] As far as the present writer knows, no evidence has ever been found that would discredit the generally accepted view that the cradle of the human race was where the Bible pictures it to have been, that is, in Southwest Asia. Moreover, evolutionists must accept the fact *that there had to be a space-time locus* at which the transition from *hominidae* to *homo sapiens* actually occurred; and that with the appearance

1. Quoted by Douglas Dewar, *The Transformist Illusion,* 125.

of *homo sapiens,* reason also appeared (as indicated by the Latin *sapiens* or *sapientia,* "wise" or "having reason"), and along with reason, conscience, which is the voice of practical reason (cf. Gen. 3:9-11). In view of these facts, it must also be recognized that all humanoidal forms existing prior to the transition were not forms of *homo sapiens.* The tendency of so many scientists to pontificate about these humanoidal "finds" makes it necessary for us to put their significance in proper perspective in order that we may not be led astray by guesses and gross exaggerations.

32. The Mendelian laws of heredity have been generally accepted in biological science. However, it must be kept in mind that these "laws" are simply descriptions of what evidently takes place in transmission through the media of the genes; they do not tell us why these transmissions take place as they do, nor do they give us any information as to the *modus operandi* of the transmissions themselves. Even the genes themselves are only hypothetical "determiners"—we are told—of heredity. This is true, of course, of practically all facets of the evolution theory: nearly all that the advocates have to tell us is *descriptive* in character, of *what* occurs, not of *why,* nor specifically of *how,* it occurs. Perhaps these are mysteries that lie beyond the scope of human comprehension? The fact is that almost every argument put forward to support evolutionism is based on *inference,* and not on concrete evidence, and practically every one of these arguments leaves the big question open, namely, is the inference necessary, that is, unavoidable, or is it academic guess-work? (According to the *Herald and Presbyter,* the phrase, "we may well suppose," occurs over eight hundred times in Darwin's two principal works, not to mention, of course, such expressions, "apparently," "probably," and the like, all of which express uncertainty: the eminent scientist, like his successors, was simply guessing.) (See Bryan, *In His Image,* 90, 91.)

33. In the final analysis, *the arrival of a new species* is to be accounted for only on the basis of variations transmitted through the chromosomes and genes: as far as we know, inheritance in man takes place in no other way. If mutations be the final "explanation" of these genetic changes, then the mutations must have occurred in chronological sequence to have produced the continuous progressive changes (demanded by the theory) into more and more neurally complex organisms, culminating in the human organism. It is only a mark of sanity to conclude that there is reason and order back of this entire process, actualizing all such changes, and that the Cosmos is the

handiwork of the Universal Mind and Will whom we call God (Psa. 19:1-6).

34. In the areas of the astronomical, geological, and geographical sciences the theory of *uniformitarianism* plays a dominant role. This theory is stated in one geology textbook as follows:

To the uprooting of such fantastic beliefs ["supernatural explanations"] came the Scottish geologist Hutton, whose Theory of the Earth, presented in 1785, marked a turning point in thought on this subject. Hutton argued that *the present is the key to the past* and that, if given *time*, the processes now at work could have produced all the geologic features of the globe. This philosophy, which came to be known as *uniformitarianism*, is now universally accepted by learned men. It demands an immensity of time.[1]

As another writer states it:

According to these modern ideas, the laws of nature have always been the same as they are today, so that the present state of nature is the explanation of its past state and of its future state too. Thus, geological formations, fossils, etc., arise today in just the same manner as they did millions of years ago. Hence the name "uniformitarianism" for this type of philosophy. And thus the concept arose that catastrophes and acts of God have nothing or little to do with the formation of the geological strata we observe today.[2]

It seems that the Holy Spirit warned against the rise of this kind of thinking "in the last days." He predicts for our benefit that in the last days mockers, who live only to satisfy their own lusts, will jeer at the notion of a Second Coming of Christ to save the redeemed and to judge the world. They will cry, "Where is the promise of his coming? for, from the day that the fathers fell asleep, all things continue as they were from the beginning of the creation" (2 Pet. 3:3-7). It strikes us that so-called "learned men" are not intelligent enough to realize that the process of creation itself lies entirely outside the possibility of a continuous uniformitarian origin of the world as we know it and of the myriad forms of life that inhabit it. Evolutionists themselves will certainly agree that there was a time when man did not exist; that, farther back, there was a time when life had not come into being; that back beyond that, there was only the astronomical (celestial) world in process of being formed (according to their theory). We are now back to our original dilemma: We must accept the existence of Power that is without beginning or end, or the "Almighty Nothing" as the First Principle. *On the basis of the metaphysical principle that there must*

1. Schuchert and Dunbar, *Outlines of Historical Geology*, 35.
2. A. E. Wilder Smith, *Man's Origin, Man's Destiny*, 49.

*be as much reality in the cause as in the effect—a principle which evolutionists are not aware of, or else ignore or even ridicule—only the God of the Bible, the theistic God, can be the First Principle of all things.* Again, *on the basis of the metaphysical principles* (1) *that being exists either potentially or actually* (*the full-grown oak tree is potentially in the acorn*), (2) *and that a potency cannot actualize itself, we must conclude that the God of the Bible is the Efficient Cause* (the Power that unites the *matter* and the *form*—the *form* being the plan which, *e.g.,* puts each tree in its specific *kind* or species—to bring the tree into actual existence) *of the Totality of created beings.* Again, we affirm that both science and theology need the disciplines of logic and metaphysics. No better example of this could be cited than the closing statement of the first of the quotations immediately above: "It [their theory] demands an immensity of time." *But as we have noted already, claims of the immensity of time become little more than question-begging devices.* If more time is needed to establish any phase of their theory, evolutionists simply hypothesize—that is, *assume*—it.

35. *The doctrine of biopoiesis* (the creation or making of life from non-living material) completely overlooks the fact that the necessary power—possibly in the arrangement of the atoms in the "parent" molecule—had to be there, before life *could have been* generated "spontaneously." Is not this a matter of pushing the problem of origin a notch farther back? How did the necessary conditions come to exist in the first place to bring into existence the first living form? What Power equipped the "parent" molecule with these necessary conditions? Who indeed, but the living and true God? Creation, we are told in Genesis, was decreed (executed) by the Logos and actualized (consummated) by the Eternal Spirit (Gen. 1:1-31; Psa. 33:6, 9; Gen. 148:1-6, Heb. 11:3).

*Man cannot have created himself or any of his kind. Man cannot even make a seed. Man cannot add to, or take away from, the total energy of the cosmos. Man cannot bring into being any creature greater than himself. Man cannot per se bring about racial distinctions. Man's role in life is to love and serve God here, that he may enjoy Him hereafter.*

36. Let us consider for a moment the problem of dating in relation to the mystery of time. *Time is indeed a mystery.* On this point Wilder Smith's excellent analysis is helpful, as follows:

585

In the beginning God is reported as having taken the "dust of the earth" and as having formed Adam from it. He then breathed the breath of life into him and Adam became a living soul. The Bible does not report Adam as having arisen as a newborn babe. According to the scriptural record, no parents were there to take care of him. So he must have been adult at his creation and have possessed immediately his five senses in full state of development so as to have been able to fend for himself from the start. Let us now consider some consequences of this creative act. Adam is standing there in all the beauty of new creation, straight from the Creator's hand. Shall we say, for the sake of argument. that he is just two breaths, or some five seconds old? His lungs have just filled themselves with the pure air of Eden. But just how old does Adam look, judging his age by our time-measuring experience? He is adult, perhaps handsome, mature. It takes, according to our way of reckoning time, some twenty to thirty years to allow a man to come to maturity, and Adam is obviously a mature man. Accordingly, we would guess Adam's age to be some twenty to thirty years. But in reality, we know he is just two breaths, or about five seconds old. This example makes it clear that where creation is concerned the laws of thermodynamics, as we know them, are turned upside down. Here the laws governing time do not function either. Adam is just five seconds old and yet looks as though he were twenty to thirty years old. What is more, at every act of creation there must be the same illusion of age. Dr. Karl Barth, the famous Swiss theologian and founder of neo-orthodoxy, maintains a similar idea of creation in his well-known saying that when God created, He created with a past. There must be this built-in illusion of the passage of time. This must be the case, for our concept of entropy—and thus of the passage of time—cannot be valid during any creative act. In a primitive sort of way, the same applies to any true synthetic act, even today. If, for instance, we measure time by the natural half life of a biologically active compound, then any synthetic act involving cancellation of the natural decay of biological activity would be in a way a reversal of "time" and decrease of entropy as far as that system is concerned. This must also be the case with respect to the creation of the cosmos and the earth. Here too, an act of creation must bring with it an illusion of age and this illusion lies in the very nature of creation *ex nihilo.* That this illusion is a built-in one may be seen from the following example: If a mixture of lead and uranium in an ore was created at the beginning, it would automatically give an illusion of age. For we know that certain isomers of lead arise at the end stage during the radioactive decay of uranium. By measuring the amount of lead in a uranium ore we can determine the ore's age. Since it takes $X$ years to form so many milligrams of lead from a given amount of uranium, by measuring the amount of lead in the ore we can determine the ore's age, for this decay rate remains constant. But after an act of creation in which an ore is made containing, for example, five grams of lead and five grams of uranium, later calculations must go awry for the following reasons: the five grams of lead will automatically *produce the illusion* of having been *derived* from the uranium over millions of years. But it was actually not derived, but created *de novo.* In reality the mixture of lead and uranium has been created as such, but after creation it cannot avoid producing the illusion that it is millions of years old. . . . An act of creation lies so much outside our present-day knowledge that we do not really know how to calculate to take it truly into account, even though all physics demands an active creation to explain the very being and order of life, atoms and of the subatomic world of particles, waves, and orbits. For this basic reason of an act of creation at the back of the cosmos, it is on principle impossible to arrive at an absolutely definitive and meaningful date for creation. Science demands an act of creation as an explanation of being, but this act of creation must produce an illusion of age and time. We must remember too, in addition to all this, that before matter and space existed, no time existed either. So, to be scientically sound, we must be very cautious in matters concerning time in general and dating in particular. . . . If there are, in fact, no fundamental reasons why time should not stop or even run backward, it is obviously going to be very difficult for us to fix a date for creation, or indeed for any other event in the very distant past. So that dogmatism on dating and methods can usually be attributed to an ignorance of fundamental issues at stake in this area of thought. This also applies to statements on the historicity, or lack of it, in biblical chronology.[1] [*Vide*, in this connection, Sir James Jeans, *The Mysterious Universe*, New Revised Edition, pp. 36, 37.]

The fact is that the dating of fossils, or of anything in the early historic or in the prehistoric past, is a very precarious business. *Man has always been prone to mulitply problems for himself unnecessarily by obtruding his notions of measured (mathematical, temporal) time into the realm of God's timelessness, that is, eternity.*

37. *Theistic evolutionism.* This is the view, stated in simplest terms, that evolution was, and is, God's method of creation. The problem involved in thinking of evolution from this point of view is, primarily, whether theistic evolution can be harmonized with the Genesis narrative of the Creation. There are educated and sincerely religious persons who hold that this view if "properly stated" (that is, within certain limitations) is not necessarily in conflict with the teaching of Genesis, if the latter is also "constructively interpreted."

(1) For example, there is a clear correspondence between the Genesis cosmogony and present-day scientific thinking, especially with reference to the order of creation: first, energy, matter, light; then, atmosphere; then, lands and seas and plant life; next, measurement of time (chronology); then, the air and water species, the beasts of the field, and finally man and woman, in the order named.

(2) It must always be kept in mind that the major aim of the Genesis Cosmogony, and indeed of the Bible as a whole, is to tell us *who* made the Cosmos, and not *how* it was made. It was what God said, that "was so," that is, "was done." (Gen. 1:3, 7, 11, 15, 21, 25; Psa. 33:6, 9; Psa. 148:6). However, the inspired writer makes no attempt whatsoever to inform us as to *how* it was done. It is crystal clear that the narrative is intended to be a *religious,* and not a *scientific,* account of the Creation.

1. A. E. Wilder Smith, *op cit.,* 150-153.

(3) In relation to theistic evolutionism, very much depends on the meaning of the word "day" (*yom*) as used in the Genesis account of the Creation. Substantial evidence can be adduced to support either of the two views of the seven "days" involved, namely, the *solar* or twenty-four hour day, or the *aeonic* day, a long period of time. Certainly, there is nothing in the Genesis account that constrains us to accept the ultra-literal view that God spoke all living species into existence at one and the same time. On the contrary, according to the narrative itself, the activity of Creation was extended over six "days" and a fraction of the seventh. This is true, however, we may see fit to interpret the word *yom*.

(4) The language of the Genesis Narrative itself seems to allow for a divinely progressive development, through the media of secondary causes, throughout the Creation. This is implicit surely in God's decrees, "Let the earth put forth grass," etc., "Let the waters swarm with swarms of living creatures," "Let the earth bring forth living creatures," etc.; and even in the earlier decrees with reference to non-living forms of being, "Let there be a firmament in the midst of the waters," "Let the waters under the heavens be gathered together into one place," "let the dry land appear," etc. The idea implicit in the original here is that of *causation,* as if to say, "let the earth *cause,* let the seas *cause,* it to be done," etc. We see no reason for rejecting the view that God whose Will is the constitution of the universe and its processes, should operate through the majesty and sovereign power of His own established decrees. After all, what science calls "laws of nature" are really the laws of God. Law is always the expression of the will of the lawgiver; hence, laws of "nature" are really the expression of the Will of the God of nature; His will is the constitution of the cosmos: "He hath made a decree which shall not pass away" (Psa. 148:1-6) until the "times of restoration of all things" (Acts 3:21) (Cf. Heb. 1:10-13, 2 Pet. 3:8-13, Rev., ch. 21).

(5) As we have noted heretofore, there are philosophers and theologians who take the position that at certain stages in the Creation, God, by *direct* action (that is, *primary,* as distinguished from *secondary,* causation) inserted ("stepwise," as it is sometimes put) new and higher powers into the Cosmic Process, the first above the inanimate world (matter-in-motion)

being the *life process* (cellular activity), then *consciousness* (the product of sensitivity), and finally *self-consciousness* (person and personality). Obviously, these are phenomena which mark off, and set apart, the successively more complex levels of being, as we know these levels empirically. On the basis of this theory, it is held that even though variations—both upward (progressive) and downward (retrogressive)—by means of *resident* forces, may have occurred on the level of plant life and that of animal life, the actualization of the first form of *energy-matter*, first *life*, first *consciousness*, and first *personality* (homo sapiens) must surely have been of the character of special creations. It is interesting to recall the fact here that Wallace, the author with Darwin of the theory of natural selection, held that there were three breaks in the progressive continuity, namely with the appearance of life, with the appearance of sensation and consciousness, and finally with the appearance of spirit. These breaks seem to correspond, in a general way, to *vegetable, animal,* and *rational* (human) life, in the order named. (Wallace, *Darwinism* 445-478. Quoted by A. H. Strong, *Systematic Theology,* 473.).

(6) Finally, it must be admitted that one of man's most common fallacies is that of trying to project his own puny concepts of time into the sphere of God's *timelessness.* God does not hurry; His timelessness is Eternity. (2 Pet. 3:8, 2 Cor. 4:18).

(Obviously, theistic evolutionism must be studied particularly in relation to the meaning of the word "day" as it occurs in the Genesis account of the Creation, and in relation to creation and constitution of man as given in Genesis 2:7. According to present plans, a complementary treatment of the Biblical doctrine of the Holy Spirit will be presented in a second book, to be entitled *The Eternal Spirit: His Word and His Works,* to be published in the near future.)

38. *The following summarizations of the status of the theory of evolution* at present writing will suffice to conclude our study here. The first is from G. T. W. Patrick, as follows:

On the whole, all the theories of organic evolution, including Darwinism, are somewhat disappointing to the student of philosophy, who is trying to understand the world of living things. There are more gaps and unexplained factors than we supposed—and they are found in very critical places. Most disappointing of all is the complete failure of any accepted theory to determine the causes of evolution itself. The fact is that evolution is a very much over-worked word. . . . Evolution means unwrapping, unrolling, or unfolding. It indicates a process in which the implicit is becoming explicit, the potential, actual. There is no evidence that evolution is in any sense an unwrapping process. On the contrary, it is distinctly of an epigenetic or upbuilding character. Even the simplest Darwinian variation, much more a mutation, is a real increment, a novelty, a new creation, a veritable plus. Neither is evolution a process in which the potential is becoming actual. We speak of the evolution of the automobile—but the latest skilled product of this art was not potential in the first crude machine. Every improvement has been a new creation, a new thought. . . . Since we do not know the causes of evolution, we do not know of any developmental potency in matter. The only way to support this proposition, would be to argue that since all life has come out of matter, it must have been contained potentially in it, where the only authority for the major premise is the etymological meaning of the word *evolution*. One might as well say that one sees in oxygen and hydrogen the promise and potency of water and all its forms, or in the behavior of apes the promise and potency of the infinitesimal calculus. Water satisfies thirst, and revives the drooping plant, and freezes at zero Centigrade. But certainly there is no promise of any of these qualities in oxygen and hydrogen. There is something more than oxygen and hydrogen in a molecule of water, namely, a certain peculiar organization with the accompanying characteristic qualities of water. Briefly, then, the meaning of evolution is that it is a creative process, something new appearing at every step of the developmental history. Every change is a transformation. The French word *transformisme* is a happier word than the English *evolution*, or the German *Entwickelung*. . . . Evolution is a history of new forms and functions. Every new form is a plus—a new creation. . . . Creation does not mean the production of something out of nothing. The architect creates a Gothis cathedral, but not the stone and mortar. The promoter creates a new organization, but he does not create the men that compose it. Creation means just this—the production of something distinctly new and unique. Reality is found, as Aristotle told us long ago, in structure, form, organization, and function—not in the mere stuff which happens to compose the material. . . . Thus Darwinism has nothing to teach us concerning either the origin or the nature of life and mind. It records only the unexplained appearance of an unending series of new events, one of which is the great event of mind. If we seek to know the origin of life and mind, we must go beyond Darwin in some deeper analysis of the process called evolution. It is not a movement from the potential to the actual. It cannot be defined as a series of orderly changes, for as far as the changes are evolutionary, they are disorderly. . . . It seems like the work of a creative imagination. It reminds ever of the work of an artist.[1]

Why should not Creation remind us of the work of an artist? Is not our God the God of Love? 1 John 4:16—"God is love; and he that abideth in love, abideth in God, and God abideth in him." And is not Love always sacrificial, always outgoing, always creative? Back of all the "scientific" aspects of our Cosmos are the aesthetic. The God of the Bible is the superb Aesthete! His very outgoingness, as Divine Love, is, in all likelihood, the very *why* of the whole Creative Process!

The following is from the pen of Dr. Radoslav A. Tsanoff:

The philosophical interpretation of evolutionism has been complicated by the fact that Darwinism explained the survival results of fit

1. *Introduction to Philosophy*, 144-147.

variations, but did not provide an explanation of the causes of variations or proceed to ultimate cosmological inferences. Regarding the heritability of variations, opinions differ. The Lamarckians have definitely lost ground, though they have never been without allies. The theory of mutations, as developed and interpreted by careful geneticists, has reached specific conclusions regarding the evolutionary results of changes in the germ plasm. But the longer pattern of evolutionary cosmology can scarcely be regarded as ascertained. Is it a pattern of strictly mechanical determination? Or does biological evolution produce results that cannot be reduced to merely antecedent causal determinants, that indicate a certain natural creative activity? Or does the stream of existence, unlike water, somehow rise higher than its source; do lower processes produce their self-transcendence, in higher types of being? Philosophy since Darwin has explored these and other theories. Many evolutionists have taken a basically materialistic position; the initial oppostion to the theory of evolution was led by those who regarded it as undermining the recognition of spiritual values. Writers like John Fiske (1842-1901) advanced a reinterpretation of evolution as God's cosmic design, the progressive realization of intelligence and spiritual powers in nature.[1]

## Arthur Kenyon Rogers writes:

The importance of natural selection as an agency is now indeed generally admitted, but also it is widely believed that it does not explain all the facts. For one thing, it is plain that selection does not *cause* advance in the first place. Selection can only take place on the basis of an advance already made; and so we now have to ask the further question: What is the cause and nature of the original variations that are afterwards selected as well as of the factor of heredity which Darwin also took for granted. Evolution is therefore not necessarily identical with Darwinism.[2] [This author, however, subscribes to the "principle" which, as he puts it, has been applied with results that "have put a new face on all our knowledge."].

Evidently, infinity in God has no reference to any kind of magnitude because God is Spirit (John 4:24). Rather, the term designates the inexhaustible Source of Power by which the cosmos was created and is sustained in its processes. Therefore, we must always keep in mind that the basic problem before us here is not one of *power,* but of *method.* Whatever the method, the Efficient Causality in operation was that of Power. And we are surely thinking "straight" when we declare our conviction that *all Power is of God.*

I think it fitting to conclude at this point with another excerpt from *The Witness,* written by my colleague Curtis Dickinson:

Modern education has undermined today's children by denying them the knowledge of this basic fact, that they are created by a loving, wise, just and merciful God. What kind of character is to be expected of the person who sees himself as the chance product of "nature"? What purpose can exist for something that is a mere step in the

1. *The Great Philosophers,* 567-568.
2. *A Student's History of Philosophy,* 451.

purposeless ladder of evolutionary development? Who am I? The ten-billionth stage of the growth of a cell that began in primordial ooze 60 billion years ago? Even the thought of such meaninglessness chills the mind! And to think that today's children are compelled to sit under such teaching practically one-third of the time, many of them continuing in public class rooms through college until they are past the twenty-second birthday. The official doctrine of the state school system is atheistic evolution, with the truth of God's creation attempted only by a small minority of brave teachers who are generally ignored. Thus the very system that is supported for the purpose of education leaves the young people without purpose and direction, and apt to follow whatever voice is the loudest.

Is it possible that the facts stated in this excerpt account for the tragic consequential fact that the United States of America is now a pagan nation? Is it too late now to pray—

"Lord God of hosts, be with us yet,
Lest we forget, lest we forget"?

\* \* \* \* \* \* \*

I would again call special attention to the book by A. E. Wilder Smith, *Man's Origin, Man's Destiny,* for a genuinely critical treatment of evolutionism and Christianity. The book may be secured from Harold Shaw, Publishers, Wheaton, Illinois, 60187, or from the Bible-Science Association, Inc., Box 1016, Caldwell, Idaho, 83605. Any of the publications by this group of scientists is well worth reading. I am grateful for the privilege of quoting from some of these publications.

I would also call attention here to a recent publication of the National Geography Society, Washington, D.C., 20036 entitled *The Marvels of Animal Behavior.* This is an eye-opener about the manifoldness of instinct in the subhuman life-world. C.C.C.

# BIBLIOGRAPHY AND SUGGESTED REFERENCE WORKS

Allport, Gordon W., *Personality: A Psychological Interpretation.* Holt, New York, 1937.

Aquinas, Thomas, *Summa Theologica.* "Translated by Fathers of the English Dominican Province." Burns Oates and Wasbourne, London.

Aristotle, *De Anima.* In *The Works of Aristotle Translated into English,* under editorship of W. D. Ross. Translation by J. A. Smith. Oxford University Press, Oxford, 1931. Also, Loeb Classical Library edition, Hett translation, Harvard University Press, Cambridge, and Heinemann, London.

——————, *Metaphysics.* Loeb Classical Library, in 2 vols. Harvard University Press, Cambridge, and Heinemann, London, Vol. I, 1947. Vol. II, 1936. Translation by Hugh Tredennick.

——————, *Physics.* Trans, by Philip H. Dickstead and F. W. Cornford, 2 Vols. Loeb Classical Library, Vo. I, Putnam, New York, and Heinemann, London 1929; Vol. II, Harvard University Press, Cambridge, and Heinemann, London, 1934.

Augustine, *Confessions,* Everyman's Library. Pusey translation. Dent, London; Dutton, New York.

——————, *De Genesi ad Litteram.* Migne Editions: *Patrologia Latina,* 1844-45; *Patrologia Graeco-Latina,* 1859-68.

Bahm, Archie J., *Philosophy: An Introduction.* Wiley, New York, 1953.

Barnett, Lincoln, *The Universe and Dr. Einstein.* Sloane, New York, 1949.

——————, —————— "The Meaning of Einstein's New Theory," *Life,* Jan. 9, 1950.

Beadle, George W., "High-Frequency Radiation and the Gene," *Science and Life in the World,* Vol. II., The George Westinghouse Centennial Forum Series, in 3 vols. McGraw-Hill, New York, 1946.

Belloc, Hilaire, "More Beasts for Worse Children," in *Cautionary Verses,* Knopf, New York, 1951.

Bergson, Henry, *Time and Free Will.* Pogson translation. Allen and Unwin, London; Macmillan, New York, 1928.

——————, *Matter and Memory.* Translated by Nancy Margaret Paul and W. Scott Palmer. Allen and Unwin, London; Macmillan, New York, 1929.

—————— ———— ——————, *Creative Evolution.* Authorized translation by Arthur Mitchell. Holt, New York, 1911, 1937.

—————— ——————, *The Two Sources of Morality and Religion.* Translation by R. Ashley Audra and Cloudesley Brereton, Holt, New York, 1935.

Berman, Louis, M.D., *Behind the Universe.* Harper, New York and London.

Bernheim, H., *Suggestive Therapeutics,* trans. by Christian A. Herter. Reprinted by the London Book Company, New York, 1947.

Biederwolf, W. E., *A Help to the Study of the Holy Spirit.* Revell, New York, 1905.

Boethius, *On the Consolation of Philosophy,* Loeb Classical Library, Trans. by H. F. Stewart. Harvard University Press, Cambridge, 1918.

Brightman, Edgar S., *A Philosophy of Religion.* Prentice-Hall, New York, 1946.

Brownville, C. Gordon, *Symbols of the Holy Spirit.* Revell, New York, 1945.

Bryan, William Jennings, *In His Image.* Revell, New York, 1945.

Burnet, John, *Early Greek Philosophy.* Fourth Edition. A. & C. Black, Ltd., London, 1930.

Butler, Joseph, *Analogy of Religion, Natural and Revealed.* Everyman's Edition, Dent, London; Dutton, New York, 1927.

593

Calkins, Raymond, *The Holy Spirit*. Abingdon, New York, 1930.
Campbell, Alexander, (On Jesus as the Logos), in *The Christian Baptist*, May 7, 1827.
————, ————, *The Campbell-Owen Debate*. Published first under the title, *The Evidences of Christianity*, by the Standard Publishing Company, Cincinnati, 1829. Recently republished by the McQuiddy Printing Co., Nashville, 1957.
Carrel, Alexis, *Man the Unknown*. Harper, New York, 1935.
Chambers, Oswald, *Biblical Psychology*. Oswald Chambers Publication Association, Fort Washington, Penn., 1962.
Chase, Stuart, *The Tyranny of Words*. Harcourt, New York, 1938.
Chesterton, G. K., *The Everlasting Man*. Doubleday Image Book, New York, 1955.
Clarke, Adam, *The Holy Spirit, with Commentary and Critical Notes*, in 6 vols. Royal Octavo Stereotyped Edition. Published by Waugh and Mason, for the Methodist Episcopal Church, at the Conference Office, 13 Crosby St., New York, 1933.
Clutton-Brock, A., "Spirit and Matter," in *The Spirit*, edited by B. H. Streeter, Macmillan, New York, 1922.
Coggins, James Caswell, *The Thrones of the Apostles*, privately published, 1947.
Cohen, Morris R. and Nagel, Ernest, *An Introduction to Logic and Scientific Method*. Harcourt, New York, 1934.
Cornford, Francis Macdonald, *Plato's Cosmology*, Harcourt, New York, 1937.
————, ————, *Plato and Parmenides*, Kegan, Paul, Trench, Trubner; London, 1939.
————, ————, *Plato's Theory of Knowledge*, Harcourt, New York, 1935.
Crawford, C. C., *Genesis*, in 4 vols. College Press, Joplin, Mo., 1966-71.
Cronin, A. J., "Why I Believe in God," *Woman's Home Companion*, June, 1950. Condensed in *Reader's Digest*, September, 1950.
Cruden, Alezander, *A Complete Concordance to the Holy Scriptures*. Winston, Philadelphia, 1949.
Cummin, James Elder, *Through the Eternal Spirit*. Revell, New York, 1896.
Davis, Watson, editor, *The Advance of Science*. Duell, New York. Out of print.
Deane, W. J., *Pulpit Commentary*: Zechariah (Vol. 32), New Edition. Funk and Wagnalls, New York.
De Broglie, Louis, *Matter and Light*. Trans. by W. H. Johnston. Dover, New York, 1946.
De Chardin, Pierre Tielhard, *The Phenomenon of Man*, Trans by Wall. Harper, New York, 1959.
————, ———— *The Divine Milieu*, Harper, and Row, New York, 1960.
————, ————, *The Future of Man*, trans. by Denny; Harper and Row, New York, 1964.
————, ————, *Hymn of the Universe*, Trans. by Bartholomew, Harper and Row, New York, 1965.
Delitzsch, F., (and C. F. Keil), *Biblical Commentary*: The Pentateuch, Vol. I. Trans, from the German by James Martin. Eerdmans, Grand Rapids.
Dewar, Douglas, *The Transformist Illusion*. DeHoff, Murfreesboro, Tenn., 1957.
DeWelt, Don, *The Power of the Holy Spirit*. College Press, Joplin, Mo., 1963.

Dewey, John, *Experience and Nature*. Open Court, Chicago, 1925.
----------, ----------, *A Common Faith*. Yale University Press, New Haven, 1934.
Dimnet, Ernest, *The Art of Thinking*. Simon and Schuster, New York, 1928.
----------, ----------, *What We Live By*. Simon and Schuster, New York, 1932.
Dods, Marcus, *The Expositor's Bible: Genesis*. Edited by Nicoll. Eerdmans, Grand Rapids.
Dummelow, J. R. (editor), *Commentary on the Whole Bible*, in one vol. Macmillan, New York, 1909.
Dungan, D. R., *Hermeneutics*. Standard, Cincinnati.
Durant, Will, *The Story of Philosophy*. Simon and Schuster, New York, 1926, 1933, 1953.
----------, ----------, *The Mansions of Philosophy*. Simon and Schuster, New York, 1929.
Du Nody, Lecomte, *Human Destiny*. Longmans, New York, 1947.
Eddington, A. S., *The Nature of the Physical World*. Macmillan, New York, 1929.
----------, ----------, *Science and the Unseen World*. Macmillan, New York, 1930.
Euripides, *Bacchae*, Loeb Classical Library. Trans. by Way, Putnam, New York, and Heinemann, London.
Fisher, George P., *The Grounds of Theistic and Christian Belief*. Scribner, New York, 1900.
Furnas, C. C., *The Next Hundred Years*. Reynal and Hitchcock, New York, 1936.
Garland, Hamlin, *Forty Years of Psychic Research*. Macmillan, New York, 1937.
Garrigou-LaGrange, Reginald, *The One God*. Tr. by Dom. Bede Rose. Herder, St. Louis and London, 1943.
----------, ----------, *The Three Ages of the Interior Life*. Herder, St. Louis and London, 1947. Trans. by Sister M. Timothea Doyle, O.P.
Gilson, Etienne, *God and Philosophy*. Yale University Press, New Haven, 1941.
Goodspeed, Edgar J., *The New Testament: An American Translation*. University of Chicago Press, 1923.
Gordon, A. J., *The Ministry of the Spirit*. Revell, New York, 1895.
Green, James B., *Studies in the Holy Spirit*. Revell, New York, 1936.
Green, William Henry, *The Unity of the Book of Genesis*. Scribner, New York, 1895.
Groves, Ernest R., *Understanding Yourself*. Emerson, New York, 1935.
Guyot, Arnold, *Creation, or the Biblical Cosmogony in the Light of Modern Science*. Scribner, New York, 1884.
Hadfield, J. Arthur, "The Psychology of Power," in *The Spirit* (edited by Streeter). Macmillan, New York, 1922.
Haldane, J. B. S., *Possible Worlds*. (Out of print).
Hamilton, Sir William, *Lectures on Metaphysics*, Herder, St. Louis and London, 1861. (Long out of print, but often quoted.)
Hare, Julius C., *The Mission of the Comforter*, Macmillan, London, 1877.
Hesiod, *Theogony*. Loeb Classical Library; *Hesiod the Homeric Humns and Homerica*. Trans. by Evelyn-White. Harvard University Press, Cambridge, and Heinemann, London.
Hill, David, *Greek Words and Hebrew Meanings*. Cambridge University Press, London; American Branch, New York, 1967.
Hocking, W. S., "A World-View," in *Preface to Philosophy: A Textbook*,

by Hocking, Blanshard, Hendel, and Randall. Macmillan, New York, 1947.

Hodgson, Leonard, The Doctrine of the Trinity. Scribner, New York, 1944.

Hogben, L. T., Science for the Citizen. Knopf, New York, 1938.

Hooton, Ernest A., Up From the Ape. Macmillan, New York, 1937.

Hoyle, Fred, The Nature of the Universe. Blackwell, Oxford, 1952.

Hubbard, L. Ron, Dianetics. Hermitage House, New York, 1950.

Hudson, Thomas Jay, The Law of Psychic Phenomena, Thirty-second Edition. McClurg, Chicago, 1909.

Illingworth, J. R., Personality: Human and Divine. Shilling edition, Macmillan, London, 1923.

Inge, W. R., God and the Astronomers. Longmans, New York, 1933.

James, William, The Meaning of Truth, Longmans, New York, 1933.

——————, ——————, "Is Life Worth Living?" International Journal of Ethics, October, 1895.

——————, ——————, Varieties of Religious Experience. Modern Library, Random House, New York, 1902.

Jastrow, J., The Subconscious. Houghton Mifflin, Boston, 1916.

Jauncey, James H., Science Returns to God. Zondervan, Grand Rapids, 1961.

Jeans, Sir James, The New Background of Science, Macmillan, New York, 1934.

——————, ——————, The Mysterious Universe. New Revised Edition, Macmillan, New York, 1943.

——————, ——————, Physics and Philosophy. Macmillan, New York, 1943.

Jerusalem Bible, The. Alexander Jones, General Editor. Doubleday, New York, 1966. (A magnificent work. C.C.)

Joad, C. E. M., God and Evil. Harper, New York, 1943.

——————, ——————, Guide to Philosophy. Random House, New York, 1936.

Johnson, Ashley S., The Holy Spirit and the Human Mind. Published by the Author, Knoxville, Tenn. 1903.

Jones, Rufus, Spirit in Man. Stanford University Press, Palo Alto, California, and Oxford University Press, London, 1941.

Kahn, Fritz, M.D., Man in Structure and Function, 2 vols. Trans. from the German and edited by George Rosen, M.D. Knopf, New York, 1946.

Knudson, Albert C., The Religious Teaching of the Old Testament. Abingdon-Cokesbury, New York, 1918.

Kuyper, Abraham, The Work of the Holy Spirit. Trans. by Henri De-Vries (from the Dutch). Eerdmans, Grand Rapids, 1941.

Laertius, Diogenes, Lives and Opinions of Eminent Philosophers, 2 vols. Loeb Classical Library. Trans. by R. D. Hicks. Putnam, New York, and Heinemann, London, 1925.

Landis, Carney, and Bolles (M. Marjorie), Textbook of Abnormal Psychology. Macmillan, New York, 1947.

Lange, John Peter, Critical, Doctrinal, and Homiletical Commentary on the Holy Scriptures: Genesis. Trans. by Tayler Lewis and A. Gosman. Scribner, New York, 1868.

Lard, Moses E., Commentary on Romans. Christian Publishing Company, St. Louis, 1875.

LeBon, Gustave, The Evolution of Matter. (Out of print).

Lebreton, Jules, S.J., History of the Dogma of the Trinity, Vol. I. Translated by Algar Thorold from the Eighth Edition. Benziger Bros., New York, 1939.

Leibniz, G. W. *Monadology*. Modern Student's Library Edition. Scribner, New York.
Lemon, Harvey Brace, *Cosmic Rays Thus Far*. (Out of print).
Lewis (Charlton T.) and Short (Charles), *Harper's Latin Dictionary*. Founded on the translation of Freund's Latin-German Lexicon, edited by E. A. Andrews. American Book Company, New York, Chicago, etc. 1879, 1907.
Liddle (Henry George) and Scott (Robert), *Greek-English Lexicon*. New Edition, revised and augmented by Henry Stuart Jones. Clarendon Press, Oxford, 1948.
Lotze, Hermann, *Mikrokosmus*. (May be found in translation in all standard philosophical editions.)
Lovejoy, Arthur O., *The Great Chain of Being*, Harvard University Press, 1950.
Lyttelton, Edith, *Our Superconscious Mind*. (Out of print).
Maclaren, Alexander, *Sermons*, (in several volumes). Eerdmans, Grand Rapids.
Manning, H. E. (Cardinal), *The Temporal Mission of the Holy Ghost*. Appleton, New York, 1866.
Maritain, Jacques, *An Introduction to Logic*. Sheed and Ward, New York, 1937.
————, ————, *An Introduction to Philosophy*. Trans. by Watkin. Sheed and Ward, New York, (no date).
Marsh, F. E., *Emblems of the Holy Spirit*. Pickering and Inglis, London, 1923.
Matheson, George, *Voices of the Spirit*. Hodder and Stoughton, London, (Out of print).
McGarvey (J. W.) and Pendleton (P. Y.), *The Fourfold Gospel*. Standard, Cincinnati.
————, ————, (Standard Bible Commentary): *Thessalonians, Corinthians, Galatians, Romans*. Standard, Cincinnati, 1916.
McKeon, Richard, *Selections from Medieval Philosophers*. Modern Student's Library, Scribner, New York, 1929.
McWilliams, J. A., *Cosmology*. Second Revised Edition. Macmillan, New York, 1939.
Messenger, Ernest C., *Evolution and Theology: The Problem of Man's Origin*. Macmillan, New York, 1932.
Michener, Wm. H., *Physics for Students of Science and Engineering*, 1947.
Milligan, Robert, *Scheme of Redemption*. Christian Publishing Co., St. Louis, 1868.
Moll, A., *Hypnotism*. (Out of print).
Monser, J. W., *Types and Metaphors of the Bible*. F. L. Rowe, Cincinnati, 1936.
Montague, W. P., "The Chances of Surviving Death," in *Basic Problems of Philosophy*, by Bronstein, Krikorian, and Wiener. Prentice-Hall, New York, 1947.
Moore, Raymond G., *Historical Geology*. First Edition. McGraw-Hill, New York, 1933.
Morrison, A. Cressy, *Man Does Not Stand Alone*. Revell, New York, 1944.
Myers, F. W. H., *Human Personality, and its Survival of Bodily Death*. 2 vols. Longmans, New York, 1904.
Murphy, Gardner, editor, *An Outline of Abnormal Psychology*. First Modern Library Edition. Random House, New York.
Murray, Andrew, *The Spirit of Christ*. Nisbet, London, 1888.
Murray, Sir James, editor, *A New English Dictionary, On Historical*

*Principles*, commonly known as *The Oxford English Dictionary*. Clarendon Press, Oxford, 1888-1928.

Negley, Glenn, *The Organization of Knowledge*. Prentice-Hall, New York, 1942.

Noble, Ruth Crosby, *The Nature of the Beast*. Doubleday, New York, 1945.

Nordenskiold, Eric, *The History of Biology*. Trans. from the Swedish by Leonard B. Eyre. Tudor Publishing Company, New York, 1936.

Nys, D., *Cosmology*, 2 vols. Translated by Sidney Raemers; Bruce, Milwaukee, 1942.

Ogburn (Wm. F.) and Nimkoff (Meyer F.), *Sociology*. Houghton Mifflin, Boston, 1946.

Otto, Rudolph, *The Idea of the Holy*. Trans. by John W. Harvey, Oxford University Press, London, 1925.

Overstreet, Harry, *The Mature Mind*. Norton, New York, 1949.

Owen, John, *A Discourse Concerning the Holy Spirit*. Presbyterian Board of Publication, Philadelphia.

————, ————, *The Holy Spirit: His Gifts and Power*. Kregel, Grand Rapids, 1954.

————, ————, *Hebrews: The Epistle of Warning*. Kregel, Grand Rapids, 1953.

Parker, Joseph, *The Paraclete*. Scribner, New York, 1883.

Petronius, *Satiricon*. Loeb Classical Library. Trans. by M. Heseltine.

Plato, *Phaedrus*, Loeb Classical Library, Trans. by H. N. Fowler. Harvard University Press, Cambridge; Heinemann, London, 1938.

————, ————, *Theaetetus*. L. C. L. Trans. by R. G. Bury. Harvard Univ. Press, Cambridge, and Heinemann, London, 1942.

————, ————, *Timaeus*. L. C. L. Trans. by R. G. Bury. Harvard Univ. Press, and Heinemann, London, 1942.

Prince, Morton, M.D., *The Unconscious*. Macmillan, New York, 1921. Excerpt in *An Outline of Abnormal Psychology*, edited by Gardner Murphy, Modern Library, Random House, New York.

Read, Grantly Dick, *Childbirth Without Fear*. Harper, New York and London, 1944.

Rees, T., *The Holy Spirit in Thought and Experience*. Scribner, New York, 1915.

Rhine, J. B., *The Reach of the Mind*. Sloane, New York, 1947.

Richardson, R., *A Scriptural View of the Office of the Holy Spirit*. Chase and Hall, Cincinnati, 1875.

Richet, Charles, *Thirty Years of Psychical Research*. Trans. from The French by Stanley DeBrath.

Robinson, A. W., *The Holy Spirit and the Individual*.

Robinson, H. Wheeler, *The Christian Experience of the Holy Spirit*. Harper, New York and London, 1928.

Rogers, Arthur Kenyon, *A Student's History of Philosophy*, Macmillan, New York, 1937.

Rotherham, J. B., *The Emphasized Bible*. Kregel, Grand Rapids, 1959.

Schuchert (Charles) and Dunbar (Carl O.), *Outlines of Geology*. Third Edition, Wiley, London, 1937.

Sharp, D. E., *Franciscan Philosophy at Oxford in the Thirteenth Century*. Oxford University Press; Humphrey Milford, London, 1930.

Simpson, George Gaylord, *The Meaning of Evolution*. Mentor Book, New American Library, New York, 1952.

Skinner, John, *The International Critical Commentary: Genesis*. Scribner, New York, 1910.

Sloan, Harold Paul, *He Is Risen*. Abingdon-Cokesbury, New York, 1954.

BIBLIOGRAPHY

Smith, A. E. Wilder, *Man's Origin, Man's Destiny*. Harold Shaw Publishers, Wheaton, Illinois, 1970.
Smith, J. Ritchie, *The Holy Spirit in the Gospels*. Macmillan, New York, 1926.
Smith, W. Robertson, *The Religion of the Semites*: *Fundamental Institutions*. Appleton, New York, 1889.
Smuts, J. C., *Holism and Evolution*. Macmillan, New York, 1926.
Sperling, Abraham, *Psychology Made Simple*. Doubleday, New York, 1957.
Spinoza, *Selections*, including the *Ethics*. Modern Student's Library, Scribner, New York, 1930.
Strong, Augustus Hopkins, *Systematic Theology* (three volumes in one). Judson Press, Philadelphia, 1912.
Sweeney, Z. T., *The Spirit and the Word*. Gospel Advocate, Nashville.
Swete, H. B., *The Holy Spirit in the New Testament*. Macmillan, London, 1910.
----------, ----------, *The Holy Spirit in the Ancient Church*. Macmillan, London, 1912.
Taylor, A. E., "The Vindication of Religion," in *Essays Catholic and Critical*, Macmillan, New York, 1950.
Thompson, W. R., F.R.S., Introduction to the latest Everyman's edition of Darwin's *Origin of Species*. Dent, London, and Dutton, New York, 1956.
Toy, C. H., *Introduction to the History of Religions*. Harvard University Press, Cambridge, 1924.
Trueblood, D. Elton, *Philosophy of Religion*. Harper, New York, 1957.
Tsanoff, Radoslav A., *The Great Philosophers*. Harper, 1953.
Ueberweg, F., *A History of Philosophy*. In 2 vols. Trans. from the Fourth German Edition by George S. Morris. Scribner, New York, 1872.
Villee, Claude A., *Biology*: *The Human Approach*. Saunders, Philadelphia, 1950.
Wells (H.G.), Huxley (Julian) and Wells (George P.), *The Science of Life*. Doubleday, New York, 1931.
Whitehead, A. N., *Science and the Modern World*. Macmillan, New York, 1926.
----------, ---------- *Process and Reality*. Macmillan, New York, 1967.
Whitelaw, Thomas, *The Pulpit Commentary*: *Genesis*. New edition. Funk and Wagnalls, New York.
Wiggam, A. E., *Exploring Your Mind*. Bobbs-Merrill, Indianapolis, 1928.
Williams, Jesse F., *A Textbook of Anatomy and Physiology*, Seventh Edition. Saunders, Philadelphia, 1943.
Williams, R. J., *The Human Frontier*. Harcourt, New York, 1946.
Xenophanes, *Fragments*. In Loeb Classical Library, *Elegy and Iambus*, Vol. I., Trans. by J. M. Edmonds. Harvard University Press, Cambridge; and Heinemann, London, 1944.
Young, Robert, *Analytical Concordance to the Bible*. Twentieth American Edition, revised throughout by Wm. B. Stevenson. Funk and Wagnalls, New York.
N.B. Some books are listed in the foregoing bibliography as "out of print," which, in all likelihood, they are. These were in my possession, however, when I prepared the first edition of this work in manuscript form. But they seem to have disappeared from my library, as books, especially old books, tend to do. Copies may be found, of course, in libraries and in secondhand bookstores. C.C.